THE LONESOME ROAD

SAUNDERS REDDING was born in Wilmington, Delaware, and received his undergraduate and graduate degrees from Brown University. He was the recipient of the Rockefeller Foundation Fellowship in 1940 which resulted in his authoring a book entitled *No Day of Triumph*. His other books include *Cavalcade, Plays of Negro Life, They Came in Chains,* and *To Make a Black Poet*. Mr. Redding was formerly a Professor of English Literature at Hampton Institute. At present he is the Ernest I. White Professor of American Studies and Humane Letters at Cornell University and also a Special Consultant to the National Endowment for the Humanities.

THE LONESOME ROAD

A Narrative History of Blacks in America

SAUNDERS REDDING

Anchor Books
Anchor Press/Doubleday
Garden City, New York
1973

THE LONESOME ROAD was originally published by Doubleday & Company, Inc., in 1958. A Dolphin paperback edition was published in 1961.

The Anchor Books edition is published by arrangement with Doubleday & Company, Inc.

Anchor Books edition: 1973

To my Father

CONTENTS

INTRODUCTION

Researched and written in the mid-1950s, *The Lonesome Road* was conceived as historical biography covering the period from the end of the eighteenth century to the middle of the twentieth. It was assumed that the story of the Negro in the United States could be told by presenting certain biographical facts and group experiences in the context of dominant social, cultural, and ideological trends of the times. It was assumed that black Americans, too, were affected by policy shifts in the national government, by the way laws worked or did not work, by the operation of the general society's system of values, and by the occasionally critical impact of ideas upon the course of events. It was assumed, finally, that the black experience could be synthesized and reflected in the lives of a few blacks who, even when obscure, were representative in what they did and felt and said in response to fundamental aspects of American life.

These assumptions were certainly valid down through 1954, when the Supreme Court declared school segregation illegal. But since that year of decision many things have happened to bring the assumptions into question. A few of these events, typical of many in their consequences, need mention. In 1956, the black people's bus boycott in Montgomery, Alabama was headlined for months in the international press. Four years later, the freedom rides and the student boycotts of restaurants, theaters, stores and other places of public accommodation generated retaliatory violence against blacks, which was also widely publicized. Four months before the assassination of President John F. Kennedy, a quarter of a million people, including a substantial number (estimates vary) of liberal-minded, concerned whites—national figures such as Senators Humphrey and Edward Kennedy and representatives of the American Jewish Congress, the National Conference of Catholics, the AFL-CIO—staged a March on Washington "for jobs and freedom," which the news media described as "the largest mass demonstration in the history of America." The next summer was the "long hot summer," when cataclysmic riots took place in city after city, where Negroes believed themselves to be—as, indeed, they mostly were—victims of exploitation and repression, of police brutality and "official" indifference and neglect. In 1967, the Kerner Commission on Civil Rights, appointed by President Johnson two years before, reported 164 racial disorders in 128 cities.

These manifestations of racial protest frequently resulted in amelioration of the conditions against which Negroes were protesting. There was a general tightening of the enforcement of existing laws against discrimination and segregation, and new laws were promulgated. Several building trades unions, prodded by OEO, The Civil Rights Commission, and similar mandated federal agencies, instituted apprenticeship training programs for underprivileged Negroes and members of other minorities, and pledged to put them in jobs. Here and there nondiscriminatory open housing was effected. Here and there school desegregation was accomplished with a minimum of difficulty, or none at all.

But, paradoxically, these victories, such as they were, coincided with the splintering of the co-ordinated civil rights movement. Cries of "black power" and "self-determination for black people" rose throughout the land, providing compelling evidence that, contrary to the preceding century and a half, the overwhelming majority of Negroes no longer rallied around those black leaders who showed the greatest promise of bringing about racial integration in the shortest time. "Race separatism," "black power," and "putting it together"—each meaning different things to different people—were the new watchwords, the new shibboleths.

Such leaders as Roy Wilkins of the NAACP, the late Whitney Young of the National Urban League and James Farmer of CORE were agreed that the struggle for the black man's rights should be carried on within the system and that the aim of the struggle was racial integration. But these leaders were repudiated. New leaders, with different goals and various means of attaining them, emerged, flourished for a longer or shorter time, and sank back into the mass. Old race-uplift organizations factionalized. The Southern Christian Leadership Conference, which the late Martin Luther King helped to found and which the Reverend Ralph Abernathy now heads, split over policies and program, giving the Reverend Jesse Jackson an excuse to form his own organization, People United to Save Humanity (PUSH). Two separate and distinct groups call themselves Black Panthers. Under the self-exiled Eldridge Cleaver, one faction advocates Third World revolutionary nationalism. The other, led by Huey Newton and Bobby Seale, both of whom have faced charges of murder, has come out in favor of local community action. The Black Muslims split. The followers of Elijah Muhammad, the founder called Prophet, proclaim their hatred of the "inferior white race" and wish to be as removed from it as their emotional bias demands and spatial reality permits. The dissidents rallied around Malcolm X in 1964 and created the Organization of Afro-American Unity with the aim of internationalizing the black struggle in the United States. The National Black Caucus, whose members got together presumably on the basis of broad mutuality in the spring of 1972, could not reach a consensus on long-term policies and programs.

There are other black organizations and individuals: Stokely Carmichael, expatriated in Africa; H. Rap Brown, in jail under a new criminal indictment; Angela Davis, recently found not guilty of capital offenses; Imani Baraka (formerly LeRoi Jones) the well-known and highly regarded poet-playwright turned activist; Floyd McKissick, creator of the still unrealized "Soul City"; Shirley Chisholm, the congresswoman from the Bedford-Stuyvesant area of Brooklyn; Julian Bond, a Georgia legislator, who could not accept the proffered vice-presidential nomination of the Democratic Party in 1968 because he was too young; Coretta King, widow of the assassinated Martin Luther King. The list of factions and those who command their allegiance is now practically endless.

And which of them is representative? One would find it impossible to fasten upon the story of any of these, relate that story in the context of a particular social, cultural or intellectual ambiance, and use it as a metaphor for the black experience. Since 1950, the story of the Negro in America has become many stories. The historical-biographical approach and the assumptions that supported it prior to 1950 will not satisfy the complex notional requirements of the history of the Negro beyond that point. A narrative synthesis of the years 1950 to the present must wait for time to provide perspective and thought to inform observation.

SAUNDERS REDDING

Part One

GLORY ENOUGH FOR A DAY

I. BOMBS BURSTING IN AIR

1. *Death in the Dark*

Everything was quiet except the sea, and that—ebbing as the purple dusk congealed to darkness—sucked back through the marshes and hissed along the narrow strip of beach with the sound of ravening mouths. The air was acrid, partly from the odor of the marsh, partly from the brine of the sea, but mostly from the sting of burned gunpowder and cordite. Though the bombardment of forty-one guns, aided by the cannons of six warships riding a stone's throw offshore, had ceased three hours ago, no breeze had risen to dispel the hot scent of the cannonade. It had lasted eleven hours, but Fort Wagner remained—slope-sided, parapeted and silent, as impregnable as ever, it seemed, in the thickening twilight. It would have to be stormed.

Shortly before seven o'clock a fog-laden breeze drifted in from the sea, and the men of the 54th Massachusetts Regiment tried to relax. It was impossible. They were raw troops, having had only a skirmish on James Island the previous day to learn from. For two years, while the battles of the Seven Days, second Bull Run, Fredericksburg, and Chancellorsville were fought and lost, certain leaders and champions of freedom had urged, pressed, harangued President Lincoln to recruit black men for war. "With every reverse to the national arms, with every exulting shout of victory raised by the slave-holding rebels, I have implored the imperilled nation to unchain against her foes her powerful black hand," cried Frederick Douglass. Charles Sumner and Samuel Pomeroy echoed him in the Senate, and Horace Greeley in the press. Carl Schurz, minister to Spain, came across the ocean: "Mr. President, all Europe is looking. . . ." And now at last that black hand was unchained, a thousand pairs of black hands. But they could not relax.

In this battle, and in what was left of the war, they would have much to contradict and more to affirm. They would have to contradict all those charges made against them: that they would not fight, for "at a crack of Old Master's whip" they would flee the field in abject terror; that even were they endowed with courage they were too ignorant to learn the arts of combat; that this was, after all, "the white man's country and the white man's war"— charges that Lincoln himself seemed to believe sufficiently to keep black men from battle. Now by their conduct in this engagement they would have to prove that they possessed all those qualities—confidence, resolution, and valor —summed up in the word "manhood." They would have to affirm their faith that the ultimate mission of this war was not only to save the Union but to free the slaves. They would have to vindicate their belief that "liberty won only by white men would lose half its lustre."

Gathered squatting and sitting in little knots to themselves, some distance from the seasoned white troops that had occupied the southern end of Morris Island for several days and that were also to be committed to this battle, the men of the 54th were not aware of the approach of their brigade commander. But suddenly a low-pitched voice called out, "Men! Men of the 54th!" They scrambled up quickly, tensely, snatching rifles and fixing bayonets, and pressed together just as General Strong, flanked by aides and orderlies, rode up. The lights of federal warships, bobbing at anchor in the channel, pulsated dimly through the drifting fog. The general clapped his white-gauntleted hands, making a sound like a pistol shot, but his voice was quiet when he spoke.

"Men of the 54th—free men. We will attack." He paused dramatically, and for a moment there was a silence as palpable as a knife thrust. His gaze swept the disordered press of men. "You will lead it," the general said. Then a cheer rose uncertainly, gathered strength, but never really swelled to the full, and years later a man of the regiment was to say that they were choked up with emotion.

With the barest gesture of salute, General Strong cantered away.

The emotion that choked up the cheers of the 54th may have been gratitude; it may have been pride; it may have been fear. It may have been all these and more, so many feelings so compacted that they could not be defined. The heart too often ravaged cannot defend itself. "I remember how it was," wrote a young man of the regiment to his father, and in the moment of knowing how it was he had wondered how many black men would have to purchase dignity with death. For he remembered also the mocks and taunts, the gibes of certain Northern Negroes grown cynical and bitter. "Sure *they* want you. They want you dead, sacrificial blacks on the altar of Union!" He remembered the jeers of not always hooligan whites, set to the cadence of a march, *the* march from camp in Massachusetts to Boston Harbor, thence shrilling to the hammering of an engine vessel, the *De Molay*, chugging past a thousand miles of terror-blasted shores:

> *In battle's wild commotion*
> *I won't at all object*
> *If a nigger should stop a bullet*
> *Coming for me direct.*
>
> *A nigger's just an ape-thing,*
> *A thing of no respect.*
> *If he should stop a Minié ball*
> *I shan't at all object.*

Lewis Douglass—the younger son of the Negro abolitionist Frederick Douglass, who with his brother Charles had been the first in the state of New York to enlist—remembered. But also he remembered his father's answer to those jeers. "Better even die than to live slaves. . . . The day dawns; the morning star is bright upon the horizon! The iron gate of our prison stands half open. One gallant rush . . . will fling it wide, and four millions of our brothers and sisters will march out to liberty." Lewis wrote to his sweetheart in faraway Syracuse, "I thought of it and felt better." But this was afterward.

Now, as the troops formed and moved forward over the hard-packed sand of the narrow causeway, no one felt good, and especially none of the men of the 54th. They had arrived on Morris Island only a couple of hours before sundown. They had had neither rest nor refreshment for two days. Moreover, a sudden severe thunderstorm had drenched them, and as they moved to the van their steaming uniforms weighed heavy as lead. There were six regiments in the 1st Brigade, commanded by General Strong, but since the plan was to commit them a regiment at a time the 54th was ordered up on the double so as to widen the distance between it and the supporting 6th Connecticut.

There was an air of suspense as they advanced the depth of a regiment. No gun spoke and no light shone from the fort less than four hundred yards ahead. Had Wagner been knocked out by the bombardment and evacuated? Soon they were almost within musket range, an excellent massed target against the fading sky and the tawny beach. Still nothing from the fort. Perhaps the rumor that went whispering sibilantly through the ranks was true. Perhaps in that hour of blackening rain and thunder the Confederates had scampered down the hidden sea face of the fort and escaped in small boats to Sumter.

But, indeed, the opposite had happened. Wagner had been heavily reinforced.

All at once the cry "Heads up!" rang out from the rear, and the column of moving men on the left pressed inward against their companions as a horseman went tearing by. There was no room for dispersion on the road between the sea and the marsh. Two more mounted men galloped past. The first was General George C. Strong. He was easily recognized by his white-gauntleted hands, with which he held the reins high and loose. It was not certain who the others were, but word came back that one was General Gilmore himself. A moment or two more and the troops were ordered to halt. They did not have long to wait. General Strong's voice spoke out. The forward men could hear well enough, but the breeze, blowing stiffly now, whipped the voice before it reached the rear, and the men back there caught only drifting tatters of it.

"Free men . . . 54th . . ." The general first expressed his regret for sending them into battle without food or rest, but ". . . hour has struck. Men . . . tonight for freedom . . ." It was the kind of pre-battle address fashionable since the days of the Caesars. It was the siren voice of glory "luring them to the bloody and inhospitable trenches" of Wagner. A little more of this and then the three horsemen, General Strong the last, rode back down the line, but slowly, fixing the troops with steady gaze, and all three holding salute, their horses sidling with their heads toward the ranks.

But speechmaking was not yet over. Colonel Shaw, the regimental commander, stepped forward. He had been until recently a captain in the 2nd Massachusetts, and had fought at Winchester and Antietam. The commission for his new command had been carried to him like a votive offering by his father from Boston to Virginia. Ordinarily Shaw's manner was uncommonly impressive, but in the dusk before the battle, survivors said later, the man shone with "angelic light." And even if this was merely the normal glorification of the heroic dead, all sources are agreed that Robert Gould Shaw was an exceptional human being. Between him and his men flowed a strong tide of feeling. He gave them his patrician-bred understanding and sympathy; they gave him gratitude and their implicit faith. He was for them a symbol of what men—and black men too —could be; of what perhaps this war was fought to prove they could become once it was over. He was a talisman. As if to prove it, the skies, lowering and threatening since the storm, cleared and a few stars winked as Shaw stepped forth. A quite spontaneous cheer went up. The men leaned to hear him. They did not need to, for the breeze that had torn General Strong's voice to tatters had no power over Shaw's. It was bugle-clear and beautiful.

It took him only a minute to make his speech. He told them that much depended on this night's work. He reminded them that an act of the Confederate Congress made the Union's Negro soldiers outlaws, denied them the protection of the captured, and that as prisoners they might be sold into slavery, summarily shot, or hanged. The military design of the assault, he said, was to breach the defenses of Charleston. But was this all, or even the main? Not by any means. Lifting his drawn sword, the colonel pointed to the emblematic pennon, which none could read in the gloam. But they did not need to do this either, for they knew what that oblong of white silk bore—the figure of Liberty. The simple command "Forward!" rang out, and the mass took stride on the shelterless narrow strip of the flat.

Before they had gone forty paces, being now within musket range, the bastion front lit up from end to end with a sheet of running flame. It was a terrific shock, for the men half believed and half hoped that the bombardment had permanently silenced the Rebel guns, sealed up the approaches to the bombproof, and sent Taliaferro's forces skedaddling for the relative safety of Cumming's Point.

With that first blast, this was proved a delusion. Men dropped like ripened fruit in a windstorm. But in that instant glow of sulphurous light before the smoke and dust rolled out, Colonel Shaw saw his first objective—a place forward where the gourd-shaped island flared out before it narrowed to a neck of land on the tip of which blazed Wagner. Urging his men to it, Shaw loosened his ranks and charged them into that murderous hail of canister, grape, and musket ball. The screams of the wounded pierced the frightful din, but as if in eerie counterpoint the voice of a corporal named Payne kept shouting, "Liberty, boys!" and a moment later from farther down the line, "Freedom, boys!" Corporal Payne was everywhere at once. The ramparts of Wagner crackled and roared, spurting the blue flames of small arms and the reddish-yellow blasts of cannon. And as if this were not enough, a crash of artillery and a storm of solid shot thundered in from the left. The Confederate batteries on Sullivan's Island had opened up, and it was like sweeping a corridor with a broom of fire. Men fell in swaths: others pushed ahead.

Indeed, there was nothing else to do and no place else

to go but ahead. For now the Rebel guns at Cumming's Point and Sumter were lobbing shells onto the sandspit, plowing up the ground in the rear of the 54th and pinning down, at least temporarily, the supporting regiments. The wider ground on which Shaw had deployed his troops was completely plastered. Somewhere off on the seaward flank, but apparently in the path of fire, General Strong realized what the situation was and ordered a double-quick charge. He did not live to see it executed; nor could it have been executed. All the 54th could do was creep into a musketry fire that was as solid as a wall of steel. The rest of the 1st Brigade, consisting of five regiments, staggered in behind.

Almost every step produced confusion. No one knew the terrain in the dark. The regiments backing up the 54th got scrambled like eggs. Colonel Barton of the New Yorkers found himself in the midst of troops from Maine. His own men had gone on ahead, where they briefly occupied some rifle pits hastily dug for the assault of seven days before. When he did find his men they were coming back with their wounded. Meantime a company of Connecticut men had got bogged down in the marshes of Vincent's Creek off to the left and, caught in the heaviest fire from Sullivan's Island, were churned to bloody mincemeat in the mud. The 2nd Brigade came in under Colonel Putnam, who kept shouting, "Forward! Forward!" and, losing his men, himself advanced so swiftly as to overtake the rear of the 54th. The hailstorm did not slacken. The din was "like a million locomotives straining on a grade." There were now three thousand men caught on a spot of land three hundred yards at its widest. Two thousand more were to come. But none of them, except those who died, stayed for long.

It seems impossible that no one on the Union side knew about the ditch. Eight days before, on July 10, the Union landing on Morris Island had been effected, and that same day an attack was pushed within six hundred yards of the fort, but the position was untenable. On July 11, General Gilmore's dispatch to General Halleck noted: "We now hold all the Island except about one mile on the north end, which includes Fort Wagner, and a battery at Cumming's Point. . . ." On the twelfth a parallel was commenced for the emplacement of siege guns a thousand yards from Wagner, and other measures were taken preliminary to the assault, timed for six days later. Since it is impossible to conceive that among these measures was none for scouting and reconnoitering the terrain, it must be supposed that in the furious, milling confusion of the infantry attack the ditch was forgotten.

There it was, several feet wide and filled with four feet of water. The glacis of the fort sloped down to it, and the glacis was Colonel Shaw's next objective. Only the musketry and grenades of the enemy could reach here. But the going was tough. The sandy slope was pitted from the bombardment, and it was dark, and darkness was the doom of this attack. With Shaw at its crest, the first wave of the 54th plunged headlong into the unseen ditch. A few men panicked and drowned, but most scrambled out, shouted warnings to those who followed, and started up the glacis. Musket fire hissed into them. Grenades screamed down. Beyond the ditch, and halted by it in utmost confusion, a company of Maine men began firing on the slope, and Captain Luis Emilio, bringing up the rear of the Negro columns, shouted out, "Don't fire on us! We're the 54th!" But his shouts were ineffective. He ordered a retreat, and some of his men slid down the scarp and waded back across the ditch.

Meanwhile the brave or reckless Colonel Shaw and about ninety men, Corporal Payne and Sergeants Lewis Douglass and John Wall among them, had clawed their way to the top. A sudden blaze of calcium light revealed them mounted on the parapet. For a shocked moment the Confederates who saw them there stopped firing as if in awe, or in tribute to such daring. How could they have come up the glacis slope through that savage storm? Yet there they were, plainly to be seen in the blaze of light, their colonel waving his sword, and next to him the color sergeant, John Wall, carrying the flag. Both were hit at the instant Lewis Douglass' sword sheath was blown off him and he, uninjured, blasted back down the scarp. Wall staggered and dropped the flag, but the wounded Sergeant

Carney caught it and slid away. Colonel Shaw, however, toppled inside the fort, and some eighty of his "reckless and insane men," said General Taliaferro's report, "who seemed to insist upon immolation," jumped in after him. There they fought hand to hand around Shaw's lifeless body until every man of them was killed.

The assault on Fort Wagner was totally repulsed and over in an hour, but the Union forces did not retire completely. Captain Emilio gathered what was left of the 1st Brigade, dug in on a line seven hundred yards from the fort, and kept up a desultory and useless fire through half the night. Scattered elements of the 2nd Brigade fronted the enemy at other points. Until two o'clock in the morning they waited for the order to renew the attack, but it never came. The sand had drunk its fill of blood. In the morning, "as the sun rose and revealed our terrible losses, what a rich harvest Death had gathered during the short struggle!" Two thousand men had fallen. Five hundred and fifty-eight of these were officers and men of the first Negro regiment recruited in the free states. When in the morning a request was made for the body of Colonel Shaw, a Rebel officer sent back the reply, "We have buried him with his niggers."

2. A Question of Identity

A little while earlier a good many people, and perhaps a majority even in the North, would have snickered with gratification at this reply. Save only the abolitionists, few felt sympathy for the Negro, and even a considerable group of abolitionists led by William Lloyd Garrison had not wanted a war to free the slaves.

> To the flag we are pledged, all its foes we abhor,
> And we ain't for the nigger, but we are for the war.

But, indeed, enthusiasm for the flag and "union forever" soon drained off in the defeats of Bull Run, Fredericksburg, and Chancellorsville. Before the winter of 1861 ran out some Northern newspapers, like the Philadelphia *Age*, were complaining that the government had "plunged the

country into a costly war to help the undeserving Negro."
Horatio Seymour, governor of New York, Franklin Pierce,
New England-born and -bred ex-President of the United
States, and James Gordon Bennett, editor of the New York
Herald, expressed—and heatedly, too—the opinion that the
North had committed a "crime" against the South and that
it should be expiated by a peace that left undisturbed all
the prerogatives of the slave power.

In short, the great body of Northerners did not care to
fight for the freedom of Negroes. When the Emancipation
Proclamation made it clear that the issue of freedom was
joined with the issue of union, a crisis developed. It was
especially acute among the working-class whites, who, already in competition with free Negroes in the Northern
labor market, saw emancipation as the start of a tidal wave
of black men that would wash them out of the labor market entirely. The crisis swelled and burst in the spring of
the Proclamation year, when Lincoln signed a draft law
whose provisions made it virtually impossible for the common run of white men to escape war service. Infuriated,
they turned upon Negroes. They destroyed Negro property. They murdered a hundred Negroes in Cleveland. At
the very time when black soldiers were dying in droves at
Wagner, black men, women, and children were lying
butchered, shot, and roasted in the ashes of an orphanage
in New York.

The Negro's recruitment into the Union Army seems to
have increased the hostility. This was irony and paradox.
Negroes had fought and several thousands of them had
died in the war for American independence, and when the
victory in that war seemed about to be undone they fought
again and died in the War of 1812, when they were invited by the hot-eyed General Andrew Jackson "to share
in the perils and divide the glory" with their "white coun-
trymen." But their feeble identification both as Americans
and as men had been destroyed in the years between the
wars. It had been destroyed quite relentlessly by the economic and social imperatives of slavery, which, combining
with an abstruse metaphysic, made the declaration, "Negroes, sir, are brute beasts," sound reasonable. No one ex-

cept Negroes themselves and a few abolitionists seriously argued against this opinion, based as it was on the "scientific calculation" that the Negro was only three-fifths human. Thus as a matter of course he was excluded from the dispensation of the natural rights of man. Thus it seemed an abomination that his freedom should be a cause of war and a defilement of humanity that he himself should fight for it, or want to.

The same reasoning had produced in the South, the place of its origin, quite other results. It created the anachronistic spectacle of masters riding off to war with black body servants to squire them. It led to the impressment of slaves to do service for the Confederate cause in arsenal, mill, and factory; as cooks, teamsters, and ambulance attendants; as builders of roads, bridges, and fortifications. It produced legislative authorization (Tennessee, 1861) to enlist free Negroes in the Army of the Confederacy. And finally it led to the adoption of a resolution by the governors of North and South Carolina, Georgia, Alabama, and Mississippi to arm the slaves to fight for the perpetuation of their own slavery.

No Southerner pretended that this resolution failed of implementation because of a revulsion of Confederate sensibilities. The evidence is that it failed under the weight of a practical consideration. "God forbid that this Trojan horse should be introduced among us!" cried a member of the Confederate Congress. But in the last grim days of the war the Trojan horse was less fearful to contemplate than total defeat, and one no longer shilly-shallied over the meaning of a foggy passage in President Davis' message (1864) to Congress: "Should the alternative ever be presented of subjugation or the employment of the slave as soldier, there seems no reason to doubt what should then be our decision." The alternative presented itself, and there was no doubt, and on March 13, 1865, Davis signed an enactment to enlist slaves in the Rebel army.

In the established pattern of thinking and feeling about the Negro, this too was logical. And having come to this decision, if the South then wooed the slave, or tried to, with wine and song, parade and drum, to fight for the continuance of his vassalage, this was no more aberrant to Southern minds than the hostility to the Negro's fighting for union and freedom was to Northern minds. That is to say, not at all. Indeed, Northern and Southern minds were one in the pattern of reason—a pattern that, operating with equal effectiveness in both sections of the country, could not have been better devised to destroy the Negro's last thin ties to humanity and drive him to the verge of madness had this been the conscious intention.

It is no wonder that in their convention of 1863 free Negroes revived and debated in gloomy wretchedness the once damned question of immigration to Africa and South America. It is no wonder that one of their leaders cried out in weary anguish, "Who am I, God? And what?"

II. BORN FREE

1. Charleston Child

There were those of his contemporaries who said that
Daniel Payne was always crying out to God. It was a habit
that he had acquired early, even perhaps by inheritance
from that Grandfather *Paine* who had fought at Bunker
Hill, whose twisted, thickened, gray-black likeness can be
seen in Trumbull's painting of that battle, and who had a
reputation for eccentricity—"he walked and talked with
God"—as well as character. The reputation was not un-
earned. Dismayed or angered by the order of General
Gates discharging black men from the Continental Army,
Paine, a free man, shipped for Virginia in the 1780s. Here
he changed the spelling of his name, married a free woman,
and begot a son called London.

By this time there were two hundred thousand slaves in
Virginia, and the state was a notorious slave-trading center. But from the beginning slavery there had created
problems and raised grave questions of control, and the
consciences of the best men of the land were never at peace
with it. Negro rebellion flared with terrifying regularity.
Miscegenation was producing a "mongrel race, unamenable
to reason and proper rearing alike." In the 1750s heavy
duties had been imposed upon slave importation, but the
furious greed of traders would not be denied, and the
duties were overridden. The liberalism for which Virginia
colonial life was said to be distinguished dried up, and
aristocratic sensibilities hardened under the scab of economic necessity. But they were set in flux again by the
humanistic ardor that boiled up in the 1770s. Virginia
aristocrats took the lead in the revolutionary struggle. They
framed the state constitution of 1776: ". . . all men are

by nature equally free and independent, and have certain inherent rights . . . namely, the enjoyment of life and liberty. . . ."

This was not all hollow sentiment. Anti-slavery societies had sprung up and were active everywhere during and just after the Revolution. In Virginia alone ten thousand slaves were emancipated, and Patrick Henry was moved to write a friend: "Is it not amazing, that at a time when the rights of Humanity are defined and understood with precision in a Country above all others fond of Liberty: that in such an Age and such a Country, we find Men, professing a Religion the most humane, mild, meek, gentle and generous, adopting a Principle as repugnant to humanity. . . . Would anyone believe that I am Master of Slaves of my own purchase!"

Like Henry, other liberal aristocrats were stung by the inconsistency—stung sufficiently hard to put through a law prohibiting the slave trade in Virginia. But slave traders were resourceful enough to get around the law. They bought slaves directly from trim "Maryland runners, the fastest vessels that ever sailed the African coast," and, posing as "gentlemen removing with their slaves to other parts," brought them into Virginia without molestation and sold them south. They bred slaves too, but this took time and money. And what was a nigger good for if he was not a slave? The question was not rhetorical. Traders kidnaped free Negroes, among them London Payne.

There is not much of a record of London Payne: cloudy dates haze over what there is, and the secondhand memory of a four-year-old across a span of sixty years is necessarily taken on trust. But Daniel Payne's testimony is that his father was still a "child" when he was kidnaped and sold south to Charleston—to a house and sign painter who was probably a "kindly" man. For though the sign painter's professional interest may have made it expedient for him to teach London to read and letter, mere expediency cannot account for letting London join an association of free Negroes called the Brown Fellowship Society and attend the midweek meetings in the newly founded African Methodist Church, where, as often as not after 1809–10, a bitter, burning ex-slave named Denmark Vesey identified the Negro race with the ancient Israelites and turned Holy Scripture to the purposes of rebellion. Expediency did not require that London Payne be let to hire out his spare time, so that his savings mounted year by year. Or perhaps he was helped by the free half-Indian woman—the mother-to-be of Daniel—he met and married. At any rate London bought his freedom for a thousand dollars the year he came of age.

So Daniel was born free on February 24, 1811, and the date was duly recorded in the metal-clasped family Bible. He was only four when his father died, and just turning eight when his mother also passed away. His memory was of having learned his letters before their deaths. His memory was of being carried on his father's shoulders from the house on Swinton Lane and along the purpling evening streets to church. He remembered his mother striding just a half a step behind, the better to hum in London's ear and help him carry the tune of the hymn he would be singing. Daniel himself could never sing a note, but in later years he was to compose religious verse, being instrumental music and robed choirs to the services of the African Methodist Episcopal Church, and to write the lyrics for sacred hymns, some of which the Church still sings today.

After the death of his parents the days grew grim in Charleston, as everywhere in the Southern seaboard states. The economic crisis brought on by the Embargo and Non-Importation acts and the new war with Britain in 1812 had just appreciably lessened when natural disasters aggravated it again. Drought one year, rain and flood the next marched in implacable alternation through the seaboard states from 1815 to 1819. In South Carolina indigo plantations failed. Rice fields reverted to swamps. Cotton had all but exhausted the soil. The day was fast approaching when Robert Hayne, a South Carolina senator, would testify, "If we fly from the city to the country, what do we behold? Fields abandoned; agriculture drooping; our slaves . . . working harder and faring worse; the planter striving with unavailing efforts to avert the ruin which is before him."

Ruin had already overcome many. In 1820 depression

rode Charleston itself like an incubus. Merchants went bankrupt. Crop loans were foreclosed. Shipyards shut down. A noticeable number of the sea-front houses that used to sing and purl with music and the gaiety of guests were boarded up and silent, and their mortgaged owners gone to live permanently in the country, there to brood over the sterile fields and the thinning ranks of slaves, and to breed into a new generation of their kind that passionate pride and contempt and resistless will to domination that, grown desperate, carried it gleefully into a hopeless war. Whites of another sort turned their faces west.

Meantime slaves were restless and defiant too, as ever in periods of economic distress, when their provisions were cut to the "scurvy sickness" level, or they were "run off," or leased out, or—fate most dreaded—sold down the river —when, in short, the master's only other option was to "be ruined to save the wretches." In the decade 1810–20 and for some time thereafter not many masters in the seaboard states could save the "wretches," whose subterranean discontent broke the surface here and there like so many erupting volcanoes: Maryland in 1811; Virginia in 1810, '11, '13; North Carolina in 1814, '15; South Carolina in 1817 and again in 1819.

This last was the year Daniel Payne, age eight, was taken to live with a Mrs. Elizabeth Holloway, who very shortly besought the Brown Fellowship Society "for aid for the helpless orphan." Aid came and was later supplemented from another source. The Minor Moralist Society was a group of free Negroes organized to provide for the material needs of colored orphans. It also ran a school, and Daniel went to it. He acquired reading, writing, and arithmetic, as well as the hunger for a knowledge no man has ever found in books alone—"Who am I, God?" Payne was past fifty when he thus addressed the Almighty, but even later he declared that he was still seeking knowledge of himself, "which, next to knowledge of God, is hardest to acquire."

But Payne's book learning was interrupted early. It was interrupted by one of those rebellious incidents in consequence of which slaveholders "never lay down to sleep

without a brace of pistols at their side," and in consequence of which the South Carolina Supreme Court held
that "A free African population is a curse. . . . This race,
however conducive they may be in a state of slavery, in a
state of freedom and in the midst of a civilized community
. . . become corruptors of slaves." And by 1822 hundreds
of slaves in Charleston and the surrounding forty miles
had been corrupted by Denmark Vesey. If rebellion was
a spreading disease—and it seemed to be—Payne's youth
alone saved him from infection. He knew Vesey well, and
Morris Brown, then Payne's "spiritual guardian" and later
his devoted friend, was Vesey's "secret counsellor."

But secret counsel was not enough to insure the success
of Vesey's ambitious plan. It had been preparing in his
head for twenty years and outside it for two. Six companies
of slaves, each under carefully selected leaders, were to be
formed. One company was to seize the arsenal in Meeting
Street, another the guardhouse, another the post at Cannon's Bridge, another Bennett's Mill, a fifth Bulkley's
farm, and the sixth was to be on orders at Vesey's house.
The day was to be a Sunday in the summer, for Sunday
crowds of Negroes on the streets of Charleston were no
unusual sight, and in the summer many whites left the city
for resorts. About five thousand Negroes, slave and free,
were involved. A few had guns, but mostly they were
armed with pikes and bayonets and daggers, which Mingo
Harth, a blacksmith co-conspirator, had forged in many
midnights. As Vesey paraphrased it from Holy Writ, the
purpose was to destroy "utterly all that was in the city,
both man and woman, young and old . . . with the edge
of the sword." Letters had been sent to the black President of the new black republic, Santo Domingo, describing
the sufferings of Negro slaves and asking aid in the enterprise.

The operation was to begin at midnight, June 16. In
mid-May the leaders began passing the word down to sub-
leaders. One of the latter, a William Paul, had more will
than wit. He was anxious to swell his corps of men. Unaware of Vesey's interdiction against house slaves, whom
he distrusted more than "drunkards and loose-tongues,"

Paul spoke to one Devany, the cook in the Prioleau household. Devany's genius was "culinary, not revolutionary," and he promptly informed his master. This was on May 25. Moving furtively so as to arouse neither the alarm of the whites nor the suspicions of the uncaught insurgents, the authorities arrested Devany and Paul. Devany knew little, and for two weeks Paul refused to talk. But red-hot copper wires driven under the nails of hand and foot will draw words from any mouth. By June 14, carried forward with all the secrecy circumstances allowed, "extensive and efficient preparations had been made for the safety and protection of the city," reported Governor Bennet, three of whose slaves were among the rebels shortly to be hanged.

Informed by grapevine of what was afoot, the companies did not rendezvous—nor, strangely, did their leaders take advantage of the avenues of escape still open to them, though they knew that arrests were being made with little discrimination. A fit of petulance, a muttered word, a sullen look, a fancied discourtesy remembered from five years before was enough to bring arrest. On June 28, though the authorities were not sure that all the rebel leaders were in their hands, trials were begun. They were over by July 9. Thirty-seven Negroes were executed, forty-three transported, and forty-eight, found guilty of being privy, were publicly lashed and discharged. If this was all, a reporter for the New York *Commercial Advertiser* did not believe it. After commenting that Charleston was getting rid of its free black population "without the aid of the Colonization Society," he reported on August 5 that "there are about fifty more in confinement . . . who will probably be strung up with as little ceremony as they string up fish in the Fulton Market."

2. And "Every Distinction"

It was not necessary for the full extent of the conspiracy to be revealed to obtain the results that followed. Events had always given substance to the fear of slave conspiracies, and the specifics against fear were the very stuff of which revolts were made. Now more specifics were proposed. They make a catalogue that sounds, but was not, fantastic. It was proposed that itinerant preachers, those "apostolic vagabonds who, with the sacred volume of God in one hand, breathing peace to the whole family of man, scatter at the same time with the other the firebrands of discord and destruction . . . among our Negroes," be found out and dispersed. It was proposed that Negroes not be allowed to "wear any silks, satins, crepes, lace, or muslin," for "every distinction should be created among whites and Negroes, calculated to make the latter feel the superiority of the former." It was proposed that the number of Negro mechanics be limited, since many of the leaders of the conspiracy were mechanics, and that the hiring out of free time should end. It was proposed that the prohibitions against slaves owning property be erected against free Negroes also. It was observed that many of the late leaders of the conspiracy could read and write, and it was concluded that literate Negroes were dangerous. Negroes, therefore, slave and free, should be prevented from learning to read and write.

But proposals were not enough. Portentous logic said that laws must follow, and they did—immediately. Hereafter conspiracy to rebel was punishable by "death without benefit of clergy." It was decreed that slaves could no longer hire out in spare time. The Negro Seaman's Act provided that sailors entering Charleston Harbor be arrested and held until their vessels sailed again. All other free Negroes entering Charleston did so under penalty of prison or the auction block. To supplement an older statute that taxed free non-native Negroes fifty dollars a year, a new law required all free Negroes above fifteen years of age to have some respectable white person as guardian, and any who failed to maintain the reputation vouched for by his guardian would be sold forthwith into slavery. Negroes were denied the right of assembly, and this drove their churches underground. It was ruled a felony to teach, or permit to be taught, reading and writing to any Negro, and this closed down Negro schools.

And to enforce these laws? By the winter of 1823,

Charleston had become an armed camp. Frederick Olmsted, later to journey there, wrote: "Police machinery such as you never find in towns under free government: citadels, sentries, passports, grapeshotted cannon, and daily public whipping of the subjects for accidental infractions of police ceremonies. I happened myself to see more direct expression of tyranny in a single day and night in Charleston, than at Naples for a week . . . there is . . . an armed force, with a military organization, which is invested with more arbitrary and cruel power than any police state in Europe."

3. *Preceptor's Farewell*

Daniel Payne, still short of his teens, did not understand all that was going on in 1822–23. The lot of a free Negro orphan child was somewhat harder than the lot of a slave child separated from his parents. Without blood relatives, cut loose from the ties that normally belong to childhood, Payne was projected into a dark, disorganized, and complicated world of fear and violence. The woman to whom he had first been sent, Mrs. Holloway, was dead. So too was Mrs. Sarah Bordeaux, an "aunt" more by courtesy than kin. Among other adults of his acquaintance, Vesey, Gullah Jack, and Monday Gell were dead by hanging. Thomas Bonneau, who had taught Payne the first two books of Euclid, was unaccounted for, simply vanished without a trace. Thinking it best to get out before it was discovered that he had encouraged the conspirators, the leader of the congregation of free blacks, "Elder" Morris Brown, fled north to Philadelphia, there shortly to become a bishop in the infant African Methodist Episcopal Church. The Church, the Brown Fellowship Society, and the Minor Moralist Society were disrupted or suppressed. The free Negroes of Charleston—collectively "a curse to any country" and an "evil exactly proportional to the numbers of such population"—lived in a wilderness of laws and regulations to which no light of hope or reason seemed able to penetrate.

In this violent disorganization of his life, and as much

from natural inclination as from imitative habit, young
Payne turned to God with an intensity of religious passion
most unusual in a boy of twelve. It was a period of seeking, he said later. The group worship—the singing, the
prayers, and the testimonies—and the formalisms of the
Church, however erratically practiced, had been a smooth
and well-trod highway direct to heaven, and most of the
people he had known marched along it. But now the road
had disappeared overnight, by terrifying magic, and he
was alone in a trackless desolation, he must find his way
alone. He made solitary prayers. From his seventh or
eighth year, sitting with his elders in weekly religious
meetings, he had "sometimes felt the spirit of God moving" through his heart. Now he implored the spirit to take
up permanent residence there.

At this time he was apprenticed to a carpenter and had
a tiny back room on the ground floor of a house just off
Swinton Lane. His room gave onto a patch of garden, ragged with a few flowers, grassless under a great magnolia
tree, and here at night he used to pray. But nothing happened for a long time. When at last something did happen, it was not in the garden, or at night. "Between twelve
and one o'clock one day, I was in my humble chamber
pouring out my prayers to the listening ears of my Saviour,
when I felt as if the hands of a man were pressing my two
shoulders and a voice speaking within my soul saying, 'I
have set thee apart to educate thyself that thou might be
an educator to thy people.'"

If this was a mystical experience, Payne nowhere re-
cords having another. Perhaps he did not need another.
This one he took for truth and, God's voice or not, Payne
gave it an obedience that, except in one moment of extreme discouragement, never slackened. For the next six
years, until he was eighteen, he lived like the ascetic he
basically was. Now and then he found a teacher courageous
enough to risk prison to help him, but mostly he taught
himself. He had advanced far enough in the carpenter's
trade to make simple things such as clotheshorses, benches,
and stools, and these he peddled from door to door on
Saturday afternoons. Other days he had fairly regular em-

ployment as a carpenter's helper. Nights after a supper of roasted sweet potato, or perhaps "a dish of black-eye peas boiled to a mush with a piece of fat," or, on a good night, "a scrap of ham or chicken" pilfered from the white folks' table by a slave woman who befriended him, Payne studied until midnight, slept until four, and studied again until six. He committed *Murray's Primary Grammar* to memory. He studied the *Columbian Orator*, as Frederick Douglass was to do in a few years, and pored over the *Self-Interpretating Bible*, whose Scotch author, the Reverend John Brown, noted in the preface his unaided conquest of Latin and Greek. Payne also studied Latin and Greek. Books were hard to come by legitimately: Payne "found" some and "borrowed" others. He studied geography, botany, zoology.

Meantime the lid of repression clamped on the brisk boiling up of slavery in 1822–23 was eased off a little. Another pot was on the fire. The tariff question of 1816 and 1824 began to simmer again in 1827. It gave off a smell offensive to Southerners, and particularly to John C. Calhoun, the most influential South Carolinian. For the better protection of his political career, he had recently abandoned his federalist views. Tariff was now a national issue, and slavery—not yet raised to that "bad eminence" by the organized agitation of "crack-brained abolitionists" and the presidential ambitions of Calhoun—was nothing compared to it. In 1828, when the "Tariff of Abominations" was passed, the North-South seam running down the back of the nation was strained almost to splitting.

Vice-President Calhoun represented the extremist view. He was for nullification and secession. Other men, including the governor of South Carolina, spoke more loudly about "the alarming extent to which the Federal Judiciary and Congress have gone toward establishing a great and consolidated government subversive of the rights of the States," but none had Calhoun's steely ambition. Senator George McDuffie might shout about resorting to arms to restore the "dignity of the South," but he did not have Calhoun's dogged, calculating, though disingenuous hate. And Charles Pinckney might declare that "the Constitution is degraded [by the tariff] to destroy one [the South] and support the other [the North]," but only Calhoun's tongue and only Calhoun's ambition and hatred were equal to annealing South Carolina, and with it the whole South, to the issue of secession.

If slavery was made an element in this issue by virtue of the first move to petition Congress to abolish it in the District of Columbia in 1828, the fact was temporarily overlooked. And so too were the slaves.

Thus it was no wonder that the Methodists also should be ignored, and that they should take advantage of it. Though the high fever of abolition had abated in them since the death of Wesley, they were still subject to "fits of the humanitarian sickness," and they still had their proselytizing zeal. They believed and said—and very persuasively, too—that the neglect of the spiritual needs of the slaves was a reflection on slaveholders. What a nuisance they made of themselves deploring the absence of suitable opportunities for giving their "inferior brethren" a Christian education and improving thereby their souls! In the midst of the congressional uproar upon which most Southern attentions were focused, one of these Methodists went quietly about his ordained business of "adapting and teaching Christian truth to the condition of persons having a humble intellect and a limited range of knowledge."

But Bishop William Capers was no emancipationist. It was no part of his idea to teach Negroes to read and write. Though he set up missions and persuaded some masters to send their slaves to them, he made it very clear that instruction would be oral, "by constant and patient reiteration," and based on biblical injunction: "Our heavenly Father commands that you, who are servants, should 'be obedient to them that are your masters according to the flesh.' . . . As you ought to understand well what is the will of God respecting you, I will read to you again this part of the Bible. 'Servants, be obedient . . .'"

Bishop Capers' mission class did not promise much, but it allowed for a certain freedom of social intercourse that Payne needed. It brought him in contact with Samuel

Weston, who gave more and other instruction than the bishop intended. Weston was the sort of Southern white man who was apotheosized in John G. Fee, who, disowned by his slaveholding family and mobbed twenty-two times for his anti-slavery views, went on to found Berea College for the education of both whites and Negroes.

Bishop Capers' dedication to his mission classes and their "beneficent" Christian influence contributed to a relaxation of the whites' fear and vigilance and made it possible for the free Negroes of Charleston to mend and patch their torn group life. For two or three years Daniel Payne attended the Cumberland Church mission class. Then at eighteen he opened a school of his own and started the work he believed God had called him to do.

It was not easy then, or ever. The first year his pupils were three freeborn children and three adult slaves. The schoolroom was in a building owned by a prosperous freeman on Tradd Street, and though Caesar Wright gave the use of it rent-free, the fifty cents a month Payne charged each pupil was scarcely enough to keep the place warm in winter. The teacher was constantly pressed for subsistence. He dressed in castoff clothing. A slave pupil brought food as often as she could manage to steal it. When Payne closed the term in May, he was tempted by an opportunity to go to the West Indies with a white man who wanted a free, intelligent Negro servant.

> *There's the proposition. Well, boy, damnit, what do you say?*
> *I would like to pray, sir.*
> *Pray if you must, but, damnit, the experience will be worth more than wages. Goddamnit, boy——*
> *You are too profane, sir.*

Payne had sixty pupils, mostly freeborn children, when he opened for the second term in the autumn of 1830. Wright's room was now too small, and Robert Howard, another free Negro, built a suitable shed in the rear of his yard on Anson Street. Here Payne kept school for the next five years. He taught grammar, arithmetic, geography, and the elements of zoology. He studied. He purchased books from friendly itinerant canvassers and, sub rosa, through Samuel Weston. Local bookstores would sell Negroes nothing. He picked herbs, shrubs, and flowers and studied them. He caught small animals, fish, and insects, examined their structures, and afterward frequently cooked and ate them. Worms, toads, and snakes he refused to eat. Much of what he did he recorded in a journal he kept from time to time.

"I bought a live alligator, made one of my pupils provoke him to bite, and whenever he opened his mouth, I discharged a load of shot from a small pistol down his throat. As soon as he was stunned, I threw him on his back, cut his throat, ripped his chest, hung him up, and studied his viscera till they ceased to move."

But an end to all this, never more than an arm's length away, was now at hand, and the hand grew tight with apprehension. Every wind brought the clamor of new alarms. In 1830 there appeared almost simultaneously in a half dozen places in the South copies of an inflammatory pamphlet addressed to "the colored citizens of the world, but in particular and very expressly to those of the United States," by a free Negro named David Walker. The following summer in Virginia Nat Turner's rebellion, thought to have been touched off by Walker's *Appeal*, raged through two bloody nights and days and brought "death in the most horrid forms" to sixty white men, women, and children. It required the mobilized military of three states to put it down. William L. Garrison founded the *Liberator* in Boston in 1831. The next year he declared that "no truth is more self-evident than that moral power, like physical, must be consolidated to be efficient." Issues of the *Liberator* mysteriously turned up in the South.

Aroused, and indeed already leaping to the first pitch of madness, the citizens of Charleston broke into the local post office to search for anti-slavery propaganda. "It will fall into the hands of niggers!" and too many Negroes could read and write. But hereafter the new South Carolina law of 1835 said, "If any free person of color or slave shall keep any school or other place of instruction for teaching any slave or free person to read or write, such free person of color shall be liable to the same fine, imprisonment, and corporal punishment as is by this act imposed and inflicted. . . ."

The long night had come. Payne closed his school. He was twenty-four, and old beyond his years. His yellow-brown, cadaverous face, under the taut skin of which the skeleton showed like brittle filigree, and his wasted-looking frame gave him the appearance of a graveyard thing. But behind his steel-rimmed glasses his eyes burned. He was full of obscure intricacies. To his students he addressed a poem, *Preceptor's Farewell*.

> *Hate sin; love God; religion be your prize;*
> *Her laws obeyed will surely make you wise,*
> *Secure you from the ruin of the vain,*
> *And save your souls from everlasting pain.*
> *O, fare you well for whom my bosom glows*
> *With ardent love, which Christ my Saviour knows!*
> *'Twas for your good I labored night and day;*
> *For you I wept and now for you I pray.*
>
> *And I! O whither shall your tutor fly?*
> *Guide thou my feet, great Sovereign of the sky.*
> *A useful life by sacred wisdom crowned,*
> *Is all I ask, let weal or woe abound!*

Wither indeed?

III. BORN SLAVE

1. *To Be Free*

The very presence of free Negroes was anathema to the slaveholding South, where, on the word of Charles Van Evrie, "Free negroism [is] not a condition . . . which the higher law of nature grants. . . . There are then only two possible conditions for the Negro—isolation or juxtaposition with the white man—African heathenism or subordination to a master. . . ." Free Negroes were "a dangerous anomaly," a "threat to the established and natural order of our society," and "an incubus upon the land." And an incubus must be exorcised by the mighty conjurations of *lex scripta, non scripta,* and *talionis.*

Thus in South Carolina, as elsewhere in the South, the free Negro was allowed very little initiative. He could not move into the next county, where, haply, there might be work. In his own county he could not engage in any occupation that required reading and writing. He could not learn or engage in certain trades, such as brewing. He could not buy or sell brew made by others. He could purchase nothing on credit. He could not vote. Free Negroes could not testify against white men or protect themselves by carrying or possessing firearms. In conformity to the opinion expressed (in 1832) by the South Carolina Court of Appeals that free Negroes "ought by law be compelled to demean themselves as inferiors, from whom submission and respect to the whites . . . is demanded," they could not even carry canes. On the other hand, the colored freeman had to carry a certificate of freedom or risk being taken up and sold, though his certificate did not permit him to join "lyceums, lodges, fire companies, or literary, moral or charitable societies." Indeed, the distinction be-

tween slave and black freeman was sometimes so slight
as to be indiscernible.

But if free Negroes seemed a dangerous anomaly to
many in the South, they also seemed to some in the North
a threat to society. A contributor to *Niles' Register* was
not alone in believing that free Negroes were "a species of
population not acceptable" to the people of Indiana, "nor
indeed to any other, whether free or slave-holding, for they
cannot rise and become like other men . . . but must always remain a degraded and inferior class of persons without the hope of much bettering their conditions."

That was written in 1818, when the number of free
Negroes in the North was relatively small. By the 1830s
the number had grown to two hundred thousand, an increase of 82 per cent, and there were highly visible concen-
trations of Negroes in Philadelphia, New York, and Boston, and west in Cincinnati. Here the English actress
Fanny Kemble, embittered and grown restless on her husband's Georgia plantation, saw them and reported in her
journal: "They are not slaves indeed, but they are pariahs,
debarred from every fellowship save with their own
despised race, scorned by the lowest ruffians. . . . They
are free, certainly, but they are also degraded, the off-scum
and the off-scouring of the very dregs of your society."

It was a society—in the late thirties and all through the
forties—daily burdened with new problems. The industrial
revolution was happening to America. Immigration was
happening. Urbanization was happening. Migration westward was happening. Touched off by the flaming words of
Garrison and blown upon by the timeless winds of social
reform, abolition fires were roaring to a blaze. That ab-
straction known, then and now, as the "American way of
life" was suffering changes of such profundity that the
American mind could not fathom them. Having subcon-
sciously adopted the German philosopher Herder's rosy
conception that a nationality is "a plant of nature . . . one
nationality with one national character," Americans had
achieved by the 1830s a fancied homogeneity of character
as stable as England's. It was a character molded and supported by three extrinsics: the Protestant faith, the desig-

nation Caucasian, and political freedom. Combined, these made "Anglo-Americans" who, in subliminal expectation of the fulfillment of De Tocqueville's prophecy, "alone will cover the immense space . . . extending from the coasts of the Atlantic to those of the Pacific."

But that homogeneity, as well as the prophecy, was threatened, and if this was for the metaphysicists and the population theorists to worry about, the fabled man in the street had his worries too. What worried and alarmed him was the threat to his economic well-being. This was personal, this was real. In the face of it there began to develop one of those periodic blights of Northern grass-roots idealism that, temporarily, made the poet Bryant's words sound ironic:

> There's freedom at thy gates and rest
> For Earth's down-trodden and oppressed,
> A shelter for the hunted head,
> For the starved laborer toil and bread.

Native-born Americans in the North resented the black freemen, who were certainly among the "Earth's down-trodden and oppressed." Thus in 1834 the *American Sentinel,* a New Jersey paper, declared that the state was "literally overrun with blacks, driven by the violence of an infuriated mob from their homes and property in Philadelphia . . . the first indication of a permanent residence [here] should, and we feel confident will, call forth rigid enforcement of the statute against admission of blacks into our boundaries." But this was far from the only statute. Across the river in Pennsylvania, and in Ohio, Illinois, Indiana, and Michigan, Negroes were denied the free franchise, were ruled vagrants on the slightest pretext, and were subject to penalties, in some cases even enslavement, "harsher than those imposed upon white people guilty of the same crimes." Up in Massachusetts itself the abolitionists grew mute with suspense and confusion while the state legislature debated a bill forbidding admission and residence to Negroes.

But neither council chamber nor court of law was the arena in which the common native-born Northern workman chose to fight his battles. He chose the labor hiring hall. He chose the street. In one he waged a war of attrition; in the other, battles of blood. Trade unions, which since the 1790s had been slowly gaining effectiveness, proscribed Negroes for the silliest of reasons: Negroes depressed wages. They could not find apprenticeships in industry. The carpenters of Philadelphia, the shoemakers of Boston, and the ship caulkers of New Bedford and New York said, "No work for niggers," and when this was ineffectual, as it sometimes was in a labor market beginning to grow cheap from oversupply, Northern workmen went into the streets with club and torch and gun. They did this in Philadelphia in 1834, as we have seen, and that same year in New York, and again in '35, '36, and '39, and in Boston, as in the West, periodically. Whereas in Philadelphia in 1820 a decided majority of the artisans were Negroes, fifteen years later only 350 of the 11,500 Negroes were employed in the skilled trades. In New York, 2386 of 3237 were common laborers or domestic servants. In Boston in 1850, when the working Negro population numbered 935, all save 46 "barbers and hairdressers" were laborers and house servants.

And even these jobs were hard to find and harder to keep when the Irish, and to a lesser degree the Germans, started coming in the 1830s. Mostly peasants who had grown weary of peasantry, the Irish swarmed in the Northern cities, where they too met opposition from the native-born. Though "street fights between natives and foreigners were common occurrences," and "Catholic convents and churches, and German *Turnverein* headquarters were sometimes attacked and destroyed," the enmity was not altogether cultural. It was also—and principally—economic. The Irish and German workers competed with native mechanics who employed against them the weapons already proved against the Negro. The immigrants were left out of labor unions. Natives refused to work with the "dirty foreigners." Forced into digging, ditching, and docking, while their women went into "service," the Irish accepted lower wages than even the Negroes and in many places forced the latter out of jobs.

In these circumstances, without any place in the economic and political order, and without any dependable means of support, Negroes in the North began to be credited with those attributes of character that the white South was busily fashioning for the defense of slavery everywhere—namely, cunning and ignorance, laziness and prodigality, mendacity and lechery, rowdyism and criminality: in short, beasts. These attributes were to constitute a race concept of such durability that a century of time and change would not entirely obliterate it. If the concept was embraced by the mind in the performance of its simplest function, rationalization, it must nevertheless be remarked that even the simplest minds do not rationalize from nothing.

And there were the Negroes, many of them fugitives from slavery, used to dependence, drained of initiative by the meagerness of rewards, public charges. There they were, proliferating in slums spreading through the waterfront districts of Cincinnati and Philadelphia, crowding each other in the fetid alleys and dead-end streets of lower east side New York, and dying (as Phillis Wheatley, the first poet among them, died) of poverty, disease, and exposure in the teeming courts of Boston. And an undue proportion turned mean and vicious, creating problems for the police and shame for their upright brothers. They attracted attention. The jails, the poorhouses, and the prisons were crowded with them, and in 1836 a Senate committee predicted that the disparity of "Negro crime would be absolutely intolerable" within a few years. The very next year, with regard to Philadelphia, the committee seemed right. Thirty-six per cent of Philadelphia crime was committed by the colored 9 per cent of her population.

2. *Runaway*

Nevertheless, freedom was North, and when Frederick Augustus Washington Bailey escaped in 1838 he headed straight for it. He went boldly by train, pretending to be a sailor and flashing an official-looking paper with the

American eagle engraved on it. Arriving in New York with scarcely money enough to feed him for a week, he found refuge with David Ruggles, secretary of the New York Vigilance Committee, and the first Negro to edit an anti-slavery magazine. New York was not heaven, Ruggles warned him—and no man knew better than Ruggles—for slave catchers were everywhere. It would be wiser for Frederick to move on. But first he had better change his name: he had too much of it. So Bailey became Johnson, Frederick Johnson; and a few days later, when Anna Murray, the free woman he had met in Baltimore, joined him, this was the name he gave her as his wife.

But New Bedford, Massachusetts, where Ruggles sent them, had a superfluity of colored Johnsons, and Frederick soon discovered that there was much confusion in those very situations where confusion was most ruinous. Prospective employers sometimes could not tell one Johnson from another. The police were not always discriminating either. On one occasion an innocent Negro had been jailed in place of another bearing the same name. If all Negroes looked alike, as the popular expression had it, at least they did not have to sound alike. Frederick began to cultivate his speech very carefully and to increase his reading skill. After a few weeks he again changed his name, adopting Frederick Douglass. Sooner than anyone dreamed, the name was to acquire a special meaning.

Not even Douglass himself suspected that he was about to begin a career that would make his name one to be conjured with in the highest councils of the country, that would bring him scorn and hatred, but also great honor and high place and international fame.

It started modestly enough, for his simple wish was to fulfill the "sweet responsibilities" of freeman, husband, and father. There were proscriptions, but he took them in stride. Pro-slavery, anti-Negro doctrine had long since reached the shipyards and docks of coastal New England, where the slave trade once had thrived, and the section had its share of slavery sympathizers. Unable to get employment at his trade of ship caulking, Douglass did odd jobs. He "sawed wood, shoveled coal, dug cellars, moved rubbish from back yards," and worked as a stevedore. But already he had heard Garrison lecture in New Bedford, had subscribed to the *Liberator*, had become a member of an informal Negro group to discuss the issues of slavery. Already he had begun to "whisper into every sympathetic white ear" that all men must be free.

What he whispered to whites he spoke out bold and clear to Negroes when they gathered in their little church and schoolhouse on Second Street. They gathered rather often, for the little brotherhood of black men was close-knit, sensitive, and probably afraid. It embraced Douglass warmly. Douglass could read, he could write and, it was soon apparent, he could speak with force, logic, and clarity; could speak so well, indeed, that the African Methodist Church wanted to license him as a preacher.

Word of such a man got around quickly in New Bedford, and when it came to the ear of William Coffin, a white abolitionist, he knew what to do with it. In 1841, Douglass was asked to address an anti-slavery convention in Nantucket. His stomach quivered and his voice quaked, but Douglass made a better speech than he thought. Moreover, he was impressive to look at. A massive mulatto, he had a strong rather than a handsome face that, seasoned by only twenty-four years, was already so deeply lined as to excuse the beard he later felt constrained to wear. His hair was as long and coarse as a lion's mane and swept back from a broad forehead. He spoke that day without gestures, without oratorical flair, "simply, yet with deep feeling." John Collins, general agent of the Massachusetts Anti-Slavery Society, had advised him, "Give us the facts; we will take care of the philosophy."

And for a time, while he gained valuable experience as a full-time lecturer for the Anti-Slavery Society, Douglass let them take care of the philosophy. He saw no reason to question it. He had no intellectual sophistication by which to test the philosophy's beguiling simplicity. Indeed, it was for him much less a philosophy than a program, and the program was also simplicity itself: immediate emancipation. How this was to be accomplished and leave undisturbed the tangled growth of legal, economic, and social relationships that, million-rooted, burrowed into every area of Southern life he completely ignored. It did not occur to him to question Garrison's artless expedient of dissolving the constitutional Union. Slavery was an unmitigated evil, the Boston abolitionist had no doubt, and Douglass' job was to depict and portray that evil. "Tell your story, Frederick," Garrison admonished him. The story was argument enough, and if it were not, then "the very look and bearing of Douglass," James Russell Lowell said, was "an irresistible logic against the oppression of his race."

Perhaps it was. But it was exactly this that caused Douglass embarrassment. As he developed ease of manner, people began to doubt that he had ever been a slave. He did not look like the well-advertised notion of one. The habit of plantation speech being now entirely gone, he did not talk like one. He did not act like one. A shrewd Yankee listener summed up the general disbelief: "He don't tell us where he came from, what his master's name was, nor how he got away. Besides, he is educated and is in this a contradiction of all the facts we have concerning the ignorance of slaves."

Add to this the fact that Douglass himself was beginning to be bored with repeating his story. He was no longer a "brand-new" and curious fact. The time had come when he could not narrate the wrongs of slavery without denouncing them. And, finally, he was beginning to harbor cautious doubts of Garrison's absolute wisdom. "New views of the subject [of slavery]," he wrote later, "were being presented to my mind." Already he had been, though unwittingly, in one political campaign over the Dorr constitution in Rhode Island and found that he liked the passion and the sound, the intellectual thrust and parry. He was beginning to think that politics had its uses in the fight against slavery. His study of the federal Constitution led him to question whether that instrument was quite the "agreement with hell" that Garrison contended, and whether it *was* part of his duty as an abolitionist to advocate its destruction.

But if these were signs pointing a new direction, Douglass tried to ignore them. He liked Garrison, even revered him, and he was grateful to the Massachusetts Anti-Slavery

Society. He did not want to invite a break. What appeared to him to be of immediate moment was the reestablishment of his credibility as a bona fide escaped slave. After all, there were charlatans abroad. Although Douglass did not know it, some of his abolitionist friends connived in the publication of spurious narratives of "escaped slaves." Douglass was scrupulous to a fault, and he was also farsighted enough to see that lies, half-truths, and fraudulent claims could destroy the abolition movement. He determined to tell his whole story; to give dates and to name people and places, and to do this in writing. It was a risky decision, for it would mark him as "Bailey, runaway slave of Thomas Auld," and expose him to recapture by any slave catcher. His friends warned against it. But the *Narrative of the Life of Frederick Douglass* was published in May 1845. Three months later, partly to escape the consequences of his confession, Douglass sailed for England.

3. *North Star*

The signs Douglass tried not to read in 1843 could not be ignored when he returned to America in 1847. They blazed brighter, more legible, and more demanding all the time. The British Isles had given him the "room" he complained of lacking in the United States, and his experiences there had broadened his thinking and deepened his insights. His speeches in England, a London critic said, had revealed him as "the master of extraordinary information" on such topics as world peace, universal manhood suffrage, women's rights, and labor. Still he was first and foremost an abolitionist. George Thompson, an English friend, chided him time and again, saying that merely to preach Negro emancipation was not enough. And, anyway, how was it to be achieved?

The appetite for politics that Douglass had not satisfied in 1841 grew to a lust for political action while, on the other hand, Garrison's position was the exact one he had taken almost ten years before in organizing the New England Non-Resistance Society. Garrison and his followers would "voluntarily exclude themselves from every legislative and judicial body, and repudiate all human politics, worldly honors, and stations and authority." Garrison condemned servile rebellions as a moral abomination. Douglass was moving toward the opposite conviction, and in 1849, galvanized by the currents already shooting from John Brown's "divine madness," was able to say that he would "welcome the intelligence tomorrow, should it come, that the slaves had risen in the South, and the sable arms which had been engaged in beautifying and adorning the South were engaged in spreading death and destruction there."

Back in Massachusetts, Douglass again suffered from lack of scope, and it was more acute now. English friends had raised twenty-five hundred dollars for him to start his own paper, and he wanted to get on with it. George Thompson had made him aware of more than the need of emancipation for slaves, and Douglass began to talk of the day when the "school-house, the workshop, the church, the college" would be as freely accessible to Negro children "as to the children of other members of the community." He thought his work as an editor might hasten that day. For a decade he had been at least one remove from "the people with whom I had suffered . . . as a slave." Now he wanted to identify himself with all phases of Negro life; to address Negro audiences, to join Negro organizations. Starting a paper for his people was a challenge he could not bolt.

Still he held off for weeks, while Garrison and Wendell Phillips bombarded him with arguments. Such a paper was not needed, they said. He, Douglass, was especially endowed as a lecturer, they said, and he should stick to it. He had no proven editorial gifts, and Phillips predicted the exhaustion of his resources and failure within three years if he started a paper. Douglass "brooded," Garrison wrote his wife, " 'like the black storm cloud over the capes' upon the future."

But Douglass, though he was "under the influence of something like slavish adoration of these good people," determined to go ahead. Late in 1847 he moved from Lynn, Massachusetts, to Rochester, New York, and in the first week of December of that year he issued the first number of the *North Star*. From then until the emancipation was an accomplished fact and the union of the states assured, the *North Star*, later known as *Frederick Douglass's Paper*, was published weekly.

Nevertheless, Douglass was reluctant to cut the ideological cord that bound him to Garrison's impractical idealism. That idealism had tested brittle against successive onslaughts of the slaveholders, who, battening on a feast of political victories since the Missouri Compromise of 1820, were even then fashioning the strategy by which to accomplish another—the admission of California as a slave state. But even in the face of this threatened overwhelming addition to the South's political force, and through all the testy and sardonic talk of restoring "to the South, through constitutional amendment, the equilibrium of power she once possessed in the Federal government," Garrisonians continued to abjure political action, to remain non-voting abolitionists and non-resisters to the aggressive Southern will. Though he did not say so at the time—and, indeed, continued to support Garrison's philosophy in the *North Star*—Douglass in fact was done with all this.

Moreover, he had to be done with it if he was to work with his own people. *They* had not been patient. They had been angry and urgent, and their frequent conventions had long and loudly proclaimed them committed to political action. As early as 1838 they had served notice that "We take our stand upon the solemn declaration, that to protect inalienable rights 'governments are constituted among men . . .' and proclaim that a government which tears away from us and our posterity the very power of consent is a tyrannical usurpation which we will never cease to oppose." Since the 1840s they had gone further. "If we must bleed, let it all come at once. . . . Brethren, arise, arise! Strike for your lives and liberties!"

Frederick Douglass had some catching up to do. He began by working for the Liberty party in the campaign of 1848. It was not much of a start, for the Liberty party had already grown so anemic on the diet of abolition that the transfusions (recommended, it might be said, by Dr.

James Russell Lowell) of the tariff, the public lands, and the Mexican War questions could not bring it back to glowing health. Besides, Douglass found politics a strange forest, and he was lost in it. There were too many parties and too many candidates. The Democrats had nominated Lewis Cass of Michigan, but he was completely cold to the slavery issue and therefore the anti-slavery Democrats were cold to him. These latter, mostly New Yorkers who called themselves Barnburners, wanted Martin Van Buren. So did the anti-slavery Whigs. On this common ground the dissident anti-slavery factions of both parties met in Buffalo in August 1848 and, declaring themselves for "free soil, free speech, free labor and free men," nominated Van Buren.

Perhaps the measure of Douglass' bewilderment was that he was at that convention, addressed it as a "noble step in the right direction," commended its choice of Van Buren and condemned Zachary Taylor, the regular Whig candidate, as a "known robber and assassin," but continued to support John P. Hale, the candidate of the Liberty party.

If there was method in this, it did not become apparent until later, when Gerrit Smith, the enduring spark plug of the Liberty party, proposed that the party's paper and the *North Star* merge, with Douglass as editor. Smith was wealthy, generous, and dedicated. The *North Star* sorely needed financial help. Negroes, for whom it was primarily intended, were too poor to support it. Besides, there were those who would not support it if they could, for some refused to ally themselves with the "race movement." Among Negroes in general there were all shades of opinion, all varieties of interest, and loyalties as diverse and unstable as the fulfillment or the violation of personal hope and ambitions could make them. But Douglass had this to learn. Meantime he accepted the help Gerrit Smith offered, renamed his paper *Frederick Douglass's Paper*, and spent the last two years of the decade trying to resuscitate the Liberty party.

This was a hopeless endeavor. The party had been swamped in the political seas of 1848, and the seas, agitated by the storms over the boundary of Texas, the territories of New Mexico, Utah, and Oregon, and the admission of California, had grown more turbulent. Danger signals flew. No one could doubt that the leaky ship of states was at hazard.

Old, ill, and embittered by frustration, John C. Calhoun, who had threatened secession over the tariff, threatened it again in 1849 if Congress admitted California as a free state. The North, he declared, must concede "to the South an equal right to the acquired territory," must vigorously enforce the Fugitive Slave Law, the breach of which was costing the South "millions in human property annually," and must "cease the agitation of the slave question."

But Calhoun and the South had no monopoly on sectional feelings: there were men of the North who welcomed disunion as heartily as ever Calhoun did. Perhaps a compromise could save the situation? Old Henry Clay thought so, and he came out of retirement to propose one. California should be admitted as a free state; Texas should give up her claim to extend her western boundary; Congress should give up the right (which had never been granted in the first place) to control the slave trade within the states and between states; Utah and New Mexico should become territories in which the decision on slavery would be left up to the people of the territories; and a more stringent fugitive slave law should be enacted. Webster of Massachusetts supported Clay of Kentucky. Flashing some of the brilliance of twenty years before, Webster spoke for the "preservation of the Union. Hear me for my cause."

The "cause" was saved, but few approved of the compromise that saved it. And the compromise itself could not for long hold up to the battering of sectional pride and prejudice and the moral indignation that immediately beset it. Southern politicians were quick to see that the admission of California as a free state upset the balance in Congress. Virginia, South Carolina, Georgia, Alabama, and Mississippi declared for secession. Northern abolitionists were not slow to realize that the new Fugitive Slave Law was a "screaming iniquity," and their cries of outrage rose from all sides. Garrison saw villainy "of an unmitigated type, treachery to the cause of liberty and humanity of the blackest shade." Senator Seward of New York, who was always the politician and whose professed political object was to defend and further the interests of Northern farmers and wage earners, regarded the compromise as a subversion of the "law of God, whence alone the laws of men can derive their sanction." Even Emerson descended from Parnassus to pronounce the compromise "a filthy enactment. . . . I will not obey it, by God!"

Passion took over.

It is not strange that Douglass missed or ignored the political significance of the compromise. Excepting the moderate Whigs, nearly everyone did. For Douglass and other free Negroes, the Fugitive Slave Law was a stunning personal blow. "It broke down," as Whittier said, "all guarantees of their personal liberty." It made it possible for an alleged runaway slave to be arrested without a warrant, taken before a commissioner or a judge who, legally bound to disallow the defendant's testimony, could take the word of the claimant and capturer as proof of the charge. Trial by jury was not required or even permitted. "Free papers" had no more value than a cynical or a venal commissioner cared to place on them. "Even free colored people who had been free all their lives felt very insecure" —insecure enough, in fact, to send whole communities scampering into self-exile in Canada. In Douglass' home town of Rochester all but two of the entire membership of the Colored Baptist Church fled.

Many Negro leaders pulled out. Henry Highland Garnet slipped away to England. Samuel R. Ward, whose "depth of thought, fluency of speech . . . and general intelligence" had impressed the leadership of the Free-Soil party, scuttled into Canada. Martin Delany, who had been associated with Douglass on the *North Star* for a time, took ship for Africa. Soon to be a bishop in the African Methodist Episcopal Church, Daniel Payne, distressed beyond the solace of religion, lamented to Douglass, "We are whipped, we are whipped! And we might as well retreat in order."

But Frederick Douglass was not whipped. He had courage that, in the instance, amounted to a reckless and foolhardy contempt for danger. For two years his house in Rochester had been the jumping-off place for slaves escaping into Canada. At one time in the early winter of 1850 as many as eleven fugitives had harbored there, and John Brown, on one of his periodic visits of solicitation in the neighborhood, made a speech to them. Now, though the danger of such activity was more than doubled, Douglass did not stop. In the very week in which the Fugitive Slave Law became effective he gave refuge to three runaways who were charged not only as fugitives but as murderers, for in making their escape they had killed a man. "I could not look upon them as murderers," Douglass said. "To me, they were heroic defenders of the rights of man. . . . So I fed them and sheltered them in my house."

Other men—and mostly white men—in Delaware, Pennsylvania, and New York, in Kentucky, Ohio, and Kansas were feeding and sheltering runaways too, and had been for years. More and more runaways required this charity. Though the Underground Railroad ran on a faster schedule after the new Fugitive Slave Law of 1850, it could not run fast enough to satisfy the North's conscience and pride. That conscience was exacerbated by the harshness of the law upon whose "faithful execution . . . depends the preservation of our much-loved Union." Pride was painfully injured by the South's verbal assaults against the North's free society and the unceasing references to Northerners as "mongrels" and "mudsills." So Northerners, each according to his nature, took baleful glee or moral joy in defying the law.

Nor was the satisfaction of conscience and pride their only excuse. Slaveholders and slave catchers had grown aggressive to the point of criminality. In Maryland a white man was lynched for proving the free status of a kidnaped Negro girl. Aprowl in Philadelphia, a Baltimore sheriff shot and killed William Smith, a free Negro, for saying that he was free. Northerners responded to such acts as these with equally criminal acts of their own. In Troy, New York, they seized a recaptured runaway and set him free. A Boston mob rescued Frederick Jenkins from the United States marshal who was about to return him to slavery, and Theodore Parker called this the "most noble deed done in Boston since the destruction of the tea in 1773." Northern mobs in Philadelphia, New York, and Syracuse matched this nobility.

With so many Negro leaders gone or grown silent, a man more self-centered, perceptive, and less scrupulous than Douglass might have tried to lay hold of authority. But neither acute perception nor ruthlessness was a quality Douglass could claim. An effort to seize power over his people was utterly beyond him, though in the circumstances he might easily have done so.

For it is true that white people generally thought of him as the outstanding Negro leader and spokesman. After 1847, when a deluge of national publicity, some of it scurrilous, swept over him in connection with his return from England, the purchase of his freedom, and an open letter addressed to his old master in the pages of Greeley's *Tribune*, he was the man to whom white people turned with questions about the Negro. Without his willing it, his opinions were suddenly influential among whites. He was quoted in and out of context everywhere. He had authority among whites. Since Negroes had little power to implement their own will and sought recourse in their white friends, it is probable that Douglass could have influenced substantially the Negro fate. But he believed in discussion. He referred questions about Negroes to Negroes themselves. He set such questions forth in his paper. He brought them up in the Negro conventions, where, more often than not, crafty strategists managed to bring about a repudiation of Douglass' own opinions.

For this was also true: Douglass had some implacable enemies among both his own people and white Garrisonian abolitionists. Charles Remond, the first Negro anti-slavery lecturer, was jealous of Douglass' reputation. Robert Purvis, a quadroon of considerable affluence, clashed with Douglass over Negro freedom as against the "rights of free Negroes." William Wells Brown accused Douglass of belittling him. Having become a favorite of Garrison, William Nell, the Negro historian, followed his inflexible patron down a tortuous byway to bitter estrangement. Garrison had never forgotten or forgiven the fact that Douglass had established a paper against his advice. He made opportunities to blast his onetime protégé in the press and from the platform. In 1853, when Julia Griffiths, an Englishwoman living in Rochester, was managing the finances of Douglass' paper, Garrison, hinting at sexual immorality, alleged that Miss Griffiths was "one whose influence had caused much unhappiness in his [Douglass'] own household" and that he "could bring a score of unimpeachable witnesses . . . to prove it."

In spite of his enemies Douglass' influence over his own people grew and spread slowly, almost imperceptibly, and in no fixed pattern. Although he gave up profitable lecture engagements to speak gratis to small, impoverished Negro groups and wrote hundreds of private letters to unknown Negroes who asked his advice, other leaders seemed more popular than he and were applauded with greater gusto at Negro meetings. In 1848 he was elected, grudgingly, president of the Colored Convention, which had been meeting sporadically for two decades, but the next year, when he proposed to organize a convention on a national basis the more effectively "to fight slavery, secure interracial cooperation . . . improve the conditions of the Negro people," other Negro leaders refused to indorse the plan. When Douglass, who advocated woman suffrage, became prominent in the feminist movement, William Nell sneered at him as an "Aunt Nancy man." Some Negro leaders were for colonization; Douglass was against it. Entranced by the dream of a "purely educational institution for Negroes," some leaders actively and acrimoniously fought Douglass' idea of "a series of workshops where colored people could learn some of the handicrafts, learn to work in iron, wood and leather, and where a plain English education could also be taught." (This was the idea that an ex-slave named Booker T. Washington was to lift straight from the pages of Douglass' *My Bondage and My Freedom* a quarter of a century later and set forth as his own.) This was the idea that Douglass outlined in great detail to Harriet Beecher Stowe.

The publication of *Uncle Tom's Cabin* in 1852 had catapulted Mrs. Stowe into international fame and given her prestige in councils and controversy far beyond her housewife's capacity and experience to support. In America, where she was backed by all the emotional force of the anti-slavery movement, the general if reluctant acceptance of female reformers such as Lucy Stone, Elizabeth Stanton, and Jane Swisshelm—"those hissing esses," a bawdy-tongued Georgian called them—and the reputation of her thunderous brother, Henry Ward Beecher, it was easy to maintain this prestige. But later in the 1850s she was going abroad to England, and in England the London *Times* had criticized *Uncle Tom* as "unrealistic": "Its effect will be to render slavery more difficult than ever of abolishment." Mrs. Stowe knew that she must be practical and realistic in England, where she had already been pledged "a considerable sum of money . . . for the permanent improvement of the free colored people." What could she offer her audiences there?

She sent for Frederick Douglass. Could he suggest anything? she inquired. He certainly could. Then would he "write out his views in the form of a letter" so that she could take it to England with her that "friends there might see to what their contributions were to be devoted"? He would indeed—and did.

". . . An industrial college—a college to be conducted by the best men, and the best workmen which the mechanic arts can afford . . . where colored youth can be instructed to use their hands. . . . Prejudice against the free colored people in the United States has shown itself nowhere so invincible as among mechanics. . . . Denied the means of learning useful trades, we are pressed into the narrowest limits to obtain a livelihood . . . and even these employments are rapidly passing out of our hands. The fact is (every day begins with the lesson and ends with the lesson) colored men must learn trades. . . ."

It seemed unlikely that Douglass' idea "could . . . be tortured into a cause for hard words" by either the British or the American people, but a segment of the American people found cause for hard words anyway. Mrs. Stowe was virulently attacked, especially by the pro-slavery press. She was accused of "misrepresenting slavery with iniquitous lies," and no one bothered to refute this old canard. But when she was charged with receiving "British gold for her own private use," and was persistently and bitterly attacked by some of the abolitionist press on this score, her brother, the Reverend Henry W. Beecher, came to her defense and very pointedly referred her maligners to Frederick Douglass, "if they would learn what she intended to do with the money." Douglass responded immediately and at length. The attacks on Mrs. Stowe soon ceased.

But Douglass' response did as much for him as for Harriet Stowe. The fortuitous linking of his name with that of the most famous woman in the world in such a way as to reveal that she had taken council with him and with him alone enormously increased his prestige. Even the most jealous and suspicious Negroes paused to take another look at the man whom Garrison had admonished them to ignore. How could they now? Douglass' stock shot up, particularly in the Negro market. By 1855, when many people were beginning to realize that the social ferment of the times was a plexus involving more than abolition and more than a single body of ideas, Douglass was the Negroes' acknowledged leader, and clothed by them with an authority such as no single Negro has since acquired.

4. *Days of the Martyr*

He was to need that authority almost immediately to win his people to a recognition that the policy of "abolition or disunion" was futile. Only by winning them from this Garrisonian nullity could he hope to get their support for a program of political action. What that program would be or what name it would bear Douglass was by no means certain. His own political allegiance had been divided. The Liberty party, which he had joined when it was organized, was split and weakened to the point of collapse by 1852. For a time he flirted with the Free-Soil party, but its principal candidates, George W. Julian and John P. Hale, ignored two direct and pertinent questions: whether a political party should regard it a duty to secure equal rights for all; and whether "slavery, so far as capable of legislation, is a naked piracy, around which there can be no legal covering." Douglass felt that he could not support the Free-Soil party. Politically he did not know where to go, but by 1854 he knew he must go somewhere and take his people with him.

For in that year it became evident that the skillful machinations of the South were increasing the power of that section out of all proportion to political equity. Stephen A. Douglas, the senator from Illinois, introduced a bill to organize the central plains into a territory, and won the support of the most radical pro-slavery sympathizers by agreeing to have the measure provide for the repeal of the Compromise of 1850. Having made this concession, he was forced to make a further one: so that the principle of popular sovereignty could work to the advantage of the slaveholders, the senator agreed to a provision that divided the territory into Kansas and Nebraska. Now the political strength of the South stood out in naked arrogance.

Though the North desperately mustered its own strength, it could not prevail against the power of the South. The Kansas-Nebraska Bill passed both houses, and Franklin Pierce, apostate New Englander that he was, signed it to the accompaniment of cheers from Southerners. Their jubilance had excuse. They had fought with feverish but calculating realism against the odds of a numerical majority in the North. They had opposed the North's moral pretensions, ethical professions, and humanitarian zeal with a simple formula of political action. Every victory had made their cause appear brighter. They had proved indomitable. With the signing of the Kansas-Nebraska Bill, it must have seemed to them that Professor George Tucker of the University of Virginia said truly when he wrote, "History is the great arbiter of right in national disputes, and the scale of justice on which she happens to light is almost sure to preponderate."

In the breakup of the old parties that followed immediately upon the passage of the Kansas-Nebraska Bill, some anti-slavery leaders saw an opportunity for political cohesion. Many Northerners whose opposition to slavery had been dormant now roused themselves, not necessarily on behalf of anti-slavery, but to stop the extension of the slave power. Northern Democrats, those same "Northern men with Southern principles" who had voted against the Wilmot Proviso and who cared little about the slavery controversy one way or the other, were chagrined by an ever tightening Southern control of the party. "Conscience Whigs" and Free-Soilers were simply adrift. Some of all these came together to form the Republican party.

Meantime the Know-Nothing or American party, which had been jerry-built out of all those elements that hated or feared foreigners and Catholics—and which Henry Wise had called "the most impious and unprincipled affiliation of bad means, for bad ends"—had spent its force. And when its Southern pro-slavery adherents gained control of it in 1855, the Northerners withdrew almost to a man and lined up with the new Republicans. Frederick Douglass, however, thought that the Liberty party, with its seamless devotion to abolition, was due for a revival. He delivered the bloc vote of the Negroes of western New York to that party in 1854, but the Liberty party, as well as its offshoot, the Radical Abolitionist, had used up its ninth life. Douglass went over to the Republicans and carried practically all the enfranchised Negroes with him.

Nor was this all he did. Though at first reluctant to solicit among his own poverty-stricken people, Douglass was soon telling them that "no sacrifice, even to life itself, [is] too much to ask for freedom." Funds were needed for a variety of purposes—to support the Republican candidate, John C. Frémont; to keep the Underground Railroad running; to promote the work of the Emigrant Aid Society, hastily organized to help establish anti-slavery men in the Kansas Territory, and for even more desperate expedients. Men and words and ballots alone would not do in Kansas. What were needed, John Brown told Douglass, were "swords and bullets, and you must help me get them."

And Douglass did. "I got up meetings and solicited aid

to be used by him for the cause, and I may say without boasting that my efforts in this respect were not entirely fruitless," wrote Douglass years later. "Deeply interested as 'Osawatomie Brown' was in Kansas, he never lost sight of what he called his greater work—the liberation of all the slaves in the United States. But for the then present he saw his way to the great end through Kansas."

But Kansas was not the way. In the inextricable linkage of violence with politics, Brown's actions in the territory were a danger and a thwart to pro-slavery sympathizers, but they were far from enough to secure the liberty of "all the slaves in the United States." They were barely enough to accomplish what had to be done in Kansas—the making of that state "a clean bed," as Lincoln put it, "with no snakes in it." There were plenty of snakes before John Brown got there. In the preceding March (1855) five thousand Missouri ruffians had crossed over into Kansas to make sure of the election of a pro-slavery legislature. Senator David Atchison had ordered them to "shoot, stab or beat any abolitionists seen at the voting places." The pro-slavery men won that election but, in October, John Brown arrived to keep them from winning another. Fanatical beyond mere ruthlessness and cruelty, he had come, he said, "to promote the killing of American slavery" and "to do the work of the Lord." The work was murder. For a year Brown was a presence in Kansas and the terror of all Missouri, his "name alone equal to an army with banners." But even this was not enough for his great purpose, and when he quit Kansas to solicit more funds in the East—to meet Theodore Parker, Salmon P. Chase, Amos Lawrence, Emerson, and Thoreau, and to renew his acquaintance with Gerrit Smith and Frederick Douglass—Brown knew it was not enough.

So also did Douglass, whose optimism had dwindled. The apparent victory of the cause in Kansas had been wholly vitiated by the Supreme Court decision in the case of Dred Scott, a slave who, having been taken into free Illinois and back again to Missouri, sued for his freedom on the ground that he had lived on free soil. The Court's decision held that masters could take their slaves anywhere in the territories. It held that the Missouri Compromise was unconstitutional. It declared, in effect, that "Negroes had no rights which white men were bound to respect." On the strength of this decision the South renewed its demands to reopen the slave trade, and for a time it looked as if those demands would be met.

It is no wonder that Douglass was discouraged. He said so to Daniel Payne, who seven years before had cried, "We are beaten!" But now, already dreaming of founding the first Negro college, where "the peace of God and the light of learning would shine," Payne demurred. "Oh, Frederick, Frederick! Take comfort. The stars are not altered in their courses." But Payne could not pull Douglass through the depression that enveloped him to the very eve of the Civil War, when at a public meeting a woman, gaunt and fleshless as a ghost, rose to ask the speaker, "Frederick, is God dead?"

John Brown, the self-appointed man of God, had answered that the year before. "God," he had said then, "cries out for blood!" Douglass could not ignore that cry altogether. He was Brown's friend and of his council. He had given comfort to Brown and aid to his plans to free the slaves. When Brown called, Douglass felt duty-bound to answer. Brown called in August of 1859.

The two men met in an abandoned stone quarry near Chambersburg, Pennsylvania. The "terrible saint" had a new and bolder plan. He would do more than run off slaves. He would seize the government arsenal at Harper's Ferry. He would kidnap prominent citizens and hold them hostage. He would make rebellion flame in all the Southern states. Douglass was appalled. For a day and a night he argued. Brown would have the whole country arrayed against him. He was "going into a steel trap" and he would never get out alive. Virginia "would blow him sky-high, rather than that he should hold Harper's Ferry an hour." But Brown was not to be stopped; he craved his martyrdom. He was beyond both reason and fear. "Come with me, Douglass," he said. "I will defend you with my life. I want you for a special purpose. When I strike, the bees will begin to swarm, and I shall want you to help hive them."

A few weeks later he struck. He seized the arsenal and virtually the town of Harper's Ferry, Virginia. He freed fifty slaves. The alarm spread quickly, and all the powers of government mobilized against him. President Buchanan sent federal troops under the command of Colonel Robert E. Lee. Virginia, Maryland, and the Carolinas called out militia. Armed with sticks and stones and squirrel guns, men and boys from Charleston streamed through the hills toward Harper's Ferry. It took three days to put down the rebellion, and only three of Brown's twenty-two men lived to see the end of it.

Meanwhile rumors sped. The seizure of the arsenal was only the first of a series of raids to be conducted by hundreds of men. The capture of "Mad-dog Brown" had only scotched the snake. Others were implicated, among them Thomas Wentworth Higginson, Theodore Parker, Samuel Howe, and Frederick Douglass. Governor Wise of Virginia charged treason and appealed to the President for federal warrants. But Parker was in Italy, Howe in England, and Higginson safe behind the bastion of his family name. Friends urged Douglass to flee. Did he suppose, innocent or not, that the South would let slip an opportunity to hang the most prominent Negro abolitionist?

Eluding by only six hours the federal officers sent to arrest him, Douglass fled to Canada. But, "Farther, farther, Frederick!" Daniel Payne urged. So, feeling that he was "going into exile, perhaps for life," Douglass sailed for England. He did not return until the eve of the Civil War.

Part Two

ALL GLORY GONE

IV. FAITH

1. *Isabella No-Name*

She was called Isabella at first, and the language spoken in her family was Dutch. But to speak of her "family" is an irony, for ten of her brothers and sisters had been sold away, and only her father, Baumfree, her mother, Bett, and her brother, Peter, remained. The parents had no surname. "Baumfree" was a moniker for tall-as-a-tree, and the father refused to have another. Though in later years the name would have fitted Isabella, in her youth it would not stick. She was variously called Bell, Bella, and Lil Bett. She belonged successively to the Hardenberghs, the Nealys, the Scrivers, and the Dumonts, and for more than a year she gave her considerable services to the Van Wageners, but she took the name of none of them.

She held John Dumont, a man of gross appetites, in fervent, idolatrous regard and bore him children, but she did not take his name either for herself or for them. When she married, probably in 1820 and probably at the age of twenty-three, her husband had no name to give her. He was called simply Tom, or Black Tom—not because of the color of his skin but because he "worked roots" or voodoo and practiced divination. The son Tom begot was called Peter, nothing more. When Peter was a young man in the city of New York he found the lack of a surname a handicap to such a devil-may-care free Negro as himself and he adopted the name of Williams—Peter Williams. He was twice booked into Tombs prison under this name, and under this name he shipped as a seaman to a foreign port in 1839 and was, save once, heard of no more.

Isabella had not only left him nameless, she had left him motherless. In one way or another she left all of her children—five, or six, or seven—motherless. There was a frigid winter spot in the blazing tropics of her soul.

She dismissed Tom, a freedman, while she was still a slave. He died in a poorhouse in 1830. Peter, the son of Tom, and the children she had by Dumont were left with Dumont when she ran away. It is true that she did not run far, or try to lose herself, but this is scarcely evidence that she missed or wanted her children.

Dumont had promised to set her free in 1826, but when the time came he was reluctant to make his promise good. In the interval since her marriage Isabella had got religion and had founded her faith in God. But she never went to church, and hers was a strange religion, compounded of Tom's weird conjure lore and Old Testament maledictions. She worshiped in secret, in "a circular arched alcove" she had constructed "entirely of willows" on an islet in a stream at the edge of the Dumont estate. Also, according to reports, hers was a terrible God —a master black magician apotheosized from every awful attribute of witchcraft, necromancy, and superstition.

She invoked this God for or against Dumont, and then she ran away. Somehow she knew that Dumont would not try to get her back. She had been an embarrassment to him, to his wife, and finally, as they grew up, to his legitimate children. When she left she did take her second child by Tom, an unnamed infant girl, but within a month or two she abandoned her to be reared by strangers in the neighboring town of New Paltz, New York.

Yet there was one curious episode.

Dumont sold the boy Peter. It was 1826. Slavery in New York State had only fourteen months to go. Peter was five and therefore still useless as a slave, but in some circles it was fashionable to train a Negro child as one would train a monkey or a dog and show off its accomplishments in the parlor. Peter's new master, Dr. James Gedney, apparently tired of this entertainment and transferred title in the boy to his brother, Solomon Gedney. Solomon in turn sold Peter to the husband of a sister, a Deep South planter named Fowler. In defiance of the law forbidding native-born slaves to be taken beyond the borders of the state, Fowler carted Peter off to Alabama.

Isabella exploded, a blazing holocaust—but ignited from what kindling and fed by what fuel it is impossible to tell. She defies analysis. Any of a number of elements in the situation might have sparked a simpler woman to maddened action—the loss of a well-loved child, a blind and twisted jealousy, a passion for fair play, a sense of intolerable humiliation—but Isabella is not explicable in terms of any of these.

She went to Dumont and charged him with perfidy. Then she went to the Gedneys' mother and in broken English screamed, "Oh, I must have my child! I will have my child!" She shrieked out maledictions upon the heads of all concerned, invoked hell and death, and cursed to action the sluggard forces of the law. And she had her child. Under delayed sentence and a bond of six hundred dollars, Solomon Gedney fetched Peter back from Alabama.

But Isabella did not really want the boy. She gave him into the keeping of a family in Wahkendall. Then she herself went to live in New York City.

2. Bathed in Holiness

Perhaps a group of thirty ex-slaves living on Manhattan Island were a little too sanguine when in the early 1830s they addressed a letter to their "Afflicted and Beloved Brothers" in the South: "We get wages for our labor. We have schools for our children. . . . We are happy to say that every year is multiplying the facilities. . . ."

Among these facilities were a theater-hotel called the African Grove, the first Negro newspaper, *Freedom's Journal*, the largest Negro church in the United States, and living space in the Five Points district—where kidnapers prowled in armed gangs and shanghaied any likely Negro, free or not, and sold him south to slavery. But kidnapers could not seriously reduce the Negro population. Negroes kept coming all the time, though a vigorous pro-slavery press thundered against them and against abolition, "this most dangerous species of fanaticism extending itself

through our society. . . . Shall we, by promptly and fearlessly crushing this many-headed Hydra in the bud, expose
the weakness as well as the folly, madness and mischief
of these bold and dangerous men?"

But in New York metaphors were not all that was
mixed, often for good but sometimes for ill. Daniel Payne,
fleeing Charleston in 1835, would stop there briefly, wan-
der in innocent curiosity into Cow Bay Alley, be "revolted"
by the brazen prostitution and open "consortium of white
drabs and drunken Negro sailors"; but, finally, through his
connection with the Methodist Episcopal Church, meet
some white teachers and preachers who would provide
him with a scholarship to study at the Gettysburg Semi-
nary and send him on his way. And on a September morning three years later Frederick Douglass would find himself
"one more added to the mighty throng which, like the
confused waves of the troubled sea, surged to and fro between the lofty walls of Broadway." After a few days "of
freedom from slavery, but free from food and shelter as
well," he too would meet a mixed group, the Vigilance
Committee, find refuge in the home of one of them, and
be given steamer fare to New Bedford.

Much of the spirit called humanitarian found focus in
New York. Assorted idealists and crackpots, hewing their
timbers from the forest of radicalism, were busy building
the New Jerusalem. Their hammers rang. The forges of
Free Enquirers, Sabbatarians, Emancipationists, Femi-
nists, Owenites, and evangelical sects of all sorts gave off
an incandescent glow. Negroes were frequently suffused in
it. Many of them attended white churches. They were
welcomed in many movements. Situated in what is now
Greenwich Village, a mixed utopian community flourished
for a time. The Manumission Society had founded the first
African Free School in 1787, and by the early 1830s there
were seven such schools taught by teachers of both races
and supported by appropriations from the state legislature
as well as from the Common Council. "It was due mainly
to [these schools] that there was produced in New York
City . . . a body of intelligent and well-trained colored
men and women."

In New York lived John Russwurm, first Negro graduate of an American college (Bowdoin, 1826). Dr. James McCune Smith, graduate of the Glasgow University, practiced medicine there "without prejudice to his white patients, who were numerous." Alexander Crummell and J. W. C. Pennington, one a graduate of Cambridge University and the other with an honorary degree from Heidelberg, frequently preached to white congregations.

New York was a haven for Isabella when she arrived in 1829. Almost the first people she met were the Elijah Piersons, a white couple of great wealth and inexhaustible mystic faith. Both were unstable; both had begun a tragic descent into unreality. Their devotion to the organized Church had been reamed out in the revival of anticlericalism in the 1820s and rendered them neurotic prey to a religious eclecticism that was almost as pagan as it was Christian. They had set out to convert the whole of New York City, after which, in their grandiose imaginings, they would convert the world. They had founded an ascetic church called Five Points House, an esoteric group known as the Retrenchment Society, and a house for fallen women named the Magdalene Society. Their own home on Bowery Hill was known as the Kingdom.

Here Isabella went to live with them. Responsive to their religious influence as well as to their kindness, she was quick to substitute their messianic mysticism for the dark and vengeful spirit of the sorcery she had learned from Black Tom. "Our God is a God of love," Pierson drummed into her time and again, "and you are one of His prophets." She had never known a God like theirs. Soon she was having religious seizures—"I feel so light and so well, I could skim around like a gull!"—and visions of great intensity—"It is Jesus!" She was also making prophecies (a practice which must have continued for some time, for Harriet Beecher Stowe, who did not meet her until the 1850s, called her the "Libyan Sybil").

All this seemed to suit Isabella's temperament, and the Piersons seemed her kind of people. They fasted periodically for days at a time, refusing water as well as bread, but Isabella outdid them. When they went preaching in the

streets (a "slight, blond" man; a "small, graceful," and
dark-haired woman), Isabella preached more fervently.
No one could match her prayers. Her voice was timbred
like a man's and guttural with the Dutch accent she never
quite unlearned. Tall and gaunt, with a strong, dark,
homely face jutting angularly below a white headcloth,
she attracted attention by her appearance and held it by
the power of a personality that no scoffers could shrink.

Under a regimen of prayer, preaching, and fasting, Sarah
Pierson's health gave way, and her husband, now mysti-
cally renamed "Elijah the Tishbite," refused to have a doctor for her. He himself would effect her recovery according
to St. James. "Is any sick among you? Let him call for the
elders of the church; and let them pray over him, anointing
him with oil in the name of the Lord: and the prayer of
faith shall save the sick, and the Lord shall raise him up."

The elders were called, among them Isabella, and they
prayed and anointed, but Sarah Pierson died.

But a stranger who had wandered into the Kingdom
some time before and announced himself as Matthias explained to a broken Pierson and a faith-faltering Isabella
that they had misunderstood the word of God. He *had*
raised Sarah up—up into eternal life. Nor was this the only
instance in which God's word had been misunderstood,
Matthias explained. He would set them right. He, Matthias, was "the Spirit of Truth" that had disappeared
from the earth at the death of Matthew in the New Testament. "The spirit of Jesus Christ entered into that Matthias, and I am the same Matthias. . . . I am he that has
come to fulfill the word."

And the word was "all things in common." Matthias,
who heretofore had been known simply as Robert Mat-
thews, who had deserted his wife and children in Albany,
and who had several times been arrested as a public nuisance, very soon had Isabella, Pierson, whose daughter now
joined him, and a well-to-do couple, the Benjamin Folgers,
completely under his spell. Pooling their considerable resources and turning them over to Matthias, these five
moved with him to Sing Sing, New York, to a country

place Matthias called Zion Hill. It began as just another experiment in communal living, a material projection of pure idealism such as blistered the American landscape in the 1830s. It ended after two years in a riotous carnival of licentiousness, adultery, and suspected murder.

For Matthias turned the Pierson fasts to feasts, their prayers to pimping. He was not long in convincing Pierson and the Folgers of the divine origin of his "matched souls" doctrine. According to this, Pierson would meet his wife again in the form of another woman: Matthias saw to it. Whatever Pierson's trysts with his own daughter signified under the doctrine, Matthias himself made open love to any woman who struck his sybaritic fancy—and Mrs. Folger did. In a ceremony that Pierson performed, Mrs. Folger became Matthias' soul mate, and Benjamin Folger himself gave her away. A few days later Elijah Pierson suffered what was called an epileptic fit, and in succeeding days a series of them, and then he died.

But the death of this once wealthy, reputable man, known down in the city for his charitable though eccentric works, did not go unnoticed by his relatives. They were suspicious. The body was exhumed and traces of arsenic found in it. Matthias was arrested and charged with murder. Isabella was implicated with him, and was also accused by the Folgers of trying to poison them. But the evidence against her in both these matters was insupportable, and she escaped indictment.

For the truth seems to be that Isabella was not aware of what went on at Zion Hill and Matthias did not corrupt her with this knowledge. He kept her hypnotically transfixed in a religious state beyond all comprehension of reality and worked on her the same spell that, for different reasons and with quite contrary results, he worked on the Piersons, the Folgers, and other members of the cult.

And Isabella remained spellbound longer. She saw Zion Hill as "bathed in holiness" even while the Folgers were testifying to its abominations. Her defense of Matthias in court was so spiritually naïve and sincere that only perfect innocence could have produced it.

3. *Sojourner*

The trial of Matthias was the beginning of a new life for Isabella. Though she was now truly religious, the ecstatic seizures ceased and the visions began to fade. She dropped back into reality like one "once blind but now made to see."

What she saw with mundane clarity was a Negro life sunk to a depth almost beyond recovery. She saw it aswarm in the fetid alleys of Five Points, where Negroes "crawled over each other like flies on a dungpile." It lurked in the shadows of the docks, the stables, and the abattoirs, where, perchance, there might be a day's work free from molestation by immigrant whites who, arriving on every ship, were given first rights in such jobs as offered. She saw Negroes trying to beat back the compacted misery of their days with nights spent in Dickens Place, where assorted whores and their pimps did a brisk trade in flesh and thievery.

For, indeed, this was the life her son became involved in. Peter was now in his teens and his sister had just turned ten, and Isabella, after years of neglecting them, tried to make a home. But Peter was man-size, boisterously genial, already hardened in petty crime. Besides, Isabella had to work.

At first she made her living polishing the brass fixtures that adorned the doors of houses along the east-side avenues. She had regular customers to whom she sometimes talked in an earnest, forthright way about God. The notoriety of the Matthias trial still clung to her, and she was regarded as a strange character. She could be seen any day except Sunday, a can of dampened ashes mixed with sand at her feet, polishing rags hanging from the waist of her kilted skirt, putting a shine on name plates, doorknobs, and hinges. But this work depended upon the weather, and eventually she took a job in domestic service.

Even so, there was little time for her home. She was a prominent member of the African Zion Church, the church militant. Here gathered all the social forces that Negroes could command. There was plenty of the old-time religion still, and there were many prayer meetings and "love feasts" where Isabella exercised her gifts for prayer and testimony, but here the "most dangerous species of fanaticism" permeated the atmosphere. When anti-slavery ministers like John Marrs and Dempsey Kennedy came to preach, what Isabella heard was less of the word of Christ and more of the battle cry of freedom. At African Zion Church she heard discussions of the questions of colonization, education, and abolition. Once in the early 1840s, William Lloyd Garrison spoke there. Through her association with the church Isabella met Charles B. Ray, the Negro abolitionist, and it was in his home that she first saw Frederick Douglass, the white and wealthy Tappan brothers, and Gerrit Smith. Strange contours shaped and deep new furrows plowed her mind. James Sturges, the English abolitionist, told her, "This [abolition] is God's work too." She did what she could, but her appearance was against the clandestine work of the Underground Railroad, in which many of the Church's members were engaged. She was better suited to public agitation, to haranguing the streetcorner rabble. She drew crowds wherever she spoke.

Meantime her son was going to the dogs. All Isabella's prayers could not save him. He professed an interest in the sea, and Isabella gave him the money to pay for a course in navigation, but he spent it on dancing lessons. She got him a job as coachman, but he sold his livery and the stable gear. Three times he went to jail—twice for theft and once for pandering—and when jail threatened for the fourth time Isabella refused to help him, and he sneaked away to sea. She never saw him again.

She had better luck with her daughter. Aged sixteen, the girl married a man named Banks and with him drifted slowly westward. A son born of their union was to be the only blood kin Isabella was ever known to love.

Once again free of responsibility to a family, Isabella poured her great vigor into "God's work." The steely shards of social reform and anti-slavery magnetized around her faith. Her fanatic tendencies blazed up again, but they were controlled by her developing intelligence and ironic insight. It was almost as if she sported with what Harriet B. Stowe was to call her "strange powers." Gradually her visions returned, but they were not now the apocalyptic visions of heaven's pearl and hell's brimstone. They were hardly visions at all, but sleeping dreams in which voices urged her to "go out into the world, gather in the flock." Sometimes it was the voice of the Reverend Charles Ray, sometimes of the Reverend Henry Garnet, sometimes of Gerrit Smith. Sometimes it seemed the voice of God. She grew impatient with the necessity to earn her living. She felt oppressed by New York, where, she said, "the rich do rob the poor, and the poor rob the poorer," and where the "truth of God is locked away" from sight.

Then one day she felt reborn. "I felt so tall within—I felt as if the power of a nation was with me." It was in the spring of 1843—the year Daniel Payne entered the active ministry of the African Methodist Episcopal Church, the year Frederick Douglass took part in "one hundred conventions." She was working for a Mrs. Whiting, who in answer to a question about her erstwhile maid replied: "She told me that she was going away and that the Lord was going to give her a new name. I thought Bell was crazy. She took a pillowcase and put her things in it, and then she left, saying she must be about her father's business. A new name indeed! And what was her father's business? Poor woman, I thought for a fact she was crazy. She said she was going east."

And she did go east. She renamed herself Sojourner Truth, and hiked slowly through Connecticut and into Massachusetts. She had set out with just enough money for a week's supply of the coarsest food: for the rest of her long life she would allow herself only enough to supply her most stringent needs. Sometimes she earned money by doing a day's work. Often money was given her. In mild weather she slept out of doors. When she needed shelter she asked for it. If she shared a family's meal she paid in coin or labor. She went undaunted everywhere. She was welcomed nearly everywhere. She seemed "sent by God," wrote a Massachusetts man.

"Sister, I send you this living messenger, as I believe

her to be one that God loves. Ethiopia is stretching forth her hands unto God. You can see by this sister that God does by his spirit alone teach his own children. . . . Please receive her and she will tell you some things. Let her tell her story without interrupting her, and give close attention, and you will see she has got the love of truth, that God helps her to pray where but few can. She cannot read or write, but the law is in her heart. She is sent by God."

Sojourner Truth had the apostolic manner. In some homes she would announce that she had come to talk about the "angelic elect," but her private conversations differed little from her public preachments. She spoke of the "nation's sins against my people." She carried a white satin banner on which was inscribed, "Proclaim Liberty Throughout All the Land unto All the Inhabitants Thereof." When she had unfurled this on the makeshift rostrum of a camp meeting ground, she would begin: "There is more den one kin' of liberty, an' I come to tell you about all kin' of liberty. . . ."

The first winter caught up with her in Northampton, Massachusetts, where she took up temporary residence. Samuel Hill, Parker Pillsbury, and the brother-in-law of Garrison, George Benson—abolitionists all—received her as one of them. When spring came she was off again, this time journeying west. Her reputation outran her. She was the first Negro woman anti-slavery speaker. Sometimes attempts were made to silence and hinder her. She was beaten with sticks and pelted with stones, and on one occasion received injuries that finally ulcerated her leg. She was beaten many times.

4. God's Pilgrim

Slavery had ceased to be a question of moral debate, though the Garrisonians continued to act as if it were. But Garrison's principle of non-resistance had never been popular outside New England—and least of all in the West, where slavery was a matter both of politics, as in the South, and of economics, as in the urban East. The question was dangerously surcharged with emotion everywhere. The best interest of Western farmers could not be served by an alliance with slavery, but there were many farmers who hated anti-slavery. Industrial capitalism and slavery were natural enemies, but capitalists joined with slave-holders to fight abolition. The New York Stock Exchange offered five thousand dollars for the head of Arthur Tappan. Midwestern industrialists hired hoodlums to break up abolition meetings. Some "Gentlemen of Property" in Cincinnati posted a notice throughout the city:

> Abolitionists. BEWARE!
> The citizens of Cincinnati, embracing every class, interested in the prosperity of the city, satisfied that the business of the place is receiving a vital stab from the wicked and misguided operations of the abolitionists, are resolved to arrest to their course.

In Cincinnati, James Birney, converted from Alabama slaveholder to Northern emancipationist, was attacked by a mob under the protection of Nicholas Longworth, the richest man in the Midwest, Jacob Burnet, formerly a judge of the Ohio Supreme Court, and Oliver Spencer, a Methodist minister. The "spirit of lawless violence" that William Jay had deplored in the East was more evident in the West. Pro-slavery sentiment was better organized, more given to deeds than to debate. The president of the new interracial college, Oberline, Asa Mahan, was stoned in Indiana. Mobbed in Kansas and hounded out of Missouri, Elijah Lovejoy was at last murdered in Illinois.

But violence triggered by any show of radicalism was only half the story. The resolute, refractory, and gentle Quakers were the other half. Their anti-slavery tradition went back more than a hundred years. It went back to Ralph Sandiford, who wrote, and Benjamin Franklin, who published A Brief Exposition of the Practice of the Times—a pamphlet "packed with brimstone." It went back to Benjamin Say, who, "to show his indignation against the practice of slavekeeping, once carried a bladder filled with blood into a meeting; and, in the presence of the whole congregation, thrust a sword . . . into the bladder, exclaiming at the same time, 'Thus shall God shed the blood of those persons who enslave their fellow creatures.' The terror of this extravagant and unexpected act produced swooning in several of the women of the congregation."

The Midwestern Quakers no longer carried blood in bladders—they knew better tricks—and their women were too busy to swoon. They were busy devising stratagems of elusion, such as the one a certain Faith Webster pulled. Caching a group of fleeing slaves on the Kentucky side of the Ohio River one dawn when daylight made further progress impossible, she returned in the evening to find slave hunters scouring the area. Faith Webster changed into such clothes as a slave woman would wear, burntcorked her pretty face, and decoyed the posse into chasing her while the slaves escaped across the river.

Miss Webster had unnumbered colleagues—Quakers and Baptists and those of no denomination—and they were all busy operating the mysterious railroad that "ran underground from Cincinnati to Canada." It was not easy to operate. It jeopardized livelihood. It put life and limb at hazard. But it ran. Whole families ran it—the Rankins, the Coffins, the Sloanes—and three hundred thousand slaves escaped.

Sojourner Truth would have joined in this work, but her appearance was just as conspicuous now as it had been ten years before. So she spoke. She spoke for abolition and for women's rights, which, thanks to Lucy Stone and Jane Swisshelm, was a subject practically inseparable from abolition in the Midwest.

"Where dere is so much racket dere mus' be somethin' out o' kilter," Sojourner told the heckling males at a women's rights convention in Akron. "I think dat 'twixt de niggers of de South and de womens of de North all a-talkin' 'bout rights, de white mens'll be in a fix pretty soon. Ef de firs' woman God ever made was strong enough to turn de worl' upside down all by her lonesome se'f dese together ought to be able to turn it back an' git it right side up again, an' now dey is askin' to do it de mens better let 'em. Dey talks 'bout dis thing in the head—what dey

call it? Intellec'. Dat's it, honeys—intellec'. Now what's
dat got to do wid us women's rights or niggers' rights? Ef
my cup won't hol' but a pint an' yourn hol's a quart,
wouldn' you be mean not to let me have my little half
measure full?"

Sojourner's ironic wit and her subtle power dominated
that meeting. The woman who chaired it, Mrs. Frances
D. Gage, later reported that Sojourner Truth "had taken
us up in her strong arms and carried us safely over
the slough of difficulty, turning the whole tide in our
favor."

But she was not able always to turn the tide.

There was much hostility in Ohio, where she made Sa-
lem and the office of Marius Robinson's *Anti-Slavery
Bugle* her headquarters for two years. (Robinson tried to
teach her to read, but "my brains is too stiff now,"
Sojourner told him.) It was 1852, when she judged her
age to be "gone sixty," but she went from Ohio town to
town speaking, soliciting subscriptions for the *Anti-Slavery
Bugle,* and occasionally even making sorties into neighboring states. She could not go into Indiana without facing
the threat of arrest, or into Illinois without the chance of
violence. But she went many times. She said she was
"God's pilgrim" and under God's protection, but that protection sometimes wilted in the hot breath blowing in
from Missouri and across the plains of Kansas, where John
Brown, drunk on the wine of his coming crucifixion, would
soon reappear to make good the defiance flung out by
Senator William Seward: "Come on, then, gentlemen of
the slave states! Since there is no escaping your challenge,
I accept it on behalf of freedom. We will engage in competition for the virgin soil of Kansas, and God give the
victory to the side that is stronger in numbers as it is in
right."

Sojourner Truth was manhandled in Kansas, and ever
afterward needed the support of a cane, which, she
avowed, also came in "mighty fine for crackin' skulls."

If this was said jocosely, the rumors, the galling jokes,
and the downright lies that followed her everywhere were
not. Nor could the portrait of her drawn by Harriet

B. Stowe modify them. The people who were Sojourner's detractors did not read the *Atlantic Monthly*. If Sojourner was for Mrs. Stowe a "Sybil," she was a "black witch" for many more, and it was said that she worshiped in graveyards. If, as Mrs. Stowe wrote, she had "power and sweetness," there were others more vociferous who said she cast spells.

The unsavory reputation that surrounded her during the exposure and trial of Matthias was revived. Some believed that she was a man masquerading as a woman for reasons that would not bear examination. The St. Louis *Dispatch* reported, "Sojourner Truth is the name of a man now lecturing in Kansas City." Her vigorous, rail-like frame, her scarred, strong face and heavy-timbred voice were deceptive, and there were those who honestly doubted her femininity. But if such doubts persisted (as late as 1877), it was not Sojourner's fault.

In 1858 she had set a Kansas anti-slavery meeting above the usual pitch of turbulence. The meeting had been rigged by the enemies of abolition. As soon as Sojourner began her speech, a man in the audience interrupted her. "Hold on," he said. "Is the speaker man or woman? The majority of persons present believe the speaker to be a man. . . . I demand that if she is a woman, she submit her breast to the inspection of some of the ladies present . . . !"

While the abolitionists gaped in shocked silence, the pro-slavery claque, stamping their feet and clapping their hands, shouted in ribald mockery, "Uncover! Uncover! You are a man!" The dazed abolitionists responded only with cries of, "No, no! For shame!"

The whole auditorium was in confusion, for there were bully boys on both sides, and Sojourner Truth, facing it from the rostrum, whence had fled the chairman and the other platform guests, waited the tumult out. When it had quieted to manageable proportions, she stepped to the edge of the platform and pounded her cane on the floor.

"My breasts," she said, "has suckled many a white baby when dey shoulda been sucklin' my own." Her voice quavered momentarily, and then rose again firmly, tranquilly.

"I dar'st show my breasts to de whole cong'agation. It ain't my shame dat I do dis, but yourn. Here den," she said, ripping her clothes from neckline to waist, "see fer yourself!" Her hard gaze sought and found the face of the man who had first attacked her. She thrust her bared breasts forward and said in angry scorn, "Mought be you'd like to suck?"

5. *"Frederick, Is God Dead?"*

But Sojourner Truth was beginning to feel the wear and tear, the slow erosion of the years. Traveling with Parker Pillsbury on one of his speaking tours through the Midwest, she suffered occasional spells of faintness. Her wounded leg ulcerated. In Battle Creek, Michigan, where she had found her daughter's son, Sammy Banks, with whom she now lived, a physician was able to arrest the infection, but it broke out again periodically and gave her great pain. Nevertheless, she refused to stop for long. She went back into Illinois, Kansas, Ohio, Indiana. She went out into New England, where she was the guest of the Stowes in Andover, Massachusetts. And there was one brief interlude, more pleasant than strenuous. She went to Tawawa Springs, Ohio, to visit Daniel Payne, who, with his wife and her two children, was making his home there.

Payne was as busy as ever. He presided over the work of the African Methodist Episcopal Church in Ohio, Indiana, and Canada. His duties had forced him to live at one time or another in Troy, New York, Philadelphia, Baltimore, Washington, and Cincinnati. In addition to his churchly work, he had organized in each place adult Negroes into study groups and started schools for their children. He himself had done most of the teaching—reading, writing, and "social and civic morality" to the adults; a more formal curriculum to the children.

Now he was engaged in a more ambitious educational venture. He was the only Negro trustee of the new Wilberforce University. It had been founded by the white Methodist Church for "the benefit of the African race."

(The exigencies of the war were to close it down in 1862, but Payne was to reopen it the very next year and become the first president of the first Negro-controlled college.) While Sojourner was his guest in 1858, he took her to visit the college on the outskirts of Xenia. How she reacted to a campus populated exclusively by the illegitimate mulatto offspring of Southern planters is not recorded, but Payne felt moved to remind her that "these also need learning and God as much as any." When he had her speak to the adults of his Moral and Mental Uplift Society, he wished that there had been a thousand "instead of twenty to hear my simple and eloquent friend."

Before the visit ended, Payne read his friend some verses, pieces of his own published in 1850, and from a book of poems by the slave George M. Horton. Sojourner's comment made him laugh wryly. "Dan," she said, "yourn be pretty, but his'n be strong." She regretted that she could not read them for herself, but the bishop made her a gift of his slim volume anyway.

This visit did Sojourner Truth good, and she left Tawawa Springs to go stumping about as usual, attending meetings and speaking.

But all the most eloquent tongues in Christendom could not have modified the momentum or changed the direction of the decade that was now fast drawing to a close. Neither North nor South had been reconciled to the Compromise of 1850. Neither made serious efforts to preserve intersectional peace. If the North's defiance of the Fugitive Slave Law further embittered the South, then the passage of the Kansas-Nebraska Act exacerbated the feelings of the North and brought about a new political alignment of Northern Whigs, Free-Soilers, and Democrats. Professedly anti-slavery, the Republican party pieced out a program attractive to many who cared nothing about the slavery issue. In 1857 the Dred Scott decision did not prove "happily a matter of but little importance," as President Buchanan had said. It was oil thrown on the fire. In 1859, John Brown staged his raid on Harper's Ferry and achieved his martyrdom. In 1860 the Republicans elected the unknown Abraham Lincoln. In that same year Frederick Douglass, deep in despair on his return from England, spoke at an anti-slavery meeting commemorating West Indian emancipation:

"They [Republicans] are men who are brave enough to trip up a man on crutches, push a blind man off the sidewalk, or flog a man when his hands are tied, but too base and cowardly to contend with one who has an equal chance of defense with themselves. The black man, excluded alike from the jury box and the ballot box, is at the mercy of his enemies. . . . All know that the election of Lincoln would destroy all the conciliatory power which this new injustice to the Negro might exert. . . . But what will the colored people and their friends do now . . . ?"

Just at this point Sojourner Truth rose slowly in the back of the hall. "Frederick," she cried, "is God dead?"

God was not dead. Eight months later He was "trampling out the vintage where the grapes of wrath" were stored.

V. MISSISSIPPI DELTA

1. *Crusade in Cuba*

The 24th Infantry of the U. S. Regular Army, colored troops, reached Santiago Bay, Cuba, on June 20, 1898. They were the first to arrive. Their ship, the *City of Washington,* cruised within sight but out of range of Morro Castle until nightfall. The next day, when American gunboats began to arrive, the *City of Washington* was ordered to feint at Morro Castle so as to draw fire from the Spanish guns, and, like a punch-drunk fighter, she lumbered in time and again. The Spanish guns consistently overshot her. It is a good thing they did, for she was no ship for the job. She was a steamer, an excursion boat, and one clean shot would have splintered her wooden decks; but she feinted at the fortress off and on for five days, while the gunboats cannonaded Morro Castle until its guns were silenced. Then the *City of Washington* landed her six hundred soldiers, who marched immediately to Siboney and made camp five miles from the front, where the Spaniards were chewing up elements of Máximo Gómez' ragged army.

The *Comal* reached Cuban waters on June 21. She was a transport. Since she carried, in addition to some Negro regulars of the 10th Cavalry, Batteries B and K of the 2nd Artillery, white troops, baggage, ammunition, rations, horses and mules, she was valuable, and an escort of gun and torpedo boats was sent to pick her up off Dry Tortugas. But in spite of shelling from Admiral Sampson's gunboats, Morro Castle was still hot when the *Comal* arrived, and she steamed sixteen miles down the bay west of Santiago. Here she spent the night making half-mile circles so as to give the horses and mules air. It was very hot, and there was no breeze. In the morning the *Comal* moved within sight of Daiquiri and lay to until the armored cruiser *New York* came in to bombard the villages along the coast above and below the town.

Under the cover of this fire the 10th Cavalry began landing operations. They were at it two days, for they had to land the equipment and swim the livestock through heavy surf to the rocky beach. Two men were lost. Batteries B and K of the 2nd Artillery stayed aboard the *Comal*, which was later joined by the *Anne* and the *Topeka*, also carrying white troops. Then the three ships moved nine miles down to Siboney, where the beach was smoother and where the engineers had built a landing dock.

Meanwhile the dismounted 10th Cavalry had pushed overland to Siboney, which they reached shortly after midnight. Here they rested, and at three-thirty in the morning set out for Las Guásimas, where the enemy occupied a hill commanding the road to Santiago. The 1st Volunteers, popularly called the Rough Riders, had been pinned down at this spot for sixteen hours. When the 10th Cavalry came up, Colonel Leonard Wood, commanding the 1st Volunteers, deployed his troops to flank the hill right and left, and ordered Troops A, B, and I of the 10th to charge the enemy position frontally. Yelling and whooping like crazy men, the Rough Riders stormed up the hill on the right and left without the loss of a single man, but the 10th, charging head on, was met by heavy fire and sustained a loss of twenty-eight men, seven of them killed.

The *Concha* took on the 14th Infantry, a battalion of the 2nd Massachusetts, the brigade headquarters—all white—and the 25th Infantry, colored, at Tampa on June 7. They totaled thirteen hundred men. Aboard ship, white and colored troops were segregated at once. The latter were assigned to the bottom deck, where bunks were arranged in tiers of four, where it was dark at high noon, and where the only air came down the canvas air shafts when they were turned to the breeze. Topside, white troops lolled on the larboard; Negro troops milled around the gear piled starboard.

The *Concha* stayed tied up at the Tampa dock until

June 15, but Negro troops were forbidden ashore except when an officer could take a whole company off to bathe and exercise. This was done twice during the eight days, and by the time the *Concha* sailed she was as ripe as an eighteenth-century pesthouse. It was unbearably hot during the crossing, and Negro troops disobeyed the order against sleeping on deck. Packs of thirty at a time took turns at it, but in seven days no man slept up there twice, and some did not sleep up there at all. They landed at Daiquiri on the twenty-second, where the Cuban troops of General Castillo met them and led them on a two-day march over a jungle trail to Las Guásimas. They arrived just in time to clean up the retreating stragglers from the hill taken by the Rough Riders and the 10th Cavalry. Then they pushed on toward El Caney.

The 9th Cavalry, nicknamed the Black Buffaloes, was short its normal complement when it was ordered from Fort Robinson, Nebraska, to Chickamauga Park, Georgia, on April 20. From Chickamauga the six hundred men marched to Chattanooga, thence went by rail to Port Tampa, arriving on May 2. Here they quartered, and General Joseph Wheeler, in command of the Fifth Army Corps, detailed three officers and six enlisted men to recruitment duty. He wanted six hundred men. The detail found the new recruits in the vicinity of Orangeburg, South Carolina, but before they could return with them the veterans of the 9th Cavalry had sailed, along with some white elements of the Fifth Army.

The 9th disembarked at Daiquiri on June 23, but the sea suddenly became too rough to land the white troops, and the transport carried them to Siboney. That night the 9th bivouacked a few miles to the rear of the Rough Riders, and the next morning a hatless and breathless courier thundered in with the news that the Rough Riders needed help at Las Guásimas. The Black Buffaloes got there too late, help having been provided by the 10th Cavalry, and returned to camp and spent the next two days building roads. On June 27 three troops of the 9th were sent to scout and patrol, while five troops stayed behind roadbuilding until June 30, when they too moved out.

2. *Santiago*

Considering that when Congress declared war on Spain the War Department was only large enough to meet the needs of a peacetime army of twenty-eight thousand men, and that it had not for over thirty years transported, even by rail, a larger contingent than a regiment; and considering the fact that nearly all that was done between April and August 1898 was done by inexperienced officers more or less scrambled up in an unwieldy organization of staff corps, the transportation of seventeen thousand men, all told, their equipment and accouterments, was commendably done.

The specific objective of these troop movements was Santiago, Cuba, and the reason the troops converged on that place was also commendable. It was not because "our rapidly-increasing power," or our "commercial needs," or because "more than either, geography determined it," as Senator Beveridge declared. It is true that all these played their parts in America's imperialist expansion and the fulfillment of her "manifest destiny" in other directions; but the common soldier did not believe that the business in Cuba was of a piece with annexing the Hawaiian Islands, or building a coaling station in Pago Pago, or establishing bases on Wake, Midway, and Howland, or organizing the first Pan-American Congress. These troops, more than half of them state militia and volunteers, believed they were in Cuba because America and Americans had been "shocked in their moral sense" by Spain's "intolerable oppression" of the Cuban people, by Spain's violation of "all the principles of justice," and because it was America's "bounden duty to carry freedom to a race of worse than slaves abroad."

The battle at Santiago was to be the first (and last) land battle in pursuit of this noble end.

In defense of the city the Spaniards held two strongly fortified perimeter positions—the village of El Caney and the hills called San Juan. These had to be cleaned out, after which it was thought that the city would fall to the attackers like a ripe mango. Three command divisions were to take part in the initial attack. The first was to be launched from El Pozo, an elevation some three miles from Santiago, from which could be seen the masked entrenchments, the barbed-wire entanglements, and the blockhouses of the San Juan hills. Northeast and to the right, on a hill overlooking all approaches to Santiago, stood the stone fort and the blockhouses of El Caney. Southwest and on the left crawled the shallow San Juan River. Due north stood the city of Santiago on the bay, and on July 1, the day of the attack, the bay grinned and glittered in the bright sun.

General Lawton's command pulled out from El Pozo first. It consisted of three regiments of infantry—the 7th and 12th, white, and the 25th, colored. Their job was to storm and capture El Caney, execute a flanking movement, and then smash against the hills of San Juan from the right. Meanwhile General Kent's division of infantry—the 71st New York and the 13th, white, and the 24th, colored—was to cross the San Juan River, follow an exposed ridge north, and thus flank the hills on the left. Finally General Wheeler's dismounted cavalrymen—the Rough Riders, white, and the 9th and 10th, colored—were to await the reduction of El Caney and then make a frontal attack on the San Juan hills.

Lawton had already gone when the artillery duel began at four-thirty. It was thought that Lawton's infantry could reduce El Caney by midmorning. But this was not the only miscalculation made that day. The American artillery opened up with black powder instead of smokeless, and the Spanish artillery, quickly getting the range, forced the cavalry out of its assembly area before eight o' clock. There was confusion. An American observation balloon floating over the cavalry ranks gave away every movement. Spanish fire converged on them anew. They made for the river, there to seek shelter under its wooded banks, but near the crossing confusion was compounded.

Kent's 71st New York had managed to reach the exposed ridge road running north, but that was all. Spanish fire had completely demoralized them. Now they were milling around in the river crossing like panicked cattle. As the dismounted cavalry approached, the 71st broke through the cavalry ranks, which could not open fast enough to give them passage. Cavalrymen were shoved right and left, and one of them was knocked down and trampled to death. General Kent, "disgusted, with tears running down his cheeks," screamed out entreaties and threats, but he could not stop the 71st's terror-stricken recoil.

The cavalry units finally gained the bed of the river and stood waist-high in the water and waited. The balloon followed them, and Spanish fire followed the balloon. Why it was there none of the men knew. Who ordered it? Who manipulated it? Once it dropped a note saying that the men in the river were being fired upon, but this was quite superfluous information.

Taking the responsibility upon himself, Lieutenant J. J. Pershing, a platoon commander, called the other platoon commanders of the 10th Cavalry together and suggested that they leave the river a platoon at a time and deploy in thin skirmish lines on the shore. His own platoon went first. Three followed. As each platoon scrambled from the river, Pershing's men crawled forward through the light cover to make room. The fire was terrific. Two officers and eleven men were killed in the first five minutes. But the farther the skirmish lines advanced over the six-hundred-yard plain, the thicker the cover grew, and Lieutenant Pershing lost only fourteen men of his platoon before it reached fairly adequate cover near the base of the first hill. Here he waited.

But this was not the attack at all, nor the way it was supposed to be. Back in the bed of the river General Wheeler and some of his staff conferred over the situation, which was not promising. Just behind them in the river a thousand men waited. Another thousand were packed at the ford. Shells burst among them, and they were restless, for it is not easy to stand still and be shot at. It was now after ten o'clock, and Lawton had not reduced El Caney. Lawton was stalled. A part of Kent's command was in retreat. There was no right flank, there was no left flank. Co-ordination of commands had been lost. Retreat or advance? If this was a question in General Wheeler's mind, he did not have to answer it.

For suddenly a horde of men, miraculously moved by the same impulse, plowed out of the river, broke forward toward the ridge road, thronged wildly over it, and started across the plain toward the first hill. They were no one's command. They were a mixed company, white and black, regulars and volunteers, and they went yelling and shouting across the plain and firing over the heads of the skirmish lines as they advanced. Little clouds of dust, thrown up by bullets, bloomed on the hillside. Pausing only momentarily for loading and firing, the line of men—here thick, there thin—swept across the plain through a sheet of Mauser shot and onto the crest of the first hill. The Spaniards retreated to the second line of defense.

At the top of the hill the Americans halted to regroup for the attack on the entrenchments and blockhouses on the second hill. The Rough Riders, with some elements of the 13th Infantry, were put in the center of the line. The 9th Cavalry, which had lost a hundred men, held down the left. Pieced out with some units of the 24th Infantry, the 10th Cavalry held the right, facing the steep southern declivity, which when they poured into it was like spooning sliced potatoes into a pan of sizzling fat. The Spanish fire doubled in intensity when the attack was resumed, and a flood of flame swept over the Americans. But the momentum of the first phase held. Within an hour the blockhouses were taken, the entrenchments overrun, and the Spanish in flight toward Santiago. It was three-thirty in the afternoon.

Meantime the fight that was to have been finished at El Caney by midmorning was still in progress. It was an orderly battle, conducted by the book. At dawn three pieces of artillery had opened up against the stone fort, the blockhouse, and the church tower, but after only one round the dynamite gun jammed, and after only seven the Hotchkiss gun was knocked out. At six-thirty the 2nd Massachusetts was committed. The only visible targets were the fort, the blockhouse, and the tower, and musket fire was ineffective against these. They could not see a single

Spanish soldier, but the Spanish saw them. As they moved through the cover of grass and stunted palm, fusillades whined and whimpered from the rifle pits and entrenchments skillfully concealed in the slopes above them. It was like fighting ghosts, but they kept at it for two hours, and then they were withdrawn.

Four companies of the 25th Infantry replaced them. An initial charge carried them within five hundred yards of the fort. Here they were stopped by barbed wire "woven close as cloth" and pinned down by fire from the fort and cross fire from the blockhouse. They had no wire nippers. Working in groups of four, they hacked through the wire entanglements with their bayonets. It took them more than an hour. The operation cost fifty-three men.

But when the work was done the rest of the 25th and all of the 4th Infantry went in. The latter went in on the left and carried to a deep escarpment that blocked further advance but gave them cover from which they poured distractive fire on the blockhouse. The 25th advanced through fire from the fort and the church tower. The charge moved in quick rushes, but it made slow progress.

The 12th Infantry was the last to go in, and it was committed at four o'clock. Compared to the advance of the 25th, its sweep forward over the dead, dark bodies of comrades was triumphant. When Corporal T. H. Jones of I Company, the 25th, saw the 12th advancing, he remarked to Sergeant Butler of H Company, "Here they come to take credit for what our blood and bullets won." In Corporal Jones's company and in H, C, and D companies not an officer was left. The 12th was moving up in battle array, and though the ropy, pitched terrain spoiled their neat order, they nevertheless gave a distinct impression of picture-book soldiers in the final chapter of a storybook war. Impulsively Sergeant Butler ordered Companies I, H, C, and D to a final charge, and in ten minutes of insane fighting they stormed and carried the fort. An officer of the 12th arrived just in time to receive the Spanish flag.

Forty minutes later the blockhouse and the church tower surrendered, and at six-thirty in the evening all resistance at El Caney came to an end.

But the Spanish were not through yet—they simply re-tired toward Santiago—and there was no sleep for some of the American troops that night. The 25th Infantry was brought forward from El Caney to help the 24th extend and strengthen the lines. The 9th Cavalry gathered the wounded and buried the dead. The 10th Cavalry brought up food and ammunition. These troops worked all night, and in the morning, as General Wheeler had anticipated, the battle was resumed.

It went on for two days longer, but with less and less animation. On July 3, Spanish General Linares asked for a truce, but Cervera, the Spanish naval commander, tried to run his fleet out of Santiago Harbor and had it smashed to bits by the American fleet in Santiago Bay. By July 4 everything was over except the formalities and the shout-ing, and the war that had been fought "to rebuke a sister nation for her inhumanity," the war that had been fought "for independence, fair play . . . and democracy, against all that was tyrannical" was done.

In the three-day land battle of that war Negro troops of the 9th and 10th Cavalry and of the 24th and 25th Infan-try suffered 22 per cent greater casualties than their white comrades in arms.

3. *Rope and Faggot*

Before the fight at El Caney one of the Negro soldiers who died in it had written to his wife, "Surely the same strong spirit and quickened conscience which took up the cause of Cuba will secure justice to the American Negro."

And so it seemed that it might. In October 1898 the *Review of Reviews* commented editorially: "One of the most gratifying incidents of the Spanish War has been the enthusiasm that the colored regiments of the regular army have aroused throughout the whole country. . . . Men who can fight for their country as did these colored troops ought to have their full share of gratitude and honor." Even the Atlanta (Georgia) *Journal* was "pleased" to note not a sin-gle dissenting voice in the chorus of praise. Perhaps moved more by this than by political considerations, President

McKinley appointed a Negro as register of the Treasury, another as recorder of deeds, and still another as collector of customs.

All the same, the forces of reaction had only been scattered, not destroyed, and they were gathering again in no time at all. The ink was scarcely dry on the pages of the *Review of Reviews* when one Negro was hanged and ten shot to death by mobs in Mississippi. That same month, October, a South Carolina rabble attacked members of the "nigger-loving family" of John R. Talbot, collector of the port at Charleston, and forced them to leave the state. A few days later in North Carolina, where the election of 1896 had put a handful of Negroes into public office, the Democrats, in solemn conclave assembled, determined that "Negroes should be made to fear the lynchers' rope for aspiring to political power."

Red shirts and white shirts, symbols of terror in Reconstruction, were brought out again. A Presbyterian minister, the Reverend A. T. Nickelway, later wrote in the *Outlook*: "It is difficult to speak of the Red Shirts without a smile. They victimized the Negroes with a huge practical joke. . . . A dozen men would meet at a cross road, on horseback, clad in red shirts of calico, flannel or silk, according to the taste of the owner and the enthusiasm of his womenfolk. They would gallop through the country, and the Negro would quietly make up his mind that his interest in political affairs was not a large one, anyhow."

If this was a practical joke, it had the grimmest consequences. On the day following the election of 1898 a mass meeting of Red Shirts and other white citizens of Wilmington, North Carolina, passed resolutions to employ only white labor, to banish the Negro editor of the *North Carolina Record*, and to destroy the *Record's* printing press. More than a dozen Negroes were killed out of hand that very night, and before the fury had spent itself the following day twenty-three "black men, women and children were shot, stabbed and beaten to death." On receipt of this news in Atlanta a young social historian named W. E. B. Du Bois cried out, "The clock is turned back!

The sixties are here again!" Twitching with horror and bitter anguish, he buried his face in his hands.

4. *"Keep Powerful Friends"*

Quite different was the reaction of Isaiah T. Montgomery when the news reached him down in Mound Bayou, Mississippi. It is reported that he said to no one in particular but to the world at large, "I told you so!" Was there a note of satisfaction in the utterance? Almost certainly. But it was not because he enjoyed blood—he had gone through three years of the Civil War and managed not to draw a drop of it; nor did he like to have Negroes shot down—he was himself a Negro. The thing was that he needed vindication.

The only Negro delegate to the Mississippi constitutional convention in 1890, Montgomery had made a speech there. "Let no one persuade us Negroes to fight a cyclone," he had said then, and the next day cast his vote with those who believed that "every political feud, every factional disturbance, and every race riot can be traced to the ignorant, presuming Negro." He was accused of the basest treachery to his people, and since then it had seemed to him that every instance of terror, every murderous act committed against Negroes in any of the various names of the "public good" somehow justified his stand.

Isaiah Montgomery was a hard man to figure.

He had been a precocious youth, quickly maturing in a precarious age. Born in 1847, the slave of Joseph Davis, elder brother of Jefferson Davis, he grew up on Hurricane Plantation. Joseph Davis taught all the Montgomerys to read, and in addition Isaiah acquired the fundamentals of accounting. At nine he was his master's office boy. At twelve he was doing all the plantation accounts, while his brother helped to supervise the work in the fields, his cousin, Ben Green, served as general mechanic, and his father, old Ben, bossed the whole enterprise.

Joseph Davis was partial to the Montgomerys. It was said that he "never lifted so much as a finger against them." They probably never gave him cause. He trusted them;

they trusted him. Many an afternoon in the slack season the master could be found sitting on the back veranda of his house talking "man to man" with the Montgomerys and Ben Green grouped on the steps below him. They talked "plantation business, land speculation and family affairs"—and especially the affairs of young Jefferson Davis, who had been to West Point and to Congress, had come back from the Mexican War a hero, and who, in 1858, a senator from Mississippi, was widely recognized, since Calhoun's death, as the leading spokesman for the South. They talked about the tightening sectional tensions. They talked about the prospects for war.

When the war came Joseph Davis was in his seventies, much too old to fight. Taking a few slaves and some livestock, he went to Montgomery, Alabama, where the capital of the new Confederacy had been established.

> *Say, darkeys, hab you seen de massa,*
> *Wid di muffstash on he face,*
> *Go long de road some time dis mornin',*
> *Like he gwine leab de place?*
>
> *He see de smoke way up de ribber*
> *Whar de Lincum gunboats lay;*
> *He took he hat an' leff berry sudden,*
> *An' I s'pose he's runned away.*
>
> *De massa run, ha, ha!*
> *De darkey stay, he, he!*
> *It mus' be now de kingdom come,*
> *An' de y'ar of jubilee.*

Undoubtedly some of the Davis slaves sang this ditty, but it is highly improbable that the Montgomerys were among them. Old Ben was left in charge of Hurricane Island plantation and of Brierfield, Jefferson Davis' plantation. He took William, his elder son, to Brierfield with him, and put Isaiah and Ben Green in charge at Hurricane. Isaiah was fourteen, Ben three years older.

But in a few weeks the tide of war rolled toward Hurricane. The bluffs on both sides of the river were fortified to protect Vicksburg against the Yankees, who soon made the city a military objective. Shoving out from their base at Memphis, scouts of Grant's army prowled the west shore of the river. Isaiah saw skirmishes between Confederate and Union patrols. He saw the gunboat *Indianola* sunk when Porter's fleet tried to run through the river defenses in 1863. Shortly after that he saw Captain Porter himself. Porter ordered both Hurricane and Brierfield evacuated. He sent old Ben, his wife, their two daughters, and their elder son north to Cincinnati. He kept Isaiah. He was struck by the boy's precocity. He made Isaiah "a prize of war."

Isaiah served Porter as cabin boy on the *Benton* and on other ships that were in the fighting. Isaiah saw the Battle of Grand Gulf. His ship stood by at the Battle of Port Gibson and made a scouting run up the Red River to Fort De Russey. It joined in the bombardment of Vicksburg and was there when that city fell. Though he served for a time as gunner's mate, Isaiah never fired a gun, pulled a lanyard, or breeched a shell, but he was painfully wounded in an accident aboard ship. Captain Porter assigned a nurse to accompany him to Mound City, Illinois. Recovering in a few weeks, Isaiah joined the rest of the Montgomerys in Ohio. He was seventeen.

But life in the North was not for the Montgomerys. Cincinnati was not their environment. Neither the sorcery of their personalities nor the combination of their skills, so effective at Davis Bend, worked to advantage there. They made a living, it is true—the women as seamstresses, the men as laborers—and they pooled their resources; but it was not the living they wanted, or the living they were used to.

Cincinnati was crowded with Negroes, among whom an inflexibly self-conscious class structure had already formed. The Montgomerys were excluded from the status their superior endowments and training argued they deserved. The city and the country around, as far north as Xenia, had been the favorite dumping ground for the mulatto offspring of Southern planters. Many of these mulattoes were doing well. They had urban skills and, often, substantial financial backing. One, a real estate operator named Henry Boyd, was worth fifty thousand dollars. Samuel Wilcox manufactured beds and employed white and Negro labor. A mulatto landscape artist had studied in Rome, and a daguerreotypist was said to be the most skillful in the entire West.

These and others like them were the free Negro aristocracy, and they guarded their status jealously. The Montgomerys were pure black. Fresh up from a slavery that had been for them warm and even rewarding in personal relations with a master class they understood and among Negroes they could command, they were nevertheless peasant. Though slavery was over for them, they looked homeward to Mississippi. The occasional letters they had from Cousin Ben Green brought tears of nostalgia to their eyes.

Ben Green himself was doing all right. He had gone to Vicksburg and set up as a mechanic. There was much to do. "Ruin and army worms is everywhere," he wrote. "About all the plantations is left or made into camps for the colored who work in the woodyards for the soldiers and have not enough to eat. Money comes in driplets but I am better off as most white and colored get no money at all." He reported that Major Compash, who once owned more than a hundred slaves, could be seen in the streets of Vicksburg peddling cakes and bread made by his wife. Farms were going to swamps and weeds because the Negro workers had deserted them. Rumor had it that a railroad was coming through from Memphis to New Orleans, and many freedmen had gone east to help build it. Perhaps things would get better, Ben Green wrote, but, "O, the good land so desolated!"

The Montgomerys went back to Mississippi in 1865, and the next year they leased Hurricane and Brierfield from their old master, Joseph Davis. Ben Green did not have to be begged to join them. In Vicksburg, Natchez, and Jackson they found some of the ex-slaves with whom they had formerly worked and brought them back to the plantations. Each male "hand" was promised rations and fifteen dollars a month. Each head of family—seven in all, making a group of forty-six people that first year—had his own hut and kitchen garden.

Things began to hum. Ben Green restored the forge and made and repaired tools. The first cotton crop was planted in the spring of 1867. In summer the army worm came, but they conquered it. In late summer they rebuilt the levee and the dock at Hurricane. That fall they picked and ginned five hundred and twenty bales of cotton. By settling-up time, just prior to Christmas, the Montgomerys had tripled their original investment, and had done so well that they agreed to buy Hurricane and Brierfield for thirty thousand dollars. Young Isaiah signed the purchase notes. He had not then attained his majority. By 1873 the Montgomerys had become the third largest cotton producers in the state, and their cotton took all the prizes at the Cincinnati Exposition.

But all was not fair weather. Planters in the vicinity of Davis Bend, many of them the "new breed" Ben Green had mentioned in his letters, objected to the Montgomerys on principle. The Montgomerys' tenants were sometimes stopped and questioned about activities on the plantations. Sometimes they were thrown into jail on trumped-up charges, putting the Montgomerys to trouble and expense to get them out again. On at least one occasion a Montgomery well was poisoned and four mules and a horse died of drinking the water. Even the old breed of planters who accepted the Montgomerys and the Montgomerys' help muttered against the new situation that seemed to be developing generally in the life of the state.

It was a situation that the vast majority of Southern whites meant to resist, for it tended to make permanent their forfeiture of political power and to subvert the social principles upon which their attitudes, their economy, and their lives had been founded. In Mississippi, as elsewhere in the South, some slaveholders resisted simply by withholding news of freedom from their slaves. Young men formed patrols to keep "slaves" confined. In May 1865, Governor Clark issued a proclamation: "Masters are still responsible as heretofore for the protection and conduct of their slaves, and they should be kept home as heretofore."

Many professed to believe that slavery still had legal existence. The only question in their minds was whether the state should adopt a policy of gradual emancipation. The answer to this was far from an unqualified and universal yea. Serving as the ears of President Johnson in 1865, Carl Schurz heard from nineteen of every twenty Southern men that Negroes would not work except under compulsion, that they could not live without a master, and that they positively "could not be adopted to a system of free labor."

But the legality of freedom was real enough. The presence of federal troops attested the fact. In November 1865 the new governor of Mississippi, Benjamin Humphreys, urged the legislature to reckon with Negro freedom as a reality. "The Negro," he said, "is free, whether we like it or not; we must realize that fact now and forever. To be free, however, does not make him a citizen, or entitle him to political and social equality with the white race. . . ."

Less than three weeks later white Mississippians did reckon with the reality, but after their own fashion. Following the hasty passage of legislation that provided, among other things, for binding out Negro children, without the consent of their parents, to former masters, and the establishment of iron-hard vagrancy regulations applying only to Negroes, the governor signed another piece of legislation called "An Act to Confer Civil Rights on Freedmen."

It was a new Black Code in twelve sections, and Carl Schurz summed up its spirit. "It is that the Negro exists for the special object of raising cotton, rice and sugar for the whites, and that it is illegitimate for him to indulge, like other people, in the pursuit of his own happiness in his own way. Although it is admitted that he has ceased to be the property of a master, it is not admitted that he has a right to become his own master. . . . There are systems intermediate between slavery as it formerly existed in the south, and free labor as it exists in the north, but more nearly related to the former than to the latter, the introduction of which will be attempted. . . ."

The Mississippi legislation was just such an attempt. All of its provisions were direct threats to the Negroes of the state, but the economic limitations it placed upon them were especially severe. All Negroes must have homes and occupations and written evidence thereof. Negroes employed for a term of service of more than a month must produce a written contract to that effect. If engaged in irregular job work, they must have licenses issued by local authorities. The licenses could be revoked at will. Failure to produce a contract or a license upon demand made Negroes liable to prison or to practical re-enslavement, and though employers could dismiss them with impunity, Negroes could not quit their employment before the time stipulated in their contracts. "Every civil officer shall, and every person may," the law said, "arrest and carry back to his or her legal employer any freedman, free Negro, or mulatto who shall have quit the service of his or her employer."

And, finally, there was a section providing that "no freedman, free Negro, or mulatto can rent or lease any lands or tenements except in incorporated cities or towns. . . ."

It was this provision that immediately jeopardized the Montgomerys. They were still leasing in 1866–68. Even before the law became effective, and even while Negroes were supposed to be under the protection of the federal military, by whom the land had been confiscated from its original owners, Negro leaseholders around Davis Bend had been thrown off the land. And now suppose the law were made to operate retroactively? The Montgomerys would be subject to eviction without compensation. Instead of working for themselves, they would have to work for others.

It was a prospect that Benjamin Montgomery, now growing old, could not face. He summoned his sons and Ben Green for a family conference. William was pessimistic. He had a wife and children and he talked gloomily of going north again to Ohio, where there was good farmland. "I tell you, Pa, the new men won't let us work for ourselves." Ben Green kept silent, as was his habit, but he shook his head disconsolately. They all looked to Isaiah.

"There's Mr. Charles Clark," Isaiah said, "and he's not one of the new men." Clark, indeed, had been a frequent guest of Joseph Davis before the war. "He's not the governor now, but he's still a power. The thing is, if you've got none yourself get somebody with power, and not be stiff-necked. Let's go see Mr. Clark."

Benjamin and Isaiah Montgomery traveled to Jackson to see Charles Clark. He talked with them in his carriage house. He saw to it that they were fed in his kitchen. Father and son returned to Davis Bend in the best of spirits. They had Clark's word for it, law or no law, they would not be molested.

"We got to keep powerful friends," Isaiah said.

There was a pattern of behavior to which slavery had trained them, and within that pattern they could operate effectively.

5. No North: No South

It soon seemed to Republicans in the North that power in the South was being used to subvert the principles of freedom and equality upon which, many Northerners now professed to believe, the war had been fought. Southern state after state passed laws that were meant to bring about the practical re-enslavement of the Negro. In no state did the Negro have freedom of movement or of person. In no state could he vote. In Mississippi, South Carolina, and Louisiana he could not buy or lease farm-land, or sell farm products. There was no use for Negroes to protest, as they did, either the laws or the men charged to administer them. All through the summer and fall of 1865 state conventions were busy fixing requirements for suffrage and hammering out constitutions to assure white supremacy. Constitutional conventions simply ignored the resolutions of Negro groups, who were inclined, as Governor Perry of South Carolina said, "to forget that this is a white man's government, and intended for white men only."

But it was evident that the radical Republicans were not in agreement with this point of view. They had inveighed against Lincoln's veto of the Wade-Davis Bill, which would have penalized the South rather harshly, and they had warned the President "that the authority of Congress is paramount and must be respected." In 1864 they had refused to seat the new senators from Louisiana because the state had denied the franchise to Negroes—and had done this in spite of even Lincoln's expressed hope that "some colored people . . . especially those who have fought gallantly in our ranks," might be let in. If, after the death of Lincoln, Johnson seemed determined to follow a program of conservative reconstruction, the radical Republicans were just as determined that he would not. Their disapproval swelled to militant anger. Thaddeus Stevens, "the first Republican madman," declared that "the very foundations of their [Southern states'] institutions must be broken up and relaid, or all our blood and treasure have been spent in vain."

When Congress convened in December 1865, the radical Republicans were set for a knockdown, drag-out fight. It was not long coming.

Though the open issue and the only issue for some was Negro suffrage and civil rights, there were other issues not strictly political in nature. Knowing politicians could not ignore them. The power of the executive had been enormously increased during the war, and that had to be curtailed, the balance between it, the legislative, and the judicial power restored. The unindemnified loss of billions in slaves and other confiscated property had to be adjusted. The runaway pace of industrialism in the North; the relative economic paralysis of the South; the future of the poor whites, whose man Johnson was; the rise of the money merchants, corporations, trusts, and monopolies— all these were involved in the problem of reconstruction and the task of binding up "the nation's wounds." All these were at issue in the fight between radical and conservative.

But it did not seem so when the radicals made their first move. Effectively controlling Congress, and led by Thaddeus Stevens and Charles Sumner, they refused to admit to Congress the South's newly elected representatives. They argued that the South had not purged and redeemed itself. They argued that the conditions of redemption had not been properly established. They argued that the re-admission of the states was not, as Lincoln had presumed and Johnson was trying to prove, an executive matter: it was legislative. To fix the conditions upon which the South might have congressional representation, Stevens pushed through a proposal to set up a Joint Committee of Fifteen with broad discretionary powers.

Meantime the new Black Codes were attacked as contrary to "elemental justice," as undoubtedly they were, and not only the radicals but the Puritan idealists contended that the federal government must step in to protect the Negro against his former master. But how? In February 1866, Congress passed a bill giving sweeping adjudicative and economic powers to the Freedmen's Bureau, a war-time emergency agency. President Johnson vetoed it. Three days later he publicly defended his veto in language so personal and intemperate that some Northern newspapers accused him of being drunk. Yet "drunk either with wine or power," a few weeks later still he also vetoed a bill designed to "protect all persons of the United States in their civil rights, and to furnish the means of their vindication."

Stung by the President's stubbornness, by his rejection of the Joint Committee of Fifteen's preliminary report (which said, in part, that "the South deliberately proposed to oppress white Unionists and freedmen"), and by his vituperative censure of the Republican party, Congress overrode the veto of the Civil Rights Bill. In June it passed the Fourteenth Amendment to the Constitution and sent it to the states for ratification.

Having shown their power, the radicals were now determined to consolidate it in the elections of 1866. The squabbles between the President and the Congress had made clear the issues, and the Republicans propagandized them. The national debt must be saved from "the inevitable repudiation" that awaited it if rebels were returned to power. Freedom must be maintained, "not for a limited time but for all time." The "Constitution must know no North, no South."

Charles Sumner was the most brilliant and persuasive

speaker in the Republican party. His altruism was as incorruptible as Stevens' vindictiveness was adamant. One was fire, the other rock. One attracted the misty-eyed idealists, the other the tough-minded pragmatists. Stevens acted; Sumner spoke—and when Sumner spoke people listened. "Thus is Equality the Alpha and the Omega, in which all other rights are embraced. Equality is the first of rights. . . . Strike at the Black Code, as you have already struck at the Slave Code. There is nothing to choose between them. Strike at once, strike hard! You have already proclaimed Emancipation; proclaim Enfranchisement also. . . ."

President Johnson had only pieces of parties behind him, and no machinery through which the pieces could operate. Moderate Republicans and Copperhead Democrats met in Philadelphia and, for what it was worth, pledged their support to him. It was not worth much, and the "Tennessee tailor" did nothing to increase its value. His choleric temper got the better of him as he stumped the Midwest. He slung personal abuse at his public enemies. Northerners heckled him, and he replied with rancor and without the dignity both his position and his policy required. Preaching tolerance for the South, he himself grew increasingly intolerant. He was again accused of drunkenness. He injured his own cause.

On the other hand, the Republicans got help not only from Northern industrialists and financiers, who envisioned the free South as a vast reservoir of cheap labor and a fertile field for investments; they got it also from certain events that supported the well-propagandized opinion that the South "menaced hate" and that no one, "white or black, who was friendly to the Union was safe" there. In the spring a Memphis riot brought death to forty-six Negroes and destruction to four of their churches and twelve of their makeshift schools. On their way to a political meeting—marching, as was the almost universal custom in those rallying days—a band of New Orleans Negroes were attacked by whites. A fusillade of shots peppered the Negroes' ranks; they were set upon by the police as well as by the spectators. When the frightened Negroes barricaded themselves in the Mechanics' Institute Hall they were shot like fish in a barrel. Fifty-eight were killed and a hundred wounded, and others were killed as they tried to flee. "It was an absolute massacre," reported General Sheridan after an investigation, ". . . murder which the mayor and police of the city perpetrated without the shadow of a necessity."

Following such incidents as these, all bloodily embellished by the Northern press and pulpit, the Republican victory came easily. The Republican Congress would have a two-thirds majority—143 to 49 in the House; 42 to 11 in the Senate. Let Johnson veto all he had a mind to!

And he had a mind to veto much, but that handy power was soon shriveled by a Congress that believed the elections to be a prescription to carry through with Reconstruction on the basis of the report of the Joint Committee of Fifteen. Even before the preceding Congress adjourned, it had tied Johnson's hands—as President, with the Tenure of Office Act; as Commander in Chief, with a decree that military orders must be channeled through the General of the Army, a new rank, to which U. S. Grant, the North's Civil War hero, was appointed.

This done, the first Reconstruction Act was passed. By its terms each of the ten states still technically in rebellion was designated as belonging to one of five military districts over each of which an officer of general rank would exercise vast civil powers. His immediate function was to prepare the states in his district for readmission to the Union by registering all citizens, black and white, and by ordering elections for conventions to adopt state constitutions providing for Negro suffrage. Once the new constitutions had received congressional approval and the states had ratified the Fourteenth Amendment, readmission to the Union would follow.

By 1868 the process had been completed in all but Virginia, Texas, and Mississippi, and these, forced to capitulate if they would avoid being ruled as conquered territories, came around in 1870, by which time the Fifteenth Amendment to the Constitution had been ratified. By which time, too, the Union League and the politicians who infested the Freedmen's Bureau were keeping the strength of the Republican party solid through a thorough control and manipulation of the Negro vote. Negroes sat in the highest councils of the reconstructed states. Sixteen, representing seven of these states, sat in the United States Congress. Two from Mississippi were elected to the Senate. Hiram Revels, one of the latter, went to Washington in 1870 to take the seat once held by Jefferson Davis.

6. *Black Man's Place*

If there was a kind of poetic justice in this, the Montgomerys did not appreciate it. Isaiah was to refer to the Negro Mississippi congressman John R. Lynch and to the Negro senators, Revels and Blanche K. Bruce, as "outlanders." He was to pass remarks about "all these new people in here," and to profess himself "mighty dissatisfied with the way things are running."

That he inquired closely into the way things were running is doubtful, else he would have known and been pleased by the fact that Hiram Revels fought in the Senate for the removal of the restrictions placed on ex-Confederates. He would have known that John R. Lynch, a member of the Mississippi legislature and Speaker of its House before he was elected to Congress in 1873, not only petitioned Congress on behalf of the old master class but opposed with all his unavailing strength the bill that increased taxes fourteenfold and resulted in the tax sale of six million acres of Mississippi farmland. (In 1873 the Montgomerys paid taxes of $2447.09.)

But Isaiah Montgomery was a jangle of contrarieties, though still in some almost organic way a pure product of his times. By training and experience he was one thing, by instinct and temperament another. He had tremendous self-esteem but in the face of his own material success, which he seemed truly to believe the doing of God, abject humility. Reared in the paternalistic pattern of slavery and in the ways of thinking that slavery encouraged, all his life his public acts and utterances marked him a believer in the innate inferiority of his race, yet as a free man he was sensitive and proud to the extent of vowing that he would starve rather than work as a menial for any white man.

He was generous and "charitable," but he did not hesitate to demand interest as high as 50 per cent on loans, and he was known to take advantage of his workers at Davis Bend by markups of 20, 30, and even 40 per cent on supplies from the commissary.

He founded a Negro colony that eventually spread over thirty thousand acres of rich Delta land, and this undoubtedly stimulated race pride and ambition and contributed to race progress. But when John R. Lynch, described as "the ablest man of his race in the South," importuned him to "work with us for the uplift of our people," Montgomery expressed such aversion to joining forces with reputable Negro leaders of Mississippi as to appear psychopathic. Nevertheless, he considered himself an ardent "race man"—though his ardor would be difficult to prove by the fact that, in the year Lynch was elected to Congress, Montgomery voted for J. L. Alcorn in the gubernatorial election, who was pledged to re-establish the "Bourbon system," and who had, consequently, been repudiated by the Negroes of the state. As the only Negro in the Mississippi constitutional convention in 1890, Isaiah Montgomery spoke and voted for Negro disfranchisement.

Were these the acts and attitudes of a self-seeker or of an uncommonly wise man? Perhaps Montgomery saw that Negro political and civil equality, forced upon the South by a vindictive and perhaps venal Congress, could not last. To see this in those times of extreme disorganization required, certainly, uncommon insight. And especially in Mississippi, where there was the greatest confusion of attitudes, trends, and forces: humanitarian zeal and inhuman hate, both personal and racial—and neither with a clear advantage; flux and counterflux; movement from the land to industry in the cities; from the cities back to the land; from the South, North; from Southeast, West. There was a ruined Southern oligarchy, and there were powerful segments of Northern capital organized to keep it ruined and to forestall the resurgence of Southern political power. If many conservative white men insisted on the necessity of satisfying the requirements of Congress, at least an equal number were opposed. Although most Democrats went along in principle with the editor who wrote that "nigger voting, holding office and sitting in the jury box are all wrong," many did not at first act on the principle they espoused. Accepting what seemed to be the inevitable instead, they spared no effort to enlist the Negro vote.

And the efforts themselves were confused. On the one hand there were unsegregated barbecues and picnics "at which Negro bands and glee clubs entertained," and on the other there were economic pressures, threats, and violence. Though the radical Republicans enjoyed the overwhelming advantage of Negro support, they regarded it as a necessary evil, and they would not countenance Negro control of the party, or allow "social equality," or encourage widespread economic opportunity for Negroes. After the withdrawal of the Freedmen's Bureau in 1870, while native Delta planters were enticing Negro workers with small social and economic advantages and declaring that "every step taken in the development of the section has been dependent upon an increased Negro population," other elements, including, naturally, the poor whites, were convinced that "every Negro that leaves the state is a blessing" and that "the South cannot hold up her head until the last Negro is gone."

While the Klan and Klan-like organizations rode through the countryside murdering Negroes and burning their schools and churches, Blanche K. Bruce, the Negro senator from Mississippi, and his wife "entertained a distinguished group which included the wives of Supreme Court justices and other officials."

Whether or not Isaiah Montgomery saw through the confusion of the 1870s and '80s, one thing he saw clearly: the Montgomerys' present security lay in their plantations on Davis Bend. Here they were removed from the political confusion of Vicksburg, Jackson, and Natchez, and they would not need, God willing, the authority their white friends no longer possessed. And if they minded carefully their own business they would not provoke the authority now in the hands of strangers. None of the Montgomerys attended the political meetings called by the enthusiastic Negroes of Vicksburg and Jackson in 1867 and '68. They did send Ben Green as an observer. Green reported trouble ahead. The positions of mob and nabob had been reversed. In December 1868 there were rumors that "Negroes throughout the South had a thorough understanding, and planned to repeat all the atrocities of Santo Domingo." Considering that the "atrocities" in Santo Domingo had come to an end fully a half century before, and considering the much-bruited "abysmal ignorance" of Negroes, the rumor was fantastic, but Mississippi gave it credence. Governor Ames appealed to the military commander of the district to keep an armed force ready.

But armed forces of sorts were even then ready and going about their business of murder. General Nathan B. Forrest, the implacable racist who had refused to recognize the Union's colored troops as soldiers and had ordered the wholesale killing of those captured at Fort Pillow, had already organized the Ku Klux Klan. There were, besides, the Knights of the Black Cross, Heggie's Scouts, and the Washington Brothers. A member of Heggie's Scouts boasted that on one occasion the Scouts killed "a hundred and sixteen niggers and threw their bodies in the Tallahatchie." Catching a group of Negroes in baptismal rites in Yockana Creek, the Klan of Lafayette County drowned thirty of them. All through the late sixties and the seventies ubiquitous bands of terrorists murdered Negro preachers and land renters, "black Republicans and some Jewish merchants."

As Isaiah Montgomery saw it, undoubtedly the best thing was isolation. He did not want to be thought involved or to be caught unprotected in the white man's world. But the isolation of Davis Bend was not quite enough. When the military commander of the district, General Ord, named old Ben Montgomery a justice of the peace, the wave of reaction of native whites to this first appointment of a Negro official washed over the Montgomerys on their plantations. Said the Jackson *Clarion*:

"General Ord has heretofore exhibited a wisdom in his administration, but we doubt not lovers of peace . . . will condemn this action as insulting to that race whom God has created the superior of the black man, and whom no monarch can make his equal." While old Ben held his breath, Isaiah assured the white neighbors on Davis Bend that his father would not hear cases involving whites; that, in fact, he did not want to be a justice of the peace anyway—but what could he do?

Back into play came that ceremonial submissiveness to whatever will was ascendant and to whatever climate of opinion prevailed.

There was of course much for the Montgomerys to do simply to mind their own business, and they minded it with unremitting care. It was Isaiah's ambition to make the plantations self-sufficient, as in the days of slavery. A commissary was built. Once a year Isaiah journeyed to Cincinnati to buy "furnishings"—the shirting, shoes, and jeans, the gaudy calicoes, the cheap candies, and the shoddy toys the workers would buy for their children at Christmas. From the plantation smokehouse came the fat back, from the cane mill the sorghum. A sawmill was built. With the help of the Freedmen's Bureau the Montgomerys salvaged some old machinery and built a cotton gin. They loaded their cotton directly onto the steamer from their own dock. In 1869 a disastrous flood swept away their dock, breached the levee, and ruined part of the crop. They had recovered by next planting time, but in harvest season the dock, which was already stacked with the first bales of cotton, was mysteriously destroyed by fire at night. Old Ben thought some careless worker had dropped ashes from his pipe. Ben Green suspected vandalism. Isaiah kept his own counsel, but when the dock was rebuilt he went to the white planters on Davis Bend and offered them its facilities free of charge. You had to "stay right" with the white folks.

In common with other planters, the Montgomerys had trouble keeping workers, for if freedom meant anything to great numbers of ex-slaves it meant freedom to move about. "Every little accident would make them get up and leave," Isaiah recalled years later, "and when there were no accidents, they'd find excuses." Not all of the excuses were simple. ("I'se jes' movin' ter town perminint so's ter save de trip dere ev'y Sa'dee.") In town and city were schools for their children, domestic work for their wives, and wage work for themselves. Competition for farm labor was keen and ruthless among river-county planters. Many of them lured workers from neighboring plantations and even from neighboring states. They painted rosy pictures and made big promises, but such deception did not pay off in the long run, for there were the railroads providing free transportation to distant places and offering the princely wage of a dollar and seventy-five cents a day. Though this was less than the two to three dollars paid blacksmiths, carpenters, and brickmasons, it was far more than the wage of farm hands.

But the city was Babylon, and slavery had taught no defense against Babylonian temptations. Idleness was the test of freedom, but idleness had to be supported. "In cat-fish season they [Negroes] fattened and did well," and in winter they got rations from the government, until General Gillem, commissioner of the Freedmen's Bureau, cut them off in 1867. The practice, he said, abetted "indolence and independence," as no doubt it did. But in that year and the following hard times struck, and even the most industrious were forced into idleness. So many Negroes died of yellow fever, cholera, and smallpox that confident forecasts were made of the Negro's complete extinction. In 1867 the Natchez *Democrat* was certain that "the child is already born who will behold the last Negro in the State of Mississippi," and the eminent clergyman, Dr. C. K. Marshall, who seems to have got direct word from heaven, foresaw with satisfaction that "On the morning of the 1st of January, 1920, the colored population will scarcely be counted . . . a few . . . here and there who may still earn precarious bread as they pass away."

The graveyards filled up in bad times, the jails in good. Fear of the law could not restrain the petty pilfering that had been so easily learned in slavery. And drunkenness was another thing, for during slavery "not to be drunk during the holidays was disgraceful" and aroused the suspicions of the masters, who freely supplied the whisky. Now any chosen day was a holiday, and there were drunkenness and quarrels and profanity, and these led straight to the lockup. Of the 1416 people who "served time" in the Vicksburg workhouse from March 1868 to the next February, 992 were Negroes, "and Negroes idling in jail are a problem."

But General Gillem had a solution. He would lease the convicts. It was a strange kind of lease that gave a planter-capitalist named Edmund Richardson control of state prisoners in 1868. Under the terms of it the state paid Richardson eighteen thousand dollars a year for the maintenance of prisoners and he could employ them as he saw fit. He saw fit to employ them not only on his own plantations but to hire them out to other planters at fifteen dollars a month a man. Richardson's contract lapsed in 1871, but five years later the almost incredible Jones Hamilton, who played with plantations, race tracks, railroads, and steamboats as a reckless boy plays with marbles, finaigued a similar agreement. Through Hamilton the Montgomerys got some convict laborers for the plantations on Davis Bend.

Skilled and tactful campaigners though they were, the Montgomerys could not ward off all the strokes of chance or impregnably defend against all the common afflictions. The production of cotton rose, but the price went down, and the cost of agricultural credit soared from 15 to 30 per cent. In 1877 a hundred bales of cotton brought only as much as fifty had brought ten years before. The land, too, was petering out. In 1878 old Ben Montgomery died, and some of the sentiment went out of the Davis Bend plantations. William again talked of leaving. But where would he go? What would he do? He was not one of those "burr-head ignoramuses" cluttering the roads in search of excitement. Good timber covered nearly a thousand acres of Brierfield, and Isaiah had plans for it. He sent William and Ben Green to Vicksburg to set up a sawmill. They turned out barrel staves, puncheons, and railroad ties.

They sold scrap lumber to the steamboats. The end of the Montgomery place on Davis Bend was near at hand.

It came when Joseph Davis' heirs disputed the Montgomerys' title to Hurricane and Brierfield. It was an easy suit to settle. When the Davis lawyers came from Jackson to see Isaiah, he did not argue. They did not bother to take their hats off in Isaiah's parlor and in the presence of his wife and three young daughters. They referred to him as a "nigger man," and reminded him that he was just a "nigger boy" when he signed the purchase notes in 1867. He was only twenty then, and even had he been white that was too young to sign a legal instrument and make it stick.

Isaiah did not even engage a lawyer. What lawyer would take a Negro's case against a white man? He did write to "Miss Varina," Jefferson Davis' wife, and he got an answer, too. Miss Varina expressed her sympathetic concern that he avoid all trouble, but the matter was out of her hands: neither she nor her husband was a party to the suit.

So Isaiah yielded without a struggle. If he yielded on a quid-for-quo basis that involved, explicitly, relinquishing the property and a fourteen-thousand-dollar equity in order to retain the good will of men who could and probably would ruin him otherwise, and, implicitly, the acceptance of white supremacy and the fact that the end of slavery brought an end to his immunity, he was responding to the reality he saw everywhere about him. He knew what was required of him in the face of it. He had no illusions. The old masters were back and accounting for every move in terms of their social responsibility, *the* social good. Wedding the rage and passion of the poor whites to the purpose of restoring the South as it was (though in that South the poor whites lived degraded and denied), they, the old planters, new capitalists, and poor whites, marched under slogans as under a cloud of banners. "Mississippi Is a White Man's Country, and by the Eternal God We'll Rule It!" "God Almighty, in farming out His privileges to mankind, drew a line as to qualifications." And the masthead of the *Mississippi Register* proclaimed, "A White Man in a White Man's Place. A Black Man in a Black Man's Place. Each According to the Eternal Fitness of Things."

Isaiah Montgomery was an artless evocation of the real present and of the predictable immediate future. He could see the superiority of white men growing ever more preponderant over colored until at last black men were squeezed into some sterile, half-forgotten corner, there to live on sufferance or to die. Isaiah did not want to die.

Accepting the thirty-five hundred dollars that was offered him "partly as a gift, partly as a reasonable share" for the crop left standing in the fields, and gathering his household goods and his wife and children, he joined his brother William and Ben Green in Vicksburg. The year was 1883. Isaiah had something over six thousand dollars in cash and part ownership of a thriving sawmill. He had acumen, energy, and a considerable deposit of good will in the patronizing thoughts of some influential white men, including those who had done him out of Davis Bend.

If he also had a will to personal power and dignity, born, paradoxically, out of his own slavery, he knew the precincts wherein it could be exercised. It took only a small gift of insight to realize that whatever power and dignity he acquired must ultimately derive from the vexed temper, the indifference, and the scorn of white men for black. This was the lesson he had learned too well ever to forget. This was the knowledge that gave meaning to his "I told you so."

7. *The Boss*

For a year and a half Isaiah devoted himself to the enterprises of the Montgomery clan. Besides the sawmill, there were now a store and a few parcels of real estate which he had taken care to buy in the neighborhood of Negro expansion. He reasoned it unlikely that either the greed or the envy of white entrepreneurs would disturb him in the possession of them there. He seems to have given little thought to anything outside the little world of family. Ridiculous, grim, and tragic things were happening on his very doorstep, as it were, but he did not

bother to lift the shade and look out of the window. In
1884 he could have been a member of the Mississippi
House or even of the Senate. The fusion system, which
aligned Negro Republicans with white Democrats, operated in all the predominantly Negro river counties, but
when the Republicans, led by the redoubtable Jim Hill,
approached him, he turned them down. When the white
Democrats themselves came later, Isaiah, deferential and
polite, said no to them too.

He wanted no part of politics. It was a white man's
country; let white men run it. John R. Lynch, once
a United States congressman, and Blanche K. Bruce, once
a United States senator, pleaded with him to work with
them for "the uplift of our people," but Isaiah would have
no part of that either. He considered Lynch and Bruce
"both foreigners, both Fred Douglass men," and he exe-
crated Frederick Douglass. Had not Douglass agents come
into Mississippi in the seventies and urged Negroes to mi-
grate to a fool's paradise in Kansas? What did Douglass
know about the uplift of the colored people in the South?
And had not his second wife been white? "The farther you
stay away from white people's politics, the better," Isaiah
said. Thus when the Colored Farmers' Alliance and Co-
operative Union began to make sounds like a political organization and to co-operate with the white National
Farmers' Alliance in 1886, Isaiah resigned.

But white folks' politics of the most corrupt kind was
tied up with the vast land grants to railroads, and Jones
Hamilton had something to do with the land grant to the
Yazoo-Mississippi Railroad, and Isaiah Montgomery had
something to do with Hamilton. Through Hamilton he
had once hired convict labor. Now through Hamilton he
met Colonel Harold Dermott, a land agent.

In 1886, Isaiah made several mysterious trips north toward Memphis, but exactly where and why no one seemed
to know. Whenever he went, he left detailed instructions
for his brother at the store and Ben Green at the sawmill.
On the fifth trip he took Ben Green, and upon their return Isaiah called the family together to announce that
he and Cousin Ben had bought from the Yazoo-

Mississippi Railroad eight hundred and forty acres of land in Bolivar County. The price? A song, Ben Green said laconically.

Though at first it seemed scarcely worth a song, in a few years it was rich in myth and legend. Legend says that, standing knee-deep in water, Isaiah flung wide his arms, exulting, "This is for my people, a place where God dwells, and liberty." Legend says that he prayed against the water that covered the land farther than the eye could see through cypress, gum, and blackjack trees, and "in the morning the water was gone." Legend has it that when the first colonists stepped off the train and faced the uncleared wilderness Isaiah addressed them in these words: "Have you not for centuries braved the miasma and hewn down forests like these at the behest of a master? Can you not do it for yourselves and your children unto successive generations, that they may worship and develop under their own vine and fig tree? Why stagger at the difficulties that confront you?"

Whatever legend says, the fact is that the swamp forest of Bolivar County was enough to stagger any man. It was completely uninhabited and, some thought, uninhabitable. Having been induced to buy tracts sight unseen at eight dollars an acre, the fainthearted fled without a second look, but others who had put all they had into the venture stayed. With saw, ax, and dynamite, all purchased from Isaiah, they cleared eighty scattered acres that first summer. Montgomery and Green brought in a sawmill and cut logs for cabins and lumber for railroad ties. When a settler's funds were exhausted, Isaiah either extended credit at 15 per cent or set the settler to work clearing more land.

The following spring the first log cabins went up, the first families moved in, and the first crop was sown. There were fifty-nine people now, including a half dozen infants and several infirm old women. The men cleared land, the women and children worked in the fields. There was trouble from depredators. Bears and coons got into the corn, "deer in herds like cattle" fed upon the sugar cane. Sometimes panthers slunk out of the forest, and "the howling of wolves was common music at nightfall." Until drainage ditches were dug and a levee erected, every rain brought flood. There was swamp fever. There was death.

Nevertheless, a townsite gradually emerged. It was bisected by the railroad. Well east of the depot and facing the tracks, Isaiah's trellised, gabled cottage went up, and in the fall of 1888 he brought his family on from Vicksburg. Also he acquired on a commission basis two thousand acres more. He built a "general mercantile emporium," a funeral parlor, and an assembly hall. In the winter he held the first series of "citizenship meetings." But the name he called them stretched a point.

The colony's government was paternalistic, its society approbational. When things did not please Isaiah he spoke about them in meeting. If Dillon Henry left his plow to spend an hour at the depot at morning train time, Isaiah gave Dillon a public dressing down. If Millie Poe ventured to shop in the white stores of Shelby, where lower prices made the five-mile trip worth while, Isaiah brought her to public shame for her disloyalty. Nothing seemed to escape Montgomery's eyes; everything came at last to his ears. He was the colony's conscience, its guide and guard. Strangers were not tolerated unless they came to take up land. Couples had to produce certificates of marriage. Illegitimacy was punished by immediate expulsion of erring mother and child. If there was no really rational moral design in all this, it was at least highly practical. "Here in this place," Isaiah told the colonists, "we are building a place of safety, a refuge."

And a refuge it seemed to be to a score of Negro families who fled there from other parts of the state in 1889. The political campaign of the year before had brought a return of intimidation, terror, and violence. The Republican grip on municipal governments was beaten loose. In Jackson, where a biracial Republican organization had held power since 1866, terrorist tactics were so successful that only one Negro even attempted to vote. ("He was an old negro and looked silly and he was not hurt, but told to hustle out in double-quick time, and he hustled.") Negroes were killed in numbers estimated as high as three hundred. But the Republicans swept the national elections of that year, and with both houses of Congress controlled by Republicans, the conviction grew in Mississippi, as elsewhere in the South, that federal control of elections would be again imposed and the Negro vote restored.

The conviction did not seem groundless in view of the introduction of Henry Cabot Lodge's Force Bill. Negro Republicans from forty Mississippi counties gathered in Jackson and boldly demanded that the Democrats adopt a fusion ticket. Failing this, they held a convention and proposed their own ticket with a slate of Negro candidates. This was too much. A bloody wave of violence swept over the river counties. Hundreds of Negroes fled. Some of those who fled to the colony in Bolivar County were allowed to remain. Isaiah lectured the new colonists on the evils of political participation.

But in his own eyes he was neither deceitful nor traitorous when, in 1890, he made his deal with the Democrats. He was silent about it, but he was as clear and simple as a mountain stream. He operated without enchantment under the only social and doctrinal imperative he knew. Mississippi, the South, the United States was the white man's country. If the Negro was to be free from molestation, from pressure and, above all, from fear in a little corner of this white man's country, then thanks to the tolerant grace of the white man.

So in 1890, when the sentiment for calling a constitutional convention swelled irresistibly in Mississippi, Isaiah Montgomery entered politics for the first and last time. His purpose was to keep his people out of politics forever. He went straight to the heart of the matter. He got in touch with the white Democratic leader. What he said to J. Z. George is quite unknown, but the sentiments that the Jackson *Clarion-Ledger* attributed to George were known to everyone. "If every Negro in Mississippi was a graduate of Harvard, and had been elected as class orator . . . he would not be as well fitted to exercise the right of suffrage as the Anglo-Saxon farm-laborer, *adscriptitius glebae,* of the South and West. Whose cross 'X,' like the broad arrow of Locksley, means force and intellect, and manhood—*virtus*."

In the nature of things Mississippian, the constitutional convention would have been all white, but there were the Republicans sitting tight in Washington, and the "bloody shirts" among them were supporting the Lodge Force Bill, and if the Negroes were to be disfranchised without "calling forth an iniquitous Federal inquisition," they must be made at least to seem to disfranchise themselves.

When John R. Lynch called a gathering of Negro Republicans to form a slate of colored convention delegates, Isaiah was there. He said he wanted to be on that slate, and the logical inference was that he wanted to be on it to "protect the rights of Negroes." He was named as the Republican candidate to the convention from Bolivar County. In the county contest that followed, he was elected easily, although he did not campaign actively. He did not have to, for he had an understanding with George that in Bolivar County the practice of fusion would be temporarily restored. George swept Isaiah in, and he was seated in the convention without protest—the only Negro delegate and the lone Republican.

The one hundred and thirty Democrats who assembled in the constitutional convention on August 12, 1890, were tired of needing the Negro vote, in sacrifice to which, the best among them knew, honor, integrity, and truth had melted like snow. "Sir, it is no secret that there has not been a full vote and a fair count in Mississippi since 1875," a delegate told the convention. "In other words we have been stuffing ballot boxes, committing perjury, and here and there in the state carrying elections by violence and fraud. . . . No man can be in favor of perpetuating the election methods which have prevailed in Mississippi since 1875 who is not a moral idiot."

But did this mean that the Negro vote was to be allowed? Certainly not. For the plain truth was that even the best men—those who did not want to "die and leave their children with shotguns in their hands, a lie in their mouths and perjury on their souls"—even these had this in common with the worst: they wanted to restore and preserve white supremacy. They wanted this so badly and with such a passionate singleness of purpose that it can only be called madness. And as for violence and fraud, they would no more be done away with than the Negro himself, for as a matter of simple fact, to the end of bringing about the legal and official repudiation of the black man as a political equal, as a citizen, and as a human being, they employed the very ends best calculated to insure that this same Negro would be fair game for the systematic depredations of planter, cotton-gin operator, and merchant, and the acceptable object of the unrestrained violence of any white man who bore a grudge.

And Isaiah Montgomery? He knew as well as any man what the purpose of both the best and the worst white men was. And he served that purpose not only because he saw the logical consequence of not serving it—the white man's intrusion upon his private domain—but also because he believed that the elimination of the Negro vote was in the best interest of the Negroes in the state and the nation; because he believed that Negro disfranchisement would bring an end to terror, violence, and race hatred, and would eventually create that salubrious emotional climate in which "the best white people will protect the colored" even against the latter's own profligacy and lawlessness. Called upon to speak as a member of the committee on franchise, Isaiah said this in effect. Then, in clear conscience, he proceeded to endorse the registration requirement, the tax requirement, and Section 244 of the constitution, which imposed a literacy requirement that not one in ten thousand Negroes could meet, and which was to serve as the model for other Southern states, all of which had completed the process of Negro disfranchisement before the battleship *Maine* was sunk in Havana Harbor. In a speech applauded by the whole white South and ex-President Cleveland, Isaiah endorsed the section the expressed intent of which was "to eliminate Negroes with or without education, and to remove no white voters from the rolls." He helped to postpone the day of the South's commitment to respect the citizenship of the Negro, and he helped to fix the traditional ways of thinking about what the Negro's place in American life is and how best to prepare for it.

And this was by no means all. For Isaiah Montgomery secured at the same time that exemption from interference in which he meant to remain undisturbed in the control of his colony of Mound Bayou and the lives lived there.

For though he was reverently called "The Honorable," a harsher, truer title would have been Boss of Mound Bayou. For years he was the mayor, and he hand-picked the three aldermen. Though the white sheriff of Bolivar County appointed the Negro deputy for Mound Bayou, Isaiah named him. Isaiah chose the town constable. He hired the first schoolteacher and guaranteed the salary of the first preacher. By 1893 there were four thousand Negroes in Mound Bayou and the colony spread over twenty thousand alluvial acres and was still growing. Isaiah owned either in whole or in part with his cousin Ben Green the cotton gin and the warehouse, the feed and fertilizer store, the lumberyard, the general merchandise emporium, the burial business. He owned uncounted first mortgages. He was turning a profit of eight thousand dollars a year on rough lumber alone, and he was reputed to be—and probably was—the only Negro in the United States who could put his hands on fifty thousand dollars "cash money" in an hour's notice.

Insulated by such power, he did not turn a hair when Ben Green was murdered. First Cousin Green, the taciturn, plodding mechanic who kept the cotton gin and the sawmill going, and who had done Isaiah's bidding for thirty years, seems to have grown dissatisfied in 1892.

Perhaps his wife had something to do with it. He had married her almost surreptitiously while Isaiah was crowning the eminence of his disfranchisement speech with a call on President Harrison and House Speaker Reed. By all accounts, Mrs. Green was a woman of exceptional strength of character, bred from three generations of freemen. At any rate, Cousin Ben grew recalcitrant. Isaiah was "head of everything." Ben Green was heard to complain that Isaiah "consistently drew off the larger share of profits" from their joint enterprises. Suddenly, in 1892, Green dissolved the partnership, and between him and Isaiah mistrust and enmity bred. One day in 1896 Ben Green was shot to death.

In a town fiercely suspicious of strangers, no one had seen a stranger. The town constable and the deputy sheriff had the assistance of the county sheriff, but no clue was ever found, and the final official word was that Ben Green had "met his death at the hands of parties unknown." He left a widow and a young son. He also left among his kindred a precedent for dying violently. Long after Isaiah himself was in his grave, the precedent would overtake a Montgomery daughter and a daughter's spouse.

Isaiah made no visible show of loss at Ben Green's death. Indeed, he was not bereft. He acquired more property, including Cousin Ben's half interest in the cotton gin, the operation of which proved too much even for the sagacious widow. He invested a piddling sum in a prosperous tristate fraternal-benefit association and persuaded its officers to build the headquarters in Mound Bayou. What better site for a Negro institution than an all-Negro town? Isaiah practically guaranteed that if it did not bother white folks, white folks would not bother it. A popular jingle had it:

> A nigger's a nigger,
> You can tell by his face;
> And he's got no business
> In a white man's place.

It was comforting to know that a white man had no business in a black man's place either.

8. Patience Is the Pay-Off

If, on the local level of Mound Bayou, Isaiah Montgomery was creating not only an environment for Negroes but a generalized Negro mentality more or less tractable to a single will, another was attempting a very similar thing on a much grander scale.

The patience to wait for the main chance, an unerring instinct for compromise, and a sure knowledge of the subtler uses of adversity had brought Booker T. Washington a long way since his slave birth in Virginia in 1856, '57, or '58. These qualities, directed by a cunning cast of mind, had carried him through Hampton Institute, brought him the especial favor of the white teachers there and of General Samuel Chapman Armstrong, the president, and had been his chief recommendations to a group of Alabama white men who, in 1881, were looking for someone to head a school they proposed to found for Negroes. Now as principal of that school, Tuskegee Institute, Washington was the best-known Negro in the South. He meant eventually to be the best-known and most influential Negro in the United States. In 1893 he was well on his way.

Booker Washington had already won the gratitude of certain whites. He had done this in the early post-Reconstruction period by assuring the white South that black men would not again aspire to, much less usurp, the place of white men. It never occurred to him or to the South that there might be a real and complex question as to what and where was the Negro's place.

On the land, traditionally held to be his tether and his domicile? Except for the fortunate handful of Negroes (only 120,000 of more than 4,000,000) who had managed to bull their way to ownership of a few paltry acres, a place on the land in the South meant a return to slavery or peonage. The Southern aristocratic ideal, the storied sense of noblesse, which had certainly moved some planters to render slavery tolerable, was now decayed. Many of the aristocrats themselves were gone, leaving the land in the care of those who took satisfaction in using the methods of slavery to control the Negro's freedom. And even for a place on the land there was increasing competition. There were poor whites and growing numbers of small dirt farmers made landless by the strangulation of the cotton market and the operation of debt and mortgage laws. They too must eat, and to eat must work—and on whatever terms they could get. And the terms, inevitably disadvantaged by the clamoring crowd of the dispossessed, were in substance and sometimes in degree the same for these whites as for the blacks: sunrise-to-sunset, tumble-down-shack, fat-back-and-molasses, pellagra-rickets-and-consumption terms. Tenant terms. Cropper terms. And as for those few landowning Negroes, their prospects were the same as for the small landowning whites—an endless accumulation of debt to the supply merchant, who demanded mortgages on the crop, the chattels, the land, and even the tools with which to cultivate it.

Many Negroes fled these terms and these prospects. Most fled northward, cityward. And did they find a place there? Scarcely. They were "an industrial superfluity." Competition with European immigrants, tough since the raw 1840s, grew subtly vicious in the closing decades of the century, and Negroes lost. Fannie B. Williams, a feature writer for the New York *Age*, reported:

"It is quite safe to say that in the last fifteen years, the colored people have lost almost every occupation that was regarded as peculiarly their own. . . . White men wanted these places and were strong enough to displace the unorganized, thoughtless and easy-going occupants. When the hordes of Greeks, Italians, Swedes, and other foreign folk began to pour into Chicago, the demand for the Negro's place began. One occupation after another that the colored people thought was theirs forever, by a sort of divine right, fell into the hands of these foreign invaders. . . . The Swedes have captured the janitor business by organizing and training the men for this work in such a way as to increase the efficiency and reliability of the service. White men have made more of the barber business than did the colored men. . . . The 'shoe polisher' has supplanted the Negro bootblack, and does business in finely appointed parlors, with mahogany finish and electric lights. Thus a menial occupation has become a well-organized and genteel business with capital and system behind it."

Negro efforts to organize and get capital and systems behind them came to nothing. Though scattered groups of Negro workmen's protectives had achieved sectional cohesion in the National Bureau of Labor, they had little strength, and some of this was drained off in the political campaign of 1884, the rest thoroughly dissipated in the campaign of 1892. President Cleveland said in his first inaugural that "there should be no pretext for anxiety touching the protection of the freedmen in their rights," and he repeated the sentiment in his second inaugural; but he kept silent while Southern states disfranchised the Negro and the Supreme Court rendered its "separate but equal" decisions, and while evidence of the drastic curtailment of the Negro's citizenship rights grew more incontestable every day.

No attention-commanding voice was raised in behalf of the Negro, but many were raised against him. None was louder than South Carolina's Ben Tillman's when it thundered, "If you want to rise, keep the nigger down!"

This injunction was heard and heeded even in the North. White craft unions refused Negroes admission. Industrialists, who did not like unions anyway, were smart enough to encourage this prejudice. What industrialists wanted was a large, uncommitted surplus of labor, and Negroes were that surplus, and so long as the industrialists had it they could scorn to negotiate with white organized labor. Used as strikebreakers, Negroes called down upon themselves a triple measure of the enmity of the white laboring man, thus closing up the evil cycle. Neither white nor black worker had any clear notion of the forces affecting his life. Each approached whatever situation confronted him from within a pattern of thought generally held to be valid: the immutable superiority of white men to black.

The voice that might have shouted an effective denial to this was stilled in 1895.

Frederick Douglass' death, one of his admirers said, presaged an even more troubled future for the Negroes, and that future was soon upon them. Within seven months of Douglass' funeral, Booker T. Washington stood before a packed throng at the Atlanta Cotton States Exposition and delivered his people over to the whims of the prejudiced, the exploitation of the venal, and the machinations of the crafty. Washington's exposition speech exploded in the national press like a pyrotechnic display in salute to the "New South." "You can be sure in the future, as in the past," he told an audience swelling with gratitude, "that you and your families will be surrounded by the most patient, faithful, law-abiding, and unresentful people that the world has ever seen." The speech was firmly based upon the premise that "the Negro enjoyed the friendship of the Southern whites." But the irony of this was evident even while Washington spoke.

At that very moment the South Carolina state convention was vigorously pushing the disfranchisement of Negroes. On that very day a North Carolina court found guiltless a white farmer who had killed a "lazy" and "abusive" colored tenant. On that day "Florida officials promised a mob at the outset of the trial of a Negro that he would be hanged." Under the headline "An Eye for an Eye," the Memphis *Commercial Appeal* described the mutilation-slaying of a Negro prisoner by a white mob. Two days after Washington's speech Wilcox County, in Washington's own state of Alabama, published its education budget for 1896. It provided salaries of $28,108 for the teachers of 2285 white children, and $3940 for the teachers of 10,745 colored children. Within the week Washington spoke, the management of the Tennessee Coal, Iron and Railroad Company announced the replacement of "eighty-seven negro laborers by others, mostly Chinese."

Within a month President Cleveland wrote Booker T. Washington: "Your words cannot fail to delight and encourage all who wish well for your race; and if our colored citizens do not from your utterances gather new hope and form new determination to gain every valuable advantage offered them by their citizenship, it will be strange indeed."

Certainly valuable advantage might be gained, but it was not of the sort President Cleveland had in mind, and it had little to do with citizenship. Indeed, it had more to do with citizenship's opposite and its denial: the exclusion of Negroes from the body politic, the ultimate civic isolation that was the Negro "place," and that made possible—and even, it seemed, desirable—an Isaiah Montgomery and a Mound Bayou. And what was strange indeed and quite apparent before Isaiah Montgomery died, and his daughter was killed like a common criminal by a white sheriff, and before Eugene Booze, the husband of another

Montgomery daughter, was murdered by parties unknown, and long, long before Mound Bayou had become, ironically, a focal point for Negro insurgency in Mississippi—what was strange was that whatever hope and determination Negroes gathered came from circumstances quite different from any Washington had foreseen or Cleveland desired: came, first, from the final resurgence of Negro political power in the fusion campaign that sent a North Carolina Negro to Congress in 1897 and returned roughly a hundred Negroes to public office "throughout the Southern land . . . where other black men were gratefully hearing the news and surging up in emulation."

And before this had quite expired a second circumstance was already in being—the quarrel with Spain over Cuba. It does not matter that it was a quarrel sought for and one that could easily have been avoided. It does not matter that the real cause was that "the taste of empire" was in the mouths of some American leaders and that, though they "envisaged now the kingdom, the power, and the glory," it had nothing to do with the Lord's Prayer. Most Negroes had not heard of Albert J. Beveridge or of Cushman K. Davis, and Negroes thought, as the common man everywhere in America thought, that the war with Spain was a crusade of righteousness, for liberty from oppression, and for "the law supreme . . . the law of God." And to Negroes—and of even more consequence to them—it was a war to complete the revolutionary struggle of a "colored people" led by the "Black Thunderbolt," Quintín Bandera, and the mulatto, General Antonio Maceo. And if the American people, including especially the white people of the South, could give such booming enthusiasm to a war for the freedom from oppression of a foreign colored people, was not this a matter from which to gather new hope?

"Surely," wrote a Negro who died at El Caney, "the same strong spirit and quickened conscience which took up the cause of Cuba will secure justice to the American Negro."

VI. A DOCTOR'S DILEMMA

1. *My People*

One day in January 1890 a neat little man hastened along Dearborn Street in Chicago. He was dressed in a black bowler hat and a black chesterfield overcoat, below the flopping tails of which his scurrying legs, oddly encased in white duck, seemed to twinkle as he walked. A small black satchel swung in his hand. His naturally pale face was flushed pink with cold and his breath frosted on the light brown, almost blond mustache that covered his upper lip.

Except that he might be driven by the cold, there was no need for so great a hurry, and he realized it and tried to slow his pace. But quickness of movement was a habit with him, and, anyway, he thought, perhaps the nurse he had engaged was not as thorough as she was recommended to be. Perhaps he should not trust her with all the last-minute preparations. He thought about the medical profession. He thought about physicians and nurses in general, and about Negro nurses in particular. Negro nurses? Where could you find one? The subject was his special demon, and lately it had been riding him without pause.

Just a month before, he had made a decision and a promise. The Reverend Louis Reynolds, pastor of the African Methodist Church, had asked him to use his influence to have Reynolds' sister admitted to a nurses' training course in one of the Chicago hospitals. Dr. Williams smiled ruefully now as he thought of it. Because he was on the surgical staff of the South Side Dispensary, where he gave clinical instruction to Chicago Medical College students, and because he was a member of the Illinois State Board of Health, people thought he had influence. But did he? He had never thought about it. Now all at once he suspected that those colleagues of his who knew his history considered him an exception, and the thought made him blush. None of them had ever mentioned race—so why should he? The students to whom he lectured had no idea that he was a Negro.

He was, it seemed, caught in a dilemma, one horn of which was his personal career in medicine, and the other a tradition of racial ties that knit itself through three generations of his family. Mixed blood had mixed and confused and lost to him some of his nearest kinsmen. Was it to confuse and lose him too? With a sudden ache he thought of his father as he had thought of him when he talked to the Reverend Mr. Reynolds. "No," he remembered having said then, pausing while the minister's eyes glinted bitterly. "I don't think I'll try to get your sister into one of those training courses. We'll do something better. We'll start a hospital of our own, and we'll train dozens and dozens of nurses."

Dr. Williams meant to make good that promise.

2. Mixed Heritage

Daniel Hale Williams was born in Hollidaysburg, Pennsylvania, in 1858, of a class so mixed in nationality and blood that some of his cousins used to say that they were of the "scrambled race." In the line that stretched immediately backward from him were a Scotch-Irish grandmother, a German-Negro grandfather, and a pure German great-grandfather. Though his own mother could prove only Negro and white blood, a heavy Indian strain showed plainly in her straight black hair, high cheekbones, and luminous eyes.

His father, also called Daniel, was a strong-minded, substantial man, proud, independent, and—for all his Caucasian ancestry, and, indeed, perhaps because of it—ambitious for the progress of Negroes, to whom he habitually referred as "my people." Before the Civil War he missed few of the national conventions by means of which Negroes sought to make their voices heard. After the war he moved his family to Annapolis, Maryland, and became a zealous member of the Equal Rights League, "arduously traveling and speaking" in its name. He wore himself out in this service and died at forty-seven, leaving his wife, Sarah Ann, with seven children and enough to live on if only she were careful.

Sarah Ann was not careful. She had difficulty handling responsibility or even recognizing that there was a responsibility to handle. Her first independent move after the death of her husband was to put the two middle girls in an expensive convent school, leave the youngest with their grandmother, and take the two older girls to Illinois. Price Williams, the older son, was twenty and already on his own in the North, teaching and reading law. Daniel, the youngest child of all, she apprenticed to a shoemaker in Baltimore. Daniel's enemies were to say later that his mother had deserted him, but this may not have been the instance they referred to, for there was another. After a year Dan gave up his apprenticeship and bummed his way to his mother in Illinois. A few months later, however, Sarah Ann, reckless, restless, and homesick, returned east without him. He was twelve. He was on his own.

But he was on his own in a section of the country particularly attractive to those Negroes who were anxious and ambitious to make good use of freedom. The South was beginning again to set rigid in its opposition to Negro social and cultural mobility. As we have seen, and as even Booker Washington was later to say, the postwar South meant for Negroes "poor dwelling houses, loss of earnings each year because of unscrupulous employers, high-priced provisions, poor school houses, short school terms . . . bad treatment generally, lynching and white-capping, fear of the practice of peonage, a general lack of police protection, and want of encouragement." In spite of black Republicans, Reconstruction and the Fourteenth Amendment, the Freedmen's Bureau and Yankee missionaries, Negroes were virtually re-enslaved in many places in the South.

The West was relatively new and absorptive and flexible. No cultural mold had been unalterably fashioned, no social pattern set. It was a cultural frontier where even sons of the South—inheritors of an ancient dream of aristocracy—learned "a democracy native to the frontier." In the Ohio Valley and farther up in the Rock River Valley, and farther still along the upper reaches of the Mississippi, gathered, as Parrington points out, "a multitude of rough libertarians [who] took seriously the doctrine of equality and proposed to put it into practice." In the 1870s the expanding West was a heady land and a hearty land. Here a man could blaze his own trail; here a man could make his way.

Or, so far as that went, a boy. Twelve-year-old Daniel Hale Williams made his way. He worked on lake steamers and saw something of the Northwest. He worked in barbershops and learned a barber's skills. He worked on river boats, and once or twice found himself in Cincinnati, where he may have seen and heard a Negro youth of about his own age—one Gussie L. Davis, who had yet to write "The Baggage Coach Ahead," "Send Back the Picture and the Wedding Ring," and other popular tunes, but who was already "stealing a knowledge of music" as he swept the classrooms of the Cincinnati Conservatory. The city in the early seventies was not much different from what the Montgomerys had known in the early sixties. It was still a mulatto mecca. Years later Dan was to reminisce about the beauty of its "high-toned" ladies.

But the life of the wanderer was no life for Dan Williams. He wanted to settle down, to get an education, to follow the admonition he had more than once heard fall from the lips of his father: "We colored people must cultivate the mind." His ambitions were vague but they tugged at him persistently nonetheless. He was often lonely. When his oldest sister, Sally, wrote asking him to join her in Edgerton, Wisconsin, where she was in the hair goods business, he went gladly. He opened his own barbershop. For a time his restlessness was eased.

Edgerton was a frontier village. There was no school, for there were as yet not enough children to justify one. Traveling lecturers avoided it, and the occasion was rare when even one of the ubiquitous clan of book canvassers set up shop for half a day in the vestibule of the Grange

Hall. Janesville, however, was only a few miles away, and Dan was impressed with it on shopping trips there with his sister. It had a population of ten thousand and was still growing. It had schools, an opera house, and a Young Men's Association. Henry Ward Beecher and Robert Ingersoll frequently lectured there. There were flourishing industries—woolen mills, shoe factories, farm-implement manufactories. There was also, Dan noted on one trip, a large barbershop run by a Negro named Anderson.

Sally too was no longer happy in Edgerton. Attractive, fair-skinned, and aged twenty-six, she was tired of spinsterhood. She had admirers in Edgerton, two of whom had quite substantial means, but she refused to have any of them. She would not "marry white, even if a white man was the last man on earth." But there were at least a few colored men in Janesville, and shortly after Dan and his sister moved there in 1876, Sally married one of them—a man named Turner—and went to live in Portage. Dan, now twenty, was again alone. In a special way, he was alone all his life.

He used to say later that in Janesville he "came to himself." This was a Janesville colloquialism that meant he became acquainted with himself and found his direction. It was not easy to come by either self-knowledge or the direction he would take. He sometimes wished he could recompose the basic ingredients of his personality, and all he knew about his direction was that it must challenge him and lead, as tradition devised, to some center in the Negro world. Finding such a road was trial and error and finally happenstance.

Harry Anderson wanted him to stick to the barber's trade with music as a side line. Anderson had not only the best and busiest shop in town, serving the town's best people, but his string orchestra played for the best people's dances, and it accompanied touring stars, among them Helena Modjeska, who came to entertain in Mayer's Opera House. Anderson had plenty of time to influence Dan. He and his Irish wife (for "in these parts colored women are in short supply"—to which Dan's response was an echo of his sister's: "But I would not marry white") took the young man into their home and treated him as if he were one of their own children, of which they had five. Beneath Dan's shy reserve lay a hunger for affection and a need to deserve it. Under the influence of the Andersons, Dan took up the guitar and learned to play the bass fiddle; he joined Anderson's orchestra and traveled with it all over Wisconsin and into the bordering states.

But a barber-musician's career was not for Dan either. Other influences poured in upon him—from Professor Haire's Academy, where he enrolled to study Latin, mathematics, and zoology; from lectures in Apollo Hall, where he heard Robert Ingersoll thunder, "Every library is an arsenal, filled with the weapons and ammunition of progress, and every fact is a *Monitor* with sides of iron and a turret of steel. . . . Nothing but truth is immortal." And from Jenkin Lloyd Jones, Welsh pastor of the Unitarian church; and from his older brother, now a successful lawyer back East, whose name kept appearing in the Negro papers. For a year after getting his high school diploma, Dan clerked and read Blackstone in a lawyer's office. But the law was not for him.

He realized this one day when he read in the Janesville *Gazette* an account of a local medical case. He knew Dr. Henry Palmer, the physician on the case, in the way a barber would know an important patron, the town's leading medical light and a civic worker who had once been mayor. Dr. Palmer was probably Janesville's most influential citizen. His opinions frequently appeared as editorials in the local paper; his every activity was news. Now he had a case of gunshot wound, and he was giving "it all his skill and knowledge," which, the paper said, "were considerable." He was "striving desperately to save a life."

From the moment he read the account Dan knew with overwhelming certainty that he had found the road he wanted to take. The only problem was to get on it. Putting aside self-doubt, beating back his natural shyness, he spoke to Dr. Palmer the next time he cut the physician's hair. Dr. Palmer may have been curiously stirred, or—though there was no question but that he took his profession with passionate seriousness—he may have been amused. But after all, the first surgeons were barbers. And why not? At any rate, within three months Dan Williams joined two white apprentices in Dr. Palmer's office, and two years later, under the lax medical standards that generally prevailed, he was qualified to enter into the practice of his profession.

Dr. Palmer had impressed upon his apprentices the fact that scientific theories were changing and medical knowledge expanding, and that the only way one could keep up with advances was by attending medical school, "taking one's lumps in hospital," and learning both theory and practice. Dr. Palmer made them feel that anyone who set up in the practice of medicine without a certified M.D. was little better than a quack.

Medical studies cost money, and Dan had none. He could not count on his mother, who had recently come into her own father's considerable property. Though he felt a warm love for his mother, as neglected children often do, he knew her for what she was—thoughtless, extravagant, selfish, and completely involved in her own life. Borrowing a hundred dollars, for which Harry Anderson stood security at the Janesville bank, and which was barely enough for books and fees, Daniel Williams went down to Chicago.

3. *Doctor in Chicago*

If Negroes thought of Cincinnati as the mulatto mecca in the 1870s, in the 1880s they were beginning to think of Chicago as the new Canaan. Lured primarily by prospects of employment, but also by the city's reputation for racial liberalism, black migrants were trickling in from the South, principally by way of the coal fields of Illinois, whence the competition of foreign labor was driving them, and the cornfields of Kansas, where in the late seventies so many had gone that conditions comparable to the "contraband camps" of the Civil War resulted. As President Hayes's policy of letting the Southern states alone came more and more to mean the consolidation of white supremacy and the unhindered imposition upon Negroes of those social terms already described—political repression, cultural isolation, and peonage—the trickle into Chicago became a stream. From about three thousand in 1870, Chicago's colored population topped ten thousand by 1880. And, indeed, the "foolish hegira," which even the influence of Frederick Douglass could not bring to a stop, was taking on serious proportions for other Northern cities, where the characteristics of the latter-day Negro ghetto began to evolve.

There was no ghetto, however, in 1883, when Daniel Hale Williams, brand-new M.D. from Chicago Medical College, opened an office at Thirty-first Street and Michigan Avenue. It was a substantial neighborhood, racially mixed, and Dan's office adjoined those of white physicians. He soon discovered that good hospital staff appointments were hard to get because "Chicago hospitals were as tightly organized as personal clubs" and they "did not welcome strangers." Toward the end of his third year in private practice one valuable appointment came his way: he was taken on to do minor surgery at the dispensary connected with Chicago Medical College and to serve as a demonstrator in anatomy to medical students there.

Meantime, such private cases in surgery as he undertook were performed in the dining rooms and kitchens of his patients' homes. He had rather more of these than his white colleagues, partly because his predominantly Negro patients had difficulty getting private rooms in hospitals, and partly because the distrust of hospitals, still commonly referred to as "butcher shops," was stronger among Negroes than among whites.

But gradually a question was projected into the mind and heart of Dan Williams. It was of such varied and complex aspects that he resisted it and refused for a time to face it. But somehow it seemed to get involved in all he did.

It was a question both of identity and of identification. He had learned from his father who and what he was, but the years of his childhood had been relatively simple. Alignments had been ordained, commitments inevitable. One was committed to Negroes because one was himself a Negro, and this was his complete and unassailable identity.

True, there were those mixed bloods, a few of Dan's relatives among them, who blurred or lost this identity, but Dan's father was not one of them. Blue-veined and blue-eyed, and with only the barest crinkle in his hair, Dan, Sr., would have no truck with that society of Negroes who, in so far as they could, withdrew from all things Negro and racial, created their own twilit and traumatic half-world, and subscribed to the proposition that white-skin was best, and brightskin far better than black, and blackskin was very bad indeed. They were a cabal as secret, designing, and exclusive as the Medici. The elder Dan Williams would have nothing to do with them. He talked constantly about his "people," by which he meant the Negro people. When he moved his family to Maryland after the war his first act was to pay his respects to George Forten, an ex-slave, a worker for the Equal Rights League, and as black a man as ever put on clothes.

An identification of such pristine simplicity was not easy for Dan, Jr., in Chicago in the eighties and nineties. His professional life was a complication. He wanted to go as far in his profession as intelligence and skill could take him, but also he had inherited a compelling sense of duty to his people. The two seemed irreconcilable.

So long as Negroes remained too poor to afford the private facilities of hospitals—or prejudice kept them out of hospitals—and so long as he devoted himself principally to their care, he could have only limited access to those avenues of new medical learning and surgical skills that hospitals provided. It seemed that he must sacrifice career to race or race to career. The idea of passing into the white race occurred to him but he rejected it. He could not deny his people the service he could give them; nor could he deprive them of whatever pride they might take in whatever success he achieved. Were they not already boasting that he was "the first Negro ever appointed to the Illinois Board of Health" and that his latest appointment "on merit as surgeon to the City Railway Company" had broken a precedent?

Unless he were to accept standards of behavior and attainments of mind lower than those he was used to, Dr. Dan Williams had no choice on the social level but to live in the world of the mixed bloods. It was a privileged world. Inhabited largely by the bastard sons and daughters of former slaveowners, but also by those who, like Dan himself, had come by their white blood legitimately, it boasted of its ancestry, its tradition of freedom, its culture. By virtue of education and the manners sedulously imitated in the "big house" and carefully passed on, like priceless gems, from parents to children, the mixed bloods could attain the better jobs on the scale running from the personal service of valet, butler, barber, and tailor to petty but secure clerkships in civil service. A few acquired independent businesses, and a very few acquired professions. There were bookkeepers, brewmasters, and undertakers, schoolteachers and journalists. They had a security undreamed of in the Negro world of common labor. They were zealous to educate their children, often at great sacrifice. They were equally zealous to guard against misalliances that might introduce a too dark strain into their white blood. They were conspicuous and self-conscious consumers not only of goods but of culture; and they were very, very careful to make ineradicably clear the difference between themselves and the common run of Negroes.

And yet this world of mixed bloods—a new world, it might be said, dropped unordained and maculate, foreboding and perverse, from the womb of genetic chance—soon developed a necessary and important dual function.

More consciously than it admitted, and not altogether insusceptible to the flattery it implied, it served as model and preceptor to the lately freed. It was, too, liaison, intercessor, and spokesman between the white world above and the black world beneath. In a sense, for all its differences from each, it complemented both.

It was no easy thing to do. The people of the mixed-blood world were often troubled and driven to despair by a sense of race duty that operated irresistibly somehow against their will and, as many of them thought bitterly, against their world's best interest. Fierce tides of hatred and self-hatred, pride and fear and love dragged many an anchor from the harbor of sanity. It is little wonder that later historians have been forced to note the high incidence of psychotic behavior: the suicides; the mad sacrificial joy with which families encouraged scions to pass over —knowing that in passing they were lost to them forever —not inevitably to a fuller, better life, but to a kind of painless limbo; the crazed pride with which mothers, for all their rigid insistence on morality and sexual virtue, gave up daughters into the arms of men because, simply, the men were white. Dan Williams himself was to be sacrificed to this pride when the mother of the mixed-blood girl he loved would not let her "marry a man identified with colored people," though the man was Dr. Dan, honorable and eminent and in appearance white almost as snow. It was a traumatic world, surely, where, as Pauli Murray reports in *Proud Shoes*, a woman was still counted sane who ranted at her neighbors thus:

"I'll tell anybody I'm a white man's child. A fine white man at that. A Southern aristocrat. If you want to know *what* I am, I'm an octoroon, that's what I am . . . and I don't have to mix with good-for-nothing niggers if I don't want to. . . . And I'll tell you another thing. My father was one of the best criminal lawyers in the South. He was in the North Carolina legislature. Before the Civil War he saved fourteen poor Negroes from the gallows free of charge. He got many colored folks out of trouble and kept 'em from rotting in jail. . . ."

However mad some of the individuals in the mixed-blood world might be, the function of that world was sane enough, and Daniel Hale Williams was soon pushing that function to the limits of consistency—and there were some who said beyond. But the fact was that Chicago was changing rapidly, and Dr. Dan saw needs where others did not. Every day brought a new quota of Negroes into the city. They were crowding into the south side, in the area of Dan's office, faster than the white people could sell and move out. By 1890 there were twenty-five thousand of them, and Chicago was beginning to lose its reputation for equality of opportunity and lack of prejudice.

The south side was becoming a ghetto, where vice and prostitution flourished. Dr. Dan's venereal cases doubled, then tripled. He did not like it. He did not like what it signified in ignorance and social degradation. The crime rate jumped. Saturdays Dr. Dan spent long after midnight bandaging battered heads, sewing up knife wounds, and probing for bullets. It was not the work he wanted to do. He felt that it was not the work that should need doing.

Among his friends he began to talk about conditions in the ghetto. Basically shy and retiring, he was no crusader in the ordinary sense. His earliest conversations on these matters were contemplative and tentative rather than persuasive. He talked about the young men who loafed all day in front of the poolrooms and the honky-tonks and the "dirty little pork and greens shops" that were squeezing up on both sides of State Street north of Forty-third. It gave him a particular wrench to see Negro girls frequenting these places and seeking distraction on street corners. These young people, for want of something better to do, Dr. Dan told his friends, were candidates for careers in crime and vice. The young men could find occasional employment only as strikebreakers—and this subjected them to violence; the young women, even when they had finished high school, could get no employment at all.

Dan soon realized that to talk to his friends was not enough. Some of them laughed at him. What had he to do with the problems of ignorant Negroes coming up from the South? He was a medical man, not a social worker, and his friends refused to take him seriously except as a physician. What they did not understand was that social problems were inextricably mixed up with a Negro physician's practice. He tried to make this clear.

There was, for instance, the case of a Negro patient who needed a hysterectomy, but no hospital would take a Negro as a private patient, and no hospital would let him operate. Could he perform a hysterectomy on a kitchen table? Should he send his patient to a charity ward? As a member of the state Board of Health, he knew what charity wards were. They were crowded, they were often filthy, they were always inadequately staffed. Even a white woman could not hope to get the care she needed in a charity ward, and if this was true for a white woman, then—— "To attack the medical problems of Negroes," Dr. Dan wrote later, "[is] necessarily to attack the problem of race."

This was a construction so realistic and so simple that Dan Williams was surprised that it had not occurred to him before.

His medical career was a matter of friendly interest to some of his white associates in the profession. He often met with them informally to discuss new medical theories and surgical techniques. Also in the Hamilton Club, a political organization behind which stood the portly power of ex-Postmaster General Walter Gresham, there was some talk of hospital staff appointments, clinic lectureships, and the like—though always as if his being a Negro were completely irrelevant. Naturally this was flattering, since the assumption seemed to be that professional competence was the sine qua non, and he was not averse to dreaming that perhaps his skill and intelligence had been enough to secure his appointment to the South Side Dispensary.

But were they enough really? Would he have got the position with the City Railway Company if the question of his race had come up and he had had to answer it? He did not think so. And could he say honestly that his appointment to the Illinois State Board of Health had nothing to do with political expediency, a matter of the Republicans hoping to make Negro voters happy?

To pretend that only his personal qualifications, without any regard for his racial background, made for success in his career was to leave out of consideration the fact that he practiced medicine principally among Negroes, and was to pretend that certain problems of medical care were not peculiar to Negroes, and was, in the final analysis, to desert Negroes altogether. Would the competence that might open doors for him under the condition of being thought an exceptional Negro also open doors for other Negroes? He did not think so. Assuming his entrance at those guarded doors of the white medical world, and assuming further his climb to eminence there, could he then bring subtle pressure to bear to fling the doors wide for all? Again he did not think so.

These were the conclusions Dr. Dan had reached when he told the Reverend Mr. Reynolds, "We'll do something better. . . . We'll get down to brass tacks."

Getting down to brass tacks meant hounding his friends, colored and white. "There must be a hospital for Negroes," he told them, "but not a Negro hospital." There was a great and decisive difference. "It must be an institution expressive of interracial good will, one where colored and white can work together, but it must be dedicated to medical service and the training of Negroes—internes, technicians, nurses, all the nurses we can train."

No one could remember seeing Dr. Williams so excited as he was during the closing months of 1890. Once his retiring personality had polarized around the idea of the hospital, he "radiated an almost sparkling magnetic force," and his appeals, though quiet, were irresistible. He formed committees of white and colored people and put them to work. He skipped from meeting to meeting and from rally to rally. He personally solicited funds. He sustained enthusiasms. He won from staff members of Mercy Hospital and the faculty of Chicago Medical College pledges of services to the embryonic institution, already named the Provident Hospital and Training School. He wanted the highest standards and the best men to maintain them, so, excepting himself in surgery and Dr. Charles Bentley in odontology, the staff he began to organize was white. Drs. W. W. Jaggard and H. T. Byford of the Medical College faculty were to be obstetrician and gynecologist, Frank Billings chief consulting physician, and the renowned Christian Fenger consulting surgeon. Within a few months a three-story building at the corner of Twentyninth and Dearborn had been selected and a first payment on it made. It had room for a dozen beds, and this seemed enough for a start.

But the start was still several months away. A great deal of money was needed, and money came slowly. Times were not good in the ghetto. The first ominous clouds of the depression that would spread over the whole land in

1893 already darkened the lives of Negroes. Besides, Dr. Dan was a busy practitioner. He could not attend all the meetings or chair all the committees. The faithful friends of the idea worked hard, but these faithful friends were practically all of the mixed-blood world, for only they had the time to give, and only they had important connections in the white world. Underprivileged Negroes, though they stood to benefit, were resentful and suspicious. Provident Hospital and Training School looked like a "half-white dickty" to-do to them.

The mistrust of Negroes wounded Dr. Dan more deeply than the prejudice and indifference of whites, but he redoubled his efforts. The founding of Provident was a challenge to the integrity of his sense of race. He would help his people whether or no. He passed over an opportunity to study with Dr. F. B. Robinson, a renowned abdominal surgeon. He talked in Negro churches; he talked at meetings in poor Negro homes; he talked to Negroes on the streets. "It will be our hospital," he told them. Grudgingly, gradually, they came to believe him.

Finally he approached Millionaire Row and got contributions ranging from two hundred to five hundred dollars from the Kohlsaats, the Armours, Marshall Field, and the Pullmans. Eighteen months after the start of the campaign the moment came to draw up the papers of incorporation. The line where Daniel Hale Williams' signature should have appeared was never filled in. At the time of the signing he was performing a hysterectomy on a Negro patient. His sterilizer was a wash boiler, his operating table a dining-room table, and his operating room a cleared space off the steaming kitchen of a home on the west side of Chicago.

4. *Our People*

The "grand opening" of the country's first interracial hospital in May 1891 was a huge success. "Everybody who was anybody," the papers said, and many who were nobodies in the ghetto community, were there. They came bringing gifts of "sheets, beds, old linen, sugar, soap, black currant jelly and loaves of bread," and some of these gifts "were kept up month by month." Wealthy white people made financial gifts too, but Provident remained just this side of extreme destitution. Though desperately needed and gratefully received, eggs, butter, and vegetables were not medicines, and books, "a Japanese screen worth $6.50," and a clothes wringer, whatever therapeutic values they might be imagined to have, were not forceps and Reverdin needles and cystoscopes. Dances, benefit dinners, and church bazaars staged by the Ladies' Auxiliary and the Provident Hospital Association did not keep the petty cash box supplied. At the end of the first year, having admitted one hundred and eighty-five patients, nearly a third of them white, Provident had a deficit of close to a thousand dollars.

But finances were not the only cause for worry. Dr. Dan wanted to add Negroes to the staff, but he did not wish to compromise the severe standards he had established. To do so would be to destroy his own concept of Provident, to play fast and loose with the reputations of the men who had consented to give their services to it, and to reduce good will to condescension and sincere sympathy to scornful patronage. He could not risk losing a competent white staff. He did not want it said that Provident was "just another nigger institution," with all the phrase implied of carelessness and irresponsibility. As a Negro physician, he was on the defensive for his people: they had yet to prove themselves.

So even applicants to the nurses' training school had to meet standards that were more than ordinarily high. The level of training Dr. Dan imposed on the school and the caliber of the men and women who gave instruction required that nursing students have "a broad intelligence already fairly trained," and those personal attributes—"punctuality, neatness, moral fitness and a gentle manner"—that might prove insurance against mediocrity and failure. Of the one hundred and seventy-five applicants the first year, Dr. Dan accepted seven. His cousin's daughter and the sister of the Reverend Mr. Reynolds were among them. They were all high school graduates. They were all light-skinned and of the mixed-blood world. What seemed to give this inexorable circumstance an unfortunate blush of policy and planning was the fact, equally inexorable, that the two Negroes on the medical staff and the one interne were also of the mixed-blood world. The only other Negro physician who had applied did not meet the standards, and he had been rejected. His name was George Hall.

In Negro life in Chicago, as elsewhere, ambitions were stirring. A harsh, aggressive species was beginning to press up, claw up through the multitude. As a class it had not yet put either a great social or a great emotional distance between itself and the throng. A protective tribal instinct operated. It operated now in the mass as it had operated during slavery to condition the relations of the great number of field slaves to the few, more privileged house servants and free people of color, most of whom were mulattoes, and most of whom the field slaves thought were in league against them. They were suspicious and resentful. George Hall was of this breed.

A dark-skinned man of genial bearing, Hall was well known and well liked in the ghetto. Here his opinions were respected, and one of his opinions was that he was just too dark for Dr. Dan Williams' taste.

It sounded plausible enough to the people in the ghetto. That the course of study at Chicago Medical College was then the stiffest in the country meant less to them than that George Hall, their friend, was a doctor the same as Dr. Dan. Medical training was medical training, without discrimination as to the level of it, and in Hall's dingy office hung a medical diploma. It was from one of the more than twenty Eclectic schools in Chicago. As a member of the Illinois State Board of Health, Williams knew what those schools were. They were still back in the pre-bacteriology, pre-antiseptic age. Their graduates could not meet the standards the head of Provident insisted upon.

But Hall had a following, and he had the powerful shibboleth of "color-struck dickties" around which to rally it. This gave him a kind of authority Dr. Dan was never to have and was never to learn to cope with. Apparently approached by some of Hall's crowd, the hospital's board, totally comprised to Negroes, grew concerned for the welfare of the Provident and the solidarity of the race. They persuaded Dr. Dan to appoint Hall to the children's clinic—"to look after measles and chicken pox, and such," Hall said bitterly. Indeed, it was no flattering appointment; another type of man would have refused it. Hall was required to call in a consultant on even the simplest cases. He was never to forget or forgive.

Hall's inclusion on the staff was eventually to wreck the medical standards and play hob with the administration of Provident's affairs, but for the time being things went on much as before. It was a struggle to keep the hospital going. Most of the patients were poor, three fourths of them required expensive surgery, and many of the accident and physical-violence cases brought in from the streets, the stockyards, and the railroads could not pay anything. Though Dr. Dan and some of the white physicians on the staff brought in their private patients and sometimes turned their fees into the hospital's general funds, as the record shows, there was never enough money. The record also shows that the finance committee regularly sent out appeals for "arnica, Pond's Extract, Brown's Ginger, plasters, camphor from your medicine chests." As the depression of 1893 deepened there were many weeks when the board and the staff met emergency expenses from their personal resources, and "more than once Dr. Dan reached into his own pocket and gave the superintendent money for the day's food."

The Chicago World's Fair brought some relief. The Chicago Negro weekly newspaper, the *Crusader*—and, indeed, Negro weeklies throughout the country—gave passionate publicity to Provident as an "interracial venture of great significance, where white and colored work together for the benefit of mankind." This appealed to Bishop Daniel Payne, who believed that "to help mankind is to love God." As gentle as always, but tottering now, and now more than ever like a graveyard thing (for he was to die in November), he came bringing a gift of five hundred dollars from his diocese in Ohio.

The aging, gray-maned Frederick Douglass, himself only two years from death, also played a part in lifting the "siege of Provident's debts." He was in Chicago as Haitian commissioner to the fair. Once recorder of deeds for the District of Columbia, once grand marshal of the United States, and lately minister to Haiti, he was still the race's spokesman and still the most famous Negro in the country. Negroes flocked to see him and to do him honor, and he urged them to contribute to Provident. An interracial hospital was his kind of thing. He did not "approve of organizations distinctively racial. . . . There are societies where color is not regarded as a test of membership, and such places I deem more appropriate for colored persons." So Negroes went to Provident and left their pennies, dimes, and dollars.

Of course Douglass himself went—and not merely because he and Dan Williams had discovered the faint possibility of a blood relationship and called each other "cousin." He went with those twin furies, Ida B. Wells and Fannie B. Williams, "whose tongues were never still on the question of equality," and he left the fifty dollars that he had solicited after a lecture in a Negro church. His visit was well advertised in advance, and "Dearborn Street was packed with every Negro in Chicago." Visibly tired, Douglass declined to make a speech, but he waved a greeting to the crowd, and the crowd shouted with one voice.

Things were easier after the summer of the fair, and Dr. Dan could give more of his attention to the practice of medicine. Chicago Medical College, which had expanded into postgraduate work and was about to be absorbed by Northwestern University, had moved to within five minutes' walking distance of Provident. Dr. Dan enrolled in a course in bacteriology. He had another opportunity to study abdominal surgery with Dr. Byron Robinson, and now he could take it. Sometimes he was the assistant, but more often he simply watched and listened as the great scowling gynecologist and "stomach man" operated and lectured. Williams absorbed medical knowledge as if his mind were a sponge. Even the cantankerous Robinson, known to be stingy of praise, spoke of him as a "skilled surgeon . . . one of the best . . . of wide experience and good judgment."

Dr. Dan had earned such mentions for his work at Provident, and as they were repeated by men of the highest professional repute it became common for physicians to crowd into the hospital's small surgery to watch him work. His manual dexterity was amazing. He was bold and ingenious, but generally he knew the full medical history in every case, and his daring and resourcefulness were grounded in a thorough knowledge of anatomy and exercised on carefully calculated risks. He was never reckless. When he made an incision he knew what he expected his knife to find.

The operation that brought him national fame and international recognition was an emergency. One day in July 1893 a tough young street fighter named Cornish was brought to Provident. He had a one-inch knife wound in the chest just left of the breastbone. It seemed superficial, but within a half hour the man was seized with a paroxysm of coughing, and within the hour he had collapsed from shock. Dr. Dan diagnosed the injury as a damaged blood vessel, perhaps the heart itself. Unless something was done, obviously the man would die.

There was no precedent to follow. In those days, even opening the thoracic cavity was considered an invitation to death. The latest authoritative work treating the subject of wounds to the heart—*Surgery*, by C. W. M. Mollin, a Fellow of the Royal Society of Surgeons—had been published but two years before, and it stated that the only treatment was "absolute rest, cold, and opium," after which the patient invariably died.

To follow this treatment now would do no harm to Dr. Dan's reputation. But if he did not follow it? If, venturing into the unknown, he challenged death with the weapons at his command? They were not today's weapons. There was no X ray. There were no sulphur drugs to fight infection. There was not even a choice of anesthesia, and blood transfusions were unknown. As he watched the patient grow steadily weaker, Dr. Dan alerted the hospital's one interne. He had decided to operate.

Besides the interne, only five professionals (four of them white) were there when medical history was made. Not one of them "but must have shuddered when Dr. Dan put the point of his knife to Cornish's inert body." It was over in a matter of time no one remembered to record, so tense was the atmosphere. The man was still alive when the last suture was made, and this was success from the medical point of view. But was it a *real* success? The answer came fifty-one days later, when, following a second operation to remove five pints of bloody serum from the chest cavity, Cornish was discharged. He lived for more than twenty years afterward. He was the first human being to survive an operation on the heart.

When the news got around Dr. Dan was besieged by medical men and reporters, but he gave only one interview. This was to the *Inter Ocean*, a newspaper controlled by Herman Kohlsaat, who was one of the first white men to contribute financially to Provident, and who, together with Marshall Field and Otto Young, would one day make possible a new, modern Provident. And even that interview said more about the interracial policy of the hospital, its mixed staff, and its nurses' training school than about Dr. Dan himself and the precedent-breaking operation he had performed.

Though Daniel Hale Williams did not know it, he was about to begin an undertaking that would have as its final result an estrangement from his people so nearly complete that a once favorite cousin would exclaim bitterly, "He wanted to be white. He wanted to be white, so let him be it!"; and that would make the furious curse of George Hall seem fulfilled at last: "I'll punish him worse than God ever will. I'll see he's forgotten before he's dead!"

And for Dan Williams, the estrangement from the lives and the struggles of his people was indeed a worse punishment than any he could have imagined coming from God.

5. *Song of Love*

The state of Negro affairs in the last decade of the nine-teenth century left something to be desired. The Demo-cratic party's victory over Reconstruction was complete. The Negro remained a source of fear and hatred in the South on the one hand, and the victim of evasion and neg-lect in the North on the other. Any effort to improve his condition seemed only to worsen it. By 1894 all but a tardy handful of Southern states had disfranchised him. By 1896 the Supreme Court had pronounced its "separate but equal" doctrine, thus assuring the continuance of the tradition of racial difference and those discriminatory practices by means of which many Southern whites could satisfy their "consuming monomania"—the perpetuation in law of an incontestable superiority to blacks. By the middle years of the last decade of the century Negroes were be-ing lynched at the rate of one every fifty-six hours.

For Southern attitudes Southern spokesmen of course were not slow to find justification in a kind of pseudo re-ality. It was a false reality created in part by the systematic exclusion of Negroes from the general cultural life and in part by an ineradicable tendency to romanticize what had been dearly loved and tragically lost—namely, a way of life, as imagination reproduced it, so aristrocratic, gracious, and precious in particulars, and so beneficent, generous, and fruitful in principles that it might well have served and even should have served as a model for all mankind. It was a pseudo reality that was sustained for long years after the North's outcries ("The South of popular story is a figment of the imagination, I tell you!") against the actuality were stilled, and long after the entire machinery of attitudes, custom, and law had been adjusted to the Southern point of view.

Since the American world accepted as unquestioned fact the "inherent and irredeemable inferiority" of the Negro, it was not necessary to keep padding the fact, ex-cept as the padding was poultice for a raw conscience. And it was poultice.

"You could ship-wreck 10,000 illiterate white Americans on a desert island, and in three weeks they would have a fairly good government, conceived and administered upon fairly democratic lines. You could ship-wreck 10,000 Negroes, every one of whom was a graduate of Harvard University, and in less than three years, they would have retrograded governmentally; half of the men would have been killed, and the other half have two wives apiece." Thus Mississippi Senator John Sharp Williams spoke the common Southern opinion in the 1890s.

This, of course, was the pained conscience at work. It was at work in all those Southern spokesmen—from John P. Kennedy (*Swallow Barn*), through Thomas Nelson Page (*Red Rock*), to Thomas Dixon (*The Leopard's Spots*)—who helped to create and tried to breathe life into the stereotypes of the Negro character, the Negro mind, and the Negro soul. That character was at once depraved, comic, and benign; that mind was at once dull and crafty; that soul was either inexplicably angelic or primally debased beyond redemption.

By reason of his exclusion from the cultural life and his inability to gain traction in the intellectual life, the Negro had no effective defense against these attributions. Sutton Griggs might publish novel after novel from a corrective point of view, and Pauline Hopkins might write books crying out in agony, "We are not like that! Dear God knows we're not like that!" but they had to peddle their books from door to door. Even Charles Chesnutt, a close friend of Dan Williams, who had won distinction as a racially unidentified writer of stories for the *Atlantic Monthly*, might write "uncompromisingly and impartially, sparing neither whites nor Negroes, Southerners nor Northerners," those soberly documented novels of Southern life, but *The House behind the Cedars*, *The Colonel's Dream*, and *The Marrow of Tradition* tended to modify the common opinion and correct the false concepts, and the white reading public paid scant attention—and a fine literary talent fizzed out like a drenched fire.

Certainly one result of the implacable resistance to the assertion of the Negro will and the Negro concept of himself was this: perhaps realizing that sometimes the battles you do not fight are the ones you win, Negroes began or seemed to begin to live up to the baleful attributions, both in their literature and in their lives. It was extremely un-healthy, as first a few and then a growing number realized. But slowly their vaunted talent for compromise, for com-pliance and conformity took over. In his famous "Atlanta Speech" in 1895, Booker Washington urged these as the characteristics that should henceforth define Negro life. Temporarily bewitched by the country's almost frenzied reception of Washington's ideas, men who were later to proclaim their dignity as Negroes and their rights as American citizens fell into line as if moved by the hand of God.

How unhealthy all this was showed up in the life of Paul L. Dunbar, who for a brief time was the most widely read poet in America. Dr. Dan first met Dunbar when the poet served as Douglass' assistant at the Chicago World's Fair. Later he was to know him better as a friend and as a patient brought hopelessly drunk to the alcoholic ward of Freedmen's Hospital in Washington. But in 1893 the poet—then twenty-one and the author of one volume—was just beginning his short, brilliant, tragic career.

White friends in his home town of Dayton, Ohio, had brought his poetry to the attention of William Dean Howells, then America's most influential man of letters. Charmed by the dialect pieces written frankly in imitation of Stephen Foster and Irwin Russell, Howells encouraged Dunbar to develop this vein. This was the vein, the critic said, that "in the charming accents of the Negro's own version of our English" most clearly defined "the range be-tween appetite and emotion, which is the limited range of the race."

But it was not really Dunbar's vein. He was not at home in it; he could not do what he wished to do in it—sing of the aspirations and depict the depths of Negro life. Yet here was the arbiter of American letters advising him to develop it. For Dunbar's second volume, *Majors and Mi-nors*, Howells wrote for *Harper's Weekly* a full-page re-view devoted solely to praise of the dialect pieces. For the third volume, *Lyrics of Lowly Life*, Howells wrote the introduction. "Paul Dunbar is the only man of pure African blood and of American civilization to feel the Negro life esthetically and express it lyrically."

But it was not Negro life. It was what the white South had seduced America into believing was Negro life, and no one knew this better than Dunbar. But he had an aging mother to provide for and a young and beautiful wife to support, and writing was all he knew to do for a livelihood. Dialect poems and stories, or the pallid romantic novels he fashioned around idealized white characters, were all the public would accept from him. He poured them out, and his publishers handsomely bound and illustrated them, at the rate of nearly one volume a year.

Fame sickened him even as he pursued it. He took to drink. It assuaged his bitterness and frustration and what a recent critic has called his "self-hatred." He drank more heavily. He disgraced himself at his public lectures, notably at Yale and at Northwestern. His wife left him. She loved him no less than he loved her, but she could no longer protect their love from shame and abasement and him from himself. No one could, not even his cherished mother, to whom he fled in 1905. In the last months of his life he somehow managed to gather his energies and turn out some of the most poignant of his lyrics in pure English, among them this:

> He sang of love when life was young,
> And Love itself was in his lays,
> But, Ah, the world, it turned to praise
> A jingle in a broken tongue.

He died in 1906 at the age of thirty-four.

6. *The Nadir*

In some areas appearances did not entirely betray those who, like Booker Washington, pretended to believe that everything was fine in the Negro situation and in race relations. Negro secondary schools and colleges were crowded. Most of them were substandard, it is true, but the white denominations that supported them and the white men and women who taught in them were sincere in their efforts on the Negro's behalf. Negro churches, such as the African Methodist Episcopal, the African Zion, and the Colored Methodist, enjoyed an unprecedented growth in membership just before the turn of the century. They could claim "23,000 churches, with unusually wide activities, and spending annually at least $10,000,000."

Some of this money went to Negro businesses, of which there were a sufficient number to make for the presence of four hundred delegates at the first convention of the National Negro Business League in 1899. The delegates represented restaurant and hotel chains, bakery companies, co-operative grocers and catering firms, and some of these were substantial, but they were hardly in a class with the Negro insurance companies, mutual aid societies, and burial associations that were organized in the same period.

Fraternal orders, such as the Masons and Odd Fellows, had long been established among Negroes in the 1890s, but new groups came into being. Negro banks, too, sprang up. Some, like the State Street Bank of Chicago, flourish still, but most collapsed after a year or two. Negroes supported orphanages, homes for the aged, and asylums for fallen women. The National Association of Colored Women, founded in 1895, set up kindergartens for the children of poor working mothers and social clubs for young girls.

Individual Negroes, too, gained recognition, and this was sometimes inflated beyond all deserving by a people who were culturally starved and hungering for heroes. Sports figures, theatrical personalities, and just "characters" were made to shine like gods. Negroes of really fine accomplishment had a way of getting absorbed by the white world, usually abroad. Henry Tanner, the painter, whose works hang in the Luxembourg, the Franklin Institute, the Chicago Art Institute, and the Metropolitan, went to Europe in 1891 and lived in France until his death in the 1930s. Sissieretta Jones and Marie Selika (whose voice and artistry were "above criticism") were so much in demand on the concert stages of Europe that one found time to visit her homeland only a few times in a half dozen years and the other never returned at all. Negro papers in the nineties tried to follow such careers, but it was rather like firing a cannon at the stars.

While the front pages of Negro papers were often roseate with success stories, the editorial pages were gray with gloom—and for reason. The lynching rate climbed steadily. The anti-Negro activities of organized labor, which refused to see the unity of interest between white and black workers, were most severe. Negroes were pitilessly lampooned in the national press.

Negro editors gloomed especially over political prospects. They remembered Reconstruction, when Negroes sat in legislative bodies in the South, and there were black sheriffs, postmasters, magistrates, superintendents of education, and officials of all kinds. "Politics," wrote John Langston, a Negro leader, "is the key to unlock all doors." But with Reconstruction finished, the doors were as tight-locked as they had ever been in slavery, and the key hung out of reach.

When Grover Cleveland, who had already served a presidential term, was again the Democratic nominee in 1892, few Negro editors saw any reason to change the opinion most of them had expressed in 1884: "If Cleveland is elected . . . it will be a cold afternoon for this country and especially for the Negro and the laboring classes." For, meantime, Cleveland had denounced the Federal Election Bill and had praised Isaiah Montgomery for helping to engineer the disfranchisement of Negroes in Mississippi. But Cleveland was elected. "Equality follows the badge of citizenship wherever found, and, unimpaired by race or color . . ." he said, hitting the proper note of exhortation in his inaugural speech. But it seemed unlikely that he himself would do anything to lift the Negro from his plight.

Only one monument to the liberalizing, fluid period of Reconstruction remained—the Freedmen's Hospital, in Washington, D.C. And even that was threatened by indifference and neglect.

7. *Freedmen's Own*

An old friend of Dr. Dan's and an early benefactor of Provident Hospital was soon to prove that the indifference and neglect were not total.

Ex-Postmaster General Walter Q. Gresham had left the Republican party to campaign for Cleveland and the Democrats, and Cleveland rewarded him by appointing him Secretary of State in the new cabinet. It was not a post in which a man would ordinarily concern himself with Negro affairs, but Judge Gresham was one of those interfering Yankees who stuck his long nose into all sorts of matters that were but disingenuously his concern. He stuck his nose into Freedmen's Hospital and Refugee Camp, and what he sniffed was foul. He pressed the Secretary of the Interior, Hoke Smith, so hard that that Southern gentleman's resistance was completely smashed and he promised to start reforms.

Then on a visit home to Chicago, Secretary Gresham sent for Dr. Dan. He told Dr. Dan that Freedmen's was going to be completely reorganized and he wanted him to apply for the executive position there. He brushed aside the physician's solicitude for Provident. That hospital was in fine condition, as Gresham well knew, with a staff as strong as any in the city, and with a small surplus of funds. "If it's service to your race you're thinking of," Gresham said, "Freedmen's needs you more than Provident."

This was a line of argument Dr. Dan could not ignore, and it had the greater strength from the fact that his mother and two younger sisters had moved to Washington just a few months before. He promised to apply.

There were other applicants, among them one who wrote, ". . . no colored physician can fill the place properly because they have less respect for their own race than a good Christian white man feels." Dr. Dan's application was supported not only by Gresham's political influence but by enthusiastic letters from the most eminent medical men in the Midwest and by his own professional distinction. He got the job.

It was the end of December 1893 and he was to assume his new duties the first day of February. He wanted to leave Provident's affairs in order. He had a large private practice to dispose of and other personal matters to attend. But friends who knew he had worked unceasingly for seven years urged him to take a vacation, and he went off reluctantly to southern Illinois. There on a hunting trip he had an accident that sent a load of buckshot through his foot. By the time he could return to Chicago and Provident, inflammation of the veins of his leg had developed. Time dragged. Three days before he was to leave for Washington he left the hospital. It was too soon. Lymph vessels and glands became involved, and the celebrated endocrinologist, Dr. Christian Fenger, had all he could do to save his colleague's life.

This unfortunate accident and Dr. Dan's delayed recovery gave George Hall an opportunity he had awaited with well-concealed impatience. The gladhand, the backslap, the bluster had won him a reputation for affability even at Provident, but his manner hid a satanic vindictiveness and a designing ambition. Though now at last, having attended evening classes at a second-rate medical school, he had a degree in allopathic medicine, he cut no figure in the professional world. His colleagues at Provident rated him a mediocre physician, and he had not been promoted.

He felt unfairly treated. He felt that his unfair treatment had the most inexcusable of reasons—his dark skin. Stored up in him were explosive quantities of professional and personal jealousy, for neither his own attainments nor the blatant attractions of a red-haired octoroon wife had won him entree to that mixed-blood world with which most of his Negro colleagues were associated by birth. Hall wanted this at least as much as he wanted professional preferment. He believed that one signalized the other. All the emotional tensions of the struggle for status, complicated by the severe intorsions of color caste within the race, worked in Dr. Hall to an intolerable degree.

The last thing he wanted was for Dr. Dan to stay at Provident, where he might continue to block his promotion. Yet at the same time he did not want his rival (for

so Hall conceived him to be) to have the Negro world-
wide recognition of the appointment to Freedmen's. Dan
Williams was not what Hall would describe as a "race
man." He did not put race above all other considerations.
He did not give Negroes the "breaks" just because they
were Negroes. If he could not block Dr. Dan's appointment, Hall thought he might at least besmirch Dr. Dan's
name.

Thus, while the latter lay critically ill, Hall, radiating
great waves of race consciousness, addressed the Negro public through the Washington paper, the *Colored American*.
He implied that Dr. Dan was stalling, that he was satisfied
with the deluge of publicity. "Freedmen's new chief," Hall
wrote, "will never assume his post there." Hall persuaded
James Blackever, a Negro politician of questionable ethics
and little power, to write the Secretary of the Interior.
Blackever enclosed a copy of Hall's newspaper diatribe,
which was, he told Hoke Smith, "written by an associate
of Dr. Williams." As for himself, he continued, he had
been in Chicago, "where I left Dr. Williams following his
everyday profession. . . . Everyone knows that he is only
baffling with the Department . . . at the expense of those
he was sent to serve."

It was easy to induce Robert S. Abbott to take up the
attack. His mind was as dark and twisted as Hall's—and
for the same tragic reasons. "Freedmen's Hospital is in
charge of an invalid who has drawn eight months salary
without performing a single week of service. . . . He is a
fitter subject for a hospital than for the management of
one." But Abbott, whose first paper came out as irregularly
as a groundhog in a variable winter, was not then the powerful editor of what was to be the most influential Negro
weekly in the world.

Dr. Dan was hurt by these attacks, not in his standing
with the federal officials, who had been kept informed, but
in that deeply personal way he was always to be hurt when
his own people accused him of disloyalty. He had no defense against such attacks. He was too modest to point out
the sacrifices he had made to establish and keep Provident
going. He told no one how drastically his income would

be reduced by taking the position at Freedmen's. Weakened by the long illness that nearly took his life, and upheld only by the hope of turning Freedmen's into "an institution in which Negroes could take pride," Daniel Hale Williams packed his instruments and his medical library and in the fall of 1894 set out for the nation's capital.

8. *Conflict in Cow Town*

Washington was a great change from Chicago. The capital city for a century and a half, it was just beginning to look like it—and this only to the eyes of the uninitiated. Reeking marshes sprawled inward from the Potomac River and infested Georgetown, Anacostia, and LeDroit Park with seasonal plagues of mosquitoes and frogs. In spring the river sometimes flooded and inundated the Negro quarter at the very foot of the Capitol. Radiating from this, the principal avenues, Pennsylvania, Massachusetts, and Connecticut, had long since claimed the embassies, the clubs of the influential and wealthy, and the ornate homes of the nouveau riche. The intersecting streets, too, had established their character. Solid rows of red brick fronts, broken here and there by architectural oddities in stoops, steps, and porches, frowned down like fortresses on tiny patches of front yards graced with fences of iron, stone, or hedge. But behind the stone and marble of the avenues and the brick of the middle-class streets, behind and between and in every crack and corner squeezed the noisome alleys and courts of the poor—some black, some white, and some few red Indians.

A little to the northwest but outside the boundaries of the city proper, the federal government had established two institutions for Negroes. Founded in the irritable frenzy of the Civil War and Reconstruction, they stood side by side. One was Freedmen's Hospital, Asylum and Refugee Camp—the very name of which signified emergency—and the other Howard University. Over the years they had come to be the twin symbols of what President Grant had called "the Government's undiminished regard" for the welfare of colored people. Over the years, without either losing or quite fulfilling their separate functions, they had mingled their identities and grown so close together in physical fact that one could not tell whether the slums of Cow Town, to which the hospital was attached on one side, made progress toward the respectability of the university or the university declined to the slums.

Actually, though, there was no mobility in Cow Town. Poverty and repression had vitiated all but the rawest instincts of survival. The sign of the slums, as the poet Dunbar pointed out, was the hospital and asylum. The inhabitants of Cow Town, ignorant and untrained, could get no handhold in a city where there were no factories, no mills, no industry of any kind, and where the jobs in domestic and personal service were traditionally pre-empted, as they had been in slavery, by an altogether different caste and class of Negroes.

This other class made the university the symbol of their lives. They had ambition. One who drove a senator's horse today aspired to carry his official messages tomorrow, and to be perhaps his clerk (for there were already a few Negro clerks in government) a year from now. In short, there was competition, struggle, and it was all the more unremitting and ruthless because positions of prestige were so few and because the competitors for them had started from the same place, with similar advantages and handicaps, and were, in a way of speaking, sprung from the same loins.

So Dr. Charles B. Purvis did not see why Dr. Daniel H. Williams had any more claim to head Freedmen's than he. A member of the university's faculty of medicine, Purvis had run the hospital for a dozen years. That he had run it badly, as a sinecure, no one seemed to detect until Judge Gresham interfered. But the two positions had given Purvis tremendous prestige in the Negro community, and he did not care to lose it. He made trouble of a nagging sort. He injected politics into the situation. He tried to rally the university trustees and faculty by declaring that the advantages the university medical students enjoyed would be lost if a non-faculty man, and a stranger to boot, ran the hospital.

But the truth is that Freedmen's was more asylum and

refugee camp than hospital when Dr. Dan took over. Housed in six buildings, five of them wooden, barracks-like structures, on three acres of ground, it had been built for an emergency and the emergency had lasted thirty years. The patients were wards of the government—the indigent, the homeless, the useless, the habitually drunk, the insane, and the blind—dumped there by the authorities of distant cities where, though native to them, they were not tolerated. Those who were able were required to render such services as cleaning the yards and buildings, and making "bedsacks, sheets, chemises, aprons, handkerchiefs," and the like.

The medical care they got was not only negligible but negligent and dangerous. Surgery was sometimes performed "by students who needed the experience." The mortality rate was more than an excessive 10 per cent. There were no trained nurses. On his first morning Dr. Dan was shocked to see a "ward mammy" take up a position between the rows of beds in the female ward, clap her hands, and shout, "All you 'leven o'clockers, take yo' medicine!" Freedmen's, a monument to the government's "undiminished regard" for the welfare of Negroes, resembled nothing so much as a medieval pesthouse. Yet to be its surgeon in chief was to attain the highest administrative post the federal government accorded Negroes. The head of Freedmen's was an important man in the Negro world, and in that world his position commanded great esteem.

The prestige value of the job meant practically nothing to Dr. Dan. He did not know how to employ it to surround himself with influential friends who might prove useful. He cared little for society. His friends were people to whom he was attracted by intrinsic qualities and professional interests. He did sometimes go to visit his "cousin," Frederick Douglass, who, in semi-retirement, quietly waited for death in nearby Anacostia, and once a week he dined with his mother and two sisters in Kingman Place, but for the most part he was so deeply involved in Freedmen's that he had no time for anything else.

His first job was to reorganize the hospital, and within a month this work was begun. He established seven departments. His reputation in the medical world, coupled with a local scarcity of professionally broadening opportunities, made it possible for him to enlist an unpaid, biracial staff of twenty of Washington's "most competent and successful" specialists. This was the kind of organization he had started with at Provident, and he extended it here. He saw an interneship program as necessary, since, excepting Provident, there was not a hospital in the United States that welcomed colored medical graduates. He refined the hospital's ties to the university medical school, which was still an evening school for students who had to work days to support themselves. He wanted to substitute a nurses' training school for the two-nights-a-week instruction in practical nursing that Purvis had installed and offered to women of pitifully inadequate background. If Dr. Dan conceived of Freedmen's as both a hospital and a center of medical training for Negroes, he also felt it was a challenge to the belief that Negroes could not "do" and learn and apply as well as whites.

There were difficulties. The annual budget of fifty-two thousand dollars was inadequate for a two-hundred-bed hospital and training center. Purvis sniped from nearby and used his still considerable influence to undermine the work. He encroached on the authority of Sarah Ebersole, whom Dr. Dan had brought on from Chicago to run the training school and nursing staff. There was, finally, the indifference of the Secretary of the Interior, a Georgian who preached white supremacy and "cared not a fig" about Freedmen's.

Nevertheless, things were accomplished. Dr. Dan's abilities won over the university administration and all of the medical faculty save Purvis. A biracial staff worked as smoothly at Freedmen's as it had at Provident. After less than a year young white medical graduates were applying for interneships, and Dr. Dan admitted the best qualified of them along with Negroes. He demonstrated and lectured in surgery. Steadily the caliber of the medical service rose to match the reputation the deprived masses of Negroes were all too prone to give anything that was theirs and racially identified with them. While surgical cases increased almost 200 per cent, the mortality rate dropped lower than 3 per cent. By 1896, Freedmen's was admitting five hundred surgical cases a year, and Dr. Dan was proving in the East his right to the reputation he had earned in the Midwest as one of the "country's greatest surgeons." Not only local medical men pressed for opportunities to watch him operate, but soon men were coming from Johns Hopkins in Baltimore and the University of Pennsylvania in Philadelphia.

In spite of the success of the biracial program, prejudice was far from dead. Some Negroes thought that Dr. Dan's knowledge and skill should be kept within the race, and that Freedmen's should admit no white patients and have neither white internes nor white members on the medical staff. Freedmen's was theirs: Dr. Dan was theirs—one of them. The whites had hospitals to which Negroes were not admitted even as patients, much less as staff physicians and surgeons. They had, too, their professional groups, like the District Medical Society to whose meetings Negroes were never invited (though it was known through the proud testimony of an eavesdropping Negro waiter that Dr. Dan's operations had been subjects of discussion there twice in three months). White medical men were simply using Freedmen's as a good thing, and Dan Williams was rather a fool to permit them to do it. Or—perhaps there was something else. Could it be that Williams was more desirous of having the approbation and acknowledgment of white people than of giving service to his own?

Whether or not such insidiously inspired talk reached the ears of Dr. Dan, he was soon to give it the lie. He had been instrumental in establishing a local group for the professional benefit of colored physicians, and though certain men like Purvis had boycotted and maligned it, the Medico-Chirurgical Society had flourished. It was a mixed group, for Dr. Dan knew that the exchange of ideas and experience with advantaged white men would be good for Negroes in the profession. But he also knew and respected that powerful defensive impulse in Negroes to have something that belonged exclusively to them. Born of the race's experience of indignity and kept strong by the galling indifference of whites, the impulse did sometimes lead to a development of initiative and racial self-respect. The Negro church systems, the militant Negro press were products of it. And perhaps, Dr. Dan wrote his friend Dr. Charles Bentley, the impulse "could be made to work to the advancement of Negro medicine."

Acting on this thought, Daniel Williams invited a representative group of Negro physicians to a meeting in Atlanta, Georgia. There they organized the National Medical Association. It was their own, and for more than half a century it was to remain the only national medical body to which Negroes could belong. Refusing the presidency, Dr. Dan consented to be the association's first vice-president. It was in this capacity that he met Booker Washington, some two or three months before the Alabama educator was hurled onto the national stage by the storm of applause that greeted his "Atlanta Speech."

The three men—George Hall, Charles Purvis, and Booker Washington—who were each in his own way to contribute to the inevitability of Daniel Hale Williams' withdrawal from Negro affairs and the race milieu had now entered his life.

9. *Washington, Farewell*

In the next two years circumstances seemed to shape right for Purvis and events to fall wrong for Dr. Dan. Frederick Douglass died in February 1895, and Judge Gresham the following May. With the passing of these two men, Dr. Dan lost the only politically powerful friends he had.

But more unhappy in its immediate consequences was the death of his only brother that same year. Price Williams, errant, jovial, braggart, had always been his mother's favorite child. At his burial her reason snapped. Dan was head of the family now, the last male in his line, and in the days that followed he contemplated resigning to devote himself to Sarah Ann's care. His two younger sisters, with whom the mother lived, were virtually helpless. It was a time of great strain and personal anxiety for the physician.

Even after his mother's reason returned, the strain did not lessen.

For, meantime, Dr. Charles Purvis had managed to create and win attention for the politics involved in Freedmen's. The time was ripe. Both major political parties had been thrown off balance by the Populist revolt of 1892, and neither had recovered fully. Populists, Democrats, and Republicans had "sought to win the Negro vote . . . and resorted to desperate means." Party lines were still blurred West and South. The Populists increased their total vote by 40 per cent in the congressional elections of 1894, while the Democrats, seriously split and unable to close ranks in the South, lost 25 per cent. The panic of 1893, which sent more than a hundred railroads into receivership, and the depression that spread through '94 and '95 put the country in a sullen mood. Politicians of both major parties knew that something must be done, or the power of doing anything might be taken out of their hands. The Democrats had no great strategist: they had only William Jennings Bryan. The Republicans had Marcus Alonzo Hanna. And Hanna had many people, including Negroes. The Democrats were routed in 1896. The Republicans swept back to power.

Purvis was a Republican who knew his way around the hustings (he had campaigned vigorously for McKinley) and the halls of Congress. There was an old congressional committee, set up to investigate "all charitable and reformatory institutions in the District," but it had grown moribund. Purvis thought the committee's work should be revived. The patronage that went to Negroes was in short supply, and one way to replenish it was to find cause to get rid of Negro Democrats in office. An investigation of Freedmen's might help to accomplish the trick. Purvis began knocking on congressional doors. He was, he said, not only a campaigning Republican, as everyone knew, but a deserving Republican, as all Negroes knew. It took him six months to get this subtlety across.

Meanwhile, however, he was not idle in other directions. In February 1897 the Washington *Bee* revealed that Dr. Purvis had been persuading Howard University medical students "to sign a paper against Dr. Williams"—perhaps, the *Bee* hinted, on pain of not being awarded their degrees. But Purvis had also put his persuasive powers to another use. Sporting as a figure of influence in the Republican party, he had convinced Dr. Dan's assistant and the director of nurses' training at Freedmen's that he, Purvis, could do for them what no one else could. Dr. William Warfield, the assistant, was incompetent; Miss Ebersole, chief of nurses, was aging and tired. Both had comfortable berths at Freedmen's, and both wished to stay on. In instance after instance during the subsequent investigation, Dr. Warfield and Miss Ebersole perjured themselves.

As the investigation dragged on and Purvis' trickery came to light, it seemed to Dr. Dan that politics of this kind soiled him personally and put his professional reputation at stake. Aided by white associates, who knew his worth to Freedmen's, he defended himself with all his force. Jeremiah Rankin, the president of Howard University, was the final key witness. He testified that Dr. Williams was "a choice man in the job, a first class surgeon," and that "everything he has done has been fully justified."

In spite of his complete exoneration by the congressional committee, Dr. Dan was tired and discouraged. Alice Johnson, the daughter of an ex-slave and the famous Jewish sculptor, Moses Jacob Ezekiel, had had her troubles too. Until the illness of her mother brought Dr. Williams into her home, she had isolated herself from society. She was proud of her father but ashamed of her illegitimacy which, since it had been no secret from her student days at Howard, was the subject of whispers and cruel taunts. Her uncommon beauty brought her insults, especially when, boarding the horsecars, she advertised her Negro blood by sitting where Negroes were forced to sit. White men followed her, molested her. She began to go heavily veiled. Finally she stayed home altogether.

The illness of her mother was the turning point in her life. She and Dr. Dan became friends. He brought her quietly among his own few social acquaintances, mostly temporary residents of Washington—the poet Dunbar, ex-Congressman John Langston and his family—and gave her a measure of protection she had never known. They had a quiet courtship. Alice hated Washington, and Dr. Dan could not be unmindful of this. Six weeks after he was exonerated he resigned from Freedmen's, and a few days later he and Alice Johnson were married. Dunbar wrote a "ditty" for the occasion.

> *Step me now a bridal measure,*
> *Work give way to love and leisure,*
> *Hearts be free and hearts be gay—*
> *Dr. Dan doth wed today.*

. . . .

> *'Tis no time for things unsightly,*
> *Life's the day and life goes lightly;*
> *Science lays aside her sway—*
> *Love rules Dr. Dan today.*

. . . .

> *So with blithe and happy hymning*
> *And with goblets harmless brimming,*
> *Dance a step— Musicians, play—*
> *Dr. Dan doth wed today.*

The bridal couple read it as their train sped toward Chicago.

10. *Dirty Work*

Chicago was glad to have Daniel Hale Williams back. He had scarcely resettled there when professional demands upon him grew so heavy that he found himself with patients in five hospitals at once. Most of his patients were white, but they had to seek him out in his ghetto office, for he had not considered breaking off his identity with his race.

As a matter of fact he was even then engaged in a correspondence with Booker Washington, who, having visited Freedmen's the year before, had written, "I was not in your hospital two minutes before I saw, as I had never seen before, what you are." He had asked Dr. Dan to "come to

Tuskegee for two or three days" to help set up "medical and nurse training departments." Exactly what the school principal had in mind the physician did not know, but his own ideas were solemn and grand. He wrote Washington about the building of a great medical center "to serve not only Tuskegee but thousands of those poor people who die for want of . . . attention."

This was too much for Washington, whose ambitions were completely organized around himself and who cared nothing for a medical center that might overshadow him and Tuskegee. Dr. Dan tried various approaches, all of them self-effacing, but Booker Washington knew that Daniel Hale Williams was a name of some luster and that it might shine more brightly than he cared to have shine the names of those associated with him. The "sage of Tuskegee" apparently had decided to drop the whole matter when Dr. Dan, still pursuing it, wrote, "When you come to Chicago, come to see us."

Booker Washington did come to Chicago in the fall of '98, but he did not see Dr. Dan. He penned a note saying that his "time was more than taken." He did not say that some of it was taken by the unctuous Dr. Hall.

The ghetto was beginning to sense itself as a cultural and ethnic unity. Striving for independence and self-respect, it nevertheless tested the flexibility of the surrounding white community by constant encroachments upon it, invading and absorbing when it could, resenting bitterly when it could not. The ghetto wanted to be two things at once: an imperium in imperio and an interrelated community of the city. It hated the repressive prejudice that threw it back upon itself, while at the same time it reveled in its self-sufficiency. A clangorous race chauvinism marked its every move, every event.

The ghetto was where Dr. Dan made his home, and where he believed in all conscience he belonged. If as a professional man he honored the obligation to offer his services to all alike, as a social being he felt a compulsive loyalty to the struggle for the community's advancement. "We need not be dependent on white people," he told his friend Charles Bentley. He resumed his place on the finance committee of Provident and his old post as chief surgeon. He gave his services free to the new Negro Old Folks' Home. The Reverend Reverdy Ransom was making the first attempt at social settlement work among Negroes, and Dr. Dan gave his support to this, contributing money to the Institutional Church and Social Settlement, and free medical care to those members who could not pay for it. With a small group of Negroes, he helped to organize the United Brotherhood Fraternal Insurance Company.

But at the same time he wanted and needed the stimulation of new ideas and new professional knowledge, and this stimulation could come only from outside the race. There were not enough forward-looking Negro doctors in Chicago to provide it. Their only opportunities to keep abreast were through an alliance with Provident and through postgraduate courses at Northwestern University. But few could afford, in either time or money, postgraduate work. Their associations with advantaged white men in the profession were one-sided and tenuous. They were admitted to the Chicago Medical Society and could attend its discussions, but listening to papers was an entirely different thing from studying problems in the morgue and the laboratory, and from watching men at work on them in surgery. And this was what Dr. Dan wanted. He resumed the associations with white men that had been cut off by four years of absence.

That he was welcomed as a contributing member of the small vanguard of medicine soon became evident. His monographs began to appear in the *Chicago Medical Journal* and in the *Journal of Obstetrics* and to be reprinted in professional publications all over the country. He performed operations before growing numbers of surgeons at Provident, at St. Luke's, and at Mercy, and the colored papers were quick to point out that he was the first and (then) the only Negro to do so. He lectured to the Chicago Medical Society and to similar groups in distant cities, always insisting, however, that Negro physicians, too, be invited to hear him. In Dallas and other Southern cities he refused "to operate in lily-white hospitals." The *North Carolina Medical Journal* wrote soliciting a paper, but this

Southern publication had been printing articles purporting to offer scientific proof that the shape of the Negro skull marked the race's inferiority. Dr. Williams took pleasure in replying that he was a Negro and "too busy just now to send an article."

He considered it an outrage to be looked upon as a Negro who had become exceptional by virtue of a skin color that indicated his white blood. "The color of the skin," he pointed out more than once, "furnishes no correct index" to anything. He believed that what colored men needed was opportunity. When opportunity came and they muffed it, he was dispirited.

Through acquaintances in Washington and through the Negro press he kept in touch with Freedmen's. Things had steadily deteriorated. The institution had been thrown to the political lions and had attracted the ambitions of men who were at once unscrupulous and mediocre. William Warfield, who had been Dr. Dan's assistant, was one of these. Though his own testimony before the congressional committee had proved him perfidious, he was perhaps less perfidious than Purvis and his political connections were just as strong; he had been chosen to run the hospital. But now the Negro press gave currency to an exciting rumor that there was to be a new national hospital for Negroes, the "modern Freedmen's." Architects' drawings were published; estimates were discussed. Dr. Dan was emboldened to write Booker Washington.

For by the early 1900s the principal of Tuskegee had become the virtual dictator of Negro affairs. He had been hoisted to this eminence by a group of powerful men— Baldwin, Carnegie, Frick, Huntington, Peabody, and Rockefeller—whose "psychology of materialism and reaction," as one historian points out, "dimmed the fervor of real American idealism" with a pretense that the alternative to the industrial control of wealth was chaos, and with the belief that private philanthropy was an adequate substitute for social justice and equality. In so far (and it was very far indeed) as Washington decried the Negro's participation in organized labor and politics, and in so far as he advocated extreme compromise in every situation that might upset the status quo, he was their man. He would help maintain the South's quiescence by keeping Negroes —the truly revolutionary force, the catalytic power—out of politics. He would hold Negroes to the "Negro's place." He would assure industry's power over a recalcitrant white labor force by delivering a cheap, docile, and plentiful supply of Negro labor. He was the man for the great industrial barons, and they did right by him. They raised him to the nth degree of power over Negro affairs. From 1895 almost until his death in 1915, Booker Washington was "the umpire in all important appointments of Negroes; the channel through which philanthropy flowed, or did not flow, to Negro institutions; the creator and destroyer of careers; the maker and breaker of [Negro] men." "He was appealed to," wrote Mary White Ovington, "on any and every subject: how many bathrooms to put in a [colored] YMCA, whether or not to start a day nursery in some town, and so on." The so-called Tuskegee machine, which Washington built with great precision out of the talents of self-seeking men, ran with devilish efficiency on the fuel of his egomania.

Daniel Williams was quite naïve in some respects, but he was not alone in his ignorance of the fact that even when the deepest interests of the race were at stake Booker Washington was strictly committed to the quid pro quo. The worldly wise and somewhat cynical Mrs. S. Laing Williams told Dr. Dan this. She was amused by his shocked reaction. "You're so *nice*," she remarked lightly, and went on to tell him how her husband, a lawyer, wanted a position with the Chicago office of the Department of Justice, and Booker Washington wanted a stop to the critical attention he was getting in the Chicago Negro paper, the *Broad Ax*. Mrs. Williams was a journalist, and she knew the *Broad Ax* editor well: indeed, most of the unsigned pieces critical of Washington were her own. Soon the paper was printing her name over pieces "glowing with praise for the Wizard of Tuskegee." Mrs. Williams' husband got the job.

But all Dr. Dan had to offer Washington was a dedication to the welfare of their "common race," and he offered it.

"It would be a calemity," he wrote (he never learned to spell with consistent accuracy any but scientific terms), "to the whole aspiring race for the new Freedmen's to be put in charge of a mediocre man." He wished it to be unmistakably clear that he did not want the job himself, but he begged Washington to use his influence to see that only the best men were considered. "Now is the time when we can do much for our young men and women who are groping in the dark for leadership. They can do little for themselves without opportunity and guidance. . . . I am appealing to you for the interest of deserving men who will never know anything of this unselfish move on your part."

There were two things wrong with this. The "*we* can do much" was a phrase likely to jar on the sensitive ear of Booker Washington; and Washington did not want people whom he helped to be ignorant of the fact. His answer to Dr. Dan was noncommittal, and the matter might have stopped there but for a stroke of chance.

The most important cog in the Tuskegee machine was Washington's private secretary. Washington admitted that Emmett J. Scott was the only Negro in the country indispensable to him. Scott knew Washington better than his chief knew himself, and he had that nice combination of cynicism and personal loyalty that his job demanded and that Washington had an expert's eye for. Now Scott fell ill with appendicitis, and Washington wired Dr. Dan to come at once. Dr. Dan went, operated, and saved Scott to his chief. Dr. Dan had a quo for Washington's quid.

"It [Freedmen's] is too important for our men of science to be dealt out through favoritism," he wrote. "I want you to understand me. My interest is sincere, it is not for preferment. . . . I so much want your interest and help in this important matter, this one grand opportunity of our time, to finally develop an exceptional institution. If it is lost or carelessly handled, it will put our doctors and nurses back 25 years."

After a whole summer of silence came Washington's reply. He had been awaiting, he said, an opportunity to see the Secretary of the Interior. Now he had seen him, and the Secretary wished from him, Washington, "recommendations for the reorganization of Freedmen's." Would Dr. Dan send him by "return mail the names of six or eight colored doctors . . . the very highest and best. . . . Of course we want to include your name."

Dr. Dan did not include his own name, understandably, since not only was his pride involved but he had told the simple truth when he said he did not want to be considered for the position. But there was another name he left off the list, and Washington's response undoubtedly upset him: "Do you not think it a good idea to put Dr. Hall's name down? . . . Of course I understand the conditions surrounding him, but sometimes I find it pays to overcome littleness with bigness and to do our whole duty regardless of how people may feel toward us."

Dr. Dan assumed that he had been called upon to submit names because, as an officer of the National Medical Association, he was in a position to know the work of Negro physicians and who were best qualified among them. His sharply worded answer was in the nature of a rebuke to one who would accept standards lower than they should be.

"In selecting the names sent you, I drew upon my knowledge of what each individual had actually done to merit recognition, and not upon newspaper notoriety. I believe the names seldom appear in the Negro press, though they are powerful factors in race progress. They are doing something. . . . 'The man who is doing something,' quietly adding to the sum total. That is the man who can get my endorsement.

"I cannot say that I consider the party you named in that class. There is so much that you do not know and have no way of knowing.

"All the Gentlemen I named are not friends of mine . . . but I do know of their ability and honor, and assure you that they are men of such standing that I would be perfectly willing to serve with them. . . . And again, I want to impress most sincerely, Mr. Washington, that I am in this for the advancement of my people, to make conditions better for them, to prepare them for serious life work. I am serious in everything I undertake. If I go into this, it is not for social prestige or outside show. . . ."

But if there was much that Booker Washington did not know, there was considerably more that Dr. Dan himself had no way of knowing. He had no way of knowing that even during the yearlong course of this correspondence Booker Washington was in constant and intimate touch with George Hall. Slipping into Chicago, Washington would see Hall and his wife, Theodocia, without letting Dr. Dan know he was in the city. He became an intimate in the Hall household. Mrs. Hall did "little things" for him, and he called her "Teddie," though "only in private." He sent little gifts, sometimes to her alone, sometimes to both. She wrote Washington: "When the Dr. [Hall, her husband] returns he will find your delightful gift awaiting him. To say he will be pleased is putting it very mildly. The Dr. indulges in a sort of hero worship for the 'Wizard of Tuskegee,' you know, a condition to which the rest of the family must also plead guilty."

"Teddie" was as skillful in the arts of ingratiation as her husband, and her husband had proved very skillful indeed.

He had used his skill at Provident during Dr. Dan's absence. He had attained only slight professional advancement there, it is true, but he was crafty and devious in a way that only his Negro colleagues understood and, in the delicate nature of co-operative relations between Negro and white, dared not expose. He got on well with the white people who counted on the supervisory council and the staff. He was more careful not to be wrong than to be right on principle. He did not press his ambitions openly, but seemed desirous only to be helpful. He smiled and flattered and went along. When a vacancy occurred on the board, he was named to it, and he greased his way onto the powerful executive committee of that body. Finally promoted to the department of gynecology, where "he was permitted to do uncomplicated surgery on hernia," he presented himself to the public as the medical rival of Dr. Dan.

Not many Negroes knew better. Booker Washington invited him to Tuskegee to lecture. He went to Georgia and South Carolina to set up clinics and to operate in them.

(Not one of the clinics lasted a year.) Once at a demonstration in Birmingham, Alabama, "a country doctor had to take over Hall's operation to save the patient's life."

But when the *Tuskegee Student*, Booker Washington's nationally distributed paper, edited by Emmett Scott, carried a laudatory article on Daniel Hale Williams, Hall wrote the principal:

"My grievance is the use the *Student* is put to, exploiting a man whose professional rivalry with me is known to you and to everyone around Tuskegee. . . . When my friends, on whom he has taken special pains to impress how important he is to you at Tuskegee, asked me about it, I said it was not true. So you can well imagine I was embarrassed beyond all measure when there appeared in the *Student* a column and a half of Appreciation of this great man!"

Of course, Dr. Dan did not know about this either. Involved as he was in many professional commitments, he was not especially aware of how "Hall was pushing himself into the [administrative] routine of Provident." Nor did he have any way of knowing that, while Hall was nourishing his own reputation for loyalty to the ghetto and to the race, he was destroying Dr. Dan's bit by bit. He did it mainly by hint and innuendo, but he was also known to remark that "That fair-complexioned fellow doesn't seem to know what race he wants to belong to," and to ask, as if in disinterested curiosity, "Do dark colored people ever go to the Williamses'?"

It was easy to make such insinuations stick. The Williamses' social acquaintances were of the mixed-blood world. Besides, Dr. Dan's professional life took him daily into the white world, and it would have been strange indeed if the white world did not sometimes figure in his social life. His white colleagues liked him as a person. Some of them did not know he was a Negro. So wide was the gap between white and black that they could not conceive of a "colored" man of such great professional skill and reputation. "I was well acquainted with him for two years before I knew he was colored," wrote Dr. J. Wyllys Andrews.

Dr. Dan was vulnerable, and Hall made the most of it. Again he wrote Booker Washington: "When I think of my unquestioned well-known stand for Tuskegee and all concerned, in Chicago and everywhere, as compared with one who has never opened his mouth in public to advocate the school or the policy of its principal, I think I have every right to seriously object . . ."

But the principal was playing some game of his own. He answered Hall, ". . . When I am in Chicago I shall hope to have the privilege of talking to you and of telling you more in detail just how I feel toward you." But in that same week he also, at long last, answered Dr. Dan: "For the present, let the whole matter concerning the party [Hall] about whom I wrote you pass out of your mind. Nothing has been said or done to obligate me to anyone else in the matter, and there is no special reason why he should be taken up just now at least."

When the special reason came, it was political.

11. *Resignation*

Having served more than three years of the term of the assassinated McKinley, Theodore Roosevelt wanted to be elected President in his own right in 1904. He had been a hero to Negroes during and just after the Spanish-American War. In a speech during his campaign for the governorship of New York, Roosevelt had quoted one of the officers who had served with him in the war, " 'Well, the 9th and 10th [Cavalry] men are all right. They can drink out of our canteens,' " and he had added on his own, "I don't think that any Rough Rider will ever forget the tie that binds us to the 9th and 10th Cavalry." Such remarks earned him a majestic reputation among Negroes: his voice drew all ears.

Once safely in the governor's mansion, however, he changed his tune. He wrote in an article for *Scribner's* magazine, "They [Negro soldiers] are, of course, peculiarly dependent on their white officers. . . . None of the white regulars or Rough Riders showed the slightest sign of weakening; but under the strain the colored infantrymen began to get a little uneasy and to drift to the rear."

Negro newspapers crackled with outrage. Teddy was a hero no longer. He was instead "a turncoat," "a treacherous friend," who, as one Negro paper put it, "grins and grins and stabs you in the back."

Roosevelt tried to regain his status with the race. Within a month after succeeding McKinley he entertained Booker Washington at lunch in the White House. Negroes were "delighted at this signal recognition," and delighted the more because it "shocked, boiled . . . and exasperated the South." Two years later Roosevelt exasperated the South again by appointing a Negro as collector of the port at Charleston and declaring that "color was no sufficient reason to keep a good man from office." He would not, he said, "close the door of hope" to any American citizen. It helped.

But, in the election of 1904, Roosevelt's Democratic opponent, Alton B. Parker, presented a claim to the Negro's allegiance. Descended from an old anti-slavery family, the New York jurist had stood up for "Negro rights," and his endorsement by a scattering of the Negro press indicated at least that Northern Negro voters were no longer "blind Republicans." In order to line up the Negro vote, Roosevelt needed the active support of Booker Washington; and Washington, of course, wanted the added power and prestige he could derive from the President.

Washington himself called on the help of George Hall, who had organized and now bossed the Chicago ghetto's Hyde Park Republican Club. Aided by Hall, Washington managed to swing the Chicago *Bee* to Roosevelt. He bought out the Chicago *Conservator*, another Negro opposition paper, and put his own men in control. Washington complained to Hall about a certain Negro reporter, and Hall replied: "If you will just leave that newspaper reporter to me, I think when I get through he will be good. He is hugging me now to save himself and I am sawing off his limb close to the tree." Hall sawed off many limbs, and Booker Washington showed proper gratitude.

For, once Roosevelt was elected, the principal of Tuskegee set about to promote Hall's name far beyond the limits of Chicago's Negro community. "Send me," he urged, "your best photograph, put in the most prominent and successful operations you have performed. I can use these in a way to be of great service." The piece his public relations staff subsequently put out appeared in thirty-five Negro newspapers, a dozen of which had national distribution.

Then, skillfully timed to ride this wave of publicity, a rumor floated up from Washington, D.C. The principal of Tuskegee was strongly endorsing a Chicago physician for surgeon in chief at the new Freedmen's. Though everyone seemed to surmise that the Chicago physician was Hall, professional men who were acquainted with him and knew his mediocrity as a surgeon and physician could scarcely credit it. Dr. Dan knew no more than the rumors and the surmises. No letters concerning Freedmen's, or anything else, had passed between him and Booker Washington for months. Long since discouraged over the misuse of "the one great opportunity of our time to be of service," Dr. Dan shut the matter from his mind.

Moreover, he was very busy. His reputation was such that he was called as far west as North Dakota to perform surgery on a mining millionaire, and east to New York to attend a bishop of the Episcopal Church. Once a year he went to lecture and hold clinics, without fee, at the Negro Meharry Medical College (in Nashville, Tennessee) and other places in the South. He was still surgeon in chief at Provident, where his operations drew crowds of other surgeons. But he was finding it increasingly difficult to work at Provident. Hall had gained administrative power there. Dr. Dan's private patients were given short shrift and treated with little discourtesies. "The operating room would not be ready [for him]. Nurses would not be detailed to him."

But the professional esteem in which Dan Williams was held increased rather than lessened. In 1908, Negro doctors from all over the country gathered at a banquet in Chicago to celebrate Dr. Dan's twenty-fifth year in medicine. There were gifts from individuals and from groups. There was a silver bowl engraved with the names of thirty-seven Chicago physicians, white and colored, but George Hall's name was not among them. He had responded to Dr. Carl Robert's invitation to join in honoring Dr. Dan, "Curse him! I'll punish him worse than God ever will. I'll see he's forgotten before he's dead!"

And the circumstance that Hall seized as the opportunity to start, he thought, his "rival's" name toward oblivion was the very circumstance that signalized at the time the highest recognition of Dr. Dan's skill.

Dr. Dan was appointed associate attending surgeon at St. Luke's, an honor no other member of his race would attain for a quarter of a century after his death. He entered upon his duties at once. Though these duties required a reorganization of his private schedule, they in no way interfered with his other work; but Hall persuaded the Provident board that Dr. Dan's acceptance of the St. Luke's appointment was "an act of disloyalty to the Negro race." The board ordered Dr. Dan to bring all of his patients, "rich and poor, black and white," to Provident. The order was absurd. In the light of Dr. Dan's career, it was an outrage.

Daniel Hale Williams resigned from Provident. He did more—he resigned from the Negro race.

12. *Resignation Rescinded*

The old man had not stirred for a long time. His nerveless hands lay helpless on the blanket that swathed his legs. His eyes were closed, but should he open them he would see across a tiny bit of lake to the woods that half encircled this retreat in northern Michigan. In the later afternoon a woman came out onto the screened porch, tipped across it, and gently snugged in a corner of the old man's blanket. It was a kind of ritual, and when she heard the usual "I'm not 'sleep," the woman smiled. She was a German woman, and she had been the old man's housekeeper since his wife died in 1921. Now it was 1926.

"I'm bringing the post," the woman said, holding up a packet of letters.

"Margaret, you're not bringing," the old man said. "You're already here. Won't you ever learn English?"

But Margaret knew English very well, for now, as she had done for several months, she opened the letters and began to read. "Dear Dr. Dan . . ." or "Dear Dan . . ." There were some twenty letters, all from fellow members of the American College of Surgeons—Coleman Buford, Cary Culbertson, William Fuller, Willie Mayo—of which the old man was a charter member. The housekeeper's voice went on and on, and suddenly Dan Williams interrupted her.

"Margaret, tomorrow," he said, "we must have that lawyer out from town. It's time I made my will."

When the will was opened five years later it was seen to contain the following bequests: medical books to the Mercy (Negro) Hospital of Philadelphia; two thousand dollars for the operating room of a new interracial hospital on Chicago's south side; five thousand dollars each to Meharry (Negro) and Howard (Negro) Medical Schools, "to be used for impoverished students"; eight thousand dollars to the National Association for the Advancement of Colored People.

Part Three

MEN IN MOTION

VII. PATHS TO THE FUTURE

1. *"Nigger Demus"*

While it was quite possible to set up limits, material and ideological, to the Negro's physical penetration of the white environment, it was something else again to curb a cultural tide. And that tide was rising. Though it had its unnoted beginnings in the preconscious days of slavery, the rise was marked by a convenient date—1879. Then it was that the Fisk Jubilee Singers set out to bring to the attention of the world those Negro songs called "spirituals." Then it was, too, that an aging Negro opened the floodgates through which poured and pounded northward, eastward, westward thousands of his people, bringing with them their sorrows and their songs, their laughter and laments, and their incomparable quality as agents of social change.

Being unlearned, Benjamin Singleton understood only a part of what he did, but the Senate committee that called him to testify in 1880 probably understood even less. Indeed, the committee saw only the political issues involved in the migration, which they thought, and tried to prove, was a Republican plot to discredit Southern Democrats and lessen Southern representation in Congress. The committee thought that "Pap" Singleton, perhaps unwittingly, was a tool in devilish hands. But, "No," the old man told them, "I was the whole cause of the migration. Nobody but me."

This of course was not the whole truth, for the whole truth involved—as Southern Democrats well knew—fraud, violence, and murder. "If I votes the Republican ticket," one Southern Negro swore in evidence, "I wakes up nex' mornin' in the graveyard." Seventeen hundred pages of testimony affirmed the likelihood of this and, without knowing it, so did Pap Singleton. "I am the Moses of the colored exodus," he declared. And he was—a leader who embodied the longings and the restless strivings of his people and who, before his work was done, led eighty thousand of them westward from "the land of night" toward the Kansas sun.

They went singing:

We have Mr. Singleton for our president. He will go on before us and lead us through. . . .
Marching along, yes, we are marching along.

Mistaking the biblical Nicodemus for Nigger Demus, they sang:

> *Nigger Demus was a slave of African birth,*
> *And was bought for a bag full of gold.*
> *He was reckoned a part of the salt of the earth,*
> *But he died years ago, very old.*
>
> *Good time coming, good time coming,*
> *Long, long time on the way. . . .*

They sang for themselves, as folk do everywhere, and no more than they themselves did others guess that the songs they sang—their rhythms and their moods—would be originative of forms and modes far above the level of "folk" and would, in time, fix the cultural identity of America for the rest of the world.

At the moment, since these were "nigger songs," they were of no account. They did not meet the sacred standards of taste fawned on by men who had come back from Europe with costly copies of the graphic masters, who had read the songs of Scott and Byron with streaming eyes, and who (for all their claim to wide learning and broad aesthetic judgment) did not sense in these songs of wandering, of labor, of sorrow, and of joy the epitome of what they themselves had made and the essence of the culture they had produced. Nor did they hear in them the sounds of the life they had begot or—since this surely was the hardest thing of all—recognize them as specifics against the very thing they most feared—the revolutionary intransigence of five million blacks. For the truth was, of course, that these songs had their provenance in the heart of time and place, and this "nigger music" laid a grip upon realities that were constantly denied. And to be appreciated, the songs and music had finally to go from the world that made them into a world that they would shape.

But since realities cannot be denied forever, it is no wonder that a young Negro who heard these songs for the first time when he was seventeen should recognize them instantly "as of me and mine," and should, when he came to write the first book of his private revolution, head each chapter with a bar of this dark music. Nor should it surpass credit that a young printer with a face like night, hearing this music in all the many-timbred sonances of a massive Negro choir, did "weep and also feel exalted as by the might of angels."

2. Less Than Enough

Though they were born in the same year, 1868, William Burghardt Du Bois and Robert Sengstacke Abbott were as different as parentage, background and training could make them. Their only point of resemblance was negative: neither looked like the "men of war" in the Negro song both loved.

Small though strong of frame and feature, Du Bois bore clear traces of his French Huguenot lineage. His forehead was broad, his nose fine-chiseled, and his lips thin in a sharply tapering amber-colored face. Abbott was so black of skin that it was once remarked that if he were cut he would "bleed ink." His ancestry was pure Ibo. His face was a flat plane over which his nose spread like thick molasses to the heaped mound of his lips. Heavy-fleshed and squat, he had the hammered-down look of primitive African statuary. Du Bois was flame blown on by jets of air. Abbott was flesh oppressed by brooding midnight. One was excitation and intellect. The other was solemnity, intuition, and lumbering brain. If neither man looked like men of war, both were to prove themselves such men.

Du Bois was the first. Descendant on his mother's side of those brown-skinned, Dutch-speaking Burghardts who had come through the western passes from the Hudson to the valley of the Housatonic, who had in time fought in the Revolution and the War of 1812, meanwhile establishing farms and families, Du Bois was reared to a sense of independence, and revolt was in his blood. His paternal grandfather, Alexander Du Bois, lived many years, and from this old man, who still gave certain words the sound of French, William heard snatches of Alexander's life.

He had been born in the Bahamas of a rich bachelor and a mulatto slave and brought to America and enrolled in the Cheshire School, but upon the death of his father, who left no will, the white Du Boises had dropped him to fend for himself. They told him he was "colored," and so he sought a colored country, Haiti, to "learn in pride the meaning of the word." He learned it. Returning to the United States, he revolted against the white Episcopal parish in New Haven and shaped more to his liking a new "colored" parish named St. Luke's.

The grandson, William, learned early that he himself was "different from other children." The difference did not matter much in Great Barrington, Massachusetts, at first. He played with white companions (there were no other Negro children) on the hills and in the river. He had a lively imagination, he could think of things to do, and he was, it seems, the leader of the town's gang of schoolboys, and perfectly at home in the town's best houses.

But when he entered high school he discovered that the parents of some of his schoolmates considered his brown skin a misfortune. He grimly determined to show them it was not. His temper quickened, hardened. The irascibility that later marked the man and was called "airs" and "insolence" must have entered him then. He excelled in his studies. He was "spurred to tireless effort." Though he did not have the physique for sports, he did well in them. Winning the first of many scholarships, he declared his wish to go to Harvard and was told that his place was in the South among "his people." He rebelled, and brooded for six months, but by a sudden "miracle of emotion" he felt "part of a mightier mission." He enrolled at Fisk.

Fisk University in Nashville, Tennessee, was his first experience of the Negro world. The whole "gorgeous color gamut" of it excited him nearly to delirium. Girls and boys of a species he had never known left him tongue-tied and dreaming "boastful dreams" of great remedies for the sickness of the world. For already he knew the world was sick. He heard the Negro folk songs and was "thrilled and moved to tears." Studying under white teachers too wise, honest, and noble to flaunt the role of missionaries, and living, learning, and larking with "darkly delicious" young men and women, if Du Bois felt that he was experiencing the best of two worlds, he did not shun the worst of either.

In two summer vacations he went deep into rural Tennessee and taught a Negro school. He saw the galling, unrewarding drudgery of Negro country life, the wrenched and wretched existence of Negro peasants. He sensed the "senseless cruelty" of a social system controlled—often exclusively controlled—by ignorant white men. He saw, he said, the race problem at nearly its lowest terms. Nothing had prepared him. In his senior year at Fisk he crammed in history, politics, and economics. Harvard offered scholarships in the South that year, and Du Bois applied for one. He was astonished when he got it.

He was twenty when he entered Harvard in the junior class. He knew what he wanted and where he could get it, and he went straight to Albert Bushnell Hart in history, William James in psychology, Santayana in philosophy, Barrett Wendell in English, and George Herbert Palmer in social problems—this last being as close, in 1888, as Harvard got to sociology. If some of his classmates also had something to offer, Du Bois did not share it. Herbert Croly, Augustus Hand, Norman Hapgood, and Robert Herrick were of the class of 1890, but Du Bois met none of them. Having come to Harvard by way of Fisk, he knew what he knew. And he knew that to accept the social limitations that a still provincial college society imposed upon Negroes, Jews, Catholic Irish, and Chinese was not to excuse them.

Besides, he did not lack social life. In nearby colleges were other Negro students, and on one memorable occasion he joined with them to perform Aristophanes' *The Birds* in a colored church. He had other satisfactions too—in the semisocial relations of the Philosophical Club, where Josiah Royce sometimes dropped in for tea; in having his papers read or cited by Wendell in English 12, and his work publicly commended by William James, at whose home he was more than once a guest. Professor Hart also had him for dinner. These giants in the Harvard faculty endorsed his application for a Rogers graduate fellowship.

But after two years of Harvard College and two years as a graduate fellow there, Du Bois was still unsatisfied. He had far more education than most young white men, but he felt that he had not had enough. At work on his master's thesis, *The Suppression of the Slave Trade*, he had conceived, however vaguely, a notion of his mission—that "mightier mission" of which he felt a part. He was going to raze the barriers of race. He saw this as "a matter of knowledge; as a matter of scientific procedure." His view of it seemed all the more valid in that day when the German ideal of scholarship was much sought after. Urged by their German-trained teachers, hundreds of American students rushed to Germany to acquire the laboratory habit of mind. Among Du Bois' own teachers, Palmer, Royce, and James had studied there. Du Bois was constantly reminded that German methods of investigating the phenomena of social existence were responsible for establishing such fields as political science, sociology, and history on a modern basis in America.

The Slater Fund "for uplifting the lately emancipated" had been established in 1882, and its income had been used to promote industrial and vocational training among Negroes. But in 1890 the chairman of its board had said: "If there is any young colored man whom we find to have . . . any special aptitude for study, we are willing to give him money from the educational funds to send him to Europe or give him an advanced education. . . . So far we have found only orators."

Whether or not this was a nasty oblique personal fling at him (since he had won prizes and attention for public speaking at Harvard), Du Bois rose as to a challenge. He applied to the Slater Fund. The chairman, ex-President Hayes, answered that he had been misquoted—that the fund had no plans for such aid. But Du Bois was not to be rebuffed. Gathering letters of recommendation from his most influential professors, and writing a clearly impudent letter of his own, he reapplied. Days of silence were followed by a fresh bombardment of letters from everyone he "knew in the Harvard Yard and places outside." Finally he was granted a fellowship "to study at least a year abroad under the direction of the graduate department of Harvard."

In 1892 he registered in the University of Berlin and was temporarily dizzied by a wealth of resources and dazzled by slants of intellectual light for which not even Harvard had prepared him. He was admitted to the seminars of Wagner and Schmoller in economics and the fiery Von Treitschke in history. The meaning of his knowledge underwent radical changes. The intellectual conformity and the conventional patterns of thought he had acquired at Harvard began to dissolve. Habitual premises were susceptible of revision; truth was not final. Having heard Von Treitschke—soon to be censured by young Wilhelm II— thunder that the European push into Africa should not be looked upon as "the advance of civilization and the tutelage of barbarians," Du Bois could no longer think of the little old woman of Windsor as a magnificent symbol of noble empire dedicated to guiding the colored peoples of the earth to Christianity and higher culture. New contours of thought began to form and alter the landscape of his mind, modify the perspectives of history. Perhaps above all he came to see the "race problem" as a world social problem and to sense its connection with the political-economic development of Europe.

Du Bois studied and also he traveled. Every break from books and lectures found him going to some new place. He went to the south of Germany, to Italy, France; east to Austria-Hungary, Czechoslovakia, Poland; north to Sweden,

Denmark, Norway. In Holland he talked with natives of Borneo, in France with Cameroon and Algerian blacks, in England with Indians. The designation "colored" came to mean "a greater, broader sense of humanity and world-fellowship."

But two years of study and travel were all he could afford; were, indeed, more than his fellowship allowed, and in 1894, sporting a beard and carrying a cane, he came back from Europe. Harvard granted him the Ph.D.

Now twenty-seven, he felt ready for his life's work, which he conceived as "putting science into sociology." He was going to face the facts, "any and all facts . . . of the racial world," and study and present them. His object was uplift and reform.

3. *Mixed Blood*

Robert Sengstacke Abbott was an altogether different breed. Though he was described as shrewd, calculating, and "tight with guile," the facts dispute the estimate. His mind was not equipped to deal with subtleties. The formal education he managed to acquire was not of much use to him. In middle life he was called a demagogue and dangerous—"like a monkey with a shotgun," Julius Rosenwald said, "who will hurt anybody." But he was more hurt than hurting, and his demagoguery, if this is what it can be called, had in it more of pathos than of calculating sense. He was not the son of his father.

Born in a cabin on the crummy edge of a Georgia plantation, Robert Abbott spent much of his life trying to live down the opprobrious term "Geechee." It was an epithet that conjured up in the Negro mind the storied attributes of the lowest slave type, the ignorant "field nigger," with a dull and stupid mind, gross habits, and primitive passions beyond control. And it was unfair. Robert's father, Tom, had been Charles Stevens' trusted boss house slave, the envy of other slaves for miles around. The esteem in which the Stevenses held him is attested by the fact that when freedom came they gave him a cabin and a plot of ground, and when he died in 1869 they buried him in their own graveyard.

And by that time, in the common opinion, Tom had deserved less. He had gone off to Savannah and abused his freedom. Nearly fifty years old and still unmarried, he had played city sport, lived by his wits and on his gracious white-folks manners, which attracted, among others, Flora Butler, a hairdresser and ladies' maid at the Savannah theater. But Flora was not a frivolous, easy woman. She would settle for nothing less than marriage to a man who had a job and "common decency." Tom pled and promised and, when they were married, took Flora to his cabin and plot of ground on St. Simon's Island. Farming, however, was beneath him. He converted the front room of his cabin into a store. In the room behind it Robert was born only five months before Tom died of "galloping consumption."

Flora was more durable. Free since childhood, she had become a skilled hairdresser and an expert seamstress, but no one on St. Simon's had a need for her services, and after the death of Tom she took her infant son and returned to Savannah, where she readily found employment among the wives of the German shopkeepers with whom she became a favorite by picking up a speaking knowledge of their language. This favoritism proved timely. She had been settled in the city only a few months when Tom Abbott's sister, alleging Flora to be an unfit mother, brought suit for the custody of the child. The Germans came to Flora's support, and one of them, John H. H. Sengstacke, engaged a lawyer who successfully defended her.

Sengstacke had had dealings with lawyers and lawsuits. His short history in America was thorny with legal tangles. White to all appearances, and German-reared, he was born the son of an immigrant father and a slave girl. When the mother died at the birth of a second child, his father took his two mulatto children to Germany to be reared by his sister. The father himself returned to the States in 1850, prospered in the mercantile trade, regularly remitted money for the support of his children, and died in 1862. He left a will that amply secured his offspring, but his white executors ignored it, for after his death no money from the estate, estimated at fifty thousand dollars, ever reached Germany. The son came to America to investigate in 1869.

John H. Hermann Sengstacke was an educated man, fluent in five languages—just the man for the job of translator for the Savannah *Morning News*. But in the course of pushing his claim to his father's estate he had to reveal the fact of his Negro blood. He was fired. Thereafter some of his father's old friends treated him with contempt. Completely unprepared for this betrayal of old loyalties and this ravishment of his personal dignity, by the time he was financially able to escape to Germany he had perforce identified himself with the Negro race, and he decided to remain. The experience of his Negroness left deep scars. Already there was something of the messiah in him, and something of the masochist. When the dwindled estate was finally settled he came to the conclusion—at once bitter torment and solace—that since he was a Negro he was lucky to salvage two or three thousand dollars, a small frame house, and a store-front building on a bluff in the western section of Savannah.

This was the man who married Flora Abbott in 1874 and gave his name not only to the seven children he begot but to his stepson as well. This was the man who, with the burning ardor of the ancient Christian convert, embraced with passion the scabrous cross of his Negroness and staggered under it with mad delight.

Ordained a minister of the Congregational Church and appointed a teacher in a rural Negro school, he also undertook to publish, edit, and sustain a Negro newspaper. As a preacher-teacher he earned altogether forty dollars a month. His church had few members, and these were so poor that they "could pay," he reported, "only one dollar towards his whole year's salary." Yet he alienated some of these and expelled others for belonging to secret societies. His school had no books, no blackboards, no pencils, no stove. He wrote his newspaper copy in longhand—all of it. "We labor under great disadvantages," he informed a friend. And indeed he did. Eventually the disadvantages became willful malignities offered to him personally. He saw the grim red finger of malice pointing at him from every quarter. He saw himself as a Negro persecuted not only by society but by individuals. The world was against the Sengstackes. The world was against him.

4. *"Everybody Always Picked on Him"*

If this was the spirit of Robert's training at home and in his father's school, it was given substance by his earliest experiences at Beach Institute. This was a day school founded by the Freedmen's Bureau but supported by the American Missionary Society. In Savannah, as in other urban centers in those days, there was a Negro color caste as rigid as iron. Mulattoes, as we have seen, were generally the privileged and the exclusive. They had their own churches, their own social clubs. Only mulattoes were normally expected to go to school beyond the second or third grade.

Robert was as black as tar. The prejudice of his light-skinned schoolmates at Beach was cruel to an extreme possible only to adolescents. They dubbed him "Liver Lips," "Tar Baby," and "Crow." Their malevolence undoubtedly generated the unconscious self-hatred that was one of the twisted, ruling passions of Abbott's life—that made him shun the color black even in clothes and cars; that made him dun Negro fraternal organizations to use the whiteball as the symbol of rejection, and plaster black Chicago with slogans urging Negroes to "Go to a White Church on Sunday."

Only Joseph and Catharine Scarborough were not unkind to him at Beach, and if this was more out of respect for their father's friendship with the Reverend John H. H. Sengstacke than friendly regard for Robert, the latter did not sense it. Indeed, he fell in love with Catharine—he was seventeen at the time—and courted her for nearly thirty years. In 1897 he asked her to marry him, but her father was "outraged" at the black man's presumption, and Catharine declined the honor. In 1918, when she had twice been widowed by ne'er-do-well mulatto husbands, Catharine finally agreed to marry him. He was by then a millionaire, but even as he prepared to go to her in Savannah she wrote that she had changed her mind.

But all this was in the future in 1886. What was in the present was the intolerable weight of obloquy and the crushing blows to his self-esteem. He did not cry out aloud. Instead he adopted a system of attitudes—not principles of conduct or principles of ethics—informed only by a defensive spirit, which served him the rest of his life. And the chief of these was patient meekness. In some ways it was as false as Uriah Heep's—and to much the same purpose.

To the disappointment of his stepfather, Robert retreated from Beach after less than two full terms. He dreamed of Hampton, in Virginia, but when his stepfather suggested Claflin University, a hundred miles from his home, he pretended enthusiasm for that place and agreed to work his way through that institution's equivalent of high school. He stayed six months. He was nineteen and still separated from his future by a vast ignorance. Another year went by before Hampton accepted him "conditionally" to study the printing craft.

At Hampton, it is reported, "everybody always picked on him." His hangdog mien and his genuine feelings of inferiority invited it. He was the butt of crude, practical, and sometimes vicious jokes. He probably resented them, but he was too patient, too hungry for acceptance, and too cowardly to protest. Driven to the other extreme at times, he tried to bluster through class recitations, but his dull mind was no help to him, and he invariably made a fool of himself.

He did no better socially. The same prejudice, though degrees milder, that plagued him at Beach prevailed at Hampton, and, inept to begin with, Robert had no success in the highly formalized and rigidly controlled social life of the campus. He was not asked to join the intimate bull sessions. He got no invitations to parties. Girls ignored him, and one of his classmates told him, half in jest, that he was "too black to associate with fair women."

Ironically enough, his black skin did bring him one distinction. Toward the end of his first year he was chosen as a member of the Hampton Quartet. But this was not because his tenor voice was the best that could be found. It was because "white people resented seeing light-complexioned boys in the group"; because Hampton's white administrators knew the emotional impact that "four black boys forlornly singing spirituals" had on white audiences; and because white audiences were the targets of the school's financial appeals. Abbott had a good voice, and he sang the sorrow songs with feeling, but not even the distinction of becoming a member of the quartet in his first year suggested that, next to Booker T. Washington, he would one day be the school's best-known graduate. It took some students five years to complete the four-year course. Abbott required seven.

He was twenty-seven when he graduated and accepted a teaching post in a school on the outskirts of Savannah. Soon he was supplementing his income with part-time work as a printer. He was not very good in either job, and both together did not provide enough for him to court Catharine Scarborough in the manner he thought she deserved. Rivalry for that lady's attentions was keen, and when she rejected his first proposal Abbott felt that the odds were against him. His rivals, though scarcely more affluent than he, were light-skinned. Perhaps if he could get money he could overcome the handicap of his color, equalize the competition. But how get money? His stepfather's example proved that money was not in teaching or preaching. Even the printer's craft offered scant returns to a black man in Georgia. Perhaps in another state—a city in the North—he could use his vocation as a steppingstone "to higher things." After presenting Miss Scarborough with a handsome gold watch in the summer of 1897, he still had enough money to support himself while he explored.

He went to Chicago. When the Hampton Quartet had sung there at the World's Fair four years earlier, Abbott had been awed by the conspicuous display of Negro wealth and achievement. Now almost at once he wrote home, "I will stay out west and try to make a fortune."

But fortunes were not easily made, and he did not know

how to begin. He managed to obtain part-time employment as a printer, but earning "real money" at his trade looked no more promising in Chicago than it had in Savannah. It did not take him long to discover that the men to emulate, the men whose names were spoken with deference along State Street and Dearborn Street, were either independent businessmen or professionals. Daniel Hale Williams was a physician and surgeon, Charles Smiley a caterer, Edward Morris a lawyer, and John Jones, who was still remembered as the first Negro to hold public office in Chicago, had been a wealthy merchant tailor. These men were of the status to which Abbott aspired. His ambition was uninformed by any idea of service or any dedication to large purposes. He wanted simply to "accomplish *something* noteworthy"; he wanted—as a later phrase had it—to be a big shot.

He tried to find ways into the closed circle of the elite. He joined the Grace Presbyterian Church where the elite went. He sacrificed necessities to buy admission to the charity balls given for the benefit of Provident Hospital and the Institutional Social Settlement. No one paid the slightest attention to him. For all that he had been a member of the Hampton Quartet and had a better than passable tenor voice, his bid to join the choir of Grace Presbyterian Church was rejected. He was black, and his speech gave him away as one of those "new-come Southern darkies" who were "spoiling things" for long-time residents of the North. Every rebuff fed his passion to "show them" and increased his torment to "make his mark," no matter how. He wrote his mother, "Tell father if he will back me, I will . . . run a paper. . . . Let me know his intentions before I begin to make up my mind as to what steps to take."

The Reverend Mr. Sengstacke, undoubtedly recalling his own costly experience, advised against the newspaper but seemed willing enough to back his stepson in another line, for in the fall of 1898 Robert enrolled in the evening classes of the Kent College of Law. Now for the first time he dropped Sengstacke as a surname and put himself on record as Robert S. Abbott. It is reported that when his stepfather heard of this he wept.

If Robert S. Abbott also wept, it was for other reasons. He had a better than average capacity for self-pity, and later he was to write of this period that he "probably would have starved to death but for the generosity of some folk who would loan me a dime now and then. Even when I did work I did not earn enough to pay back rent, repay loans and eat. . . ."

Somehow, though, he managed to get through law school, only to be advised by the light-skinned lawyer Edward Morris, to whom he went for encouragement and help, that he was "too dark to make any impression on the courts in Chicago." As a matter of fact, Abbott failed to pass the Illinois bar. He was told that Indiana was easier, and he moved to Gary. He went on to Topeka, Kansas. The story was the same. When he returned to Chicago in 1903, all he had to show for five years of painful effort was a contract as Chicago distributor of the national Negro weekly, the *Kansas Plaindealer*. He was thirty-three, and all the pathways to fulfillment seemed blocked against him, but he was as obdurate as stone.

He did not look like a man in whom the fires of worldly ambition burned with corroding intensity. Stubby, dour-faced, he affected semiclerical garb, poor but neat: patched white shirt with celluloid collar and white string tie, a blue suit turning green with age, shoes lined with paper. Indeed, he seemed the exact copy of a pastor of a small, earnest fundamentalist sect. He did not play cards, or smoke (though he was to acquire the habit of fifty-cent cigars later), or drink.

Excluded from the "best" society, he shunned the worst, and made his acquaintances among that emerging middle class of decent domestic servants, small tradesmen, part-time lawyers, and night-time doctors who were becoming extremely vocal on such subjects as race discrimination, Negro rights, and Negro solidarity, and who, under the leadership of Louis B. Anderson and George Hall, were learning the uses of political power even as they slowly acquired it. Abbott joined their social groups, earned a part of his precarious living doing their printing jobs on borrowed presses, and took part in their discussions. They liked him, and he liked them. Among them he did not have to live down his blackness; he had rather to live up to it. Other qualities began to peep from beneath the cloak of his patient humility. He had gratitude. He could be depended on. He had insinuating kindliness of spirit. He counted among these people—counted enough for them to exert their political influence to get him a job in a printing firm that did the work of the city government.

It was among this middle-class-in-emergence, too, that he again broached the idea of starting a newspaper. The more intelligent could not see it, and would not help him, and told him so. There were already three Negro newspapers in Chicago—the *Conservator*, the *Broad Ax*, and the *Illinois Idea*—and none of them was a financial success. There was no need for yet another paper. But Abbott thought otherwise, and he backed his thinking with an inspired argument—his friends and acquaintances had no voice. The social historian, Roi Ottley, notes that existing papers "were primarily vehicles for the editors to expound their views . . . and advance their personal political ambitions." Abbott's acquaintances were never mentioned in them. Their births, their weddings, their deaths were unheralded. Their churches, their clubs, and their community activities existed in a murmurless limbo. Abbott would give them a voice. This was the idea that drew nourishment from the subterranean depths of personal frustration, and around it his fumbling intelligence, his oceanic patience, and his legendary stubbornness fixed as inexorably as fate.

So, his only capital twenty-five cents and a tongue ready with promises, Robert Sengstacke Abbott launched the first issue of the paper for which he did not even originate the name. The date was May 5, 1905, and the Chicago *Defender* would not miss a weekly issue for fifty years. At the age of thirty-seven Abbott had at last found his métier. His manner, his methods, and his mission would evolve and change with time.

5. *Race War*

Meanwhile, although W. E. B. Du Bois' purposes had lengthened and his pace accelerated, he had not changed the direction he took in 1894. He still believed that "the Negro problem was . . . a matter of systematic investigation and intelligent understanding," and that "the world was thinking wrong about race, because it did not know."

But investigation, no matter how systematic, was not enough. The experience of two years as a teacher at Wilberforce, a third year spent on a study of Negroes in Philadelphia for the University of Pennsylvania, and seven years on a more comprehensive study at Atlanta University, where he had gone to join the faculty in 1897, taught Du Bois that. The world was thinking wrong, but the South itself compounded the error in action. In growing indignation, even while the "Atlanta University Studies" were being distributed and quoted among scholars throughout the world, Du Bois watched the spread of the very evils his studies were meant to expunge. Jim Crow laws, spreading disfranchisement, and swollen lynching rates aroused him to passionate protest and then to organized opposition. The year and the month the Chicago *Defender* was founded, Du Bois issued a call for "aggressive action on the part of men who believe in Negro freedom and growth." Twenty-nine colored men responded. They met in Niagara Falls, Canada, in July, and demanded free speech, a free, unsubsidized press, manhood suffrage, and an end to distinctions based on color and race.

Though these demands were as germane to American idealism as the Constitution itself, a cannonade of criticism roared through the press, white and Negro. While the *Outlook,* then the most influential weekly magazine, barked of radicalism and hinted at subversion, and the New York *Evening Post* spoke of a congregation of "malcontents," sections of the Negro press, largely controlled by Booker Washington, boomed forth a personal scurrility calculated to riddle the reputation of Du Bois. He was accused of being "ashamed of his race," and "wanting to be white," and "envious" of Booker Washington.

These attacks were renewed the next year when the "men of Niagara" met at Harper's Ferry, and the year after that, when they met in Boston. Snarled the dean of Howard University, Kelly Miller, who might have gone along with Du Bois had he been invited to, "We may expect a further session at Appomattox, so prone is the poetic temperament to avail itself of episodal and dramatic situations."

But there were to be no further sessions of the Niagara Movement, though dramatic situations seemed to explode everywhere—and they were not "episodal," and in no way digressive. They were of a trend that had proved increasingly dynamic since the Spanish-American War. They resulted from clashes of personality, of ideas, and especially of social forces that seemed beyond the control of men, and certainly beyond the control of any one man, even though that man should be Theodore Roosevelt, President of the United States.

Well into his second term Roosevelt's attitude toward the race problem grew callous. The evidence was that he not only permitted the civil degradation of Negroes to proceed without protest but, taking his cue from Booker Washington, emphasized the Negroes' shortcomings and put the blame for their condition on themselves. Thus the vast slums that fouled the air of cities were not even in part the result of segregation, unemployment, and the venal exploitation of landlords, but of Negro shiftlessness. Negro family disorganization, juvenile delinquency, and crime were not in part the natural consequence of the neglect of public agencies to do corrective social work and to provide parks, playgrounds, and swimming pools such as could be found everywhere for whites.

In Roosevelt's second term only a few Negroes realized that the President's "friendship was neither consistent nor sustained," but many were to realize it in 1906, when, scorning to hold a hearing, he discharged without honor a battalion of the Negro 25th Regiment on the charge that it had "shot up the town" of Brownsville, Texas. Taken on the word of one lone army inspector, this action was so arbitrary and unfair that Senator "Pitchfork" Ben Tillman, as rabid a racist as ever pounded the hustings, defined it as an "executive lynching."

Senator Tillman's sensibilities were not as shocked as he pretended.

On a strumpet's false charge that she had been raped by a Negro, the white people of Springfield, Illinois, went surging through the Negro section of the city setting fires to dwellings, looting stores, and howling, "Abraham Lincoln may have freed you, but we'll show you where you belong!" For three days the arson, the mayhem, and the murder went on to the encouraging shrieks of a thrice-convicted female criminal named Kate Howard, even then at liberty under bond. Seventy people were killed and injured. Two hundred Negroes fled to Chicago, and an equal number to places unknown.

Ben Tillman did not say a word.

But a distinguished journalist named William English Walling did in "Race War in the North," an article that appeared in the *Independent*. ". . . Either the spirit of Lincoln and Lovejoy must be revived and we must come to treat the Negro on a plane of absolute political and social equality, or Vardaman and Tillman will soon have transferred the race war to the North. . . . Yet who realizes the seriousness of the situation, and what large and powerful body of citizens is ready to come to their [Negroes'] aid!"

Though the body of such citizens showed neither so large nor so powerful as it was later to be, the spirit of the abolitionists was revived in the grandson of one of them. Wrote Oswald Garrison Villard, "We call upon all believers in a democracy to join in a National conference for the discussion of present evils, the voicing of protests, and the renewal of the struggle for civil and political liberty." Jane Addams, John Dewey, William Dean Howells, Mary White Ovington, Joel Spingarn, Moorfield Story, and the men of Niagara answered that call, and the Niagara Movement was absorbed in the first meeting of what came to be known as the National Association for the Advancement of Colored People.

Du Bois, who had complained of the throttling and the buying of the Negro press, now had a sounding board. It was called the *Crisis*. Ostensibly the organ of the NAACP, Du Bois was its first editor, and soon there issued from it words of such clarity and sense, thunders of such wrath, and screeches of such derisive laughter that its audience of one thousand quickly grew to ten, then fifty, then one hundred thousand.

"Sympathize with the great Peace movement . . . sympathize with world-wide efforts for moral reform and social uplift, but before them all we must place those efforts which aim to make humanity not the attribute of the arrogant and exclusive only, but the heritage of all men. . . ."

"Let every black American gird up his loins. The great day is coming. We have crawled and pleaded for justice and we have been cheerfully spit upon and murdered and burned. We will not endure it forever. If we are to die, in God's name let us perish like men and not like bales of hay."

"In Virginia eighteen counties celebrated *Colored Tuberculosis Day*."

But neither Du Bois nor the organization he represented was content with words, however sensible, or angry, or droll. Far from it. Believing that the denial of rights was not only unjust but, as Du Bois wrote, "a menace to our free institutions," the NAACP first set up a Legal Redress Committee. Within six months its lawyers, headed by Arthur B. Spingarn, were in court fighting the disfranchisement of Negroes in Maryland, the "grandfather clause" in Oklahoma, and Negro peonage in Georgia and Alabama. Within a year it had defended Negroes accused of crimes ranging from petty larceny to rape and murder. Within that length of time also the NAACP had opened branches in seven cities, where officers and members busied themselves "to widen industrial opportunities for Negroes, to encourage the law-abiding spirit, and to cooperate in civic improvements." By 1911 its voice was heard overseas, where Du Bois was sent to the International Congress of

Races, and where he took the opportunity to smudge the rosy picture of American race relations that Booker Washington had painted for foreign galleries the year before.

"The keynote of Mr. Washington's propaganda for the last fifteen years [has been that] it is not well to tell the whole story of wrong and injustice . . . but rather one should emphasize the better aspects. . . . It is a dangerous fallacy into which Mr. Washington and his supporters fall. They assume that the truth—the real facts concerning a social situation at any particular time—is of less importance than the people's feeling concerning those facts. There could be no more dangerous social pragmatism."

Nor was it only "radicals" like Du Bois who saw it this way. With such conservative names as Mrs. W. H. Baldwin, W. T. Schieffelin, and L. Hollingsworth Wood behind it, the National Urban League was far from radical, but its officers saw it this way. When it was formed in 1911, its purpose was to press for opportunities for Negroes that had too long been denied them. Its slogan was "Not Alms but Opportunity." The Urban League exerted itself to open the doors of Northern industry, to pry loose the lid of segregation and discrimination in Northern housing and recreation, and it dared to challenge Northern civic and economic management on the issue of Negro employment.

Booker Washington was listed among the League's sponsors, but it was apparent that he was not pleased with its activities in the North. He had caused to be reprinted in his own paper, the *Tuskegee Student*, an editorial from the Beaumont (Texas) *Enterprise:* "Negroes can do more for themselves and for humanity by working in the fields of the South. . . . The Negro who will work and who will keep his place can find more real happiness in the South than he will ever find in cities of the North." And he had sent Robert R. Moton, the man who would eventually succeed him as principal of Tuskegee, throughout the South to urge Negroes "to remain with the white men of the South."

But the truth was that Washington's "soft-speaking conformity and sheer opportunism" had not paid off in solid gains. In Washington's South, 2,000,000 Negroes were still illiterate farm hands and sharecroppers. While the Negro population in the rural South had increased to 6,250,000 by 1910, only 90,000 owned farms. Only 50,000 held membership in national and international unions, and in unions of common labor—in which category Negroes were mostly employed—there were none at all. Fifty-one and four tenths per cent of all Negro women and 49.3 per cent of all Negro children between the ages of ten and fifteen worked, but only 16 per cent of white women and 22.5 per cent of white children were employed. The death rate of 34.2 per 1000 was twice the figure for whites. Of every 10,000 Negroes, 98 were annually convicted of crime, compared to 12 of every 10,000 for whites.

Failing to show the results claimed for them, the soft conformities met opposition, solid and implacable, and there seemed to be little the conformists could do about it. It is true that Washington seduced and brought over to his side some Negro newspapers, including the New York *Age*, the Chicago *Broad Ax*, and, as we have seen, the Chicago *Conservator*, but his touch was noxious. No sooner had a paper come under his influence than it began to wither and die. No sooner had he deflated opposition in one place than it ballooned in another. As the election of 1912 approached, there was no holding down opposition any place.

It was not a good time for Mr. Washington. Formerly straw boss for Roosevelt and currently messenger boy for Taft, Washington was obligated to both the Progressive Republican and the Old Guard candidate. He had strong reasons for attempting the impossible job of supporting both men—Taft because he was the choice of the monied interests who donated so liberally to Tuskegee; and Roosevelt because he proclaimed himself on the side of the Negro majority, and Washington could not resist a majority. But there were those Negroes who could not see either candidate. Taft had played "safe and silent" on the question of civil rights. Roosevelt had turned his head while the representatives of eight million Negroes were barred from his splinter convention.

Du Bois and the "radicals" did not hesitate. "We sincerely believe," said Du Bois' *Crisis* editorial, "that even in the face of promises disconcertingly vague, and in the face of the solid caste-ridden South, it is better to elect Woodrow Wilson President of the United States and prove once and for all if the Democratic Party dares to be democratic when it comes to black men. It has proven that it can be in many Northern states and cities. Can it be in the nation? We hope so and we are willing to risk a trial."

There followed, naturally, attack and defense. The Indianapolis *Freeman* declared, "Because a man comes from Harvard and Heidelberg [sic] to boot, does not mean that he is prepared for leadership in a general way. . . . We make a mistake in trying to have him [Du Bois] as a leader of the race." The Richmond *Planet* believed that "Dr. Washington's policy is to move in the line of least resistance. The colored people do not believe that Dr. Washington has the fortitude or inclination to bare his breast to opposition. . . ." Galled because it had been accused of selling out to Booker Washington, the New York *Age* printed without comment a letter to the editor:

". . . [Dr. Du Bois'] greatest public work has been the publication of 'The Souls of Black Folk,' which has been rightly styled by the white press as the 'lamentations of a black man who wants to be white.' . . . 'Deeds! not words,' was the cry of Clarius Marius before the Nobles in the Roman Senate. . . . 'Deeds! not words,' was the cry of Abraham Lincoln at the dedication of the National Cemetery at Gettysburg, and the theme of Booker T. Washington in all his writings and all his lectures has been the tradition of all those whom he has proven himself worthy to succeed: 'Deeds! and not words.' "

As befits a minister, the Reverend Dr. William Moses was more temperate. "In my opinion, the colored people of America can, and should, and are slowly uniting under the unquestioned leadership of Dr. Du Bois. . . . He never sounds a false note on any question; nor gives any uncertain sound. He rings out clear and true. And American prejudice and racial discrimination shudder at his very name."

But the editor of the Atlanta *Independent*, who was

also the Negro Republican boss of Georgia, did not agree.

"He [Du Bois] is a former citizen of our town. We know the man. . . . He never took time to register or vote and to put into practice what he advocated until 1908. . . . The Negroes of this country would like to know whether he voted [in 1908] for the party of disfranchisement against the party of enfranchisement for money or principle. . . . The Negro people would like to know and have him explain how he expects to cure disfranchisement, Jim Crowism and race proscription by voting for the Democratic party. . . ."

Even some sections of the white press entered the controversy.

6. *Moods of Despair*

One Negro editor, however, stayed conspicuously aloof. Robert S. Abbott had not made up his mind on this and many other issues, and until his mind was made up not even the persuasive powers of his friend, Dr. George Hall, could move him. Abbott refused to be bought. As a matter of fact, when Hall tried, not too subtly, to buy into the *Defender* in the interest of Booker T. Washington, he was repulsed with an asperity that threatened their friendship. Abbott was slow, Abbott was stubborn, but he was not, he said, "a pure-born fool." In truth, the growth of the *Defender* in both circulation and influence bore him out.

Contrary to the belief of some, not all the credit for this growth was due to the often questionable and always sensational ways and works of J. Hockley Smiley, whom Abbott had hired in 1910. Though meagerly gifted himself, Abbott knew talent when he saw it, and he could make talent work for him. He used this knack to advantage so long as he lived. Smiley had the talents and the techniques of a Hearst. It was he who introduced the glaring red headlines, who thought up the slogans ("With Drops of Ink We Make Millions Think") and the elaborate, circulation-pulling hoaxes. It was Smiley who departmentalized the paper into theater, sports, and society sections, and he who recruited Pullman porters, dining-car waiters, and performers on the Negro vaudeville circuit to carry weekly bundles of the *Defender* east to New York and Boston, south to Atlanta and Birmingham, and west to Seattle and Los Angeles.

But the editorial page belonged to Abbott, and much of the credit for the *Defender's* growth must go to the editorials. This is not to say that Abbott wrote them. He seldom wrote them in their final form, for his prose was often ungrammatical and clumsy; but his ideas informed the editorials, and in them his consciousness, it might be said, prevailed.

It was a consciousness that was cunning without being the least subtle. It did not work from design but through instinct, and often, therefore, it plunged—like a man falling through space—past all the levels of logic to plop at last against the bedrock of personal experience. Whatever position he took, he took on this bedrock ground, and whatever position he took, he held tenaciously. He was almost never known to change his mind, even when he was demonstrably in error.

For instance, when he was a member of the Chicago Commission on Race Relations it was brought forcibly home to him that the *Defender's* campaign to lure Negroes from the South was doing more harm than good. The facts with which the commission dealt showed clearly that the hysterical South–North migration caused a great leap in all the depressing statistics—unemployment, delinquency, crime—and a tragic upsurge of anti-Negro feeling North and South. Mentioning the *Defender* by name, the commission itself urged "greater care and accuracy in reporting incidents involving whites and Negroes, the abandonment of sensational headlines and articles on racial questions, and more attention to means and opportunities of [Negroes] adjusting themselves and their fellows into more harmonious relations with their white neighbors. . . ." But, in 1914, Abbott had taken the position that migration to the North was the Negro's salvation, and in 1919 he refused to abandon it. When disastrous riots flared up all the summer and fall of the latter year, Abbott "did not view them as unmitigated evil."

If he seldom changed his mind, even more rarely did he change his heart. He was emotionally rigid and complex. He felt his black skin to be not only a severe handicap in the Negro world—which, of course, it was—but a source of personal shame. In spite of the most concrete evidence to the contrary—his wealth, prestige, and influence—he was convinced that his intrinsic worth as a person could be certified only by the acceptance of mulattoes. Nevertheless, he felt an obsessive loyalty to blackskin people per se. He reflected their moods instinctively and their minds so perfectly that they saw their composite image in the pages of the *Defender*. He was "for the masses, not the classes." He wanted them to "solidify, throw off the shackles. Rise!" and any small instance of rising—a high school graduation, a black boy on a white athletic team, a Negro victory in the prize ring or in any other contest against a white opponent —any immaterial instance was enough for columns of praise and joy.

Yet—strange duality!—no instance whatever was testimony to his own intrinsic worth. Only intimate social concourse with mulattoes could provide that; only, say, a light-skinned wife could make him worth while and respectable in his own eyes. When finally he married at the age of fifty he took to wife a woman whom he did not love but who was indistinguishable from white. When this unhappy affair ended in divorce he took a second wife who was "white in fact," and who, accompanying him to "white" places of entertainment, did not seem to mind the ridiculous gibberish he spoke in the impossible hope of being mistaken for a foreigner. It is strangely characteristic that, though he gave only casual and token assistance to the black Abbotts and completely ignored them in his will, he contributed regularly to the mulatto Sengstackes, was for years a dependable source of income for their white relatives in Germany, and saw to it that some of the white direct descendants of his father's master were educated.

Though these abiding indices to his character were evident in 1912, Abbott had at that time made up his mind on no public issues and on only one policy for his paper. The *Defender* would not fight Negroes and the editor's own private enemies. It would concentrate its fire on the common foe, the whites. Abbott wanted to unify "the black population for aggressive counter-action," and if this required him to vilify even well-meaning whites, then he would vilify. Of course this was wrong on the face of it, but "give the skunks hell," Abbott would say, and in his book of rules nearly every white man was a skunk, including the good philanthropist friend of the Negro, Julius Rosenwald, who was not the only white man to think that Abbott was a mindless "monkey with a shotgun, who will hurt anybody."

Anybody, that is, except Negroes—who certainly were hurt enough by the white press; and anything except the struggle in which even the semiliterate masses believed themselves engaged. Week after endless week the *Defender's* slogan for that struggle was "American Race Prejudice Must Be Destroyed." The proof of its destruction would rest, Abbott himself wrote (with a habitually greater regard for sense than syntax), in "the opening of all trades and trade unions to blacks. . . . Representation in the President's Cabinet. Engineers, firemen and conductors on all American railroads, and all jobs in government. Representation in all departments of the police forces over the entire United States; Federal legislation to abolish lynching and full enfranchisement of all American citizens."

Though Du Bois probably had the *Defender* in mind when he said that "some of the best colored papers are so wretchedly careless in their use of the English language . . . that when they see English they are apt to mistake it for something else," it is highly unlikely that he also included the *Defender* in his condemnation of those colored weeklies that did not "stand staunch for *principle*." That year, 1914, nearly every Negro paper in the country blasted Du Bois at one time or another, but not the *Defender*. Abbott hated and feared divisive argument among Negroes, and Abbott realized that he and Du Bois were fighting the same war on the same side.

Many Negroes did not realize, except sporadically, that Du Bois was on their side. The man had an unhappy predilection for making enemies. He was impatient, especially of ignorance; he was temperamentally unsuited to mingling with the masses. He was called "race traitor" more than once because it was thought he sounded like one. He was as caustically critical of Negroes as of whites. "Jeremiads were needed to redeem [the Negro] people," he said, and jeremiads he gave them. Abbott on the other hand gave them panegyrics and made excuses for their wrongdoing. Neither man realized that he reflected a deepening mood of frustration and despair.

There were reasons for this mood.

7. *Exodus*

No sooner had Woodrow Wilson been inaugurated than it became apparent that a constant progress in demagoguery in the South had led to a recovery of those extremes of sectionalism and race hatred that were thought to have been buried with Reconstruction. Within months Cole Blease was shouting to wild applause, "Whenever the Constitution comes between me and the virtue of the white women of the South, I say to hell with the Constitution!" No sooner had Congress convened than it put into the legislative hopper a confusion of bills brazenly designed to prohibit Negroes from holding commissions in the armed forces, to choke off immigration of Negroes from the West Indies, and to facilitate the segregation of Negroes in the civil service. Indeed, segregation in the civil service was accomplished without legislation, by executive order of the President. If this was in the pattern of "absolute fair dealing" and an example of "advancing the interests of the Negro race" that Wilson had promised before his election, it was not testified to by Negroes. A few liberal white papers in the North deplored this "perfidious action," but the South, which had a political-power potential three times greater than the North's, applauded it. And went beyond. Curfew laws, applicable only to Negroes, were revived in Georgia, Alabama, and Florida. Police brutality and mob law took over.

Then, in 1915, Booker Washington died. Washington's influence among Negroes had waned of late, and Du Bois probably spoke for thousands when he said, "In stern justice we must lay to the soul of this man a heavy responsibility for the consummation of Negro disfranchisement, the decline of the Negro college and public school, and the firmer establishment of color caste in this land."

Nevertheless, Washington's death was an incalculable loss. Whether he spoke well or ill in Negroes' behalf, he did speak—and in councils of influence. Whether Negroes agreed or disagreed with his policies, and even though many of them scorned the uses to which he put his intelligence, they believed that in his heart Washington meant his people well, and they knew that only when they came from his mouth might their appeals be heard. If Washington's "imperturbable good nature" had inclined him to keep silent on the subject of their rights, it had all the same won them time and leniency in which to go on fighting for those rights. As the New York *Times* said, "Washington was far from being the Negroes' acknowledged leader," but he was still the only Negro leader the whites acknowledged. "Who now will speak!" lamented the Richmond *Planet*. Who indeed?

And speaking, what say—either as advice or in exhortation? For not only did the race problem grow more complex, but its complexity was compounded at its very heart in the South when the guns began to yammer along the Marne and when natural disasters brought in their train a load of economic tensions and uncertainties.

First of all, the war-stimulated European demand for cotton in 1914 had seemed the knock of opportunity for which the South had listened vainly since 1853. When it came cotton acreage was recklessly expanded forthwith. Cotton mills were thrown up everywhere. White tenants, sharecroppers, and small farmers, their wives and children swarmed to the mill towns like plagues of locusts. For the first time since the Civil War the surplus of Southern white labor was absorbed.

Then in 1915 the boll weevil came again in clouds, and apparently to stay. What the weevil left, floods destroyed in two tragic years in succession. Destruction of the cotton crop wiped out collateral, and planters' credit dwindled.

For want of cotton, mills closed down. Rural Negroes, the vast majority, were caught in this squeeze, and what they did to extricate themselves set a current flowing toward consequences that might have been foreseen. They crowded into Southern cities, where they were soon in such numbers as to make the laboring poor whites, traditionally committed to enmity for blacks, fearful of a glut on the labor market and the debasement of their wages. Tensions rose and registered their rise on the most sensitive of social barometers. In 1915 sixty-seven Negroes were lynched, thirty-two of them within the corporate limits of Southern towns.

When the boll weevil was brought under subjugation and the recovery made from floods, was there a reversion to the former state of things, to that peace—uncongenial, uneasy, uneven though it was—that, putting the best face on it, might be said to have prevailed since the demise of Reconstruction? Not at all. When cotton could grow again (and in a twinkle soared to forty cents) and the gins were ready to roar and the mills to pound, it was discovered that growing cotton and running mills needed Negroes, and needed them more desperately than Negroes needed "soft air, sunshine and sowbelly." And Negroes in thousands were gone—north!

The earliest realization of their departure brought a sigh of relief in some Southern quarters. The Negro's going, the Nashville *Banner* said, would "rid the South of the entire burden and all the brunt of the race problem, and make room for and create greater inducements for white immigration." Like many another Southern paper, the *Banner* was not expert in analysis. How could the South, where wages averaged only twenty-three dollars a week, lure white migrants who could earn three times as much in the North? How, even—and this was soon to be the crucial question—could the South keep its Negro field hands and laborers when word was being whispered among them of the big money in the North? In "Chi," in "Deestroy" and in Pittsburgh eighty dollars for a six-day week was quite common, and time and a half for Sundays. Add also the fact that each week there passed from black hand to hand copies of the Chicago *Defender*, haranguing:

". . . For the same reason that an unchecked rat has been known to jeopardize the life of a great ship, a mouse's nibble of a match to set a mansion aflame, I've concluded to carve a slice of liver or two from that bellowing ass who, at this very moment no doubt, somewhere in the South, is going up and down the land, telling the natives *why* they should be content . . . to remain in that land—to them— of *blight*; of *murdered* kin, *deflowered* womanhood, *wrecked* homes, *strangled* ambitions, *make-believe* schools, raving 'gun parties,' *midnight* arrests, *rifled* virginity, *trumped up* charges, *lonely* graves, where owls hoot, and where friends dare not go! Do you wonder at the thousands leaving the land where every foot of ground marks a tragedy, leaving the graves of their fathers and all that is dear, to seek their fortunes in the North? And you who say their going is to seek better wages are insulting the truth, dethroning reason, and consoling yourselves with a groundless allegation."

Surely the language and the order of its elements were Abbott's.

Though Du Bois was calmer, he too knew how to harangue, and he did month after month. "We might as well face the facts squarely: if there is any colored man in the South who wishes to have his children educated and who wishes to be in close touch with civilization and who has any chance or ghost of a chance of making a living in the North it is his business to get out of the South as soon as possible. . . . The same reasons that drive the Jews from Russia, the peasants from Austria, the Armenians from Turkey, and the oppressed from tyranny everywhere should drive the colored man out of the land of lynching, lawlessness and industrial oppression. . . . The only effective protest that the Negroes *en masse* can make against lynching and disfranchisement is through leaving the devilish country where these things take place."

Given the whole course and context of Southern history, it is no wonder that the common white men of the South, seeing their dreams of wealth threatened by this disaffection, should again resort to those measures they had hitherto employed to control the Negro. If the common men did not pause to consider that these means might frustrate the end they sought, there were those uncommon white men who did. "There is no secret about what must be done if Georgia would save herself from threatened disaster," wrote the editor of the Atlanta *Constitution*. "There must be no more mobs. . . . We must be fair to the Negro. We have not shown that fairness in the past, nor are we showing it today, either in justice before the law . . . or in other directions." The Montgomery *Advertiser* warned, "While our very solvency is being sucked out from underneath we go on about our affairs as usual—our police officers raid poolrooms for 'loafing Negroes' . . . keep them in barracks all night, and next morning find that many [are] valuable assets to their white employers: suddenly [the Negroes] have left and gone."

This response to the logic of the circumstances came too late. By 1916 a half million Negroes had "left and gone." By that year, too, even some of the more stable minds of the South had moved from hope to frustration and from restlessness to despair. The organs through which these more stable minds spoke did not make a complete about-face to the common man's reactionism, but they did praise *The Birth of a Nation*, a film infamous for invoking the common white man's hatred of the black; and they kept silent while United States marines killed blacks in Haiti; and they were alarmingly unanimous in their refusal to say that the burning alive of an "impudent Negro before thousands of men, women and children" in Waco, Texas, was anything but an enlightening spectacle calculated "to teach Negroes a lesson."

The South was soon brought to the discovery that the Negro was learning other lessons from other teachers. Ray Stannard Baker, writing in *World's Work* in 1916, first brought it to attention: ". . . There are more than four hundred and fifty newspapers and other publications in America devoted exclusively to the interests of colored people. . . . The utter ignorance of white Americans as to what is really going on among the colored people of the country is appalling—and dangerous."

Until then most white people were unaware of themselves and their public policies as Negroes saw them. When they did become aware, they reacted in several ways, all of them predictable. Early in 1917 an Associated Press dispatch, datelined Pine Bluff, Arkansas, informed the public that "Chancellor John M. Elliott today issued an injunction restraining John D. Young, Jr., Negro, and 'any other parties' from circulating the Chicago *Defender*, a Negro publication, in Pine Bluff or Jefferson County. The injunction was granted at the instance of Mayor Mack Hollis. . . ."

At the same time Du Bois began receiving so many letters of the substance of the following that his office kept a file of them:

"I would be glad to continue to serve you as agent as willing, but you are aware of the fact that the crackers or the Ku Klux will beat a colored man for giving the *Crisis* away in some sections of this country. I wish to stop here a little longer as I make good wages in railroad service. . . . As long as I can stay in peace I decided I would discontinue. . . ."

Scattered here and there were Southern Negro editors, too, who in order to "stay in peace" did what one of them in Tennessee confessed to doing: "I went straight to the white folks in this section and knocked on the door of their conscience and they received me, and assured me of their loyal support."

Aggressive Negro leaders believed the attitude expressed by the Tennessee editor to be more harmful than the opposition of white people. With Booker Washington dead, they decided the time had come to forgo the luxury of divided opinion and to weld Negroes into a unity that had seemed impossible so long as Washington lived. To achieve this, they called a conference at Amenia, New York, in 1916 and resolved, among other things, "that antiquated subjects of controversy, ancient suspicions and factional alignments must be eliminated and forgotten if [the] or-

ganization of the race and [the] practical working understanding of its leaders are to be achieved."

If both Abbott and Du Bois were overoptimistic as to
the unity brought about by the Amenia conference, and
if the organization of the race did not immediately result,
there was no way of telling from the Negro publications,
which more and more white people were reading and
which presented an unbroken front of social disaffection,
of defiance to established custom, and of racial militance.
The monstrous aspect of this phenomenon, undeniably in
view by the spring of 1917, inspired fresh fears in the
majority of Southerners who were still committed to the
old beliefs and habits and to the conviction that unquestioned submission to them was necessary to the safety of
the South and the well-being of the country.

So it was not surprising that a Southern sheriff named
Moon, armed with a pearl-handled pistol and papers certified by the attorney general of Georgia, should journey
from Waycross to Chicago, burst unceremoniously into the
office of the *Defender*, and claim the authority to arrest its
editor. But Abbott knew just enough law, and he was surrounded by just the right number of hard-bitten men of
his staff, to disallow this.

It is not surprising either that James F. Byrnes, mantling
his native section in the seamless robes of patriotism,
should declare in Congress that "would-be Negro leaders
. . . are antagonistic to the United States"; that he
should be the prime mover in trying to get one of those
leaders, A. Philip Randolph, sentenced to two and a half
years in prison; and that, eventually, he should call upon
the United States Attorney General to institute sedition
proceedings against W. E. B. Du Bois and Robert S. Abbott.

It was already a crime in South Carolina, Mississippi,
and Georgia to read the *Defender*. It was almost as much
as a Negro's life was worth to be caught with a copy of
the *Crisis* in a Southern community. And in at least one
instance it was death to be discovered a "migration agent"
—as many Negroes, in the pay of Northern industry, were

—even if one paid the license fee, which ran to a thousand dollars in Birmingham and Jacksonville.

The pump and heave of racial animus was not confined to the South. Some ten thousand Negroes had been invited, some as strikebreakers, to East St. Louis, Illinois, in 1916, and then had stayed on to become non-union laborers in the city's war-swollen industries. The whites did not like it or them. After a series of "racial incidents" throughout the spring came an explosion of such violence as to leave at least a hundred Negroes dead, a half million dollars in property damage, and six thousand Negroes homeless. A young Russian Jew who witnessed the three-day riot commented, "The Russians at least gave the Jews a chance to run while they were trying to murder them. The whites of East St. Louis fired the homes of black folk and either did not allow them to leave the burning houses or shot them the moment they dared attempt to escape the flames."

Two months later, disarmed, as one official report put it, "when it was feared that they would use their weapons to defend themselves" against the attacks and insults of Houston's citizenry, Negro soldiers of the 24th Infantry seized the forbidden arms and in one wild night killed seventeen whites. The trial of these soldiers was a farce that ended as it was bound to end—with fourteen Negroes hanged for mutiny and murder and forty-one imprisoned for life.

Du Bois wrote that "there was never a period in the history of the American Negro when he has been more discouraged and exasperated."

The fact was not evident from the record of Negro registration when America entered the war.

8. Walk Together, Children

The record was made in the face of persistent rumors that President Wilson had said that the war was "a white man's war." Negroes rushed to volunteer in such numbers that within five days of the declaration quotas of Negro military outfits were oversubscribed. There were ten thousand Negroes in the four Regular Army units, and another ten thousand in the National Guard when the War Department ordered a halt to Negro enlistment. "No more," it said, "need apply." This in itself was enough to make the President's rumored remark seem painfully credible, but then a few days later Colonel Charles Young, the highest-ranking Negro officer and a graduate of West Point, was summarily retired. "High blood pressure," the army medical board declared. "Prejudice. A miserable ruse," the Negroes said. Ruse or not, it worked to prevent Young's promotion to general rank. To prove his health, the colonel rode horseback in full field equipment from his home in Ohio to Washington, D.C. Abashed by this evidence, coupled with Negro protest, the army recalled him. But he was not destined to wear a general's star. He was assigned as military attaché in Haiti, where he fumed out the war.

The President's remark, if he made it, was bitterly modified after registration for the draft began in July. It quickly became apparent that something was wrong, and whatever it was had this final result: 51.65 per cent of all Negro registrants were placed in Class 1, as against 32.53 per cent of whites, and 30 per cent of Negro registrants were actually inducted, as compared to 26 per cent of whites. It looked very much as though draft boards were guided by the forthright precepts of Willard D. Mc-Kinstrey, editor of the Watertown (New York) *Times*, who had written:

"It seems a pity to waste good white men in battle with such a foe. The cost of sacrifice would be nearly equalized were the job assigned to Negro troops. . . . An army of a million could probably be easily recruited from the Negroes of this country without drawing from its industrial strength or commercial life. . . . We will be sacrificing white blood . . . and drawing our skilled labor when unskilled labor was available."

Given this thinking, which, though it did not operate to the extent some might wish or Negroes thought, operated flagrantly enough to draw repeated protests and to lead, finally, to the dismissal of the whole Atlanta draft board, to whom the equitable percentage of exemptions was thirteen for Negroes and seventy-two for whites—given this thinking, it seemed to a conclave of Negro leaders something less than reasonable to deny "the right of our best [Negro] men to lead troops of their race in battle, and to receive officers' training in preparation for such leadership."

Already in April the government had said that such training would not be given to Negroes, since "it was illegal under the law to train them in camps with white officers," and since there were no camps for Negro officers. Speaking, he thought, out of the new unity of Negroes, Joel Spingarn proposed the establishment of a separate camp, but there were objections to this—and from an unexpected quarter. Not only did a cadre of Southern whites inveigh against a waste of funds in training a "people who cannot make good officers," but Robert S. Abbott declared himself against "this Jim Crow officers' camp." Du Bois rebuked him.

"Where in heaven's name do we Negroes stand? If we organize separately for anything—'Jim Crow!' scream all the Disconsolate; if we organize with white people— 'Traitors! Pressure! They're betraying us!' yell all the Suspicious. If, unable to get the whole loaf we seize half to ward off starvation—'Compromise!' yell all the Scared. If we let the half loaf go and starve—'Why don't you *do* something?' yell these same critics. . . . Just now we demand Negro officers for Negro regiments. We cannot get them by admission to the regular camps because the law of the land, or its official interpretation, wickedly prevents us. Therefore give us a separate camp for Negro officers."

Abbott fell into line.

Du Bois was not alone in wanting to know where the Negro stood. State and federal governments asked the same question. German propaganda and intrigue were at work, and, though the government's fear of Negro disloyalty had no basis in fact, it had every justification in reason. Just where did Negroes stand, then? Just what were their objectives? the Attorney General of the United States wanted to know. "We are seeking to have the Constitution thoroughly and completely enforced," answered

Du Bois. "We are not trying by this war to settle the Negro problem," said the Secretary of War. "True enough," replied Du Bois, "but you are trying to settle as much of it as interferes with winning the war."

The War Department yielded to the pressure and set up a Negro officers' training camp at Fort Des Moines, Iowa. A thousand "college-trained and college-worthy" Negro men were sent there under the command of Colonel C. C. Ballou. One of this officer's first official acts was to call the Negro officer candidates together and tell them that they "need not expect democratic treatment." To add insult to willful injury, when the Negro 92nd Division was organized Ballou, raised to the rank of major general, was given command. He promptly issued a bulletin that read, "White men made the Division, and they can break it just as quickly if it becomes a troublemaker. . . . Don't go where your presence is not desired."

The presence of Negroes seemed not to be desired anywhere. The very month the Des Moines camp was set up, special trains were run to a place in Tennessee called Macon Road Bridge, five miles east and south of Memphis, and five thousand men, women, and children looked on while a Negro was burned alive. The Memphis *News-Scimitar* reported, "This is the first time in the record of lynching that the mob lynched in broad daylight and did not seek to hide their identity or wear masks."

Seventeen other Negroes were lynched between May and September.

And in October, the very month when six hundred and thirty-nine Negro officers were commissioned at Fort Des Moines, the drum major of the 15th New York Infantry was severely beaten because he did not think or know enough to remove his jaunty field cap when he tried to buy a paper from a white newsdealer in Spartanburg, South Carolina. The 15th, camped on the edge of the town, seethed. This was not the first incident, or the most outrageous, or the last; but it was the one that focused the attention.

Noble Sissle was no ordinary drum major. He was a music maker—as public to Negroes as an advertising calendar, and almost equally so to a sophisticated segment of Northern whites, who were just beginning to appreciate "jig bands playing nigger jazz." Sissle was one of those who had brought this jazz from God-knows-where to the East, and from the Renaissance in Harlem to the Rondo in the Village he had played its strange, inverted chords and compounded its earthy rhythms, as inscrutably sad and yet as profoundly unsentimental as Shakespearean tragedy, in a musical vernacular as fluid and far-ranging as dreams, defiance, and irony could make it. Though scarcely understood, Sissle's music was known, and was, indeed, beginning to be celebrated by a sizable coterie of Northern whites. The news of his unprovoked beating made headlines in the press.

The country was already in a condition bordering on hysteria. The war clouded everything, so that nothing was clear, nothing was simple. Hate rode hard upon the heels of fear. Negro soldiers especially were touchy. Already they had rioted and killed in other places, and now, though several days had passed since the beating, reports said they proposed to riot in Spartanburg. Colonel William Hayward, commanding the 15th, reported to the War Department his fear of "a violent eruption." The War Department felt that something should be done.

Actually it could make one of two choices, neither of them good. It could keep the regiment at Spartanburg and thus invite the eruption so much feared; or it could send the regiment, half trained, overseas. Secretary of War Baker chose the second. Redesignated the 369th Infantry, the 15th sailed from Hoboken in December 1917.

Du Bois wrote: "Close ranks! . . . Let us, while this war lasts, forget our special grievances and close our ranks shoulder to shoulder with our own white fellow citizens. . . . We make no ordinary sacrifice, but we make it gladly and willingly with our eyes lifted to the hills."

His syntax as clumsy as ever, Abbott wrote: "I say with absolute certainty that without a shadow of a doubt . . . we are Americans always!"

The men of the 369th Infantry were destined to be the first American troops to move up to the fighting front.

VIII. AFRICAN FANTASY

1. *Les Enfants Perdus*

The really big offensive that would plow through the Vosges Mountains, carry to the west bank of the Rhine, and end the war began on the night of September 25, 1918. At six-thirty in the evening of that day the 1st Battalion of the 369th New York Infantry moved out of the first line of Sous Secteur Beauséjour. It was the last of the three battalions to move, and it moved out in groups of half a platoon, in single file, with a distance of fifty paces between each group. The move was not particularly hazardous. There was still some artillery fire, but the German attack of seven infantry divisions, which was the last such attack of this war, had been temporarily discouraged and repulsed, and the 2nd and 3rd Battalions of the 369th had moved out in broad daylight three hours earlier.

The 369th was fighting as an organized part of the 161st French Division under General Lebouc. Its morale was high. The men were proud of the name the French had given them, *Les enfants perdus*. Just before they had gone into the front line of Sous Secteur Beauséjour on September 12 they had seen copies of Lincoln Eyre's dispatch in the New York *World* describing the "Battle of Henry Johnson." This event had occurred nearly five months before and had been headlined in the American press at the time, but the men of the 369th had been at the front for one hundred and thirteen days and had seen no newspapers. They were proud that Henry Johnson and Needham Roberts—men of their own outfit, Negroes—were the first Americans to be awarded the Croix de Guerre.

Now as the 1st Battalion, Major Arthur Little in command, slogged out in the dark toward the new front, the half-platoon groups closed, still in single file, on the shoulder of the road. They made a line nearly a tenth of a mile long, and in this order they threaded their way through the gummy jam of men and vehicles all bound for various rendezvous close behind the new front. The rendezvous for the 1st Battalion was Ravin des Pins. They were due at ten o'clock, and they made it only because an afternoon reconnaissance had uncovered a trail that led off the road and across the mutilated country. Even so, it was a tough three-hour march. No sooner were they disposed on the sheltered slope of their ravine than the great guns spoke. It was 11:00 P.M. The Battle of the Meuse-Argonne had started.

The artillery engagement, which lasted six hours, seemed to go well. At 5:00 A.M. the first assault teams started over. These teams consisted of several Moroccan battalions of the 161st French Division, and the 2nd and 3rd Battalions of the 369th. From where the 1st Battalion waited, it looked like a black man's war, but men in battle or about to go into battle can know very little, and all they could see from the south bank of the Dormoise River was the steep slope of the hill rising on the north bank and, finally, 3rd Battalion men crawling up the hill, silhouetting suddenly against the sky line, and disappearing instantly, as if by magic. It was evening before they saw the last line go up and over, for German artillery had pinned the first groups down for more than ten hours.

Not until it crossed the river on the night of September 26 did the 1st get its orders. At dawn it was to begin an advance in a northeast direction to Bellevue Ridge, a hill rising abruptly from the plain of the Argonne country, there to relieve a French battalion positioned somewhere on the crest and along the north face of the hill. As soon as practicable after making the relief, they would go in alone on the town of Sechault, take it, reorganize, and then, supported by the 2nd Battalion, press through the woods called Petits Rosiers. They were to dig in north of the woods and await further orders. The whole distance of their advance from the Dormoise River was to be just over seven kilometers. It did not look bad on the situation maps, and it did not sound bad in the orders.

It continued to look good as the 1st came down the hill on the north bank of the river and out onto the flat ground. But appearances were deceptive. Initially pinned down for nearly eleven hours, the Moroccans and the 2nd and 3rd Battalions had broken through the night before and had thereby incurred the risk of all night infantry attacks—they had by-passed some German positions. Before the 1st could penetrate the plain to the depth of half a kilometer the by-passed pockets put up a stiff resistance, and it required a half day's dogged fighting to clean them out, while, meantime, German artillery pounded the plain. The 1st lost eighteen of its two hundred and sixty men in this mop-up, and ten more in the broad light of early afternoon as it relieved Favre's battalion on Bellevue Ridge. From here Sechault was still more than a kilometer away, and enemy artillery raked the area that stretched before it.

But the 1st was under orders to take Sechault on September 27, and this was the afternoon of that day. At three o'clock they started down the ridge that they had relieved at two. From the northeast came a constant pounding of artillery. They went down in companies, each company with a section of two machine guns, at fifteen-minute intervals. This took an hour. If the town was to be won by dark they had not more than three hours to accomplish it. There was no artillery support. The only cover in a kilometer of flat land was a drainage ditch a scant fifty yards from the southern edge of the town, and before they could take this they would have to drive the enemy out of it and subdue a German gun mounted just behind it. The gun, shooting canister, had a clear field of fire.

The men wriggled forward on their bellies. A few yards in, the first man was hit. He rose, was hit again, turned slowly, took one eternal step, and then fluttered down, arms flaying, like a stricken bird. Other men rose by reflex and some of them were hit. A battery of Austrian 88s drummed fire from beyond the woods four kilometers north of the town. They were guns without courtesy, and they were not called Whiz-Bangs for nothing. When you heard their shells they had already arrived and exploded. At 4:40 P.M. Major Little sent back a request for artillery support. It never came.

And even before he could have expected it the major got support of another kind. He had decided to send in Company C as an assault wave to overrun the ditch and the gun and after a two-minute interval to pile the other companies in on the right and left. He so informed Lieutenant MacClinton, who commanded Company C. The German outwork, which ran from east to west, was not two hundred yards long, and the three companies of the 1st Battalion were on a line that overlapped each end of the outwork by a city block. There could not be many Germans in the ditch. Major Little counted on a rush creating an element of surprise.

He had just sent Sergeant Davis crawling across the plain with this advice to the company commanders when he looked up to see staggering from the rear through that field of fire the remnants of a company of the 2nd Battalion. It was a completely foolhardy thing to do, but in their dazed and disorganized condition—their commander, Captain Clark, having been killed—they could not be expected to realize this. Ordered held in support until the town should be taken and the assault on the woods begun, they had bivouacked on the eastern spur of Bellevue Ridge. Here an enemy plane had spotted them and enemy artillery found them. Within minutes their strength had been reduced by nearly a third. It seemed better to move up than to be chewed up without a chance to resist. And here they were, a hundred and fifty men loping drunkenly into a spattering rain of fire toward a place they were not supposed to be. The major cursed in amazement.

The enemy must have been amazed too, for suddenly there was no fire at all from the ditch, only the sound of artillery growling overhead. The cessation of fire probably would have lasted only a moment, but in that moment the major ordered Company C in. Bayonets fixed, they rushed in yelling, and the enemy, numbering about fifty, swarmed pell-mell out of the ditch and into the nearest streets of the town.

From the shelter of the ditch, where the men were packed like sand, Major Little ordered a detail to search for the wounded and sent forward three two-man patrols. Only one of these six men returned, but on the basis of the report this man gave the major sent a dispatch to regimental command. It was 6:00 P.M. "The town [Sechault] is filled with M.G. snipers. . . . Cannot tell you how soon we can go forward. Shall we halt when too dark to see?"

Halting did not depend on the descent of night alone.

Sechault was just a small town in the center of a great plain, but it had been designed as if for the special advantage of the enemy. The north—south streets, some nearly as wide as Parisian boulevards, ran straight through without a break. The Germans had set up machine guns to command these streets. Three hundred yards north of the town they had established machine-gun posts protected by sandbags. Two and a half or three kilometers beyond this defensive line a thick woods darkened the horizon. The woods swarmed with the enemy and trembled with the roar and recoil of artillery. Altogether there must have been a dozen guns, some of them 155s, in and north of the woods. The enemy meant to contest every foot of ground. If they could not blunt the edge of this spearhead in this sector it would be all over, and they knew it.

At six-twenty two companies of the 1st began a house-to-house advance through the eastern and western edges of the town. They pressed to take advantage of the remaining daylight. Company B met little resistance, and within less than an hour occupied a house on the northeast edge of Sechault. But it was slow, hard work for Company D and fifteen men were killed doing it. Every house in the western section had to be flushed from cellar to attic, and some of the cellars were saturated with gas. At seven thirty-five Major Little reported again to regimental command: "Appearance of a counter attack from the north. . . . Forming to meet it."

But this meant getting through the town in force and finding cover beyond it. In the only unhit stone house in the center of the town a command post was set up. Here the major got bad news. He was isolated.

The 163rd and the 363rd French Infantry were to have been echeloned to his left and right rear and to come in support when needed. But the Frenchmen had simply got lost, disappeared. Two hours of scouting failed to find them. Informed of this situation, the regimental commander, Colonel William Hayward, sent Major Little the following message: "You will have to exercise your own best judgment on the spot." He had lost half of his own battalion and another third of the men who had staggered onto the field before Sechault. What was his own best judgment?

At a few minutes past eight o'clock the bombardment started again. The enemy lobbed shells over the woods and into the town. It was a creeping barrage that raked the town from south to north. The only way to meet it was to move forward, dig in, protect a makeshift line with outposts, and hope for the best. By the major's reckoning, the outpost farthest from the enemy's machine guns would be a scant hundred yards. It was dark, and darker as it began to rain.

"We are not conducting a holding action, men," the major told his officers. "This is an offensive. Let's go."

They went. They began to find ditches. An irregular pattern of unconnected ditches was all around the north side of the town. A flare caught some of the men as they advanced and machine-gun fire whanged into them. Lieutenants Holden, Hutley, and Winston were wounded. Captain Cobb and twenty-two men were killed. Some of the ditches were refuse pits, stinking of human offal, but the living men lay tight in them—a dozen here, fifteen or twenty there, and so on. The enemy tried to coax them to expose themselves. As soon as one flare drifted down, another swooshed up. At 2:00 A.M. a patrol from the lost 163rd French Infantry stumbled into one of the outposts a quarter of a mile northwest of the irregular center, and liaison with support had been established at last. The rain, the flares, and the enemy fire kept up more or less continuously all night.

In the morning General Lebouc himself took personal command of the action in this sector of the northwest front, the arc of which the Germans had extended for a distance no one on the Allied side had estimated. The 3rd Battalion was now sent up to join the other two battalions of the 369th. They were to take the woods and march on to Les Petits Rosiers. They tried. From the 7:00 A.M. H-hour until 2:00 P.M., when the first line reached the edge of the woods, they tried. Major Little reported: "Cannot get through woods without artillery." This time he got artillery, and reported later: "The French artillery fire referred to consisted of about a half dozen shots. The 1st Batt. has about 137 men and 7 officers. The 2nd Batt. has about 100 men and 3 officers. The 3rd Batt. has about 300 men and 9 or 10 officers. . . . I hope that a relief can be made."

The 363rd French Infantry came as relief the next day. At six on the morning of September 30, artillery gave the woods a shelling that lasted two hours. At eight o'clock the 363rd started an advance that carried through the woods and reached Les Petits Rosiers that afternoon.

For five days more the 369th New York stayed alerted at Sechault, after which they moved to the rear and camped in the vicinity of Minaucourt. Too weary to be jubilant at the rumored news that Austria and Turkey had demanded an armistice, they rested for a week. On October 14 they started fighting their way through the Vosges Mountains and down again to Belfort Gap and Bischwiller and the front-line trenches of Secteur Collardelle, which they reached on October 16. Twelve days later they fought their last fight in the war and lost three killed, eight wounded, and one missing. The missing man was later found buried in a grave the Germans had dug and marked. On November 5, with the war sputtering out, they withdrew to Belfort, and on November 12 a document, addressed to Headquarters 369th Infantry U. S. Army, reached them and was read:

"After having boldly stopped the enemy, you have attacked them for months with indefatigable faith and energy, giving them no rest.

"You have won the greatest battle in History and saved the most sacred cause, the liberty of the world.

"Be proud of it.

"With immortal glory you have adorned your flags.

"Posterity will be indebted to you with gratitude.

"The Marshal of France, Commander in Chief of the Allied Armies, Foch."

It sounded fine, and the ceremony of pinning the Croix de Guerre to the regimental colors of the 369th New York Infantry was a fine and impressive sight. But only seven hundred and twenty-five officers and men of the original three thousand were there to see it. The rest were either wounded or dead.

2. *Black Star's Zenith*

The boys came marching home again to Harlem, Brooklyn, and the Bronx. To the music of a dozen bands they marched under the Victory Arch, up Fifth Avenue to 110th Street, and then west to Lenox Avenue. Now the head of the column was approaching 135th Street. At every dozen paces after 116th, some mother saw her son, some woman her man, some child its father, and rushed into the street, there to clasp and cling and hang in the ranks like burrs. But it was a parade still. Though it cast off its pomp, it kept the spirit and the starch. The men stepped jaunty as ever. Their rifles kept the proper angle. Their grins were wide.

Unnoticed on the curb as the parade swept by stood a little, rotund black man whose quick-darting eyes glistened like a captive bird's. Jerking a crumpled handkerchief from his coat pocket, he took off his gray velour hat and wiped his forehead. The weather was cold. Indeed, February 17, 1919, was one of the bitterest days of the year, but the little man's face dripped with perspiration. He wiped his eyes, for they too were wet, though whether with perspiration or tears he could not have said. He trembled visibly at one moment, but the very next he stood rigidly tight, breathing in short, quick gasps, lest the emotions that surged and rocked so painfully in him should tear him apart. He had the bitter, ironic sense that even if this happened, no one would notice. Almost no one had noticed him since he left the British West Indies three years ago. And he wanted notice. But now all eyes were fastened on the marchers. Heroes, he thought sarcastically, returning from the white man's war. All throats except his own were shouting a joyous welcome home.

The little man grunted. Home! They had no home. Where was their government? Where was their President? Where their ambassadors, their army, navy, men of big affairs? Fools, fools! he groaned. If Europe is for Europeans, then Africa shall be for the black peoples of the world. The other races have countries of their own, he thought, and it was time for the four hundred million blacks to claim Africa as theirs.

Quite suddenly the ugly little man, whose name was Marcus Garvey, felt tired. His face was dripping sweat again. He must get away. Pressing, elbowing, kneeing back through the crowd, he apologized to no one, though he was conscious of barking shins and smashing toes. People were packed from curb to building line. Black people were everywhere, leaning from windows above the street, gawking and shouting from fire escapes, peering down from rooftops. Boys clung crazily in the bare trees in the center of the avenue.

Marcus Garvey fought his way to the corner of 135th Street and turned west. The street was empty. A few steps brought him to the door of a crumbling brownstone house from which a flag fluttered on a staff at a second-story window. He looked up at the black star centered in a red and green field. This was the flag *they* should be marching under, and not that stupid and alien bunting representing a white man's land. This was *their* flag.

Africa for the sons of Ham! Up, you mighty race!

Garvey climbed the stairs to the second floor, unlocked a door, and went in. The neat and crowded room was hot and stuffy and smelled of stale food, but he did not open a window. The less he heard of the shouts, the music, and the marching feet from Lenox Avenue, the better. Slowly, as if fearing he might break, he lowered himself into the chair at the big desk. He dropped his head and wound his arms about it on the desk top. When Amy Ashwood, his secretary, came in an hour later, she found him sitting thus, his thick shoulders heaving with sobs.

3. *"Oh, Kinsmen!"*

Marcus Garvey was born in the tiny town of St. Ann's Bay, Jamaica, British West Indies, in August 1887. There he grew up under as obdurate a full-blooded black man as ever cursed his enemies and in a tradition as proud as history and folk myth could devise. His father's father had been a Maroon, had shed his blood and spilled the blood of others for freedom, and had bequeathed to his descendants the prestige of his deeds and station. Marcus Garvey's father had kept that prestige intact; indeed, had added to it. The only master stone- and brickmason in the town, he acquired a small fortune. He owned the only private library in St. Ann's. Even the white schoolmaster and the Anglican priest borrowed books from him. Though he lent, he scorned the borrower. Most blacks, however, had no use for books, and for them he felt harsh pity. Even after a series of disastrous court actions had lost him nearly everything except his homesite and reduced him almost to the level of the other blacks, he pitied them. For the whites and mulattoes, who had brought the actions, he mixed hate with scorn. He died when Marcus, his youngest son, was sixteen.

The boy had got a start by then. He had been to school and, he claimed, was graduated from the Church of England High School. He had also learned the printer's trade, and at the age of seventeen he went to Kingston to follow it. His mother died very shortly afterward. In the seven or eight subsequent years, unencumbered by family responsibility, Marcus Garvey followed his trade in Costa Rica, Panama, Ecuador, Nicaragua, Honduras, Colombia, and Venezuela. In Limón he worked briefly for the United Fruit Company and learned something of the plight of Negro field workers. He started a newspaper, *La Nacionale*, protesting that "no white person would ever regard the life of a black man equal to that of a white man." The paper failed. In Colón he started another, *La Prensa*. That failed. "Sickened with fever and sick at heart," his wife wrote later, "over appeals from his people for help," he returned to Jamaica. Less than a year later he was off to London.

England was the bright sun of the colonial world, but already in 1912 there were those who could discern sunspots—though the magnetic storms they presaged would be many years abrewing. African and West Indian, East Indian and Egyptian students and workers, all of them extreme nationalists, were Garvey's friends. He learned a great deal about his "heart's people" and his "native land."

Reading at Birkbeck College and at the British Museum ended his systematic education, but he continued to learn, and particularly from Duse Mohammed, a Nubian-Egyptian who published the *Africa Times and Orient Review* and made speeches in Hyde Park advocating Egyptian home rule. Garvey too made speeches in Hyde Park. In London he met American Negroes who told him that their lot at home was poor. He read Booker Washington's *Up From Slavery*—"and then my doom . . . of being a race leader dawned upon me." Seeing the war clouds gather and congeal over Sarajevo in 1914, he hastened home to Jamaica. He did not intend to fight the white man's war. He itched to start the black man's.

That summer he organized and issued the first manifesto for the Universal Negro Improvement and Conservation Association and African Communities League:

"To establish a Universal Confraternity among the race; to promote the spirit of race pride and love; to reclaim the fallen of the race; to administer to and assist the needy; to assist in civilizing the backward tribes of Africa; to strengthen the imperialism of independent African States; to establish Commissionaries or Agencies in the principal countries of the world for the protection of all Negroes irrespective of nationality; to promote a conscientious Christian worship among the native tribes of Africa; to establish Universities, Colleges and Secondary Schools for the further education and culture of the boys and girls of the race; to conduct a world-wide commercial and industrial intercourse."

But obviously Jamaica was not large enough for such ambitious undertakings. An unknown foreigner, Garvey went to New York in March 1916. Three years later, though he had made speeches in thirty-eight of the states, founded a paper, the *Negro World*, harangued from a stepladder draped in red, green, and black from every street corner in Harlem, and claimed a membership of two thousand for UNIA, he was still relatively obscure.

He had erred badly, partly from ignorance, partly from passion. In Jamaica he had grown up under a color-caste system in which the blacks were separated from the mulattoes by a wider social and economic gulf than that between mulattoes and whites. He had felt as great a resentment of mulattoes as of whites, and his experiences in Central America had not modified it. He carried his resentment to England; he brought it to the States.

Here he tried to exploit it, but no such dipartite Negro race structure operated—or at least was not acknowledged to operate—here. Garvey, therefore, attracted only Harlem's West Indians and a tiny core of the utterly dispossessed in the hinterlands. And even among these he had the doubtful status of a curiosity.

But, by the winter of 1919, Garvey had seen his error and had modified his resentment enough to take steps to correct it. He employed William Ferris, a mulatto graduate of Harvard, to edit his paper. Ferris brought in Hubert H. Harrison, William Pickens, John Bruce, and Eric Walrond, the first three of whom had been identified with race-uplift movements long before Garvey left Jamaica.

Both the tone and the character of the paper changed radically. It outdid the Chicago *Defender* with a program of race pride and unity, and the *Crisis* with a program of race redemption. It was printed in Spanish and French as well as English, and soon it was going to subscribers in all the Caribbean Islands, in Central America, and in British and French possessions in Africa. It proclaimed "One Aim, One God, One Destiny" for the Negro race, which, said

J. A. Rogers, one of the paper's writers and an incurable mythologist, included not only Dumas, Pushkin, and Browning, as the world generally knew, but Beethoven ("the world's greatest musician was without doubt a dark mulatto"), Ethiopians ("that is, Negroes, who gave the world the first idea of right and wrong"), and Jean Baptiste Bernadotte ("a colored man, founder of the present royal house of Sweden. Enlisting as a private in Napoleon's army he rose to be field-marshal. In 1818 he ascended the throne of Sweden as Charles XIV").

Facts or myths, Negroes were ready to believe them. They were ready to believe anything that would seal up the seepage of dignity and pride that "the brave exploits of colored soldiers" in the war had raised to a high level. A fresh outbreak of mass intolerance was draining it off. The Ku Klux Klan—its body and its spirit—had come back to life with greater vitality than ever. By the spring of 1919 it was active in every Southern state except Virginia. Exploiting war weariness with talk of "dangerous entangling alliances," the Klan's Americanism program attracted citizens in Massachusetts, Connecticut, and New York. Indiana, Illinois, and Michigan knew the like. It was against Catholics, Jews, and all foreigners.

In the North it circularized a proposal that "agents be sent among the colored population to emphasize the desirability of returning to the ancestral homeland [Africa]." In the South the official word was, "We would not rob the colored population of their rights, but we demand that they respect the rights of the white race in whose country they are permitted to reside." They tried to enforce respect by means of the knout, the torch, the gun. Seventy-six Negroes, some still in the uniforms of the United States Army, were lynched in 1919. In the awful "red summer" of that year Negroes and whites did each other to death in Longview, Texas; Elaine, Arkansas; Chester, Pennsylvania; and in the nation's capital. A twelve-day riot in Chicago left twenty-two Negroes and sixteen whites dead and more than five hundred of both races injured.

The high toll of whites in affairs of this kind was a new thing altogether. A new kind of Negro was exacting it.

Wartime experiences had changed him. He had held jobs from which he had formerly been restricted. He had won at least a legal victory over residential segregation. His children had gone to school with white children, and he himself had had his choice of seats on streetcars and trains, in theaters and some restaurants in the North.

But especially had the army experiences abroad scoured new contours in his mind and reshaped the patterns of his thought. He had seen white boys from Dixie salute Negro officers. He had discovered that white men die, whether cravenly or bravely, as easily as black. In France and Belgium he had broken the taboos, even the most sacred, and the world had not collapsed about his head. And either abroad or in the North he had heard of a thing called Bolshevism—or so Congressman James F. Byrnes seemed to think. Speaking before the House in August 1919, Byrnes declared it palpable that Negro leadership "appeals for the establishment in this country of a Soviet government" and the "incendiary utterances of would-be Negro leaders . . . are responsible for racial antagonism in the United States."

Byrnes succeeded in moving Attorney General Palmer Mitchell to action and to words. Three months later the Justice Department reported that "there can no longer be any question of a well-concerted movement among a certain class of Negro leaders . . . to constitute themselves a determined and persistent source of radical opposition to the Government and to the established rule of law and order." And this, apparently, was satisfactorily documented by, "First, an ill-governed reaction toward race-rioting. Second, the threat of retaliatory measures in connection with lynching. Third, more openly expressed demands for social equality. . . . Fourth, the identification of the Negro with such radical organizations as the I.W.W. and an outspoken advocacy of the Bolshevik doctrine."

In the first three instances the Attorney General was almost as right as weather, but in the final instance he was as wrong as Byrnes. Bolshevism was not for Negroes. It was godless. It was supported by a dogma and explained in a jargon that the common run of Negroes made no effort to understand. It advocated ideas—among them the idea of a forty-ninth Negro state—abhorrent to Negroes. But first of all and most of all Bolshevism was not democracy, and American Negroes were possessed of an abiding faith in democracy.

This was true even of those who seemed deeply moved by the promises of Communism. And there were promises. A group of American Negroes went to the Third Congress of the Third International to hear them. When Claude McKay, the Negro poet, addressed the Fourth Congress of the International, some Americans doubtless recalled a poem he had written in the desperate dog days of 1919:

> If we must die, let it not be like hogs
> Hunted and penned in an inglorious spot,
> While round us bark the mad and hungry dogs,
> Making their mock at our accursed lot. . . .
> Oh, Kinsmen! We must meet the common foe;
> Though far outnumbered let us still be brave,
> And for their thousand blows deal one death blow!
>
> . . . .
>
> Like men we'll face the murderous cowardly pack,
> Pressed to the wall, dying, but fighting back.

Vengeful and radical this may have been, but Communist it was not, as even Congressman Byrnes should have known. The bitterness could not hide the simple human impulse behind it or obscure the fact that the bitterness itself was the consequence of the abnegation of those principles under the aegis of which the war had been fought and a million men had died. "Make the world safe for democracy!" But what world—and whose?

4. Black Star's Decline

Marcus Garvey thought he had the answer. Almost nightly the curious gathered to hear him shout it out in the big auditorium he had bought in Harlem. "We will draw up the banner of democracy on the continent of Africa!" Garvey was flamboyant and dramatic. He could whirl like a dervish and beat his breast like a Jeremiah.

He wept on occasion, but not now from personal frustration: he wept publicly from fullness of spirit. The crowds that came to hear him swelled in number and in pride. They were no longer simply curious. From one branch with a handful of members, UNIA grew to twenty branches with, Garvey claimed, two million members scattered throughout the whole colored world.

"We have died for five hundred years for an alien race. The time has come for the Negro to die for himself," Garvey shouted. "Race is greater than law! Wake up, Ethiopia! Wake up, Africa! Let us work toward the one glorious end of a free, redeemed and mighty nation. Up, you mighty race! You can accomplish what you will."

Money poured in, ten million dollars in the three years from 1919 to 1921, his widow reported later. "Africa for Africans," cried Garvey, and "Back to Africa," the headlines of his paper screamed. In the pages of the *Crisis*, Du Bois cautioned, "Do not invest in the conquest of Africa. Do not take desperate chances in flighty dreams." A relative newcomer named A. Philip Randolph called Garvey "charlatan" and "fool," and the best-known Negro leaders agreed with him.

But Garvey now had the ear of the great dark host of the naïve, the disillusioned, and the dispossessed. He filled the air with obloquy of the NAACP, the Urban League, and similar organizations, which, he warned, belonged to upper-class Negroes whose leaders were "weak-kneed and cringing . . . sycophant to the white man." These " 'Uncle Tom' Negroes must give way to the 'new' Negro, who is seeking his place in the sun." His followers cheered.

They cheered even more when Garvey projected an all-Negro steamship company, incorporated it as the Black Star Line, and with their money bought a rusty ship. No matter that on her first voyage to Cuba the ship foundered just off Newport News and jettisoned her cargo to keep afloat. There were other things to cheer about: the organization of the Negro Factories Corporation "to build and operate factories in the big industrial centers of the United States, Central America, the West Indies, and Africa to manufacture every marketable commodity"; the recapitalization of the Black Star Line for ten million dollars, and the purchase of two other ships. The Factories Corporation built no factories and the ships plied no trade routes, but this did not matter either to a people caught up in a roaring vortex of race consciousness.

For by this time, 1920, Garvey had founded the African Orthodox Church and created the Court of Ethiopia. Though the first rejected the concept of a white God and soon had its Primate, priests, catechists, and seminarians, and its images of God, Christ, and the Virgin Mary shaped to Negro likeness, the second was more spectacular. Garvey himself assumed only the modest title of Provisional President-General of Africa, but the ranked orders of the Court's nobility glittered with titles and glistened in the barbaric splendor of royal garb. There were dukes and duchesses, lords and earls and dames, high potentates, knights commanders of the Distinguished Order of the Nile, magnificoes, and squads and squadrons of lesser folk—the African Legion, the Black Eagle Flying Corps, the Universal Black Cross Nurses, and the Universal African Motor Corps. All these made a brilliant show at the first UNIA convention, which attracted, the New York *Tribune* estimated, "25,000 Negro delegates from all parts of the world."

But if Negroes were attracted by the show, certain elements in the white race were attracted by something else again.

Garvey had long since taken the position that "political, social and industrial America will never become so converted as to be willing to share up equitably between black and white." He believed that "as long as the white population was numerically superior the blacks could never hope for political justice or social equality." In effect he recommended that they forgo these goals. The step from this to African resettlement and race nationalism was logical enough, and on this ground he was content to rest for a while.

Then as one by one, and finally in concert, the leaders of the less infectious Negro organizations attacked him for opposing his isolationism to their integrationism, the anti-mulatto bias he had learned as a boy and had never comfortably suppressed broke out anew. He publicly scorned and reviled mulatto leaders, who were "always seeking excuse to get out of the Negro race." They were "time-serving, boot-licking agencies of subserviency to the whites," the "pets of some philanthropists of another race."

Such aspersions, at first merely retaliatory, inevitably suggested a logical progression of their own, and Garvey made conscious drift toward it. "It is only the so-called 'colored' man who talks of social equality," he said late in 1921. "Some Negroes believe in social equality. They want to intermarry with the white women of this country, and it is going to cause some trouble later on. Some Negroes want the same jobs you have," he admonished whites. "They want to be Presidents of the nation."

He was now poised for the last short jump. In 1922 he made it. "I believe in a Pure Black Race. . . . It is the duty of both the white and black races to thoughtfully and actively protect the future of the two people, by vigorously opposing the destructive propaganda and vile efforts of the miscegenationists of the white race, and their associates, the hybrids of the Negro race."

No one can pick the point at which a man's destiny first joins with his will to move him toward the end the gods have ordained, but this seemed to be the point for Garvey. His sentiments—the complete abdication of Negro rights in America, the espousal of race purity—won him the applause and the support of organized white reactionaries. More than once the platform of Garvey's Liberty Hall was graced by the presence of Earnest Sevier Cox, faithful champion of white supremacy. John Powell, organizer of the Anglo-Saxon Clubs of America, spoke there. In January 1922, Garvey went to Atlanta, Georgia, to confer with the most powerful of all Klansmen, Edward Young Clarke, and shortly thereafter issued the following statement: "I regard the Klan, the Anglo-Saxon Clubs and the White American Societies as better friends of the race than all other groups of hypocritical whites put together."

Hitherto Negro leaders had tried to ignore or merely to

belittle Garvey, but they could no longer afford the luxury of silent contempt. He was the Nemesis of all they stood for—widening opportunities, equality, integration, the fulfillment of American democracy. Also it was soon apparent that Garvey had made enemies of men who but lately were his friends and followers. Thus while the Negro leaders bombarded the little Jamaican from editorial page and platform, former Garveyites, led by Edgar M. Gray and Richard Warner, not only aroused fear in some of the faithful for their investments in the Black Star Line but went to New York's district attorney, Edwin P. Kilroe.

It seems that the business affairs of the line were, as George Schuyler punned, "on the shady side." It seems that the line's funds were sometimes used to pay the debts of the UNIA, a different concern altogether. It seems that capital was indiscriminately deposited to the personal accounts of various officials, that stock had been diluted with water, and that the mails were used to defraud. Kilroe was sufficiently impressed to confer with the postal authorities. Toward the end of February 1922, Garvey and three of his associates were indicted on twelve counts of using the mails to defraud. This was the first blow in a barrage so persistent as finally to beat Garvey back to the obscurity of Jamaica. He had scarcely rallied from it when the second came.

James W. H. Eason, once a high official in UNIA but now broken with Garvey, was known to be organizing a nationwide opposition movement. Never a good one for tolerating his enemies, the Jamaican went all out against Eason. Garvey's paper and Garvey's agitators railed at this "arch-foe" for months. In New Orleans to address a chapter of his anti-Garvey group in the first week of January 1923, Eason was beaten, stabbed, and shot to death. Two of Garvey's minions—his "chief of police" and a "patrolman" in the premature Universal Police Corps—were charged with the crime.

It was never proved that Garvey had ordered this murder—and, indeed, his policemen were eventually freed—but few of his growing crowd of enemies seemed to doubt it, especially when a day or two later his wife, pushing a long-pending divorce action, published "lurid charges of cruelty and misconduct" against him. The anti-Garvey papers, which included the most influential Negro papers, made the most of both affairs. A. Philip Randolph and Chandler Owen, editors of the *Messenger*, drummed up their slogan "Garvey Must Go" to such effect that Harlem street meetings and Negro gatherings generally demanded the alien's deportation. A highly respected Episcopal minister, known as a temperate man, the Reverend Dr. Robert Bagnall, described Garvey as "a sheer opportunist and demagogic charlatan . . . egotistic, tyrannical, intolerant, cunning, shifty . . . avaricious, without regard for veracity, a lover of pomp and tawdry finery and garish display."

On January 15, 1923, a group of prominent Negroes who called themselves the Committee of Eight, but who spoke for many others, addressed an open letter to the Attorney General of the United States, Harry M. Daugherty. The letter charged Garvey as an "unscrupulous demagogue, who has ceaselessly and assiduously sought to spread among Negroes distrust and hatred of all white people," and respectfully pleaded that the Attorney General "vigorously and speedily push the government's case against Marcus Garvey for using the mails to defraud."

Garvey was brought to trial in May. Whether because a little reading of law in England had given him an exaggerated notion of his own legal competence, or whether it was simply that the irrepressible showman in him took over, Garvey dismissed his attorney at the end of the first day of trial. Thereafter for nearly a month he strutted and fumed under the indulgent eye of Judge Julian Mack and before the jury in a courtroom packed with his admiring followers. It was a megalomaniacal display of spectacular interest, but it had the effect of strengthening the government's case, which was so weak that any able lawyer might have destroyed it. Judge Mack urged Garvey to employ counsel. Even unfriendly newspapers warned him that it was foolish to "add his strength to that of his enemies."

But Garvey was hardheaded, and he ignored advice. Though his final address to the jury was very moving, he had done himself too much harm, and on June 18 he was sentenced to five years in federal prison.

He seemed, however, a greater, more commanding hero than ever to his die-hard followers. Their fortunes and their numbers, too, were low, and it took them three months to raise twenty-five thousand dollars' bond. Nevertheless, they showed their spirit when, the night after Garvey's release, at a monster rally in Liberty Hall, they pledged a hundred thousand dollars for his defense.

Garvey's own spirit had never faltered. A few weeks after his release on bond he opened complicated negotiations for a resettlement scheme with the Liberian government, but these were hampered and finally shut down by the objections of both Britain and the United States. Next he organized yet another steamship line, the Black Cross, and bought yet another ship, the *General G. W. Goethals*. But on its first voyage it was impounded in Kingston, Jamaica. Garvey had lost his touch, his time had run out, his luck had changed. A federal grand jury indicted him for perjury and income-tax evasion. In February 1925 the appeal from the mail-fraud conviction was disallowed. Shackled like a common felon, he was sent to Atlanta Penitentiary. From there he tried to direct the vital force that he perhaps more than any other man had brought into being. But it was hopeless. That force was already finding other channels, already boring its resistless way in a dozen directions through the Negro psyche.

When he was pardoned by President Coolidge after two years, Garvey re-entered a world that had all but forgotten him, but through which his spirit still blustered like a germinating wind. He went back to Jamaica, but the West Indies were still too small. He went to England, where in 1940 he died, too wretched to remember how profoundly he had stirred the race consciousness of colored people throughout the world, and too senile to realize how firmly he had anchored the pride and passion of America's "new" Negro in the hurrying wave of the future.

5. *Jazz Age*

Dating from Marcus Garvey there was a new Negro. He was far from happy to have things done to him, with him, and for him. He had jettisoned many of the old beliefs, the old attitudes, the old habits of mind—and particularly the habit of excusing himself *because* he was colored. His values and his standards of attainment had taken a great leap. In less than a decade he seemed to spring into manhood's full growth of initiative and self-reliance. It was this that marked the "Bolshevism," "incendiarism," and the "ill-governed reaction to race-rioting" so widely noted and deplored, and so greatly misunderstood to be the result of subversive influences.

This new sense of self and race, which the Negro philosopher, Alain Locke, described as a spiritual emancipation, found expression in a variety of dynamic ways in the years following the war.

Heretofore generally simple in their culture, and never having had any truly seminal principle of social and economic development, Negroes now reorganized and gave new direction to their lives in every area. The Friends of Negro Freedom functioned locally and nationally "to protect Negro tenants and organize forums through which to educate the masses." The American Negro Labor Congress was founded in 1925, the same year that A. Philip Randolph, at last irrevocably setting his own course, was joined by Chandler Owen to form the National Association for the Promotion of Labor Unionism among Negroes. In 1926 the Colored Housewives' League began encouraging Negro women to spend money only in places where there was some prospect that they or their men could also earn it. As early as 1927 in some of the larger cities boycotts operated sporadically against stores that refused to employ Negroes. Naturally the Colored Merchants' Association supported this activity, but it also served as an information and buying center for small business. Negro big business had its own informal clearing-house, through which one could learn that such enterprises as Walker's Beauty Preparations, the Atlanta Life Insurance Company, the North Carolina Mutual Company, the Dunbar Theatre Corporation, and a small handful of other concerns were truly million-dollar institutions—and rated so by Dun and Bradstreet.

But setting up as independent of the white economy, though it would seem the strongest proof of self-direction, was illusory at best, and was but one side of the matter marking the ascendancy of race pride in the new Negro. There was also a bold and intellectually conscious reappraisal of the formula that composed the "old nigger"—the social and cultural mimicry, the conformity to white folks' presumptions, the responsiveness to white folks' thoughts, the artful aping of white folks' ways. Said Langston Hughes in 1928, "We are not any longer concerned with telling white people only what they want to hear." And if the truth, at once revealing and vindicating, was to come, Negroes could not afford to be so concerned.

And the truth would come, and did—in Du Bois' *Darkwater* (1920) and *The Gift of Black Folk* (1924), volumes of essays and poems that spoke of the Negroes' "own selves and the dwelling place of their fathers" and the "inner ferment of [their] souls." In *Survey Graphic's* special issue (1925) on "The New Negro" edited by Alain Locke. In the *Book of Negro Spirituals* (1926), edited by the Johnson brothers, who felt that at long last the spirituals could be rightly heard and sung and truly loved. The next year the younger brother, James Weldon, published *God's Trombones*, and the year after that a new edition of his novel, *The Autobiography of an Ex-Coloured Man*, treating boldly the theme of miscegenation, in which the miscegenate was neither fool nor beast. In the historical studies of Carter G. Woodson, *A Century of Negro Migration* (1928), and Charles Wesley, *Richard Allen: Apostle of Freedom* (1930), and in *What the Negro Thinks* (1929)—a book that did much to right the wrong uses to which Robert R. Moton, its author, had put his influence in the days before the First World War. In articles in the *Modern Quarterly*, *American Mercury*, *The Nation*, and *New Masses*; and in periodicals, pamphlets, and broadsides too numerous to mention by men too many to name.

And all this revelation and vindication elicited response from white academic circles in which the hereditary notions of what the Negro was had scarcely been disturbed for two hundred years—from Park and Detweiler at Chicago; Boas and Tannenbaum at Columbia; Dollard and Powdermaker at Yale; Seligman at N.Y.U.; and Odum, Vance and Woofter at Chapel Hill, North Carolina.

But most of all—and certainly with greater immediate impact—this new Negro was revealed and vindicated by the race passion, bitter defiance, and hot-questing pride of the younger men. By Claude McKay's *Harlem Shadows* (1922) and Jean Toomer's *Cane* (1923), through which gushed a tide of love for a heritage too long despised:

> *O Negro slaves, dark purple ripened plums,*
> *Squeezed, and bursting in the pine-wood air,*
> *Passing, before they stripped the old tree bare*
> *One plum was saved for me,*
> *One seed becomes*
>
> *An everlasting song, a singing tree,*
> *Caroling softly souls of slavery,*
> *What they were, and what they are to me,*
> *Caroling softly souls of slavery.*

By Water White's *Fire in the Flint* (1924) and *Flight* (1926), after which the author turned to writing of a factual kind, as in *Rope and Faggot: A Biography of Judge Lynch*. By Countee Cullen's *Color* (1925), and Langston Hughes's *Weary Blues* (1926), and Rudolph Fisher's *Walls of Jericho* (1928).

Also from the bold, cold, cynical music of a hundred jazz musicians, and from the subtle ironies and satire of the blues, which now could be heard performed by Negro stage folk in night clubs and in musicals on Broadway itself. In 1921, *Shuffle Along* opened at a downtown theater; then *Runnin' Wild*, which introduced the "Charleston"; *Chocolate Dandies*, with Josephine Baker, *Dixie to Broadway*, with the incomparable Florence Mills, and *Africana*, with Ethel Waters and Bojangles Robinson, followed quickly.

And all this, too, eliciting its appropriate response. For not only was there the sanction and encouragement of H. L. Mencken and Waldo Frank, and the serious criticism of Paul Rosenfeld and V. F. Calverton, but there was the creative use to which white writers, dramatists, and composers put the new Negro revelations. Eugene O'Neill wrote *The Emperor Jones* and *All God's Chillun Got Wings*. In 1927, Paul Green won the Pulitzer prize with *In Abraham's Bosom*, a play of Negro life. Marc Connelly's *The Green Pastures* opened on Broadway in 1930 and ran continuously for five years. DuBose Heyward's novels, *Porgy* and *Mamba's Daughters*, were both successfully adapted to the stage. George Gershwin's "Rhapsody in Blue" began its eternal haunting of the world.

These men and others and their works established the Negro on the highest level of appreciation he had ever known. No wonder Alain Locke rejoiced that the new Negro "had attained an objectivity and an expressiveness" unthinkable to the old. No wonder Langston Hughes gloated that the Negro was at last liberated and now "stood free on the mountain top" of pride.

But eventually from his mountaintop the Negro came to see quite clearly encroaching on his new freedom and preying on his new-discovered pride the ancient fears, and he came to understand that the fears were conjured up by the very things designed to lay them—free inquiry and analysis, and new ideas that, assiduously pursued and applied, might conceivably upset the old status quo. Also he saw growing, partly in reaction to the exhausting psychological and economic demands of the late war and partly from disenchantment with the less than righteous peace, a kind of fateful involvement in the spectacle of the "new era of economy," which, nearly all agreed, the 1920s were. Though some warnings sounded and some consciences revolted at the crasser manifestation of economic progress, Babbitt did not seem a bad fellow to most. The calamity howlers, the dissenters, and the prophets of doom, like John Maynard Keynes, Roger W. Babson, and

John Dos Passos, were simply interesting crackpots. Obviously the only calamity was a putting iron named "Calamity Jane," and the only doom—a pleasant one—that promised by the Four-Square Gospel as expounded by a charmer named Aimee Semple McPherson.

It was boom time. "It was sex time and drink time." The jazz age, which the new Negro fathered, named, and gave a voice, was an age of momentous trifles: the new Negro was a bauble in it. He became a commercialized fad. His talents were likely to be sold and his integrity rifled by slick gangster types who, for one thing, dominated a few of the theaters, more of the music outlets, and practically all of Harlem—a place loudly trumpeted as "Nigger heaven." There could be found the exotic, the primitive, the virile. There life had "surge and sweep and pounding savagery." There Gaiety was king—but Harlem was not for Negroes.

> We cry among the skyscrapers
> As our ancestors
> Cried among the palms in Africa
> Because we are alone,
> It is night,
> And we're afraid.

Disillusioned and fear-driven, those Negroes fled who could. Langston Hughes set out by way of Russia to see the world once more. Alain Locke went to Italy, Paul Robeson to England, Cullen, Toomer, and McKay to France.

IX. AMERICAN CHAPTER

1. *Bust*

Those young "new" Negroes who fled were an infinitesimal and lucky minority of the race. Obviously the majority had no place to go save from the South to the North and perhaps back again—increasingly a two-way passage into frustration and futility. As early as 1926–27, when warnings of economic disaster seemed no more than faint whispers against the wind, thousands of Negroes lost the jobs to which industry had admitted them during the prewar boom. They were already in a depression, but it grew worse for them and gradually, almost imperceptibly at first, for everybody.

As the boom declined to bust, neither farm in the South nor factory in the North had places for Negroes. Even the employment traditionally theirs was taken away. North and South, labor unions generally excluded black workers and made common cause against them. One large Southern railroad, pressured by the Railway Brotherhoods, whittled down its Negro firemen from 80 per cent before 1918 to 10 per cent in 1930. Nearly half the skilled Negro workers in the country were displaced by August 1929, and by 1931 Negroes made up half the unemployed population in such cities as New York, Chicago, St. Louis, Memphis, and Atlanta.

In Southern cities it became common to see white men doing jobs they had formerly despised—digging gutters, cleaning streets, collecting garbage. Domestic service and service industries found less and less for Negroes to do and more and more of them clamoring to do it. By 1930 roughly a million Negroes were "on the turf," as they put it. At the beginning of the first full year of the depression the median income of Negro families in the North was less than half that of white families, and in the South the Negro city family earned $326 a year to the white family's $1339. The disparity widened as the depression grew.

As a natural consequence of this, the work of the old-line Negro uplift organizations began to fall off just at the time when that work was needed most. The depression increased racial tension. It sanctified the vaunted purposes of the Klan and the Anglo-Saxon League as nothing else could short of a holy crusade. In the eyes of many theirs was a holy crusade. They would save America from the Jews, who "controlled the nation's wealth"; from Catholics, whose chief American representative was a politically ambitious Irishman named Al Smith, who got "his orders from the pope"; from Negroes, who were "an inherently inferior people"; and from the Communists, who were again thought to be "making dangerous inroads" in the colored population.

The Klan and the Anglo-Saxon League would save America without ever realizing that among the forces that threatened to destroy her was intolerance, and that intolerance was most conspicuously in their employ. Discrimination increased at an appalling rate, and especially anti-Negro discrimination—partly no doubt because it gave many idle and ignorant whites something to do, and vicious whites a good excuse for doing it. In this time of double trouble the National Urban League, the NAACP, and the American Negro Labor Congress had fewer defensive resources. Membership in all these groups suffered drastic curtailment. The *Crisis*' subscriptions fell to thirty-five thousand from a peak of a hundred thousand. Some Urban League centers closed. The American Negro Labor Congress shut down altogether.

Much of the little money Negroes managed to get was put to uses that gave greater emotional satisfaction at the same time that they promised more immediate practical returns than the long-range programs of the race leaders. Cults proliferated. Some were brazenly charlatan, offering in exchange for "consecrated dimes" the most esoteric nonsense. Others, like Father Divine's Peace Movement, set up free employment agencies and day nurseries, opened restaurants where substantial meals were served for ten or fifteen cents, established a chain of stores where food and clothing could be bought at cost, and provided communal living quarters for the faithful. All this was paid for under a system by which those of the cult's profession turned over everything they had and hoped to have to Father ("God" himself) Divine.

Such cults, however, were for suckers, in the common phrase, and the sophisticated black urbanite invested his pennies in the daily numbers lottery, which returned a fantastic 500 per cent to the lucky. Few were lucky except the numbers barons, who in the deepest trough of the depression as likely as not prowled the dark ghettos in Dusenbergs, Rolls-Royces, and sixteen-cylinder Lincolns, while their kept women, sleekly glittering with expensive baubles, sometimes managed to get a foot in and "almost to push through the doors to polite Negro society."

But life beyond those doors was mostly make-believe. Even by the middle of the second decade Negro polite society was less than it had been, and the impending economic crisis was to rend its standards of morality, manners, and taste almost beyond repair. It had once had an important function, authority, and support, but now its function was gone, its authority—thanks in part to Marcus Garvey—dissipated, and its support dried up. In the past several years its own emotional climate, "the dry rot of indifference and the mould of intolerance," had eaten away the communications the class had once maintained between the races. It had no skill to restore them. Though with thinner and thinner warrant its older elements continued to look upon themselves as saviors and benefactors of the race, the younger, more energetic and thoughtful of those born around the century's turn had long since begun to question the class's right to the immunity and privilege it claimed—immunity from the hazards of the day-to-day struggle, the privilege of pretending to direct it. The intensive social reshuffling of the postwar years and the spirit, more than the specifics, of Garveyism had created apostates from the class. Among them were Walter White, who had given up a financially secure career in a prosperous Georgia insurance firm to risk his future with the NAACP; and Lester Granger, who had left the sure if devious road to political preferment in New Jersey for the niggardly wage and obscurity of social work; and Asa Philip Randolph.

2. *Apostle*

A. Philip Randolph had come a long distance from Crescent City, Florida, where he was born in 1889, and a far way in thought since the days when he had "liked the prestige and sociability" of his father's calling. It had not been an easy journey. However commanding and sociable the position of a minister in the African Methodist Church, it was not financially rewarding. Young Randolph delivered papers, did odd jobs, and, as he grew bigger, worked summers as a railroad section hand to pay his way through high school at Cookman Institute in Jacksonville. In 1906 he went to New York.

Here appeared the first signs of what he would be later. He could not keep a job because he was constantly arousing his fellow workers to agitate for better labor conditions. He ran an elevator and was fired. He worked as a porter and promptly tried to organize the porters of the Edison Company, and was again promptly fired. On his third trip as a waiter on a coastal steamer he was overheard haranguing the steward's crew about conditions in their quarters. He was run off the boat.

At this rate it took him nearly a decade to finance and finish the irregular course of study he was taking at New York's City College, and even then he found no immediately receptive market for his training and his talents. He took up Shakespeare, employed a speech teacher who drilled him in the accents of Oxonian speech, and gave reading recitals in churches and clubs in and around Harlem. But this was only for a living. He became converted to socialism and was one of a small handful of Negroes so inclined who nightly could be found on Harlem street corners inveighing against the principles of private enterprise, the disease of capitalism.

Meantime he had met Chandler Owen, another apostate from the Negro upper class. Owen was brilliant, an intellectual dragonfly whose wit darted at likely surfaces with tongues of poisonous scurrility. He came later to be called the "Negro Mencken." Randolph, on the other hand, having abandoned the religious faith of his father somewhere along the way, apparently had no adequate leaven for the soul. He was heavy-spirited, humorless, "over-earnest." He lived a great deal within himself, and it was difficult to penetrate the formidable barrier of his reserve.

Owen, though, must have done it, for the two of them became intimate associates almost at once, and in 1917 founded a monthly magazine, the *Messenger*, which flaunted from its masthead: "The only radical Negro magazine in America." And so it seemed to most readers. "The principle of social equality," the editors declared in an early issue, "is the only sure guarantee of social justice." Within a few months of its founding the Justice Department indicted the magazine in these terms: "The *Messenger* . . . is by long odds the most able and dangerous of all the Negro publications." Randolph and Owen printed the condemnation as advertising.

Their magazine was fearlessly forthright, perhaps foolhardy. It turned topsy-turvy the standards of the black bourgeoisie. It preached socialism. The solution for the race problems, it said, "will not follow the meeting of white and Negro leaders in love feasts. . . . Industry must be socialized, and land must be nationalized. . . . The people must organize, own and control their press. The church must be converted into an educational forum. The stage and screen must be controlled by the people." And as if this were neither plain nor enough to effect their radical purposes: "*Lastly, revolution must come.* By that we mean a complete change in the organization of society. Just as absence of industrial democracy is productive of riots and race clashes, so the introduction of industrial democracy will be the longest step toward removing that cause. When no profits are to be made from race friction, no one will longer be interested in stirring up race prejudice. . . . The capitalist system must go and its going must be hastened by the workers themselves."

When America entered the war Randolph protested the "hypocrisy of the slogan 'making the world safe for democracy.'" He refused to serve in the war on grounds of conscience. "I am fundamentally and morally opposed to the war," he said. "I am a pacifist so far as national wars are concerned." He went about the country expressing these sentiments to Negroes.

In Cleveland in the summer of 1918 agents of the Department of Justice snatched him from the platform where he was speaking and threw him in jail. It was, plainly, a denial of his right of free speech, a persecution for conscience, and when Randolph was released he might have found the hair shirt of the martyr a becoming fit had he decided to wear it. But his instincts were right, and he passed up this opportunity for self-exploitation. He was not the man for "cheap personal note and glory." He was the man for a "true, good cause." If he was personally ambitious the fact was not apparent. Indeed, quite the opposite must have been the case. Years later it was said of him that he was "almost a god to the great mass of Negro workers."

In 1925 he found his true, good cause in the efforts of a small scattering of Pullman porters to form an effective labor union. These efforts had begun in 1909, but in spite of the common cause the Pullman conductors had made with the porters, the efforts had been dawdling and less than halfhearted. The company, naturally, did not favor unions, and the tradition of Negroes, unbroken since the days of Booker T. Washington, was to cultivate the favor of those who dispensed economic opportunities. Besides, the porters' contact with the upper-middle-class traveling public had steeped them in middle-class prejudices. It pleased them to serve "monied men," bankers, and industrial tycoons. It put little cash in their pockets, but it made them feel like moneyed men themselves, and even if one is only vicariously a tycoon he is likely to be against labor unions.

Thus the efforts to organize dozed and waked fitfully

until 1918, when the War Labor Conference Board decided that Pullman employees had the right to organize and select their own representatives for collective bargaining. No sooner had the right been granted than the Pullman conductors formed their own separate union and bothered with the porters no more.

But by this time Booker Washington was four years dead and a new Negro spirit was in the ascendancy. By this time the slumbrous mass of old porters, among whom there were still ex-slaves, had been yeasted by younger men who were reasonably conscious of the benefits of collective bargaining. It was a matter of simple deduction. Unionized railroad workers got benefits. The "Big Four" Brotherhoods won victory after victory. The Order of Sleeping Car Conductors demanded and got shorter hours and higher pay. The company was no less anti-union, and particularly no less anti-Negro union. It did not recognize that a porters' union had any place or any necessity. "The laborer," it said, "can work or quit on the terms offered; that is the limit of his rights."

The terms offered were very poor. Whereas other Pullman carrier employees had a standard work month of two hundred and forty hours, porters worked four hundred hours. If they exceeded this before they had traveled ten thousand miles in a month, it did not count as overtime. Their work month was computed in hours plus miles. Even though they put in three to four hours in the yards preparing cars for trips, regular time did not begin for them until the train left the station. The highest wage they could hope for in 1918 was fifty-nine dollars a month, and this only after having worked forty-five years. The company expected them to eke out their wages with tips.

Nevertheless, Pullman porters were of the industrial elite and the economically advantaged among Negroes. They wore uniforms, not overalls; carried valises, not lunch pails. In the Negro social community they stood just below professionals, civil service employees, and businessmen. Their rank was important in the community and they were proud of it. Their place in the Negro community was strategic.

Pullman porters traveled. In the North and West they were the only Negroes with whom thousands of white people came into contact. If only some of them were conscious of helping to shape white opinion about Negroes, nearly all of them were careful to serve as models of the best Negro behavior. This was a social responsibility, which, having assumed, they generally lived up to. They were moral, upright, churchgoing. In short, they were self-consciously middle-class. But there was a hitch. Unions were for the laboring class. Some porters did join the Railway Men's International Benevolent Industrial Association in 1918, since it sounded less like a union—and was in fact much less than a union; but even the association suffered a severe loss of membership after the porters' wages were increased by an average of two dollars a month in 1920.

When in that same year Pullman presented its own company union plan, most porters were naïvely grateful. The company combined its union with the Porters' Benefit Association, a sort of picnic-outing group, and called it the Pullman Employee Representation Plan. Pullman gave it all the trappings of a fraternal lodge, including insignia, and promised the porters not only protection during illness and at death but bargaining rights as well. Indeed, Pullman went so far as to call for an election of delegates to a wage conference in 1924, where it soon became apparent that the new union's rights were paper rights, and the wage increase the company granted did not meet even the minimal expectations of the delegates. In conference the porter-delegates "suffered from a sort of psychological paralysis in the presence of white men." They feared that they might lose their jobs. They attributed the stingiest concession to the company's generosity and were extremely grateful. Only one of them, a man named Ashley Totten, who was already "in bad," spoke out. Only he realized that what the porters needed was a leader of courage and intelligence, preferably a man not employed by the company.

A. Philip Randolph was just the man. Already known for his activities on behalf of labor, he was deeply interested in the porters' problems. It seemed to him that they represented the problems common to all Negro labor. More, in fact. The porters' world was a microcosm of the Negro world, with its crosscurrents and dissensions. It had the same considerable though disingenuous identification with the white middle class. It too lacked the ability to appraise and therefore to modify its relation to the surrounding world. There was the same complex of relationships between the exploited and the exploiters; the same association of ideas; the same fairly definite patterns of thought.

If in his earlier years Randolph had believed that the solvent for all this was socialism, he had now apparently changed his mind and was on the side of orthodoxy rather than revolution. He had opposed Marcus Garvey on the grounds that Negroes were Americans, though black, and that America was their home, and that here they would have to live and work out their salvation. "If the Negro's American hope dies," Randolph was saying now, "then democracy's hope dies everywhere."

When the small founding core of porters asked him to become general organizer of the Brotherhood of Sleeping Car Porters in 1925, Randolph accepted. He was under no illusions as to the intensity of the struggle he faced. It began at once.

The company had all the advantages. It had experience in dealing with dissident labor groups. It had unlimited resources, a variety of methods. It had successfully publicized itself as the friend of Negroes, in proof of which it pointed to the fact that, with sixteen thousand on its pay roll, it was the largest single employer of Negro labor in the country. Unions were far from the order of the day even among whites in the early postwar years, and the company could count on a considerable anti-union sentiment among porters, and on at least a normal degree of perfidy, self-interest, and fear. Moreover, Pullman had an aggressive anti-labor policy, which it pursued adamantly in 1926–27, when an economic recession that cut into profits also increased the potential supply of Negro porters.

The company's initial strategy was to ignore the

Brotherhood's existence. Under this cloak it called to-gether its "bully-boy" district superintendents and secretly ordered them to find reasons to discharge any porter known to be affiliated with the new union. In exchange for assignments to choice runs, becoming welfare workers or other sub-officials in the Benefit Association, some porters were persuaded to turn stool pigeons. District super-intendents in the Far West, in the Kansas-Missouri area, and in the Pennsylvania district were especially tough. Many porters were discharged without a hearing or the right of appeal. Some of these were replaced by Mexicans and Filipinos.

Still pretending to ignore the Brotherhood, the com-pany attacked Randolph. His public record was not an impenetrable armor. He had not fought in the war and was called a slacker. In 1920 he had campaigned for Sec-retary of State of New York on the Socialist ticket and was therefore a "Communist." Since he was not and had never been in the employ of the Pullman Company, he was an "outside agitator."

It was easy enough to find anti-union employees to sup-port these attacks. One of these wrote to the Chicago *Defender*, whose editor was, as usual, slow in making up his mind, "Mr. Randolph is a liar with a deceitful and seem-ingly fraudulent intent. I advise Pullman porters to be-ware of mere orators and scholars who bark but never bite and who belong to the correspondence school of labor leaders." Another, in a letter to the New York *Age* in 1928, deplored the fact that the preceding year "marked the dissolution of the Negro porter's monopoly," and went on to say that a "sinister influence has been hovering over this happy group of workers, preaching to them the doc-trine of hatred and discontent against this Big Father of Industry that furnished employment to many thousands of colored men and women. . . . Under his [Ran-dolph's] leadership we have been supplanted by 200 Filipinos and 300 Mexicans."

The mailed fist of the Pullman Company could also be felt in the attack of a white group, the Industrial Defense Association, which declared that Randolph believed in "miscegenation, free love, atheism, and fermented class hatred by advocating an economic system on the Russian plan . . ."; that he supported the idea of "having Negroes use force and violence," and "the domination of black, brown and yellow races in the world's affairs."

Randolph met these personal aspersions with as much dignity as he could muster. "I knew that slanderers would attempt to blacken my character with infamy," he said at one point. "I knew that among the wicked, corrupt and unenlightened . . . I would be branded as a disturber of peace, as a madman, fanatic, a Communist." But he was mainly interested in defending the Brotherhood, in building its membership, and in giving substance to the idea that the cause of white labor and black labor was a common cause. Though he won endorsements of the union from the American Federation of Labor, the Amalgamated Clothing Workers, and the Big Four Brotherhoods, the Pullman Company still pretended that the Brotherhood of Sleeping Car Porters did not exist, the Association of Railroad Executives refused to recognize it, the Railroad Labor Board would not protect it, and the Interstate Commerce Commission declined to investigate its most pressing grievances.

An able writer, Randolph publicized the union's cause in the *Messenger*, which he had made the official organ, and in more widely distributed magazines like *Opportunity* and *Survey Graphic*. He toured the country, explaining, protesting, defending. A clear and logical speaker, he sometimes found it expedient to rely not only on the arts of oratory but on a racialist appeal as well. "By all the gods of sanity and sense, Brotherhood men are a crucial challenge to the Nordic creed of the white race's superiority. For only white men are supposed to organize for power, for justice and freedom."

When the Watson-Parker Bill creating a new Labor Mediation Board became law in 1927, Randolph set to work to have the Brotherhood displace the Employee Representation Plan as the bargaining agency for the porters. Though the board found for the Brotherhood, the company claimed that there was nothing to negotiate; it "knew of no dispute between itself and its porters and maids."

But there was solid ground for dispute, as Pullman well knew, and by 1928, with more than half the porters and maids in membership, Randolph thought he had the means to bring the company to the forum. He would call for a strike vote. He did not want to strike. What he wanted was to make an indisputable show of union strength. What he hoped was that, at the simple threat to strike, the government's Mediation Board would step in, as the President could order it to do under the Railway Labor Act of 1926. It was in this hope that he had headed a delegation of union officials to call upon President Coolidge early in January. Though "Silent Cal" was as noncommittal as ever, the strike vote was taken in April. Of a total of 7300 union members, 6053 voted for and only 17 against. The results gratified Randolph.

Still the company took no official notice, and the government would not, since it did not see the strike vote as a threat to essential transportation. Indeed, Randolph himself contributed to this view. As days went by and the company made no gesture of recognition, the man's confidence was shaken. Persistent rumors reached him of porters backing off from the possible consequences of their vote, of their being afraid to strike under any circumstances. A strike by Negroes, Randolph realized, was a complete reversal of the psychology of a people who had got most of their industrial opportunities as strikebreakers. He began to hedge. "A strike vote is not a strike," he said, for the benefit of the disquieted porters, citing cases in which unions had "taken strike votes without striking."

He sensed how deep a conflict there was between his union ideas and the interracial labor pattern. The factors in the old amiable relationship between "master and man" were powerful still. Could he weaken them? Though the company held fast to the odd notion that it was entitled to gratitude for employing Negroes at all, perhaps the porters could be made to see that the company's obligations under the ancient tradition of noblesse oblige had been long abandoned, and that though they were absolutely dependent upon the company as the source of their daily bread, they should no longer be dealt with arbitrarily, by whim. Dare he call a strike? And how soon? Already Perry W. Howard, Republican National Committeeman, and other "prominent men of color [who] had hired their souls for Pullman gold to lie and deceive" were busy undermining the union idea. Would this first effort to win dignity and power for Negroes in the ranks of organized labor end only in outright defeat or bitter anticlimax?

Meantime, for all its official refusal to recognize that a threat existed, the company had not been idle. The firing of Negro porters increased. Quite suddenly Filipinos became a highly visible element in Pullman service even on the east coast. Pinkerton police were put on call to "avert trouble of any sort." Negroes who had wanted to be Pullman porters all their lives were easy to find, and the company not only found them but discovered them so eager that it could hold them on a stand-by basis without pay. As operating porters signed in for runs, they were required to say whether or not they intended to strike should a strike call come. Thus faced with the immediate prospect of loss of job and of dire consequences to home and family, even most of those who had voted to strike chose to stay with the company. No wonder that a few days before the strike date the company could issue a confident announcement: "The Pullman Company is prepared to maintain its service to the public, is not losing any sleep over the situation and does not anticipate that any of its patrons will be inconvenienced. The company is fully conversant with the activities of certain outside agitators to cause defection in the ranks of its porters, a large majority of whom are not in sympathy with the movement and will remain on the job."

President Coolidge maintained his silence; the Mediation Board sat tight. The conduct of both was "strange and unjustifiable." Though the President had had the board intercede in a dispute when only six hundred of the KC, NM & O Railroad's several thousand employees voted to strike, it was the board's declared judgment in the case of the porters, whose strike vote was all but unanimous, "that at this time an emergency . . . does not exist." Randolph thought it obvious that the board and "perhaps the President himself" had been warned that board intercession "was going to stir up the Negroes of this country and make them cocky, so that they would feel their power and that this would cause business interests to have trouble with their Negro workers."

The company seemed fully prepared to break a strike. Already weakened and its financial resources sapped by the company's summary dismissal of unionized porters, the union was further weakened by the defection of members right and left. A few days before the strike date Randolph, desperate and discouraged, asked advice of William Green, president of the AFL. The two men met in Washington. Green had the reputation of being a bumbler and, however sincere, frequently misguided; but on this occasion he came directly to the painful point. The porters were Negroes, he said, and by reason both of race and occupation in a "submarginal category." The public patience would not support a strike by such workers. Moreover, economic conditions did not favor it. Apparently Green had given the situation much thought, and he rumbled on, uttering opinions that, because of their inexorable truth, were all the harder to take. As the old labor leader talked, the distance that separated white men from black and black from the realization of their democratic heritage stretched before Randolph immeasurably, like an impassable morass.

"It is my firm conviction," Green said at last, "that the best interest of all workers concerned would be served through a postponement of strike action and the substitution therefor of a campaign of education and public enlightenment regarding the justice of your case and the seriousness of your grievances."

The word "postponement" fooled neither man. The strike was off.

The Brotherhood's retreat was the signal for its enemies to redouble their attacks. Internal dissension, repressed during the struggle with the company, broke out publicly. Porters who had voted to strike but who had also told the company bosses they would not strike began to say now that they would have struck—if. Already fear on the one hand and dismissals on the other had reduced the union's membership by half between the time of announcing the strike vote and voting to strike; and now what was left was cut in half again—to 2368 within six months. Word came from the Pullman Company that it would "probably look with more favor" on the union if Randolph, "a known Socialist, and an outsider," were dropped. But a hard core of union officials knew a trick when they saw one, and they knew, too, the integrity, the selflessness, and the courage of their man. They would not hear of Randolph's dismissal. Union morale dropped like a lowered curtain, dues dwindled. The official organ of the Brotherhood, the *Messenger*, was forced to cease publication. Union headquarters gave up its telephone; it gave up its electric light. It was said that the Brotherhood was dying.

And its funeral gift? A check for ten thousand dollars made out to Randolph and signed by a man Randolph suspected of acting for the Pullman Company, a man he scarcely knew. He could think of no other explanation. The check came in a letter, and the letter was too pat. I⁴ said that Randolph had "done all any person could be expected to do and now that the cause was lost," the writer urged him, Randolph, to take this gift as a reward and "take a trip to Europe." It must have been a great temptation. Office rent was coming up. His own house rent was due. Randolph returned the check by registered mail.

3. *Victory?*

Though as a matter of administrative necessity the union officials were made privy to what must be called—and was in fact commonly called—Pullman's attempt to bribe Randolph, the only public reference he himself made to it was general, even oblique. "Believing that money was all powerful," he said, "our detractors boasted glibly that we would soon be in the vest pocket of Pullman. But they reckoned without cognizance of the force of the idealism of the New Negro. They knew not of the rise of a newer spirit within the race which placed principles, ideals, and convictions above dollars. Happily, the Brotherhood is demonstrating to black men and women, and incidentally to Pullman officials, that money is not everything, but that the spirit and the will of a people for justice is unconquerable."

Nevertheless, word of the incident got around and was added to until rumor became conviction that Randolph could live in velvet for the rest of his life if he cared to accept money for giving up the effort to organize the porters. But instead—and this was perhaps the greater part of it—he chose to stay on without an adequate or a regular salary and at great personal sacrifice to endure the fight. This belief helped, but not as much as it might have had Randolph's modesty allowed him to exploit it. And he needed all the help he could get if he was to make anything of Green's advice to wage "a campaign of education and public enlightenment."

For it soon became evident that the "respectable elements" of the Negro race did not like the idea of a labor crusade. Though the National Urban League favored unionization, local branches, more or less autonomous, shied away. Their drives for funds were directed at local corporations and industries, and these were naturally anti-union. The Chicago Urban League was especially hostile: Pullman contributed substantially to it.

The NAACP endorsed the union, and James Weldon Johnson, the NAACP's chief executive officer, persuaded the Garland Fund to give ten thousand dollars to the Brotherhood, but the NAACP membership generally was strictly class-conscious bourgeoisie and thought it had little in common with the laboring class. Several leading Negro newspapers, including the St. Louis *Argus*, the Chicago *Whip*, and the Pittsburgh *Courier*, opposed the union and attacked Randolph personally—and the company distributed free copies of these papers in its workers' quarters. But the lash of the *Whip* lost most of its sting when the only Negro congressman, Oscar De Priest, declared that he was an "eye-witness to the passing of fifty-five per cent of the *Whip*'s stock to Daniel J. Schuyler, one of the attorneys for the Pullman Company." The *Argus* could scarcely claim impartiality of observation and judgment when in the same issue in which it carried an anti-porter-union blast it also carried a half-page ad for the Pullman Company. And the *Courier* was certainly suspect since, until 1928, it had staunchly supported the Brotherhood.

But the Negro church was the chief enemy of the union and of Randolph, and if the Negro masses were to be enlightened it must be brought about in part at least under the auspices of the church. No one knew this better than Randolph. Whatever the church's shortcomings—and they were many, of which an uneducated ministry was the first—it was the supreme cohesive agent; it was the base on which the Negro social structure stood. It had the oldest tradition, the largest following, the greatest power and prestige. But the great rout of the Negro ministry was ignorant of the union's functions, and it was against the union. It remembered that in his earliest days Randolph had criticized the Negro church, and that he was said to be an ungodly man. Something would have to be done to change or modify the church's attitude.

Though usually a direct man, Randolph knew that indirection had its uses. Nor had he been a minister's son quite for nothing. First he sought to awaken the church's awareness of its identification with the working class and to associate the principles of unionism with religious loyalties. Thanks to James Weldon Johnson and the Garland Fund, the Brotherhood now again had an official organ, the *Black Worker*. Its cover page blossomed with a biblical catch phrase: "Ye shall know the truth, and the truth shall set you free." Randolph's exhortations to labor action and labor solidarity bristled with religious admonishments:

"Let not your hearts be troubled neither let them be afraid, comes the injunction from the prophet of a new world brotherhood, and is a challenge and a promise to the work-weary, worn and oppressed millions by the heartless hands of capitalists, imperialists, in our modern industrial society. Fight on brave souls! Long live the Brotherhood! Stand upon thy feet and the God of Truth and Justice and Victory will speak unto thee."

"Son of man, stand upon thy feet and I will speak unto thee. . . . Such a call to black men and women has come to fight for the cause of Truth and Righteousness. . . . We, as a great race, shall not fail, for the God of Power and Progress will aid."

Inelegant as these were, they came to be more and more effective.

Brotherhood officials did not overlook the fact that, for all its structural independence, the Negro church still looked up to the white church, still saw it as a model, still felt secure in following its lead. Moreover, Green's advice had not been to educate the Negro public only, for that was not the public that used sleeping cars for overnight trips and parlor cars for day trips. The white public, too, must be made to see the justice of the porters' case and the seriousness of their grievances.

Randolph enlisted the interest of the Methodist Federation for Social Science, and its *Social Service Bulletin* published a report on the problems of Pullman porters. In 1929 the Federal Council of Churches of Christ in America had its department of research and education make a study of the occupational status of porters and publish its findings in an official paper. The white Congregational Ministers Union of Chicago endorsed the Brotherhood. Powerful Catholic groups and various synods of the Lutheran Church did the same. The Negro ministry dared not let it be said that white churchmen were more helpful to a "race cause" than they. Influential Negro ministers began to fall into line. By 1932 there was scarcely a colored church in the country whose doors were not flung open to the union's program of education.

The program was pushed with determined vigor. The union held "labor institutes" up and down the country, and surprising numbers of people attended them—four hundred at Mount Carmel Baptist in St. Louis; fifteen hundred at the Metropolitan Community Church in Chicago, two thousand at the Abyssinia Baptist Church in New York.

The white press was beginning to find the activities of the Brotherhood worth news and editorial space. The *Na-*

tion commented: "The men who punch our pillows and shine our shoes and stow our bags bear no little responsibility for the industrial future of the race." Randolph was widely reported to say, "The old policy of defending Negroes' rights is well nigh bankrupt and is of limited value. Fundamentally rights don't mean a thing if you can't exercise them. The solution, then, is for the Negro to take the offensive and carry the fight for justice, freedom and equality to the enemy. No minority group, oppressed, exploited and discriminated against, can win its rights and its place in the sun on the defensive."

If this sounded as if Randolph had forsworn the ideal of interracial unity in the labor struggle, it was because he had learned the strength of the biracial labor tradition. It was because he had to start where he could, which was with a challenge that his people could understand, and then go as far as he could, which was to affiliate his union with the AFL. In the Federation's yearly conventions, in its committees, and in private talks and public talks Randolph hammered away at the point: "Labor has paid dearly for its own lack of democracy, for capital kept labor weakened for decades by the use of masses of unorganized and 'unaccepted' workers. . . . Labor never can win fully until it opens its doors freely and equally to all workers."

In 1934 the Railway Labor Act was amended to outlaw company unions and to guarantee collective bargaining. It was the break the Brotherhood had waited for. With nearly a half million dollars put up by porters and maids, Randolph made a final great effort for members, and by 1935 more than eight thousand Pullman workers were paying dues to the Brotherhood. In that same year the union won a jurisdictional dispute with the Porters' Employee Representation Plan, now severed from the company, and Pullman, forced to it by the amended law, acknowledged the existence of the Brotherhood for the first time in the ten-year struggle.

Still the company was far from giving in to what it called the union's "exorbitant" demands. It delayed. It frustrated. It fought against the intercession of the national Mediation Board and, when this failed, it requested one postponement after another. The company reasoned that Negroes could be outmaneuvered and easily discouraged. But public opinion had been considerably modified by the pro-labor, pro-underdog policies of President Roosevelt's government, and both the public and the press were against the "vested interests." Pullman could delay only so long.

Finally in April 1937 it agreed to sit down with Randolph and the Mediation Board, but even then it stubbornly resisted negotiating a contract. Not until August 25 —exactly twelve years from the day Randolph took up the fight—did the company sign an agreement. It called for an increase of two million dollars in annual wages, a reduction averaging one third in the number of hours a porter worked, and a cut in the distance he had to travel in a month from eleven thousand to seven thousand miles.

When news of this victory broke, Negroes all over the country celebrated at dances, dinners, picnics, boat rides. Only Randolph seemed preoccupied. Only he seemed to realize that this was at best a Pyrrhic victory. If it demonstrated the Negro's ability to organize on racial lines and move forward toward democratic goals, it proved as well the continuing necessity to do this, and it demonstrated that there were still goals that white America would never willingly leave undefended to the attainment of the race. It proved, in its final measure, that caste-class division was no less than ever a threat to the moral structure of democracy. Would nothing awaken the American people to the potency of this threat except a translation into physical terms—a physical "organization of the Negro people for power, for justice and freedom"?

These were the thoughts that preoccupied A. Philip Randolph. But he need not have brooded, for the organization of the Negro people for power and justice had already taken place in a few metropolitan centers, notably Harlem. And now such an organization was in development countrywide. Nor could one who watched closely fail to note the performance of a group intelligence and the operation of an entirely new spirit of calculation.

4. *Untrod Path*

It might be said to have started in the late winter and early spring of 1933, by which time it was evident that Franklin D. Roosevelt had brought to the White House a new concept of the functions of federal government. With extraordinary moral courage and (since he was no theorist or scholar) with an instinctive feel for the empirical, he was testing his concept vigorously. There was no lack of situations to test it in. When he took office on March 4 the banks of twenty-two states and the District of Columbia were closed, and the nationwide banking system was at the point of collapse. On March 5, Roosevelt closed all the banks, and four days later rushed a bill to Congress designed to allow the sound banks to reopen and to furnish them with currency. Next he turned his attention to the agricultural situation, and within two weeks drew up a singular bill for the relief of farmers. It was based on the unheard-of principle of granting subsidies to farmers in return for crop reductions. With this bill the President sent a message to Congress. "I tell you frankly that it is a new and untrod path, but I tell you with equal frankness that an unprecedented condition calls for the trial of new means. . . ."

The message might well have been sent with all the bills that were jammed through Congress in the first one hundred days, and it might well have been blazoned on the office walls of all the ad hoc agencies created to administer them. Before Roosevelt's first term had run a year John Maynard Keynes, the British economist earlier known to the American people as a calamity howler, wrote to the President: "You have made yourself the trustee for those in every country who seek to mend the evils of our condition by reasoned experiment within the framework of the existing social system. If you fail, rational change will be greatly prejudiced throughout the world, leaving orthodoxy and revolution to fight it out."

But no matter how it might look to Keynes three thousand miles away, to many people at home it began to look as though the "framework of the existing social system" was already crumbling and revolution already triumphant.

At its base level the New Deal was a program of social reconstruction. Roosevelt himself was a reformist. He was a precedent breaker and an experiment maker in a big way. And of course he met increasing opposition—from Wall Street for revising the rules by which financiers played their amazingly intricate game; from industry for encouraging labor; and, most pointedly for our story, from the South for "wooing the Northern Negro vote."

It was a successful wooing. Even though the New Deal did not and could not keep all the glowing promises of the courtship, it did begin an equalizing process quite contrary to the will of reaction. "A minimum of the promises we can offer to the American people," Roosevelt said, "is the security of all the men, women and children of the nation."

He seemed to mean it. Wages and hours legislation worked to the advantage of a quarter of a million Negroes, half of them in the South. When an investigation revealed that the relief provided by the Agricultural Adjustment Administration was going to Southern farmers rather than to the workers and tenants for whom some of it at least was intended, the program was modified to permit checks to go directly to farm laborers, the majority of whom were Negroes. "Like any assistance to the Negro which is not controlled by the white landowners," wrote Thomas Woofter, a Southern liberal who helped administer the program, "this met with suspicion and some active opposition. . . ." What were those people in Washington up to?

Having first hailed the advent of Roosevelt as a Second Coming, the white South all at once began to find him and all he stood for bad beyond measure, and the South's spokesmen in and out of Congress were thunderously loud in saying so.

But it was quite otherwise with Negroes. Their vote for Roosevelt had been represented by only a few dissidents in 1932, but it rose to 65 per cent of the total Negro vote in 1944. In the years between, Negroes were reminded that the Republican party under Hoover had replanted the seeds of lily-white Republicanism, and each time they were reminded their impetus toward the Democratic party was renewed. In 1936 they sent to Washington from Illinois the first Negro Democrat ever to sit in the national government, and he has been followed by a Negro Democrat ever since. Adam C. Powell went as a Democrat to Congress from the 22nd New York District in 1945, and he has been in Congress ever since.

The revolutionary spirit of the New Deal encouraged surprising political and economic changes on the state and municipal level too, even in parts of the South. Though the changes were of little consequence numerically, they nevertheless indicated possibilities of greater change, and they helped further to document a circumstance that was to have ponderable effect in the 1940s and '50s—the circumstance of the physical organization of the Negro people for power and justice. Economic boycott opened job opportunities for Negroes in chain stores located in Negro neighborhoods in Durham, Memphis, and Atlanta. The Southern Bell Telephone Company and certain automobile agencies in Nashville and Louisville hired Negro salesmen. A dozen major Southern cities took on Negro policemen. Greensboro and Winston-Salem, North Carolina, and Richmond, Virginia, elected Negro city councilmen. Kentucky and West Virginia, Maryland and Missouri seated Negroes, only one Republican among them, in state legislatures.

But Wendell Willkie's wholly unexpected nomination as the Republican presidential candidate threatened to bring an end to what was called the "perfidious bond" between the Negro and the New Deal. Obviously a man of great sincerity and, for all his rural, rumpled presence, shining like Galahad, Willkie was almost as attractive to Negroes as Roosevelt was. Moreover, he was a Republican, a fact that had considerable weight with many Negroes in whom the memory of a traditional allegiance to the party of Lincoln was strong, and for whom rallying to the banner of the Democrats was an irritant to conscience.

Nor were Negroes, generally, unaware of the preponderance of Southern Democratic power in the Congress. Seventeen major committees in the Senate and twenty-five in the House were controlled by Southerners, and in both chambers they employed cynical devices to block legislation designed to benefit Negroes. So far as these latter were concerned, Byrnes and Smith of South Carolina, Cox and Russell of Georgia, and Bilbo of Mississippi were a pox pustulating on the fair body of the New Deal and polluting the blood stream of democracy.

Thus when Wendell Willkie told Negroes, "I want your support," they were attentive. "But irrespective of whether Negroes go down the line with me or not," Willkie said, "they can expect every consideration. They will get their fair proportion of appointments, their fair representation on policy-making bodies. They'll get the same consideration as other citizens."

The Democrats, though, could cite past performance. "Our Negro citizens," said the New Deal platform of 1940, "have participated actively in the economic and social advances launched by this Administration, including fair labor standards, social security benefits . . . work relief projects . . . decent housing. . . . We have aided more than half a million Negro youths in vocational training, education, employment. . . . We shall continue to strive for . . . safeguards against discrimination."

The New Deal's record on Negroes was in fact exceptional, and among those who helped to establish and publicize that record were men who somehow seemed to move in an aura of unassailable personal integrity—Harold Ickes, W. W. Alexander, Clark Foreman, and Aubrey Williams. Clearly if Negroes were discriminated against in some of the government-sponsored programs, it was the fault not of these policy makers but of local administrators in the South. In the North and Midwest there was little or no discrimination in the administration of FHA, CCC, and NYA.

Nor was this all. Perhaps of final, overriding importance was the fact that the New Deal guaranteed its consideration of Negroes by employing Negro officials whose duty it was to see that their people got consideration. It is true that some old-line Negro politicians and others criticized these race relations advisers as "vote bait" who "perform[ed] no useful service to the agencies in which they are employed or to the people whose special interests they are supposed to serve." But such strictures sounded like jealousy, and their effect—assuming that they had effect—was nullified by the fact that Southern whites also criticized the Negro consultants, though on other grounds, and by the circumstance that many race relations officers had given up secure and rewarding private employment for the headaches and multiple uncertainties of appointive posts.

It was in one of these posts that Ralph Bunche made an inconspicuous beginning to an illustrious career in world affairs. William Hastie, later the first Negro governor of the Virgin Islands, and later still (and now) a judge of the U. S. Circuit Court of Appeals, held one. Mary McLeod Bethune gave up the presidency of a college to direct the Negro work of NYA, under which some sixty-five thousand Negro youths were enabled to stay in high school and college. Frank Horne helped to create the liberal racial policies of the Federal Housing Authority. Robert Weaver, Ira Reid, Abram Harris, Rayford Logan, James Evans, Campbell Johnson—the whole catalogue would fill a page —deserved and got the gratitude of Negroes and the respect of the people with whom they worked.

By 1940 only three major departments—Treasury, State, and War—had no race relations officers, but even for these the pressure of events and the strength of a cohesive minority were soon to make them necessary.

Nevertheless, there remained an important area in which the race relations experts were completely ineffectual. As the country converted itself into the "arsenal of democracy" and American manufactory geared to the production of munitions, the anti-Negro bias of industry and organized labor reared almost as high and as implacable as Everest. Five million whites who were unemployed in 1939 were all absorbed by 1940, but a million and a half Negroes were still fretting under enforced idleness in 1941. NYA had trained eighty-five thousand Negro youths specifically for defense work, but that training was going to waste. The Office of Production Management set up a Negro employment and training branch, but the situation was not relieved. The National Advisory Committee decried industry's failure to hire Negroes. Secretary of the Navy Knox warned naval ordnance plants against refusing Negroes employment and against condoning anti-Negro attitudes of white employees, who, Knox said, should be "subject not only to immediate dismissal but may be prevented from obtaining employment in other establishments engaged in war production." In September 1940 the President's message to Congress cried shame on racial discrimination.

Yet in cities all over the country industry lamented "extreme shortages of skilled workers," while skilled Negro workers walked the streets. An official government report stated that between January and March 1941 the U. S. Employment Service placed 1066 workers in "selected essential occupations" in the electrical equipment industry, but only 5 were Negroes; 8769 workers in the aircraft industry, but only 13 were Negroes; 35,000 in machine shop and tooling, foundry and forging, but only 245 were Negroes. The report concluded, "Not only are non-white workers not receiving many skilled and semi-skilled jobs in a great many defense establishments, but they are receiving very few jobs of any type, even unskilled."

While Negro organizations such as the NAACP and the Urban League did what they could (which was not much, since their resources had not recovered from the drain of the depression, and since neither—one being legalistic and the other admonitory and educational in its approach— had a quick opening offensive against the old enemy in this new emergency); and while the race relations experts conducted surveys, wrote advices, and here and there cracked the shell of prejudice; and while the President addressed a memorandum to Messrs. Knudsen and Hillman, co-directors of OPM, declaring in strong terms that the government could not countenance discrimination against American citizens in defense production and that the doors of employment must be opened "to all loyal and

qualified workers regardless of race"—while all this was
building into a national issue with overtones of scandal,
A. Philip Randolph brooded.

It was said that for hours and even days at a time, as
1940 clanked into 1941, he shut himself away in his office,
saw no one save his secretary, answered no phone calls. He
had been little in the public eye since 1937. That seemed
to be the way he wanted it.

Then one day in the early winter of 1941 the clerical
staff at Brotherhood headquarters and the knots of off-duty
Pullman porters, who habitually congregated there, were
startled to see Randolph burst from his office, stride
swiftly through the hall, and, impatient of the creaking
elevator, dash down the three flights to the street. Hatless
and coatless in the freezing January weather, he hailed a
cab. A few minutes later he entered the office of an old
colleague, Frank Crosswaith, chairman of the Harlem
Labor Union. To Crosswaith, Randolph outlined his plan
for an effective new use of the "organization of a people."

The idea was not new. It had originated with old Jake
Coxey, who in 1894 called up a host of the unemployed
and marched to Washington to demand that something
be done about their plight. It had been used again in
1932, when fifteen thousand veterans of World War I
formed a "Bonus Expeditionary Force," part of which strag-
gled into the national capital demanding immediate payment of a bonus of a thousand dollars a man. All
the same, such a march was a bold thing for Negroes to
contemplate.

For three months the Negro March-on-Washington
committee of Randolph, Crosswaith, Walter White, Lester Granger, Rayford Logan, and Henry Craft went quietly about the business of making plans. But no matter
that eventually was to involve so many could be kept
secret for long. Before the committee had planned it, the
March-on-Washington movement had a national press.
Randolph was the spokesman. "The administration leaders
in Washington will never give the Negro justice until they
see masses—ten, twenty, fifty thousand Negroes on the
White House lawn! . . . July first is March day." The

number that was prepared to march from all sections of the country, he said, was a hundred thousand.

Washington was only mildly apprehensive at first, but as the scope of the plans for the march gained definition in the press, apprehension increased. Fiorello LaGuardia, mayor of New York and head of Civilian Defense, was sent to deal with the march committee, and he was quickly followed by Aubrey Williams, director of NYA, but since neither man had the authority to make concessions, both failed. Then Mrs. Roosevelt herself came to New York. "You know where I stand," she told Randolph, "but the attitude of the Washington police, most of them Southerners, and the general feeling of Washington itself are such that I fear that there may be trouble if the march occurs." But Randolph was resolute. Nor did his resolution falter when the emissaries, each having failed singly, came back as a group; nor when President Roosevelt, grown properly disturbed now, summoned him to a conference in which the Secretaries of War and Navy also sat.

Randolph wanted firm assurance that positive steps would be taken against discrimination, especially in defense production. He argued that there was no time to send legislation grinding through the Congress, even if that body could be supposed to support it. He suggested an executive order, though no such order affecting Negroes had been issued since Lincoln's time. Mr. Stimson reasoned. Mr. Knox bellowed. Mr. President hemmed and hawed. Mr. Randolph gave courteous thanks and left.

Just a week before "M-day" the President sent for Randolph and the March-on-Washington committee and showed them the draft of an executive order. The committee rejected it. The order outlawed discrimination in defense industries only: it must outlaw discrimination in government as well. After a conference lasting several hours a satisfactory draft was drawn, and the next day it was issued.

Executive Order 8802 decreed that "there shall be no. discrimination in the employment of workers in defense industries and in Government because of race, creed, color, or national origin. . . ." It set up a committee on fair employment practices to investigate violations of the decree. The order drew heated opposition from the South, where it was called an "insidious social fiat" and interpreted as an encroachment upon the most cherished of Southern patterns—segregation. Governor Dixon of Alabama said it was a "meddling with the racial policies of the South," and promptly attended a meeting where it was proposed to create a League for White Supremacy. "The time to act is now," the Supremacists declared. "An organization should be formed, so strong, so powerful, so efficient, that this menace to our national security and our local way of life will rapidly disappear. It can be done. It should be done. Alabama must lead the way."

If in the circumstances these sentiments were so extravagant as to seem burlesque, one of the original members of the Fair Employment Practices Committee adopted them and added to them. "All the armies of the world," said Mark Ethridge, "both of the United Nations and the Axis, could not force upon the South the abandonment of racial segregation." Then he resigned.

The South simply went on ignoring Executive Order 8802.

But not only the South. Defiance of the order was widespread. Though the Fair Employment Practices Committee lacked enforcement powers, anything it did was thought to be politically damaging to the New Deal. Eventually the President was prevailed upon to take away the committee's status as an independent agency responsible to himself and to make it responsible to the War Manpower Commission, which was dependent upon a Southern-dominated Congress for funds. A punctured balloon could have withered no faster. Randolph protested to President Roosevelt once, twice, repeatedly—in vain.

Early in the summer of 1942 he issued a call for a mass gathering of New York Negroes—this to be "the first of a series . . . to be duplicated in every city in the North having a considerable Negro population." Twenty thousand people flocked to Madison Square Garden to hear speeches by Walter White, Lester Granger, Frank Crosswaith, and "Mother Mary" McLeod Bethune, all of whom received loud and sustained applause. Randolph spoke not a word, "although the thousands had been drawn by his magnetism." But in the end, when he rose to dismiss them with a gesture, a silence fell deep as night. "It was a moment of reverence," one who was there said later; and later still a white observer, Edwin R. Embree, wrote that Randolph was "almost a god to the great mass of Negro workers."

But "almost a god" was not enough for a people who wanted heroes.

Nor were the angers and dissatisfactions with the world at large the only conducements to the physical organization of the Negro people that already was beginning to seem inviolable. Angers and dissatisfactions are but negative after all, and they cannot of themselves supply a people's will to do and to be. Because not one Negro in, say, ten thousand would ever know the meaning of accomplishment and success, the need was all the greater (and the gratification, when it came, scarcely less) to identify with the positive personal triumphs of one of their own kind, and to see in this rare one the apotheosis of all they themselves could never be.

5. A Big Man Goes Far

For this a giant of a fellow named Paul Robeson seemed to have the potential. He had been known to Negroes and the country at large since 1917, when syndicated sports writers began putting his name in headlines: "Dashing Robeson . . ." "Rutgers Blanks Fordham; Robeson, Giant Negro, Plays Leading Role for Jersey Eleven." He was nineteen years old at the time, a junior at Rutgers, and about to be elected to Phi Beta Kappa. In his senior year he was on Walter Camp's All-American.

For a while after that the headlines in the white papers disappeared. Robeson graduated from Rutgers and went on to study law at Columbia. He supported his studies and, later, a wife by playing professional football. The Negro papers found his exploits with the Milwaukee Badgers excellent copy.

There were two brief flurries of headlines in the na-

tional press during this period. One came when it was rumored that a group of sportsmen had "confidentially
pledged a million dollars" to back Robeson as the "prospective heavyweight champion of the world." But Robeson was not interested in the prize ring, so nothing came
of this. The second came when, having graduated at the
top of his law school class, and having been urged on by
a wife forceful and ambitious in ways not easy to explain,
he accepted a position in a prominent white New York
law firm. The white press's reaction to this was mixed.
The Negro press was jubilant.

But writing briefs for cases involving railroads, banks,
and hundreds of thousands of dollars hardly seemed calculated to help Robeson fulfill the "service to his people"
of which his father had used to speak. The Reverend William Drew Robeson had been a great influence in the lives
of his three sons, the eldest of whom was a physician and
the middle one a minister. Paul told a friend of those days,
"I want to plead the case of the misunderstood and oppressed peoples before the highest courts of the land. I
want to help create laws which will guard their homes and
children; I want to legislate those laws. I want to speak
out so the whole world will hear!"

There were ways of pleading the case of the oppressed,
but Robeson seemed in no hurry to find them. He had, he
admitted, a lazy streak. He seldom sought for things to do,
but he could work with great concentration and brilliance
once he was committed. In the law firm he felt as he used
to feel in his college classes and on the athletic field—the
need to excel *because* he was a Negro. He prepared brilliant briefs, but white associates were chosen to defend
them in court. He knew why this was so: a Negro lawyer
simply did not represent important white clients before a
court of law. He began to experience real frustration for
the first time in his life, and he had not developed the
equipment to deal with it.

His wife sensed his bafflement. She was blindly ambitious in many directions, but experience had taught her
discernment, and she had inherited from her Jewish-
Negro stock a passionate sense of reality. She knew her

husband, knew his temperament, knew his talents. She was too ambitious to entertain the prospect of his frittering his life away in a picayune civil practice, which was the fate of so many Negro lawyers; too realistic to encourage him to resign with nothing else in view; and too sensible not to cast about for a means to his greater fulfillment. Meantime she drew him into the fields of her intellectual and social interests—amateur politics, amateur music, amateur theatricals—where she roved with all the inquisitiveness of a scientist and the ardor of a votary.

By now 1924 had come and, as we have seen, the viable interest in the Negro and in Negro life as subjects for serious art was beginning to flower. Eugene O'Neill had already had great success with *The Emperor Jones* and was currently at work on *All God's Chillun Got Wings*. *Porgy* and *Scarlet Sister Mary*, novels of Negro folk life, were soon to climb high on the best-seller lists, but not quite so high as those books about Negro life in Harlem, *Nigger Heaven*, *Home to Harlem*, and *The Blacker the Berry*.

Much of Harlem was as synthetic as bathtub gin, but there were some genuine people living there, and the cultural tide of the 1920s washed more than flotsam and jetsam onto the banks of the Harlem River. Writers and artists and actors came in on that tide, bringing new and sometimes wild ideas, and an abundance of life.

The James Weldon Johnsons gave a party for Claude McKay just before he sailed for Russia in 1922. McKay had recently published a book of poems of which Johnson was to write, "There is nothing in American literature that strikes a more portentous note than these sonnet-tragedies. . . ." But the party itself struck a portentous note. McKay had been Max Eastman's associate editor of the *Liberator*, and until lately the executive editor with Michael Gold. He had had white friends and associates of the Mike Gold stamp for some time, and he had been in the habit of taking "some of them up to the cabarets and cozy flats of Harlem. I did not invite my white friends to the nice homes of the Negro elite," he wrote later, "simply because I did not have an entree."

The Johnsons gave him and his friends that entree.

Soon no party given by the Negro elite was complete unless it included half a dozen white guests, liberals of one stripe or another. And the more liberal the better. And the more active in the arts the better still. The Eastmans, Carl Van Vechten, Eugene O'Neill, Cleon Throckmorton, Susan Glaspell, and Theodore Dreiser were quite active indeed.

This, then, was the eclectic and dynamic circle into which Eslanda Robeson drew her impressionable husband. Her lively energies were not dissipated in the circle's gay party life. They bubbled up in community activities and in volunteer social and charity work, which she pursued in that spirit of noblesse oblige that is so conspicuous an element in the home learning of upper-class Negroes.

Paul too could be counted upon for work of the same sort, in the same spirit. All through his boyhood and four years of college he had given recitations and "rendered" solos in his father's church. He had a notable flair for dramatic reading, he had a superb but untrained bass voice, and he could be counted on to use them in some struggling mission church's crisis of money raising. He refereed basketball games in parish houses and at the YMCA. He sponsored a neighborhood boys' club. In 1924 he found himself committed to act in an amateur production of Ridgely Torrence's play, *Simon the Cyrenian*, at the Harlem YWCA.

Mrs. Robeson was not one for hiding her husband's light under a bushel. She was convinced of the range of his untrained talents. At one party or another she had met members of the Provincetown Playhouse coterie, and she brought some of them to watch her husband perform in Torrence's play. Later Kenneth MacGowan said, "Some magic emanated from the man," and James Light spread the word in MacDougal Street that Robeson was "a born actor." Before Robeson knew what was happening to him, O'Neill the playwright, Light the director, and Robert Edmond Jones the scene designer had fixed upon him to play Jim Harris in *All God's Chillun Got Wings*.

The announcement of this brought on a wind of controversy and a rainfall of protest. *All God's Chillun* was that kind of play. It dealt in somber, realistic terms with the melancholy married life of a mixed couple. The papers protested playing a Negro opposite a white actress. O'Neill issued a statement to the press. "Prejudice . . . is the last word in injustice and absurdity. . . . All we ask is a square deal. A play is written to be expressed through the theater, and only on its merits in a theater can a final judgment be passed on it with justice. We demand this hearing."

Robeson was once again in the headlines of the white press. He was to stay in headlines almost continuously for the next twenty years.

In the spring of 1925 he gave his first concert of Negro spirituals at the Greenwich Village Theater, and Alexander Woollcott lauded him as "the finest musical instrument wrought by nature in our time." Later that year he went to London and played *The Emperor Jones* to great applause at the Ambassadors' Theater. He returned briefly to the States and found himself a much-sought-after celebrity, courted by whites and feted by Negroes—practically all of whom identified with him as he identified with them. He was one of them. He was, he said in a public speech at the time, their "instrument."

Back in Europe again, he saw a lot of Claude McKay, who had just returned from his second trip to Russia full of enthusiasm and unstinting of praise. "Russia now has her opportunity. Russia has had the courage to tear down old rotten walls." It was the kind of thing many Western intellectuals were saying in the 1920s. The Robesons heard it on every hand.

Robeson made a triumphant concert tour of the States in 1927 and then went back to England, which was to be his home for the next four years. From here his music and his personality radiated all over the Continent. He gave command performances. Always and everywhere he sang the sorrow songs of his people. Indeed, they were all he knew at the time. The London *Daily Express* proclaimed him "more than a great actor and a great singer. He is a great man, who creates the soul of a people in bondage and shows you its true kinship with the fettered soul of man. We became like little children as we surrendered to his magical genius."

This piece and others in the same vein were widely reprinted in the United States. American Negroes were strengthened in their belief that Robeson was their "instrument," their ambassador to the world.

When he sang "Ol' Man River" in the first American revival of *Show Boat*, Edna Ferber, the author of the book, wrote, "I have never seen an ovation like that given any figure of the stage, the concert hall, or the opera. . . . That audience stood up and howled. They applauded and shouted and stamped. . . . The show stopped. He sang it again. The show stopped. They called him back again and again. . . ."

That was in the spring of 1933.

Meanwhile, though it was evident that something had happened to the social climate of America because of the depression of the 1930s, a far subtler change had been occurring in the intellectual atmosphere since the lush days of the 1920s. In that boom time some intellectuals had found the American environment uncongenial and, rather than "suffer death on the cross of American industrialmaterialism," fled to Europe. But the world-wide depression had driven them home again, where, in an air now acid with poverty, their ideas were even less viable than before.

They were a lonely lot, as all idealists and utopia-seekers are likely to be, and now also they were deprived of the sense of a commonly shared intellectual adventure they had known in the bistros on the Left Bank of Paris. Playwrights without producers, writers without an audience, artists without a market, they were sharply aware of the illness of a society that thwarted their creative drives. They had a heightened perception of the "dreadful deficiencies of capitalistic democracy"—in witness to which were the shut-down factories, the staggering bread lines, the millions of unemployed. They felt helpless to effect a cure, and they were certain that it could not cure itself.

Could socialism? For a time a few professed to think so. Technocracy? Some flirted with the idea of it until it was pointed out that technocracy was merely "mechanistic positivism reorganized." Then quite suddenly the intellectuals discovered the brilliance of dialectical materialism. Here was a new adventure! If in the final analysis Marx's dialectical materialism could also be defined as mechanistic positivism, it should only be remarked that American intellectuals had not come—and in the early 1930s were still years from coming—to the final analysis of Marxism. For the present it was enough that it recreated a sense of sharing in an intellectual excitement of a kind a dying capitalistic democracy could not supply. Moreover, at least in their imaginings, it identified them with the dimly felt aspirations of the voiceless millions for whom they, the idealists, had always felt concern. Marxism was a saving grace.

Especially did it seem so to the Negro intellectual, to whom it appealed with special force. His deprivation was more than the chance result of a capitalistic democracy in its death throes. His deprivation and isolation were of the very structure of that democracy. His emotional heritage, transmitted through a long line of dissenting radicals and newly incremented by every generation, was a compulsive will to a comradeship of struggle, to abolish differences of caste and class and, above all, race.

And Marxism offered that and more. It offered not only liberation but brotherhood. Richard Wright was "amazed to find that there did exist in this world an organized search for the truth of the lives of the oppressed and the isolated. . . . It was not the economics of Communism, nor the great power of trade unions, nor the excitement of underground politics that claimed me; my attention was caught . . . by the possibility of uniting scattered but kindred people into a whole. . . . I felt that . . . it linked white life with black, merged two streams of common experience."

Like Wright, the Robesons were "impressed by the scope and seriousness" of the Communists' activities. They were certainly active. They had formed Leagues for the Defense of this and that. They were for the survival of "the people's art," for the Negro Youth Congress, for

James Ford, a Negro, as Vice-President of the United States. Their efforts seemed so all-out and self-denying that Wright, even before he joined the party, resolved to tell "the common [Negro] people of the self-sacrifice of Communists who strove for unity among them." Soon the Robesons were attending those hot little gatherings where the outraged compassion of fellow travelers confessed to impulses so ennobling as to seem the doctrines of a new and great religion.

The Robesons returned to England and the Continent in 1934 and remained abroad five years. Again Paul saw Claude McKay, who was still inexhaustible on the subject of Russia, and who took him to meet Max Eastman in Nice, Glenway Wescott in Villefranche, and Frank Harris in Cimiez. Mrs. Robeson settled down to study at the London School of Economics, and, probably through her, Paul became acquainted with Harold Laski and some of his like-minded colleagues.

As the guest of the Dean of Canterbury one weekend, Robeson was treated to a strange and impressive discourse on Christianity, the one brotherhood of man, and the USSR. "All I hear of the Russian program grips and inspires me," said the Very Reverend Hewlett Johnson. "If what we hear is true, it is majestic in range, practical in detail, scientific in form, Christian in spirit. Russia would seem to have embarked upon a task never yet attempted by modern or ancient State."

A week later Robeson was in Russia, and within that same year he returned there as a guest of the Russian state. Meanwhile he had learned the language. He had read avidly—Exupéry, Gide's play *Oedipe*. He made a picture in Russia. He made proper speeches: "All I can say is the moment I came here I realized that I had found what I had been seeking all my life. . . ." "All the people of this portion of the globe must be proud when Stalin speaks of the cultures of the different nationalities of the Soviet Union as 'socialist in content and national in form.'"

After this second visit to Russia, Robeson was not the same. He seemed much older. At thirty-six there had been about him still a boyish charm, a natural ease and grace

of manner—the mark, one supposes, of a mind that, however troubled, is innocent and free. At thirty-seven he
seemed plundered of innocence and of things native to
his spirit. The zestful geniality that had characterized his
relations with the world was strained. He was no longer
the "magnificent primitive" pictured by Alexander Woollcott. He seemed to be enduring a torturous conflict of
conscience and a harrowing obliteration of the ideas by
which he had lived—the ideas that were embedded in the
structure of his character and that had had no little influence on his personal success. He was like one struggling
toward a reconciliation with himself.

Forsaking his old haunts and giving up the great financial rewards of London's fashionable West End theaters,
he joined the Unity Theatre group, which, its brochure
said, was "open to all members of the Labour and Trade
union movement and to those who are in sympathy with
our aims and objectives." He was no longer interested in
being merely an entertainer. A way "to plead the case of
the misunderstood and oppressed" had found him. He attended various "progressive congresses" and supported
groups promoting cultural relations with Russia. He was
taken up by the London *Daily Worker* and the *New
Statesman.*

In his spare time he acquired a smattering of Chinese,
competent Spanish, and a thorough mastery of Yiddish.
Sometimes for expense money, but often for no money at
all, he gave concerts for "workingmen's gatherings" in Birmingham, Glasgow, and Dublin, in Manchester and Mar-
seille. He was always at the service of the British Negro
colony in Camden Town. In Stockholm, Copenhagen, and
Oslo his concerts "developed into anti-fascist demonstra-
tions." He sang not only Negro spirituals but the Jewish
"people's" songs in Yiddish, the Chinese "people's" songs
in Cantonese, songs expressive of "the new spirit of Soviet
Russia" in Russian, and the songs of the Spanish Republic
in Spanish. In 1938 he went to Barcelona and to the
Madrid front to sing for the soldiers of the Republic.

These activities were faithfully reported in the American press, and especially in the Negro press, and they had

the stamp of American approval. Fear and hatred of fascism were growing, and Negroes felt they had greater warrant than most Americans to hate fascism. Robeson himself had said that "fascism is no less the enemy of colored peoples than of Jews." He was in England when Mussolini's Fascist legions invaded Ethiopia. In Germany he had seen the Nazi Brown Shirts when they were as yet but local bully boys, but in the summer of 1936 he saw them again—a force disciplined in terror—in Lisbon on their way to join Franco in Spain. In 1938 came Munich, and after Munich only the thoughtless and the blind did not see that fascism was a threat to freedom everywhere.

The imminence of war in Europe forced Robeson to return to America in the summer of 1939. He arrived just in time to subscribe to the sentiments of a letter addressed to "All Active Supporters of Democracy and Peace." Though dated two weeks before the Hitler-Stalin Pact, it was published the very week the pact was announced, and it bore the signatures of four hundred names well known in American intellectual and artistic circles. It rejected "the fantastic falsehood that the USSR and the totalitarian states are basically alike." It said that the Soviet Union "continues as always to be a bulwark against war and aggression, and works unceasingly for a peaceful international order." Just weeks later Russia attacked neutral Finland.

Robeson did not act like one of those whose idealism had been betrayed by the Hitler-Stalin Pact. He was not one of the thousands who publicly questioned or criticized the Russian turnabout. Perhaps an ironic sensibility, or an urge to sacrifice in some aberrant act of atonement his moral consciousness as well as his privileged position, operated in him. When the Nazi-Communist pact was broken and Hitler marched against Russia in 1941, Robeson delivered a speech in which he said, in part, "I am awfully happy and optimistic because fascism has at last come to grips with the one power [Communism] that will show it no quarter."

What he thought when America too came to violent grips with fascism is not recorded, but to be pro-Russian then was not to be anti-American democracy. Robeson was generous of his talents on the home front. He sang to thirty thousand people at the Watergate in Washington, D.C., to the workers of the American Aviation Plant, to a convention of the National Maritime Union, which, incidentally, bestowed an honorary membership on him. His programing was different from what his American audiences were used to. He sang the spirituals still, though not so many, and principally he sang pieces like "Joe Hill," "Peat Bog Soldiers," "Cradle Song of the Poor," and the "Song of Kazakstan."

Imperceptibly, in the way the mind is slowly shaped or altered by the accidents of day-to-day perception and experience, a peculiar estrangement had developed between Robeson and his people. They still flocked to hear him sing, still believed he was fighting their fight, still told themselves he was one of them. But he was no longer their instrument. He was sincere, but his sincerity seemed striving to overreach itself, to be more than it was, to be a substitute for every other moral and personal force. His human warmth was gone, his sense of humor was gone, or shut away. This was not *the* Robeson. This was another man bearing the same name.

He opened in the Theatre Guild production of *Othello* in October 1943. It was a great artistic success, though Michael Gold, who reviewed it for the *Daily Worker*, made it sound like a political rally of the proletarian left. Before the Broadway run ended, Robeson was honored by the National Federation for Constitutional Liberties for his "outstanding contribution toward building international unity within our country and throughout the world." The NFCL had been certified subversive. Before the Broadway run ended, an organization that Robeson had helped to found, the Council of African Affairs, was placed on the government's list of Communist-front organizations. Before the play left Broadway another organization with which he was connected, the National Negro Congress, was brought under suspicion when Mrs. Eleanor Roosevelt, ordinarily so generous of her patronage, refused to sponsor a concert in its behalf. Later the National Negro Congress was added to the government's list.

By the time the play's provincial tour ended in June 1945 the war in Europe was over, and in Asia nearly so, but, said Frederick Lewis Allen, "no sooner had America started to relax" than it was "borne in upon us, with increasing ominousness, that Soviet Russia in her turn was bent upon world conquest" and that "Communism was a deadly threat to institutions at home."

By the time the play's tour was over Paul Robeson had become co-chairman of the National Committee to Win the Peace, and a member of the national executive committee of the Independent Committee of the Arts, Sciences and Professions, both of which the New York *Times* reported "linked with left-wing and Communist activities," and both of which also went on the government's subversive list.

Accused of belonging to thirty-four Communist-front groups in 1946, Robeson was called before a Joint Committee on Un-American Activities of the California legislature. He testified, "Real racial equality is almost not an American conception. . . . If Mr. Truman is going to raise the underprivileged one-third of the nation, or the Negro one-tenth, he'd better establish a dictatorship in the South." He testified, "I think the best country in the world to test the principles of Marxism might be the America of today."

Edgar G. Brown, director of the Negro Council, appeared before the same committee the next day. He had no great importance as a race leader, but he spoke the troubled mind of Negroes. "Ninety-nine and nine-tenths per cent of the Negroes in the United States believe in the American system," he testified. "Any implication in yesterday's testimony by Paul Robeson that American Negroes would welcome an authoritarian regime to insure equalitarianism as in Russia is the biggest lie." He testified, "I do not consider Paul Robeson as a real spokesman or representative campaigner for Negroes. He is no hero now."

6. *The Better Man Wins*

One night in the early summer of 1935, the year the Russians were entertaining Paul Robeson as a guest of the state, a tawny Negro boy sat awaiting the end of the ceremonious preliminaries that would send him into his first important boxing match. He sat quietly, his shoulders slouched, his face hooded by a towel draped over his head. Opposite him in the ring sat his opponent, a man six and a half feet tall and weighing close to three hundred pounds, grimacing and fidgeting on his stool as if he itched in places he could not scratch. The Negro boy seemed completely unaware of him, of the blaze of lights, of the sixty thousand people who packed the vast stadium, of the several million who, the papers would say, sat huddled over radios across the great land.

Celebrities were now being introduced from the ring. Flash bulbs popped. Fight officials and trainers and seconds passed back and forth along the apron of the ring. The Negro boy, who had just turned twenty-one, and whose ring name was Joe Louis, scarcely stirred. "You lis'nin' to me, Chappie? Now you hear me good," his trainer said softly into the boy's ear. The boy grunted. "A tree liak this here you got to chop down," the trainer went on. "Cain't do no fancy whittlin'. No knife work. Ax him. You hear me, Chappie?" The boy grunted again and now, as the announcer moved to the center of the ring and reached for the suspended microphone, stood up, suddenly, marvelously alert.

Harry Balogh, the announcer, had been carefully instructed and rehearsed. Powerful segments of the American press had not wanted this fight. The Scripps-Howard chain of newspapers had opposed it from the beginning, and lately William Randolph Hearst, whose wife's pet charity, the Milk Fund, stood to benefit from it, had urged calling it off. Trouble was brewing between Italy and Ethiopia, and that "trouble could find focus in the prize ring at Yankee Stadium." American Negroes had already formed the Council of Friends of Ethiopia and had sent a delegation to denounce Italy before the League of Nations. It was foolhardy at this time, Hearst felt, to match a Negro against an Italian, especially when the Italian seemed certain to lose. The bout would exasperate passions, and "among whites there was talk of an aftermath of rioting."

"Ladies and gentlemen," the announcer said into the microphone, "tonight we have gathered here to watch a contest of athletic skill. We are Americans. That means that we have come from homes of many different faiths, and that we represent a lot of different nationalities. In America we admire the athlete who can win by virtue of his skill. Let me then ask you to join me in the sincere wish that regardless of race, color, or creed, the better man may emerge victorious. Thank you."

It is estimated that fifty million people listened to the blow-by-blow broadcast of the Louis-Carnera fight. When it ended in the sixth round, with the Italian a bloody, stumbling hulk, ten million Negroes heard for the first time a voice that when it spoke hereafter would quicken all the numbness of their patient years and sound through all the ranges of their hope. It said, "I glad I win." It was a coarse, thick voice unused to speech. On the night when they first heard it Negroes in Harlem, as in every ghetto in the country, sent up a "terrific roar. . . . Pandemonium broke loose. Tens of thousands marched through the streets." They laughed and sang and wept for joy. Some went to church to pray.

7. *Folk Epic*

The life of Joe Louis has something of the quality of an American folk epic. A mingling of three old indigenous strains—peasant-class black, master-class white, nomadic red—he was born on an Alabama tenant farm in 1914, the fifth child of his illiterate parents. By the time the seventh was born the father, Monroe Barrow, was breaking under the strain of never ending debt and wrenching less than a living from a worn-out cotton farm. He crumpled up completely while Joe was still a toddler, and the sheriff came and took him to the home for Negro feeble-minded near Mobile. Neither his wife nor his children ever saw him again. There was no money for sentimental journeys.

There was no money period. Mrs. Barrow seldom saw a dollar from one year to the next. She and the older children worked the land, and Joe was helping at the age of four. The cotton they raised was just enough to keep them poorly housed. They raised collard greens and beans and a stand of corn for food. Relatives scarcely more prosperous donated salt pork. The Barrows lived in the pattern prescribed by early postbellum history—matriarchal family, poverty, illiteracy. Though on Sundays they went regularly to church, where Mrs. Barrow renewed her trust in God, on weekdays there was little time for school. Joe did not learn to talk till he was six, or read till he was nine. The Barrows were so ragged that their clothes whistled in every wind.

Things got a little better when a widower began to call on Lillie Barrow. Patrick Brooks had several children of his own, but he was hard-working and ambitious, and he had it in his mind to "leave out for Dee-stroy" as soon as he was able. There was money there and a man had a "better go" for it. While he nursed this dream toward reality he wooed, and when word came that Monroe Barrow had died in the distant asylum Lillie married Patrick Brooks. After her son had become heavyweight champion of the world she was horrified to learn that she had been misinformed about Monroe's death. He did not die until November 1938. Joe wired money for a costly funeral.

Leaving his own younger children with his new wife, Pat Brooks went to Detroit and got a job at Ford's. He was following a pattern that was by then classic in its simplicity. He would send for his family when he had saved enough. This took two years. All the Barrows and Brookses reached Detroit in 1924. Joe was ten. He just could write his name, and his speech was so thick that he had difficulty making himself understood. Four or five years in elementary school helped some, but not much. The kind of learning he went there to get simply confused him and strangled the expressions of his personality. He switched to a vocational school. At the end of one marking period his teacher noted on the report card that Joe was "good in manual training. This boy should be able to do something with his hands."

Joe was already doing many things with his hands, and with his whole lithe, handsome body. For one thing, he was protecting himself in the human jungle where the Barrows lived. Also he worked after school delivering ice, selling papers, and collecting scrap metal. There were a lot of Barrow-Brookses, and they were poor—though far from poverty-shocked—and Pat Brooks's job at Ford's went "a-glimmering" when the depression struck. For almost a year they were on relief, incurring a debt that Joe Louis felt morally bound to repay in 1935. He thanked the Welfare Board, but he said, "They's others you can he'p now." He was living up to the family code of poor but decent. "I wants all my chil'ren to be decent," Mrs. Brooks used to say. She worked at decency, she embellished it and made it shine. She kept the children in school as long as she could. She even had Joe taking violin lessons on a pitifully cheap violin once a week.

One day when Joe was going for a lesson he met an ex-schoolmate. Thurston McKinney, who was two or three years older, had long since quit school and had become the amateur light heavyweight boxing champion of Michigan. He fought for merchandise checks, and when the merchandise turned out to be something he did not need or want, he sold it for cash, pocket money. He was in search of a sparring partner the day he met Joe. He joshed Joe about the violin—"It ain't nothin' for a man to do"—and persuaded him to fill in as a sparmate. They went to the Brewster Center Gymnasium. Joe was completely ignorant of the fine points of boxing, and McKinney toyed with him for a while; but Joe's reflexes were perfect, and his body seemed to have an intelligence independent of his mind, a sentience that never registered in his face. Suddenly he caught McKinney with a right and the older boy would have fallen had not Joe rushed in to hold him up. "You way too good for school, man," McKinney said.

It was summer, and in the fall Joe did not return to

school—was, in fact, already working as a six-dollar-a-week lathe operator at Briggs. Jobs of any kind were scarce in 1931, and Joe knew he was lucky. The day after the encounter with McKinney he gave up the violin too, and joined the Brewster Center Boxing Club. There was a little racket about this at home. "But, Ma," Joe said, "a guy kin be decent an' a fighter both."

Joe was both. For the next three years, during which he got a job at Ford's, he fought for merchandise checks. His wages went to his mother for the common pool. In 1932 he won the Detroit Golden Gloves. In 1933 he barely missed becoming national amateur light heavyweight champion. In 1934 he made it.

That was the year a man named John Roxborough first took an active interest in Joe Louis. A mulatto lawyer, physically as glossy-smooth as new chrome, but mind-scored and complicated beyond belief, living professionally on the slippery edges of the underworld, Roxborough was an American archetype machined by those attitudes that operated to exclude him from sharing in the decenter large prospects society offered to white men of half his talents, training, and ambition. He was cunning, he was callous, and he was involved in transactions that were shady.

Still he could not quite put down or cast off a hundred years of careful breeding, or uproot all the thousand precepts planted by his forebears. He had scruples still, and particularly strong ones on matters of race. If in privacy he lived beyond the reach of them, he, nevertheless, was very careful that other Negroes should not. He sent—that is, financed—many worthy Negro boys through college, admonishing them, "You've got to help the race." He donated to Negro social welfare. He did boys' work at the Negro Y. He found jobs for worthy Negro youths either with friends or in one of the legitimate enterprises—insurance companies, real estate—he controlled. Not the least complex thing about John Roxborough was a romantic sense of mission. This was strangely wedded to an instinct for the main chance.

In pursuit of his interest in Joe Louis, Roxborough

called in a friend from Chicago. He had a habit of employing fronts, even in legitimate affairs, and Julian Black was
to be a front. "I've found a boy, a fighter," Roxborough
said, and began laying down the rules for a game Black
did not even know he was going to play. "No fakes,
no falls," Roxborough said. "Joe's not to have bouts that
aren't contested strictly on merit."

But Black knew about Negroes in boxing, he had managed several, nearly all of whom, he knew, had been asked
at one time or another to fake or fall. Otherwise they did
not last long as fighters; or if they were really good and
lasted, they were never allowed to reach the top of the
heavyweight division. Jack Johnson had spoiled that.
Black spoke of this, and called the names of Langford,
Godfrey, and Wills.

Though Roxborough had never managed fighters, he
knew all this too, but the difference was that he thought
this knowledge could be put to redeeming use. He remembered that when Jack Johnson won the world's heavyweight championship Jack London, reporting that fight
from far-off Australia, expressed the hope that "somewhere
in America might be found a man to crush this impudent
black." There was a frantic search for a "white hope," and
Jim Jeffries came out of retirement to meet Johnson in
what was advertised to be "the greatest battle of the century." Jack London reported that fight too for the New
York *Herald.* "Fight?" he wrote. "There was no fight. . . .
It was a monologue delivered to twenty thousand spectators by a smiling Negro." The New York *World* commented: "That Mr. Johnson should so lightly and
carelessly punch the head off Mr. Jim Jeffries must have
come as a great shock to every devoted believer in the supremacy of the Anglo-Saxon race." This was raillery, of
course, but next day, when rioting broke out country-wide,
it seemed something else again. The New York *Herald* reported, "Half Dozen Dead as Crowds Attack Negroes.
Reign of Terror Here."

"This fighter's a good boy," Roxborough said. "Not
smart-alecky. Modest."

"I've never seen a good fighter yet who was modest, especially a spook," Black said.

"This boy is. We've just got to make white people know it."

"The way things are, that's going to take some doing."

"I know the kind of boy he is," Roxborough said. "I've watched him. I've asked around. You find out what Jack Blackburn thinks of him as a fighter."

"I don't think Blackburn'll be for training a colored heavyweight in earnest," Black said.

"See," Roxborough said. "And, Julian, I want him trained for real, in earnest. I've got plans."

Though a Negro himself, and once a great welterweight, Jack Blackburn objected at first, for reasons he considered overwhelming. Negro heavyweights earned little money; they were used mainly to help build the reputations of white fighters; and "*They* ain't never goin'a let another colored boy wear 'at crown." But he consented at last, and Joe Louis was trained for real. Julian Black became the manager of record. Behind all three stood Roxborough, putting his lawless cunning to work for the furtherance of an altogether lawful, proud, and beneficent end—the making of a Negro boy into an American hero.

There was plenty to work with. Joe Louis had the physical equipment of all great boxers. His "rhythm," Jack Blackburn said, "showed he was jus' nat'ally a fighter." His timing and co-ordination were flawless, his strength and power exceptional. But Jack Johnson—and Sam Langford and Joe Jeannette—had all these too, and in great degree, and they were not enough. Joe Louis had something more. He had traits of temperament, of personality, and of character so different from those usually ascribed to figures in the world of sports as to make him seem a strange mutation. Even after his private life was largely absorbed in his public career he retained a quality so modest and guileless that some of the keenest observers called him "dumb," "stupid," and "insensitive."

But Joe Louis was none of these. He was not articulate, but he was extremely sensitive—and especially to those nuances of fear and rage and hope that sped like messages of doom or redemption through the air his people breathed. Toward the end of his first year as a professional boxer, when it was quite evident that Negro fans were already rearing him to the status of race hero, a reporter talked to him. Joe had just knocked out Charley Massare, "one of the greatest heavyweight prospects since Dempsey," and in his dressing room in the Chicago Stadium he was cooling out, while a squad of policemen guarded his door against a mob of Negroes clamoring to see him. "Joe," the reporter asked, "do you hear that?" "Yeah," Joe replied impassively, "I hears it." "Well, what do you think, Joe? They're calling for you." There was a moment's silence. "I thinks if I evah does somethin' to let my people down, I wanna die."

Certain constellations in his mind and character were fixed. Probably without being aware of it, he had assumed a responsibility for discharging some of the burden of obloquy and shame and struggle his people bore. He was —or, thanks to John Roxborough, was made—perceptive to the least change in the running current of race relations. In 1935, when anti-Jewish feeling, whipped up beyond control by unscrupulous race baiters in Harlem, exploded in a riot that destroyed more than two million dollars' worth of Jewish and white property, Joe Louis was mindful to point out that the promoter who "brang me to the bigtime" was Mike Jacobs. Already a man to be seen (and more to be seen than heard, since he was after all what he was), Joe appeared at many race-uplift rallies, including one for Philip Randolph's Pullman porters.

Finally, unlike many of limited learning and an even more limited experience of the right to self-respect, Louis was sensitive to the demands of human dignity and pride. In the very last fight of his first professional year he knocked out Lee Ramage, who was the latest "greatest heavyweight prospect." Joe had been a three-to-one underdog in the fight. When it was over he spoke on a local radio hookup. He said, "He [Ramage] was sho' a tough customer. I never seen so many gloves flyin' at me as he sent to my face. I tried to box him, but I soon learn . . .

he knows too much boxin'." Later he said, "I wanna win good an' lose good."

The proof of losing good came sooner than Joe Louis and almost everyone else in America expected. To say that the Carnera fight had made him overconfident and even somewhat cocky is to point out that Louis had at least a normal complement of frailties. He was young, he took pride in his prowess. He had had twenty-six professional fights and had won all of them, twenty-three by knockouts, when he climbed into the ring against Schmeling in 1936. Sports writers like Grantland Rice, Allison Danzig, and Bill Cunningham had hung enough superlatives on him to founder the humility of a saint. Even the New York *Times* seemed to concede that Louis was invincible. The Schmeling fight proved that he was not.

The German was anxious to regain the heavyweight title he had lost three years before. Joe Louis stood in his way. He was determined to crush Joe Louis. Having once lost to Max Baer, a Jew, Schmeling was in disgrace at home, where Hitler was already beginning the most wicked persecution of a people the world has ever known. But few Americans then understood the mad emotional structure of Nazism—the satanic hate and rage with which it inspired its disciples; the will to discipline it imposed. When Schmeling, training at Napanoch, made typical Nazi racist remarks about "superior" and "inferior" peoples, few sensed behind them the dark power of the German's psychological commitment. Twice, meantime, he had watched Louis fight, and he had studied for hours all the Louis fight pictures. He declared that he had found a weakness, and he planned and trained with cold, grim efficiency to exploit it.

Louis, on the other hand, apparently thought of the German as just another fighter and the match with him as just another fight. He trained routinely. Self-complacency had crept over him so gradually that he did not realize how careless he had become, how dull his fighter's instincts, how negligent his fighter's mind. He behaved as though he believed the newspapers, none of which conceded he could lose. He had his twenty-second birthday at his training camp in Lakewood and he celebrated it with a party. He played a lot of golf with Joe Williams, a sports writer assigned to the camp by the *World-Telegram*. Williams reported admiringly that it was "amazing any man could be so unconcerned . . . as Louis" in the weeks before an important fight.

Joe was unconcerned—and that was the way he remained all through the training period. He seemed not to realize how much of the pride of his people depended upon his skill and power; that he was their very symbol of equality. For the first and only time in his professional career his emotional machinery failed to respond to the spark of his Negroness and to the goad of his racial experience.

So Max Schmeling defeated him the night of June 17, 1936. The German *had* found a weakness. In the fourth round his right fist, zinging over Louis' lowered left, crashed against his opponent's chin. The "Brown Bomber" went down. Though he was up at the count of three, and though he still had enough to keep the German wary, he fought in a daze. His defense was as thin as tissue paper. He took a terrific beating. Round after round Schmeling's right fist did its methodical work of destruction until that work was done. In the twelfth round Louis was knocked out with a punch as clean and true as a rifle shot. He had "lost good." But the German would not even concede him this. In an article in the *Saturday Evening Post* some weeks later, while pictures of the fight were being billed in Germany as *The Typical Nazi Triumph* and *The Great Nordic Victory*, Schmeling accused Louis of deliberately hitting low.

No one recorded what Schmeling said in his German-language broadcast to the Fatherland immediately after the fight, but all remembered that it had ended with an exuberant "Heil Hitler!" Turning from the microphone to the writers who crowded his dressing room, Schmeling upbraided them in a heavy accent. "You should have known better. I would not have taken this fight if I did not think that I, a white man, could beat a colored man. *Ja?*" A few minutes later he had a felicitous cable from Goebbels, and he waved it over his head.

Meanwhile Joe Louis lay still half dazed in his dressing room across the corridor. His managers, Roxborough and Black, his trainer, and a few still incredulous newsmen were with him. He could remember little about the fight, and as his head cleared he kept asking over and over, "What happen'?" It was Jack Blackburn, the trainer, who told him, trying to make the telling neither less nor more than it should be. "You got tagged, Chappie. An' when you git tagged right, that's all—there ain't no more." There was a deeper silence in the quiet room. "You got in a low one too," Blackburn said, "but you didn't know what you was doin'." Louis struggled upright then. "Roxy," he said, "you go tell him I'm sorry. I don' wanna foul nobody." Without a word Roxborough left for Schmeling's dressing room.

An hour later, when Louis and his handlers were leaving the stadium, a reporter asked whether they would protest the blow Schmeling landed after the bell ending the fifth round. "He beat me fair," Louis said, and that was that.

The Negro race went into mourning. That night the bars and restaurants in Harlem closed early and many cabarets did not open at all. South-side Chicago stayed indoors. It was said that Paradise Valley, Detroit's Negro section, "whimpered like a runned-over puppy." Everywhere in the colored world Joe Louis' defeat was felt to be a calamity as tragic and as irrevocable as a sudden, unlooked-for death. Indeed, it was a death—the death of a hero. The ideal attributes of the hero—imperious skill, indomitable strength, invincible courage—could no longer be vested in one of their own. They believed that they had fastened their hopes on unattainable goals. They were thrown back—or they felt thrown back, which was much the same thing—to an acceptance of the white man's evaluation of the race. Pride could not anchor in attributes they had, but only in attributes they aspired to have. Schmeling's shattering fists, they felt, had smashed more than the body of a black man: they had crushed the pride of a race.

But at the very time when Joe Louis seemed least so, he was most heroic. He was back in training before the bruises were gone from his body. By mid-July, scarcely a month after his defeat, a match had been arranged with

Jack Sharkey, who had once beaten Schmeling for the title. The Schmeling fight, the newspapers said, had "exploded the Louis myth." The German, the newspapers said, had "taken it out of him." Watching Louis train, sports writers commented that the defeat had "affected Louis badly." He was slow, he was deliberate, he was self-conscious even against sparmates in the training ring.

The newspapers reported many things about him, including the fact that he gave but grudging support to the American Olympic Committee, who solicited him for funds to help American athletes travel to the games in Germany. He was changed. He was now, Paul Gallico wrote (and implied much more) in the *Reader's Digest*, "A mean, mean man." He was also a "has-been." Ten days before the match with Sharkey, Allison Danzig reported that "Almost to a man, they [the fight experts] agree that Louis is trying his comeback far too early and against far too shrewd a campaigner in Sharkey."

Louis knocked out Sharkey in three rounds. He won three more fights in that year and three the next before he defeated James J. Braddock for the heavyweight championship in 1937.

Though these victories had much to do with restoring Louis to public esteem, his character and deportment in and out of the ring had everything to do with keeping him there. The things he did and the things he refused to do became, more and more, the subjects of editorial comment. He fought for charity more often than the four previous heavyweight champions combined. Before a fight his silence was impenetrable; his post-fight remarks were without presumptuousness. "I was lucky"; "I glad I win"; "I know I been in a fight."

He had no disdainful words for an opponent, "no matter how pitiful [the opponent's] exhibition or how dirty his fighting." He refused to endorse a nationally advertised brand of cereal because he did not eat it, and he turned down five thousand dollars to endorse a cigar because he did not smoke. Roi Ottley, a well-known newsman, tells of overhearing the following dialogue between two Negroes. "If we had more Negroes like Joe Louis," said one, "things would be better for us." "Sure 'nuff," replied the other, "but if we had more white folks like Joe, things would be better still."

But if Joe seemed once more a paragon to his own people, he was scarcely less a model to whites. All the latter had seen and heard and read of him, quite aside from his athletic prowess, added up to those ennobling moral characteristics—honorableness and honesty, modesty and generosity—with which men will endow their heroes when heroes give them half a chance. Joe Louis gave them better than half a chance, and whites, too, took pride in him—in the oft-repeated boast that only in this country was such a career possible for him; in the belief that the American environment alone could imbrue him in the "American" virtues. Joe Louis had achieved that rare metamorphosis from Negro to American.

So—save perhaps a few scattered colonies of Germanophiles, who were extremely confident—all of America came up to the night of Louis' return match with Schmeling in 1938 in a state of high, apprehensive excitement. Some of the excitement was patriotic. It was not that the seventy thousand people who packed Yankee Stadium already recognized German National-Socialism as an international evil. No doubt some had read in *Mein Kampf* Hitler's exhortations to a "Germany, mistress of the globe by the victorious sword of a master race." Though at least two hundred Jews bearing anti-Nazi slogans picketed the stadium, and though only three months before Hitler had begun the occupation of Austria, not many in America took Hitler and his rantings seriously until after Munich, and Munich was still three months in the future. No. The excitement of patriotism amounted to this: the heavyweight championship of the world was a national possession, and Joe Louis, American, was to fight Max Schmeling, German, to keep the title here.

But it was not quite that simple for Joe Louis and fourteen million Negroes. They were very much aware of the new racism and of the moral sickness with which Germany seemed bent on infecting the world. Negro newspapers had recently reprinted their hot condemnations of Hitler's and Goebbels' refusal to shake hands with the American Negro athletes who had "swept to scintillating victories" in the Olympic games in 1936. Negroes were reminded, too, that Schmeling had accused Louis of deliberately fighting foul, and had scorned him as a "black fellow" and a "stupid amateur" in such a way as to sear all colored people in the acid of his contempt. To Negroes, Schmeling was not just a German; he was Nazism's embodiment, and when Joe Louis stepped into the ring against him the outcome would somehow prove whether the concept of superior-inferior races or the concept of racial equality would prevail.

Considering the mixed emotions, the apprehensive excitement, the vague but real sense of crisis, the jingo atmosphere (a thousand German nationals were present in a body), the fight itself was an anticlimax.

Just as the referee finished his instructions to the fighters someone shrieked, "Joe, remember Hitler sent him! Hitler sent him!"

The bell rang. Scarcely had the fighters met when Joe Louis' left hand flashed out and sent Schmeling reeling against the ropes. A right hand crunched against the German's jaw and he went down. The crowd rose instantly. Far out in the dark reaches of the stadium, among the cheaper seats, a cry went up, "Oh, Joe! Oh, Joe! Oh, Joe!" and as Schmeling rose, blood streaming from his mouth, the whole stadium seemed to take up the cry. "Oh, Joe! Oh, Joe!" There was another drumfire of blows so vicious that the German whimpered in pain and many at the ringside winced to hear him. The German went down again. The shouts changed. "Back to Hitler! Back to Hitler!" The mixed emotions were now one emotion, the seventy thousand voices one voice. Schmeling struggled to his hands and knees, rose swaying and glassy-eyed. The punch that sent him down for the last time spattered blood over the press row.

Nat Fleischer, the boxing authority, summed up the spirit that prevailed in Yankee Stadium that night: "The heavyweight championship of the world remained in America . . . the barrage that swept Schmeling to such swift disaster [enabled] an American youth to retain for his country the heavyweight title."

8. "Ain't Fightin' for Nothin'"

But there were other fights for other causes. The rehabilitation of Louis' self-esteem, though it uplifted other Negroes too, was not enough. As a professional boxer, he was proud to be champion; as a man, he was frustrated by the very real inadequacies that kept his personality half submerged. He hired a tutor. He tried to master the mysteries of grammatical speech. He tried to build a satisfactory family life—and failed.

As a Negro, he was troubled. Establishing a fund for the Federal Council of Churches of Christ in America, he wrote, "Before I retire, I want to put up one more fight—the best of my career—to help my people." In 1940, though scarcely prepared for it intellectually, he campaigned for Wendell Willkie, delivering practically the same speech to Negroes in a dozen cities. "I am a fighter, not a politician. This country has been good to me, and has given me everything I have, and I want it to be good to you and give you everything you need. I am for Willkie because I think he will help my people. I think my people ought to be for him too."

On January 9, 1942, he defended his title against Buddy Baer and turned his purse over to the Navy Relief Fund. Before the fight, when a reporter asked him how it felt to be "fighting for nothing," Louis shot back, "Ain't fightin' for nothin'. Fightin' for my country." Willkie spoke briefly from the ring: "Thank you, Joe Louis, in the name of the United States Navy and the American people. Thank you for your magnificent contribution and generosity in risking for nothing a title you have won through blood, sweat and toil."

Three days later—just five weeks after Pearl Harbor—Joe Louis enlisted as a private in the army, and Paul Gallico, who had once called Joe Louis Barrow "a mean, mean man . . . just emerging from the pit," was moved to write in *Liberty* magazine: "Citizen Barrow has set us a lesson. Can we learn it, we are saved. Should we ignore it, we shall reap what we deserve."

Part Four

AND LONG ENDURE

X. "YOU CAN'T TELL WHICH OF THEM JOES"

America had already fought this war longer than she had fought any war against a foreign foe. It had started in December 1941, and many men had died on alien seas, in strange lands where they had never thought to be, and in the screaming air. Now it was early spring of 1945, and the only sure thing was that, though the fighting and the dying would go on, the things for which the war was being fought could not be won in blood alone. This was the one solid, unshakable certainty in a war in which nothing else —neither its shape nor its dimensions, its tactics nor its weapons—remained for long the same.

This war had a genius of its own, and that genius not only wrought changes in the current of each battle, but in contingency after grave contingency and the shifting alterations of the mind to meet them, it changed rules and customs and, sometimes, the stubborn heritage of men's home-grown thoughts. Yet the decisions and the acts that marked these changes were for the most part so strangely low-keyed when they came as to make them seem almost the normal course of things, and to indicate perhaps that, for all the hard necessity of them, a conscience and a will had gone before. Only after decisions had been made and acts fulfilled did men look back and recognize the strangeness—and not always then.

Thus the *Stars and Stripes*, an army newspaper, reported with great casualness, "The plan of mixing white and colored troops in fighting units, a departure from previous U. S. Army practice, is operating successfully." This was printed on April 6, 1945, four full months after General George Patton had packed white troops on Negro-manned tanks and rushed them to the Ardennes to fight and die together. It was a month after the fight at Remagen where, fighting in mixed companies of armored infantry, eight hundred men had died. And it was two weeks after an incident in a woods near a German town called Wessel.

The Germans were in the blasted woods. The trees were mostly naked of branches, and the trunks of the trees were barked and splintered, and the floor of the woods was knee-high in the debris from the trees. A road divided the woods. It was a dirt road, pocked with small craters, and though it had once had real military value, it had little now. Indeed, when the main striking force of the American Third Army drove north in February and early March, this road had not been used. It simply went north to Wessel, a town taken by elements of the 17th Airborne, who had dropped from the sky, and the town where K Company of the 349th Infantry Regiment was headed on March 24 when it was stopped by the Germans who held the woods. K Company was scheduled to be re-equipped in Wessel and trucked from there to join the regiment farther north.

There should have been no battle. It was an accident, and it had no bearing on the big pattern of the war. The real fighting was going on way north of Wessel, and Wessel itself was four miles from the woods. With a small exception, this was Allied territory for thirty miles around.

The exception was the woods, and the Germans had no business in it, and no one either then or afterward had any clear idea of why they were in it, or what some of them were doing dressed in American uniforms, or why it should be that of the eighteen who were finally captured at least a half dozen spoke English with no trace of accent. Undoubtedly they were saboteurs who had been dropped behind the lines. But why in that place? What was there to sabotage?

K Company, commanded by a temporary major and consisting of three platoons, came down the road at about ten o'clock in the morning. The weather was unusually fine for the time of year, and the men were relaxed, tramping along in lines of four at an unsoldierly eighty-five paces a minute—there was no hurry—and taking a civilian-like care to avoid the muddy holes in the road. K was one of those companies newly reorganized on the new integrated basis, and it had a platoon of Negroes mixed in with two platoons of whites. Most of the Negroes had been service-of-supply troops—ordnance men, truckers, engineers, and signalers—eight weeks before, but when the new policy was handed down they were among the many thousands of Negroes who had applied for transfer to combat. So many had applied that to take all of them would have disrupted the vital functions of supply, and the number taken was finally limited to three thousand. These were some of them. They were as proud as they could be, but they felt that they were on trial, and they could not wait to join the regiment and get into combat.

The last lines of the company had passed two or three hundred yards into the shade cast on the road by the woods when one of the Negro GIs said to the sergeant walking beside him, "I seen something move in them woods," and pointed to the left. The sergeant was not impressed. "I tell you, Sarge, I seen something move." "Okay," the sergeant said, "you got my permission to go see."

The men who heard this exchange laughed, and all the nearest men slowed down and watched the soldier who had seen something move cross the road, jump the ditch, and scramble up the steep bank on the other side. A shot whanged out. The soldier tumbled forward and out of sight. Before the men in the road could recover from their surprise, machine-gun and rifle fire came pouring out of the woods on both sides. Some men broke back along the road clear of the woods, but most hit and hugged the ground. The sergeant shouted, "Goddamn, there is something in them woods! Men with guns!" The steel kept zinging back and forth over their heads and into the trees. Up forward, the major, prone with the rest, raised himself to a low crouch and looked around.

There were three things they could do. They could make a dash for the clear road more than a tenth of a mile ahead; they could make a dash for the clear road several hundred yards behind; they could stay where they were until darkness came.

There was an alternative that the major refused to consider, for the last thing he wanted was a fight. The heaviest weapons his men had were Browning automatic rifles, and there were only eight of them. The stuff that was coming at them—harmlessly enough so long as they stayed down— seemed no heavier, but there was no way of knowing how many of the enemy there were to send it. Also, the Negroes were a question. They were new to his command. He had never seen them in combat, and, though he considered himself a man without prejudice, the major half believed what he had heard. He just did not know what kind of soldiers they would make. He just did not know what kind of *men* they were.

Crouching, the major looked up and down the road. The men had hurled themselves down just as they were, in lines of four, but now they were separating, crawling on their bellies, some toward the ditch on one side and some toward the ditch on the other side of the road. No one was in panic. The men crawled a few feet and then lay quietly awhile and crawled again, cursing the unseen enemy in the woods and waiting for the major to make up his mind.

But it was not entirely up to the major to decide how the situation was to be met, for even as he tried to estimate it the men became targets for a new, more intense burst of fire. Some of the enemy on the left had made their way to the embankment and, protected behind it, were firing down on the road. The Americans returned the fire blindly. The most they hoped for was to prevent the Germans from getting pot shots at them. The major shouted, "Watch the right too! Watch the right!" Some of the men swung round on their bellies and watched the right.

Meanwhile a lieutenant, who with about a dozen men had sprinted clear of the woods with the first burst of fire, had an idea. He told the men who were with him about it, and then he sent a soldier forward to tell the major. The lieutenant and his men would leave the road, skirt the woods on the right for a likely distance, and then go into the woods to see what they could see.

When the major sent back word to try it, the lieutenant ordered his men to fix bayonets, and they went into the field at the edge of the woods, which, bending sharply outward here, stretched for a quarter of a mile. At three or four hundred yards, pausing to get some sense of the enemy's location by the sound of his fire, they ventured in. Underbrush and debris made the going difficult. The men spread out, but kept each other in sight among the trees, and went as quietly as they could. They must have effected a measure of surprise, for well back from the road they came upon five Germans huddled over a spring in a small clearing. Apparently they had left their weapons up on the line. They surrendered at once. One of the Negroes in the lieutenant's command shouted jubilantly, "We got us some Krauts!" That was the end of surprise. Germans could be heard crashing toward them from the direction of the road. The Americans had to fight a retreat through the trees. One of the prisoners escaped.

When they got back to the road an American lay dead in the road and the others were fighting from the ditches. A few grenades on either side would have made a great difference. The men in the ditch on the right were firing over the heads of their own men in the ditch on the left, and vice versa, and each of these lines had its back to the Germans who were firing on it. As a military matter, the situation was completely ridiculous. The stalemate was so thorough that the major could leave the ditch without great risk and go down the road to the edge of the woods to question the scouting party.

It did not occur to him to question the prisoners. He himself did not speak German. Schooled as he was in the ordinary ways of his National Guard, civilian-insurance-broker background, it did not cross his mind that an ordinary German might speak English. That he did question the prisoners was an accident of his emotions. When he got from the lieutenant nothing as to the number and disposition of the enemy, nothing more valuable than the bare report of the skirmish in the woods, the major looked at the prisoners and remarked with evident annoyance, "Well, it's a sure thing these s.o.b.'s won't escape."

The reaction was immediate. Two of the prisoners, not understanding and perhaps thinking themselves addressed, stiffened; the third drew his elbows in and spread his hands; and the fourth, grinning, said, "But Captain, we do not wish to escape." His English was perfect.

The major stared at him, and at all of them, really seeing them for the first time. They were not the "syphilitic old bastards" from the bottom of the barrel the Germans were supposed to be using now. They were younger than he, and he had just turned thirty. Suddenly he saw them as persons, and a feeling of human comradeship might have stirred in the major under other circumstances. He was that kind of man. But the man was submerged in the soldier, and the soldier was intent on his military problem. The major's youthful face grew rigid with responsibility. He questioned the English-speaking prisoner closely.

How many Germans were in the woods? A handful on one side, fewer on the other. What did he call a handful? Perhaps twenty-five or thirty on the left, not so many on the right—that morning some had been sent out to reconnoiter for a route to rejoin other German forces. Didn't they know there were no other German forces within fifty miles? A shrug. Well, what weapons did they have there in the woods? Rifles and perhaps five machine guns and two mortars. The mortars and three of the machine guns were on the left. Since they were badly outnumbered, would they surrender? Those on the right probably, but those on the left—no; they were SS; they were Nazi.

"You're not Nazi?"

The spokesman prisoner looked at the hand-spreading prisoner, and they both grinned. The major searched them for identification. They had none.

On the basis of this information the major decided to try to clear the woods. The word was passed along. Both sides of the woods would have to be cleared simultaneously, and the major meant to drive in front and rear. He divided and disposed his men for this purpose. A quarter of them were sent across the open field along the edge of the woods on the right, and another quarter skirted the woods on the left. At a given signal they were to go in with the object of getting behind the enemy. The rest of the men, facing the Germans from the road, were to go in after the enemy was engaged in the woods.

It sounded like a cinch, but it was not. There could be no secrecy in the preparations, and what the Germans could not see happening they could make intelligent guesses about, and when the attack came they were ready—especially those on the left. The Americans had to come to them. They had to tunnel through underbrush, climb over fallen trees. The shouts they raised as they went in, like Arkansas farmers on a rat hunt, soon turned to curses of rage and frustration. They lost contact with one another, and it was each man for himself. Machine-gun and rifle fire streaked through the trees; mortar bursts sent debris flying. There may have been only twenty-five or thirty of the enemy, but it seemed at least a hundred—and all hidden, all firing without showing themselves. It was like fighting in the dark passages of an abandoned mine filled with rotting timbers and hung with the webs of monstrous steel-spinning spiders, and exploding on all sides with charges of powder. The woods pinged and hammered and roared.

The men on the right finished first, stumbled out to the road with eleven prisoners, collected themselves, and rushed in on the left. They managed to keep together pretty well and to fight effectively as a team. Coming to the rear of a mortar and some riflemen spread out in the underbrush before it, they killed several of the enemy and took two prisoners. It ended quickly after that. The firing diminished to single shots and then to silence. The men who were scattered all through the woods now began to shout, somewhat tremulously, inquiringly, to find one another. Gradually the shouts converged, and finally one hundred and thirty-seven Americans came out of the woods almost together.

They brought four prisoners with them, but they were too dazed to remark that the prisoners wore American battle jackets and helmets. Including the soldier who had seen something move and the one who had got it on the road, eleven of the company had been killed, but no one mentioned the fact; no one asked questions. They looked a mess. It was incredible that they should have got so ragged and grimed and smudged with dirt. Their emotions were in a state too. They were too stupefied from the shock of the crazy battle to do anything but stand there in the road and stare about with glazed eyes. They did not seem to know what to do with themselves, or with the prisoners, or with the dead man who lay sprawled down the road. They seemed to be waiting for something to happen, and nothing happened for a long time.

Then, suddenly, a Negro soldier was afflicted with laughter. He doubled over and stumbled drunkenly in the middle of the road in a paroxysm of laughter. He tried to smother it, but every time he got it under control his eyes would light instantly on someone's face and he was off again. In slowly gathering wonderment the men looked at him. The major was the first to recover. He took the soldier by the arm and shook him. "What are you laughing at, soldier? Hold it now," the major said. "Hold it, soldier," he repeated more sternly as the man looked at him and broke out again.

"You too, Major," the Negro said, tears streaming. "Major, sir," he said, his voice beginning to whoop again, "I swear to God an' hope to die if you can tell which of them Joes is white and which is colored! Look at 'em, Major. I swear to God . . ."

Grinning sheepishly, the men looked at each other, and some began to laugh. The major laughed, the men laughed, and even some of the prisoners laughed. The road rang with the sound of it rising, rippling, and gathering to a hilarious roar. When it had spent itself the major, frowning, said, "Okay. Okay, soldiers. We've still got work to do. The war's not over yet."

XI. MORNING FAIR

1. *Strategy*

Back home in America the Negro's political, economic, and social position was better than it had ever been before. It was far from ideal, but, among other things, the Supreme Court had ruled it unconstitutional to exclude him from white Democratic party primaries; his employment opportunities were greater; his wage differential had been practically eliminated; he was increasingly active in organized labor. Some of the bars to his advancement in the military were down.

Even the South seemed to realize that the physical struggle against fascism had subjected the traditional pattern of race relations and attitudes to considerable strain, and while some Southerners reacted to this in their accustomed ways, the best minds of the South moved to meet it. Liberals like Ralph McGill of Georgia and Virginius Dabney of Virginia, together with a handful of ministers and educators, took the initiative in a program of "new morality to give assurance [to Negroes] of our sincere goodwill and desire to cooperate."

If cynicism suggested that the manifestations of this "new morality" were compelled by the inexorable logic of history and a perception of America's new place in the world, rather than created in the integrity of the hearts of men, so much the better. Perhaps America had grown more realistic, even as the world had shrunk. Good will had often in the past proved an uncertain commodity in the market of race relations, and however much Negroes respected it, they were no longer willing to depend upon it. The war had joined their fate to that of minority and colonial peoples throughout the world, and the new touchstones of race destiny and of the destiny of all men were economic and political. If practical politics and economics were inspired by kindliness, well and good; but they should first be informed by simple reason and a reasonable concern for the safety of the world. Negroes believed with Lester Granger, head of the Urban League: "The United States must hold to the elemental principles of cooperation. . . . Back of all that is planned or achieved is the fact that henceforth it is one world or none."

So it was not that Negroes rejected good will. It was never quite worthless, and, in fact, it had brought about many a measure beneficial to them. The shocked mourning over the death of President Roosevelt would have been less deep except that Negroes deeply felt the loss of his humanitarian interest. They respected the good will shown by the Department of State when it accredited several Negroes to the organizational meeting of the United Nations, and they applauded the Preamble and Article I of the UN Charter, which reaffirmed a belief in human rights and "fundamental freedom for all without distinction as to race. . . ."

But Negroes knew that if the charter meant what it said, that if democracy would be fulfilled—and, indeed, if it would be saved—then the instruments of democratic government—the executive, the legislative, and the judicial —must join an attack on the inequities inherent in racial segregation. As they approached the halfway mark of the twentieth century Negroes by and large looked beyond solicitude to strength, beyond men to the measures they proposed, beyond messiahs to machinery, and beyond good will to strategy.

The strategy was scarcely new: the NAACP had devised it long ago. It was simply applied on a new and broader front and directed by a new, rigidly disciplined and yet resilient mind.

2. *Nobody's Fool*

Until he was twenty-one Thoroughgood Marshall had no idea of becoming a lawyer. Entirely without self-consciousness before that time, he gave little thought to *becoming* anything. He simply was. And what he was amounted to a yeasty mixture of brash assertiveness, a sharp and sportive sense of humor, an instinct for people, an amused irreverence for the "solemn finer things of life," and mercenary ambitiousness. At forty-five he retained his sense of humor and his gregariousness, but all else had changed. At forty-five he had defended in a hundred courts of law the finest concepts of human dignity and equality of civil rights, had won twelve of fourteen cases on these issues before the highest court in the land, and was everywhere acknowledged to be the leading civil rights lawyer of his time. The transformation was less accidental than providential.

Marshall was born in Baltimore in 1908—that prophetic year when a group of deeply troubled whites conceived the idea of the NAACP—and into a class that was then still making a slow and sometimes painful transition from staid color-conscious mulatto aristocrats to race-conscious bourgeoisie. His mother was a public-school teacher; his father chief steward of a country club. Both—as such things are calculated—were at least half white. The census takers never knew what to make of Marshall's paternal grandmother. Was she white or colored? Her answer was that she could not say. She had been raised in a Negro home in Virginia, and that was all she knew.

On both sides of the Marshall family there was a tradition of rebellion, but personal achievement and family position had attenuated it long before Thoroughgood reached the age of discovery. During his boyhood it showed up chiefly in his father's disputatiousness. William Marshall argued about everything and anything, but he did not bluster. He believed in facts. Much of his leisure time was spent looking them up and cramming them in and using them to challenge the logic of even the most commonly accepted ideas. There was not much that he would take for granted. Thoroughgood, his younger son, inherited his disputatious bent and his loud, commanding voice. Often the strangers who passed along the street where the Marshalls lived must have wondered what such loud-mouthed Negroes were doing in such an obviously genteel Negro neighborhood.

The Marshalls lived a happy, comfortable life. Compared to the lives of Negroes in neighborhoods south and east of them, it was very comfortable indeed. But in the years just before and after the First World War few Negroes on Druid Hill Avenue bothered to compare—except perhaps to confirm the general opinion that poverty, disease, and crime were due to shiftlessness. Apparently even William Marshall took this for granted. For fear that improvidence was not demonstrably an inborn trait, it was his idea that his boys should avoid contact with it in all its forms. Thoroughgood was sent to the school where his mother taught, where she could keep an eye on him. Since he was endowed with more than the normal supply of intellectual curiosity, he galloped through his studies, especially those he liked. At home he did his share of chores. But curiosity and gregariousness are a hard combination to control, and now and then he slipped away and prowled the east and south side's bitter streets, where, probably, he mistook the visible insignias of despair for something else again. He had still to reach the age of discovery.

He graduated from high school and entered college in 1926. Lincoln University, in Pennsylvania, was one of the half dozen really choice colleges for Negroes. Its students and alumni called it the "black Princeton." It had been founded by a Princeton graduate, it sported Princeton's colors as its own, and its faculty was staffed almost exclusively with Princeton men. It was a good school, more strict for learning than most, but very loose on social control, and completely indifferent to falderal and academic glitter.

Its students came from everywhere, including Asia and Africa, and represented the economic classes from laboring poor to semi-idle rich. Though Lincoln men talked a great deal about making "big money" (it was a period of financial boom), and though the educational ambitions of most of them were geared to one or another of the independent professions (called rackets) that seemed to guarantee this end, a display of wealth brought a man no more respect than poverty brought scorn. "Don't tell us who your daddy is," incoming freshmen were told, "show us what you are."

Nearly everybody worked. Rich and poor competed not only for academic honors but for summer jobs as waiters, kitchen help, and bellhops at resorts along the Eastern coast. Lincoln men were as boisterous as gamins, as ebullient as fizz, and as alert as startled foxes.

In this raucous community of three hundred, young Marshall quickly found his place. He could "kid" and "crack wise" as effectively as any. He was louder and brasher than most.

By the middle of his sophomore year he began to discover things other than the raw pleasures of late adolescence, the thrill of learning under competent instructors, and—as a member of the Forensic Society—the challenge of debate. Beneath the crude manners, which Lincoln men made a point of flaunting like flags, and the blatant cynicism in their talk of the big money, beneath the selfish ambitions projected in their boastful dreams blazed a furious zeal for the concept of racial equality, burned a bitter hatred of injustice, smoldered a lava flow of race consciousness that alternately anguished and exalted them. Never in the presence of their white instructors—for these feelings were confused by pride and shame as well, and must never be exposed to whites—but in nightly bull sessions they expressed themselves without restraint or pretense.

It was the era of the "new Negro." The Harlem renaissance was at its height, and Lincoln men were extravagantly proud of the successes of Paul Robeson, the literary acclaim of the new, young Negro poets and writers, the musical-comedy renown of Florence Mills. But Garvey's release from prison and his deportation in 1927 was an occasion for the white press to review his amazing exploits in a vein of comic scorn, and Lincoln bull sessions were often bitter with denunciations of "niggers who cut the hog." Many a bull session lasted all night.

Marshall began to discover who and what he was. Race consciousness grew to bud. He read all the books by or about Negroes he could lay his hands on. Sociology, history, fiction, and poetry were pouring from the press in unbelievable quantity. He read Julia Peterkin and Carl Van Vechten and was skeptical. He read Jerome Dowd's *The American Negro* and felt challenged. He read Carter Woodson's *The Negro in American History* and was uplifted. He read Du Bois. "To be sure," he read, "behind the thought lurks the afterthought—suppose, after all, the World is right and we are less than men?" Marshall was troubled, and his private war of impulses raged.

But his high-spirited sense of life could not be dampened for long. Once he began to discover himself, a fundamental integrity fixed the abiding elements of his character in a pattern which, though still incomplete—and for all the surface that overlay it—could scarcely be mistaken. "Don't let his loud mouth fool you," Marshall's acquaintances said; "he's nobody's fool." He was not only honest but frank to the point of insult. His temper was volatile. He hated sham. He had a natural affinity for the underdog, for arguing the unpopular side ("just to exercise his brains"), and for fighting against the odds. He would one day be satisfied with nothing less than complete dedication. Without willing it or intending it, he would one day find composed within himself a pride and passion of race and a shame and hatred of racial inequality that marked him a "new Negro." At twenty-one the most he lacked was self-discipline and the proper channel for his energies. Before another year had passed, he was on his way to both.

Marshall was graduated cum laude from Lincoln in 1930, and in the fall of that year enrolled in the law school at Howard University. He had by this time married a bright young coed from the University of Pennsylvania, and money, never plentiful at any time, was pitifully scarce. The young couple lived in Baltimore, where everything was a shade cheaper than in Washington, and Marshall commuted to the university. He was up every morning at five for the long day ahead. Classes and study occupied most of it, but there was a wife to provide for and tuition to pay. He worked in the law library at night, and he squeezed in odd jobs when he could. Frequently it was long after midnight when he got home. It was not an easy life, but it was an absorbing one.

Howard University was experiencing a regeneration. Its first Negro president, Mordecai Johnson, had set out willfully to destroy the reputation for social glamor that, while it brought the university a kind of prestige, had sapped its intellectual and spiritual vitality for half a century. A man of vision and tremendous drive, Dr. Johnson was one of those Negroes who believed that the ferment of the times, the shifting patterns of thought and behavior, the skeptical inquiry and rebellion of the middle-class intellectual against old dogmas, the loosening of conventions, the to-hell-with-it disillusionment of the masses—in short, the change, the doubt, the fear and chaos that characterized the great depression—presented an opportunity for the social reparation of the Negro, if only the Negro would seize it. Johnson believed that the business of education was to incite beneficial change and to help solve the problems that change brings. An institution of learning, while it protected the good and valuable in older traditions, must at the same time encourage that "higher individualism" that constantly makes for new and greater values.

He had attracted to the university men of similar thought and of undeniable intellectual stature. Their ideas and their learning flowed back and forth through the university like the waves of an alluvial tide. Alain Locke, the spiritual father of the Negro renaissance, was there in philosophy, E. E. Just in the natural sciences, Franklin Frazier in sociology, Charles Burch and Sterling Brown in literature, Rayford Logan in history, and Ralph Bunche in government and politics. But especially significant for the direct influence they had on Thurgood Marshall (he had legalized the diminutive by this time) were Charles Houston, dean of the law school, and William Hastie and James Nabrit. In two years Houston converted Howard Law from a second- or third-rate school into a first-rate school of a very special kind.

While not exclusively committed to a narrow specialization, the law school was thoroughly dedicated to the enlargement of the Negro's civil rights. Houston himself frequently represented the NAACP in cases involving these rights, and so did Nabrit, and so did Hastie, a former editor of the *Harvard Law Review*, who joined the faculty in 1930. Howard Law had become a kind of legal laboratory, where officials of the NAACP met with the faculty and some of the brighter advanced students to plan offensive strategies against racial inequalities, especially in education. In the first case tried in Virginia in 1932–33, court action by day was followed by planning at night in the Howard Law Library. It was during this time that Thurgood Marshall came to the attention of Walter White, chief executive of the NAACP. White wrote in his autobiography of:

". . . a lanky, brash young senior law student who was always present. I used to wonder at his presence and sometimes was amazed at his assertiveness in challenging positions [taken] by Charlie [Houston] and the other lawyers. But I soon learned of his great value to the case in doing everything he was asked, from research on obscure legal opinions to foraging for coffee and sandwiches. This law student was Thurgood Marshall who later became special counsel of the Association and one whose arguments were listened to with respect by the U. S. Supreme Court."

But before he became special counsel for the NAACP, Marshall went into private practice in Baltimore. He did not expect to make much money, but he did hope to provide a modest living for his wife. He barely managed. His clients were poor in everything except frustrated rage at the injustices of dispossessions, evictions, police brutality, and excessive penalties for slight offenses. Marshall, who had "learned what rights were," threw himself into these cases with a zeal that the prospect of large fees could not possibly have stimulated. He took many of them without the slightest expectation of a fee. He became known in Baltimore and the surrounding county as the "little man's lawyer." He became known as a crusader in the war for human rights.

It was a war for more than the rights of Negroes (for as a matter of fact some of his clients were white, though usually alien and poor). "What's at stake here is more than the rights of my client," he argued in his first important case, brought to compel the University of Maryland to admit a Negro student. "What's at stake is the moral commitment stated in our country's creed."

This was no shot in the legal dark. It was just beginning to dawn on him—and he had not yet put it into words—that the test of democracy, no less than of the moral power of justice, lay in the people's will to accept the equal application of the laws. He was just beginning to take on with certitude and passion his race's role as the catalyst in the slow-working moral chemistry of America.

When Charles Houston turned Howard Law School over to the capable direction of William Hastie and became special counsel of the NAACP in 1935, he invited Thurgood Marshall to become his assistant. It meant for Marshall a regular though penny-pinching salary. But it also meant devoting all of his time and intelligence to the kind of legal work he loved and joining an organized, co-operative effort to attain ends which, he felt, must no longer be compromised. Houston was too frank not to confess that it would also mean exhausted patience, discouragement, privation, and even physical danger. Marshall accepted with alacrity. In 1938, his health severely strained, Houston resigned, and Thurgood Marshall succeeded him. Special counsel for the NAACP had never been a sinecure. In the 1930s it was probably the most demanding legal post in the country.

3. *Bridgeheads*

As we have seen, the Administration of President Roosevelt greatly stimulated the new growth of the old idea of social reform. The decade of the thirties was the decade of the rehabilitation of the "common man," and especially of that "one third" of the American common men who were "ill-fed, ill-housed and ill-clothed." The federal housing program got under way, the federal government in the role of social welfare agent came to be the accepted thing, and the Congress voted, for purposes of relief, vast programs of public works. Security was the word for all this, and the bringers of the word differed from one another as radically as Upton Sinclair, Francis Townsend, and Huey Long. Reflected even in the shallow surface of popular entertainment, and apparently affecting everyone, reform was in the air.

True, its periodic resurrection was as much a part of America's history as the Fourth of July, but heretofore social reform had been thought of in terms of charitable, voluntary action. Now it was thought of in terms of governmental and legal action. The NAACP saw an advantage. In the seventy-fifth anniversary year of the Emancipation it undertook a great and arduous offensive against racially discriminatory practices and laws.

The very first brief Marshall prepared in his new job was in a suit brought against the University of Missouri to admit a Negro to the law school. The suit differed radically from the Maryland case, and it had far greater significance. When Lloyd Gaines, the plaintiff, applied for admission to the university he was denied on the grounds that a state provision to finance the graduate and professional training of Negroes in schools outside the state constituted equality. Many Southern states had a similar provision, and Negroes had taken advantage of it, and no one had questioned the constitutionality of it. The lower courts upheld the state's contention that it was "contrary to the constitution, laws and public policy of the State to admit a Negro as a student in the University of Missouri." The NAACP carried the case to the Supreme Court.

Marshall based his argument squarely on that clause in the Fourteenth Amendment which forbids the state to deny any person under its jurisdiction the equal protection of the laws. The United States Supreme Court was asked to decide on the applicability of this clause to the case at hand. On December 12, 1938, it ruled six to two that "equality of education must be provided within the borders of the State." It was a broad decision that not only reaffirmed an earlier opinion that "separation [of the races] is legal only when it provides equality between the races," but opened the way for legal action to compel the equalization of school funds, teachers' salaries, and school facilities of all kinds.

If many thought the decision was broad enough to sweep away discrimination in education all over the South, Marshall himself had no such illusion. Two years with the NAACP had given him some experience of the South's fanatic will to resist. He knew that the struggle had only started, and that each strong point must be stormed in a separate action. The most he hoped for at that time was that legal assault after assault (he was prepared "to fight till doomsday") would so burden the South with the expense of providing separate but truly equal education as to weaken her resistance. He had not yet begun his brooding absorption in the abstract meanings of democracy. He was still committed only to the concrete measures of democracy and to the legal steps that would make these measures full. And these quite aside, there were fronts of elemental civil rights and justice still to defend.

There was, for instance, the right of Negroes to serve on juries.

In 1940, when a Negro physician of Dallas, Texas, dared to presume that a summons to jury duty addressed to him was really meant for him, he was kicked down the courthouse steps. Marshall flew to Texas. He had at least an assault case, if he cared to prosecute it. But he was after something more. He lingered in Dallas only long enough to learn the facts and to marvel at the tensions that the kicking incident had caused, and then he went on to Austin. Unannounced until his actual arrival at the capital itself, he presented himself for a conference with Governor James Allred.

The governor at first seemed offended by such brashness, but he soon got over it. Marshall neither looked nor sounded like an agitator. He talked to the governor with quiet sincerity. His whole, somewhat easygoing manner bespoke the belief that a reasonable man will be moved by reason. Within the hour Allred "ordered out the Texas Rangers to defend the right of Negroes to jury service."

But that right had to be protected time after time in state after state until at last, in 1943, Marshall won certification of it in a Supreme Court decision that held the exclusion of Negroes from jury rolls in violation of the due-process clause, and therefore unconstitutional.

Other and earlier struggles, in Texas and elsewhere, were proving less decisive, and Marshall had to fight some of his predecessors' battles all over again—again to win victories that were incomplete. In 1917 the Supreme Court had voided ordinances restricting Negro residence to specified sections of cities, but private restrictive covenants had kept Negroes in ghettos and slums. The Supreme Court did not frown upon such covenants until the 1940s. The "grandfather clauses," too, were repugnant to the Constitution, and had been so declared in 1915, but the white Democratic primary was an effective bar to the Southern Negro's exercise of the franchise. Not until 1944 did Marshall win a victory over it. And in some places even then, the whites' threats of violence and economic reprisal—and where not these, then the Negro's force-grown lethargy and ignorance—effected what was no longer legally allowed.

But the sulphur and brimstone reek of violence was not unknown to Thurgood Marshall. The town of Hugo, Oklahoma, smoked with it for a time in 1941, when Marshall went there to fight for the cause of simple justice. A Negro odd-jobs man named Lyons had been charged with the murder of a white family of four and with setting fire to their house to hide his crime. All the evidence seemed to indicate the guilt of another person or persons. The Negroes of the town thought so anyway. "Because Lyons is colored and defenseless, he's been framed like a picture," they told the NAACP. Marshall was sent to defend him.

When he arrived the hostility of the whites had aroused such fear in Negroes that many of them had smuggled in arms from Tulsa and Oklahoma City. They had taken elaborate precautions for Marshall's safety. He was to have a protective guard; a different sleeping place was arranged for each night. But Marshall, six feet tall and weighing close to two hundred pounds, was next to impossible to hide in a town so small, and, if the whites were determined to harm him, quite impossible to protect by such means as the Negroes had. He was gregarious, he was inquisitive. He had his client to see, questions to ask, prospective witnesses—whites among them—to interview. He dismissed his bodyguard. For almost a week he moved about the county-seat town as though he were completely ignorant of its subterranean passions.

By the time the trial opened all the townspeople knew who Marshall was and what he was doing there. They packed the courtroom. They seemed as curious as hostile. Marshall's preliminary presentation of the case seemed to melt the town's icy conviction of the defendant's guilt. He was a model of quiet dignity, easy decorum, and courtesy in the courtroom. He did not rant and rave. He did not browbeat witnesses. But he did not pull his legal punches either.

His main defense hinged on the fact that his client had been intimidated, but he developed testimony that strongly implied the guilt of others, including powerful local white members of a state-wide bootleg ring. He hinted at the venal corruption of some local officials. He proved that Lyons had been beaten after his arrest, and Marshall called this "police brutality." He drew an admission that the scorched and bloody bones of the victims had been piled on the body of the accused in an effort to make him confess, and Marshall called this "sadism" and "torture." But far from increasing hostility, he coaxed the townspeople and the jury toward an awareness of pride and beauty in doing justice. He believed, and was later to say, that "even in the most prejudiced communities, the majority of the people have some respect for truth and some sense of justice, no matter how deeply hidden it is at times." On the last day of the trial the superintendent of schools, who had been in constant attendance, dismissed classes for half a day so that the white high school students could go and "hear that Nigrah lawyer" sum up.

Marshall did not get an acquittal. The jury and the town could not so abruptly sever all the complex emotional ties that bound them to the unforbearing past, nor quite yet admit of a complete victory of conscience over ancient consciousness and custom. But he won a partial victory for justice. The accused was sentenced to life imprisonment rather than to death—as he surely would have been had the jury and the town believed him guilty.

One townsman, however, did break with the past. The father of the woman allegedly slain by Lyons took up the fight for the Negro's freedom. The fight was lost, but an attitude was won. Four years later, in 1945, the slain woman's father, white native of Oklahoma, became president of the local branch of the NAACP.

4. The Conscience of the Country

After nearly two hundred and fifty years of dubious battle in the fields of conscience, an attitude seemed generally to have been won and a change seemed generally to be coming to the moral climate of America. Both the attitude and the change "were marked," said Frederick Lewis Allen, "by a broader and broader answer" to the question, " 'Who is my neighbor?' " They were marked by an increasing regard for human needs, by a strengthening conviction of the interdependence of peoples, by a growing prevalence of the one-world idea, and, again to quote Allen, "by an expanding acceptance in America . . . of 'the commitment to equality.' "

Nineteen forty-five was the year when integration was begun in the army and seemed assured in the future of other branches of the armed services. It was the year when New York and Massachusetts, soon to be followed by Wisconsin and Oregon, set up Fair Employment Practices agencies; the year a Negro became a vice-president of an international union in CIO; and the year a Negro was first mentioned (and a few months later chosen) as governor of the Virgin Islands. It was the year of the organization of the United Nations.

Few men in American public life reacted so directly to all this as the secretary and the special counsel of the NAACP. Probably no two men in America felt it to be so direct a challenge to the democratic ideal. Both Walter White and Thurgood Marshall had long since anchored the program of the NAACP in the proposition that democracy is capable of infinite improvement; both had anchored their belief in the thesis that the Negro's very presence in America had helped to quicken and extend the American idea of democracy. The changed attitude and the changing moral climate, then, were a challenge to more than the abstract principle. They were a challenge to the work to which White and Marshall had devoted their lives. They moved to confront the challenge with a new, bold idea: the idea that racial segregation is abhorrent to the concept and the ideal structure of democracy.

As a social idea, this was easy to credit; as a legal principle, it would be difficult to affirm. As a social proposition, all history proved it, and its truth was reflected in all the indices—education, employment, politics, health, housing, and crime—one cared to cite. As a doctrine of American law, all legal precedent was against it.

But Marshall had not had a dozen matchless years of experience in civil law for nothing. He believed that the equalitarian concepts embodied in the Declaration of Independence and the constitutional proscription of distinctions based on race and color should be made to apply. If as a matter of law it could be proved that segregation per se is inequality, constitutional guarantees would take care of the rest. He believed it could be proved. He had not, as he said, been a Negro all his life for nothing either.

So there began five years of intensive preparation. This included not only lower-court hearings attacking inequalities in the salaries of Negro teachers, in educational opportunities, in employment, in travel accommodations, and in the exercise of the ballot—thus establishing precedents and erecting a body of confirmable opinion item by item; but it also included periodic conclaves the likes of which had never before been convened for such purposes.

For days at a time, year after year, social scientists, psychologists, historians, legal experts, and educators—white and colored, and all volunteers—met in New York to wrestle with every aspect of the problem that Marshall and his staff thought likely to be raised in a court of law. Less frequently, in the days just before an actual hearing, the staff of NAACP lawyers—most of them, too, volunteers—

would hold moot court in the Howard Law School library, with faculty members acting as judges. "They're going to try everything in the book," Marshall said, referring to the opposition. "Our job is to stay ahead of them."

But even keeping up with "them" required tremendous emotional, intellectual, and sheer physical energy. The "commitment to equality" was not so evident in the South. That it was there, especially among white college and university students, was indicated in various opinion polls, but the South's most powerful and vociferous leaders professed to see any breach in the legal wall protecting "immemorial custom" as threatening the South with an "inundating black tide" that would "destroy the South's precious way of life."

Though Marshall laughed without noticeable bitterness at such immoderate outbursts, he knew the complex snarl of emotions they revealed. He knew his own emotional involvement, hide it as he might from all but his closest associates. He appreciated the fact that if he was amazed and revolted by the opposition's grim focus on racial prejudice, the opposition could not be expected to sympathize with his equally grim focus on destroying the interpretations of the law that supported it. In one Southern court after another, local, state and federal—thirteen times in five years—he argued that "injury results to the human personality subjecting or subjected to" civil inequalities. But the argument was still tangential. He did not try to prove it yet. He was content for the time merely to prove that inequalities existed. He worked eighteen and twenty hours a day. He traveled fifty thousand miles a year. In 1950 he was able to establish the legal bridgehead from which to launch the offensive against segregation itself.

The bridgehead was established on two cases: Sweatt vs. Painter, and McLaurin vs. Oklahoma State Regents. In the first, the state of Texas had responded to a Negro's application to the state law school by hastily founding a separate law school for Negroes under the "separate but equal" doctrine. Arguing the case before the United States Supreme Court, Marshall took the position that not only the "quantitative differences between the white and Negro law schools with respect to such matters as the number of faculty members, the size of the library and the scope of the curricula," but those "more important factors, incapable of objective measurement"—the reputation of the faculty, the experience of the administration, "the status and influence of the alumni"—proved the inequality of the Negro law school. Sweatt, Marshall argued, was entitled to his "full constitutional rights," to a legal education equal in every way to that "offered by the State to students of other races."

The Supreme Court agreed with him and ordered Sweatt admitted to the university.

In the second case another, broader, and more salient point was at issue. The plaintiff McLaurin had been admitted to the University of Oklahoma, so there was no question of the equality of faculty, facilities, and curricula. But McLaurin had been forced to sit apart from other students in classroom and library, and generally to study and live on a segregated basis. The point was whether such "State-imposed segregation destroys equality of educational benefits."

The Supreme Court held that it did.

XII. MR. SMITH GOES TO WASHINGTON

On Sunday, May 16, 1954, Negroes singly and in groups began arriving in Washington. There were not enough of them to be particularly conspicuous, but still there were a great many, most of them strangers to the capital. Although newspapers throughout the country had been speculating on the likelihood, no one except the justices of the Supreme Court really knew that Monday, May 17, was to be the day when what had been called "the noblest prerogative of democracy" either would be forsworn for the immediate present or assumed for all time. Except the justices, no one knew that Monday would bring the decision as to whether "segregation and a determination to hold some men inherently unequal to others" would prevail or be destroyed in law. Yet on Sunday a thousand or more Negroes from all parts of the country streamed toward the place of decision as if drawn there by instinct.

Some of the lawyers who represented them had been in Washington for nearly a week. They had calculated on the last Monday of the Court's present session, and tomorrow was it. In their six-room headquarters suite of the Wardman-Park Hotel, where none of them except Greenberg, Pinsky, and Weinstein, who were Jews, and Ming and Robinson, who were fair-complexioned enough to pass for white, could have stayed during the first hearing in 1952, they spent their time rehashing all the arguments. One moment they would decide that the decision would be rendered for them, and the very next that it would be rendered against them.

They tried to divert themselves with penny-ante poker, and with talk about the baseball season just getting under way. Thurgood Marshall told some of his longest, funniest stories. But nothing diverted them for long. Somebody would remember a precedent that might possibly have been pushed in argument, and somebody else would mention an authority who might have been more extensively cited. But in fact the brief that had been prepared for the second hearing, now ten months in the past, was as thorough as the great learning of two dozen scholars and the legal knowledge of as many lawyers could make it. It ran to two hundred and thirty-five close-printed pages, and it had cited all the pertinent precedents and quoted all the relevant authorities. The truth of the matter was that the lawyers were as nervous as cats.

Their clients were much less nervous. They were less sophisticated and far less knowledgeable than the lawyers. The nice and tricky questions of constitutionality and legal precedents scarcely troubled them. Indeed, most of them were so artless that the warnings of their leaders and even the unhappy past had not prepared them really to credit the fact that what the world knew to be morally wrong might be declared legally right. They had, Marshall had said, "no conception of a *legal* means of denying them what is theirs of right."

Most of those who arrived on Sunday—a clear, fine day —were more curious than troubled. Many of them did not know where the Supreme Court was, though they intended to be there when the time came. Many of them had no place to stay. Some—and probably a majority—did not know that Washington had lately been made an "open city" and that its places of public accommodation were available to all alike. They sought out other Negroes and inquired where the "colored" section and "colored" restaurants and "places where the colored stayed" were. There was a run-down Negro motel a mile or two south across the Virginia line, and some went there. There was a better motel "for colored" north across the Maryland line, and some went there. Some spent Sunday night in the railroad station; some in the bus station. A group of seven from South Carolina were especially lucky. They met a minister formerly of their state, and he invited them to his evening church service and got members of his church to take them in for the night.

The first man to reach the Supreme Court building on Monday morning arrived there at one o'clock. He was Arthur Smith, a Negro aged seventy-six, and he had come down on the midnight train from his home in Baltimore. He was no stranger to the city. For forty-one years he had commuted to his job as a messenger in the State Department, and he knew his way about. He realized that he could not get into the building until the doors opened at nine o'clock, or into the courtroom itself until eleven, but he had come for the first hearing in 1952, and for the reargument in 1953, and both times he had come too late. He did not intend to be late this time. He carried a cushion under his arm and two fat sandwiches in his sagging topcoat pocket.

He walked up and down in front of the building and along East Capitol Street for a while. He wondered how long it would be before he would be able to discern the first faint glimmer of dawn. He had some notion of watching it come up. Finally he grew tired of walking and climbed the courthouse steps, placed his cushion in the shadow of a balustrade, and sat down. In a moment he was asleep. At just before three he was awakened by a guard shining a light in his face and inquiring what he was doing there. Smith told him. Proud but deferential, he showed the guard his twenty-five-year service pin and the inscription on the gold watch his fellow employees had given him when he retired. He talked at some length. Satisfied, the guard moved on.

Shortly after that Mr. Smith had a companion in his vigil, who told him his name was Crosby Ewing. He had been in the city since evening of the day before, but "the darnedest thing," he told Mr. Smith, "after all the trouble of finding a place to sleep, doggone if I didn't wake up in the middle of the night worrying that I'd miss what I came for."

The two men talked. Mr. Smith was garrulous, and he boasted a little. He said he had once lived on the same street in Baltimore where the "head lawyer's" mother now lived. He said he must have seen the head lawyer many a time without ever suspecting "that little ol' boy in knee pants would some day be a great leader of our people." After it was over today, he said, if he got a chance he was going to make himself known to Thurgood Marshall and congratulate him. Ewing asked Mr. Smith if he would do this no matter how it turned out, "even if we lose?" Mr. Smith said he would. They were silent for a while.

"But suppose we do lose? What'll we colored do then? Just suppose now," Ewing warned, as if he dared Mr. Smith to think that such a supposition could possibly be true.

"We'll endure it," Mr. Smith said casually, pulling out the sandwiches and offering his companion one. He took the wax paper from the top half of his sandwich and then he said, "Then we'll come back as many times as we have to. It ain't going to be forever. That's the thing about it. A time'll come when we won't have to endure no more." Then he bit into his sandwich.

"You sound mighty sure," Crosby Ewing said.

"Ain't you?" Mr. Smith replied.

Long before eight o'clock there was a sprinkling of people on the courthouse steps and standing among the columns of the marble portico. When the hour struck the first queue formed, and when the doors slid back at nine o'clock there were five long queues. Black and white, young and old shuffled into the great main hall. Here for two hours more they waited, mostly in silence, for the splendid hall awed them. Then the courtroom doors themselves were opened and the courtroom filled up. The two sections of seats, the side aisles, and the Ionic colonnade were filled in a twinkling.

At eleven forty-five some of the lawyers for both sides came in and took the front benches on the left. There was an instant craning of necks and a hushed sibilance of whispering as the audience recognized this face or that. There were states' attorneys general with members of their staffs, some private lawyers, and the Negro lawyers, undifferentiated as to seating, and, so far as a disinterested visitor might discover at sight, undivided. Thurgood Marshall was there, big, rumpled, restlessly turning his head right and left.

Promptly at noon the red velvet curtains parted behind the nine chairs on the dais, the sitting audience rose at once, and the Chief Justice of the United States, followed by eight black-robed associate justices, filed in. They sat down. The audience sat. One of the justices began to read from a sheaf of papers on the long desk before him. When he had finished, another read from another sheaf of papers. Three decisions were read before the Chief Justice himself began to read in a rather high-pitched voice. Just as he uttered the first words there was a discreet rush from somewhere, and a half dozen reporters, who had been taken by surprise in the pressroom below, scrambled to the press tables next the aisles. The Chief Justice went on reading. He finished at one-five in the afternoon.

As the audience rose to leave in hushed silence, there was not a Negro among them who did not feel his allegiance to democracy strengthened and his faith in the American dream renewed.

Mr. Smith did not have the opportunity to see Thurgood Marshall afterward, but at the end of the week he clipped an editorial from a Negro paper, added a single word of his own, and addressed both to the NAACP. The editorial said, "The conscience of America has spoken through its constitutional voice. . . ." The word Mr. Smith added was "Amen."

Thurgood Marshall said, "The war's not over yet. We've still got work to do."

A NOTE OF THANKS AND
A PARTIAL LIST OF SOURCES

No one who undertakes a book of this kind could ever even initially suppose himself completely independent of the assistance and co-operation of others. His debt grows as his work proceeds, and my debt is substantial. I wish to acknowledge how much I owe to the dozens of people who, like Ralph Bunche, Greene Buster, Thurgood Marshall, and A. Philip Randolph, took time to answer numerous letters, to talk and in general to bear with my importunities.

In the Congressional Library in Washington, the Founders Library at Howard University, the Free Library in Wilmington, Delaware, and in the distinguished Schomburg Collection in New York I had the generous help of the librarians. But I am especially indebted to the entire staff of the Huntington Library at Hampton Institute, where I was given private space and where most of this work was done. The reference and research librarians, Mrs. Addie Cross and Miss Yvette Cameron, were particularly helpful by finding obscure references and unearthing mines of material which certainly broadened my knowledge and deepened, I trust, my perception of American history and Negro life in America.

Though I followed my own bent, the discerning criticisms of Mr. Lewis Gannett and Mr. George Shively saved me from many errors of thought and expression. They could not save me from all. Such errors as remain are entirely mine.

Finally, without time and freedom from committee and other assignments that take so much of the energy of college teachers these days, this book would have been much longer in the writing and, conceivably, might not have been written at all. President Alonzo G. Moron and Dean William H. Martin, of Hampton Institute, have my grateful thanks.

A list of sources that were especially helpful follows:

Adams, James Truslow. *The March of Democracy: The Rise of the Union.* New York, 1932.

Allen, Frederick Lewis. *The Big Change: America Transforms Itself 1900–'50.* New York, 1952.

———. *Since Yesterday: The Nineteen-Thirties in America.* New York, 1940.

Allen, James S. *Reconstruction: The Battle for Democracy.* New York, 1937.

Aptheker, Herbert. *American Negro Slave Revolts.* New York, 1943.

——. *Essays in the History of the American Negro.* New York, 1945.

——. *The Negro in the Civil War.* New York, 1938.

——. *To Be Free.* New York, 1948.

Baker, Ray Stannard. *Following the Color Line.* New York, 1908.

Beard, Charles A., and Mary R. *The Rise of American Civilization.* 2 vols. New York, 1933.

Blesh, Rudie, and Janis, Harriet. *They All Played Ragtime.* New York, 1950.

Bontemps, Arna, and Conroy, Jack. *They Seek a City.* New York, 1945.

Bowers, Claude G. *The Tragic Era.* New York, 1929.

Brawley, Benjamin. *The Negro Genius.* New York, 1937.

——. *A Social History of the Negro.* New York, 1921.

Brazeal, Brailsford R. *The Brotherhood of Sleeping Car Porters.* New York, 1946.

Brown, Hallie Q. *Pen Pictures of Pioneers of Wilberforce.* Xenia (Ohio), 1937.

Buckler, Helen. *Doctor Dan: Pioneer in American Surgery.* Boston, 1954.

Buckmaster, Henrietta. *Let My People Go.* New York, 1941.

Butcher, Margaret Just. *The Negro in American Culture.* New York, 1956.

Cash, W. J. *The Mind of the South.* New York, 1941.

Coan, Josephus Alexander. *Daniel Payne, Christian Educator.* Philadelphia, 1935.

Conrad, Earl. *Harriet Tubman.* Washington, 1943.

Cronon, Edmund David. *Black Moses: The Story of Marcus Garvey.* Madison, 1955.

Curti, Merle. *The Growth of American Thought.* New York, 1943.

Dabney, Virginius. *Liberalism in the South.* Chapel Hill, 1932.

Detweiler, Frederick G. *The Negro Press in the United States.* Chicago, 1922.

Drake, St. Clair, and Cayton, Horace. *Black Metropolis.* New York, 1945.

Du Bois, W. E. Burghardt. *Black Reconstruction in America.* New York, 1935.

——. *Color and Democracy.* New York, 1945.

——. *Darkwater.* New York, 1920.

——. *Dusk of Dawn.* New York, 1940.

——. *The Negro Church.* Atlanta, 1903.

——. *The Philadelphia Negro.* Philadelphia, 1899.

——. *The Souls of Black Folk.* Chicago, 1903.

Dumond, Dwight Lowell. *America in Our Time, 1896–1946.* New York, 1947.

Eaton, Clement. *Freedom of Thought in the Old South.* Durham, 1940.

Embree, Edwin. *American Negroes: A Handbook.* New York, 1942.

——. *Brown Americans.* New York, 1944.

——. *13 Against the Odds.* New York, 1945.

Fauset, Arthur Huff. *For Freedom.* Philadelphia, 1937.

——. *Sojourner Truth: God's Faithful Pilgrim.* Chapel Hill, 1938.

Fite, Emerson David. *Social and Industrial Conditions During the Civil War.* New York, 1910.

Fleischer, Nat. *Black Dynamite.* Vol. 2. New York, 1938.

Fleming, Walter L. " 'Pap' Singleton, The Moses of the Colored Exodus." *The American Journal of Sociology,* July, 1909.

Foner, Philip S. *The Life and Writings of Frederick Douglass.* 3 vols. New York, 1954.

Frazier, E. Franklin. *The Negro Family in the United States.* Chicago, 1939.

Furr, Arthur. *Democracy's Negroes.* Boston, 1947.

Gallagher, Buell G. *American Caste and the Negro College.* New York, 1938.

Ginzberg, Eli, et al. *The Negro Potential.* New York, 1956.

Graham, Shirley. *Paul Robeson: Citizen of the World.* New York, 1946.

——. *There Was Once a Slave: The Heroic Story of Frederick Douglass.* New York, 1947.

Hawk, Emory. *Economic History of the South.* New York, 1934.

Hesseltine, William B. *The South in American History.* New York, 1943.

Ingersoll, Ralph. *Top Secret.* New York, 1946.

Jenkins, William Sumner. *Pro-Slavery Thought in the Old South.* Chapel Hill, 1935.

Johnson, Charles S. *Growing Up in the Black Belt.* Washington, 1941.

——. *The Negro College Graduate.* Chapel Hill, 1938.

Johnson, James Weldon. *Along This Way.* New York, 1933.

——. *Black Manhattan.* New York, 1930.

Kardiner, Abram, and Ovesey, Lionel. *The Mark of Oppression.* New York, 1951.

Karsner, David. *John Brown: Terrible 'Saint.'* New York, 1934.

Kennedy, Louise Venable. *The Negro Peasant Turns Cityward.* New York, 1930.

Kerlin, Robert T. *Voice of the Negro.* New York, 1920.

Little, Arthur W. *From Harlem to the Rhine.* New York, 1936.

Logan, Rayford. *The Negro in American Life and Thought.* New York, 1954.

——. *The Negro and the Post-War World.* Washington, 1945.

Mandelbaum, David G. *Soldier Groups and Negro Soldiers.* Berkeley, 1952.

McGinnis, Frederick A. *A History of Wilberforce University.* Wilberforce (Ohio), 1941.

McKay, Claude. *A Long Way From Home.* New York, 1937.

McKay, Martha Nicholson. *When the Tide Turned in the Civil War.* Indianapolis, 1929.

Morrison, Samuel Eliot, and Commager, Henry Steele. *The Growth of the American Republic.* New York, 1930.

Moton, Robert Russa. *What the Negro Thinks.* New York, 1929.

The Negro in Virginia. (WPA Writers Project.) New York, 1940.

Nichols, Lee. *Breakthrough on the Color Front.* New York, 1954.

Ottley, Roi. *The Lonely Warrior.* Chicago, 1955.

——. *New World A-Coming.* Boston, 1943.

Ovington, Mary White. *The Walls Came Tumbling Down.* New York, 1947.

Page, Thomas Nelson. *The Old South.* New York, 1892.

Powdermaker, Hortense. *After Freedom.* New York, 1939.

Pyle, Ernie. *Brave Men.* New York, 1943.

Quarles, Benjamin. *Frederick Douglass.* Washington, 1948.

——. *The Negro in the Civil War.* Boston, 1954.

Reid, Ira DeA. *In a Minor Key.* Washington, 1940.

Reuter, Edward Byron. *The American Race Problem.* New York, 1927.

Richardson, Benjamin. *Great American Negroes.* New York, 1945.

Richardson, Clement (ed.). *The National Cyclopedia of the Colored Race.* Montgomery (Alabama), 1919.

Robeson, Eslanda Goode. *Paul Robeson, Negro.* New York, 1930.

Rogers, J. A. *World's Great Men of Color.* 2 vols. New York, 1947.

Rollin, Frank A. *Martin R. Delany.* Boston, 1868.

Rose, Arnold. *The Negro in America.* New York, 1944.

Schlesinger, Arthur M., Jr. *The Age of Jackson.* Boston, 1946.

Schoenfeld, Seymour J. *The Negro in the Armed Forces.* Washington, 1945.

Scott, Emmett J. *The American Negro in the World War.* Washington, 1919.

——. *Booker T. Washington.* New York, 1916.

Shulman, Milton. *Defeat in the West.* New York, 1948.

Silvera, John D. *The Negro in World War II.* New York, 1949.

Soper, Edmund Davison. *Racism: A World Issue.* New York, 1947.

Spero, Sterling D., and Harris, Abram L. *The Black Worker: The Negro and the Labor Movement.* New York, 1931.

Sterner, Richard, et al. *The Negro's Share.* New York, 1943.

Tannenbaum, Frank. *Darker Phases of the South.* New York, 1924.

This Is Our War. (Dispatches from Negro War Correspondents in World War II.) Baltimore, 1945.

Tyler, Alice Felt. *Freedom's Ferment*. Minneapolis, 1944.

Washington, Booker T. *The Negro in Business*. Boston, 1907.

——. *The Negro in the South*. Philadelphia, 1907.

——. *Up From Slavery*. New York, 1901.

Weaver, Robert C. *Negro Labor*. New York, 1946.

Weinberg, Albert K. *Manifest Destiny: A Study of Nationalist Expansion in American History*. Baltimore, 1935.

Wesley, Charles H. *Richard Allen: Apostle of Freedom*. Washington, 1935.

Wharton, Vernon Lane. *The Negro in Mississippi, 1865–1890*. Chapel Hill, 1938.

White, Walter. *A Man Called White*. New York, 1948.

——. *A Rising Wind*. New York, 1945.

Williams, Charles H. *Sidelights on Negro Soldiers*. Boston, 1923.

Williams, George W. *Negro Troops in the Rebellion: 1861–1865*. New York, 1888.

Wilson, Joseph T. *The Black Phalanx: A History of the Negro Soldiers of the U.S. in the Wars of 1775–1812, 1861–1865*. Hartford, 1888.

Woodson, Carter G. *A Century of Negro Migration*. Washington, 1918.

——. *The Education of the Negro Prior to 1861*. Washington, 1919.

——. *History of the Negro Church*. Washington, 1921.

——. *The Mind of the Negro As Reflected in Letters Written During the Crisis 1800–1860*. Washington, 1926.

——. *The Negro in Our History*. Washington, 1921.

——. *The Negro Professional Man and the Community*. Washington, 1934.

Woodward, C. Vann. *The Strange Career of Jim Crow*. New York, 1955.

Yank—The G I Story of the War. (Dispatches from *Yank* correspondents.) New York, 1947.

NEWSPAPERS, MAGAZINES & SPECIAL SOURCES

Afro-American Newspaper. Baltimore.
Century Magazine.
Chicago Bee.
Chicago Defender.
Chicago Whip.
Crisis Magazine.
Crusader. Chicago.
Journal & Guide. Norfolk.
Journal of Negro History.
Messenger Magazine.
Negro World.
New Masses.
New Republic.

New York *Age*.
Opportunity Magazine.
Pittsburgh *Courier*.
Report of the Gillem Board, War Department. November, 1945.
Small Unit Actions. Historical Division, U. S. War Department.
Study of the Negro in Military Service, by Jean Byers. (Mimeographed copy for "departmental use.") January, 1950.
Survey Graphic.

INDEX

金色夜叉
こん じき や しゃ

新潮文庫　　　　　　　　　　　お - 5 - 1

昭和四十四年十一月　十　日　発　行
平成　二　年十一月二十五日　三十一刷

著　者　　尾お　崎ざき　紅こう　葉よう

発行者　　佐　藤　亮　一

発行所　　株式
　　　　　会社　新　潮　社

　　　郵便番号　　　　一六二
　　　東京都新宿区矢来町七一
　　　電話　業務部〇三(三二六六)五一一一
　　　　　　編集部〇三(三二六六)五四四〇
　　　振替東京四─八〇八番

価格はカバーに表示してあります。

乱丁・落丁本は、ご面倒ですが小社通信係宛ご送付
ください。送料小社負担にてお取替えいたします。

印刷・錦明印刷株式会社　製本・株式会社大進堂
Printed in Japan

ISBN4-10-107401-1　C0193

新潮文庫最新刊

藤本和子訳
J・ゴアズ

狙撃の理由

11月の冬の日、鹿狩りに出かけたフレッチャーが狙撃された。卑劣な暴力に森の静かな生活を奪われた男の犯人追跡を描く長編小説。

安西水丸
村上春樹 著

ランゲルハンス島の午後

カラフルで夢があふれるイラストと、その隣に気持ちよさそうに寄りそうハートウォーミングなエッセイでつづる25編。

柳田邦男 著

「死の医学」への序章

精神科医・西川喜作のガンとの闘いの軌跡をたどりながら、末期患者に対する医療のあり方を考える。現代医学への示唆に満ちた提言。

安部公房 著

方舟さくら丸

地下採石場跡の洞窟に、核シェルターの設備を造り上げた〈ぼく〉。核時代の方舟に乗れる者は、誰と誰なのか? 現代文学の金字塔。

フリーマントル
池央耿 訳

クレムリン・キス

CIA工作担当官フランクリンとMI-6新米工作員ブリンクマンが、モスクワを舞台に展開するソ連中央委員の政治亡命の大作戦!

泉麻人 著

B級ニュース図鑑

教科書や年鑑には決して載らないトホホな事件を採集・整理し、90年代の文脈において検証する文庫書下ろし時空積分コラム。

新潮文庫最新刊

星新一著 **ありふれた手法**

かくされた能力を引き出すための計画。それはよくある、ありふれたものだったが……。ユニークな発想が縦横無尽にかけめぐる30編。

田辺聖子著 **姥うかれ**（うば）

女には年齢の数だけ花が咲く、花の数だけ夢が咲く。愛しのシルバーレディ歌子サン、大活躍！『姥ざかり』『姥ときめき』の続編。

筒井康隆著 **歌と饒舌の戦記**

思想も、宗教も、国家の目標もない金満日本の虚妄を戦争シミュレーションと饒舌で痛罵。『文学部唯野教授』の饒舌体の原点をなす。

灰谷健次郎著 **砂場の少年**

35歳で臨時採用の教師になった男はどのような教育を実践するのか――子どもと大人の真の関係の在り方を問う文庫書下ろし長編小説。

三浦綾子著 **夕あり朝あり**

天がわれに与えた職業は何か――クリーニングの〈白洋舎〉を創業した五十嵐健治の、熱烈な信仰に貫かれた波瀾万丈の生涯。

吉村昭著 **鯨の絵巻**

太地で古式捕鯨の最後の筆頭刃刺を務めた男や、夜の奄美でハブを追う捕獲人など、動物を相手に生きる人間の哀歓をさぐる短編集。

森　鷗外　著　　阿部一族・舞姫

許されぬ殉死に端を発する阿部一族の悲劇を通して、権威への反抗と自己救済をテーマとした歴史小説の傑作「阿部一族」など10編。

森　鷗外　著　　山椒大夫・高瀬舟

人買いによって引き離された母と姉弟の受難を描いて、犠牲の意味を問う「山椒大夫」、安楽死の問題を見つめた「高瀬舟」等全12編。

夏目漱石　著　　吾輩は猫である

明治の俗物紳士たちの語る珍談・奇譚、小事件の数かずを、迷いこんで飼われている猫の眼から風刺的に描いた漱石最初の長編小説。

夏目漱石　著　　坊っちゃん

四国の中学に数学教師として赴任した直情径行の青年が巻きおこす珍騒動。ユーモアと人情の機微にあふれ、広範な愛読者をもつ傑作。

国木田独歩　著　　武蔵野

詩情に満ちた自然観察で、武蔵野の林間の美をあまねく知らしめた不朽の名作「武蔵野」など、抒情あふれる初期の名作17編を収録。

岡本かの子　著　　老妓抄

明治以来の文学史上、屈指の名編と称された表題作をはじめ、いのちの不思議な情熱を追究した著者の円熟期の名作9編を収録する。

堀 辰雄 著　　燃ゆる頬・聖家族

秩序と明晰さを愛するフランス文化の伝統と日本文学の深い造詣を融和させて、洗練された抒情の世界を創り上げた著者の初期作品集。

徳田秋声 著　　あらくれ

盲目的な好悪と利欲のままに様々な男と関係し流転を重ねる女を主人公に、純粋客観の立場で女性描写の妙を発揮した自然主義小説。

二葉亭四迷 著　　浮雲

秀才ではあるが世事にうとい青年官吏の苦悩を描写することによって、日本の知識階級の姿をはじめて捉えた近代小説の先駆的作品。

樋口一葉 著　　にごりえ・たけくらべ

明治の天才女流作家が短い生涯の中で残した名作集。人生への哀歓と美しい夢が織りこまれ、詩情に満ちた香り高い作品8編を収める。

倉田百三 著　　出家とその弟子

恋愛、性欲、宗教の相剋の問題について、親鸞とその息子善鸞、弟子の唯円の葛藤を軸に「歎異鈔」の教えを戯曲化した宗教文学の名作。

菊池 寛 著　　父帰る・屋上の狂人

個人主義思想と肉親の情との相剋を描く「父帰る」、高い所へ登りたがる狂った青年のまき起こす騒動の「屋上の狂人」等代表的戯曲8編。

第六項に該当する語は次のようなものである。

恰も→あたかも 　　　　適れ→あつぱれ 　　　　他→あれ
那箇→あれだけ 　　　　那麼→あんな 　　　　奈何に→いかに
雖も→いへども 　　　　被入る→いらっしゃる 　…居る→…ゐる
…乎→…か 　　　　　　怎る→かかる 　　　　且→かつ
…旁…→がてら 　　　　箇許→かばかり 　　　　管はない→かまはない
彼此→かれこれ 　　　　屹度→きっと 　　　　行らない→くだらない
妓→ここ 　　　　　　維に→ここに 　　　　箇の・這→この
這麼→こんな 　　　　有繋→さすが 　　　　扨→さて
然れば→されば 　　　　而も→しかも 　　　　因で→そこで
而して→そして 　　　　爾→その 　　　　　　那様→そんな
衝と→っと 　　　　　詰らない→つまらない 　奈何・如何→どう
迚も→とても 　　　　甚麼→どんな 　　　　莫れ→なかれ
勿れ→なかれ 　　　　被成・為る→なさる 　胡→なぞ
何為ろ→なにしろ 　　　仍→なほ 　　　　　約り・許り→ばかり
儻と→はたと 　　　　唯管→ひたすら 　　　　亦→また
迄→まで 　　　　　　儘→まま 　　　　　最う→もう
設し→もし 　　　　…乎→…や 　　　　　旋り→やがて
衣様・猶且→やはり 　　較・良→やや 　　　　設し→よし
縦んば→よしんば 　　陸に→ろくに 　　　　故と→わざと

文字づかいについて

新潮文庫の日本文学の文字表記については、なるべく原文を尊重するという見地に立ち、次のように方針を定めた。

一、口語文の作品は、旧仮名づかいで書かれているものは現代仮名づかいに改める。

二、文語文の作品は旧仮名づかいのままとする。

三、一般には当用漢字以外の漢字も使用し、音訓表以外の音訓も使用する。

四、難読と思われる漢字には振仮名をつける。

五、送り仮名は、なるべく原文を重んじて、みだりに送らない。

六、極端な宛て字と思われるもの及び代名詞、副詞、接続詞等のうち、仮名にしても原文を損うおそれが少ないと思われるものを仮名に改める。

本書は文語文で書かれているため、前記の方針により、旧仮名づかいのままとした。

振仮名も旧仮名づかいによる。ただし、漢字の字音による語および固有名詞は、古い字音仮名づかいによらず、現代の字音による仮名を振る。(例えば、「蒼々茫々」「執着」を「サウサウバウバウ」「シフチヤク」とせず、「そうそうぼうぼう」「しゅうちゃく」とする)

目　次

金色夜叉
こん
じき
や
しや

前　編

第　一　章

未だ宵ながら松立てる門は一様に鎖籠めて、真直に長く東より西に横はれる大道は掃きたるやうに物の影を留めず、いと寂くも往来の絶えたるに、例ならず繁き車輪の轍は、或は忙かりし、或は飲過ぎし年賀の帰来なるべく、疎に寄する獅子太鼓の遠響は、はや今日に尽きぬる三箇日を惜むが如く、その哀切に小き膓は断れぬべし。

元日快晴、二日快晴、三日快晴と誌されたる日記を潰して、この黄昏より凩は戦出でぬ。今は「風吹くな、なあ吹くな」と優き声の宥むる者無きより、憤をも増したるやうに飾竹を吹靡けつつ、乾びたる葉を粗なげに鳴らして、吼えては走行き、狂ひては引返し、揉みに揉んで独り散々に騒げり。微曇りし空はこれが為に眠を覚されたる気色にて、銀梨子地の如く無数の星を顕して、鋭く冱えたる光は寒気を発つかと想はしむるまでに、その薄明に曝さるる夜の街は殆ど氷らんとすなり。

人この裏に立ちて寥々冥々たる四望の間に、争か那の世間あり、社会あり、都あり、町ある
ことを想得べき、九重の天、八際の地、始めて混沌の境を出でたりといへども、万物未だ尽く化
生せず、風は試に吹き、星は新に輝ける一大荒原の、何等の旨意も、趣味も無くて、唯
濫に邂ひ横はれるに過ぎざる哉。日の中は宛然沸くが如く楽み、謳ひ、酔ひ、戯れ、歓ひ、笑ひ、
語り、興ぜし人々よ、彼等は儚くも夏果てし子の形を飲めて、今将何処に如何にして在るかを
疑はざらんとするも難からずや。多時静なりし後、遙に拍子木の音は聞えぬ。その響の消ゆる頃
忽ち一点の燈火は見え初めしが、揺々と町の尽頭を横截りて失せぬ。再び寒き風は寂き星月夜を
擅に吹くのみなりけり。唯有る小路の湯屋は仕舞を急ぎて、廂間の下水口より噴出づる湯気は
一団の白き雲を舞立てて、心地悪き微温の四方に溢るるとともに、垢臭き悪気の盛に迸るに遭
へる綱引の車あり。勢ひで角より曲り来にければ、避くべき違無くてその中を駆抜けたり。

「うむ、臭い」

車の上に声して行過ぎし跡には、葉巻の吸殻の捨てたるが赤く見えて煙れり。

「もう湯は抜けるのかな」

「へい、松の内は早仕舞でございます」

車夫のかく答へし後は、語絶えて、車は驀直に走れり、紳士は二重外套の袖を轟と搔合せて、横縞の華
獺の衿皮の内に耳より深く面を埋めたり。灰色の毛皮の敷物の端を車の後に垂れて、
麗なる浮波織の蔽膝して、提灯の徽章はTの花文字を二個組合せたるなり。行き行きて車はこの

小路の尽頭を北に折れ、稍広き街に出でしを、僅に走りて又西に入り、その南側の半程に箕輪と記したる軒燈を掲げて、剥竹を飾れる門構の内に挽入れたり。玄関の障子に燈影の映しながら、格子は鎖固めたるを、車夫は打叩きて、

「頼む、頼む」

奥の方なる響動の劇きに紛れて、取合はんともせざりければ、二人の車夫は声を合せて訪ひつつ、格子戸を連打にすれば、やがて急足の音立てて人は出で来ぬ。

円髷に結ひたる四十ばかりの小く痩せて色白き女の、茶微塵の糸織の小袖に黒の奉書紬の紋付の羽織着たるは、この家の内儀なるべし。彼の忙しげに格子を啓るを待ちて、紳士は優然と内に入らんとせしが、土間の一面に充満たる履物の杖を立つべき地さへあらざるに遅へるを、彼は虚さず勤篤に下立ちて、この敬ふべき賓の為に辛くも一条の道を開けり。かくて紳士の脱捨てし駒下駄のみは独り障子の内に取入れられたり。

（一）の 二

箕輪の奥は十畳の客間と八畳の中の間とを打抜きて、広間の十個処に真鍮の燭台を据ゑ、五十目掛の蠟燭は沖の漁火の如く燃えたるに、間毎の天井に白銅鍍の空気ランプを点したれば、四辺は真昼より明に、人顔も眩きまでに耀き遍れり。三十人に余んぬる若き男女は二分に輪作りて、今を盛と歌留多遊を為るなりけり。

蠟燭の焔と炭火の熱と多人数の熱蒸と混じたる一種の温気は

殆ど凝りて動かざる一間の内を、莨の煙と燈火の油煙とは更に縺れて渦巻きつつ立迷へり。込合へる人々の面は皆赤きなりて、白粉の薄剝げたるあり、髪の解れたるあり、衣の乱次ぐ着頽れたるあり。女は粧ひ飾りたれば、取乱したるが特に著るく見ゆるなり。男はシャツの腋の裂けたるも知らで胴衣ばかりになれるあり、羽織を脱ぎて帯の解けたる尻を突出すもあり、十の指をば四まで紙にて結ひたるもあり。さしも息苦き温気も、咽ばさるる煙の渦も、皆狂して知らざる如く、寧ろ喜びて罵り喚くる声、笑頽るる声、捩合ひ、踏破く轟き、一斉に揚ぐる響動など、絶間無き騒動の中に狼藉として戯れ遊ぶ為体は三綱五常も糸瓜の皮と地に塗れて、唯これ修羅道を打覆したるばかりなり。

海上風波の難に遭へる時、若干の油を取りて航路に澆げば、浪は奇くも忽ち鎮りて、船は九死を出づべしとよ。今この如何とも為べからざる乱脈の座中をば、その油の勢力をもて支配せる女王あり。猛びに猛ぶ男たちの心もその人の前には和ぎて、終に崇拝せざるはあらず。女たちは皆猜みつつも畏を懐けり。中の間なる団欒の柱側に座を占めて、人の打騒ぐを興あるやうに涼き目を瞔りて、躬は淑かに引緒へる娘あり。粧飾より相貌まで水際立ちて、凡ならず媚を含めるは、色を売るものの仮の姿したるにはあらずやと、始めて彼を見るものは皆疑へり。一番の勝負の果てぬ間に、宮といふ名は普く知られぬ。娘も数多居たり。醜きは、子守の借着したるか、茶番の姫君の戸惑せるボン飾して、小豆鼠の縮緬の羽織を着たるが、人の打騒ぐを興あるやうに涼き目を瞔りて、躬は仮の姿したるにはあらずやと、始めて彼を見るものは皆疑へり。娘も数多居たり。醜きは、子守の借着したるか、茶番の姫君の戸惑せるかと覚きもあれど、中には二十人並、五十人並優れたるもありき。服装は宮より数等立派なるは

数多あり。彼はその点にては中の位に過ぎず。貴族院議員の愛娘とて、最も不器量を極めて遺憾なしと見えたるが、最も綺羅を飾りて、その起肩に紋御召の三枚襲を被きて、帯は紫根の七糸に百合の折枝を繞金の盛上にしたる、人々これが為に目も眩れ、心も消えて眉を顰めぬ。この外種種色々の絢爛なる中に立交らひては、宮の装は纔に暁の星の光を保つに過ぎざれども、彼の色の白さは如何なる美き染色をも奪ひて、彼の整へる面は如何なる麗き織物よりも文章ありて、醜き人たちは如何に着飾らんともその醜きを蔽ふ能はざるが如く、彼は如何に飾らざるもその美きを害せざるなり。

袋棚と障子との片隅に手炉を囲みて、蜜柑を剥きつつ語ふ男の一個は、彼の横顔を恍惚と遙に見入りたりしが、遂に思懐へざらんやうに呻き出せり。

「好い、好い、全く好い！　馬士にも衣裳と謂ふけれど、美いのは衣裳には及ばんね。物それ自らが美いのだもの、着物などはどうでも可い、実は何も着てをらんでも可い」

「裸体なら猶結構だ！」

この強き合槌撃つは、美術学校の学生なり。

網曳にて駈着けし紳士は恰く休息の後内儀に導かれて入来りつ。その後には、今まで居間に潜みたりし主の箕輪亮輔も附添ひたり。席上は入乱れて、ここを先途と激き勝負の最中なれば、彼等の来れるに心着きしは稀なりけれど、片隅に物語れる二人は逸早く目を側めて紳士の風采を視たり。

広間の燈影は入口に立てる三人の姿を鮮かに照せり。色白の小き内儀の口は瘡の為に引歪みて、その夫の額際より緒禿げたる頭顱は滑かに光れり。妻は尋常より小きに、夫は勝れたる大兵肥満にて、彼の常に心遣ありげの面色なるに引替へて、生きながら布袋を見る如き福相したり。

紳士は年歯二十六七なるべく、長高く、好き程に肥えて、色は玉のやうなるに頬の辺には薄く紅を帯びて、額厚く、口大きく、腮は左右に蔓りて、面積の広き顔は稍正方形を成せり。緩く波打てる髪を左の小鬢より一文字に撫付けて、少しは油を塗りたり。濃からぬ口髭を生して、小からぬ鼻を金縁の目鏡を挟み、五紋の黒塩瀬の羽織に華紋織の小袖を裾長に着做したるが、六寸の七糸帯に金鎖子を垂れつつ、大様に面を挙げて座中を眴したる容は、実に光を発つらんやうに四辺を払ひて見えぬ。この団欒の中に彼の如く色白く、身奇麗に、しかも美々しく装ひたるはあらざるなり。

「何だ、あれは？」

例の二人の一個はさも憎さげに呟けり。

「可厭な奴！」

唾吐くやうに言ひて学生はわざと面を背けつ。

「お俊や、一寸」と内儀は群集の中よりその娘を手招きぬ。

お俊は両親の紳士を伴へるを見るより、慌忙に起ちて来れるが、顔好くはあらねど愛嬌深く、いと善く父に肖たり。高島田に結ひて、肉色縮緬の羽織に撮みたるほどの肩揚したり。顔を赧め

つつ紳士の前に跪きて、慇懃に頭を低れば、彼は總に小腰を屈めしのみ。

「どうぞ此方へ」

娘は案内せんと待構へけれど、紳士はさして好ましからぬやうに頷けり。　母は歪める口を怪しげに動して、

「あの、見事な、まあ、御年玉を御戴きだよ」

お俊は再び頭を低げぬ。紳士は笑を含みて目礼せり。

「さあ、まあ、いらつしやいまし」

主の勧むる傍より、妻はお俊を促して、紳士を遇ふことの極めて鄭重なるを訝り方に伴れぬ。　妻は其処まで介添に附きたり。　二人は家内の紳士を案内して、客間の床柱の前なる火鉢在る方に伴れぬ。

りて、彼の行くより坐るまで一擧一動も見脱さざりけり。　その行く時彼の姿はあたかも左の半面を見せて、團欒の間を過ぎたりしが、無名指に輝ける物の凡ならず強き光は燈火に照添ひて、始ど正しく見る能はざるまでに眼を射られたるに呆れ惑へり。　天上の最も明なる星は我手に在りと言はまほしげに、紳士は彼等の未だ曾て見ざりし大さの金剛石を飾れる黄金の指環を穿めたるなり。

お俊は骨牌の席に復ると伸く、密に隣の娘の膝を衝きて口早に呟きぬ。　彼は忙々しく顔を擡げて紳士の方を見たりしが、その人よりはその指に耀く物の異常なるに駭かされたる体にて、

「まあ、あの指環は！　一寸、金剛石？」

お俊の説明を聞きて彼は漫に身毛の弥立つを覚えつつ、

「三百円だつて」

「大きいのねえ」

「さうよ」

鰡の目ほどの真珠を附けたる指環をだに、この幾歳か念懸くれども未だ容易に許されざる娘の胸は、忽ち或事を思ひ浮べて攻蕀の如く轟けり。彼は惘然として殆ど我を失へる間に、電光の如く隣より伸来れる猿臂は鼻の前なる一枚の骨牌を引攫へば、

「あら、貴女どうしたのよ」

「まあ！　好いのねえ」

お俊は苛立ちて彼の横膝を続けさまに拊きぬ。

「可くつてよ、可くつてよ」

彼は始めて空想の夢を覚して、及ばざる身の分を諦めたりけれども、一旦金剛石の強き光に焼かれたる心は幾分の知覚を失ひけんやうにて、さしも目覚かりける手腕の程も見る見る漸く四途乱になりて、彼は敢無くもこの時よりお俊の為に頼み難き味方となれり。

「可くつてよ、可くつてよ、以来もう可くつてよ」

かくしてかれよりこれに伝へ、甲より乙に通じて、

「金剛石！」

「うむ、金剛石だ」

「金剛石??」

「成程金剛石！」

「まあ、金剛石よ」

「あれが金剛石？」

「見給へ、金剛石」

「あら、まあ金剛石??」

「可懐い金剛石」

「可恐い光るのね、金剛石」

「三百円の金剛石」

瞬く間に三十余人は相呼び相応じて紳士の富を謳へり。

彼は人々の更に己れの方を眺むるを見て、その手に形好く葉巻を持たせて、右手を袖口に差入れ、少し懈げに床柱に靠れて、目鏡の下より下界を見遍すらんやうに目配してゐたり。

かかる目印ある人の名は誰しも問はであるべきにあらず、洩れしはお俊の口よりなるべし。彼は富山唯継とて、一代分限ながら下谷区に聞ゆる資産家の家督なり。同じ区なる富山銀行はその父の私設する所にして、市会議員の中にも富山重平の名は見出さるべし。

宮の名の男の方に持噪さるる如く、富山と知れたる彼の名は直に女の口々に誦ぜられぬ。あはれ一度はこの紳士と組みて、世に愛たき宝石に咫尺するの栄を得ばや、と彼等の心々に冀はざ

るは希なりき。人若し彼に咫尺するの栄を得ば、當にその目の類無く楽さるるのみならで、その鼻までも菫花の多く擬ぐべからざる薫香に薫ぜらるるの幸を受くべきなり。

男たちは自から荒められて、女の挙りて金剛石に心率さるを、或は妬く、或は浅ましく、多少の興を冷さざるはあらざりけり。用意深く、心様も幽く振舞へるを、崇拝者は益々懐びて、我等の慕ひ参らする効はあるよ、独り宮のみは騒げる体も無くて、その清き眼色はさしもの金剛石と光を争はんやうに、偏にこの君を奉じて孤忠を全うし、美と富との勝負を唯一戦に決して、紳士の憎き面の皮を引剝かん、と手葉煉引いて待ちかけたり。されば宮と富山との勢はあたかも日月を並懸けたるやうなり。宮は誰と組み、富山は誰と組むらんとは、人々の最も懸念するところなりけるが、鬮の結果は驚くべき予想外にて、目指されし紳士と美人とは他の三人とともに一組になりぬ。

始め二つに輪作りし人数は この時 合併して一の大なる団欒に成されたるなり。しかも富山と宮とは隣合に坐りければ、夜と昼との一時に来にけんやうに皆狼狽ぎて、忽ちその隣に自ら社会党と称ふる一組を出せり。彼等の主義は不平にして、その目的は破壊なり。又その前面には一人の女に内を守らしめて、屈強の男四人左右に遠征軍を組織し、左翼を狼藉組と称し、右翼を蹂躙隊と称するも、実は金剛石の鼻柱を挫かんと大童になれるに外ならざるなり。則ち彼等は専ら腕力を用ゐて或は組の果報と安寧とを妨害せんと為るなり。果せる哉、件の組はこの勝負に蓬き大敗を取りて、人も無げなる紳士もさすがに鼻白み、美き人は顔を緋めて、座にも堪ふべからざるばかりの面皮を欠されたり。この一番にて紳士の姿は不知見えずなりぬ。男

ちは万歳を唱へけれども、女の中には掌の玉を失へる心地したるもの多かりき。

狼藉され、蹂躙されし富山は、余りにこの文明的のならざる遊戯に怖をなして、密に主の居間に逃

帰れるなりけり。

鬘を被ひたるやうに梳くれて、環の隻挽げたる羽織の紐は、手

長猿の月を捉へんとする状じて摇曳と垂れり。主は見るよりさも慌てたる顔して、

「どう遊ばしました。おお、お手から血が出てをります」

彼はやにはに煙管を捨てて、忽にすべからざらんやうに急遽と身を起せり。

「ああ、酷い目に遭つた。どうもああ乱暴ぢや為様が無い。火事装束ででも出掛けなくつちやと

ても立切れないよ。馬鹿にしてゐる！頭を二つばかり撲れた」

手の甲の血を吮ひつつ富山は不快なる面色して設の席に着きぬ。予て用意したれば、海老茶の

紋縮緬の裌の傍に七宝焼の小判形の大手炉を置きて、蒔絵の吸物膳をさへ据ゑたるなり。主は

手を打鳴して婢を呼び、大急に銚子と料理とを誂へて、

「それはどうも飛でもない事を。外に何処もお怪我はございませんでしたか」

「そんなに有られて耐るものかね」

為う事無さに主も苦笑せり。

「唯今絆創膏を差上げます。何しろ皆書生でございますから随分乱暴でございませう。故々御招

申しまして甚だ恐入りました。もう彼地へは御出陣にならんが宜うございます。何もございませ

「んがここで何卒御寛り」

「ところがもう一遍行つて見やうかとも思ふの」

「へえ、又いらつしやいますか」

物は言はで打笑める富山の腮は、愈展れり。早くもその意を得てや破顔せる主の目は、薄の切疵の如くほとと有か無きかになりぬ。

「では御意に召したのが、へえ？」

富山は益笑を満へたり。

「ございましたら、さうでございませうとも」

「何故な」

「何故も無いものでございます。十目の見るところちやございませんか」

富山は頷きつつ、

「さうだらうね」

「あれは宜うございませう」

「一寸好いね」

「まづその御意でお熱いところをお一盞。不満家の貴方が一寸好いと有仰る位では、余程尤物と思はなければなりません。全く寡うございます」

あたたかいりきた倉皇入来れる内儀は思ひも懸けず富山を見て、

「おや、此方にお在あそばしたのでございますか」

彼は先の程より台所に詰きりて、中入の食物の指図などしてみたるなりき。

「酷く負けて逃げて来ました」

「それは好く逃げていらっしゃいました」

例の歪める口を窄めて内儀は空々しく笑ひしが、忽ち彼の羽織の紐の偏、断れたるを見尤めて、環の失せたりと知るより、慌てて驚きて起たんとせり、如何にとなればその環は純金製のものなればなり。富山は事も無げに、

「なあに、宜い」

「宜いではございません。純金では大変でございます」

「なあに、可いと言ふのに」と聞きも訖らずで彼は広間の方へ出でて行けり。

「時にあれの身分はどうかね」

「さやう、悪い事はございませんが……」

「が、どうしたのさ」

「が、大した事はございませんです」

「それはさうだらう。然し凡そどんなものかね」

「旧は農商務省に勤めてをりましたが、唯今では地所や家作などで暮してゐるやうでございます。鳴沢隆三と申して、直隣町に居りますが、極手堅く小体に遣

どうか小金も有るやうな話で、

「はあ、知れたもんだね」

我は顔に顱を掻撫づれば、例の金剛石は燦然と光れり。

「それでも可いさ。然し嫁れやうか、嗣子ぢやないかい」

「さやう、一人娘のやうに思ひましたが」

「それぢや窮るぢやないか」

「私は悪い事は存じませんから、一つ聞いて見せうで」

程無く内儀は環を捜得て帰来けるが、誰が悪戯とも知らで耳掻の如く引展されたり。主は彼に向ひて宮の家内の様子を訊ねけるに、知れる一遍は語りけれど、娘は猶能く知るらんを、後に招きて聴くべしとて、夫婦は頻に臠を佾めけり。

富山唯継の今宵ここに来りしは、年賀にあらず、骨牌遊にあらず、娘の多く聚れるを機として、嫁選せんとてなり。彼は一昨年の冬英吉利より帰朝するや否や、八方に手分して嫁を求めけれども、器量望の太甚しければ、二十余件の縁談皆意に称はで、今日が日までもなほその事に齷齪し て已まざるなり。当時取急ぎて普請せし芝の新宅は、未だ人の住着かざるに、はや日に黒み、或 所は雨に朽ちて、薄暗き一間に留守居せし老夫婦の額を鳩めては、寂しげに彼等の昔を語るのみ。

第 二 章

骨牌の会は十二時に遊びて終りぬ。十時頃より一人起ち、二人起ちて、見る間に人数の三分の一強を失ひければ、猶飽かで残れるものは景気好く勝負を続けたり。富山の姿を隠したりと知らざる者は、彼敗走して帰りしならんと想へり。宮は会の終まで居たり。彼若疾く還りたらんには、恐く踏留るは三分の一弱に過ぎざりけんを、と我物顔に富山は主と語合へり。

彼に心を寄せし輩は皆彼が夜深の帰途の程を気遣ひて、我願くは何処までも送らんと、絶か念ひに念ひけれど、彼等の深切は無用にも、宮の帰る時一人の男附添ひたり。その人は高等中学の制服を着たる二十四五の学生なり。金剛石に亜い<ruby>では<rt>ダイアモンド</rt></ruby>彼の挙動の目指れしは、座中に宮と懇意に見えたるは彼一人なりければなり。この一事の外は人目を牽くべき点も無く、彼は多く語らず、又は躁がず、始終慎くしてゐたり。終までこの両個の同伴なりとは露顕せざりき。さあらんに彼等の打連れて門を出づるを見て、始めて失望せしもの寡か<ruby>は余所々々<rt>よそ</rt></ruby>しさに過ぎたればなり。らず。

宮は<ruby>鳩羽鼠<rt>はとばねずみ</rt></ruby>の<ruby>頭巾<rt>づきん</rt></ruby>を<ruby>被<rt>かぶ</rt></ruby>りて、<ruby>濃浅黄地<rt>こいあさぎぢ</rt></ruby>に白く<ruby>中形<rt>ちゆうがた</rt></ruby>模様ある毛織の<ruby>シオール<rt>よそほ</rt></ruby>を<ruby>絡<rt>まと</rt></ruby>ひ、学生は焦茶の<ruby>外套<rt>ぐわいとう</rt></ruby>を着たるが、身を<ruby>窄<rt>すぼ</rt></ruby>めて吹来る<ruby>凩<rt>こがらし</rt></ruby>を<ruby>遣過<rt>やりすご</rt></ruby>しつつ、遅れし宮の<ruby>迢着<rt>たちおく</rt></ruby>れを待ちて言出せり。

「宮さん、あの<ruby>金剛石<rt>ダイアモンド</rt></ruby>の<ruby>指環<rt>ゆびわ</rt></ruby>を<ruby>穿<rt>は</rt></ruby>めてゐた奴はどうだい、<ruby>可厭<rt>いや</rt></ruby>に気取つた奴ぢやないか」

「さうねえ、だけれど衆があの人を目の敵にして乱暴するので気の毒だったわ。隣合つてゐたもんだから私まで酷い目に遭されてよ」

「うむ、彼奴が高慢な顔をしてゐるからさ。実は僕も横腹を二つばかり突いて遣つた」

「まあ、酷いのね」

「ああ云ふ奴は男の目から見ると反吐が出るやうだけれど、女にはどうだらうね、あんなのが女の気に入るのぢやないか」

「私は可厭よ」

「芬々と香水の匂ひがして、金剛石の金の指環を穿めて、殿様然たる服装をして、好いに違無いさ」

学生は嘲むが如く笑へり。

「私は可厭だわ」

「可厭なものが組になるものか」

「組は闇だから為方が無いわ」

「闇だけれど、組に成つて可厭さうな様子も見えなかつたもの」

「そんな無理な事を言つて！」

「三百円の金剛石ぢや到底僕等の及ぶところにあらずだ」

「知らない！」

宮はシオールを揺上げて鼻の半まで掩隠しつ。

「ああ寒い！」

男は肩を竦めて直と彼に寄添へり。宮は猶黙して歩めり。

「ああ寒い!!」

宮はなほ答へず。

「ああ寒い!!!」

彼はこの時始めて男の方を見向きて、

「どうしたの」

「ああ寒い」

「あら可厭ね、どうしたの」

「寒くて耐らんからその中へ一処に入れ給へ」

「どの中へ」

「シォールの中へ」

「可笑い、可厭だわ」

男は逸早く彼の押へしシォールの片端を奪ひて、その中に身を容れたり。宮は歩み得ぬまでに笑ひて、

「あら貫一さん。これぢや切なくて歩けやしない。ああ、前面から人が来てよ」

かかる戯を作して憚らず、女も為すままに信せて咎めざる彼等の関繋は抑も如何。事情ありて

十年来鴫沢に寄寓せるこの間貫一は、此年の夏大学に入るを待ちて、宮が妻せらるべき人なり。

第 三 章

間貫一の十年来鴫沢の家に寄寓せるは、怙る所無くて養はるるなり。母は彼の幼かりし頃世を去りて、父は彼の尋常中学を卒業するを見るに及ばずして病死せしより、彼は哀嘆の中に父を葬るとともに、己が前途の望をさへ葬らざる可からざる不幸に遭へり。父在りし日さへ月謝の支出の血を絞るばかりに苦き痩世帯なりけるを、当時彼なほ十五歳ながら間の戸主は学ぶに先ちて食ふべき急に迫られぬ。

幼き戸主の学ぶに先ちては食ふべきの急、食ふべきに先ちては葬すべき急、猶これに先ちては看護医薬の急ありしにあらずや。自活すべくもあらぬ幼き者の如何にしてこれ等の急を救得しか。固より貫一が力の能ふべきにあらず、鴫沢隆三の身一個に引承けて万端の世話せしに因るなり。孤児の父は隆三の恩人にて、彼は聊かその旧徳に報ゆるが為に、菅にその病めりし時に扶助せしのみならず、常に心着けては貫一の月謝をさへ間支弁したり。かくて貫き父を亡ひし孤児は富める後見を得て鴫沢の家に引取られぬ。隆三は恩人に報ゆるにその短き生時を以て慊らず思ひければ、とかくはその忘形見を天晴人と成して、彼の一日も忘れざりし志を継がんとせるなり。

亡き人常に言ひけるは、苟くも侍の家に生れながら、何の面目ありて我子貫一をも人に侮らす

べきや。彼は学士となして、願くは再び四民の上に立たしめん。貫一は不断にこの言を以て誡め
られ、隆三は会ふ毎にまたこの言を以て囁たれしなり。彼は言ふ違だに無くて、暴に歿りけれ
も、その前常に口にせしところは明かに彼の遺言なるべきのみ。

されば貫一が鴫沢の家内に於ける境遇は、決して厄介者として陰に在りなんこそ幸は多からんよ、
はあらざりき。憖ひ継子などに生れたらんよりは、かくて在りなんこそ幸は多からんよ、
と知る人は噂し合へり。隆三夫婦は実に彼を恩人の忘形見として取扱ひけるなり。さば
かり彼の愛せらるるを見て、彼等は貫一を娘の婿にせむとすならんと想へる者もありしかど、
当時彼等は構へてさる心ありしにはあらざりけるも、彼の篤学なるを見るに及びて、漸くその心
は出で来て、彼の高等中学校に入りし時、彼等の了簡は始めて定りぬ。

貫一は篤学のみならず、性質も直に、行も正かりければ、この人物を以つて学士の冠を戴かん
には、誠に獲易からざる婿なるべし、と夫婦は私に喜びたり。この身代を譲られたりとて、他姓
を冒して得謂はれぬ屈辱を忍ばんは、彼の肩し為ざるところなれども、美き宮を妻に為るを得
ば、この身代も屈辱も何か有らんと、彼はなかなか夫婦に増したる懽を懐きて、益学問を励みた
り。宮も貫一をば憎からず思へり。されど恐くは貫一の思へる半には過ぎざらん。彼は自らその
色好を知ればなり。世間の女の誰か自らその色好の幾何値するかを当然に知れるなり。彼の美しさを以
るに在り。謂ふ可くんば、宮は己が美しさの幾何値するかを当然に知れるなり。彼の美しさを以
てして総に箇程の資産を嗣ぎ、類多き学士風情を夫に有たんは、決して彼が所望の絶頂にはあら

ざりき。彼は貴人の奥方の微賤より出でし例寡からざるを見たり。又は富人の醜き妻を厭ひて、美き妾に親むを見たり。才だにあらば男立身は思のままなる如く、女は色をもて富貴を得べしと信じたり。なほ彼は色を以て富貴を得たる人たちの若干を見たりしに、その容の己に如かざるものの多きを見出せり。剰へ彼は行く所にその美しさを唱はれざるはあらざりき。なほ一件最も彼の意を強うせし事あり。そは彼が十七の歳に起りし事なり。当時彼は明治音楽院に通ひたりしに、ヴァイオリンのプロフェッサаなる独逸人は彼の愛らしき容を見たるより仇なる恋にはあらで、女夫の契を望みしなり。殆ど同時に、院長の某は年四十を踰えたるに、先年その妻を喪ひしをもて再び彼を娶らんとて、密に一室に招きて切なる心を打明かせし事あり。

この時彼の小き胸は破れんとするばかり轟けり。半は嘗て覚えざる可憐の為に、半は遽に大なる希望の宿りたるが為に。彼はここに始めて己の美しさの寡とも奏価以上の地位ある名流をその夫に直ひすべきを信じたるなり。彼を美く見たるは彼の教師と院長とのみならず、牆を隣れる男子部の諸生の常に彼を見んとて打騒ぐをも、宮は知らざりしにあらず。

若かのプロフェッサаに添はんか、或は四十の院長に従はんか、彼の栄誉ある地位は、学士を婿にして鴫沢の後を嗣ぐの比にはあらざらんをと、一旦抱ける希望は年と共に太りて、彼は始終昼ながら夢みつつ、今にも貴き人又は富める人は名ある人の己を見出して、玉の輿を舁せて迎に来るべき天縁の、必ず廻到らんことを信じて疑はざりし彼のさまでに深く貫一を思はざりしは全くこれが為のみ。されども決して彼を嫌へるにはあらず、彼と添はばさすがに楽からんとは

念へるなり。　如此く決定にそれとは無けれど又有りとし見ゆる箒木の好運を望みつつも、彼は怠らず貫一の己を愛してゐたり。　貫一は彼の己を愛する外にはその胸の中に何もあらじとのみ思へるなりけり。

第　四　章

漆の如き闇の中に貫一の書斎の枕時計は十時を打ちぬ。　彼は午後四時より向島の八百松に新年会ありとて未だ還らざるなり。

宮は奥より手ランプを持ちて入来にけるが、机の上なる書燈を點し了れる時、　婢は台十能に火を盛りたるを持来れり。　宮はこれを火鉢に移して、

「さうして奥のお鉄瓶も持つて来ておくれ。　ああ、　もう彼方は御寝になるのだから」

久しく人気の絶えたりし一間の寒は、今俄に人の温き肉を得たるを喜びて、直ちに咬まんとするが如く膚に薄れり。　宮は慌忙く火鉢に取付きつつ、目を挙げて書棚に飾れる時計を見たり。

夜の闇く静なるに、燈の光の独り美き顔を照したる、限無く艶なり。　松の内とて彼は常より着飾れるに、化粧をさへしたれば、露を帯びたる花の梢に月のうつろへるが如く、背後の壁に映れる黒き影さへ香滴るるやうなり。

金剛石と光を争ひし目は惜気も無く瞠りて時計の秒を刻むを打目戍れり。

火に翳せる彼の手を

見よ、玉の如くなり。さらば友禅模様ある紫縮緬の半襟に縮まれたる彼の胸の中に彼は今如何なる事を思へるかを想へ。彼は憎からぬ人の帰来を待佗ぶるなりけり。一時又寒の太甚きを覚えて、彼は時計より目を放つとともに起ちて、火鉢の対面なる貫一が砌の上に座を移せり。こは彼の手に縫ひしを貫一の常に敷くなり、貫一の敷くをば今夜彼の敷くなり。

若やと聞着けし車の音は漸く近きて、益蠢きて、竟に我門に停りぬ。宮は、疑無しと思ひて起たんとする時、客はいと酔ひたる声して物言へり。貫一は生下戸なれば甞て酔ひて帰りし事あざれば、宮は力無く又坐りつ。時計を見れば早や十一時に垂んとす。門の戸引啓けて、酔ひたる足音の土間に踏入りたるに、宮は何事とも分かず唯慌ててランプを持ちて出でぬ。台所より婢も、出合へり。

足の踏所も覚束無げに酔ひて、帽は落ちなんばかりに打傾き、ハンカチイフに裹みたる折を左に撃げて、山車人形のやうに揺々と立てるは貫一なり。面は今にも破れぬべく紅に熱して、舌の乾くに堪へかねて連に空唾を吐きつつ、

「遅かつたかね。さあ御土産です。還つてこれを細君に遣る。何ぞ仁なるや」

「まあ、大変酔つて！　どうしたの」

「酔つて了つた」

「あら、貫一さん、こんな所に寐ちや困るわ。さあ、早くお上りなさいよ」

「かう見えても靴が脱げない。ああ酔つた」

仰様に倒れたる貫一の脚を掻抱きて、宮は辛くもその靴を取去りぬ。

「起きる、ああ、今起きる。さあ、起きた。起きたけれど、手を牽いてくれなければ僕には歩けませんよ」

宮は婢に燈を把らせ、自らは貫一の手を牽かんとせしに、彼は踉きつつ肩に縋りて遂に放さりければ、宮はその身一つさへ危きに、やうやう扶けて書斎に入りぬ。

裀の上に异下されし貫一は頰るる体を机に支へて、打仰ぎつつ微吟せり。

「君に勧む、金縷の衣を惜むなかれ。君に勧む、須く少年の時を惜むべし。花有り折るに堪へなば直に折る須し。花無きを待つて空く枝を折ることなかれ」[二]

「貫一さん、どうしてそんなに酔つたの？」

「酔つてゐるでせう。ねえ、宮さん、非常に酔つてゐるでせう」

「然矣、苦いほど酔つてゐる。苦いでせう」

「酔つてゐるわ。こんなに酔つてゐるに就いては大いに訳が有るのだ。さうして又宮さんなるものが大いに介抱して可い訳が有るのだ。宮さん！

「可厭よ、私は、そんなに酔つてゐるちや。不断嫌ひの癖に何故そんなに飲んだの。誰に飲まされたの。端山さんだの、荒尾さんだの、白瀬さんだのが附いてゐるながら、酷いわね、こんなに酔して。

十時にはきつと帰ると云ふから私は待つてゐたのに、もう十一時過よ」

「本当に待つてゐてくれたのかい、宮さん。謝、多謝！　若それが事実であるならばだ、僕はこのまま死んでも恨みません。こんなに酔されたのも、実はそれなのだ」

彼は宮の手を取りて、情に堪へざる如く握緊めつ。

「二人の事は荒尾より外に知る者は無いのだ。荒尾が又決して喋る男ぢやない。それがどうして知れたのか、衆が知つてゐて……僕は実に驚いた。四方八方から祝盃だ祝盃だと、十も二十も一度に猪口を差されたのだ。祝盃などを受ける覚は無いと言つて、手を引籠めてゐたけれど、なかなか衆聴かないぢやないか」

宮は窃に笑を帯びて余念なく聴きゐたり。

「それぢや祝盃の主意を変へて、仮初にもあゝ云ふ美人と一所に居て寝食を倶にすると云ふのが既に可羨い。そこを祝すのだ。次には、君も男児なら、更に一歩を進めて、妻君に為るやうに十分運動したまへ。十年も一所に居てから、今更人に奪られるやうな事があつたら、独り間貫一個人の恥辱ばかりではない、我々朋友全体の面目にも関する事だ。我々朋友ばかりではない、延いて高等中学の名折にもなるのだから、是非あの美人を君が妻君にするやうに、これは我々が心を一にして結の神に禱つた酒だから、辞退するのは礼ではない。受けなかつたら却つて神罰が有ると、弄謔とは知れてゐるけれど、言草が面白かつたから、片端から引受けて呷々遣付けた。

宮さんと夫婦に成れなかつたら、はははははは高等中学の名折になるのだと。恐入つたものだ。何分宜く願ひます」

「可愛よ、もう貫一さんは」

「友達中にもさう知れて見ると、立派に夫婦にならなければ、弥よ僕の男が立たない義だ」

「もう極つてゐるものを、今更……」

「さうでないです。この頃翁さんや姨さんの様子を見るのに、どうも僕は……」

「そんな事は決して無いわ、邪推だわ」

「実は翁さんや姨さんの了簡はどうでも可い、宮さんの心一つなのだ」

「私の心は極つてゐるわ」

「さうかしらん？」

「さうかしらんて、それぢや余りだわ」

貫一は酔を支へかねて宮が膝を枕に倒れぬ。宮は彼が火の如き頬に、額に、手を加へて、

「水を上げませう。あれ、又寐ちや……貫一さん、貫一さん」

この時は宮が胸の中にも例の汚れたる希望は跡を絶ちて彼の美き目は他に見竟に愛の潔き哉、その力を貫一の寐顔に鍾めて、富も貴きも、乃至有ゆる利慾のるべきもののあらざらんやうに、その膝に覚ゆる一団の微温の為に溶されて、彼は唯妙に香き甘露の夢に酔ひて前後をも知念は、その膝に覚ゆる一団の微温の為に溶されて、彼は唯妙に香き甘露の夢に酔ひて前後をも知らざるなりけり。

諸の可忌き妄想はこの夜の如く眼を閉ぢて、この一間に彼等の二人よりは在らざる如く、彼は世間に別人の影を見ずして、又この明なる燈火の光の如きものありて、特に彼等をのみ照すやう

に感ずるなり。

第五章

　或日箕輪の内儀は思も懸けず訪来りぬ。その娘のお俊と宮とは学校朋輩にて常に往来したりけれども、未だ家と家との交際はあらざるなり。彼等の通学せし頃さへ親々は互に識らで過ぎたりしに、今は二人の往来も漸く踈くなりけるに及びて、俄にその母の来れるは、如何なる故にか、と宮も両親も怪き事に念へり。

　凡そ三時間の後彼は帰行きぬ。

　先に怪み／＼家内は彼の来りしよりもその用事の更に思懸けざるに驚けり。貫一は不在なりしかばこの珍き客来のありしを知らず、宮もまた敢て告げずして、二日と過ぎ、三日と過ぎぬ。その日より宮は少く食して、多く眠らずなりぬ。貫一は知らず、宮はいよ／＼告げんとは為ざりき。

　この間に両親は幾度と無く談合しては、その事を決しかねてゐたり。

　彼の陰に在りて起れる事、又は見るべからざる宮の様子の常に変れる人の心に浮べる事どもは、貫一の知る因もあらねど、片時もその目の忘れざる宮の様子を見出さんは難き事にあらず。さも無かりし人の顔の色の遽に光を失ひたるやうにて、振舞など別けて力無く、笑ふさへいと打湿りたるを。宮が居間と謂ふまでにはあらねど、彼の箪笥手道具等置きたる小座敷あり。ここには火燵の炉

を切りて、用無き人の来ては遽にここに冬籠する所にも用ゐらる。彼は常にここに居て針仕事するなり。倦めば琴をも弾くなり。彼が手玩と見ゆる狗子柳のはや根を弛み、真の打傾きたるが、鮟鱇切の水に埃を浮べて小机の傍に在り。庭に向へる胱懸窓の明きに敷紙を披げて、宮は膝の上に紅絹の引解を載せたれど、針は持たで、懶げに火燵に靠れたり。

彼は少く食して多く眠らずなりてよりは、好みてこの一間に入りて、深く物思ふなりけり。両親は仔細を知れるにや、この様子をば怪まんともせで、唯彼の為ろままに委せたり。

この日貫一は授業始の式のみにて早く帰来にけるが、下座敷には誰も見えで、火燵の間に宮の咳く声して、後は静に、我が帰りしを知らざるよと思ひければ、忍足に窺寄りぬ。襖の僅に啓きたる隙より差覗けば、宮は火燵に倚りて硝子障子を眺めては俯目になり、又胸痛きやうに仰ぎては太息吐きて、忽ち物の音を聞澄すが如く、美き目を瞠するは、何をか思凝すなるべし。人の窺ふと知らねば、彼は口もて訴ふるばかりに心の苦悶を、猶彼の為んやうを見んとしたり。宮は少時ありて火燵に入りけ

貫一は異みつつも息を潜めて、斜に内を窺ひつつ貫一は眉を顰めて思惑へり。さばかり案じ煩ふべき事を如何なれば我に明さざるならん。その故のあるべく覚えざるとともに、案じ煩ふ事のあるべきをも彼は信じ得ざるなりけり。

柱に身を倚せて、斜に内を窺ひつつ貫一は眉を顰めて思惑へり。彼は如何なる事ありてさばかり案じ煩ふならん。遂に橋に打俯しぬ。

かく又案じ煩へる彼の面も、自ら俯きぬ。間はずして知るべきにあらずと思定めて、再び内を差覗きけるに、宮は猶打俯してゐたり。何時か落ちけむ、蒔絵の櫛の零れたるも知らで。人の気勢に驚きて宮の振仰ぐ時、貫一は既にその傍に在り。彼は慌てて思頬るる気色を蔽はんとしたるが如し。

「ああ、吃驚した。　何時御帰んなすつて」

「今帰つたの」

「さう。　些も知らなかつた」

宮はおのれの顔の頬に眺めらるるを眩ゆがりて、

「何をそんなに視るの、可厭、私は」

されども彼は猶目を放たず、宮はわざと打背きて、裁片畳の内を撈せり。

「宮さん、お前さんどうしたの。ええ、何処か不快のかい」

「何ともないのよ。　何故？」

かく言ひつつ　益　急に撈せり。　貫一は帽を冠りたるまま火燵に片肱掛けて、斜に彼の顔を見遣りつつ、

「だから僕は始終水臭いと言ふんだ。さう言へば、直に疑深いの、神経質だのと言ふけれど、それに違無いぢやないか」

「だつて何ともありもしないものを……」

「何ともないものが、惘然考へたり、鬱いでゐるものか。病気かい、心配でもあるのかい。言つて聞したつて可いぢやないか」

宮は言ふところを知らず、總に膝の上なる紅絹を手弄るのみ。

「病気なのかい」

彼は僅に頭を掉りぬ。

「それぢや心配でもあるのかい」

彼はなほ頭を掉れば、

「ちやどうしたと云ふのさ」

宮は唯胸の中を車輪などの廻るやうに覚ゆるのみにて、誠にも詐にも言出すべき術を知らざりき。彼は犯せる罪の終に秘む能はざるを悟れる如き恐怖の為に心慄けるなり。如何に答へんとさへ惑へるに、傍には貫一の益詰らんと待つよと思へば、身は搾らるるやうに迫来る息の隙を、得も謂はれず冷かなる汗の流れ流れぬ。

「それぢやどうしたのだと言ふのに」

貫一の声音は漸く苛立ちぬ。彼の得言はぬを怪しと思へばなり。宮は驚きて不覚に言出せり。

「どうしたのだか私にも解らないけれど、……私はこの二三日どうしたのだか……変に色々な事を考へて、何だか世の中がつまらなくなつて、唯悲くなつて来るのよ」

呆れたる貫一は瞬もせで耳を傾けぬ。

「人間と云ふものは今日かうして生きてゐても、何時死んで了ふか解らないのね。かうしてゐれ
ば、可楽な事もある代に辛い事や、悲しい事や、苦しい事なんぞが有つて、二つ好い事は無し、これ
ば考るほど私は世の中が心細いわ。不図さう思出したら、毎日そんな事ばかり考へて、可厭な心
地になつて、自分でもどうか為たのかしらんと思ふけれど、私病気のやうに見えて？」

目を閉ぢて聽なし貫一は徐に眠を開くとともに眉を顰めて、

「それは病気だ！」

宮は打萎れて頭を垂れぬ。

「然し心配する事は無いさ。気に為ては可かんよ。可いかい」

「ええ、心配しはしません」

異く沈みたるその声の寂しさを、如何に貫一は聽きたりしぞ。

「それは病気の所為だ、脳でも不良のだよ。そんな事を考へた日には、一日だつて笑つて暮せる
日は有りはしない。固より世の中と云ふものはさう面白い義のものぢやないので、又人の身の上
ほど解らないものは無い。それはそれに違無いのだけれど、衆が皆そんな事を起して御覧な、
世界中御寺ばかりになつて了ふ。儚いのが世の中と覚悟した上で、その儚い、つまらない中で切
ては楽を求めやうとして、究竟我々が働いてゐるのだ。考へて鬱いだところで、つまらない世の
中に儚い人間と生れて来た以上は、どうも今更勿方が無いぢやないか。だから、つまらない世の
中を幾分か面白く暮さうと考へるより外は無いのさ。面白く暮すには、何か楽が無ければならな

い。一事かうと云ふ楽があつたら決して世の中はつまらんもの
と云ふものが無いのだね。この楽があればこそ生きてゐると思ふ程の楽は無いのだね」

宮は美き目を挙げて、求むるところあるが如く偸に男の顔を見たり。

「きつと無いのだね」

彼は笑を含みぬ。されども苦しげに見えたり。

「無い？」

宮の肩頭を捉りて貫一は此方に引向けんとすれば、為すままに彼は緩く身を廻したれど、顔の
みは可羞く背けてゐたり。

「さあ、無いのか、有るのかよ」

肩に懸けたる手をば放さで連に揺るるを、宮は銕の槌もて撃懲さるるやうに覚えて、安き心も
あらず。冷なる汗は又一時流出でぬ。

「これは怪しからん！」

宮は危みつつ彼の顔色を候ひぬ。常の如く戯るるなるべし。その面は和ぎて一点の怒気だにあ
らず、寧ろ唇頭には笑を包めるなり。

「僕などは一件大きな大きな楽があるので、世の中が愉快で愉快で耐らんの。一日が経つて行く
のが惜くて惜くてね。僕は世の中がつまらない為にその楽を捨へたのではなくて、その楽の為に
この世の中に活きてゐるのだ。若しこの世の中からその楽を取去つたら、世の中は無い！　貫一

といふ者も無い！　僕はその楽と生死を倶にするのだ。宮さん、可憐いだらう」

宮は忽ち全身の血の氷れるばかりの寒さに堪へかねて打顫ひしが、この心の中を覚られじと思

へば、弱る力を励して、

「可憐いわ」

「可憐ければ、お前さんの事だから分けてあげやう」

「何卒」

「ええ悉皆遣つて了へ！」

彼は外套の衣兜より一袋のボンボンを取出して火燵の上に置けば、余力に袋の口は弛みて、紅

白の玉は珊々と乱出でぬ。こは宮の最も好める菓子なり。

第　六　章

その翌々日なりき、宮は貫一に勧められて行きて医の診察を受けしに、胃病なりとて一瓶の水

薬を与へられぬ。貫一は信に胃病なるべしと思へり。　患者は必ずさる事あらじと思ひつつもその

薬を服したり。　懊悩として愛に堪へざらんやうなる彼の容体に幾許の変も見えざりけれど、その

心に水と火の如きものありて相剋する苦痛は、益々募りて止まざるなり。

貫一は彼の憎からぬ人ならずや。　怪むべし、彼はこの日頃さしも憎からぬ人を見ることを懼れ

ぬ。見ねばさすがに見まほしく思ひながら、面を合すれば冷汗も出づべき恐怖を生ずるなり。彼の情有る言を聞けば、身をも斫らるるやうに覚ゆるなり。宮は彼の優き心根を見るることを恐れたり。宮が心地勝れずなりてより、彼に対する貫一の優しさはその平生に一層を加へたれば、彼は死を覚むれども得ず、生を求むれども得ざらんやうに、悩乱してほとほとその堪ふべからざる限に至りぬ。

遂に彼はこの苦を両親に訴へにやあらん、一日母と娘とは遽に身支度して、忙々しく車に乗りて出でぬ。彼等は小からぬ一個の旅鞄を携へたり。

大風の凪ぎたる迹に孤屋の立てるが如く、侘しげに留守せる主の隆三は独り碁盤に向ひて碁経を抜きゐたり。齢はなほ六十に遠けれど、頭は鬢き白髪にて、長く生ひたる髯などろも六分は白く、容は痩せたれど未だ老の衰も見えず、眉目温厚にして頗る古井波無きの風あり。彼は徐に長き髯を撫でて片笑みつつ、

「二人はの、今朝新聞を見ると急に思着いて、熱海へ出掛けたよ。何でも昨日医者が湯治が良いと言うて切に勧めたらしいのだ。いや、もう急の思着で、脚下から鳥の起つやうな騒をして、十二時三十分の滊車で。ああ、独り寂いところ、まあ茶でも淹れやう」

貫一は有る可からざる事のやうに疑へり。

「はあ、それは。何だか夢のやうですな」

「はあ、私（わし）もそんな塩梅（あんばい）で」

「然（しか）し、湯治は良いでございませう。幾日ほど逗留（とうりゅう）のお心算（つもり）で？」

「まあどんなだか四五日と云ふので、些（こ）の着（きちゃく）のままで出掛けたのだが、なあに直に飽きて了（しま）うて、四五日も居られるものか、出養生より内養生の方が楽だ。何か旨い物でも食べやうぢやないか、二人で、なう」

貫一は着更（きがえ）へんとて書斎に還りぬ。宮の遺したる筆の蹟（あと）などあらんかと思ひて、求めけれども見えず。彼の居間をも尋ねけれど在らず。急ぎ出でしなればさもあるべし、明日は必ず便あらんと思醗せしが、さすがに心楽まざりき。彼の六時間学校に在りて帰来れるは、心の痩するばかり美き俤に饑ゑて帰来れるなり。彼は空く饑ゑたる心を抱きて慰むべくもあらぬ机に向へり。

「実に水臭いな。幾許急いで出掛けたって、何とか一言ぐらゐ言遣いて行きさうなものぢやないか。一寸其処（そこ）に行つたのぢやなし、四五日でも旅だ。第一言遣く、言遣かないよりは、湯治に行くなら行くと、始に話が有りさうなものだ。急に思着いた？　急に思着いたって、急に行かなけ　ればならん所ぢやあるまい。俺の帰るのを待つて、話をして、明日行くと云ふのが順序だらう。四五日ぐらゐの離別には顔を見ずに行つても、あの人は平気なのかしらん。女と云ふ者は一体男よりは情が濃であるべきなのだ。それが濃でないと為れば、愛してをらんと考へるより外は無い。豈（あに）にあの人が愛してをらんとは考へられん。又万々そんな事は無い。けれども十分に愛してをると云ふほど濃ではないな。

元来あの人の性質は冷淡さ。それだから所謂『娘らしい』ところが余り無い。自分の思ふやう
に情が濃でないのもその所為か知らんて。子供の時分から成程さう云ふ傾向は有つてゐたけれ
ど、今のやうに太甚くはなかつたやうに考へるがな。子供の時分にさうであつたなら、今ぢや猶
更でなければならんのだ。それを考へると疑ふよ、疑はざるを得ない！

それに引替へて自分だ、自分の愛してゐるのは実に非常なもの、殆ど……殆どではない、全く
だ、全く溺れてゐるのだ。自分でもどうしてこんなだらうと思ふほど溺れてゐる！

これ程自分の思つてゐるのに対しても、も少し情が篤くなければならんのだ。或時などは実に
水臭い事がある。今日の事なども随分酷い話だ。これが互に愛してゐる間の仕草だらうか。深く
愛してゐるだけにかう云ふ事を為れると実に憎い。

小説的かも知れんけれど、八犬伝の浜路だ、信乃が明朝は立つて了ふと云ふので、親の目を忍
んで夜更けに逢ひに来る、あの情合でなければならない。いや、妙だ！自分の身の上も信乃に似
てゐる。幼少から親に別れてこの鳴沢の世話になつてゐて、其処の娘と許婚……似てゐる、似て
ゐる。

然し内の浜路は困る、信乃にばかり気を揉んで、余り憎いな、そでない為方だ。これから手紙
を書いて思ふさま言つて遣らうか。憎いは憎いけれど病気ではあるし、病人に心配させるのも可
哀さうだ。

自分は又神経質に過るから、思過を為るところも大きにあるのだ。それにあの人からも不断言

はれる、けれども自分が思過であるか、あの人が情が薄いのかは一件の疑問だ。

時々さう思ふ事がある、あの人の水臭い仕打の有るのは、多少か自分を侮つてゐるのではあるまいか。

自分は此家の厄介者、あの人は家附の娘だ。そこで自ら主と家来と云やうな考が始終有つて、……否、それもあの人に能く言れる事だ、それくらゐから始から許しはしない、好いと思へばこそかう云ふ訳に、……さうだ、さうだ、それを言出すと自分は慴られるのだ、一番それを悩むよ。勿論そんな様子の些少でも見えた事は無い。自分の僻見に過ぎんのだけれども、気が済まないから愚痴も出るのだ。然し、若もあの人の心にそんな根性が爪の垢ほどでも有つたらば、自分はこの縁は切つて了ふ。立派に切つて見せる！　自分は愛情の俘とはなつても、未だ奴隷になる気は無い。或はこの縁を切つたなら自分はあの人を忘れかねて焦死に死ぬかも知れん。切れずに措くものか。死なんまでも発狂するかも知れん。かまはん！　どうならうと切れて了ふ。

それは自分の僻見で、あの人に限つてはそんな心は微塵も無いのだ。その点は自分も能く知つてゐる。けれども情が濃でないのは事実だ、冷淡なのは事実だ。だから、冷淡であるから情が濃でないのか。自分に対する愛情がその冷淡を打壊すほどに熱しないのか。或は熱し能はざるのが冷淡の人の愛情であるのか。これが、研究すべき問題だ」

彼は意に満たぬ事ある毎に、必ずこの問題を研究せざるなけれども、未だ曾て解釈し得ざるなりけり。今日はや如何に解釈せんとすらん。

（六）の　二

翌日果して熱海より便はありけれど、僅に一枚の端書をもて途中の無事と宿とを通知せるに過ぎざりき。宛名は隆三と貫一とを並べて、宮の手蹟なり。貫一は読了ると斉しく片々に引裂きて捨ててけり。宮の在らば如何にとも言解くなるべし。彼の親く言解かば、如何に打腹立ちたりとも貫一の心の釈けざることはあらじ。宮の前には常に彼は惱をも、恨をも、憂をも忘るるなり。

今は可懷き顔を見る能はざる失望に加ふるに、この不平に遭ひて、しかも言解く者のあらざれば、彼の惱は野火の飽くこと知らで燎くやうなり。

この夕隆三は彼に食後の茶を薦めぬ。一人佗しければ留めて物語はんとてなるべし。されども貫一の屈托顔して絶えず思の非ぬ方に馳する気色なるを、

「お前どうぞ為なすつたか。うむ、元気が無いの」

「はあ、少し胸が痛みますので」

「それは好くない。劇く痛みでもするかな」

「いえ、なに、もう宜いのでございます」

「それぢや茶は可くまい」

「頂戴します」

かかる浅ましき惱を人に移さんには、甚だ謂無き事なり、と自ら制して、書斎に帰りて慰ひ心を

傷めんより、人に対して姑く憂を忘るるに如かじと思ひければ、彼は努めて寛がんとしたれども、動もすれば心は空になりて、主の語を聞逃さむとす。

今日文の来て細々と優き事など書聯ねたらば、如何に我は嬉からん。なかなか同じ処に居て飽かず顔を見るに易へて、その楽は深かるべきを。さては出行きし恨も忘られて、二夜三夜は遠かりて、せめてその文を形見に思続けんもをかしかるべきか。

彼はその身の卒に出行きしを、如何に本意無く我の思ふらんかは能く知るべきに。我を可憐しと思へる人の何故にさは為さるにやあらん。かくまでに情篤からぬ恋の世に在るべきか。疑ふべし、疑ふべし、と貫一の胸は又乱れぬ。主の声に驚かされて、彼は忽ちその事を忘るべき吾に復れり。

「ちと話したい事があるのだが、や、誠に妙な話で、なう」

笑ふにもあらず、聟むにもあらず、稍自ら嘲むに似たる隆三の顔は、燈火に照されて、常には見ざる異き相を顕せるやうに、貫一は覚ゆるなりき。

「はあ、どういふ御話ですか」

彼は長き鬢を忙しく揉みては、又顧の辺より徐に撫下して、先打出さん語を案じたり。

「お前の一身上の事に就いてだが」

彼は又遅ひぬ、その鬢は虹に苦しむ馬の尾のやうに揮はれつつ、総にかく言ひしのみにて、

「いよいよお前も今年の卒業だつたの」

貫一は遽に敬はるる心地して自と膝を正せり。

「で、私もまあ一安心したと云ふもので、幾分かこれでお前の御父様に対して恩返しも出来たやうな訳、就いてはお前も、益勉強してくれんでは困るなう。未だこの先大学を卒業して、それから社会へ出て相応の地位を得るまでに仕上げなければ、私も鼻は高くないのだ。どうか洋行の一つも為せて、指折の人物に為たいと考へてゐるくらゐ、未だ未だこれから両肌を脱いで世話をしなければならんお前の体だ、なう」

これを聞ける貫一は鉄繩をもて縛られたるやうに、身の重きに堪へず、心の転た苦きを感じたり。その恩の余りに大いなるが為に、彼はその中に在りてその中なる平生を省みたるなり。

「はい。非常な御恩に預りまして、考へて見ますと、口では御礼の申しやうもございません。愚父がどれ程の事を致したか知りませんが、なかなかこんな御恩返を受けるほどの事が出来るものでは有りません。愚父の事は措きまして、私は私で、この御恩はどうか立派に御返し申したいと念つてをります。愚父の亡りましたあの時に、此方で引取つて戴かなかつたら、私は今頃何に成つてをりますか、それを思ひますと、世間に私ほど幸なものは恐く無いでございませう」

彼は十五の少年の驚くまでに大人びたる己を見て、その着たる衣を見て、その坐れる褥を見て、漫に涙を催せり。

やがて美き宮と共にこの家の主となるべきその身を思ひて、実に七千円の粧

鑢(二)を随へて、百万金も購ふ可からざる恋女房を得べき学士よ。彼は小買の米を風呂敷に提げて、その影の如く痩せたる犬とともに月夜を走りし少年なるをや。

「お前がさう思うてくれれば私も張合がある。就いては改めてお前に頼みがあるのだが、聴いてくれるか」

「どういふ事ですか、私で出来ます事ならば、何なりと致します」

彼はかく潔く答ふるに憚らざりけれど、心の底には危むところ無きにしもあらざりき。人のかかる言を出す時は、多く能はざる事を強ふる例なればなり。

「外でも無いがの、宮の事だ、宮を嫁に遣らうかと思って」

これに就いては私も種々と考へたけれど、せめて乱さんと彼は慌忙に語を次ぎぬ。

「これに就いては私も種々と考へたけれど、大きに思ふところもあるので、いつそあれは遣って了うての、お前はも少しの事だから大学を卒業して、四五年も欧羅巴(エウロバ)へ留学して、全然仕上げたところで身を固めるとしたらどうかな」

汝の命を与へよと迫らるる事あらば、その時の人の思は如何なるべき！可恐きまでに色を失へる貫一は空く隆三の面を打目成るのみ。　彼は太く困じたる体にて、長き髯をば揉みに揉みたり。

「お前に約束をして置いて、今更変換を為るのは、何とも気の毒だが、これに就いては私も大きに考へたところがあるので、必ずお前の為にも悪いやうには計はんから、可いかい、宮は嫁に遣

る事にしてくれ、なう」

待てども貫一の言を出ださざれば、主は寡からず惑へり。

「なう、悪く取つてくれては困るよ、あれを嫁に遣るから、それで我家とお前との縁を切つて了ふと云ふのではない、可いかい。大した事は無いがこの家は全然お前に譲るのだ、お前は矢張私の家督よ、なう。で、洋行も為せやうと思ふのだ。必ず悪く取つては困るよ。約束をした宮をの、何かお前に不足でもあるやうに聞えるけれど、決して余所へ遣ると云へば、其処はお前が能く承知してくれんければ困る。又お前にしても、学問を仕上げて、なう、天晴の人物に成るのが第一の希望であらう。そのてさうした訳ではないのだから、其処はお前が能く承知してくれんければ困る。又お前にしても、宮と一所になる、ならんはどれ程の事でもないのだ。なう、さうだらう、不服と思ふから私も頼むのだ。お前に頼が有ると言うたのはこの事だ。

志を遂げさへ為れば、宮と一所になる、ならんはどれ程の事でもないのだ。なう、さうだらう、不服と思ふから私も頼むのだ。お前に頼が有ると言然しこれは理窟で、お前も不服かも知れん。不服と思ふから私も頼むのだ。お前に頼が有ると言うたのはこの事だ。

従来もお前を世話した、後来も益世話をせうからなう、其処に免じて、お前もこの頼は聴いてくれ」

貫一は戦く唇を咬緊めつつ、故ら緩舒に出せる声音は、怪くも常に変れり。

「それぢや翁様の御都合で、どうしても宮さんは私に下さる訳には参らんのですか」

「さあ、断つて遣れんと云ふ次第ではないが、お前の意はどうだ。私の頼は聴かずとも、又自分の修業の邪魔にならうとも、そんな貪着は無しに、何でもかでも宮が欲しいと云ふのかな」

「…………」

「さうではあるまい」

「…………」

得言はぬ貫一が胸には、理に似たる彼の理不尽を憤りて、責むべき事、詰るべき、罵るべき、言ふべき事、辱むべき事の数々は沸くが如く充満ちたれど、彼は神にも勝れる恩人なり。理非を問はずその言には逆ふべからずと思へば、血出づるまで舌を咬みても、敢て言はじと覚悟せるなり。

彼は又思へり。恩人は恩を枷に如此く遍れども、我はこの枷の為に屈せらるべきも、彼は如何なる斧を以てか宮の愛をば割かんとすらん。宮が情は我が思ふままに濃ならずとも、我を棄つるが如きさばかり薄き情にはあらざるを。彼だに我を棄てざらんには、枷も理不尽も恐るべきかは、頼むべきは宮が心なり。頼まるるも宮が心也と、彼は可憐宮を思ひて、その父に対する愠を和げんと勉めたり。

我は常に宮が情の濃ならざるを疑へり。あだかも好しこの理不尽ぞ彼が愛の力を試むるに足るなる。善し善し、盤根錯節に遇はずんば。

「嫁に遣ると有仰のは、何方へ御遣しになるのですか」

「それは未だ確とは極らんがの、下谷に富山銀行と云ふのがある、それ、富山重平な、あれの息子の嫁に欲いと云ふ話があるので」

それぞ箕輪の骨牌会に三百円の金剛石を炫かせし男にあらずやと、貫一は陰に嘲笑へり。されど又余りにその人の意外なるに駭きて、やがて又彼は自ら笑ひぬ。これ必ずしも意外ならず、苟くも吾が宮の如く美きを、目あり心あるものの誰かは恋ひざらん。独り怪しとも怪きは隆三の意なる哉。我十年の約は軽々く破るべきにあらず、猶謂無きは、一人娘を出して嫁せしめんとする戯るるにはあらずや、心狂へるにはあらずや。貫一は寧ろかく疑ふをば、事の彼の真意に出でしを疑はんより遲かるべしと信じたりき。

彼は競争者の金剛石なるを聞きて、一度は汚され、辱められたらんやうにも忿を作せしかど、既に勝負は分明にして、我は手を束ねてこの弱敵の自ら僵るるを看んと思へば、心稍落ちぬ。

「は、はあ、富山重平、聞いてをります、偉い財産家で」

この一言に隆三の面は熱くなりぬ。

「これに就いては私も大きに考へたのだ、何に為ろ、お前との約束もあるものなり、又私たちは段々取る年であつて見れば、その老後だの、それ等の事を考へて見ると、この鴫沢の家には、お前も知つての通り、かうと云ふ親類も無いで、何かに就けて誠に心細いわ、なう。私たちは追々年を取るばかり、お前たちは若しと云ふもので、ここに可頼い親類が有れば、どれ程心丈夫だか知れんて、なう。そこで富山ならば親類に持つても可愧からん家柄だ。気の毒な思をしてお前との約束を変易するのも、私たちが一人娘を他へ遣つて了ふのも、究竟は銘々の為に行末好かれと思ふより外は無いの

だ。

それに、富山からは切つての懇望で、無理に一人娘を貰ふと云ふ事であれば、息子夫婦は鳴沢の子同様に、富山も鳴沢も一家のつもりで、決して鳴沢家を疎には為るまい。娘が内に居なくなつて不都合があるならば、どの様にもその不都合の無いやうには計はうからと、なう、それは随分事を分けた話で。

決して慾ではないが、良い親類を持つと云ふものは、人で謂へば取も直さず良い友達で、お前にしてもさうだらう、良い友達が有れば、万事の話合手になる、何かの力になる、なう、謂はば親類は一家の友達だ。

お前がこれから世の中に出るにしても、大相な便宜になるといふもの。それやこれや考へて見ると、内に置かうよりは、遣つた方が、誰の為彼の為ではない。四方八方が好いのだから、私も決心して、いつそ遣らうと思ふのだ。

私の了簡はかう云ふのだから、必ず悪く取つてくれては困るよ、なう。私だとて年刻も無く事を好んで、何為に若いものの不為になれと思ふものかな。お前も能く其処を考へて見てくれ。

私もかうして頼むからは、お前の方の頼も聴かう。今年卒業したら直に洋行でもしたいと思ふなら、又さう云ふ事に私も一番奮発しやうではないか。明日にも宮と一処になつて、私たちを安心さしてくれるよりは、お前も私もも少しのところを辛抱して、いつその事博士になつて喜ばしてくれんか」

彼はさも思ひのままに説完せたる面色して、寛に髯を撫でてゐたり。

貫一は彼の説進むに従ひて、漸くその心事の火を覩るより明なるを得たり。彼が千言万語の舌を弄して倦まざるは、畢竟利の一字を掩はんが為のみ。貧する者の盗むは世の習ながら、貧せざるもなほ盗まんとするか。我も穢れたるこの世に生れたれば、穢れたりとは自ら知らで、或は穢れたる念を起し、或は穢れたる行を為すことあらむ。されど自ら穢れたりと知りて自ら穢すべきや。妻を売りて博士を買ふ！　これ豈穢れたるの最も大なる者ならずや。

世は穢れ、人は穢れたれども、我は常に我恩人の独り汚に染みざるを信じて疑はざりき。過ぐれば夢より淡き小恩をも忘れずして、貧き孤子を養へる志は、これを証して余あるを。人の浅ましきか、我の愚なるか、恩人は酷くも我を欺きぬ。今は世を挙げて皆穢れたるよ。悲めばとて既に穢れたる世をいかにせん。我はこの時この穢れたる世に唯一つ穢れざるものあり。喜ぶべきものあるにあらずや。貫一は可憐き宮が事を思へるなり。

我の愛か、死をもて脅すとも得て屈すべからず。宮が愛か、某の帝の冠を飾れると聞くが世界無双の大金剛石をもて賭はんとすとも、争でか動し得べき。我と彼との愛こそ泥の中に輝く玉の如きものなれ、我はこの一つの穢れざるを抱きて、この世の渾て穢れたるを忘れん。

貫一はかく自ら慰めて、さすがに彼の巧言を憎し可恨しとは思ひつつも、枉げてさもあらぬ体に聴きゐたるなりけり。

「それで、この話は宮さんも知つてゐるのですか」

「薄々は知つてゐる」

「では未だ宮さんの意見は御聞にならんので？」

「それは、何だ、一寸聞いたがの」

「宮さんはどうと申してをりました」

「宮か、宮は別にどうといふ事は無いのだ。御父様や御母様の宜いやうにと云ふので、宮の方には異存は無いのだ、あれにもすつかり訳を説いて聞かしたところが、さう云ふ次第ならばと、漸く得心がいつたのだ」

「はい」

「断じて詐なるべしと思ひながらも、貫一の胸は跳りぬ。

「はあ、宮さんは承知を為ましたので？」

「さう、異存は無いのだ。で、お前も承知してくれ、なう。一寸聞けば無理のやうではあるが、その実少しも無理ではないのだ。私の今話した訳はお前にも能く解つたらうが、なう」

「はい」

「その訳が解つたら、お前も快く承知してくれ、なう。なう、貫一」

「はい」

「それではお前も承知をしてくれるな。それで私も多きに安心した。悪い事は何れ又寛緩話を為やう。さうしてお前の頼も聴かうから、まあ能く種々考へて置くが可いの」

「はい」

第七章

熱海は東京に比して温きこと十余度なれば、今日漸く一月の半を過ぎぬるに、梅林の花は二千本の梢に咲乱れて、日に映へる光は玲瓏として人の面を照らし、路を埋むる幾斗の清香は凝りて掬ぶに堪へたり。梅の外には一木無く、処々の乱石の低く横はるのみにて、地は坦に甃を鋪きたるやうの芝生の園の中を、玉の砕けて迸り、練の裂けて飜る如き早瀬の流ありて横さまに貫けり。

後に負へる松杉の緑は麗れる空を攅してその頂に方りて爛げに懸れる雲は眠るに似たり。習との風もあらぬに花は頻に散りぬ。散る時に軽く舞ふを鶯は争ひて歌へり。

宮は母親と連立ちて入来りぬ。彼等は橋を渡りて、船板の牀几を据ゑたる木の下を指して緩く歩めり。彼の病は未だ快からぬにや、薄化粧したる顔色も散りたる萜のやうに衰へて、足の運も怠げに、動すれば頭の低るるを、思出しては努めて梢を眺むるなりけり。彼の常として物案すれば必ず唇を咬むなり。彼は今頻に唇を咬みたりしが、

「御母さん、どうしませうねえ」

いと好く咲きたる枝を飽かず見上げし母の目は、この時漸く娘に転りぬ。

「どうせうたつて、お前の心一つぢやないか。初発にお前が適きたいといふから、かう云ふ話にしたのぢやないかね。それを今更……」

「それはさうだけれど、どうも貫一さんの事が気になつて。御父さんはもう貫一さんに話を為すつたらうか、ねえ御母さん」

「ああ、もう為すつたらうとも」

宮は又唇を咬みぬ。

「私は、御母さん、貫一さんに顔が合されないわね。だから若し適くのなら、もう逢はずに直と行つて了ひたいのだから、さう云ふ都合にして下さいな。私はもう逢はずに行くわ」

声は低くなりて、美き目は湿へり。彼は忘れざるべし、その涙を拭へるハンカチイフは再び逢はざらんとする人の形見なるを。

「お前がそれ程に思ふのなら、何で自分から適きたいとお言ひなのだえ。さう何時までも気が迷つてゐては困るぢやないか。一日経てば一日だけ話が運ぶのだから、本当にどうとも確然極めなくては可けないよ。お前が可厭なものを無理にお出といふのぢやないのだから、断るものなら早く断らなければ、だけれど、今になつて断ると云つたつて……」

「可いわ。私は適くことは適くのだけれど、貫一さんの事を考へると情無くなつて……」

貫一が母の寝覚にも苦むところなれば、娘のその名を言ふ度に、犯せる罪をも歌はるる心地して、この良縁の喜ぶべきを思ひつつも、さすがに胸を開きて喜ぶを得ざるなり。彼は強ひて宮を慰めんと試みつ。

「お父さんからお話があつて、貫一さんもそれで得心がいけば、済む事だし、又お前が彼方へ適

つて、末々まで貫一さんの力になれば、お互の仕合と云ふものだから、其処を考へれば、貫一さ

んだつて……、それに男と云ふものは思切が好いから、お前が心配してゐるやうなものではない

よ。これなり週はずに行くなんて、それはお却つて善くないから、丁と話をして、

さうして清く別れるのさ。この後とも末長く兄弟でしなければならないのだもの。

いづれ今日か明日には御音信があつて、様子が解らうから、早く支度に掛

らなければ」

宮は牀几に倚りて、半は聴き、半は思ひつつ、膝に散来る萢を拾ひては、おのれの唇に代へて

連に咬砕きぬ。

鶯の声の絶間を流の音は咽びて止まず。

宮は何心無く面を挙るとともに稍隔てたる木の間隠に男の漫行する姿を認めたり。彼は忽ち眼

を着けて、木立は垣の如く、花は幕の如くに遮る隙を縫ひつつ、姑くその影を逐ひたりしが、遂

に誰をや見出しけん。慌忙く母親に呼けり。彼は急に牀几を離れて五六歩進行きしが、彼方より

も見付けて、逸早く呼びぬ。

「其処に御出でしたか」

その声は静なる林を動して響きぬ。宮は聞くと斉く、恐れたる風情にて牀几の端に竦りつ。

「はい、唯今し方参つたばかりでございます。好くお出掛でございましたこと」

母はかく挨拶しつつ彼を迎へて立てり。宮は其方を見向きもやらで、彼の急足に近く音を聞け

り。

母子の前に顕れたる若き紳士は、その誰なるやをも説かずもあらなん。目覚く大なる金剛石の指環を輝かせるよ。柄には緑色の玉を獅子頭に彫みて、象牙の如く瑩潤に白き杖を携へたるが、その尾をもて低き梢の花を打落し打落し、

「今お留守へ行きまして、此処だといふのを聞いて追懸けて来た訳です。熱いぢやないですか」

宮はやうやう面を向けて、さて淑に起ちて、恭く礼するを、唯継は世にも嬉しげなる目して受けながら、なほ飽くまでも倨り高るを忘れざりき。その張りたる腮と、への字に結べる薄唇と、尤異き金縁の目鏡とは彼が尊大の風に魃からざる光彩を添ふるや疑ひ無し。

「おや、さやうでございましたか、それはまあ。余り好い御天気でございますから、ぶらぶらと出掛けて見ました。真に今日はお熱いくらゐでございます。まあこれへお掛遊ばして」

母は牀几を払へば、宮は路を開きて傍に佇めり。

「貴方がたもお掛けなさいませな。今朝です、東京から手紙で、急用があるから早速帰るやうに——と云ふのは、今度私が一寸した会社を建てるのです。外国へ此方の塗物を売込む会社。これは去年中からの計画で、いよいよこの三四月頃には立派に出来上る訳でありますから、私も今は随分忙しい体で、なにしろ社長ですからな。それで私が行かなければ解らん事があるので、呼びに来た。で、翌の朝立たなければならんのであります」

「おや、それは急な事で」

「貴方がたも一所にお立ちなさらんか」

彼は宮の顔を偸視つ。宮は物言はん気色もなくて又母の答へぬ。

「はい、難有う存じます」

「それとも未だ御在京ですか。宿屋に居るのも不自由で、面白くもないぢやありませんか。来年あたりは一つ別荘でも建てませう。何の難は無い事です。地面を広く取つてその中に風流な田舎家を造るです。食物などは東京から取寄せて、それでなくては実は保養には成らん。家が出来てから寛緩遊びに来るです」

「結構でございますね」

「お宮さんは、何ですか、かう云ふ田舎の静な所が御好なの？」

宮は笑を含みて言はざるを、母は傍より、

「これはもう遊ぶ事なら嫌はございませんので」

「ははははは誰もさうです。それでは以後盛に御遊びなさい。どうせ毎日用は無いのだから、田舎でも、東京でも西京でも、好きな所へ行つて遊ぶのです。船は御嫌ですか、ははあ。船が平気だと、支那から亜米利加の方を見物がてら今度旅行を為つて来るのも面白いけれど。日本の内ちや遊山に行いたところで知れたもの。どんなに贅沢を為たからと云つて」

「御帰山になつたら一日赤坂の別荘にお出下さい。梅が好いのであります。それは大きな梅林が有つて、一本々々種の違ふのを集めて二百本もあるが、皆老木ばかり。この梅なんどは全で為方が無い！　こんな若い野梅、薪のやうなもので、庭に植ゑられる花ぢやない。これ

で熱海の梅林も凄まじ。是非内のをお目に懸けたいでありますね、一日遊びに来て下さい。御馳走を為ますよ。お宮さんは何が所好ですか、ええ、一番所好なものは？」

彼は陰に宮と語らんことを望めるなり、宮はなほ言はずして可羞しげに打笑めり。

「で、何日御帰でありますか。明朝一所にはなりませんか。此地にさう長く居なければならんと云ふ次第ではないのでせう、そんなら一所にお立ちなすつたらどうであります」

「はい、難有うございますが、少々宅の方の都合がございまして、二三日内には音信がございます筈で、その音信を待ちまして、実は帰ることに致してございますものですから、折角の仰せですが、はい」

「ははあ、それぢやどうもな」

唯継は例の倨りて天を睨むやうに打仰ぎて、杖の獅子頭を撫廻しつつ、少時思案する体なりしが、やをら白羽二重のハンカチイフを取出して、片手に一揮揮るよと見れば鼻を拭へり。菫花の香は咽ばさるるばかりに薫じ遍りぬ。

宮も母もその鋭き匂に驚けるなり。

「ああと、私これから少し散歩しやうと思ふのであります。これから出て、流に沿うて、田圃の方を。私未だ知らんけれども、余程景色が好いさう。御一所にと云ふのだが、大分跡程が有るから、貴方は御迷惑でありませう。二時間ばかりお宮さんを御貸し下さいな。私一人で歩いてもつまらない。お宮さんは胃が不良のだから散歩は極めて薬、これから行つて見ませう、ねえ」

彼は杖を取直してはや立たんとす。

「はい。難有うございます。お前お供をお為かい」

宮の遅ふを見て、唯継は故に座を起てり。

「さあ行つて見ませう、ええ、胃病の薬です。さう因循してゐては可けない」

つと寄りて軽く宮の肩を拊ちぬ。宮は忽ち面を紅めて、如何にとも為ん術を知らざらんやうに立惑ひてゐたり。母の前をも憚らぬ男の馴々しさを、憎しとにはあらねど、己の伈なきやうに懟づるなりけり。

得も謂はれぬその仇無さの身に浸遍るに堪へざる思は、漫に唯継の目の中に顕れて異き独笑となりぬ。この仇無き嬌しらしき、美き娘の柔き手を携へて、人無き野道の長閑なるを語ひつつ行かば、如何ばかり楽からんよと、彼ははや心も空になりて、

「さあ、行つて見ませう。御母さんから御詐が出たから可いではありませんか、ねえ、貴方、宜いでありませう」

母は宮の猶羞づるを見て、

「お前お出かい、どうお為だえ」

「貴方、お出かいなどと有仰つちや可けません。お出なさいと命令を為すつて下さい」

宮も母も思はず笑へり。唯継も後れじと笑へり。

又人の入来る気勢なるを宮は心着きて窺ひしに、姿は見えずして靴の音のみを聞きけり。梅見る

人か、あらぬか、用ありげに忙しく踏立つる足音なりき。

「ではお前お供をおしな」

「さあ、行きませう。直其処まででありますよ」

宮は小き声して、

「御母さんも一処に御出なさいな」

「私かい、まあお前お供をおしな」

母親を伴ひては大いに風流ならず、頗る妙ならずと思へば、唯継は飽くまでこれを防がんと、

「いや、御母さんには却つて御迷惑です。道が良くないから御母さんにはとても可けすまい。実際貴方には切つてお勧め申されない。御迷惑は知れてゐる。何も遠方へ行くのではないのだから、御母さんが一処でなくても可いぢやありませんか、ねえ。私折角思立つたものでありますから、それでは一寸其処までで可いから附合つて下さい。貴女が可厭だつたら直に帰りますよ、ねえ。それはなかなか好い景色だから、まあ私に騙されたと思つて来て御覧なさいな、ねえ」

この時忙しげに聞えし靴音ははや止みたり。人は出去りしにあらで、七八間彼方なる木蔭に足を停めて、忍びやかに様子を窺ふなるを、此方の三人は誰も知らず。イめる人は高等中学の制服の上に焦茶の外套を着て、肩には古りたる象皮の学校鞄を掛けたり。彼は間貫一にあらずや。再び靴音は高く響きぬ。その蹣なると近きとに驚きて、三人は始めて音する方を見遣りつ。

花の散りかかる中を進来つつ学生は帽を取りて、

「姨さん、参りましたよ」

母子は動顛して殆ど人心地を失ひぬ。母親は物を見るべき力もあらず呆れ果てたる目をば空く瞶りて、少時は石の如く動かず、宮は、あはれ生きてあらんより忽ち消えてこの土と成らんことの、せめて心易さを思ひつつ、その淡白き唇を咬裂かんとすばかりに咬みて咬みて止まざりき。

想ふに彼等の驚愕と恐怖とはその殺せし人の計らずも今生きて来れるに会へるが如きものならん。気も不覚なれば母は譫語のやうに言出せり。

「おや、お出なの」

宮は些少なりともおのれの姿の多く彼の目に触れざらんやうにと冀へる如く、木蔭に身を側めて、打過む呼吸を人に聞かれじとハンカチイフに口元を掩ひて、見るは苦けれども、見ざるも辛き貫一の顔を、俯したる額越しに窺ひては、又唯継の気色をも気遣へり。

唯継は彼等の心々にさばかりの大波瀾ありとは知らざれば、聞及びたる鳴沢の食客の来れるよと、例の金剛石の手を見よがしに杖を立てて、誇りかに梢を仰ぐ腮を張れり。

貫一は今回の事も後に知れり、彼の唯継なる事も知れり、既にこの場の様子をも知らざるにはあらねど、言ふべき事は後にぞ犖と言はん、今は姑く色にも出さじと、裂けもしぬべき無念の胸をやうやう鎮めて、苦き笑顔を作りてゐたり。

「宮さんの病気はどうでございます」

宮は耐りかねて窃にハンカチイフを咬緊めたり。

「ああ、大きに良いので、もう二三日内には帰らうと思つてね。お前さん能く来られましたね。学校の方は？」

「教場の普請を為るところがあるので、今日半日と明日明後日と休課になつたものですから」

「おや、さうかい」

唯継と貫一とを左右に受けたる母親の絶体絶命は、過ちて野中の古井に落ちたる人の、沈みも果てず、上りも得為ず、命の綱と危くも取縋りたる草の根を、鼠の来りて噛むに遭ふと云へる比喩に最能く似たり。如何に為べきかと或は懼れ、或は惑ひたりしが、終にその免るまじきを知りて、彼はやうやう胸を定めつ。

「丁度宅から人が参りましてございますから、甚だ勝手がましうございますが、私等はこれから宿へ帰りますでございますから、いづれ後程伺ひに出ますでございますが……」

「ははあ、それでは何でありますか、明朝は御一所に帰れるやうな都合になりますな」

「はい、話の模様に因りましては、さやう願はれるかも知れませんので、いづれ後程には是非何ひまして、……」

「成程、それでは残念ですが、私も散歩は罷めます。帰つてお待申してゐますから、後に是非お出下さいよ。宜いですか、お宮さん、それでは後にきつとお出なさいよ。誠に今日は残念でありますな」

彼は行かんとして、更に宮の傍近く寄来て、

「貴方、きつと後にお出なさいよ、ええ」

貫一は瞬も為で視てゐたり。宮は窘して彼に会釈さへ為かねつ。娘気の可羞にかくあるとのみ

思へる唯継は、益寄添ひつつ、舌怠きまでに語を和げて、

「宜いですか、来なくては可けません。　　私待つてゐますから」

貫一の眼は燃ゆるが如き色を作して、宮の横顔を瞪着けたり。彼は懼れて傍目をも転らざりけ

れど、必ずさあるべきを想ひて独り心を慄かせしが、猶唯継の如何なることを言出でんも知られ

ずと思へば、とにもかくにもその場を繕ひぬ。母子の為には幾許の幸なりけん。彼は貫一に就

いて半点の疑ひをも容れず、唯懸くまでも妬き宮に心を遺して行けり。

その後影を透すばかりに目成れる貫一は我を忘れて黙く佇めり。両個はその心を測りかねて、

言も出でず、息をさへ凝して、空く早瀬の音の喧きを聴くのみなりけり。

やがて此方を向きたる貫一は、尋常ならず激して血の色を失へる面上に、多からんとすれども

能はずと見ゆる微少の笑を漏して、空く早瀬……唇を咬みぬ。

「宮さん、今の奴はこの間の骨牌に来てゐた金剛石だね」

宮は俯きて唇を咬みぬ。母は聞かざる為して、折しも啼ける鶯の木の間を窺へり。貫一はこの

体を見て更に嘲笑ひつ。

「夜見たらそれ程でもなかつたが、昼間見ると実に気障な奴だね、さうしてどうだ、あの高慢ち

きの面は！」

「貫一さん」母は卒に呼びかけたり。

「はい」

「お前さん翁さんから話はお聞きでせうね、今度の話は」

「はい」

「ああ、そんなら可いけれど。不断のお前さんにも似合はない、そんな人の悪口などを言ふもの

ぢやありませんよ」

「はい」

「さあ、もう帰りませう。お前さんもお草臥だらうから、お湯にでも入つて、さうして未だ御午

餐前なのでせう」

「いえ、滊車の中で鮨を食べました」

三人は倶に歩始めぬ。貫一は外套の肩を払はれて、後を捻向けば宮と面を合せたり。

「其処に花が粘いてゐたから取つたのよ」

「それは難有う!!!」

　　　　第　八　章

打霞みたる空ながら、月の色の匂滴るるやうにして、微白き海は縹渺として限を知らず、譬へ

ば無邪気なる夢を敷けるに似たり。寄せては返す波の音も眠げに怠りて、吹来る風は人を酔はし
めんとす。打連れてこの浜辺を逍遙せるは貫一と宮となりけり。

「僕は唯胸が一杯で、何も言ふことが出来ない」
五歩六歩行きし後宮はやうやう言出でつ。

「堪忍して下さい」

「何も今更謝ることは無いよ。一体今度の事は翁さん姨さんの意から出たのか、又はお前さんも
得心であるのか、それを聞けば可いのだから」

「………」

「此地へ来るまでは、僕は十分信じてをつた、お前さんに限つてそんな了簡のあるべき筈は無い
と。実は信じるも信じないも有りはしない、夫婦の間で、知れきつた話だ。昨夜翁さんから悉く話があつて、その上に頼むといふ御言だ」

差含む涙に彼の声は顫ひぬ。

「大恩を受けてゐる翁さん姨さんの事だから、頼むと言はれた日には、僕は済まないけれど翁さんを恨んでゐ
飛込まなければならないのだ。翁さん姨さんの頼なら、無論僕は火水の中へでも飛込む精神だ。火水の中へなら飛込むがこの頼ばかりは僕も聴くことは出来ないと思つた。火水の中へ飛込めと云ふよりは、もつと無理な、余り無理な頼ではないかと、僕は済まないけれど翁さんを恨んでゐ
る。

さうして、言ふ事も有らうに、この頼を聴いてくれれば洋行さして遣るとお言ひのだ。い……いかに貫一は乞食士族の孤児でも、女房を売つた銭で洋行せうとは思はん！」

貫一は蹐跼りて海に向ひて泣けり。宮はこの時始めて彼に寄添ひて、気遣しげにその顔を差覗きぬ。

「堪忍して下さいよ、皆私が……どうぞ堪忍して下さい」

貫一の手に縋りて、忽ちその肩に面を推当つると見れば、彼も泣音を洩すなりけり。波は漾々として遠く烟りて、月は朧に一湾の真砂を照して、空も汀も淡白き中に、立尽せる二人の姿は墨の滴りたるやうの影を作れり。

「それで僕は考へたのだ、これは一方には翁さんが僕を説いて、お前さんの方は姨さんが説得しやうと云ふので、無理に此処へ連出したに違無い。翁さん姨さんの頼と有つて見れば、僕は不承知を言ふことの出来ない身分だから、唯々と言つて聞いてゐたけれど、宮さんは幾多でも剛情を張つて差支無いのだ。どうあつても可厭だとお前さんへ言通せば、この縁談はそれで破れて了ふのだ。僕が傍に居ると邪魔を為ると思ふものだから、遠くへ連出して無理往生に納得させる計だなと考着くと、さあ心配で心配で僕は昨夜は夜一夜寐はしない、そんな事は万有るまいけれど、種々言はれる為に可厭と言はれない義理になつて、若や承諾するやうな事があつては大変だと思つて、家は学校へ出る積で、僕はわざわざ様子を見に来たのだ。

馬鹿な、馬鹿な！　貫一ほどの大馬鹿者が世界中を捜して何処に在る！！　僕はこれ程自分が大

馬鹿とは、二十五歳の今日まで知……知……知らなかった」

宮は可悲と可懼はれて少く声さへ立てて泣きぬ。

憤を抑ふる貫一の呼吸は漸く乱れたり。

「宮さん、お前は好くも僕を欺いたね」

宮は覚えず慄けり。

「病気と云つてここへ来たのは、富山と逢ふ為だらう」

「まあ、そればつかりは……」

「おおそればつかりは？」

「余り邪推が過ぎるわ、余り酷いわ。何ぼ何でも余り酷い事を」

泣入る宮を尻目に掛けて、

「お前でも酷いと云ふ事を知つてるのかい、宮さん。これが酷いと云つて泣く程なら、大馬鹿者にされた貫一は……貫一は血の涙を流しても足りはは為んよ。お前が得心せんものなら、此地へ来るに就いて僕に一言も言はんと云ふ法は無からう。家を出るのが突然で、その暇が無かつたなら、後から手紙を寄来すが可いぢやないか。出抜いて家を出るばかりか、何の便も為んところを見れば、始から富山と出会る手筈になつてゐたのだ。或は一所に来たのか知れはしない。宮さん、お前は奸婦だよ。姦通したも同じだよ」

「そんな酷いことを、貫一さん、余りだわ、余りだわ」

彼は正体も無く泣頽れつつ、寄らんとするを貫一は突退けて、

「操を破れば奸婦ぢやあるまいか」

「何時私が操を破つて？」

「幾許大馬鹿者の貫一でも、おのれの妻が操を破る傍に付いて見てゐるものかい！　貫一と云ふ歴とした夫を持ちながら、その夫を出抜いて、余所の男と湯治に来てゐるのを聞いて、富山さんが後から尋ねて来たのだわ」

「さう言はれて了ふと、私は何とも言へないけれど、富山さんと逢ふの、約束してあつたのと云ふのは、それは全く貫一さんの邪推よ。　私等が此地に来てゐるのを聞いて、姦通してゐないと云ふ証拠が何処に在る？」

「何で富山が後から尋ねて来たのだ」

宮はその唇に釘打たれたるやうに再び言は出でざりき。　貫一は、かく詰責せる間に彼の必ず過を悔い、罪を詫びて、その身は未か命までも己の欲するままならんことを誓ふべしと信じたりしなり。　よし信ぜざりけんも、心陰に望みたりしならん。　如何にぞや、彼は露ばかりもさせる気色は無くて、引けども朝顔の垣を離るまじき一図の心変を、貫一はなかなか信しからず覚ゆるまでに呆れたり。

宮は我を棄てたるよ。　我は我妻を人に奪はれたるよ。　恨は彼の骨に徹し、憤は彼の胸を劈きて、我命にも換へて最愛みし人は芥の如く我を悪めるよ。　ほとほと身も世も忘れたる貫一は、あは

れ奸婦の肉を啖ひて、この熱腸を冷さんとも思へり。　忽ち彼は頭脳の裂けんとするを覚えて、苦痛に得堪へずして尻居に僵れたり。

宮は見るより驚く違もあらず、諸共に砂に塗れて掻抱けば、閉ぢたる眼より乱落つる涙に浸れる灰色の頬を、月の光は悲しげに彷徨ひて、迫れる息は凄く波打つ胸の響を伝ふ。　宮は彼の背後より取縋り、抱緊め、撼動して、戦く声を励せば、励す声は更に戦きぬ。

「どうして、貫一さん、どうしたのよう！」

貫一は力無げに宮の手を執れり。　宮は涙に汚れたる男の顔をいと懇に拭ひたり。

「呀、宮さんかうして二人が一処に居るのも今夜ぎり、僕がお前に物を言ふのも今夜ぎりだよ。　一月の十七日、宮さん、善く覚えてお置き。　来年の今月今夜は、貫一は何処でこの月を見るのだか！　一月の十七日、宮さん、再来年の今月今夜……十年後の今月今夜……一生を通して僕は今夜を忘れん、忘れるものか、死んでも僕は忘れんよ！　可いか、宮さん、一月の十七日だ。　来年の今月今夜になつたならば、僕の涙で必ず月は曇らして見せるから、月が……月が……月が……曇つたらば、宮さん、貫一は何処かでお前を恨んで、今夜のやうに泣いてゐると思つてくれ」

宮は挫くばかりに貫一に取着きて、物狂う咽入りぬ。

「そんな悲しい事をいはずに、ねえ貫一さん、私も考へた事があるのだから、それは腹も立たうけれど、どうぞ堪忍して、少し辛抱してゐて下さいな。　私はお肚の中には言ひたい事が沢山あるの

だけれど、余り言難い事ばかりだから、口へは出さないけれど、唯一言いひたいのは、私は貴方の事は忘れはしないわ――私は生涯忘れはしないわ」

「聞きたくない！　忘れんくらゐなら何故見棄てた」

「だから、私は決して見棄てはしないわ」

「何、見棄てない？　見棄てないものが嫁に帰るかい、馬鹿な！　二人の夫が有てるかい」

「だから、私は考へてゐる事があるのだから、も少し辛抱してそれを――私の心を見て下さいな。きつと貴方の事を忘れない証拠を私は見せるわ」

「ええ、狼狽へてくだらんことを言ふな。食ふに窮つて身を売らなければならんのだか、何を苦んで嫁に帰るのだ。内には七千円も財産が在つて、お前は其処の一人娘ぢやないか、さうして婿まで極つてゐるのぢやないか。その婿も四五年の後には学士になると、末の見込も着いてゐるのだ。しかもお前はその婿を生涯忘れないほどに思つてゐると云ふぢやないか。それに何の不足が有つて、無理にも嫁に帰かなければならんのだ。天下にこれくらゐの理の解らん話が有らうか。どう考へても、嫁に帰くべき必用の無いものが、無理に算段をして嫁に帰かうと為るには、必ず何ぞ事情が無ければ成らない。遠慮は要らない。さあ、さあ、宮さん、遠慮することは無いよ。一旦夫に定めた

婿が不足なのか、金持と縁を組みたいのか、主意は決してこの二件の外にはあるまい。言つて聞かしてくれ。遠慮は要らない。さあ、さあ、宮さん、遠慮することは無いよ。一旦夫に定めたものを振捨てるくらゐの無遠慮なものが、こんな事に遠慮も何も要るものか」

「私が悪いのだから堪忍して下さい」

「それぢや婿が不足なのだね」

「貫一さん、それは余りだわ。そんなに疑ふのなら、私はどんな事でもして、さうして証拠を見せるわ」

「婿に不足は無い？　それぢや富山が財があるからか、して見るとこの結婚は慾からだね、僕の離縁も慾からだね。で、この結婚はお前も承知をしたのだね、ええ？　翁さん姨さんに迫られて、余儀無くお前も承知をしたのならば、僕の考で破談にする方は幾許もある。僕一人が悪者になれば、翁さん姨さんを始めお前の迷惑にもならずに打壊して了ふことは出来る、だからお前の心持を聞いた上で手段があるのだが、お前も適って見る気は有るのかい」

貫一の眼はその全身の力を聚めて、思悩める宮が顔を鋭く打目成れり。五歩行き、七歩行き、十歩を行けども、彼の答はあらざりき。貫一は空を仰ぎて太息したり。

「宜い。もう宜い。お前の心は能く解つた」

今ははや言ふも益無ければ、重ねて口を開かざらんかと打按じつつも、彼は乱るる胸を寛うせんが為に、強ひて目を放ちて海の方を眺めたりしが、なほ得堪へずやありけん、又言はんとして顧れば、宮は傍に在らずして、六七間後なる波打際に面を掩ひて泣けるなり。

可悩しげなる姿の月に照され、風に吹れて、あはれ消えもしぬべく立ち迷へるに、淼々たる海の端の白く頽れて波と打寄せたる、艶に哀を尽せる風情に、貫一は憤をも恨をも忘れて、少時

は画を看る如き心地もしつ。更に、この美き人も今は我物ならずと思へば、なかなか夢かとも疑へり。

「夢だ夢だ、長い夢を見たのだ！」
彼は頭を低れて足の向ふままに汀の方へ進行きしが、泣く泣く歩来れる宮と互に知らで行合ひたり。

「宮さん、何を泣くのだ。お前は些も泣くことは無いぢやないか。空涙！」
「どうせさうよ」
殆ど聞得べからざるまでにその声は涙に乱れたり。

「宮さん、お前に限つてはさう云ふ了簡は無からうと、僕は自分を信じるほどに信じてゐたが、それぢややつぱりお前の心は慾だね、財なのだね。如何に何でも余り情無い、宮さん、お前はそれで自分に愛相は尽きないかい。

好い出世をして、さぞ栄耀も出来て、お前はそれで可からうけれど、財に見換へられて棄てられた僕の身になつて見るが可い。無念と謂はうか、口惜いと謂はうか、宮さん、僕はお前を刺殺して――いつそ死んで了ひたいのだ。それを怺へてお前を人に奪れるのを手出しも為ずに見てゐる僕の心地は、どんなだと思ふ、どんなだと思ふよ！ 自分さへ好ければ他はどうならうともお前はかまはんのかい。一体貫一はお前の何だよ。何だと思ふのだよ。鳴沢の家には厄介者の居候でも、お前の為には夫ぢやないかい。僕はお前の男妾になつた覚は無い

よ、宮さん、お前は貫一を玩弄物にしたのだね。平生お前の仕打が水臭い水臭いと思つたも道理だ、始から僕を一時の玩弄物の意で、本当の愛情は無かつたのだ。さうとは知らずに僕は自分の身よりもお前を愛してゐた。お前の外には何の楽も無いほどにお前の事を思つてゐた。それ程までに思つてゐる貫一を、宮さん、お前はどうしても棄てる気かい。

それは無論金力の点では、僕と富山とは比較にはならない。彼方は屈指の財産家、僕は固より一介の書生だ。けれども善く宮さん考へて御覧、ねえ、人間の幸福ばかりは決して財で買へるものぢやないよ。幸福と財とは全く別物だよ。人の幸福の第一は家内の平和だ、家内の平和は夫婦が互に深く愛すると云ふ外は無い。お前を深く愛する点では、富山如きが百人寄つても到底僕の十分の一だけでも愛することは出来まい、富山が財産で誇るなら、僕は彼等の夢想すること

も出来ぬこの愛情で争つて見せる。夫婦の幸福は全くこの愛情の力、愛情が無ければ既に夫婦は無いのだ。

己の身に換へてお前を思つてゐる程の愛情を有つてゐる貫一を棄てて、夫婦間の幸福には何の益も無い、寧ろ害になり易い、その財産を目的に結婚を為るのは、宮さん、どういふ心得なのだ。然し財といふものは人の心を迷はすもので、智者の学者の豪傑のと、千万人に勝れた立派な男子さへ、財の為には随分曲い事も為るのだ。それを考へれば、お前が偶然気の変つたのも、或は無理も無いのだらう。からして僕はそれは咎めない、但もう一遍、宮さん善く考へて御覧な、その財が──富山の財産がお前の夫婦間にどれ程の効力があるのかと謂ふことを。

い、僕は鳴沢の財産を譲つてもらはんでも、俵で置いてあつたつて、一度に一俵食へるものぢやな雀が米を食ふのは僅か十粒か二十粒だ、俵で置いてあつたつて、一度に一俵食へるものぢやな
い、僕は鳴沢の財産を譲つてもらはんでも、十粒か二十粒の米を欠いて、お前に餒い思を為せるやうな、そんな意気地の無い男でもない。若し間違つて、その十粒か二十粒の米の工面が出来なかつたら、僕は自分は食はんでも、決してお前に不自由は為せん。宮さん、僕はこれ……これ程までにお前の事を思つてゐる！」

貫一は霽する涙を払ひて、

「お前が富山へ嫁く、それは立派な生活をして、栄耀も出来やうし、楽も出来やう、けれどもあれだけの財産は決して息子の嫁の為に費さうとて作られた財産ではない、と云ふ事をお前考へなければならんよ。愛情の無い夫婦の間に、立派な生活が何だ！　栄耀が何だ！　世間には、馬車に乗つて心配さうな青い顔をして、夜会へ招れて行く人もあれば、自分の妻子を車に載せて、それを自分が挽いて花見に出掛ける車夫もある。富山へ嫁けば、家内も多ければ人出入も、劇しく、従つて気兼も苦労も一通の事ぢやなからう。その中へ入つて、気を傷めながら愛してもゐらん夫を持つて、それでお前は何を楽に生きてゐるのだ。さうして勤めてゐれば、末にはあの財産がお前の物になるのかい。よしんばあの財産がお前の自由になるとしたところは今の雀の十粒か二十粒に過ぎんのぢやないか。富山の奥様と云へば立派かも知れんけれど、食ふところは今の雀の十粒か二十粒に過ぎんのぢやないか。何十万と云ふ金がどうなる、女の身に何十万の金で面白く費へるかい。雀に一俵の米を一度に食へと云ふやうなものぢやないか。男を持たなければ女の身は立ててないものなら、一生の苦楽他人へと云ふやうなものぢやないか。何十万と云ふ金がどうなる、女の身に

に頼るで、女の宝とするのはその夫ではないか。何百万の財が有らうと、その夫が宝と為るに足らんものであつたら、女の心細さは、なかなか車に載せて花見に連れられる車夫の女房には及ばんぢやあるまいか。

聞けばあの富山の父と云ふものは、内に二人外に三人も妾を置いてゐると云ふ話だ。財の有る者は大方そんな真似をして、妻は些の床の置物にされて、責任も重く、苦労も多く、苦ばかりで楽は無いと謂つてゐながらその愛されてゐる妾よりは、可い。お前の嫁く唯継だつて、固より所望でお前を迎ふのだから、当座は随分愛しも為るだらうが、それが長く続くものか、財が有るから好きな真似も出来る、他の楽に気が移つて、直にお前の恋は冷されて了ふのは判つてゐる。その時になつて、お前の心地を考へて御覧、あの富山の財産がその苦を拯ふかい。家に沢山の財が在れば、夫に棄てられて床の置物になつてゐても、お前はそれで楽かい、満足かい。

僕が人にお前を奪られる無念は謂ふまでも無いけれど、三年の後のお前の後悔が目に見えて、心変をした憎いお前ちやあるけれど、やつぱり可哀さうでならんから、僕は真実で言ふのだ。僕に飽きて富山に惚れてお前が嫁くのなら、僕は未練らしく何も言はんけれど、宮さん、お前は唯立派なところへ嫁くといふそればかりに迷はされてゐるのだから、それは過つてゐる、それは実に過つてゐる、愛情の無い結婚は究竟自他の後悔だよ。今夜この場のお前の分別一つで、お前の一生の苦楽は定るのだから、宮さん、お前も自分の身が大事と思ふなら、又貫一が不便だと

思つて、頼む！　頼むから、もう一度分別を為直してくれないか。

七千円の財産と貫一が学士とは、二人の幸福を保つには十分だよ。今でさへも随分二人は幸福ではないか。男の僕でさへ、お前が在れば富山の財産などを可憐いとは更に思はんのに、宮さん、お前はどうしたのだ！　僕を忘れたのかい、僕を可愛くは思はんのかい」

彼は危きを拯はんとする如く犇と宮に取着きて匂滴るる頸元に沸ゆる涙を濺ぎつつ、蘆の枯葉の風に揺るるやうに身を顫せり。宮も離れじと抱緊めて諸共に顫ひつつ、貫一が臂を咬みて咽泣に泣けり。

「嗚呼、私はどうしたら可からう！　若し私が彼方へ嫁つたら、貫一さんはどうするの、それを聞かして下さいな」

「それぢや断然お前は嫁く気だね！　これまでに僕が言つても聴いてくれんのだね。ちええ、膓の腐つた女！　姦婦！！」

その声とともに貫一は脚を挙げて宮の弱腰をはたと蹴たり。地響して横様に転びしが、なかなか声をも立てず苦痛を忍びて、彼はそのまま砂の上に泣伏したり。貫一は猛獣などを撃ちたるやうに、彼の身動も得為ず弱々と僵れたるを、なほ憎さげに見遣りつつ、

「宮、おのれ姦婦、やい！　貴様のな、心変をしたばかりに間貫一の男一匹はな、失望の極発狂して、大事の一生を誤つて了ふのだ。学問も何ももう廃だ。この恨の為に貫一は生きな

から悪魔になって、貴様のやうな畜生の肉を啖つて遣る覚悟だ。富山の令……令夫……令夫人！もう一生お目には掛らんから、その顔を挙げて、真人間で居る内の貫一の面を好く見て置かない。かい。長々の御恩に預つた翁さん媼さんには一目会つて段々の御礼を申上げなければ済まんのでありますけれど、仔細あつて貫一はこのまま長の御暇を致しますから、随分お達者で御機嫌よろしう……宮さん、お前から好くさう言つておくれ、よ、若し貫一はどうしたとお訊ねなすつたら、あの大馬鹿者は一月十七日の晩に気が違つて、熱海の浜辺から行方知れずになつて了つたと、……」

宮はやにはに蹶起きて、立たんと為れば脚の痛に脆くも倒れて効無きを、漸く這寄りて貫一の脚に縋付き、声と涙とを争ひて、

「貫一さん、ま……ま……待つて下さい。貴方これから何処へ……何処へ行くのよ」

貫一はさすがに驚きけり、宮が衣の抜けて雪可く露せる膝頭は、夥しく血に染みて顔ふなりき。

「や、怪我をしたか」

寄らんとするを宮は支へて、

「えゝ、こんな事はかまはないから、貴方は何処へ行くのよ、話があるから今夜は一所に帰つて下さい、よう、貫一さん、後生だから」

「話が有ればここで聞かう」

「こゝぢや私は可厭よ」

「えゝ、何の話が有るものか。さあここを放さないか」

「私は放さない」

「剛情張ると蹴飛すぞ」

「蹴られても可いわ」

貫一は力を極めて振断れば、宮は無残に伏転びぬ。

「貫一さん」

貫一ははや幾間を急行きたり。宮は見るより必死と起上りて、脚の傷に幾度か仆れんとしつつ

も後を慕ひて。

「貫一さん、それぢやもう留めないから、もう一度、もう一度……私は言遺した事がある」

遂に倒れし宮は再び起つべき力も失せて、唯声を頼に彼の名を呼ぶのみ。漸く朧になれる貫一

の影が一散に岡を登るが見えぬ。宮は身悶して猶呼続けつ。やがてその黒き影の岡の頂に立てる

は、此方を目成れるならんと、宮は声の限に呼べば、男の声も遙に来りぬ。

「宮さん！」

「あ、あ、貫一さん！」

首を延べて胸せども、目を瞠りて眺むれども、声せし後は黒き影の掻消す如く失せて、それか

と思ひし木立の寂しげに動かず、波は悲き音を寄せて、一月十七日の月は白く愁ひぬ。

宮は再び恋き貫一の名を呼びたりき。

中　編

第　一　章

新橋停車場の大時計は四時を過ぐること二分余、東海道行の列車は既に客車の扉を鎖して、機関車に煙を噴せつつ、三十余輛を聯ねて蜿蜒として横はりたるが、真承の秋の日影に夕栄して、窓の硝子は燃えんとすばかりに耀けり。駅夫は右往左往に奔走して、早く早くと喚くを余所に、大踏歩の寛々たる老欧羅巴人は麦酒樽を窃みたるやうに腹突出して、桃色の服着たる十七八の娘の日本の絵日傘の柄に、橙色のリボンを飾りたるを小脇にせると推並び、おのれが乗物の顔して急ぐ気色も無く過ぎる後より、蚤取眼になりて遅れじと所体崩して駈来る女房の、嵩高なる風呂敷包を抱くが上に、四歳ほどの子を背負ひたるが、何処の扉も鎖したるに狼狽ふるを、車掌に強曳れて漸く安堵せる間も無く、青洟垂せる女の子を率ゐて、五十余の老夫のこれも戸惑して往きつ復りつせし揚句、駅夫に曳れて室内に押入れられ、如何なる罪やあらげなく閉てらるる扉に袂を介まれて、もしもしと救を呼ぶなど、未だ都を離れざるにはや旅の哀を見るべし。

五人一隊の若き紳士等は中等室の片隅に円居して、その中に旅行らしき手荷物を控へたるは一人よりあらず、他は皆横浜までとも見ゆる扮装にて、紋付の袷羽織を着たるもあれば、精緻の背広なるもあり、袴着けたるが一人、大島紬の長羽織と差向へる人のみぞフロックコオトを着て、待合所にて受けし餞別の瓶、凾などを網棚の上に片附けて、その手を摩払ひつつ窓より首を出して、停車場の方をば、求むるものありげに望見たりしが、やがて藍の如き晩霽の空を仰ぎて、

「不思議に好い天気に成った、なあ。この分なら大丈夫じゃ」

「今晩雨になるのも又一興だよ、ねえ、甘糟」

黒餅に立沢瀉の黒紬の羽織着たるがかく言ひて示すところあるが如き微笑を洩せり。甘糟と呼れたるは、茶柳条の仙台平の袴を着けたる、この中にて独り頬鬚の厳きを蓄ふる紳士なり。

甘糟の答ふるに先ちて、背広の風早は若きに似合はぬ皺嗄声を振搾りて、

「甘糟は一興で、君は望むところなのだらう」

「馬鹿言へ。甘糟の痒きに堪へんことを僕は丁と洞察してをるのだ」

「これは憚様です」

大島紬の紳士は黏着いたるやうに欹れたり身を遽に起して、

「風早、君と僕はね、今日は実際犠牲に供されてゐるのだよ。佐分利と甘糟は厠て横浜を主張してゐるのだ。何でもこの間遊仙窟を見出して来たのだ。それで我々を引張つて行つて、大いに気焔を吐く意なのさ」

「何じゃい、何じゃい！　君達がこの二人に犠牲に供されたと謂ふのなら、僕は四人の為に売られたんじゃ。それには及ばんと云ふのに、是非浜まで見送ると言うので、気の毒なと思うてをつたら、僕を送るのを名として君達は……怪しからん事だぞ。学生中からその方は勉強しをつた君達の事ぢやから、今後は実に想遣らるるね。ええ、肩書を辱めん限は遣るも可からうけれど、注意はしたまへよ、本当に」

この老実の言を作すは、今は四年の昔間貫一が兄事せし同窓の荒尾譲介なりけり。彼は去年法学士を授けられ、次いで内務省試補に挙げられ、踰えて一年の今日愛知県の参事官に栄転して、赴任の途に上れるなり。その齢と深慮と誠実との故を以つて、彼は他の同学の先輩として推服するところたり。

「これで僕は諸君へ意見の言納じゃ。願くは君達も宜く自重してくれたまへ」

佐分利は幾数回頷きて、面白く発りし一座も忽ち白けて、頻に燻らす巻葉の煙の、急駛せる車の逆風に扇らるるが、飛雲の如く窓を逃れて六郷川を掠むあるのみ。

「いやさう言れると慄然とするよ、実は鰤停車場で例の『美人クリイム』(こは美人の高利貸を戯称せるなり)を見掛けたのだ。あの声で蜥蜴咳ふかと思ふね、毎見ても美いには驚嘆する。全で淑女の扮装だ。就中今日は冶してをつたが、何処か旨い口でもあると見える。那奴に搾られちや克はん、あれが本当の真綿で首だらう」

「見たかつたね、それは。尻て御高名は聞及んでゐる」

と大島紬の猶続けんとするを遮りて、甘糟の言へる。

「おお、宝井が退学を吃つたのも、其奴が債権者の重なる者だと云ふぢやないか。酷い奴だ！　鬼神のお松だ。佐分利、木乃

さうだね。黄金の腕環なんぞ嵌めてゐると云ふぢやないか。余程好い女だ

はその劇なるを知りながら係つたのは、大いに冒険の目的があつて存するのだらうけれど、

伊にならんやうに褌を緊めて掛るが可いぜ」

「誰か其奴には尻押が有るのだらう。亭主が有るのか、或は情夫か、何か有るのだらう」

「それに就いては小説的の閲歴があるのさ、情夫ぢやない、亭主がある、此奴が君、我々の一世

敏嘆声は卒然としてこの問を発せるなり。

紀前に鳴らした高利貸で、赤樫権三郎と云つては、いや無法な強慾で、加ふるに大々的嬌物と来て

ゐるのだ」

「成程！　積極と消極と相触れたので爪に火が熔る訳だな」

大島紬が得意の譴浪に、深沈なる荒尾も已むを得ざらんやうに破顔しつ。

「その赤樫と云ふ奴は貸金の督促を利用しては女を弄ぶのが道楽で、此奴の為に汚された者は随

分意外の辺にも在るさうな。そこで今の『美人クリイム』これもその手に罹つたので、原は貧乏

士族の娘で堅気であつたのだが、老猾この娘を見ると食指大いに動いた訳で、これを俘にしたさ

に父親に少しばかりの金を貸したのだ。期限が来ても返せん、それを何とも言はずに、後から後

からと三四度も貸して置いて、もう好い時分に、内に手が無くて困るから、半月ばかり仲働に貸してくれと言出した。これはよしんば奴の胸中が見え透いてゐたからとて、勢ひ辞りかねる人情だらう。今から六年ばかり前の事で、娘が十九の年老猾は六十ばかりの禿顱の事だから、まさかに色気とは想はんわね。そこで内へ引張つて来て口説いたのだ。女房といふ者は無いので、怪しげな饗妾然たる女を置いてをつたのが、その内にいつか娘は妾同様になつたのはどうだい！」

固唾を嚥みたりし荒尾は思ふところありげに打頷きて、

「女といふ者はそんなものじやて」

甘糟はその面を振仰ぎつつ、

「驚いたね、君にしてこの言あるのは。荒尾が女を解釈せうとは想はなんだ」

「何故かい」

佐分利の話を進むる折から、凜車は遽に速力を加へぬ。

佐「聞えん聞えん、もつと大きな声で」

甘「さあ、御順にお膝繰だ」

佐「荒尾、あの葡萄酒を抜かんか、喉が渇いた。これからが佳境に入るのだからね」

甘「中銭があるのは酷い」

佐「蒲田、君は好い莨を吃つてゐるぢやないか、一本頂戴」

甘「いや、図に乗ること。僕は手廻の物を片附けやう」

佐「甘糟、燐児を持つてゐるか」

甘「そら、お出だ。持参いたしてをりまする仕合で」

佐分利は居長高になりて、

「些と点けてくれ」

　葡萄酒の紅を啜り、ハヴァナの紫を吹きて、佐分利は徐に語を継ぐ、

「所謂一朶の梨花海棠を圧してからに、娘の満枝が、後には親父の方から帰れ帰れ言つても、帰らんだらう。当座は莽つて帰りたがつた娘が、侍形気の親父は非常な立腹だ。子でない、親でないと云ふ騒になつたね。すると禿の方から、妾だから不承知なのだらう、籍を入れて本妻に直すからくれろといふ談判になつた。それで逢つて見ると娘も、阿父さん、どうか承知して下さいは、親父の益す意外の益す不服だ。けれども、天魔に魅入られたものと親父も愛相を尽して、唯いつかこの商売が面白くなつて来て、この身代我物と考へて見ると、一人の親父よりは金銭の方が大事だ、といふ不敵な了簡が出た訳だね」

　一人の娘を阿父さん彼自身より十歳ばかりも老漢の高利貸にくれて了つたのだ。それから満枝は益す禿の寵を得て、内政を自由にするやうになつたから、定めて生家の方へ貢ぐと思の外、極の給の外は塵葉一本償らん。これが又禿の御意に入つたところで、女め熟ら高利の塩梅を見てゐる内に、いつかこの身代我物と考へて見ると、一人の親父よりは金

　段々様子が知れたもので、後には親父の方から帰れ帰れ言つても、これは無論親父には内証だったのだが、

「驚くべきものじゃね」

荒尾は可忌しげに呟きて、稍不快の色を動せり。

「そこで、敏捷な女には違無い、自然と高利の呼吸を呑込んで、後には手の足りん時には禿の代理として、何処へでも出掛けるやうになつたのは益す驚くべきものだらう。丁度一昨年辺から禿は中気が出て未だに動けない。そいつを大小便の世話までして、女の手一つで盛に商売をしてるのだ。それでその前年かに親父は死んだのださうだが、板の間に薄縁を一板敷いて、その上で往生したと云ふくらゐの始末だ。病気の出る前などはろくに寄せ付けなんださうだがな、残刻と云つても、どう云ふのだか余り気が知れんぢやないかな──然し事実だ。で、禿はその通の病人だから、今ではあの女が独で腕を揮つて益す遣つてゐる。これ則ち『美人クリイム』の名ある所以さ。

年紀かい、二十五だと聞いたが、さう、漸う二三とよりは見えんね。あれで可愛い細い声をして物柔に、口数が寡くつて巧言をいふこと、恐るべきものだよ。銀貨を見て何処の国の勲章だらうなどと言ひさうな、誠に上品な様子をしてゐて、書替だの、手形に願ふのと、急所を衝く手際の婉曲に巧妙な具合と来たら、実に魔薬でも用ゐて人の心を瘁すかと思ふばかりだ。僕も三度ほど瘁されたが、柔能く剛を制すで、高利貸には美人が妙！　那彼に一国を預ければ頓ちクレオパトラだね。那彼には滅される気色にて、

風早は最も興を覚えたる気色にて、

「では、今はその禿顱は中風で寐たきりなのだね、一昨年から？　それでは何か虫があるだらう。

有る、有る、それくらゐの女で神妙にしてゐるものか、無いと見せて有るところがクレオパトラよ。然し、壮な女だな」

「余り壮なのは恐れる」

佐分利は頭を抑へて後様に靠れつつ笑ひぬ。次いで一同も笑ひぬ。

佐分利は二年生たりしより既に高利貸の大火坑に堕ちて、今はしも連帯一判、取交ぜ五口の債務六百四十両円の呵責に膏を取るる身の上にぞありける。次いでは甘糟の四百円、大島紬氏は卒業前にして百五十円、後に又二百円、無疵なるは風早と荒尾とのみ。

漂車は神奈川に着きぬ。彼等の物語をば笑しげに傍聴したりし横浜商人体の乗客は、幸に無聊を慰められしを謝すらんやうに、懇に一揖してここに下車せり。暫く話の絶えける間に荒尾は何をか打案ずる体にて、その目を空く見据ゑつつ漫語のやうに言出でたり。

「その後誰も間の事を聞かんかね」

「間貫一かい」と斂嘆声は問反せり。

「おお、誰やらぢやつたね、高利貸の才取とか、手代とかしてをると言うたのは蒲「さうさう、そんな話を聞いたつけね。然し、間には高利貸の才取は出来ない。あれは高利を貸すべく余り多くの涙を有つてゐるのだ」

我が意を得つと謂はんやうに荒尾は頷きて、猶も思に沈みゐたり。　佐分利と甘糟の二人はその

頃一級先ちてありければ、間とは相識らざるなりき。

荒「高利貸と云ふのはどうも妄ちやらう。全く余り多くの涙を有つてをる。惜い事をした、得難

い才子ちやつたものね。あれが今居らうなら……」

彼は忍びやかに太息を泄せり。

「君達は今逢うても顔を見忘れはすまいな」

風「それは覚えてゐるとも。あれの嶄然と外皆の鄙った所が目標さ」

蒲「さうして髪の辮毛の具合がな、愛嬌が有つたちやないか。デスクの上に頬杖を拄いて、かう

下向になって何時でも真面目に講義を聴いてゐたところは、何処かアルフレッド大王に肖てゐた

さ」

荒尾は仰ぎて笑へり。

「君は毎も妙な事を言ふ人ぢやね。アルフレッド大王とは奇想天外だ。僕の親友を古英雄に擬し

てくれた御礼に一盃を献じやう」

蒲「成程、君は兄弟のやうにしてをつたから、始終憶ひ出すだらうな」

「僕は実際死んだ弟よりも間の居らなくなったのを悲む」

愁然として彼は頭を俛れぬ。大島紬は受けたる盃を把りながら、更に佐分利が持てる猪口を借

りて荒尾に差しつ。

「さあ、君を慰める為に一番間の健康を祝さう」

荒尾の喜は実に溢るるばかりなりき。

「おお、それは辱ない」

盈々と酒を容れたる二つの猪口は、彼等の目より高く挙げらるると斉く憂と相撃てば、紅の雫の漏るが如く流るるを、互に引くより早く一息に飲乾したり。これを見たる佐分利は甘糟の膝を揺して、

「蒲田は如才ないね。面は醜いがあの呼吸で行くから、往々拾ひ物を為るのだ。ああ言れて見ると誰でも些と憎くないからね」

甘「遠は交際官試補！」

佐「試補々々！」

荒「試補々々立つて泣きに行く……」

風「馬鹿な！」

言を改めて荒尾は言出せり。

「どうも僕は不思議でならんが、停車場で間を見たよ。　間に違無いのじや」

「唯の今陰ながらその健康を禱りし蒲田は拍子を抜して彼の面を眺めたり。

「ふう、それは不思議。他は気が着かなんだかい」

「始は待合所の入口の所で些と顔が見えたのじや。余り意外ぢやつたから、僕は思はず長椅子を起つと、もう見えなくなつた。それから有間して又偶然見ると、又見えたのじや」

甘「探偵小説だ」

荒「その時も起ちかけると又見えなくなって、それから切符を切って歩場へ入るまで見えな
かったのじゃが、入って少し来てから、どうも気になるから振返って見ると、傍の柱に僕を見て
黒い帽を揮つとる者がある、それは間よ。帽を揮つとつたから間に違無いぢやないか」

　横浜！　横浜！　と或は急に、或は緩く叫ぶ声の窓の外面を飛過するとともに、響は雑然として
起り、迸り出づる、群集は玩具箱を覆したる如く、場内の彼方より轟く鐸の音はこの響と混雑と
の中を貫きて奔注せり。

☆昨七日イ便の葉書にて（飯田町局消印）美人クリイムの語にフェアクリイム或はベルクリイムの傍訓有
度との言を貽られし読者あり。ここにその好意を謝するとともに、聊か弁ずるところあらむとす。おのれ
も始め美人の英語を用ゐむと思ひしかど、かかる造語は慰に理詰ならむよりは、出まかせの可笑しを響あら
むこそ可かめれとバイスクリイムとも思着きしなり。意は美アイスクリイムなるを、ビ、アイ、バイの
格にて試みしが、さては説明を要すべき欸冗しさを嫌ひて、更に美人の二字にびじ訓を付せしを、校合者
の思僻めてん字は添へたるなり。陋しげなるびじクリイムの響の中には嘲弄の意も籠らむとてなり。なほ
高論を請ふ（三〇・九・八附読売新聞より）

第 二 章

柵の柱の下に在りて帽を揮りたりしは、荒尾が言の如く、四年の生死を詳悉にせざりし間貫一にぞありける。彼は親友の前に自の影を晦し、その消息をさへ知らせざりしかど、陰ながら荒尾が動静の概略を伺ふことを怠らざりき、こ回の参事官たる事も、午後四時発の列車にて赴任する事をも知るを得しかば、余所ながら暇乞もし、二つには栄誉の錦を飾れる姿をも見んと思ひて、群集に紛れてここには来りしなりけり。

何の故に間は四年の音信を絶ち、又何の故にさしも懐に忘れざる旧友と相見て別を為さざりしか。彼が今の身の上を知らば、この疑問は自ら解釈せらるべし。

柵の外に立ちて列車の行くを送りしは独り間貫一のみにあらず、そこもとに聚ひし老若貴賤の男女は皆個々の心をもて、愁ふるもの、楽むもの、虞ふもの、或は何とも感ぜぬものなど、品変れども目的は一なり。数分時の混雑の後車の出づるとともに、一人散り、二人散りて、彼の如く久う立尽せるはあらざりき。やがて重き物など引くらんやうに彼の漸く踵を旋せし時には、推重るまでに柵際に聚ひし衆は殆ど散果てて、駅夫の三四人が箒を執りて場内を掃除せるのみ。遽に急ぎて、蓬莱橋口より出でんと、貫一は差込る涙を払ひて、独り後れたるを驚きけん、品変あだかも石段際に寄るところを、誰とも知らで中等待合の内より声を懸けぬ。

「聞さん！」

慌てて彼の見向く途端に、黄金の腕環の気爽に燿ける手なる絹ハンカチフに唇辺を掩いて束髪の婦人の小腰を屈むるに会へり。艶なる面に得も謂はれず愛らしき笑をさへ浮べたり。

「や、赤樫さん！」

婦人の笑もて迎ふるには似ず、貫一は冷然として眉だに動かさず。

「好い所でお目に懸りましたこと。急にお話を致したい事が出来ましたので、まあ、些と此方へ」

婦人は内に入れば、貫一も渋々跟いて入るに、長椅子に掛れば、止む無くその側に座を占めたり。

「実はあの保険建築会社の小車梅の件なのでございますがね」

彼は黒樺文繻の帯の間を捜りて金側時計を取出し、手早く収めつつ、

「貴方どうせ御飯前でゐらつしやいませう。ここでは、御話も出来ませんですから、何方へかお供を致しませう」

紫紺塩瀬に消金の口金打ちたる手鞄を取直して、婦人はやをら起上りつ。迷惑は貫一が面に顕れたり。

「何方へ？」

「何方でも、私には解りませんですから貴方のお宜い所へ」

「私にも解りませんな」

「あら、そんな事を仰有らずに、私は何方でも宜いのでございます」

荒布革の横長なる手鞄を膝の上に掻抱きつつ貫一の思案せるは、その宜き方を択ぶにあらで、倶に行くをば躊躇せるなり。

「まあ、何にしても出ませう」

「さやう」

貫一も今は是非無く婦人に従ひて待合所の出会頭に、入来る者ありて、その足尖を挫げよとも踏付けられぬ。驚き見れば長高き老紳士の目尻も異く、満枝の色香に惑ひて、これは失敬、意外の龜相をせるなりけり。彼は猶懲りずまにこの目覚き美形の同伴をさへ暫く目送せり。

二人は停車場を出でて、指す方も無く新橋に向へり。

「本当に、貴方、何方へ参りませう」

「私は、何方でも」

「貴方、何時までもそんな事を言つてゐらしつてはきりがございませんから、好い加減に極めやうでは御坐いませんか」

「さやう」

満枝は彼の心進まざるを暁れども、勉めて吾意に従はしめんと念へば、さばかりの無遇をも甘

んじて、

「それでは、貴方、鰻鱺は上りますか」

「鰻鱺？　遣りますよ」

「鶏肉と何方が宜うございます」

「何方でも」

「余り御挨拶ですね」

「何為ですか」

この時貫一は始めて満枝の面に眼を移せり。百の媚を含みて睨へし彼の眸は、未だ言はずして既にその言はんとせる半をば語尽したるべし。彼の為人を知りて畜生と疎める貫一も、さすがに艶なりと思ふ心を制し得ざりき。満枝は貝の如き前歯と隣れる金歯とを露して片笑みつつ、

「まあ、何為でも宜うございますから、それでは鶏肉に致しませうか」

「それも可いでせう」

三十間堀に出でて、二町ばかり来たる角を西に折れて、唯有る露地口に清らなる門構して、光沢消硝子の軒燈籠に鳥と標したる方に、人目にはさぞ解あるらしう二人は連立ちて入りぬ。いと奥まりて、在りとも覚えぬ辺に六畳の隠座敷の板道伝に離れたる一間に案内されしも宜なり。

懼れたるにもあらず、困じたるにもあらずして貫一の容さへ可愼しげに黙して控へたるは、かかる所にこの人と共にとは思懸けざる為体を、又全くさにあらざるにもあらざらん気色にて貫

がに胸の安からぬなるべし。通し物は逸早く満枝が好きに計ひて、少頃は言無き二人が中に置れたる葛盆は子細らしう一炷の百和香を燻らせぬ。

「間さん、貴方どうぞお楽に」

「はい、これが勝手で」

「まあ、そんな事を有仰らずに、よう、どうぞ」

「内に居つても私はこの通なのですから」

「嘘を有仰いまし」

かくても貫一は膝を崩さで、巻莨入を取出せしが、生憎一本の莨もあらざりければ、手を鳴さんとするを、満枝は先じて、

「お間に合せにこれを召上りましな」

麻蝦夷の御主殿持とともに薦むる筒の端より焼金の吸口は仄に耀けり。歯は黄金、帯留は黄金、指環は黄金、腕環は黄金、時計は黄金、今又煙管は黄金にあらずや。黄金なる哉、金、金！　知る可し、その心も金！　と貫一は独り可笑しさに堪へざりき。

「いや、私は日本莨は一向可かんので」

言ひも訖らぬ顔を満枝は熟と視て、

「決して穢いのでは御坐いませんけれど、つい心着きませんでした」

懐紙を出してわざとらしくその吸口を捫拭へば、貫一も少く慌てて、

「決してさう云ふ訳ぢやありません、私は日本莨は用ゐんのですから」

満枝は再び彼の顔を眺めつ。

「貴方、嘘をお吐きなさるなら、もう少し物覚を善く遊ばせよ」

「はあ？」

「先日鰻淵さんへ上つた節、貴方召上つてゐらしつたではございませんか」

「はあ？」

「瓢箪のやうな恰好のお煙管で、さうして羅宇の本に些と紙の巻いてございました」

「あ！」と叫びし口は頓に塞がざりき。満枝は仇無げに口を掩ひて笑へり。この罰として貫一は直に三服の吸付莨を強ひられぬ。

とかくする間に盃盤は陳ねられたれど、満枝も貫一も三盃を過し得ぬ下戸なり。女は清めし猪口を出して、

「貴方、お一盞」

「可かんのです」

「又そんな事を」

「今度は実際」

「それでは麦酒に致しませうか」

「いや、酒は和洋とも可かんのですから、どうぞ御随意に」

酒には礼ありて、おのれ辞せんとならば、必ず他に侑めて酌せんとこそあるべきに、甚しい哉、彼の手を束ねて、御随意にと会釈せるや、満枝は心憎しとよりはなかなかに可笑しと思へり。

「私も一向不調法なのでございますよ。折角差上げたものですからお一盞お受け下さいましな」

貫一は止む無くその一盞を受けたり。はやかく酒になりけれども、満枝が至急と言ひし用談に及ばざれば、

「時に小車梅の件と云ふのはどんな事が起りましたな」

「もうお一盞召上れ、それからお話を致しますから。まあ、お見事！　もうお一盞」

彼は忽ち眉を攅めて、

「いやそんなに」

「それでは私が戴きませう、恐入りますがお酌を」

「で、小車梅の件は？」

「その件の外に未だお話があるのでございます」

「大相有りますな」

「酔はないと申上げ難い事なのですから、私少々酔ひますから貴方、憚様ですが、もう一つお酌を」

「酔つちや困ります。用事は酔はん内にお話し下さい」

「今晩は私酔ふ意なのでございますもの」

その媚ある目の辺は漸く花桜の色に染みて、心楽しげに稍身を寛に取成したる風情は、実に匂など零れぬべく、熟しとて紺の絹精緻の被風を脱げば、羽織は無くて、粲然としたる紋御召の袷に黒樗文絹の全帯、華麗に紅の入りたる友禅の帯揚して、鬢の後れの被る耳際を搔上ぐる左の手首には、早蕨を二筋寄せて蝶の宿れる形したる例の腕環の爽に晃き渡りぬ。常に可忌しと思へる物をかく明々地に見せつけられたる貫一は、得堪ふまじく苦りたる眉状して密に目を藪しつ。彼は女の貴族的に装へるに反して、黒紬の紋付の羽織に藍千筋の秩父銘撰の袷着て、白縮緬の兵児帯も新からず。

彼を識れりし者は定めて見咎むべし。彼の面影は尠からず変りぬ。愛らしかりしところは皆失せて、四年に余る悲酸と憂苦と相結びて、常に解けざる色は、自ら暗き陰を成してその面を藪へり。挑むとも折るべからざる堅忍の気は、沈鬱せる顔色の表に動けども、嘗て宮を見しやうの優き光は再びその眼に輝かずなりぬ。見ることの冷に、言ふことの謹めるは、彼が近来の特質にして、人はこれが為に狎るるを憚りなば、自もまた親みを求めざるほどに、同業者は誰も誰も偏人として彼を遠ざけぬ。焉んぞ知らん、貫一が心には、さしもの恋を失ひし身のいかで狂人たらざりしかを怪むなりけり。

彼は色を正して、満枝が独り興に乗じて盃を重ぬる体を打目戍れり。

「もう一盞戴きませうか」

笑を漾ふる眸は微醺に彩られて、更に別様の媚を加へぬ。

「もう止したが可いでせう」

「貴方が止せと仰有るなら私は止します」

「敢て止せとは言ひません」

「それぢや私酔ひますよ」

答無かりければ、満枝は手酌してその半を傾けしが、見る見る頬の麗く紅になれるを、彼は手もて掩ひつつ、

「ああ、酔ひましたこと」

貫一は聞かざる為して莨を燻らしゐたり。

「間さん、……」

「何ですか」

「私今晩は是非お話し申したいことがあるので御坐いますが、貴方お聴き下さいますか」

「それをお聞き申す為に御同道したのぢやありませんか」

満枝は嘯むが如く微笑みて、

「私何だか酔つてをりますから、或は失礼なことを申上げるかも知れませんけれど、お気に障へては困りますの。然し、御酒の上で申すのではございませんから、どうぞそのお意で、宜うございますか」

「撞着してゐるぢやありませんか」

「まあそんなに有仰らずに、高が女の申すことでございますから」

こは事難うなりぬべし。克はぬまでも多少は累を免れんと、貫一は手を拱きつつ俯目になり

て、力めて関らざらんやうに持成すを、満枝は擦寄りて、

「これお一盞で後は決してお強ひ申しませんですから、これだけお受けなすつて下さいましな」

貫一は些の言も出さでその猪口を受けつ。

「これで私の願は届きましたの」と、あはや出でんとせし唇を結びて、　貫一は纔に苦笑して止みぬ。

「易い願ですな」

「はい」

「貴方失礼ながら、何でございますか、鰐淵さんの方に未だお長くゐらつしやるお意なのですか。

然し、いづれ独立あそばすので御坐いませう」

「勿論です」

「さうして、まづ何頃彼方と別にお成りあそばすお見込なのでございますの」

「資本のやうなものが少しでも出来たらと思つてゐます」

満枝は忽ち声を飲めて、物思はしげに差俯きて、莨盆の縁をば弄べるやうに煙管もて刻を打ちて

ゐたり。折しも電燈の光の遽に晦むに驚きて顔を挙れば、又旧の如く一間は明うなりぬ。彼は煙

管を捨てて猶暫し打案じたりしが、

「こんな事を申上げては甚だ失礼なのでございますけれど、何時まで彼方にゐらつしやるよりは、早く独立あそばした方が宜いでは御坐いませんか。もし明日にもさうと云ふ御考でゐらつしやるならば、私……こんな事を申しては……烏滸がましいので御坐いますが、大した事は出来ません

けれど、都合の出来るだけは御用達申して上げたいのでございますが、さう遊ばしませんか」

意外に打れたる貫一は箸を扣へて女の顔を屹と視たり。

「さう遊ばせよ」

「それはどう云ふ訳ですか」

実に貫一は答に窮せるなりき。

「訳ですか？」と満枝は口籠りたりしが、

「別に申上げなくてもお察し下さいましたな。私だつて何時までも赤樫に居たいことは無いぢやございませんか。さう云ふ訳なのでございます」

「全然解らんですな」

「貴方、可うございますよ」

可恨しげに満枝は言を絶ちて、横膝に莨を拈りゐたり。

「失礼ですけれど、私はお先へ御飯を戴きます」

貫一が飯桶を引寄せんとするを、はたと扣へて、

「お給仕なれば私致します」

「それは憚様です」

満枝は飯桶を我が側に取寄せしが、茶椀をそれに伏せて、彼方の壁際に推遣りたり。

「未だお早うございますよ。もうお一盞召上れ」

「もう頭が痛くて克はんですから赦して下さい。腹が空いてゐるのですから」

「お餒いところを御飯を上げませんでは、さぞお辛うございませう」

「知れた事ですわ」

「さうでございませ。それなら、此方で思つてゐることが全で先方へ通らなかつたら、餒いのに御飯を食べないのよりか寧に辛うございますよ。そんなにお餒じければ御飯をお附け申します
から、貴方も只今の御返事をなすつて下さいませな」

「返事と言はれたつて、有仰ることの主意が能く解らんのですもの」

「何故お了解になりませんの」

「解らんぢやありませんか。親い御交際の間でもない私に資本を出して下さる。さうしてその訳
はと云へば、貴方も彼処を出る。解らんぢやありませんか。どうか飯を下さいな」

「解らないとは、貴方、お酷いぢやございませんか。ではお気に召さないのでございますか」

「気に入らんと云ふ事は有りませんが、縁も無い貴方に金を出して戴く……」

「あれ、その事ではございませんてば」

「どうも非常に腹が空いて来ました」

「それとも貴方外にお約束でも遊ばした御方がお在なさるのでございますか」

彼終に鋒鋩を露し来れるよと思へば、貫一は猶解せざる体を作して、

「妙な事を聞きますね」

と苦笑せしのみにて続く言もあらざるに、満枝は図を外されて、やや心惑へるなりけり。

「さう云ふやうなお方がお在なさらなければ、……私貴方にお願があるのでございます」

貫一も今は屹と胸を据ゑて、

「うむ、解りました」

「ああ、お了解になりまして?!」

嬉しと心を言へらんやうの気色にて、彼の猪口に余せし酒を一息に飲乾して、その盃をつと貫一に差せり。

「又ですか」

「是非!」

発に乗せられて貫一は思はず受くると斉く盆々注れて、下にも置れず一口附くるを見たる満枝が

歓喜!

「その盃は清めてございませんよ」

一々底意ありて忽諸にすべからざる女の言を、彼はいと可煩くて持余せるなり。

「お了解になりましたら、どうぞ御返事を」

「その事なら、どうぞこれぎりにして下さい」

僅にかく言ひ放ちて貫一は厳かに沈黙しつ。満枝もさすがに酔を冷まして、彼の気色を候ひたり

しに、例の言寡なる男の次いでは言はざれば、

「私もこんな可恥い事を、一旦申上げたからには、このままでは済されません」

貫一は緩かに頷けり。

「女の口からからう云ふ事を言出しますのは能々の事でございますから、それに対するだけの理由を有仰つて、どうぞ十分に私が得心の参るやうにお話し下さいましたな、私座興でこんな事を申したのではございませんから」

「御尤です。私のやうな者でもそんなに言つて下さると思へば、決して嬉くない事はありません。ですから、その御深切に対して裵まず自分の考量をお話し申します。けれど、私は御承知の偏屈者でありますから、衆とは大きに考量が違つてをります。

第一、私は一生妻といふ者は決して持たん覚悟なので。御承知か知りませんが、元、私は書生でありました。それが中途から学問を罷めて、この商売を始めたのは、放蕩で遣損つたのでもなければ、敢て食窮めた訳でも有りませんので。書生が可厭さに商売を遣らうと云ふのなら、未だ外に幾多も好い商売は有りますさ、何を苦んでこんな極悪非道な、白日盗を為すと謂はうか、病人の喉口を干すと謂はうか、命よりは大事な人の名誉を殺して、その金銭を奪取る高利貸などを

択むものですか」

聴居る満枝は益す酔を冷されぬ。

「不正な家業と謂ふよりは、もう悪事ですな。それを私が今日始めて知つたのではない、知つて身を堕したのは、私は当時敵手を殺して自分も死にたかつたくらゐの無念極る失望をした事があつたからです。その失望と云ふのは、私が人を頼にしてをつた事があつて、その人達も頼まれなければならん義理合になつてをつたのを、不図した慾に誘れて、約束は違へる、義理は捨てして私は見事に売られたのです」

「実に頼少い世の中で、その義理も人情も忘れて、罪も無い私の売られたのも、原はと云へば、金銭からです。仮初にも一匹の男子たる者が、金銭の為に見易へられたかと思へば、その無念と火影を避けんとしたる彼の目の中に遽に耀けるは、なほ新なる痛恨の涙の浮べるなり。

いふものは、私は一……一生忘れられんです。

軽薄でなければ、詐、詐でなければ利慾、愛相の尽きた世の中です。それほど可厭な世の中なら、何為一思に死んで了はんか、と或は御不審かも知れん。私は死にたいにも、その無念が障になつて死切れんのです。売られた人達を苦めるやうなそんな復讐などは為たくはありません、唯自分だけで可いから、一旦受けた恨！それだけは屹と霽さなければ揩かん精神。片時でもその恨を忘れることの出来ん胸中といふものは、我ながらさう思ひますが、全で発狂してゐるやうです。さうし

それで、高利貸のやうな残刻の甚い、殆ど人を殺す程の度胸を要する事を毎日扱つて、さうし

て感情を暴してゐなければとても堪へられんので、発狂者には適当の商売です。そこで、金銭ゆ
ゑに売られもすれば、辱められもした、金銭の無いのも謂はば無念の一つです。その金銭が有つ
たら何とでも恨が霽されやうか、とそれを楽に義理も人情も捨て掛つて、今では名誉も色恋も
無く、金銭より外には何の望も持たんのです。又考へて見ると、慾ひ人などを信じるよりは金銭
を信じた方が間違が無い。人間よりは金銭の方が寧か頼になりますよ。頼にならんのは人の心で
す！

先かう云ふ考でこの商売に入つたのでありますから、実を申せば、貴方の貸して遣らうと有仰
る資本は欲しいが、人間の貴方には用が無いのです」

彼は仰ぎて高笑しつつも、その面は痛く激したり。

満枝は、彼の言の決して諳ならざるべきを信じたり。彼の偏屈なる、実にさるべき所見を懐け
るも怪むには足らずと思へるなり。されども、彼は未だ恋の甘きを知らざるが故に、心狭くもこ
の面白き世に偏屈の扉を閉ぢて、詐と軽薄と利欲との外なる楽あるを暁らざるならん。やがて我
ぞを教へんと、満枝は斬く望を失はざるなりき。

「では何でございますか、私の心もやはり頼にならないとお疑ひ遊ばすのでございますか」

「疑ふ、疑はんと云ふのは二の次で、私はその失望以来この世の中が嫌で、総ての人間を好まん
のですから」

「それでは誠も誠も――命懸けて貴方を思ふ者がございましても？」

「勿論！　別して惚れたの、思ふのと云ふ事は大嫌です」

「あの、命を懸けて慕つてゐるといふのがお了解になりましても」

「高利貸の目には涙は無いですよ」

今は取付く島も無くて、満枝は暫し憫然としてゐたり。

「どうぞ御飯を頂戴」

打萎れつつ満枝は飯を盛りて出せり。

「これは恐ります」

彼は啖ふこと傍に人無き若し。満枝の面は薄紅になほ酔は有りながら、酔へる体も無くて、唯目を挙げて女の顔を見たるのみ。

「貴方も上りませんか」

かく会釈して貫一は三盃目を易へつ。やや有りて、

「間さん」と、呼れし時、彼は満口に飯を哺みて遽に応ふる能はず、唯打案じたり。

「私もこんな事を口に出しますまでには、もしや貴方が御承知の無い時には、とそれ等を考へまして、もう多時胸ををつたのでございます。それまで大事を取つてをりながら、かう一も二も無く奇麗にお謝絶を受けては、私実に面目無くて……余り悔うございますわ」

あたたし慌忙くハンカチイフを取りて、片手に恨泣の目元を掩へり。

「面目無くて私、この座が起たれません。間さん、お察し下さいまし」

貫一は冷々に見返りて、

「貴方一人を嫌つたと云ふ訳なら、さうかも知れませんけれど、私は総ての人間が嫌なのですから、どうぞ悪からず思つて下さい。貴方も御飯をお上んなさいな。おお！　さうして小車梅の件に就いてのお話は？」

泣赤めたる目を拭ひて満枝は答へず。

「どう云ふお話ですか」

「そんな事はどうでも宜うございます。間さん、私、どうしても思切れませんから、さう思召して下さい。で、お可厭ならお可厭で宜うございますから、私がこんなに思つてゐることを、どうぞ何日までもお忘れなく……きつと覚えてゐらつしやいましよ」

「承知しました」

「もつと優い言をお聞せ下さいましな」

「私も覚えてゐます」

「もつと何とか有仰りやうが有りさうなものではございませんか」

「御志は決して忘れません。これなら宜いでせう」

満枝は物をも言はずつと起ちしが、飜然と貫一の身近に寄添ひて、「お忘れあそばすな」と言ふさへに力籠りて、その太股を絶かに撮れば、貫一は不意の痛に覆らん

とするを支へつつ横様に振払ふを、満枝は早くも身を開きて、知らず顔に手を打鳴して嬋を呼ぶなりけり。

第　三　章

赤坂氷川の辺に写真の御前と言へば知らぬ者無く、実にこの殿の出づるに写真機械を車に積みて随へざることあらざれば、自ら人目を遉れず、かかる異名は呼るるにぞありける。子細を明めずしては「将棊の殿様」の流かとも想はるべし。あらず！　才の敏、学の博、貴族院の椅子を占めて優に高かるべき器を抱きながら、五年を独逸に薫染せし学者風を喜び、世事を拋ちて愚なるが如く、累代の富を控へて、無勘定の雅量を肆にすれども、なほ歳の入るものを計るに正に出づるに五倍すてふ、子爵中有数の内福と聞えたる田鶴見良春その人なり。

氷川なる邸内には、唐破風造の昔を摸せる館と相並びて、帰朝後起せし三層の煉瓦造の巽きまで目慣れぬ式なるは、この殿の数寄にて、独逸に名ある古城の面影を偲びてここに象れるなりとぞ。これを文庫と書斎と客間とに充てて、万足らざる無き閑月日をば、書に耽り、画に楽み、彫刻を愛るや、音楽に嘯るや、近き頃よりは専ら写真に遊びて、齢三十四に逮べども頑として未だ娶らず。その居るや、行くや、出づるや、入るや、常に飄然として、絶えて貴族的容儀を修めざれど、自らなる七万石の品格は、面白う眉秀でて、鼻高く、眼爽に、形の清に揚れるは、皎として

玉樹の風前に臨めるとも謂ふべくや、御代々御美男にわたらせらるるとは常に藩士の誇るところなり。

　かかれば良縁の空からざること、蝶を捉へんとする蜘蛛の糸より繁しといへども、反顧だに為ずして、例の飄然忍びては酔の紛れの逸早き風流に慰み、内には無妻主義を主張して、人の諫などぶつに用ゐざるなりけり。さるは、かの地に留学の日、陸軍中佐なる人の娘と相愛して、末の契も堅く、月下の小舟に比翼の櫂を操り、スプレイの流を指して、この水の終に涸るる日はあらんとも、我が恋の燄の消ゆる時あらせじ、と互の誓詞に詐はあらざりけるを、帰りて母君に請ふことありしに、いと太う驚かれて、こは由々しき家の大事ぞや。あな、可疎しの吾子が心やと、涙と共に畏くも我が田鶴見の家をばなでう禽獣の檻と為すべき。夷狄は□よりも賤むべきに、

搔口説きて、悲し歎きの余は病にさへ伏したまへりしかば、殿も所為無くて、心苦う思ひつつも、猶行末をこそ頼めと文の便を度々に慰めて、彼方も在るにあられぬ三年の月日を、憂きは死ななんと味気なく過せしに、一昨年の秋物思ふ積りやありけん、心自から弱りて、存へかねし身の苦悩を、御神の恵に助けられて、導かれし天国の杳として原ぬべからざるを、いとど可懐しの殿の胸は破れぬべく、ほとほと知覚の半をも失ひて、世と絶つの念益す深く、今は無尽の富も世襲の貴きも何にかはせんと、唯懐を亡き人に寄せて、形見こそ仇ならず書斎の壁に掛けたる半身像は、彼女が十九の春の色を苦に手写して、嘗て貽りしものなりけり。

　殿はこの失望の極放肆遊惰の裏に聊か懐を遣り、一具の写真機に千金を擲ちて、これに嬉戯す

ること少児の如く、身をも家をも外にして、遊ぶと費すとに余念は無かりけれど、家令に畔柳元
衛ありて、その人迂ならず、善く財を理し、事を計るに由りて、かかる疎放の殿を戴ける田鶴見
家も、幸に些の破綻を生ずる無きを得たりき。

彼は貨殖の一端として密に高利の貸元を営みけるなり。千、二千、三千、五千、乃至一万の巨
額をも容易に支出する大資本主たるを以て、高利貸の大口を引受くる輩のここに便らんとせざる
はあらず。されども慧き畔柳は事の密なるを策の上と為して利の為に誘はれず、始よりその
藩士なる鰐淵直行の一手に貸出すのみにて、他は皆彼の名義を用ゐて、直接の取引を為さざれば、
同業者は彼の那辺にか金穴あるを疑はされども、その果して誰なるやを知る者絶えてあらざるな
りき。

鰐淵の名が同業間に聞えて、威権をさをさ四天王の随一たるべき勢あるは、この資本主の後楯
ありて、運転神助の如きに由るのみ。彼は元田鶴見の藩士にて、身柄は謂ふにも足らぬ足軽頭に
過ぎざりしが、才覚ある者なりければ、廃藩の後出でて小役人を勤め、転じて商社に事へ、一時
或は地所家屋の売買を周旋し、万年青を手掛け、米屋町に出入し、何れにしても世渡の茶を濁さ
ずといふこと無かりしかど、皆思はしからで巡査を志願せしに、上官の首尾好く、竟には警部に
まで取立てられしを、中ごろにして金これ権と感ずるところありて、奉職中蓄へ得たりし三百余
円を元に高利貸を始め、世間の未だこの種の悪手段に慣れざるに乗じて、或は欺き、或は嚇し、
或は賺し、或は虐げ、總に法網を潜り得て辛くも縄附たらざるの罪を犯し、積不善の五六千円に

達せし比、あだかも好し、畔柳の後見を得たりしは、虎に翼を添へたる如く、現に彼の今運転せ
る金額は殆ど数万に上るとぞ聞えし。

畔柳はこの手より穫るゝ利の半は、これを御殿の金庫に致し、半はこれを懐にして、鰐淵もこ
れに因りて利し、金は一にしてその利を三にせる家令が六臂の働は、主公が不生産的なるを補ひ
て猶余ありとも謂ふべくや。

鰐淵直行、この人ぞ間貫一が捨鉢の身を寄せて、牛頭馬頭の手代と頼まれ、五番町なるその家
に四年の今日まで寄寓せるなり。貫一は鰐淵の裏二階なる八畳の一間を与へられて、名は雇人な
れども客分に遇はれ、手代となり、顧問となりて、主の重宝大力ならざれば、四年の欠きに弥れ
ども主は彼を出すことを喜ばず、彼もまた家を構ふる必要無ければ、敢て留るを厭ふにもあらで、
手代を勤むる傍、若干の我が小額をも運転して、自ら営む便もあれば、今懇ひにこゝを出でゝ痩
臂を張らんよりは、然るべき時節の到来を待つには如かじと分別せるなり。彼は當に手代として
能く働き、顧問として能く慮るのみをもて、鰐淵が信用を得たるにあらず、彼の齢を以てして、
色を近けず、酒に親まず、浪費せず、遊惰せず、勤むべきは必ず勤め、為すべきは必ず為して、
己を衒はず、他を貶めず、恭謹にしてしかも気節に乏からざるなど、世に難有き若者なり、と鰐
淵は寧ろ心陰に彼を畏れたり。

主は彼の為人を知りし後、如此き人の如何にして高利貸などや志せると疑ひしなり、貫一は己
の履歴を詐りて、如何なる失望の極身をこれに墜せしかを告げざるなりき。されども彼が高等中

学の学生たりしことは後に顕れにき。他の一事の秘に至りては、今もなほ主が疑問に存すれども、そのままに年経にければ、改めて穿鑿もせられで、やがては、暖簾を分けて屹とし たる後見は為てくれんと、鰐淵は常に疎ならず彼が身を念ひぬ。直行は今年五十を一つ越えて、妻なるお峯は四十六なり。夫は心猛く、人の憂を見ること、犬の嚔の如く、唯貪りて釁くを知らざるに引易へ、気立優しとまでにはあらねど、鬼の女房ながらも尋常の人の心は有てるなり。彼も貫一の偏屈なれども律義に、愛すべきところとては無けれど、憎ましきところとては猶更にあらぬを愛して、何くれと心着けては、彼の為に計りて善かれと祈るなりける。

いと幸ありける貫一が身の上哉。彼は世を恨むる余その執念の駆るままに、人の生ける肉を喰ひ、以つて聊か逆境に暴されたり し枯腸を癒さんが為に、三悪道に捨身の大願を発起せる心中には、百の呵責も、千の苦艱も固より期したるを、なかなかかかる寛なる温き信用と、かかる温き憐愍とを彼らんは、抵羊の乳を得んとよりも彼は望まざりしなり。憂の中の喜なる哉、彼はこの喜を如何に喜びけるか。今は呵責をも苦艱をも敢て悪まざるべき覚悟の貫一は、この信用の終には慾の為に剝がれ、この憐愍も利の為に啻まるる時の目前なるべきを固く信じたり。

（三）の　二

　蓙は毒を以て制せらる。鰐淵が債務者中に高利借の名にしおふ某党の有志家某あり。彼は三年来生殺の関係にて、元利五百余円の責を負ひながら、奸智を弄し、雄弁を揮ひ、大胆不敵に樺へ

て出没自在の計を出し、鰐淵が老巧の術といへども得て施すところ無かりければ、同業者のこれに係りては、逆撲を吃ひて血反吐を噴されし者尠からざるを、鰐淵は弥よ憎しと思へど、彼に対しては鋲桿も折れぬべきに持余しつるを、克はぬまでも棄措くは口惜しければ、せめては令見の為にも折々釘を刺して、再び那奴の翅を展べしめざらんに如かずと、昨日は貫一の瞭らず厳談せよと代理を命ぜられてその家に向ひしなり。

彼は散々に飜弄せられけるを、劣らじと罵りて、前後四時間ばかりその座を起ちも遣らで壮に言争ひしが、病者に等き青二才と侮りし貫一の、陰忍強く立向ひて屈する気色あらざるより、有合ふ仕込杖を抜放し、おのれ還らずば生けては還さじと、二尺余の白刃を危く突付けし凄じきを、その鼻頭に待ひて慄よ動かざりける折柄、来合せつる壮士三名の乱挙に囲まれて門外に突放され、少しは傷など受けて慄く帰来にけるが、これが為に彼の感じ易き神経は甚く激動して夜もすがら眠りけり。かかることありし翌日は夥く脳の慄るるとともに心乱れ動きて、その慣りし後を慣り、悲みし後を悲まされば已まず、為に必ず一日の勤を廃するは彼の病なりき。故に彼は折に触れつつその体の弱く、その情の急なる、到底この業に不適当なるを感ぜざること無し。彼がこの業に入りし最初の一年は働より休の多かりし由を言ひて、今も鰐淵の笑ふことあり。次の年より彼の学びてこれを忍得るの故は、爾来終天の失望と恨との一日も忘るる能はざるが為に、その苦は漸く慣れけれど、彼の心は決してこの悪を作すに慣れざりき。唯能く忍得るを学びたるなり。

悶の余勢を駆りて他の方面に注がしむるに過ぎず。彼はその失望と恨とを忘れんが為には、以外の堪ふまじき苦悶を辞せざるなり。されども彼は今もなほ往々自ら為せる残刻を悔い、或は人の加ふる侮辱に堪へずして、神経の過度に充奮せらるる為に、一日の調摂を求めざるべからざる微恙を得ることあり。

朗に秋の気澄みて、空の色、雲の布置匂はしう、金色の日影は豊に快晴を飾れる南受の縁障子を隙して、爽なる肌寒の蓐に長高く瘦せたる貫一は横はれり。蒼く濁れる頰の肉よ、髯へる横顔の輪廓よ、曇の懸れる眉の下に物思はしき眼色の凝りて動かざりしが、やがて崩るるやうに頰杖を倒して、くゝれる枕嚢に重き頭を落すとともに寝返りつつ掻巻引寄せて、拡げたりし新聞を取りけるが、見る間もあらず投遣りて仰向になりぬ。折しも誰ならん、階子を昇来る音す。貫一は凝然として目を塞ぎたり。紙門を啓けて入来れるは主の妻なり。貫一の慌てて起上るを、そのままにと制して、机の傍に坐りつ。

「紅茶を淹れましたからお上んなさい。少しばかり栗を如でましたから」
手籃に入れたる栗と盆なる茶器とを枕頭に置きて、

「気分はどうです」

「いや、なあに、寝てゐるほどの事は無いので。これは色々御馳走様でございます」

彼は会釈して珈琲茶碗を取上げしが、

「旦那は何時頃お出懸になりました」

「今朝は毎より早くね、氷川へ行くと云つて」

言ふも可疎しげに聞えけれど、さして貫一は意も留めず、

「はあ、畔柳さんですか」

「それがどうだか知れないの」

お峯は苦笑しつ。明なる障子の日脚はその面の小皺の読まれぬは無きまでに照しぬ。髪は薄けれど、櫛の歯通りて、一髪を乱さず円髷に結ひて顔の色は赤き方なれど、いと好く磨きて清に滑なり。鼻の辺に薄痘痕ありて、口を引窄むる癖あり。歯性悪ければとて常に湿めたるが、かかるをや烏羽玉とも謂ふべく殆ど耀くばかりに麗し。茶柳条のフラネルの単衣に朝寒の羽織着たるが、御召縮緬の染直しなるべく見ゆ。貫一はさすがに聞きも流されず、

「何為ですか」

お峯は羽織の紐を解きつ結びつして、言はんか、言はざらんかを遅へる風情なるを、強ひて問はましき事にはあらじと思へば、貫一は籃なる栗を取りて剝きゐたり。

「あの赤樫の別品さんね、あの人は悪い噂が有るぢやありませんか、聞きませんか」

「悪い噂とは？」

貫一は覚えず首を傾けたり。曩の夜の事など思合すなるべし。

「男を引掛けては食物に為るとか云ふ……」

「さうでせう」

「一向聞きますまいな。那奴男を引掛けなくても金銭には窮らんでせうから、そんな事は無からうと思ひますが……」

「だから可けない。お前さんなんぞもべ、いろしや組の方ですよ。金銭が有るから為ないと限つたものですか。さう云ふ噂が私の耳へ入つてゐるのですもの」

「はて、な」

「あれ、そんな剣きやうをしちや食べるところは無い、此方へお貸しなさい」

「これは憚様です」

お峯はその言はんとするところを言はんとには、墨々と手を束ねて在らんより、事に紛らしつ語るの便あるを思へるなり。彼は更に栗の大いなるを択みて、その頂よりナイフを加へつ。

「些と見たつてそんな事を為さうな風ぢやありませんか。お前さんなんぞは堅人だから可いけれど、本当にあんな者に係合ひでもしたら大変ですよ」

「さう云ふ事が有りますかね」

「だつて、私の耳へさへ入る位なのに、お前さんが万更知らない事は無からうと思ひますがね。あの別品さんがそれを遣ると云ふのは評判ですよ。金澤さん、鷲爪さん、それから芥原さん、皆その話をしてゐましたよ」

「或はそんな評判があるのかも知れませんが、私は一向聞きません。成程、ああ云ふ風ですから、

それはさうかも知れません」

「外の人にはこんな話は出来ません。長年気心も知り合つて家内のお前さんの事だから、私もお話を為るのですけれどね、困つた事が出来て了つたの——どうしたら可からうかと思つてね」

お峯がナイフを執れる手は漸く鈍くなりぬ。

「おや、これは大変な虫だ。こら、御覧なさい。この虫はどうでせう」

「非常ですな」

「虫が付いちや可けません！　栗には限らず」

「さうです」

お峯は又一つ取りて剝き始めけるが、心進まざらんやうにナイフの運は愈よ等閑なりき。

「これは本当にお前さんだから私は信仰して話を為るのですけれど、此処きりの話ですからね」

「承知しました」

貫一は食はんとせし栗を持ち直して、屹とお峯に打向ひたり。聞く耳もあらずと知れど、秘密を語らんとする彼の声は自から潜りぬ。

「どうも私はこの間から異いわいと思つてゐたのですが、どうも様子がね、内の夫があの別品さんに係合を付けてゐるやしないかと思ふの——どうもそれに違無いの！」

彼ははや栗など剝かずなりぬ。貫一は揺笑して、

「そんな馬鹿な事が、貴方……」

「外の人ならいざ知らず、附いてゐる女房の私が……それはもう間違無しよ！」

貫一は熟と思ひ入りて、

「旦那はお幾歳でしたな」

「五十一、もう爺ですわね」

彼は又思案して、

「何ぞ証拠が有りますか」

「証拠と云つて、別に寄越した文を見た訳でもないのですけれど、そんな念を推さなくたつて、もう違無いの！！」

息巻くお峯の前に彼は面を俯して言はず、静に思廻らすなるべし。お峯は心着きて栗を剥き始めつ。その一つを終ふるまで言を継がざりしが、さて徐に、

「それはもう男の働とか云ふのだから、妾も楽も可うございます。これが芸者だとか、囲者だとか云ふのなら、私は何も言ひはしませんけれど凡の代物ぢやありはしませんわね。それだから私は実に心配で、心火なら可いけれど、なかなか心火どころの洒落た沙汰ぢやありはしません。あんな者に係合つてゐた日には、末始終どんな事になるか知れやしない、それが私は苦労でね。内の夫もあのくらゐ利巧で居ながらどうしたと云ふのでせう。今朝出掛けたのもどうも異いの、確に氷川へ

行つたんぢやないらしい。だから御覧なさい。この頃は何となく治れてゐますわね、さうして今朝なんぞは羽織から帯まで仕立下し渾成で、その奇麗事を謂つたら、何が日にも氷川へ行くのにあんなに瀟した事はありはしません。もうそれは氷川でない事は知れきつてゐるの」

「それが事実なら困りましたな」

「あれ、お前さんは未だそんな気楽なことを言つてゐるよ。事実ならつて、事実に違無いと云ふのに」

貫一の気乗せぬをお峯はいと歯痒くて心苛つなるべし。

「はあ、事実とすれば弥よ善くない。あの女に係合つちや全く妙でない。御心配でせう」

「私は悋気で言ふ訳ぢやない、本当に旦那の身を思つて心配を為るのですよ、敵手が悪いからね

え」

「然し、何にしろ御心配でせう」

「さうして、それは何頃からの事でございます」

「ついこの頃ですよ、何でも」

「それに就いて是非お頼があるんですがね、折を見て私も篤り言はうと思ふのです。就いてはこれといふ証拠が無くちや口が出ませんから、何とか其処を突止めたいのだけれど、私の体ぢや戸外の様子が全然解らないのですもの
ね」

思ひ直せども貫一が腑には落ちざるなりけり。

「御尤も」

「で、お前さんと見立ててお頼があるんです。どうか内々様子を探つて見て下さいな。お前さんが寝てお在でないと、実は今日早速お頼があるのだけれど、折が悪いのね」

行けよと命ぜられたるとなんぞ択ばん、これ有る哉、紅茶と栗と、と貫一はその余に安く売られたるが独り可笑かりき。

「いえ、一向差支ございません。どういふ事ですか」

「さう？　余りお気の毒ね」

彼の赤き顔の色は耀くばかりに懽びぬ。

「御遠慮無く有仰つて下さい」

「さう？　本当に可いのですか」

お峯は彼が然諾の爽なるに遇ひて、紅茶と栗とのこれに酬ゆるの薄儀に過ぎたるを、今更に可愧く覚ゆるなり。

「それではね、本当に御苦労で済まないけれど、氷川まで行つて見て来て下されば、それで可いのですよ。畔柳さんへ行つて、旦那が行つたか、行かないか、若し行つたのなら、何頃行つて何頃帰つたか、なあに、十に九まではきつと行きはしませんから。その様子だけ解れば、それで可いのです。それだけ知れれば、それで探偵が一つ出来たのですから」

「では行つて参りませう」

彼は起ちて寝衣帯を解かんとすれば、

「お待ちなさいよ、今俥を呼びに遣るから」

かく言捨ててお峯は忙く階子を下行けり。

迹に貫一は繰返し繰返しこの事の真偽を案じ煩ひけるが、服を改めて居間を出でんとしつつ、

「女房に振られて、学士に成損つて、後が高利貸の手代で、お上さんの秘密探偵か！」

と端無く思ひ浮べては漫に独り打笑れつ。

　　　第　四　章

　貫一は直に俥を飛して氷川なる畔柳のもとに赴けり。その居宅は田鶴見子爵の邸内に在りて、裏門より出入すべく、館の側面を負ひて、横長に三百坪ばかりを木槿垣に取廻して、昔形気の内に幽しげに造成したる二階建なり。構の可愼う目立たぬに引易へて、木口の撰択の至れるは、館の改築ありし折その旧材を拝領して用ゐたるなりとぞ。

　貫一も彼の主もこの家に公然の出入する身なれば、玄関側なる格子口より訪るるを常とせり。彼は戸口に立寄りけるに、鰐淵の履物は在らず。はや帰りしか、来ざりしか、或は未だ見えざるにや、とにもかくにもお峯が言にも符合すれども、直にこれを以て疑を容るべきにあらずなど思ひつつ音なへば、応ずる者無くて、再びする時聞慣れたる主の妻の声して、連に婢の名を呼

びたりしに、答へざりければやがて自ら出で来て、

「おや、さあ、お上んなさい。丁度好いところへお出でした」

眼のみいと大くて、病勝ちに痩衰へたる五体は燈心の如く、見るだに惨々しながら、声の明にして張ある、何処より出づる音ならんと、一たびは目を驚かし、一たびは耳を驚かすてふ、貫一が一種の化物と謂へるその人なり。年は五十路ばかりにて頭の霜繁く夫よりは姉なりとぞ。

貫一は屋敷風の、恭き礼を作して、

「はい、今日は急ぎまするので、これで失礼を致します。主人は今朝ほど此方様へ伺ひましたでございませうか」

「いいえ、お出はありませんよ。実はね、ちとお話が有るので、お目に懸りたいと申してをりましたところ。唯今御殿へ出てをりますので、些と呼びに遣りませうから、暫くお上んなすつて」

言はるるままに客間に通りて、端近く控ふれば、彼は井の端なりし婢を呼立てて、速々主の方へ走らせつ。

茣盆を出し、番茶を出せしのみにて、納戸に入りける妻は再び出で来らず。この間は貫一は如何にこの探偵一件を処置せんかと工夫してゐたり。やや有りて婢の息促き還来にける気勢せしが、やがて妻の出でて例の声を振ひぬ。

「さあ唯今些と手が放せませんので、御殿の方に居りますから、どうか彼方へお出なすつて。其処ですよ。婢に案内を為せます。あの豊や！

暇乞して戸口を出づれば、勝手元の垣の側に二十歳かと見ゆる物馴顔の婢の待てりしが、後さ

まに帯鈎ひつつ道知辺す。垣に沿ひて曲れば、玉川砂礫を敷きたる径ありて、出外るれば子爵家の構内にて、三棟並べる塗籠の背後に、桐の木高く植列ねたる下道の清く掃いたるを行窮れば、板塀続らせる下屋造の煙突より忙しげなる煙立昇りて、折しも御前籠昇入るるは通用門なり。貫一もこれを入りて、余所ながら過来し厨に、酒の香、物煮る匂頻りて、奥よりは絶えず人の通ふ乱響したる、来客などやと覚えつつ、畔柳が詰所なるべき一間に導かれぬ。

（四）の　二

畔柳元衛の娘静緒は館の腰元に通勤せるなれば、今日は特に女客の執持に召れて、高髷、変裏に粧を改め、お傍不去に鞠略あらせじと冊くなりけり。かくて邸内遊覧の所望ありければ、先づ西洋館の三階に案内すとて、迂廻階子の半を昇行く後姿に、その客の如何に貴婦人なるかを窺ふべし。豊ならではと見ゆるまでに結做したる円髷の漆の如きに、珊瑚の六分玉を点じたれば、更に白襟の冷豔なる類ふべき無く、貴族泉の繊高緒綿の五紋なる単衣を曳きて、帯は海老色地に装束切摸の色紙散の七糸を高く負ひたり。淡紅色紋綯の長襦袢の裾は上履の歩に緩く匂こぼして、絹足袋の雪に嫋々なる山茶花の開く心地す。

この麗き容は見返り勝に静緒は壁側に寄りて二三段づつ先立ちけるが、彼の俯きて昇れるに、櫛の蒔絵のいと能く見えければ、ふとそれに目を奪はれつつ一段踏み失ねて、凄き響の中にあなや僵れんと為たり。幸に怪我は無かりけれど、彼はなかなか己の怪我などより貴客を驚かせ

し狼藉をば、得も忍ばれず満面に慚ぢて、

「どうも飛んだ麁相を致しまして……」

「いいえ。貴方本当に何処もお傷めなさりはしませんか」

「いいえ。さぞ吃驚遊ばしたでございませう、御免あそばしまして」

こ度は薄氷を踏む想して一段を昇る時、貴婦人はその帯の解けたるを見て、

「些とお待ちなさい」

進寄りて結ばんと結するを、心着きし静緒は慌てて驚きて、

「あれ、恐入ります」

「可うございますよ。さあ、熟として」

「あれ、それでは本当に恐入りますから」

争ひ得ずして竟に貴婦人の手を労せし彼の心は、溢るるばかり感謝の情を起して、次いではこの優しさを桜の花の薫あらんやうにも覚ゆるなり。彼は女四書の内訓に出でたりとて屡ば父に聴さるる「五綵服を盛にするも、以つて身の華と為すに足らず、貞順道に率へば、乃ち以つて婦徳を進むべし」の本文に合ひて、かくてこそ始めて色に矜らず、その徳に爽かずとも謂ふべきなれ。

愛でたき人にも遇へるかなと絶に思入りぬ。

三階に着くより静緒は西北の窓に寄り行きて、効々しく緑色の帷を絞り硝子戸を繰揚げて、

「どうぞ此方へお出あそばしまして。ここが一番見晴が宜いのでございます」

「まあ、好い景色ですことね！　富士が好く晴れて。おや、大相木犀が匂ひますね、お邸内に在りますの？」

貴婦人はこの秋霽の朗に潤くして心往くばかりなるに、夢など見るらん面色して佇めり。窓を争ひて射入る日影は斜にその姿を照して、襟留なる真珠は焚ゆる如く輝きぬ。塵をだに容さず澄みに澄みたる添景の中に立てる彼の容華は清く鮮に見勝りて、玉壺に白き花を挿したらん風情あり。

静緒は女ながらも見惚れて、不束に眺入りつ。

その目の爽にして滴るばかり情の籠れる、その眉の思へるままに画き成せる如き、その口元の莟ながら香に立つと見ゆる、その鼻の似るものも無くと好く整ひたる、肌理濃に光をさへ帯びたる、色の透るばかりに白き、難を求めなば、髪は濃くて瑩沢に、頭も重げに束ねられて、面の痩の過ぎたる為に、髪際の少く打乱れたると、立てる容こそ風にも堪ふまじく繊弱なれど、自ら愁ふ底寂きと、頸の細きが折れやしぬべく可傷きとなり。

されどかく揃ひて好き容量は未だ見ずと、静緒は心に驚きつつ、踏外せし麁忽ははや忘れて、常は顧らるる貌ありな見据うる流眄はその物を蚤はんと眤ふが如く、吾を失へる顔は間抜けて、おびただし蚩かり。彼は己の間抜けがら、草の花の匂無きやうに、この貴婦人の傍には見劣せらるること夥かり。彼は己の間抜けたりとも知らで、返す返すも人の上を思ひて止まざりき。

実にこの奥方なれば、金時計持てるも、指環を五つまで穿せるも、よし馬車に乗りて行かんとも、何をか愧づべき。真珠の襟留せるも、婦の徳をさへ虧かでこの嬋娟に生れ得て、しかもこの富めるに遇へる、天の恵と世の幸とを併せ

享けて、残る方無き果報のかくも痛き人もあるものか。美きは貧くて、売らざるを得ず、富める
は醜くて、買はざるを得ず、二者は惜はぬ世の習なるに、女ながらもかう生れたらんには、その
幸は男にも過ぎぬべしなど、若き女は物羨の念強けれど、妬しとは及び難くて、静緒は心に畏
るるなるべし。

彼は貴婦人の貌に耽りて、その歎待にとて携へ来つる双眼鏡を参らするをば気着かでありて、
やがて双眼鏡は貴婦人の手に在りて、措くを忘らるるまでに愛でられけるが、目の及ばぬ遠き
限は南に北に眺尽されて、彼はこの鏡の凡ならず精巧なるに驚ける状なり。

こは殿の仏蘭西より持ち帰られし名器なるを、漸く取出して薦めたり。形は一握の中に隠るるば
かりなれど、能く遠くを望み得る力はほとほと神助と疑ふべく、筒は乳白色の玉もて造られ、催
に黄金細工の金具を施したるのみ。

「那処に遠く些の小楊枝ほどの棒が見えませ、あれが旗なので、浅黄に赤い柳条の模様まで昭
然見えて、さうして旗竿の頭に鳶が宿つてゐるが手に取るやう」

「おや、さやうでございますか。何でもこの位の眼鏡は西洋にも多度御座いませんさうで、招魂
社のお祭の時などは、狼煙の人形が能く見えるのでございます。私はこれを見まする度にさやう
思ひますのでございますが、かう云う風に話が聞えましたらさぞ宜うございませう。余り近くに
見えますので、音や声なんぞが致すかと想ふやうでございます」

「音が聞えたら、彼方此方の音が一所に成つて粉雑になつて了ひませう」

かく言ひて斉く笑へり。

静緒は客遇に慣れたれば、可羞しげに見えながらも話を求むるには拙からざりき。

「私は始めてこれを見せて戴きました折、殿様に全然騙されましたのでございます。鼻の前に見えるだらうと仰せられますから、さやうにございますと申上げますと、見えたら直にその眼鏡を耳に推付けて見ろ、早くさへ耳に推付ければ、音でも声でも聞えると仰せられますので……」

淀無く語出づる静緒の顔を見入りつつ貴婦人は笑ましげに聴たり。

「私は急いで推付けましたのでございます」

「まあ！」

「なに、ちつとも聞えは致しませんのでございますから、さやう申上げますと、推付けやうが悪いと仰せられまして、御自身に遊ばして御覧なさるのでございますよ。何遍致して見ましたか知れませんのでございますけれど、何も聞えは致しませんので。さやう致しますると、お前では可かんと仰せられまして、御供を致してをりました御家来から、御親類方も御在でであらつしやいましたが、皆為つて御覧遊ばしました」

貴婦人は怺へかねて失笑せり。

「あら、本当なのでございますよ。それで、未だ推付けやうが悪い、もつと早く早くと仰せられるものでございますから、御殿に居ります速水と申す者は余り急ぎましたので、耳の此処を酷く打ちまして、血を出したのでございます」

彼の歓べるを見るより静緒は椅子を持来りて薦めし後、さて語り続くるやう。

「それで誰にも聞えないのでございます。さやう致しまするど、殿様は御自身に遊ばして御覧で、なるほど聞えない。どうしたのか知らんなんて、それは、もう実にお真面目なお顔で、わざと御考へあそばして、仏蘭西に居た時には能く聞えたのだが、日本は気候が違ふから、空気の具合が眼鏡の度に合はない、それで聞えないのだらうと仰せられましたのを、皆本当に致して、一年ばかり釣られてをりましたのでございます」

その名器を手にし、その耳にせし人を前にせる貴婦人の興を覚ゆることは、殿の悪作劇を親く睹たらんにも劣らざりき。

「殿様はお面白い方でゐらつしやいますから、随分そんな事を遊ばしませうね」

「それでもこの二三年はどうも御気分がお勝れ遊ばしませんので、お険いお顔をしてゐらつしやるのでございます」

書斎に掛けたる半身の画像こそその病根なるべきを知れる貴婦人は、卒に空目遣して物の思はしげに、例の底寂う打湿りて見えぬ。

やや有りて彼は徐に立ち上りけるが、この回は更に邇きを眺めんとて双眼鏡を取り直してけり。彼方此方に差向くる筒の当所も無かりければ、偶ま唐楪葉のいと近きが鏡面に入り来て一面に蔓りぬ。粒々の実も珍く、何の木かとそのまま子細に視たりしに、葉蔭を透きて人顔の見ゆるを、心とも無く眺めけるに、自から得忘れぬ面影に肖たるところあり。

貴婦人は差し向けたる手を緊と据ゑて、目を拭ふ間も忙しく、なほ心を留めて望みけるに、枝葉の遮りてとかくに思ふまゝならず。漸くその顔の明に見ゆる隙を求めけるが、別に相対へる人あ
りて、髪は黒けれども真額の螢々禿げたるは、先に挨拶に出でし家扶の畔柳にて、今一人なるその人こそ、眉濃く、外眦の昂れる三十前後の男なりけれ。得忘れぬ面影に肖たりとは未や、得忘れぬその面影なりと、ゆくりなくも認めたる貴婦人の鏡持てる手は兢々と打顫ひぬ。

行く水に数画くよりも儚き恋しさと可懐しさとの朝夕に、なほ夜昼の別も無く、絶えぬ思はその外ならざりし四年の久しきを、熱海の月は朧なりしかど、一期の涙に宿りし面影は、なかなか消えもやらで身に添ふ幻を形見にして、又何日は必ずと念懸けつゝ、雨にも風にも君が無事を祈りて、心は毫も昔に渝らねど、君が恨を重ぬる別の事なるやと思ひに思ふのみにて別れて後の事は知らず、如何なる労をやさまでは積みけん、齢よりは面瘁して、異うも物々しき分別顔に老いにけるよ。

幸薄く暮さるゝか、着たるものゝ見好げにもあらで、なほ書生なるべき姿なるは何にか身を寄せらるゝならんなど、思は置所無く湧出でゝ、胸も裂けぬべく覚ゆる時、男の何語りてや打笑む顔の鮮に映れば、貴婦人の目よりは涙すゞろに玉の糸の如く流れぬ。今は堪へ難くて声も立ちぬべきに、始めて人目あるを暁りて失したりと思ひたれど、所為無くハンカチイフを緊く目に掩てたり。

静緒の驚駭は謂ふばかり無く、

「あれ、如何がしました」

「いえ、なに、私は脳が不良ものですから、余り物を瞶めてをると、どうかすると眩暈がして涙

の出ることがあるので」

「お腰をお掛け遊ばしまし、少しお頭をお摩り申上げませう」

「いえ、かうしてをると、今に直に癒ります。憚ですがお冷を一つ下さいましな」

静緒は蟇地に行かんとす。

「あの、貴方、誰にも有仰らずにね、心配することは無いのですから、本当に有仰らずに、唯私が嘲をすると言つて、持つて来て下さいましよ」

「はい、畏りました」

彼の階子を下り行くと斉く貴婦人は再び鏡を取りて、葉越の面影を望みしが、一目見るより漸含む涙に曇らされて、忽ち文色も分かずなりぬ。彼は静無く椅子に崩折れて、縦まに泣乱したり。

（四）の三

この貴婦人こそ富山宮子にて、今日夫なる唯継と倶に田鶴見子爵に招れて、男同士のシャンペンなど酌交す間を、請うて庭内を遊覧せんとて出でしにぞありける。

子爵と富山との交際は近き頃よりにて、彼等の孰も日本写真会々員たるに因れり。自ら宮の除物になりて二人の興に入れるは、想ふにその物語なるべし。富山はこの殿と親友たらんことを切望して、ひたすらその意を獲んと力めけるより、子爵も好みて交るべき人とも思はされど、勢ひ疎じ難くして、今は会員中善く識れるものの最たるなり。　爾来富山は益す傾慕して措かず、家に

ツィシアンの模写と伝へて所蔵せる古画の鑑定を乞ふを名として、曩に芝西久保なる居宅に請じ

て疎ならず響く事ありければ、その返とて今日は夫婦を招待せるなり。

会員等は富山が頻に子爵に取入るを見て、皆その心を測りかねて、大方は彼為にするところあ

らんなど言ひて陥み合へりけれど、その実敢て為にもせんともあらざるべし。彼は常にその友を

択べり。富山が交るところは、その地位に於て、その名声に於て、その家柄に於て、或はその資

産に於て、孰の一つか取るべき者ならざれば決して取らざりき。されば彼の友とするところは、

それらの一つを以て優に彼以上に価する人士にあらざるは無し。実に彼は美き友を有てるなり。

さりとて彼は未だ曾てその友を利用せし事などあらざれば、こたびも強に有福なる華族を利用せ

んとにはあらで、友として美き人なれば、かく勉めて交は求むるならん。故に彼はその名簿の中

に一箇の憂を同うすべき友をだに見出さざるを知れり。抑も友とは楽を共にせんが為の友にし

て、若し憂を同うせんとには、別に金銭ありて、人の助を用ず、又決して用るに足らずと信

じたり。彼の美き友を択ぶは固よりこの理に外ならず、寛に彼の択べる友は皆美けれども、尽く

これ酒肉の兄弟たるのみ。知らず、彼はこれを以てその友に満足すとも、なほこれをその妻に於

けるも然りと為すの勇あるか。彼が最愛の妻、その一人を守るべき夫の目を眛めて、陥みても

猶余ある高利貸の手代に片思の涙を灑ぐにあらずや。

宮は悄に人無しと思へば、限知られぬ涙に掻きむて、熱海の浜に打俯したりし悲歎の足らざる

をここに続がんとすなるべし。階下より仄に足音の響きければ、やうやう泣顔隠して、わざと頭

を支へつつ室の中央なる卓子の周囲を歩みたり。やがて静緒の持来りし水に漱ぎ、懐中薬など服して後、心地復りぬとて又窓に倚りて外方を眺めたりしが、

「ちよいと、那処に、それ、男の方の話をしてお在の所も御殿の続きなのですか」

「何方でございます。へゝ、へい、あれは父の詰所で、誰か客と見えまする」

「お宅は？　御近所なのですか」

「はい、お邸内でございます。これから直に見えまする、あの、倉の左手に高い樅の木がございませう、あの陰に見えます二階家が宅なのでございます」

「おや、さうで。それではこの下から直とお宅の方へ行かれますのね」

「さやうでございます。お邸の裏門の側でございます」

「ああさうですか。では些とお庭の方からお邸内を見せて下さいましな」

「お邸内と申しても裏門の方は誠に穢うございまして、御覧あそばすやうな所はございませんです」

宮はここを去らんとして又葉越の面影を窺へり。

「付かない事をお聞き申すやうですが、那処にお父様とお話をしてゐらつしやるのは何地の方ですか」

彼の親達は常に出入せる鰐淵の高利貸なるを明さざれば、静緒は教へられし通りを告るなり。

「他は番町の方の鰐淵と申す、地面や家作などの売買を致してをります者の手代で、間とか申し

「はあ、それでは違ふか知らん」

宮は聞えよがしに独語ちて、その違へるを訝るやうに擬しつつ又其方を打目成れり。

「番町はどの辺で？」

「五番町だとか申しました」

「お宅へは始終見えるのでございますか」

「はい、折々参りますのでございます」

この物語に因りて宮は彼の五番町なる鰐淵といふに身を寄するを知り得たれば、この上は如何にとも逢ふべき便はあらんと、獲難き宝を獲たるにも勝れし心地せるなり。されども彼の眼に睨まれんとも、互の面を合せて、言は交さずとも切て別れんは本意無からずや。若し彼の眼に睨まれんとも、互の面を合せて、言は交さずとも切て別れんは相知らばやと、四年を恋に燃ゆる如く動きぬ。

さすがに彼の気遣へるは、事の危きに饑ゑたる彼の心は燃ゆる如く動きぬ。附添さへある寶の身にして、賤きものに遇はるる手代風情と、しかもその邸内の径に相見て、万一不慮の事などあらば、我等夫婦は抑や幾許り恥辱を受くるならん。人にも知られず、我身一つの恥辱ならんには、この面に唾吐けるも厭はじの覚悟なれど奇遇は寒つるに惜き奇遇ながら、逢瀬は今日の一日に限らぬものを、事の破を目に見て愚に躁るべきや。ゆめゆめ今日は逢ふべき機ならず、辛くとも思止まんと胸は据ゑつ

つも、彼は静緒を賺して、邸内を一周せんと、西洋館の後より通用門の側に出でて、外塀際なる礫道を行けば、静緒は斜に見ゆる父が詰所の軒端を指して、

「那処が唯今の客の参つてをります所でございます」

実に唐檀葉は高く立ちて、折しく一羽の小鳥来鳴けり。宮が胸は異うつと塞りぬ。

楼を下りてここに来たるは僅少の間なれば、よもかの人は未だ帰らざるべし、若しここに出で来らば如何にすべきなど、さすがに可恐きやうにも覚えて、歩は運べど地を踏める心地も無く、静緒の語るも耳には入らで、さて行くほどに裏門の傍に到りぬ。

遊覧せんとありしには似で、貴婦人の目を挙れども何処を眺むるにもあらず、俯き勝に物思はしき風情なるを、静緒は怪くも気遣くて、

「まだ御気分がお悪うゐらつしやいますか」

「いいえ、もう大概良いのですけれど、未だ何だか胸が少し悪いので」

「それはお宜うございません。ではお座敷へお帰りあそばしました方がお宜うございませう」

「家の中よりは戸外の方が未だ可いので、もう些と歩いてゐる中には復りますよ。ああ、此方がお宅ですか」

「はい、誠に見苦しい所でございます」

「まあ、奇麗な！　木槿が盛ですこと。白ばかりも淡白して好いぢやありませんか」

畔柳の住居を限として、それより前は道あれども、賓の足を容るべくもあらず、納屋、物干場、

井戸端などの透きて見ゆる疎垣の此方に、樫の実の夥しく零れて、片側に下水を流せる細路を鶏の遊び、犬の睡れるなど見るも憖に、静緒は急ぎ返さんとせるなり。貴婦人もはや返さんとするとともに恐懼は忽ちその心を襲へり。

この一筋道を行くなれば、もしかの人の出来るに会はば、遁れんやうはあらで明々地に面を合すべし。さるは望まざるにもあらねど、静緒の見る目あるを如何にせん。固より恨を負へる我が身なれば、言はぬ顔してあるべきも、争でかの人の見付けて驚かざらん。

懸けらるべしとは想はねど、さりとてなかなか道行く人のやうには見過されざるべし。ここに宮を見たるその驚駭は幾計我を怪むならん。仇に遇ふにだに堪へざるなりけり。必ずかの人の凄う激せるを見ば、宮はこれを想ふにだに堪へざるなりけり。かく思ひ浮ぶると斉しく身内は熱して冷き汗を出し、足は地に吸はるるかとばかり竦みて、脇道もあらば避けんと、静緒に間へば有らずと言ふ。知りつつもこの死地に陥りたるを悔いて、遣る方も無く惑へる宮が面色の穏からぬを見尤めて、静緒は窃に目を側めたり。彼はいとどその目を懼るるなるべし。今は心も漫に足を疾むれば、土蔵の角も間近になりて其処をだに無事に過ぎなば、と切に急がるる折しも、人の影は突としてその角より顕れつ。宮は眩きぬ。

これより帰りてともかくもお峯が前は好きやうに言繕へ、さて篤と実否を糺せし上にて私に為んやうも有らんなど貫一は思案しつつ、黒の中折帽を稍目深に引側め、通学に馴されし疾足を駆りて、塗籠の角より斜に桐の並木の間を出でて、礫道の端を歩み来れり。

四辺に往来のあるにあらねば、二人の姿は忽ち彼の目に入りぬ。一人は畔柳の娘なりとは疾く知られけれど、顔打背けたる貴婦人の眩く着飾りたるは、子爵家の客なるべしと纔に察せらるるのみ。互に歩み寄りて一間ばかりに近けば、貫一は静緒に向ひて慇懃に礼するを、宮は傍に能ふ限は身を窄めて密に流眄を凝らしたり。その面の色は惨として夕顔の花に宵月の映へる如く、その冷なるべきもほとほと、相似たりと見えぬ。脚は打顫ひ打顫ひ、胸は今にも裂けぬべく轟くを、覚られじとすれば猶打顫ひ猶轟きて、貫一が面影の目に沁むばかり見ゆる外は、生きたりとも死にたりとも自ら分かぬ心地してき。貫一は帽を打着て行過ぎんとする際に、ふと目鞘の走りて館の賓なる貴婦人を一瞥せり。端無くも相互の面は合へり。宮なるよ！　姦婦なるよ！　銅臭の肉蒲団なるよ！

とかつは驚き、かつは憤り、はたと睨めて動かざる眼には見る見る涙を湛へて、窃に歯咬をなしたり。可懐しさと可恐しさと可耻しさとを取集めたる宮が胸の内は何に喩へんやうも無く、あはれ、人目だにあらずば抱付きても思ふままに苛まれんをと、心のみは憧れながら身を如何とも為難ければ、せめてこの誠は通ぜよかしと、見る目に思を籠むるより外はあらず。

貫一はつと踏出して始の如く足疾に過行けり。宮は附人に面を背けて、唇を咬みつつ歩めり。

驚きに驚かされし静緒は何事とも弁へねど、推すべきほどには推して、事の秘密なるを思へば、賓の顔色のさしも常ならず変りて可悩しげなるを、問出でんも可や否やを料りかねて、唯可慎う引添ひて行くのみなりしが、漸く庭口に来にける時、

「大相お顔色がお悪くてゐらつしやいますが、お座敷へお出あそばして、お休み遊ばしましては如何でございます」

「そんなに顔色が悪うございますか」

「はい、真蒼でゐらつしやいます」

「ああさうですか、困りましたね。それでは彼方へ参つて、又皆さんに御心配を懸けると可けませんから、お庭を一周しまして、その内には気分が復りますから、さうしてお座敷へ参りませう。然し今日は大変貴方のお世話になりまして、お蔭様で私も……」

「あれ、飛んでもない事を有仰います」

貴婦人は、その無名指より繍眼児の押競を片截にせる黄金の指環を抜取りて、懐紙に包みたるを、

「失礼ですが、これはお礼のお証に」

静緒は驚き怖れたるなり。

「可うございますから取つて置いて下さい。その代り誰にもお見せなさらないやうに、阿父様にも阿母様にも誰にも有仰らないやうに、ねえ」

「はい……かう云ふ物を……」

受けじと為るを手籠に取らせて、互に何も知らぬ顔して、木の間伝ひに泉水の亀梁橋近く寄る時、書院の静なるに夫の高笑するが聞えぬ。

宮はこの散歩の間に努めて気を平げ、色を歛めて、ともかくも人目を遁れんと計れるなり。されどもこは酒を窃みて酔はざらんと欲するに同かるべし。

彼は先に遭ひし事の胸に鏤められたらんやうに忘るる能はざるさへあるに、なかなか朽ちも果ざりし恋の更に萠出でて、募りに募らんとする心の乱は、堪ふるに難き痛苦を齎して、一歩は一歩より、胸の逼ること急に、身内の血は尽くその心頭に注ぎて余さず熬らるるかと覚ゆるばかりなるに、かかる折は打寛ぎて意に任せて我が家に独り居たらんぞ可き。人に接して強ひて語り、強ひて笑ひ、強ひて楽まんなど、あな可煩しと、例の劇く唇を咬みて止まず。

築山陰の野路を写せる径を行けば、踏処無く地を這ふ葛の乱れ生ひて、草藤、金綿草、紫茉莉の色々、茅萱、穂薄の露滋く、泉水の末を引きて綯々水を卑きに落せる汀なる胡麻竹の一叢茂れるに隠顕して苔蒸す石組の小高きに四阿の立てるを、やうやう辿り着きて貴婦人は艱しげに憩へり。

彼は静緒の柱際に立ちて控ふるを、

「貴方もお草臥でせう、あれへお掛けなさいな。未だ私の顔色は悪うございますか」

その色の前にも劣らず蒼白めたるのみならで、下唇の何に傷きてや、少く血の流れたるに、彼は太く驚きて、

「あれ、お唇から血が出てをります。如何あそばしました」

ハンカチイフもて抑へければ、絹の白きに柘榴の花弁の如く附きたるに、貴婦人は懐鏡取

出して、咬むことの過ぎし故ぞと知りぬ。実に顔の色は頗も凄しと見るまでに変れるを、庭の内をば幾囘して我はこの色を隠さんと為らんと、彼は心陰に己を嘲るなりき。

忽ち女の声して築山の彼方より、

「静緒さん、静緒さん！」

彼は走り行き、手を鳴して応へけるが、やがて木隠に語らふ気勢して、返り来ると斉く賓の前に会釈して、

「先程からお座敷ではお待兼でゐらつしやいますさうで御座いますから、直に彼方へお出あそばしますやうに」

「おや、さうでしたか。随分先から長い間道草を食べましたから」

道を転じて静緒は雲帯橋の在る方へ導けり。橋に出づれば正面の書院を望むべく、はや所狭きまで盃盤を陳ねたるも見えて、夫は席に着きのたり。

此方の姿を見るより子爵は縁先に出でて麾きつつ、

「そこをお渡りになつて、此方に燈籠がございませう、あの傍へ些」とお出で下さいませんか。一枚像して戴きたい」

写真機は既に好き処に据ゑられたるなり。子爵は庭に下立ちて、早くもカメラの覆を引被ぎ、かれこれ位置を取りなどして、

「さあ、光線の具合が妙だ！」

いでや、事の様を見んとて、慢々と出来れるは富山唯継なり。片臂を五紋の単羽織の袖の内に張りて、鼻の下の延びて見ゆるやうの笑を浮べつつ、片手には葉巻の半燻りしを撮み、

「ああ、おまへ其処に居らんければ可かんよ、何為歩いて来るのかね」

子爵の慌てたる顔はこの時毛繻子の覆の内よりつと顕れたり。

「可けない！那処に居て下さらなければ可けませんな。何、御免を蒙る？　——可けない！」

「いや、貴方は巧い言をお覚えですな。お手間は取せませんは余程好い」

「この位に言つて願はんとね、近頃は写してもらふ人よりは写したがる者の方が多いですからね。さあ、奥さん、まあ、彼方へ。静緒、お前奥さんを那処へお連れ申して」

唯継は目もて示して、

「お前、早く行かんけりや可かんよ、折角かうして御支度をなすつて下すつたのに、是非願ひな。あの燈籠の傍へ立つのだ。この機械は非常に結構なのだから是非願ひな。何も羞含むことは無いとも、始終内で遣つてをるのに、あれで可いのさ。姿勢は私が見て遣るから早くおいで。燈籠へ倚掛つて頼杖でも拄い

「お手間は取せませんから、どうぞ」

「結構、結構」と子爵は頷けり。

は無いぢやないか、何羞含む訳ぢやない？　さうとも羞含むことは無いとも、始終内で遣つてをるのに、あれで可いのさ。姿勢は私が見て遣るから早くおいで。空を眺めてゐる状なども可いよ。ねえ、如何でせう」

心は進まねど強ひて否むべくもあらねば、宮は行きて指定の位置に立てるを、唯継は望み見て、

「さう棒立ちになつてをつちや可かんぢやないか。何ぞ持つてをる方が可いか知らんて」

かく呟きつつ庭下駄を引掛け、急ぎ行きて、その想へるやうに燈籠に倚しめ、頬杖を拄しめ、

空を眺めよと教へて、袂の皺めるを展べ、裾の綻を引直し、さて好しと、少く退きて姿勢を見る

とともに、彼はその面の可悩げに太くも色を変へたるを発見して、直に寄り来つ、

「どうしたのだい、おまへ、その顔色は？　何処か不快のか、ええ。非常な血色だよ。どうした」

「少しばかり頭痛がいたすので」

「頭痛？　それぢやかうして立つてをるのは苦いだらう」

「いいえ、それ程ではないので」

「苦いやうなら我慢をせんとも、私が訳を言つてお謝絶をするから」

「いいえ、宜うございますよ」

「可いかい、本当に可いかね。我慢をせんとも可いから」

「宜うございますよ」

「さうか、然し非常に可厭な色だ」

彼は眷々として去る能はざるなり。待ちかねたる子爵は呼べり。

「如何ですか」

唯継は慌忙く身を開きて、

「一つこれで御覧下さい」

鏡面に照して二三の改むべきを注意せし後、子爵は種板を挿入るれば、唯継は心得てその邇を避けたり。

第　五　章

遊佐良橋は郷里に在りし日も、出京の遊学中も、頗る謹直を以て聞えしに、却りて、日本周航会社に出勤せる今日、三百円の高利の為に斃さるると知れる彼の友は皆驚けるなり。或ものは結婚費なるべしと言ひ、或ものは外を張らざるべからざる為の遺繚なるべしと言ひ、或ものは隠遊の風流債ならんと説くもありて、この不思議の負債とその美き妻とは、遊佐に過ぎたる物が二つに数へらるるなりき。されどもこは謂ふべからざる事情の下に連帯の印を仮せしが、形の如く腐れ込みて、義理の余毒の苦を受くると知りて、彼の不幸を悲むものは、交際官試補なる法学士蒲田鉄弥と、同会社の貨物課なる法学士風早庫之助とあるのみ。

空を眺むる宮が目の中には焚ゆらんやうに一種の表情力充満ちて、物憂さの支へかねたる姿もわざとならず。色ある衣は唐松の翠の下蔭に章を成して、秋高き清遠の空はその後に舗き、四脚の雪見燈籠を小楯に裾の辺は寒咲躑躅の茂に隠れて、近きに二羽の鶩の汀に養るなど、寧ろ画にこそ写さまほしきを、子爵は心に喜びつつ写真機の前に進み出で、今や鏡面を開かんと構ふる時、貴婦人の頬杖は忽ち頽れて、その身は燈籠の笠の上に折重なりて岸破と伏しぬ。

凡そ高利の術たるや、渇者に水を売るなり。渇の甚しく堪へ難き者に至りては、決してその肉を割きてこれを換ふるを辞せざるべし。故に前後の不覚に渇する者能くこれを買ふべし、その渇の癒るに及びては、玉漿を盛るに異る無し。この急に乗じてこれを売る、一杯の水もその値玉漿を割きてこれを換ふるを辞せざるべし。

彼は約の如く下水の倍量をばその鮮血に搾りその活肉に割きて以て返さざるべからず。噫、世間の最も不敵なる者高利を貸して、これを借るは更に最も不敵なる者と為さざらんや。ここを以て、高利は借るべき人これを借りて始めて用ゐるべし。さらずばこれを借るの覚悟あるべきを要す。

これ風早法学士の高利貸に対する意見の概要なり。　遊佐は実にこの人にあらず、又この覚悟とても有らざるを、奇禍に罹れる哉と、彼は人の為ながら常にこの憂を解く能はざりき。

近きに郷友会の秋季大会あらんとて、今日委員会のありし帰さを彼等は三人打連れて、遊佐が家へ向へるなり。

「別に御馳走と云つては無いけれど、松茸の極新いのと、製造元から貰つた黒麦酒が有るからね、鶏でも買つて、寛り話さうぢやないか」

遊佐の声は朗々として聴くに快く、この設にとて途に求めしなり。

蒲田の声は朗々として聴くに快く、

蒲「それは結構だ。さう泊が知れて見ると急ぐにも当らんから、どうだね、イ・ゲ・エ・ム。君はこの頃風早と対に成つたさうだが、長足の進歩ぢやないか。然し、どうもその長足のちやうはてう

（貂）足らず、続ぐにフロックを以つて為るのぢやないかい。この頃は全然フロックが止つた？

ははははは、それはお目出度いやうな御愁傷のやうな妙な次第だね。まあ、それで大分話せるやうになりました」

風早は例の皺嘆声して大笑を発せり。

蒲「へへへ、この頃の僕の後曳の手際も知らんで」

風「更に一段の進境を示すには、竪杖をして二寸三分クロオスを裂かなければ可けません」

蒲「三たび臂を折つて良医となるさ。あれから僕は竪杖の極意を悟つたのだ」

遊「君の後曳も口ほどではないよ。この間那処の主翁がさう言つてゐた、風早さんが後曳を三度なさると新いチョクが半分失る……」

これを聞きて、こたびは遊佐が笑へり。

蒲「穿得て妙だ」

風「チョクの多少は業の巧拙には関せんよ。遊佐が無闇に杖を取易へるのだつて、決して見とも好くはない」

蒲田は手もて遽に制しつ。

蒲「もう、それで可い。他の非を挙げるやうな者に業の出来た例が無い。悲い哉君達の球も蒲田に

風「八十で底止だね」

風「八十の事があるものか」

蒲「それでは幾箇（いくつ）で来るのだ」

「八十五よ」

「五とは情無い！　心の程も知られける哉（かな）」

「何でも可いから一ゲエム行かう」

「行かうとは何だ！　願ひますと言ふものだ」

「語（ことば）も訛らざるに彼は傍腹（そばばら）に不意の肱突（ひぢつき）を吃（くら）ひぬ。

「あ、痛（いた）！　さう強く撞（つ）くから毎々（まいまい）球が溢（こぼ）げ出すのだ。風早の球は暴（あら）いから癇癪玉（かんしゃくだま）と謂（い）ふのだし、遊佐は馬鹿に柔いから蒟蒻玉（こんにゃくだま）。それで、二人の撞くところは電公と蚊帳（かみなり）が押択（もんちゃく）してゐるやうなものだ」

風「ええ、自分がどれほど撞けるのだ」

蒲「さう、多度（たんど）も行かんが、天狗の風早（かざはや）に二十遣るのさ」

二人は劣らじと静（あらが）ひし末、直に一番の勝負を、いざいざと手薬煉（てぐすね）引きかくるを、遊佐は　引分けて、

「それは飲んでからに為やう。夜が長いから後で寛（ゆっく）り出来るさ。帰って風呂にでも入つて、それから徐々（やをや）始めやうよ」

往来繁き町を湯屋（ゆや）の角より入れば、道幅その二分の一ばかりなる横町の物売る店も雑（まじ）りながら閑静に、家並整へる中程に店蔵の質店と軒ランプの並びて、格子木戸の内を庭がかりにしたる門

に楪葉の立てるぞ遊佐が居住なる。

彼は二人を導きて内格子を開きける時、彼の美き妻は出で来りて、伴へる客あるを見て稍打惑

へる気色なりしが、遽に笑を含みて常の如く迎へたり。

「さあ、どうぞお二階へ」

「座敷は？」と夫に尤められて、彼はいよいよ困じたるなり。

「唯今些」と塞つてをりますから」

「ぢや、君、二階へどうぞ」

「鰐淵から参つてをりますよ」

「来たか！」

「是非お目に懸りたいと言つて、何と言つても帰りませんから、座敷へ上げて置きました、些と

お会ひなすつて、早く還してお了ひなさいましよ」

「松茸はどうした」

妻はこの暢気なる問に驚かされぬ。

「貴方、まあ松茸なんぞよりは早く……」

「待てよ。それからこの間の黒麦酒な……」

「麦酒も松茸もございますから早くあれを還してお了ひなさいましよ。私は那奴が居ると思ふと

不快な心持で」

遊佐も差当りて当惑の眉を顰めつ。二階にては例の玉戯（ビリアァド）の　争（あらそひ）なるべし、さも気楽に高笑する

を妻はいと心憎く。

少間ありて遊佐は二階に昇り来れり。

蒲「浴に一つ行かうよ。手拭を貸してくれ給へな」

遊「ま、待ち給へ、今一処に行くから。時に弱って了った」

実に言ふが如く彼は心穏かならず見ゆるなり。

風「まあ、坐りたまへ。どうしたのかい」

遊「坐ってもをられんのだ、下に高利貸が来てをるのだよ」

蒲「那物（あいつ）が来たのか」

遊「先から座敷で帰来を待ってをつたのだ。困つたね！」

彼は立ちながら頭を抑へて緩く柱に倚れり。

蒲「何とか言つて逐返して了ひ給へ」

遊「なかなか逐返らんのだよ。陰忍した皮肉な奴でね、那奴（あいつ）に捉つたら耐らん」

蒲「二三円も叩き付けて遣るさ」

遊「もうそれも度々なのでね、他は書替を為せやうと掛つてゐるのだから、延期料を握つたのち

や今日は帰らん」

　風早は聴けるだに心苦くて、

「蒲田、君一つ談判してやり給へ、ええ、何とか君の弁を揮つて」

「これは外の談判と違つて唯金銭づくなのだから、素手で飛込むのぢや弁の奮ひやうが無いよ。それで忽語すると飛んで火に入る夏の虫となるのだから、まあ君が行つて何とか話をして見たまへ。僕は様子を立聞して、臨機応変の助太刀を為るから」

　いと難しと思ひながらも、かくては果てじと、遊佐は気を取直して下り行くなりけり。

　風「気の毒な、萎れてゐる。あれの事だから心配してゐるのだ。君、何とかして拯つて遣り給な」

　蒲「一つ行つて様子を見て来やう。なあに、そんなに心配するほどの事は無いのだよ。遊佐は気が小さいから可かない。ああ云ふ風だから益す脚下を見られて好い事を為れるのだ。高が金銭の貸借だ、命に別条は有りはしないさ」

「命に別条は無くても、名誉に別条が有るから、紳士たるものは懼れるだらうぢやないか」

「ところが懼れない！　紳士たるものが高利を貸したら名誉に関らうけれど、高い利を払つて借りるのだから、安利や無利息なんぞを借りるから見れば、寧に以つて栄とするに足れりさ。紳士たりといへども金銭に窮らんと云ふ限は無い、窮つたから借りるのだ。借りて返さんと言ひは為まいし、名誉に於て傷くところは少しも無い」

「恐入りました、高利を借りやうと云ふ紳士の心掛は又別の物ですな」

「で、仮に一歩を譲つて、譲つて、高利を借りるなどは、紳士たるもののいとも慚づべき行と為

るよ。さほど慚づべきならば始から借りんが可いぢやないか。未

だ借りざる先の慚づべき心を以つてこれに対せんとする能はざるなりだらう。宋の時代であつ

たかね、何か乱が興つた。すると上奏に及んだものがある、これは師を動かさるるまでもない、

一人の将を河上へ遣して、賊の方に向つて孝経を読ませられた事ならば、賊は自から消滅せん、

好いぢやないか。これを笑ふけれど、遊佐の如きは真面目で孝経を読んでゐるのだよ、既に借り

てさ、天引四割と吃つて一月隔に血を吮れる。そんな無法な目に遭ひながら、未だ借りざる先の

紳士たる徳義や、良心を持つてゐて耐るものか。孝経が解るくらゐなら高利は貸しません、彼等

は銭勘定の出来る毛族さ」

得意の快弁流るる如く、彼は息をも継せず説来りぬ。

「濡れぬ内こそ露をもだ。遊佐も借りんのなら可いさ、既に借りて、無法な目に遭ひながら、な

ほ未だ借りざる先の良心を持つてゐるのは大きな慨だ。それは勿論借りた後といへども良心を持

たなければならんけれど、借りざる先の良心と、借りたる後の良心とは、一物にして一物ならず

だよ。武士の魂と商人根性とは元是一物なのだ。それが境遇に応じて魂ともなれば根性ともなる

のさ。で、商人の魂と商人根性といへども決して不義不徳を容さんことは、武士の魂と敢て異るところは無

い。武士にあつては武士魂なるものが、商人にあつては商人根性なのだもの。そこで、紳士も高利

などを借りん内は武士の魂よ、既に対高利となつたら、商人根性にならんければ身が立たな

い。

究竟は敵に応ずる手段なのだ」

「それは固より御同感さ。けれども、紳士が高利を借りて、栄と為るに足れりと謂ふに至つては

……」

蒲田は恐縮せる状を作して、

「それは少し白馬は非ずだつたよ」

「時に、もう下へ行つて見て遣り給へ」

「どれ、一ヒ深く探る蛟鰐の淵と出掛けやうか」

「空拳を奈んだらう」

一笑して蒲田は二階を下りけり。風早は独り臥し起きつ安否の気遣れて苦き無聊に堪へざる折

から、主の妻は漸く茶を持ち来りぬ。

「どうも甚だ失礼を致しました」

「蒲田は座敷へ参りましたか」

彼はその美き顔を少く赧めて、

「はい、あの居間へお出で、紙門越に様子を聴いてゐらつしやいます。どうもこんなところを皆

様のお目に掛けまして、実にお可恥くてなりません」

「なあに、他人ぢやなし、皆様子を知つてゐる者ばかりですから構ふ事はありません」

「私はもう彼奴が参りますと、惣毛竪つて頭痛が致すのでございます。あんな強慾な事を致す

ものは全く人相が別でござります。それは可愛に陰気な靭々した、底意地の悪さうな、本当に探偵小説にでも在りさうな奴でござりますよ」

急足に階子を鳴らして昇り来りし蒲田は、

「おいおい風早、不思議、不思議」

と上端に坐れる妻の背後を過ぎて絶かその足を踏付けたり。

「これは失礼を。お痛うござりましたら。どうも失礼を」

骨身に沁みて痛かりけるを妻は赤くなりて推怵へつつ、さり気無く挨拶せるを、風早は見かねたりけん、

「不相変麁相かしいね、蒲田は」

「どうぞ御免を。つい慌てたものだから……」

「何をそんなに慌てるのさ」

「落付れる訳のものではないよ。下に来てゐる高利貸と云ふのは、誰だと思ふ」

「君のと同じ奴かい」

「人様の居る前で君の、とは怪しからんぢやないか」

「これは失礼」

「僕は妻君の足を踏んだのだが、君は僕の面を踏んだ」

「でも仕合と皮の厚いところで」

「怪しからん！」

妻の足の痛は忽ち下腹に転りて、彼は得堪へず笑ふなりけり。

風「常談どころぢやない、下では苦しんでゐる人があるのだ」

蒲「その苦しめてゐる奴だ、不思議ぢやないか、間だよ、あの間貫一だよ」

敵寄すると聞きけんやうに風早は身構へて、

「間貫一、学校に居た?!」

「さう！　驚いたらう」

彼は長き鼻息を出して、空く眼を睜りしが、

「本当かい」

「まあ、見て来たまへ」

別して呆れたるは主の妻なり。彼は鈍ましからず胸の跳るを覚えぬ。同じ思は二人が面にも顕

るるを見るべし。

「下に参つてゐるのは御朋友なのでございますか」

蒲田は忙しげに頷きて、

「さうです。我々と高等中学の同級に居つた男なのですよ」

「まあ！」

「尻て学校を罷めてから高利貸を遣つてゐると云ふ話は聞いてゐましたけれど、極温和い男で、

高利貸などの出来る気ちやないのですから、そんな事は嘘だらうと誰も想つてをつたのです。と

ころが、下に来てゐるのがその間貫一ですから驚くちやありませんか」

「まあ！　高等中学にも居た人が何だつて高利貸などに成つたのでございませう」

「さあ、そこで誰も嘘と想ふのです」

「本にさうでございますね」

少き前に起ちて行きし風早は疑を霽して帰り来れり。

「どうだ、どうだ」

「驚いたね、確に間貫一！」

「アルフレッド大王の面影があるだらう」

「エッセクスを逐払はれた時の面影だ。然し彼奴が高利貸を遣らうとは想はなかつたが、どうし

たのだらう」

「さあ、あれで因業な事が出来るだらうか」

「因業どころではございませんよ」

　主の妻はその美き顔を皺めたるなり。

蒲　「随分酷うございますか」

妻　「酷うございますわ」

　こたびは泣顔せるなり。　風早は決するところ有るが如くに余せし茶をば遽に取りて飲干し、

「然し間であるのが幸だ、押掛けて行つて、昔の顔で一つ談判せうぢやないか。我々が口を利くのだ、奴もさう阿漕なことは言ひもすまい。次手に何とか話を着けて、元金だけか何かに負けさして遣らうよ。那奴なら恐れることは無い」

彼の起ちて帯締直すを蒲田は見て、

「まるで喧嘩に行くやうだ」

「そんな事を言はずに自分も些と気凛とするが可い、帯の下へ時計の垂下つてゐるなどは威厳を損じるぢやないか」

「うむ、成程」と蒲田も立上りて帯を解けば、主の妻は傍より、

「お羽織をお取りなさいました」

「これは慥様です。些と身支度に婦人の心添を受けるところは堀部安兵衛といふ役だ。然し芝居でも、人数が多くて、支度をする方は大概取つて投げられるやうだから、お互に気を着ける事だよ」

「馬鹿な！　間如きに」

「急に強くなつたから可笑い。さあ。用意は好いよ」

「此方も可い」

二人は膝を正して屹と差向へり。

妻「お茶を一つ差上げませう」

蒲「どうしても敵討の門出だ。互に交す茶盃か」

第 六 章

座敷には窘める遊佐と沈着きたる貫一と相対して、莨盆の火の消えんとすれど呼ばず、彼の傍に茶托の上に伏せたる茶碗は、嘗て肺病患者と知らで出せしを恐れて除物にしたりしをば、妻の取出してわざと用ゐたるなり。

遊佐は、憤、を恐べる声音にて、

「それは出来ぬよ。勿論朋友は幾多も有るけれど、書替の連帯を頼むやうな者は無いのだから。さう無理考へて見給へ、何ぼ朋友の中だと云つても外の事と違つて、借金の連帯は頼めないよ。さう無理を言つて困らせんでも可いぢやないか」

貫一の声は重きを曳くが如く底強く沈みたり。

「敢て困らせるの、何のと云ふ訳ではありません。利は下さらず、書替は出来んと、それでは私の方が立ちません。何方とも今日は是非願はんければならんのでございます。連帯と云つたところで、固より貴方がお引受けなさる精神なれば、外の迷惑にはならんのですから、些の名義を借りるだけの話、それくらゐの事は朋友の誼として、何方でも承諾なさりさうなものですが。究竟名義だけあれば宜いので、私の方では十分貴方を信用してをるのですから、決してその連帯者

に掛らうなどとは思はんのです。ここで何とか一つ廉が付きませんと、私も主人に対して言訳が

ありません。利を受取る訳に行かなかつたから、書替をして来たと言へば、それで一先句切が付

くのでありますから、どうぞ一つさう願ひます」

遊佐は答ふるところを知らざるなり。

「何方でも可うございます、御親友の内で一名」

「可かんよ、それは到底可かんのだよ」

「到底可かんでは私の方が済みません。さう致すと、自然御名誉に関るやうな手段も取らんけれ

ばなりません」

「どうせうと言ふのかね」

「無論差押です」

遊佐は強ひて微笑を含みけれど、胸には犇と応へて、はや八分の怯気付きたるなり。彼は悶え

て挽断るばかりにその髭を拈り拈りて止まず。

「三百円やそこらの端金で貴方の御名誉を傷けて、後来御出世の妨碍にもなるやうな事を為るの

は、私の方でも決して可好くはないのです。けれども、此方の請求を容れて下さらなければ已む

を得んので、実は事は穏便の方が双方の利益なのですから、更に御一考を願ひます」

「それは、まあ、品に由つたら書替も為んではないけれど、君の要求は、元金の上に借用当時か

ら今日までの制規の利子が一ケ年分と、今度払ふべき九十円の一月分を加へて三百九十円かね、

それに対する三月分の天引が、百十七円強、それと合して五百円の証書面に書替へろと云ふのだらう。又それが連帯債務と言ふだらうけれど、一文だつて自分が費つたのでもないのに、この間九十円といふものを取られた上に、又改めて五百円の証書を書かされる！　余り馬鹿々々しくて話にならん。此方の身にも成つて少しは斟酌するが可いぢやないか。一文も費ひもせんで五百円の証書が書けると想ふかい」

空嘯きて貫一は笑へり。

「今更そんな事を！」

遊佐は陰に切歯をなしてその横顔を睨付けたり。

彼も遣れ難き義理に迫りて連帯の印捺きしより、太く己に懲りてければ、この際人に連帯を頼みて、同様の迷惑を懸くることもやと、断じて貫一の請求を容れざりき。さりとて今一つの請求なる利子を即座に払ふべき道もあらざれば、彼の進退はここに谷るとともに貫一もこの場は一寸も去らじと構へたれば、今は唯身に受くべき謂無き貴苦を受けて、かくまでに悩まされく一分時毎に窮する外は無くて、今は唯身に受くべき謂無き貴苦を受けて、かくまでに悩まさるる不幸を恨み、翻りて一点の人情無き賤奴の虐待を憤る胸の内は、前後も覚えず暴れ乱れてほど引裂けんとするなり。

「第一今日は未だ催促に来る約束ぢやないのではないか」

「先月の二十日にお払ひ下さるべきのを、未だにお渡が無いのですから、何日でも御催促は出来

るのです」

遊佐は拳を握りて顫ひぬ。

「さう云ふ怪しからん事を！　何の為に延期料を取つた」

「別に延期料と云つては受取りません。期限の日に参つたのにお払が無い、そこで空く帰るその日当及び僀代として戴きました。ですから、若しあれに延期料と云ふ名を附けたらば、その日の取立を延期する料とも謂ふべきでせう」

「貴、貴様は！　最初十円だけ渡さうと言つたら、十円では受取らん、利子の内金でなしに三日間の延期料としてなら受取る、と言つて持つて行つたぢやないか。それからついこの間又十円
……」

「それは確に受取りました。が、今申す通り、無駄足を踏みました日当でありますから、その日が経過すれば、翌日から催促に参つても宜い訳なのです。まあ、過去つた事は措きまして……」

「措けんよ。過去りは為めんのだ」

「今日はその事で上つたのではないのですから、今日の始末をお付け下さいまし。ではどうあつても書替は出来んと仰有るのですな」

「出来ん！」

「で、金も下さらない？」

「無いから遣れん！」

貫一は目を側めて遊佐が面を熟と候へり。その冷に鋭き眼の光は異く彼を襲ひて、坐に熱する怒気を忘れしめぬ。遊佐は忽ち吾を復れるやうに覚えて、身の危きに処るを省みたり。一時を快くする暴言は竟に曳れ者の小唄に過ぎざるを暁りて、手持無沙汰に鳴を鎮めつ。

「では、何ごろ御都合が出来るのですか」

機を制して彼も劣らず和ぎぬ。

「さあ、十六日まで待つてくれたまへ」

「慥と相違ございませんか」

「十六日なら相違ない」

「それでは十六日まで待ちますから……」

「延期料かい」

「まあ、お聞きなさいまし、約束手形を一枚お書き下さい。それなら宜うございませう」

「宜い事も無い……」

「不承を有仰るところは少しも有りはしません、その代り何分か今日お遣し下さい」

かく言ひつつ手鞄を開きて、約束手形の用紙を取出せり。

「銭は有りはせんよ」

「僅少で宜いので、手数料として」

「又手数料か！ ぢや一円も出さう」

「日当、傭代なども入つてゐるのですから五円ばかり」

「五円なんと云ふ金円は有りはせん」

「それぢや、どうも」

彼は遽に躊躇して、手形用紙を惜めるやうに拈るなりけり。

「ええ、では三円ばかり出さう」

折から紙門を開きけるを弗と貫一の腿ふる目前に、二人の紳士は徐々と入来りぬ。案内も無くかかる内証の席に立入りて、彼等の各心得顔なるは、必ず子細あるべしと思ひつつ、彼は少く座を動ぎて容を改めたり。　紳士は上下に分れて二人が間に坐りければ、貫一は敬ひて礼を作せり。

蒲　「どうも暗から見たやうだ、見たやうだと思つてゐたら、間君ぢやないか」

風　「余り様子が変つたから別人かと思つた。久く会ひませんな」

貫一は愕然として二人の面を眺めたりしが、忽ち身の熱するを覚えて、その誰なるやを憶出せるなり。

「これはお珍い。　何方かと思ひましたら、蒲田君に風早君。久くお目に掛りませんでしたが、いつもお変無く」

蒲　「その後はどうですか、何か当時は変つた商売をお始めですな──儲りませう」

貫一は打笑みて、

蒲「儲りもしますが、間違つてこんな事になつて了ひました」

彼の竟も愧づる色無きを見て、二人は心陰に呆れぬ。侮りし風早もかくては与し易からずと思へるなるべし。

蒲「儲けづくであるから何でも可いけれど、二人は心陰に呆れぬ。然し思切つた事を始めましたね。君の性質で能くこの家業が出来ると思つて感服しましたよ」

「真人間に出来る業ちやありませんな」

これ実に真人間にあらざる人の言なり。二人はこの破廉恥の老面皮を憎しと思へり。

蒲「酷いね、それぢや君は真人間でないやうだ」

「私のやうな者が慾ひ人間の道を守つてをつたら、とてもこの世の中は渡れんと悟りましたから、学校を罷めるとともに人間を罷めて了つて、この商売を始めましたので」

風「然し真人間時分の朋友であつた僕等にかうして会つてゐる間だけは、依旧真人間で居てもらひたいね」

風早は親しげに放笑せり。

蒲「さうさう、それ、あの時分浮名の噧かつた、何とか云つたけね、それ、君の所に居つた美人さ」

貫一は知らざる為してゐたり。

風「おおおおあれ？　さあ、何とか云つたつけ」

よしその旧友の前に人間の面を紅めざる貫一も、ここに到りて多少の心を動かさざるを得ざりき。

蒲「ねえ、間君、何とか云つた」

「そんなつまらん事を」

蒲「この頃はあの美人と一所に、可愛い」

「もう昔話は御免下さい。それでは遊佐さん、これに御印を願ひます」

彼は矢立の筆を抽きて、手形用紙に金額を書入れんとするを、

風「ああ些と、その手形はどう云ふのですね」

貫一の簡単にその始末を述ぶるを聴きて、

「成程御尤、そこで少しお話を為たい」

蒲田は姑く助太刀の口を噤みて、皺嗄声の如何に弁ずるかを聴かんと、吃余の葉巻を火入に挿して、威長高に腕組して控へたり。

「遊佐君の借財の件ですがね、あれはどうか特別の扱をして戴きたいのだ。君の方も営業なのだから、御迷惑は掛けませんさ、然し旧友の頼と思つて、少し勘弁をしてもらひたい」

彼も答へず、これも少時は言はざりしが、

「どうかね、君」

「勘弁と申しますと？」

「究竟君の方に損の掛らん限は減けてもらひたいのだ。　知つての通り、　元金の借金は遊佐君が連帯であつて、　実際頼れて印を貸しただけの話であるのが、　測らず倒れて来たといふ訳なので、そ(つま)れは貸主の目から見れば、そんな事はどうでも可いのだから、取立てるものは取立てる、其処は(そこ)能く解つてゐる、からして今更その愚痴を言ふのぢやない。　然し朋友の側から遊佐君を見ると、飛んだ災難に罹つたので、如何にも気の毒な次第。　ところで、　図らずも貸主が君と云ふので、轍(て)(じふ)(し)(四)鮒の水を得たる想で我々が中へ入つたのは、　営業者の鰐淵として話を為るのではなくて、　旧友の間として、実は無理な頼も聴いてもらひたいのさ。　夙て話は聞いてゐるが、あの三百円に対して(あひだ)(かね)は、借主の遠林が従来三回に二百七十円の利を払つて在る。　それから遊佐君の手で九十円、　合計(とをばやし)(これまで)三百六十円と云ふものが既に入つてゐるのでせう。　して見ると、君の方には既に損は無いのだ、であるから、この三百円の元金だけを遊佐君の手で返せば可いといふ事にしてもらひたいのだ」

貫一は冷笑せり。

「さうすれば遊佐君は三百九十円払ふ訳だが、これが一文も費はずに空に出るのだから随分辛い(くう)話、君の方は未だ未だ利益になるのをここで見切るのだからこれも辛い。　そこで辛さ競を為るの(つら)だが、君の方は三百円の物が六百六十円になつてゐるのだから、立前にはなつてゐる、此方は三(だてまへ)百九十円の全損だから、ここを一つ酌量してもらひたい、ねえ、　特別の扱で」

「全でお話にならない」(まる)

秋の日は短しと謂はんやうに、貫一は手形用紙を取上げて、用捨無く約束の金額を書入れたり。

一斉に彼の面を注視せし風早と蒲田との眼は、更に相合うて瞋れるを、再び彼方に差向けて、いとど厳しく打目戌れり。

風「どうかさう云ふ事にしてくれたまへ」

貫「それでは遊佐さん、これに御印を願ひませう。日限は十六日、宜しうございますか」

この傍若無人の振舞に蒲田の怺へかねたる気色なるを、風早は目授して、

「聞君、まあ少し待つてくれたまへよ。恥を言はんければ解らんけれど、この借金は遊佐君には荷が勝過ぎてゐるので、利を入れるだけでも方が付かんのだから、長くこれを背負つてゐた日には、体も一所に沈没して了ふばかり、実に一身の浮沈に関る大事なので、僕等も非常に心配してゐるやうなものの、力が足らんで如何とも手の着けやうが無い。対手が君であつたのが運の尽きざるところなのだ。旧友の僕等の難を拯ふと思つて、一つ頼を聴いてくれ給へ、全然損を掛けやうと云ふのぢやないのだから、決してさう無理な頼ぢやなからうと思ふのだが、どうかね、君」

「私は鰐淵の手代なのですから、さう云ふお話は解りかねます。遊佐さん、では、今日はまあ三円頂戴してこれに御印をどうぞお早く」

遊佐はその独に計ひかねて覚束なげに頷くのみ。言はで忍びたりし蒲田の怒はこの時衝くが如く、

「待ち給へと言ふに！　先から風早が口を酸くして頼んでゐるのぢやないか、銭貸が門に立つたのぢやない、人に対するには礼と云ふものがある、可然き挨拶を為たまへ」

「お話が、お話だから可然き御挨拶の為やうが無い」

「黙れ、間！　貴様の頭脳は銭勘定ばかりしてゐるので、人の言ふ事が解らんと見えるな。誰が、その話に可然な挨拶を為ろと言つた。友人に対する挙動が無礼だから節めと言つたのだ。高利貸な、ら高利貸のやうに、身の程を省みて神妙にしてをれ。盗人の兄弟分のやうな不正な営業をしてゐ、ながら、かうして旧友に会つたらば頼い顔の一つも為ることか、世界漫遊でもして来たやうな見、識で、貴様は高利を貸すのをあつぱれ名誉と心得てゐるのか。恥を恥とも思はんのみか、一枚の、証文を鼻に懸けて我々を侮蔑したこの有様を、荒尾譲介に見せて遣りたい！　貴様のやうな畜生、に生れ変つた奴を、荒尾はやはり昔の間貫一だと思つて、この間も我々と話して、貴様の安否を、苦にしてな、実の弟を殺したより、貴様を失つた方が悲いと言つて鬱いでゐたぞ。その一言に対、しても少しは良心の眠を覚せ！　真人間の風早庫之助と蒲田鉄弥が中に入るからは決して迷惑を、掛けるやうな事は為んから、今日は順く帰れ、帰れ」

「受取るものを受取らなくては帰れもしません。貴下方がそれまで遊佐さんの件に就いて御心配、下さいますなら、かう為すつて下さいませんか、ともかくもこの約束手形は遊佐さんから戴きま、して、この方の形はそれで一先附くのですから、改めて三百円の証書をお書き下さいまし、風早、君と蒲田君の連帯にして」

「うん、宜い」

蒲田はこの手段を知るの経験あるなり。

「ではさう為つて下さるか」

「うん、宜い」

「さう致せば又お話の付けやうもあります」

「然し気の毒だな、無利息、十個年賦は」

「ええ？　常談ぢやありません」

　さすがに彼の一本参りしを、蒲田は誇りかに嘲笑しつ。

風「常談は措いて、いづれ四五日内に篤と話を付けるから、今日のところは、久しぶりで会つた

僕等の顔を立てて、何も言はずに帰つてくれ給へな」

「さう云ふ無理を有仰るで、私の方も然るべき御挨拶が出来なくなるのです。　既に遊佐さんも御

承諾なのですから、この手形はお貰ひ申して帰ります。　未だ外へ廻るで急ぎますから、お話は後

日寛り伺ひませう。　遊佐さん、御印を願ひますよ。　貴方御承諾なすつて置きながら今になつて遅

遅なすつては困ります」

蒲「疫病神が戸惑したやうに手形々々と煩い奴だ。　俺が始末をして遣らうよ」

　彼は遊佐が前なる用紙を取りて、

蒲「金壱百拾七円……何だ、百拾七円とは」

遊「百十七円？　九十円だよ」

蒲「金壱百拾七円とこの通り書いてある」

かかる事は能く知りながら彼はわざと怪しむなりき。

遊「そんな管は無い」

貫一は彼等の騒ぐを尻目に掛けて、

「九十円が元金、これに加へた二十七円は天引の三割、これが高利の定法です」

音もせざれど遊佐が胆は潰れぬ。

「お……ど……ろ……いたね！」

蒲田は物をも言はず件の手形を二つに引裂き、遊佐も風早もこれはと見る間に、猶も引裂き引

裂き、引捩りて間が目先に投遣りたり。彼は騒げる色も無く、

「何を為るのです」

「始末をして遣つたのだ」

「遊佐さん、それでは手形もお出し下さらんのですな」

彼は間が非常手段を取らんとするよ、と心陰に櫃を作して、

「いやさう云ふ訳ぢやない……」

蒲田は仗と膝を前めて、

「いや、さう云ふ訳だ！」

彼の鬼臉なるをいと稚しと軽しめたるやうに、間はわざと色を和げて、

「手形の始末はそれで付いたか知りませんが、貴方も折角中へ入つて下さるなら、も少し男らし

い扱をなさいましな。私、如き畜生とは違つて、貴方は立派な法学士

「おお俺が法学士ならどうした」

「名実が相副はんと謂ふのです」

「生意気なもう一遍言つて見ろ」

「何遍でも言ひます。学士なら学士のやうな所業を為さい」

蒲田が腕は電光の如く躍りて、猶言はんとせし貫一が胸先を諸摑に無図と捉りたり。

「間、貴様は……」

挽向けたる彼の面を打目成りて、

「取つて投げてくれやうと思ふほど憎い奴でも、かうして顔を見合せると、白い二本筋の帽子を冠つて煖炉の前に膝を並べた時分の姿が目に附いて、嗚呼、順い間を、と力抜がして了ふ。貴様

これが人情だぞ」

鷹に遭へる小鳥の如く身動し得為で押付けられたる貫一を、風早はさすがに憫然と見遣りて、

「蒲田の言ふ通りだ。僕等も中学に居た頃の間と思つて、それは誓つて迷惑を掛けるやうな事は為んから、君も友人の誼を思つて、二人の頼を聴いてくれ給へ」

「さあ、間、どうだ」

彼は忽ち吭迫りて言ふを得ず、蒲田は稍強く緊めたるなり。

「友人の誼は友人の誼、貸した金は貸した金で自から別問題……」

「さあ、もっと言へ、言つて見ろ。言つたら貴様の呼吸が止るぞ」

貫一は苦しさに堪へて振釈かんと挼けども、嘉納流の覚ある蒲田が力に敵しかねて、なかなか

その為すに信せたる幾分の安きを頼むのみなりけり。　遊佐は驚き、風早も心ならず、

「おい蒲田、可いかい、死にはしないか」

「余り、暴くするなよ」

蒲田は哄然として大笑せり。

「かうなると金力よりは腕力だな。ねえ、どうしてもこれは水滸伝にある図だらう。惟ふに、凡

その国利を護り、国権を保つには、国際公法などは実は糸瓜の皮、要は兵力よ。万国の上には立法

の君主が無ければ、国と国との曲直の争は抑も誰の手で公明正大に遺憾無く決せらるるのだ。こ

こに唯一つ審判の機関がある、曰く戦！」

風「もう釈してやれ、大分苦しさうだ」

蒲「強国にして辱められた例を聞かん、故に僕は外交の術も嘉納流よ」

遊「余り酷い目に遭せると、僕の方へ報つて来るから、もう舎してくれたまへな」

他の言に手は弛めたれど、蒲田は未だ放ちも遣らず、

「さあ、間、返事はどうだ」

「吭を緊められても出す音は変りませんよ。間は金力には屈しても、腕力などに屈するものか。

憎いと思ふならこの面を五百円の紙幣束でお撲きなさい」

「金貨ちや可かんか」

「金貨、結構です」

「ちや金貨だぞ！」

油断せる貫一が左の高頬を平手打に絶か吃すれば、呀と両手に痛を抑へて、少時は顔も得挙げざりき。蒲田はやうやう座に復りて、

「急には此奴帰らんね。いつそここで酒を始めやうちやないか、さうして飲みかつ談ずると為う」

「さあ、それも可からう」

独り可からぬは遊佐なり。

「ここで飲んぢや旨くないね。さうして形が付かなければ、何時までだつて帰りはせんよ。酒が仕舞になつてこればかり遣られたら猶困る」

「宜い、帰去には僕が一所に引張つて好い処へ連れて行つて遣るから。ねえ、間、おい、間と言ふのに」

「はい」

「貴様、妻君有るのか。おお、風早！」

と彼は横手を拍ちて不意に叫べば、

「ええ、吃驚する、何だ」

「憶出した。間の許婚はお宮、お宮」

「この頃はあれと一所かい。鬼の女房に天女だけれど、今日ちゃ大きに日済などを貸してゐるかも知れん。ええ、貴様、そんな事を為しちゃ可かんよ。けれども高利貸などは、これで却つて女子には温いとね、間、さうかい。彼等の非義非道を働いて暴利を貪る所以の者は、やはり旨いものを食ひ、好い女を自由にして、好きな栄耀がして見たいと云ふ、唯それだけの目的より外に無いのだと謂ふが、さうなのかね。我々から考へると、人情の忍ぶ可からざるを忍んで、経営惨憺と努めるところは、何ぞ非常の目的があつて貨を殖へるやうだがな、譬へば、軍用金を聚めるか、お家の宝を質請するとか。単に己の慾を充さうばかりで、あんな思切つて残刻な仕事が出来るものではないと想ふのだ。許多のガリガリ亡者は論外として、間貫一に於いては何ぞ目的が有るのだらう。こんな非常手段を遣るくらゐだから、必ず非常の目的が有つて存するのだらう」

秋の日は忽ち黄昏れて、稍早けれど燈を入るるとともに、用意の酒肴は順を逐ひて運び出されぬ。

「おっと、麦酒かい、頂戴。鍋は風早の方へ、煮方は宜くお頼み申しますよ。うう、好い松茸だ。京でなくてはかうは行かんよ——中が真白で、庖丁が軋むやうでなくては。今年は不作だね、癩せてゐて、虫が多い、あの雨が障つたのさ。間、どうだい、君の目的は」

「唯貨が欲いのです」

「で、その貨をどうする」

「つまらん事を！　貨はどうでもなるぢやありませんか。どうでもなる貨だから欲い、その欲い

貨だから、かうして催促もするのです。さあ、遊佐さん、本当にどうして下さるのです」

風「まあ、これを一盃飲んで、今日は機嫌好く帰つてくれ給へ」

蒲「そら、お取次だ」

蒲（わたくし）「私は酒は不可のです」

「折角差したものだ」

「全く不可（いかん）のですから」

差付けらるるを推除（おしの）くる機（はずみ）に、コップは脆（もろ）くも蒲田の手を脱（はな）れば、莨盆（たこぼん）の火入（ひいれ）に抵（あた）りて発矢（はつし）と

割れたり。

「何を為る！」

貫一も今は悚（こら）へかねて、

「どうしたと！」

やをら起たんと為るところを、蒲田が力に胸板（むないた）を衝（つ）かれて、一耐（ひとたまり）もせず仰様（のけさま）に打僵（うちたふ）れたり。狂気の如く駆寄（かけよ）る貫一、蒲田

はこの隙（ひま）に彼の手鞄を奪ひて、中なる書類を手信（てばや）に攫出（つかみだ）せば、

「身分に障るぞ！」と組み付くを、利腕（きゝうで）捉（とら）へて、

「黙れ！」と捩伏（ねぢふ）せ、

「さあ、遊佐、その中に君の証書が在るに違無いから、早く其奴（そいつ）を取つて了ひ給へ」

これを聞きたる遊佐は色を変へぬ。風早も事の余に暴なるを快しと為ざるなりき。貫一は驚き
て、撥返さんとさんと右に左に身を揉むを、蹈跨りて挽揚げ挽揚げ、蒲田は声を励して、

「この期に及んで！躊躇するところでないよ。早く、早く、早く！風早、何を考へとる。さ
あ、遊佐、ええ、何事も僕が引受けたから、かまはず遣り給へ。証書を取って了へば、後は細工
はうりうり僕が心得てゐるから、早く探したまへと言ふに」

手を出しかねたる二人を睨廻して、蒲田はなかなか下に貫一の悶ゆるにも劣らず、独り業を沸
して、効無き地鞴を踏みてぞゐたる。

風「それは余り遣過ぎる、善くない、善くない」

「善いも悪いもあるものか、僕が引受けたからかまはんよ。遊佐、君の事ぢゃないか、何を懵然
してゐるのだ」

彼はほとほと慄きて、寧ろ蒲田が腕立の紳士にあるまじきを諌めんとも思へるなり。腰弱き彼
等の与するに足らざるを憤れる蒲田は、宝の山に入りながら手を空うする無念さに、貫一が手も
折れよとばかり損上れば、

「ああ、待つた待つた。蒲田君、待つてくれ、何とか話を付けるから」

「ええ瞋い。君のやうな意気地無しはもう頼まん。僕が独で遣って見せるから、後学の為に能
く見て置き給へ」

かく言捨てて蒲田は片手して己の帯を解かんとすれば、時計の紐の生憎に絡るを、躁りに躁り

て引放さんとす。

風「独でどうするのだよ」

彼はさすがに見かねて手を仮さんと寄り進みつ。

蒲「どうするものか、此奴を踏縛つて置いて、僕が証書を探すわ」

「まあ、余り穏でないから、それだけは思ひ止り給へ。今間も話を付けると言つたから」

「何か此奴の言ふ事が！」

間は苦き声を搾りて、

「きつと話を付けるから、この手を釈してくれ給へ」

風「きつと話を付けるな――此方の要求を容れるか」

間「容れる」

詐とは知れど、二人の同意せざるを見て、蒲田もさまではと力挫けて、身を起すとともに貫一は落散りたる書類を掻聚め、鞄を拾ひてその中に挟込み、さて慌忙く座に復りて、

「それでは今日はこれでお暇をします」

蒲田が思切りたる無法にこの長居は危しと見たれば、心に恨は含みながら、陽には克はじと閉口して、重ねて難題の出でざる先にとかくは引取らんと為るを、

「待て待て」と蒲田は下司扱に呼掛けて、

「話を付けると言つたでないか。さあ、約束通り要求を容れん内は、今度は此方が邀さんぞ」

膝推向けて迫寄る気色は、飽くまで喧嘩を買はんとするなり。

「きつと要求は容れますけれど、嚮から散々の目に遭されて、何だか酷く心持が悪くてなりませんから、今日はこれで還して下さいまし。これは長座をいたしてお邪魔でございました。それでは遊佐さん、いづれ二三日の内に又上つてお話を願ひます」

忽ち打つて変りし貫一の様子に蒲田は冷笑して、

「間、貴様は犬の糞で仇を取らうと思つてゐるな。　遣つて見ろ、そんな場合には自今毎でも蒲田が現れて取挫いで遣るから」

「間も男なら犬の糞ぢや仇は取らない」

「利いた風なことを言ふな」

風「これさ、もう好加減にしないかい。　間も帰り給へ。近日是非篤と話をしたいから、何事もその節だ。さあ、僕が其処まで送らう」

遊佐と風早とは起ちて彼を送出せり。主の妻は縁側より入り来りぬ。

「まあ、貴方、お蔭様で難有う存じました。もうもうどんなに好い心持でございましたらう」

「や、これは。些と壮士芝居といふところを」

「大相宜い幕でございましたこと。お酌を致しませう」

件の騒動にて四辺の狼藉たるを、彼は効々しく取形付けてゐたりしが、二人はやがて入来るを

見て、

「風早さん、どうもお蔭様で助りました、然し飛んだ御迷惑様で。さあ、何も御坐いませんけれど、どうぞ貴下方御竟り召上つて下さいまし」

妻の喜は溢るるばかりなるに引易へて、遊佐は青息吟きて思案に昏れたり。

「弱つた！　君が、ああして取集めてくれたのは可いが、この返報に那奴どんな事を為るか知れん。明日あたり突然と差押などを吃せられたら耐らんな」

「余り蒲田が手酷い事を為るから、僕も、さあ、それを案じて、慱々してゐたぢやないか。嘉納流も可いけれど、後前を考べて遣つてくれなくては他迷惑だらうぢやないか」

「まあ、待ち給へと言ふことさ」

蒲田は袂の中を捜りて、揉皺みたる二通の書類を取出しつ。

遊「それは何だ」

風「どうしたのさ」

何ならんと主の妻も鼻の下を延べて覦へり。

「何だか僕も始めてお目に掛るのだ」

彼は先づその一通を取りて披見るに、鰐淵直行に対する債務者は聞きも知らざる百円の公正証書贋本なり。

二人は蒲田が案外の物持てるに驚かされて、各息を凝して睥れる眼を動さず。蒲田も無言の間

に他の一通を取りて抜けば、妻はいよいよ近きて差覗きつ。　四箇の頭顱はランプの周辺に蛾に寄る池の鯉の如く犇と聚れり。

「これは三百円の証書だな」

一枚二枚と繰り行けば、債務者の中に鼻の前なる遊佐良橘の名をも署したり、蒲田は弾機仕掛のやうに躍り上りて、

「占めた！　これだこれだ」

驚喜の余り身を支へ得ざる遊佐の片手は鴨の鉢の中にすつばと落入り、乗出す膝頭に銚子を薙倒して、

「僕のかい、僕のかい」

「ど、ど、どう、どう」と証書を取らんとする風早が手は、筋の活動を失へるやうにて幾度も捉へ得ざるなり。

「まあ！」と叫びし妻は忽ち胸塞りて、その後を言ふ能はざるなり。　蒲田は手の舞ひ、膝の踏むところを知らず、

「占めたぞ！　占めたぞ!!　難有い!!!」

証書は風早の手に移りて、遊佐とその妻と彼と六の目を以て子細にこれを点検して、その夢ならざるを明めたり。

「君はどうしたのだ」

風早の面はかつ呆れ、かつ喜び、かつ懼るるに似たり。やがて証書は遊佐夫婦の手に渡りて、打拡げたる二人が膝の上に、これぞ比翼読なるべき。更に麦酒の満を引きし蒲田は「血は大刀に滴りて拭ふに遑あらざる」意気を昂げて、

「何と凄からう。奴を損伏せてゐる中に脚で掻寄せて袂へ忍ばせたのだ――早業さね」

「やはり嘉納流にあるのかい」

「常談言つちや可かん。然しこれも嘉納流の教外別伝さ」

「遊佐の証書といふのはどうして知つたのだ」

「それは知らん。何でも可いから一つ二つ奪つて置けば、奴を退治る材料になると考へたから、早業をして置いたのだが、思ひきやこれが覘ふ敵の証書ならんとは、全く天の善に与するところだ」

風「余り善でもない。さうしてあれを此方へ取つて了へば、三百円は踏めるのかね」

蒲「大踏め！　少し悪党になれば踏める」

風「然し、公正証書であつて見ると……」

蒲「あつても差支無い。それは公証人役場には証書の原本が備付けてあるから、いざと云ふ日にはそれが物を言ふけれど、この正本さへ引揚げてあれば、間貫一いくら地動波動したつて『河童の皿に水の乾いた』同然、かうなれば無証拠だから、矢でも鉄砲でも持つて来いだ。然し、全然踏むのもさすがに不便との思召を以つて、そこは何とか又色を着けて遣らうさ。まあまあ君達は

安心してゐたまへ。蒲田弁理公使が宜く樽俎の間に折衝して、遊佐家を泰山の安きに置いて見せ
る。嗚呼、実に近来の一大快事だ!」

人々の呆るるには目も掛けず、蒲田は証書を推戴き推戴きて、

「さあ、遊佐君の為に万歳を唱へやう。奥さん、貴方が音頭をお取んなさいましよ──いいえ、
本当に」

小心なる遊佐はこの非常手段を極悪大罪と心安からず覚ゆるなれど、蒲田が一切を引受けて見
事に埒開けんといふに励されて、さては一生の怨敵退散の賀と、各漫に前む膝を聚めて、長夜
の宴を催さんとぞ犇いたる。

　　第七章

茫々たる世間に放れて、蚤く骨肉の親むべき無く、況や愛情の温むるに会はざりし貫一が身は、
一鳥も過ぎざる枯野の広きに塊然として、横はる石の如きものなるべし。彼が鴫沢の家に在りける
日宮を恋ひて、その優き声と、柔き手と、温き心とを得たりし彼の満足は、何等の楽をも以外に
求むる事を忘れしめき。彼はこの恋人をもて妻とし、生命として慊らず、母の一部分となし、妹
の一部分となし、或は父の、兄の一部分とも為して宮の一身は彼に於ける愉快なる家族の団欒に
値せしなり、故に彼の恋は青年を楽む一場の風流の麗き夢に似たる類ならで、質はその文に勝
るものなりけり。彼の宮に於けるは都ての人の妻となすべき以上を妻として、寧ろその望むとこ

ろ多きに過ぎずやと思はしむるまでに心に懸けて、自はその至当なるを固く信ずるなりき。彼は

この世に一人の宮を得たるが為に、万木一時に花を着くる心地して、曩の枯野に夕暮れし石も今
将た水に温み、霞に酔ひて、長閑なる日影に眠る如く覚えけんよ。その恋のいよいよ急に、いよ
いよ濃になり勝れる時、人の最も憎める競争者の為に、しかも頓く宮を奪はれし貫一が心は如何
なりけん。身をも心をも打委せて許ることを知らざりし恋人の、忽ち敵の如く己に反きて、空く
他人に嫁するを見たる貫一が心は更に如何なりけん。彼はここに於いて曩に半箇の骨肉の親むべ
きなく、一点の愛情の温むるに会はざりし凄寥を感ずるのみにて止らず、失望を添へ、恨を累ね
て、かの塊然たる野末の石は、霜置く上に凩の吹誘ひて、皮肉を穿ち来る人生の酸味の到頭骨に
徹する一種の痛苦を悩みて已まざるなりき。実に彼の宮を奪れしは、その曽て与へられし物を取
去られし上に、与へられざりし物をも併せて取去られしなり。

彼は或はその恨を拋つべし、なんぞその失望をも忘れざらん。されども彼は永くその痛苦を去
らしむる能はざるべし、一旦太くその心を傷けられたるかの痛苦は、永くその心の存在と倶に存
在すべければなり。その業務として行はざるべからざる残忍刻薄を自ら強ふる痛苦は、能く彼の
痛苦と相剋して、その間聊か思を遣るべき余地を窘み得るに慣れて、彼は漸く忍ぶべからざるを
忍びて為し、恥づべきをも恥ぢずして行ひけるほどに、勁敵に遇ひ、悪徒に罹りて、或は弄ばれ
或は欺かれ、或は脅され、勢毒を以つて制し、暴を以つて易ふるの已むを得ざるより、一はその
道の習に薫染して、彼は益す懼れず貪るに至れるなり。同時に例の不断の痛苦は彼を撐つやうに

募ることありて、心も消々に悩まさるる毎に、醒醐利を趁ふ力も失せて、彼はなかなか死の安きを懐はざるにあらず。唯その一旦にして易く、又の空き死を遂げ了らんをば、いと効為しと思返して、よし遠くとも心に期するところは、なでう一度前の失望と恨とを露して、胸裡の涼きこと、氷を砕いて明鏡を磨くが如く為ざらん、その夕べ我は正に死ぬべきと私に慰むるなりき。

貫一は一ばかの痛苦を忘るる手段として、一はその妄執を散ずべき目的をもて、かくは高利を貪れるなり。知らず彼がその夕にして瞑せんとする快心の事とは何ぞ。彼は尋常復讐の小術を成して、宮に富山に鳴沢に人身的攻撃を加へて快を取らんとにはあらず、今少く事の大きく男らしくあらんをば企図せるなり。然れども、痛苦の劇く、懐旧の恨に堪へざる折々、彼は熱き涙を握りて祈るが如く嘆ちぬ。

「唉、こんな思を為るくらゐなら、いっそ潔く死んだ方が遥かに勝だ。死んでさへ了へば万慮空くこの苦艱は無いのだ。それを命が惜くもないのに死にもせず……死ぬのは易いが、死ぬことの出来んのは、どう考へても余り無念で、この無念をこのままに胸に納めて死ぬことは出来ないのだ。人に言はせたら、高が一人の女の宮に換へる貨が有つたら何が面白いのだ。今俺の貯へた貨は、高が一人の女の宮に換へる価はあると謂ふだらう。俺には無い！　第一貨などを持つてゐるやうな気持さへ為んぢやないか。失望した身にはその望を取復すほどの宝は無いのだ。唉、その宝は到底取復されん。宮が今罪を詫びて夫婦になりたいと泣き付いて来たとしても、一旦心を変じて、身まで瀆された宮は、決して旧の宮ではなければ、もう間の宝ではない。間の宝は五年前の宮だ。その宮は宮の自身さ

へ取復す事は出来ぬのだ。返す返す恋いのは宮だ。かうしてゐる間も宮の事は忘れかねる、けれど、それは富山の妻になつてゐる今の宮ではない、噫、鴫沢の宮！　五年前の宮が恋い。俺が百万円を積んだところで、昔の宮は獲られんのだ！　思へば貨もつまらん。少いながらも今の貨が熱海へ追つて行つた時の鞄の中に在つたなら……え！！

頭も打割るるやうに覚えて、この以上を想ふ能はざる貫一は、ここに到りて自失し了るを常とす。かかる折よ、熱海の浜に泣倒れし鴫沢の娘と、田鶴見の庭に逍遙せし富山が妻との姿は、双貫一が身辺を彷徨して去らざるなり。彼はこの痛苦の堪ふべからざるをも為して、ほとほと前後を顧ずして他の一方に事を為すより、往々その性の為す能はざるに任せて、仮さざること仇敵の如く、債務を蹇りて酷を極むるなり。退いてはこれを悔ゆるも、又折に触れて激すれば、忽ち勢に駆られて断行するを得べく、素より彼は正を知らずして邪を為し、是を喜ばずして非を為す苦をもその間に忘るるを得べく、己を枉げてこれを行ふ心苦しさは俯して愧ぢ、仰ぎて懼れ、天地の間に身を置くとき、猶潤きを覚ゆるなれど、かの痛苦に較べては、竟に忍ぶものにあらざれば、總じてその容るる空間だに猶潤きを覚ゆるなりけり。

一向に神を労し、思を費して、日夜これを暢るに違あらぬ貫一は、肉痩せ、骨立ち、色疲れて、宛然死水などのやうに沈鬱し了んぬ。その攪めたる眉と空く凝せる目とは、体力の漸く衰ふるに反して、精神の愈よ興奮するとともに、思の益す繁く、益す乱るるを、従ひて耎り、従ひて解か

んとすれば、なほも繁り、なほも乱るるを、竟に如何に為ばや、と心も砕けつつ打悩めるを示せり。更に見よ、漆のやうに鮮潤なりし髪は、後脳の辺に若干の白きを交へて、額に催せし皺の一筋長く横はれるぞ、その心の窄れる髣ならざるべき、況んや彼の面を蔽へる蔭は益々暗きにあらずや。

吁、彼はその初一念を遂げて、外面に、内心に、今は全くこの世からなる魔道に墜つるを得たりけるなり。貪欲界の雲は凝り歩々に厚く護り、離恨天の雨は随所直に灑ぐ、一飛一躍出でては人の肉を啖ひ、半生半死入りては我と腸を劈く。居る所は陰風常に廻りて白日を見ず、行けども無明の長夜今に到るまで一千四百六十日、逢へども可懐き友の面を知らず、交れども曾て情の蜜より甘きを知らず、花咲けども春日の麗なるを知らず、楽来れども打背きて歓ぶを知らず、道あれども履むを知らず、善あれども与するを知らず、福あれども招くを知らず、恵あれども享くるを知らず、空く利欲に耽りて志を喪ひ、偏に迷執に弄ばれて思を労らす、吁、彼は終に何をか成さんとすらん。間貫一の名は漸く同業者間に聞えて、恐るべき彼の未来を属目せざるはあらずなりぬ。

かの堪ふべからざる痛苦と、この死をも快くせんとする目的とあるが為に、貫一の漸く頼なる厳談酷促は自から此処に彼処に債務者の怨を買ひて、彼の為に泣き、彼の為に憤るもの寡からず、同業者といへども時としては彼の余に用捨無きを咎むるさへありけり。独り鰐淵はこれを喜びて、強将の下弱卒を出さざるを誇れるなり。彼は己の今日あるを致せし辛抱と苦労とは、未だ如

此くにして足るものならずとて、屢ばその例を挙げては貫一を嗤し、飽くまで彼の意を強ひせんと勉めき。これが為に慰めらるとにはあらねど、その行へる残忍酷薄の人の道に欠けたるを知らざるにあらぬ貫一は、職業の性質既に不法なればこれを営むの非道なるは必然の理にて、己の為すところは都ての同業者の為すところにて、己一人の残刻なるにあらず、高利貸なる者は、世間一様に如此く残刻ならざるべからずと念へるなり。故に彼は決して己の所業のみ独り怨を買ふべきにあらずと信じたり。

実に彼の頼める鰐淵直行の如きは、彼の辛うじてその半を想ひ得る残刻と、終に学ぶ能はざる譎詐とを左右にして、始めて今日の富を得てしなり。この点に於ては彼は一も二も無く貫一の師表たるべしといへども、その実さばかりの残刻と譎詐とを擅にして、なほ天に畏れず、人に憚らざる不敵の傲骨あるにあらず。彼は密に警めて多く夜出でず、内には神を敬して、得知れぬ教会の大信徒となりて、奉納寄進に財を吝まず、唯これ身の無事を祈るに汲々として、自ら安ずるところと仕へ奉る御神の冥護を辱なみて措かざるなりき。貫一は彼の如く残刻と譎詐とに勇ならざりけれど、又彼の如く敬神と閉居とに怯ならず、身は人と生れて人がましく行ひ、一も曾て犯せる事のあらざりしに、天は却りて己を罰し人は却りて己を詐り、終生の失望と遺恨とは濫に断腸の斧を揮ひて、死苦の若かざる絶痛を与ふるを思ひては、彼はよし天に人に憤るところある

第　八　章

用談果つるを俟ちて貫一の魚膠無く暇乞するを、満枝は暫しと留置きて、用有りげに奥の間にぞ入りたる。その言の如く暫し待てども出で来ざれば、又巻莨を取出しけるに、手炉の炭は狼の糞のやうになりて、いつか火の気の絶えたるに、檀座に毛糸の敷物したる石笠のランプの燄を仮りて、貫一は為む事無しに煙を吹きつつ、この赤樫の客間を夜目ながら眴しつ。

袋棚なる置時計は十時十分前を指せり。違棚には箱入の人形を大小二つ並べて、その下は七宝焼擬の一輪挿、蠟石の飾玉を水色縮緬の三重の褥に載せて、床柱なる水牛の角の懸花入は松に隼の勧工場蒔絵金々として、花を見ず。鋳物の香炉の悪古びに玄ませたると、羽二重細工の花筐とを床に飾りて、雨中の富士をば引攪旋したるやうに落墨して、金泥精描の臕竜は目貫を打つたかとばかり雲間に躍ける横物の一幅。頭を回らせば、欄間に黄海大海戦の一間程なる水彩画を掲げて座敷の隅には二鉢の菊を据ゑたり。

やや有りて出来れる満枝は服を改めたるなり。糸織の衿懸けたる小袖に納戸小紋の縮緬の羽織着て、七糸と黒繻子との昼夜帯して、華美なるシオウルを携へ、髪など撫付けしと覚く、面も見違ふやうに軽く粧ひて、

「大変失礼を致しました。些と私も其処まで買物に出ますので、実は御一緒に願はうと存じま

無礼なりとは思ひけれど、口説れし誼に貫一は今更腹も立て難くて、

「ああさうですか」

満枝はつと寄りて声を低くし、

「御迷惑でうらっしやいませうけれど」

聴き飽きたりと謂はんやうに彼は取合はで、

「それぢや参りませう。貴方は何方までお出なのですか」

「私は大横町まで」

二人は打連れて四谷左門町なる赤樫の家を出でぬ。伝馬町通は両側の店に燈を列ねて、未だ宵なる景気なれど、秋としも覚えず夜寒の甚ければ、往来も稀に、空は星あれどいと暗し。

「何といふお寒いのでございませう」

「さやう」

「貴方、間家さん、貴方そんなに離れてお歩き遊ばさなくても宜いぢやございませんか。それではお話が遠きませんわ」

彼は町の左側をこたびは貫一に擦寄りて歩めり。

「これぢや私が歩き難いです」

「貴方お寒うございませう。私お鞄を持ちませう」

「いいや、どういたして」

「貴方恐入りますが、もう少し御緩りお歩きなすつて下さいましな、私呼吸が切れて……」

已む無く彼は加減して歩めり。満枝は着重るショウルを揺上げて、

「疾から是非お話致したいと思ふ事があるのでございますけれど、その後些ともお目に掛らない、ものですから。聞さん、貴方、本当には偶にはお遊びにいらしつて下さいましな。些といらしつて下さいましな」

達而のやうな事は再び申上げませんから。私もう決して先

「は、難有う」

「お手紙を上げましても宜うございますか」

「何の手紙ですか」

「御機嫌伺の」

「貴方から機嫌を伺はれる訳が無いぢやありませんか」

「では、恋い時に」

「貴方が何も私を……」

「恋いのは私の勝手でございますよ」

「然し、手紙は人にでも見られると面倒ですから、お辞をします」

「でも近日に私お話を致したい事があるのでございますから、私はこれ程困つた事はございませんの。で、是非貴方に御相談を願はうと存じまして、……」

唯見れば伝馬町三丁目と二丁目との角なり。貫一はここにて満枝を撤かんと思ひ設けたるなれ

ば、彼の語り続くるをも会釈為ずして立住りつ。

「それぢや私はここで失礼します」

その不意に出でて貫一の闇き横町に入るを、

「あれ、貴方、其方からいらっしやるのですか。この通をいらっしやいましたね、わざわざ、そ

んな寂しい道をお出なさらなくても、此方の方が順ではございませんか」

満枝は離れ難なく二三間追ひ行きたり。

「なあに、此方が余程近いのですから」

「幾多も違ひは致しませんのに、賑かな方をいらっしやいましよ。私その代り四谷見附の所まで

お送り申しますから」

「貴方に送って戴いたって為やうが無い。夜が更けますから、貴方も早く買物を為すってお帰り

なさいまし」

「そんなお為転を有仰らなくても宜うございます」

かく言争ひつつ、行くにもあらねど留るにもあらぬ貫一に引添ひて、不知不識其方に歩ませら

れし満枝は、やにはに立竦みて声を揚げつ。

「ああ！　間さん些と」

「どうしました」

「路悪へ入つて了つて、履物が取れないのでございますよ」

「それだから貴方はこんな方へお出でなさらんが可いのに」

彼は渋々寄り来れり。

「憚様ですが、この手を引張つて下さいました。ああ、早く、私転びますよ」

シオウルの外に援を求むる彼の手を取りて引寄すれば、女は踊きつつ泥濘を出でたりしが、力や余りけん、身を支へかねて撞と貫一に靠れたり。

「ああ、危い」

「転びましたら貴方の所為でございますよ」

「馬鹿なことを」

彼はこの時扶けし手を放たんとせしに、釘付などにしたらんやうに曳けども振れども得離れざるを、怪しと女の面を窺へるなり。満枝は打背けたる顔の半をシオウルの端に包みて、握れる手をば弥よ固く緊めたり。

「さあ、もう放して下さい」

益す緊めて袖の中へさへ曳入れんとすれば、

「貴方、馬鹿な事をしては可けません」

女は一語も言はず、面も背けたるままに、その手は益放たで男の行く方に歩めり。

「常談しちや可かんですよ。さあ、後から人が来る」

「宜うございますよ」

独語つやうに言ひて、満枝は弥寄添ひつ。貫一は怜へかねて力任せに吽と曳けば、手は離れ

ずして、女の体のみ倒れかかりぬ。

「あ、痛！　そんな酷い事をなさらなくても、其処の角まで参ればお放し申しますから、もう少

しの間どうぞ……」

「好い加減になさい」

と密かに引払ひて、寄らんとする隙もあらせず摩脱くるより足を痛めて津守坂を驀直に下りた

り。

姿も終に見えず。

やうやう昇れる利鎌の月は乱雲を芟りて、迥き楢の頂に怙く掛れり。一抹の闇を透きて士官

学校の森と、その中なる兵営と、その隣なる町の片割とは、懶く寝覚めたるやうに覚束なき形を

顕しぬ。坂上なる巡査派出所の燈は空く血紅の光を射て、下り行きし男の影も、取残されし女の

　　（八）の　二

片側町なる坂町は軒並に鎖して、何処に隙洩るる火影も見えず、旧砲兵営の外柵に生茂る群松は

颯々の響を作して、その下道の小暗き空に五位鷺の魂切る声消えて、夜色愁ふるが如く、正に十

一時に垂んとす。

忽ち兵営の門前に方りて人の叫ぶが聞えぬ、間貫一は二人の曲者に囲はれたるなり。一人は黒の中折帽の鍔を目深に引下し、鼠色の毛糸の袵巻に半面を裹み、黒足袋に木裏の雪踏を履き、六分強なる色木の弓の折を杖にした州ネルの下穿高々と尻褰して、黒キャリコの紋付の羽織の下に紀り。他は盲縞の股引腹掛に、唐棧の半纏着て、茶ツックの深靴を穿ち、衿巻の頬冠に鳥撃帽子を頂きて、六角に削成したる檳榔子の逞きステッキを引抱き、いづれも身材貫一よりは低けれど、血気腕力兼備と見えたる壮佼どもなり。

「物取か。恨を受ける覚は無いぞ！」

「黙れ！」と弓の折の寄るを貫一は片手に障へて、

「僕は間貫一といふ者だ。恨があらば尋常に敵手にならう。物取ならば財はくれる、訳も言はずに無法千万な、待たんか！」

答は無くて揮下したる弓の折は貫一が高頬を発矢と打つ。眩きつつも迯行くを、猛然と追迫る檳榔子は、件の杖もて片手突に肩の辺を曳と突いたり。踏み耐へんとせし貫一は水道工事の鉄道に跌きて仆るるを、得たりと附入る曲者は、余に躍りて貫一の仆れたるに又跌き、一間ばかりの彼方に反跳を打ちて投飛されぬ。入替りて一番手の弓の折は貫一の背を袈裟掛に打据ゑければ、起きも得せで、崩折るるを、畳みかけんとする隙に、手元に脱捨てたりし駒下駄を取るより早く、彼の面を望みて投げたるが、丁と中りて癈むその時、貫一は蹴起きて三歩ばかりも迯れしを打転けし檳榔子の躍り蒐りて、拝打に下せる杖は小鬢を掠り、肩を辷りて、鞄持つ手を断れ

んとすばかりに撲ちけるを、辛くも忍びてつと退きながら身構しが、目潰吃ひし一番手の怒を作して奮進し来るを見るより今は危しと鞄の中なる小刀撈りつつ馳出づるを、報く肉薄せる二人が筈は雨の如く、所嫌はぬ滅多打に、彼は敢無くも昏倒せるなり。

檳「どうです、もう可いに為ませうか」

弓「此奴おれの鼻面へ下駄を打着けよった、ああ、痛」

衿巻掻除けて彼の撫でたる鼻は朱に染みて、西洋蕃椒の熟えたるに異らず。

檳「おお、大変な腫ですぜ」

貫一は息も絶々ながら緊と鞄を掻抱き、右の逆手に小刀を隠し持ちて、この上にも狼藉に及ばば為んやう有りと、油断を計りてわざと為す無き体を装ひ、直呻きにぞ呻きゐたる。

弓「憎い奴じゃ。然し、随分撲ったの」

檳「ええ、手が痛くなつて了ひました」

弓「もう引揚げやう」

かくて曲者は間近の横町に入りぬ。辛うじて面を擡げ得たりし貫一は、一時に発せる全身の疼痛に、精神漸く乱れて、屡ば前後を覚えざらんとす。

後　編

第　一　章

翌々日の諸新聞は坂町に於ける高利貸遭難の一件を報道せり。中に間貫一を誤りて鰐淵直行と為るもありしが、負傷者は翌日大学第二医院に入院したりとのみは、一様に事実の真を伝ふるなりけり。されどその人を誤れる報道は決して何等の不都合をも生ぜざるべし。彼等を識らざる読者は湯屋の喧嘩も同じく、三ノ面記事の常套として看過すべく、何の違かその敵手の誰々なるをか問はん。識れる者は恐くは、貫一も鰐淵も一つに足腰の利かずなるまで撃蹈されざりしを本意無く思へるなるべし。又或者は彼の即死せざりしをも物足らず覚ゆるなるべし。下手人は不明なれども、察するに貸借上の遺趣より為せる業ならんとは、諸新聞の記せる如く、人も皆思ふところなりけり。

直行は今朝病院へ見舞に行きて、妻は患者の容体を案じつつ留守せるなり。夫婦は心を協せて貫一の災難を悲み、何程の費をも容まず手宛の限を加へて、少小の癒をも遺さざらんと祈るなり

き。

股肱と恃み、我子とも思へる貫一の遭難を、主人はなかなかその身に受けし闇打のやうに覚えて、無念の止み難く、かばかりの事に屈する鰐淵ならね令見の為に、彼が入院中を目覚くも厚く賄ひて、再び手出しもならざらんやう、陰ながら卑怯者の息の根を遏めんと、気も狂く力を竭せり。

彼の妻は又、やがてはかかる不慮の事の夫の身にも出で来るべきを思過して、若しさるべからんには如何にか為べき、この悲しさ、この口惜さにては止まじと思ふに就けて、空可恐し胸の打騒ぐを禁め得ず。奉公大事ゆゑに怨を結びて、憂き目に遭ひし貫一は、夫の禍を転じて身の仇とせし可憐さを、日頃の手柄に増して浸々難有く、かれを念ひ、これを思ひて、絶に心弱くのみ成行くほどに、裏に愧づること、懼るること、疚きことなどの常に抑へたるが、忽ち涌立ち、跳出でて、その身を貴むる痛苦に堪へざるなりき。

年久く飼るる老猫の凡そ子狗ほどなるが、棄てたる雪の塊のやうに長火鉢の猫板の上に蹲りて、前足の襲落して爪頭の灰に埋るるをも知らず、駒をさへ掻き入れて熟睡したり。妻はその夜の騒擾、次の日の気労に、血の道を悩める心地にて、慵々となりては驚かされつつありける耳元に、格子の鐸の轟きければ、はや夫の帰来かと疑ひも果てぬに、紙門を開きて顕せる姿は、年紀二十六七と見えて、身材は高からず、色やや蒼き痩顔の険しげに口髭遅く、髪の生ひ乱れたるに深と紺ネルトンの二重外套の襟を立てて、黒の中折帽を脱ぎて手にしつ。高き鼻に鼈甲縁の眼鏡

を挿みて、稜ある眼色の中に喜を漾へて、面色の中に喜を漾へて、稜ある眼色は見る物毎に恨あるが如し。

妻は思設けぬ面色の中に喜を漾へて、

「まあ直道かい、好くお出だね」

片隅に外套を脱捨つれば、彼は黒綾のモオニングの新からぬに、濃納戸地に黒縞の穿袴の寛なるを着けたり、清ならぬ護謨のカラ、カフ、鼠色の紋繻子の頸飾したり。妻は得々起ちて、その外套を柱の折釘に懸けつ。

「どうも取んだ事で、阿父さんの様子はどんな？　今朝新聞を見ると愕いて飛んで来たのです」

容体はどうです」

彼は時儀を叙ぶるに追ばずして忙しげにとかく問出でぬ。

「ああ新聞で、さうだつたかい。なあに阿父さんはどうも作りはしないわね」

「はあ？　坂町で大怪我を為つて、病院へ入つたと云ふのは？」

「あれは聞さ。阿父さんだとお思ひなの？　可厭だね、どうしたと云ふのだらう」

「いや、さうですか。でも、新聞には歴然とさう出てるましたよ」

「それぢやその新聞が違つてるのだよ。阿父さんは先之病院へ見舞にお出掛だから、間も無くお帰来だらう。まあ寛々してお在な」

かくと開ける直道は余の不意に拍子抜して、喜びも得為ず噁然たるのみ。

「ああ、さうですか、間が遣られたのですか」

「ああ、間が可哀さうにねえ、取んだ災難で、大怪我をしたのだよ」

「どんなです、新聞には余程劇いやうに出てゐましたが」

「新聞に在る通だけれど、不具になるやうな事も無いさうだが、全然快くなるには三月ぐらゐは

どんな事をしても要るといふ話だよ。誠に気の毒な、それで、阿父さんも大抵な心配ぢやない

の。まあ、ね、病院も上等へ入れて手宛は十分にしてあるのだから、決して気遣は無いやうなも

のだけれど、何しろ大怪我だからね。左の肩の骨が少し攫けたとかで、手が緩縦になつて了つた

の、その外紫色の疵だの、蚯蚓腫だの、打切れたり、擦毀したやうな負傷は、お前、体一面なの

さ。それに気絶するほど頭部を撲れたのだから、脳病でも出なければ可いつて、お医者様もさう

言つてお在だそうだけれど、今のところではそんな塩梅も無いさうだよ。何しろその晩内へ舁込

んだ時は半死半生で、些の虫の息が通つてゐるばかり、私は一目見ると、これはとても助るまい

と想つたけれど、割合に人間といふものは丈夫なものだね」

「それは災難な、気の毒な事をしましたな。まあ十分に手宛をして遣るが可いです。さうして阿

父さんは何と言つてゐるました」

「何ととは？」

「間が闇打にされた事を」

「いづれ敵手は貸金の事から遺趣を持つて、その悔し紛に無法な真似をしたのだらうつて、大相

腹を立ててお在なのだよ。全くね、間はああ云ふ不断の大人い人だから、つまらない喧嘩なぞを

為る気遣はなし、何でもそれに違は無いのさ。それだから猶更気の毒で、何とも謂ひやうが無い」

「間は若いから、それでも助るのです、阿父さんであつたら命は有りませんよ、阿母さん」

「まあ可厭なことをお言ひでないな！」

浸々思入りたりし直道は徐にその恨き目を挙げて、

「阿母さん、阿父さんは未だこの家業をお廃めなさる様子は無いのですかね」

母は苦しげに鈍り鈍りて、

「さうねえ……別に何とも……私には能く解らないね……」阿母さん、間があんな目に遭つたのは、決して人事ぢやありませんよ」

「もう今に応報は阿父さんにも……」

「お前又阿父さんの前でそんな事をお言ひでないよ」

「言ひます！　今日は是非言はなければならない」

「それは言ふも可いけれど、従来も随分お言ひだけれど、あの気性だから阿父さんは些もお聴きではないぢやないか。とても他の言ふこととなんぞは聴かない人なのだから、まあ、もう少しお前も目を瞑つておいて、よ」

「私だつて親に向つて言ひたくはありません。大概の事なら目を瞑つてゐたいのだけれど、実にこればかりは目を瞑つてゐられないのですから。始終さう思ひます。私は外に何も苦労といふも無い、唯これだけが苦労で、考出すと夜も寝られないのです。外にどんな苦労が在つても可

いから、どうかこの苦労だけは没して了ひたいと熟く思ふのです。　噫、こんな事なら未だ親子で乞食をした方が寧に可い」

彼は涙を浮べて倆きぬ。　母はその身も倶に責めらるる想して、或は可憐く、或は可忌く、この苦き位置に在るに塋へかねゐつつ、言解かん術さへ無けれど、とにもかくにも言はで已むべき折ならねば、辛じて打出しつ。

「それはもうお前の言ふのは尤だけれど、お前と阿父さんとは全で気合が違ふのだから、万事考量が別々で、お前の言ふ事は阿父さんの肚には入らず、ね、又阿父さんの為る事はお前には不承知と謂ふので、その中へ入つて私も困るわね。内も今では相応にお財も出来たのだから、かう云ふ家業は廃めて、楽隠居になつて、孫の顔でも見たい、とさう思ふのだけれど、ああ云ふ気の阿父さんだから、そんなことを言出さうものなら、どんなに慍られるだらうと、それが見え透いてゐるから、漫然した事は言はれずさ、お前の心を察して見れば可哀さうではあり、さうかと云つて何方をどうすることも出来ず、陰で心配するばかりで、何の役にも立たないながら、これでなかなか苦いのは私の身だよ。

さぞお前は気も済まなからうけれど、とても今のところでは何と言つたところが、応と承知をしさうな様子は無いのだから、慫ひ言合つてお互に心持を悪くするのが果だから、……それは、お前、何と云つたつて親一人子一人の中だもの、阿父さんだつて心ぢやどんなにお前が便だか知れやしないのだから、究竟はお前の言ふ事も聴くのは知れてゐるのだし、阿父さんだつて現在の

子のそんなにまで思つてゐるのを、決して心に掛けないのではないけれども、又阿父さんの方にも其処には了簡があつて、一概にお前の言ふ通にも成りかねるのだらう。

それに今日あたりは、間の事で大変気が立つてゐるところだから、お前が何か言ふと却つて善くないから、今日は窃として措いておくれ、よ、本当に私が頼むから、ねえ直道」

実に母は自ら言へりし如く、板挾の難局に立てるなれば、ひたすら事あらせじと、誠の一図に直道を諭すなりき。彼は涙の催すに堪へずして、鼻目鏡を取捨てて目を推拭ひつつ猶咽びゐたり

しが、

「阿母さんにさう言れるから、私は不断は怺へてゐるのです。今日ばかり存分に言はして下さい。今日言はなかつたら言ふ時は有りませんよ。間のそんな目に遭つたのは天罰です、この天罰は阿父さんも今に免れんことは知れてゐるから、言ふのなら今、今言はんくらゐなら私はもう一生言ひません」

母はその一念に脅されけんやうにて漫寒きを覚えたり。　潸打去みて直道は語を継ぎぬ。

「然し私の仕打も善くはありません、阿父さんの方にも言分は有らうと、意見をしても用ゐない、こんな汚れた家業を為るのを見てゐるのが可厭だ、と親を棄てて別居してゐると云ふのは、如何にも情合の無い話で、実に私も心苦いのです。決して人の子たる道ではない、さぞ不孝者と阿父さん始阿母さんもさう思つてお在でせう」

「さうは思ひはしないよ。お前の方にも理はあるのだから、さうは思ひはしないけれど、一処に居たらさぞ好からうとは……」

「それは、私は猶の事です。こんな内に居るのは可厭だ、別居して独で遣る、と我儘を言つて、どうなりかうなり自分で暮して行けるのも、それまでに教育して貰つたのは誰のお陰かと謂へば、皆親の恩。それもこれも知つてゐながら、阿父さんを踏付にしたやうな行を為るのは、阿母さん能々の事だと思つて下さい。私は親に悖ぶのぢやない、阿父さんと一処に居るのを嫌ふのぢやないが、私は金貸などと云ふ賤い家業が大嫌なのです。人を悩めて己を肥す──浅ましい家業です!」

身を顕はして彼は涙に掻沮れたり。母は居久らぬまでに惑へるなり。

「親を過すほどの芸も無くて、生意気な事ばかり言つて実は面目も無いのです。然し不自由を辛抱してさへ下されば、両親ぐらゐに乾いた思はきつと為せませんから、清く暮したいぢやありませんか。まして非道をして捭へた貨、世の中は貨が有つたから、それで可い訳のものぢやありませんよ。無理に仕上げた身上は一代持たそんな貨が何の頼になるものですか、必ず悪銭身に附かずです。無理に仕上げた身上は一代持たずに滅びます。因果の報う例は恐るべきものだから、一日でも早くこんな家業は廃めるに越した事はありません。噫、末が見えてるのに、情無い事ですなあ!

積悪の応報覿面の末を憂ひて措かざる直道が心の眼は、無残にも怨の刃に劈れて、路上に横

死の恥を暴せる父が死顔の、犬に蹴られ、泥に塗れて、古蓆の陰に枕せるを、怪くも歴々と見て、恐くは我が至誠の鑑は父が未然を宛然映し出して謬らざるにあらざるかと、事の目前の真にあらざるを知りつつも、母は驚き、途方に昏れたる折しも、門に俥の駐りて、格子の鐶の鳴るは夫の帰来か、次手悪しと胸を轟かして、直道の肩を揺り動しつつ、声を潜めて口早に、

「直道、阿父さんのお帰来だから、泣いてゐちや可けないよ、……よ、今日は後生だから何も言はずに……」

はや足音は次の間に来りぬ。母は慌てて出迎に起てば、一足遅れに紙門は外より開れて主直行の高く幅たき軀は岸然とお客の肩越に顕れぬ。

　（一）の　二

「おお、直道か珍いの。何時来たのか」

かく言ひつつ彼は艶々と緑みたる鉢割の広き額の陰に小く点せる金壺眼を心快げに瞪きて、妻が例の如く外套を脱するままに立てり。お峯は直道が言に稜あらんことを慮りて、さり気無く自ら代りて答へつ。

「もう少し先でした。貴君は大相お早かつたちやありませんか、丁度好ございましたこと。さうして間の容体はどんなですね」

黒一楽の三紋付けたる綿入羽織の衣紋を直して、彼は機嫌好く火鉢の傍に歩み寄る時、直道は漸く面を抗げて礼を作せり。

「いや、仕合と想うたよりは怪くての、まあ、ま、あの分なら心配は無いて」

「お前、どうした、ああ、妙な顔をしてをるでないか」梭欄の毛を植ゑたりやとも見ゆる口髭を掻拈りて、太短なる眉を簪むれば、聞ゐる妻は呀とばかり、刃を踏める心地も為めり。直道は屹と振仰ぐとともに両手を胸に組合せて、居長高になりけるが、父の面を見し目を伏せて、さて徐に口を開きぬ。

「今朝新聞を見ましたところが、阿父さんが、大怪我を為つたと出てをつたので、早速お見舞に参つたのです」

白髪を交へたる茶褐色の髪の頭に置余るばかりなるを撫でて、直行は、

「何新聞か知らんけれど、それは間の間違ぢやが。俺ならそんな場合に出会うたて、唯々打れちやをりやせん。何の先は二人でないかい、五人までは敵手にしてくれるが」

直道の隣に居たる母は密に彼のコオトの裾を引きて、言を返させじと心着るなり。これが為に彼は少しく遅ひめぬ。

「本にお前どうした、顔色が良うないが」

「さうですか。余り貴方の事が心配になるからです」

「何じや？」

「阿父さん、度々言ふ事ですが、もう金貸は廃めて下さいな」

「又！　もう言ふな。言ふな。廃める時分には廃めるわ」

「廃めなければならんやうになつて廃めるのは見ともない。今朝貴方が半死半生の怪我をしたといふ新聞を見た時、私はどんなにしても早くこの家業をお廃めなさるやうに為せなかつたのを熟く後悔したのです。幸に貴方は無事であつた、から猶更今日は私の意見を用ゐて貰はなければならんのです。今に阿父さんも間のやうな災難を必ず受けるです。それが可恐いから廃めると謂ふのぢやありません、正しい事で争つて殞す命ならば、決して辞することは無いけれど、金銭づくの事で怨を受けて、それ故に無法な目に遭ふのは、如何にも恥曝しではないですか。一つ間違へば命は失はなければならん、不具にも為されなければならん、阿父さんの身の上を考へると、私は夜も寝られんのですよ。

こんな家業を為んでは生活が出来んのではないし、阿父さん阿母さん二人なら、一生安楽に過せるほどの資産は既に有るのでせう、それに何を苦んで人には怨まれ、世間からは指弾をされて、無理な財を拵へんければならんのですか。何でそんなに金が要るのですか。誰にしても自身に足りる以外の財は、子孫に遺さうと謂ふより外は無いのでせう。貴方には貴方が一人子、その私は一銭たりとも貴方の財は譲られません！　欲くないのです。さうすれば、貴方は今日無用の財を貯へる為に、人の怨を受けたり、世に誹られたり、さうして現在の親子が讐のやうになつて、貴方にしてもこんな家業を決して名誉と思つて楽んで為つてゐるのではないのではないでせう。

私のやうなものでも可愛いと思つて下さるなら、財産を遺して下さる代に私の意見を聴いて下さい。

意見とは言ひません、私の願です。一生の願ですからどうぞ聴いて下さい」

父が前に頭を低れて、軽く抗げぬ彼の面は熱き涙に蔽るるなりき。

些も動ずる色無き直行は却つて微笑を帯びて、語をさへ和げつ。

「俺の身を思うてそんなに言うてくれるのは嬉しけど、お前のはそれは杞憂と謂ふんじや。俺と違うてお前は神経家ぢやからそんなに思ふんぢやけど、世間と謂ふものはの、お前の考へとるやうなものではない。学問の好きな頭脳で実業を遣る者の仕事を責むるのは、それは可かん。人の怨の、世の誚のと言ふけどの、我々同業者に対する人の怨などと云ふのは、面々の手前勝手の愚痴に過ぎんのじや。世の誚と云ふのは、多くは嫉、その証拠は、働の無い奴が貧乏しとれば慇まるじや。何家業に限らず、財を拵へる奴は必ず世間から何とか攻撃を受くる、さうぢやらう。財の有る奴で評判の好えものは一人も無い、その通じやが。お前は学者ぢやから自ら心持も違うて、財などをさう貴いものに思うてをらん。学者はさうなけりやならんけど、世間は皆学者ではないぞ、可えか。実業家の精神は唯財じや、世の中の奴の慾も財より外には無い。それほどに、のう、人の欲がる財じや、何ぞ好えところが無くてはならんぢやらう。何処が好えのか、何でそんなに好えのかは学者には解らん。

お前は自身に供給するに足るほどの財があつたら、その上に望む必要は無いと言ふのぢやな、自身に足るほどの物があつたら、それで可えと満足しそれが学者の考量じやと謂ふんじやが。

て了うてからに手を退くやうな了簡であつたら、国は忽ち亡るぢや——社会の事業は発達せんぢや。さうして国中若隠居ばかりになつて了うたと為れば、お前どうするか、あ。慾にきりの無いのが国民の生命なんぢや。

俺にそんなに財を拵へてどうするか、とお前は不審するじやね。俺はどうも為ん、財は余計にあるだけ愉快なんぢや。究竟財を拵へるが極めて面白いんぢや。お前の学問するのが面白い如く、俺は財の出来るが面白いんぢや。お前に本を読むのを好々加減に為い、一人前の学問が有つたらその上望む必要は有るまいと言うたら、お前何と答へる、あ。

お前は能うこの家業を不正ぢや、汚いのと言ふけど、財を儲くるに君子の道を行うてゆく商売が何処に在るか。我々が高利の金を貸す、如何にも高利ぢや、何為高利か、可えか、無抵当ぢや、そりや。借る方に無抵当といふ便利を与ふるから、その便利に対する報酬として利が高いのぢやらう。それで我々は決して利の高い金を安いと詐つて貸しはせんぞ。無抵当で貸すぢやから利が高い、それを承知で皆借るんぢや。そんな高利を借りても急を拯にや措れんくらゐの困難が様々にある今の社会ぢや、高利貸を不正と謂ふなら、その不正の高利貸を作つた社会が不正なんぢや。なんぼ貸したうて借る者が無けりや、我々の家業は成立ちは為ん。その必要を見込んで仕事を為るが則ち営業の魂なんぢや。必要の上から借る者があるで、貸す者がある。利が高うて不当と思ふなら、始から借らんが可え、そんな高利を借りても急を拯はにや措れんくらゐの困難が様々にある今の社会ぢや、その必要を見込んで仕事を為るが則ち営業の魂なんぢや。財といふものは誰でも愛して、皆獲やうと念うとる、獲たら離すまいと為とる、のう。その財

を人より多く持たうと云ふぢやもの、尋常一様の手段で行くものではない。合意の上で貸借して、それで儲くるのが不正なら、総ての商業は皆不正でないか。学者の目からは、金儲する者は皆不正な事をしとるんじや」

太くもこの弁論に感じたる彼の妻は、屡ば直道の顔を偸視て、あはれ彼が理窟もこれが為に挫けて、気遣ひたりし口論も無くて止みぬべきを想ひて私に懼べり。

直道は先づ厳に頭を掉りて、

「学者でも商業家でも同じ人間です。人間である以上は人間たる道は誰にしても守らんければなりません。私は決して金儲を為るのを悪いと言ふのではない、いくら儲けても可いから、正当に儲けるのです。人の弱みに付込つて高利を貸すのは、断じて正当でない。そんな事が営業の魂などとは……！　あれは先は二人で、しかも不意打を吃したのでせう、卑劣極る奴等だ貴方はあの所業を何とお考へなさる。男らしい遣趣返の為方とお思ひなさるか。卑劣極る奴等だと、さぞ無念にお思ひでせう？」

彼は声を昂げて逼れり。されども父は他を顧めて何等の答をも与へざりければ、再び声を鎮めて、

「どうですか」

「勿論」

「勿論？　勿論ですとも！　何奴か知らんけれど、実に陋い根性、劣な奴等です。然し、怨を返

すといふ点から謂つたら、奴等は立派に目的を達したのですね。さうでせう、設ひその手段は如何にあらうとも」

父は騒がず、笑を含みて赤き髭を弄りたり。

「卑劣と言れやうが、陋いと言れやうが、思ふさま遣趣返をした奴等は目的を達してさぞ満足してをるでせう。それを撲殺しても遣りたいほど悔いのは此方ばかり。

阿父さんの営業の主意も、彼等の為方と少しも違はんぢやありませんか。間の事に就いて無念だと貴方がお思ひなさるなら、貴方から金を借りて苦められる者は、やはり貴方を恨まずにはゐませんよ」

又しても感じ入りたるは彼の母なり。かくては如何なる言をもて夫はこれに答へんとすらん、我はこの理の観察当然なるに口を開かんやうも無きにと、心慌てつつ夫の気色を密に窺ひたり。

彼は自若として、却つてその子の善く論ずるを心に愛づらんやうの面色にて、転た微笑を弄するのみ。されども妻は能く知れり、彼の微笑を弄するは、必ずしも、人のこれを弄するにあらざる時に於いて屢するを。彼は今それか非ぬかを疑へるなり。

蒼く羸れたる直道が顔は可忌くも白き色に変じ、声は甲高に細りて、膝に置ける手頭は連りに震ひぬ。

「いくら論じたところで、解りきつた理窟なのですから、もう言ひますまい。言へば唯阿父さんの心持を悪くするに過ぎぬのです。然し、従来も度々言ひましたし、又今日こんなに言ふのも、

皆阿父さんの身を案じるからで、これに就いては陰でどれほど私が始終苦心してゐるか知つてお在は無からうけれど、考出すと勉強するのも何も可厭になつて、呀、いつそ山の中へでも引籠んで了はうかと思ひます。阿父さんはこの家業を不正でないとお言ひなさるが、実に世間でも地獄の獄卒のやうに憎み賤んで、附合ふのも恥にしてゐるのですよ。世間なんぞはかまふものか、と貴方はお言ひでせうが、子としてそれを聞かされる心苦しさを察して下さい。貴方はかまはんと謂ふその世間も、やはり我々が渡つて行かなければならん世間です。私はそれが何より悲い。此方に大見識があつて、それが世間と衝突して、その為に憎まれるとか、棄てられるとか謂ふなら、世間は終には容れられなくなるのは、男の面目ではありませんよ。私はそれが何より悲い。此方に大見識があつて、それが世間と衝突して、その為に憎まれるとか、棄てられるとか謂ふなら、世間は私を棄てんでも、私は親子の名誉、家の名誉と思ふのです。今我々親子の世間から疎れてゐるのは、自業自得の致すところで、不名誉の極です！」

眼は痛恨の涙を湧して、彼は覚えず父の面を睨みたり。直行は例の嘘けり。

直道は今日を限と思入りたるやうに言を止めず。

「今度の事を見ても、如何に間が恨まれてゐるかが解りませう。貴方の手代でさへあの通ではありませんか、して見れば貴方の受けてゐる恨、憎はどんなであるか言ふに忍びない」

父は忽ち遮りて、

「善し、解つた。能う解つた」

「では私の言を用ゐて下さるか」

「まあ可え。解つた、解つたから……」

「解つたとお言ひなさるからはきつと用ゐて下さるのでせうな」

「お前の言ふ事は能う解つたさ。然し、爾は爾たり、吾は吾たりじや」

直道は怏へかねて犇と拳を握れり。

「まだ若い、若い。書物ばかり見とるぢや可かん、少しは世間も見い。なるほど子の情として親の身を案じてくれる、その点は空には思はん。お前の心中も察する、意見も解つた。然し、俺は俺で又自ら信ずるところあつて遣るんぢやから、折角の忠告ぢやからと謂うて、枉げて従ふ訳にはいかんで、のう。今度間があゝ云ふ目に遭うたから、俺は猶更劇しい目に遭はうと謂うて、心配してくれるんか、あ?」

はや言ふも益無しと観念して直道は口を開かず。

「そりや辱いが、ま、当分俺の軀は俺に委して置いてくれ」

彼は徐に立上りて、

「些とこれから行て来にやならん処があるで、寛りして行くが可え」

忽忙と二重外套を打被ぎて出づる後より、帽子を持ちて送れる妻は密に出先を間へるなり。彼

「俺が居ると面倒ぢやから、些と出て来る。可えやうに言うての、還してくれい」

彼は大いなる鼻を蹙めて、

「へえ？　そりや困りますよ。　貴方、私だつてそれは困るぢやありませんか」

「まあ可えが」

「可くはありません、私は困りますよ」

お峯は足摩して迷惑を訴ふるなりけり。

「お前なら居ても可え。さうして、もう還るぢやらうから」

「それぢや貴方還るまでゐらしつて下さいな」

「俺が居ては還らんからじやが。　早う行けよ」

さすがに争ひかねてお峯の渋々停めるを、見も返らで夫は蓦地に門を出でぬ。母は直道の勢に怖れて先にも増してさぞや苛まるんと想へば、虎の尾をも履むらんやうに覚えつつ帰り来にけり。唯見れば、直道は手を拱き、頭を低れて、在りけるままに凝然と坐したり。

「もうお中食だが、お前何をお上りだ」

彼は身転も為ざるなり。重ねて、

「直道」と呼べば、始めて覚束なげに顔を挙げて、

「阿母さん！」

その術無き声は謂知らず母の胸を刺せり。彼はこの子の幼くて善く病める枕頭に居たりし心地をそのままに覚えて、ほとほとつと寄らんとしたり。

「それぢや私はもう帰ります」

「あれ何だね、未だ可いよ」

異くも遽に名残の惜れて、今は得も放たじと心牽るるなり。

「もうお中食だから、久しぶりで御膳を食べて……」

「御膳も吭へは通りませんから……」

第　二　章

主人公なる間貫一が大学第二医院の病室にありて、昼夜を重傷に悩める外、身辺に事あらざる暇に乗じて、富山に嫁ぎたる宮がその後の消息を伝ふべし。

一月十七日をもて彼は熱海の月下に貫一に別れ、その三月三日を択びて富山の家に興入したりき。その場より貫一の失踪せしは、鳴沢一家の為に物化の邪魔払たりしには疑無かりけれど、家内は挙りてさすがに騒動しき。その父よりも母よりも宮は更に切なる誠を籠めて心痛せり。彼はただに棄てざる恋を棄ててにし悔に泣くのみならず、寄辺あらぬ貫一が身の安否を慮りて措く能はざりしなり。

気強くは別れにけれど、やがて帰り来んと頼めし心待も、終に空なるを眺りし後、さりとも今一度は仮初にも相見んことを願ひ、又その心の奥には、必ずさばかりの逢瀬は有るべきを、おのれと契りけるに、彼の行方は知られずして、その身の家を出づべき日は潮の如く迫れるに、遣方

も無く漫惑ひては、常に鈍う思ひ下せるト者にも問ひて、後には廻合ふべきも、今はなかなか文に便ならじと教へられしを、筆持つは篤なる人なれば、長き長き怨言などは告来さんと、それのみは掌を指すばかりに待ちたりしも、疑ひしト者の言は不幸にも過たで、宮は彼の怨言をだに聞くを得ざりしなり。

とにもかくにも今一目見ずば動かじと始に念ひ、それは怜はずなりてより、せめて一筆の便聞かずばと更に念ひしに、事は心と渾て違ひて、さしも願はぬ一事のみは玉を転ずらんやうに何等の障も無く捗取りて、彼が空く貫一の便を望みし一日にも似ず、三月三日は怨ち頭の上に跳り来れるなりき。彼は終に心を許し肌身を許せし初恋を擲ちて、絶痛絶苦の悶々の中に一生最も楽かるべき大礼を挙げ畢んぬ。

宮は実に貫一に別れてより、始めて己の如何ばかり彼に恋せしかを知りけるなり。彼の出でて帰らざる恋しさに堪へかねたる夕、宮はその机に倚りて思ひ、その衣の人香を嗅ぎて悶え、その写真に頬摩して憧れ、彼若し己を容れて、ここに優き便をだに聞せなば、親をも家をも振捨てて、直に彼に奔るべきものをと念へり。結納の交されし日も宮は富山唯継を夫と定めたる心はつゆ起らざりき。されど、己は終にその家に適くべき身たるを忘れざりしなり。彼は別れし後の貫一をばさばかりほとほと自らその緒を索むる能はざるまでに宮は心を乱しぬ。恋托びつつも心を貫かんとにはあらず、由無き縁をり慕ひて止まざりしかど、過を改め、操を守り、覚悟してその恋を全うせんとは計らざりけるよ。

真に彼の胸に惇める覚悟とてはあらざりき。恋托びつつも心を貫かんとにはあらず、由無き縁を

組まんとしたるよと思ひつつも、強ひて今更否まんとするにもあらず、彼方の恋しきを思ひ、こなたの富めるを愛み、自ら決するところ無く、為すところ無くして空き迷に弄ばれつつ、終に移すべからざる三月三日の来るに会へるなり。

この日よ、この夕よ、更けて床盃のその期に迫びても、怪むべし、宮は決して富山唯継を夫と定めたる心は起らざるにぞありける、止この人を夫と定めざるべからざる我身を忘れざりしかど。彼は自ら謂へり、この心は始より貫一に許したるを、縁ありて身は唯継に委すなり。故に身は唯継に委すとも、心は長く貫一を忘れず、かく謂へる宮はこの心事の不徳なるを知れり。されどこの不徳のその身に免るる能はざる約束なるべきを信じて、寧ろ深く怪むにもあらざりき。

如此にして宮は唯継の妻となりぬ。

花賀君は彼を愛するに二念無く、彼を遇するに全力を挙げたり。宮はその身の上の日毎輝き勝るるままに、いよいよ意中の人と私すべき陰無くなりゆくを見て、愈よ楽まざる心は、夫の愛を承くるに怖くて、唯機械の如く事ふるに過ぎざりしも、唯継は彼の言ふ花の姿、温き玉の容を一向に愛で悦ぶ余に、冷かに空き器を抱くに異らざる妻を擁して、殆ど憎むべきまでに得意の願を撫づるなりき。彼が一段の得意は、二箇月の後最愛の妻は妊りて、翌年の春美き男子を挙げぬ。

宮は我とも覚えず浅ましがりて、産後を三月ばかり重く病みけるが、その癒ゆる日を竢たで、初つ子はいと弱くて肺炎の為に歿りにけり。

子を生みし後も宮が色香はつゆ移はずして、自ら可悩き風情の添りたるに、夫が愛護の念は

益〻深く、寵は人目の見苦きばかり弥〻加るのみ。

始より唯その色を見て、打沈みたる生得と独合点して多く間はざるなりけり。彼はその妻の常に楽まざる故を毫も暁らず、

かく怜まれつつも宮が初一念は動かんともせで、難有き人の情に負きて、ここに嫁ぎし罪をさへ歎きて止まざりしに、思はぬ子まで成せし過は如何にすべきと、躬らその容し難きを憾ちて悲むこと太甚かりしが、実に親の所憎にや墻へざりけん。その子の失せし後、彼は再び唯継の子をば生まじ、と固く心に誓ひしなり。二年の後、三年の後、四年の後まで異くも宮はこの誓を全うせり。

次第に彼の心は楽まずなりて、今は何の故にその嫁ぎたるかを自ら知るに苦めるなりき。機械の如く夫を守り置物のやうに内に据られ、絶えて人の妻たる効も思出もあらで、空く籠鳥の雲を望める身には、それのみの願なりし裕なる生活も、富める家計も、土の如く顧るに足らず、却てこの四年が間思ひに思ふばかりにて、熟海より行方知れざりし人の姿を田鶴見の邸内に見てしまで、彼は全く音沙汰をも聞かざりしなり。生家なる鴫沢にては薄々知らざるにもあらざりしかど、さる由無き事を告ぐるが如き愚なる親にもあらねば、宮のこれを知るべき便は絶れたりしなり。計らずもその夢寐に忘れざる姿を見たりし彼が思は幾計なりけんよ。驚かず、驚かず、饑たる者の貪り食ふらんやうに、彼はその一目にして四年の求むるところを求めんとしたり。既に自ら心事の不徳を以つて許せる身を投じて、唯快く万事を彼の慾に換へて已まん、と深くも念じたり。

はこの日より益急になりて、

だかくも儚き身の上と切なき胸の内とを独自ら愬へんとてなり。

五番町なる鰐淵といふ方に住める由は、静緒より聞きつれど、むざとは父も通はせ難く、道は遠からねど、独り出でて彷徨ふべき身にもあらぬなど、克はぬ事のみなるに苦かりけれど、安否を分かざりし幾年の思に較ぶれば、はや嚢の物を捜るに等しかるをと、その一筋に慰められつつも彼は日毎の徒然を憂きに堪へざる余、我心を遣る方無く明すべき長き長き文を書かんと思立ちぬ。そは折を得て送らんとにもあらず、又逢うては言ふ能はざるを言はしめんとにもあらで、止

　　(二)　の　二

宮は貫一が事を忘れざるとともに、又長く熱海の悲き別を忘るる能はざるなり。更に見よ。歳廻来る一月十七日なる日は、その悲き別を忘れざる胸に熔して、彼の悔を新にするにあらずや。

「十年後の今月今夜も、僕の涙で月は曇らして見せるから、月が曇つたらば、貫一は何処かでお前を恨んで、今夜のやうに泣いてゐると想ふが可い」

掩へども宮が耳は常にこの声を聞かざるなし。彼はその日のその夜に会ふ毎に、果して月の曇るか、あらぬかを試しに、曾てその人の余所に泣ける微もあらざりければ、さすがに恨は忘られしかと、それには心安きにつけて、諸共に今は我をも思はでや、さては何処に如何にしてなど、更に打歎かるるなりき。

例のその日は四たび廻りて今日しも来りぬ。　晴れたりし空は午後より曇りて少く吹出でたる風

のいと寒く、凡ならず冷ゆる日なり。宮は毎よりも心煩きこの日なれば、かの筆採りて書続けんと為たりしが、余に思乱るればさるべき力も無くて、いとどしく紛れかねてゐたり。

益す寒威の募るに堪へざりければ、遽に煖炉を調ぜしめて、彼は西洋間に徙りぬ。尽く窓帷を引きたる十畳の間は寸隙もあらず裹まれて、火気の漸く春を蒸すところに、宮は体を胖に友禅縮緬の長襦袢の褄を蹈抜きて、緋の紋緞子張の楽椅子に凭りて、心の影の其処に映るを眺むらんやうに、その美き目をば唯白く坦なる天井に注ぎたり。

夫の留守にはこの家の主として、彼は事ふべき舅姑を戴かず、気兼すべき小姑を抱へず、足手絡の幼きも未だ有らずして、一箇の仲働と両箇の下婢とに万般の煩きを委せ、一日何の為すべき事も無くて、出づるに車あり、膳には肉あり、しかも言ふことは皆聴れ、為すことは皆悦ばる夫を持てるなど、彼は今若き妻の黄金時代をば夢むる如く楽めるなり。実に世間の娘の想ひに想ひ、望みに望める絶頂は正に己のこの身の上なる哉、と宮は不覚胸に浮べたるなり。

嗟乎、おのれもこの身の上を願ひに願ひし余に、再び得難き恋人を棄てにしよ。されども、この身の上に窮めし楽も、五年の昔なりける今日の日に窮めし悲しに易ふべきものはあらざりしよ。おのれのこの身の上を願ひしは、その恋人と倶に同じき楽を享けんと願ひしに外ならざるを。若し身の楽と心の楽とを併享くべき幸無くて、必ずその一つを択ぶべきものならば、孰を取るべきかを知ることの晩かりしを、遣方も無く悔ゆるなりけり。

この寒き日をこの燠き室に、この焦るる身をこの意中の人に並べて、この誠をもてこの恋しさを語らば如何に、と思到れる時、宮は殆ど裂けぬべく胸を苦く覚えて、今の待つ身は待たざる人を待つ身なる、その口惜しさを悶えては、在るにも在られぬ椅子を離れて、歩み寄りたる窓の外面を何心無く打見れば、いつしか雪の降出でて、薄白く庭に敷けるなり。一月十七日なる感は面を何心無く打見れば、いつしか雪の降出でて、薄白く庭に敷けるなり。一月十七日なる感はいと劇しく動きて、宮は降頻る雪を聴くが如く佇めり。折から唯継は還来りぬ。静に啓けたる闇の響は絶えに物述べる宮の耳には入らざりき。氷の如く冷徹りたる手をわりなく懐に差入れらるるに驚き、咄嗟と見向かんとすれば、後より緊と抱へられたれど、夫の常に飴める香水の薫は

隠るべくもあらず。

「おや、お帰来でございましたか」

「寒かつたよ」

「大相降つて参りました、さぞお困りでしたらう」

「何だか知らんが、むちやくちやに寒かつた」

宮は楽椅子を夫に勧めて、躬は燠炉の薪を燠べたり。今の今まで貫一が事を思窮めたりし心には、夫なる唯継にかく事ふるも、なかなか道ならぬやうにて屑からず覚ゆるなり。窓の外に降る雪、風に乱るる雪、楮に宿れる雪、庭に布く雪、見ゆる限の白妙は、我身に積める人の怨の丈かとも思ふに、かくてあることの欷しさ、切なさは、脂を搾らるるやうにも忍び難かり。されども、この美人の前にこの雪を得たる夫の得意は限無くて、その脚を八文字に踏展け、漸く燠まれる

頤（おとがひ）を突反（つきそ）らして、

「ああ、降る降る、面白い。かう云ふ日は寄鍋（よせなべ）で飲むんだね。寄鍋が好い。

それから珈琲（カッフィ）を一つ拵（こしら）へてくれ、コニャックを些（ちっ）と余計に入れて」

宮の行かんとするを、

「お前、行かんでも可いぢやないか、要る物を取寄せてここで拵へなさい」彼の電鈴（でんりん）を鳴して、火の傍に寄来ると斉（ひと）しく、唯継はその手を取りて小脇に挟（はさ）みつ。宮は懼（よろこ）べる

気色も無くて、彼の為すに任するのみ。

「おまへどうした、何を鬱いでゐるのかね」

引寄せられし宮はほとほと仆（たふ）れんとして椅子に支（ささ）へられたるを、唯継は鼻も摩るばかりにその顔を差覗きて余念も無く見入りつつ、

「顔の色が甚（はなは）だ悪いよ。雪で寒いんで、胸でも痛むか、頭痛でもするんか、さうも無い？どうしたんだね。それちや、もっと爽然（はっきり）してくれんぢや困るぢやないか。さう陰気だと情合が薄いやうに想はれるよ。一体お前は夫婦の情が薄いんぢやあるまいかと疑ふよ。ええ？そんなこと

は無いかね」忽ち闇（やみ）の啓（ひら）くと見れば、仲働の命ぜし物を持来（もちきた）れるなり。人目を憚（はば）らずその妻を愛するは唯継が常なるを、見苦しと思ふ宮はその傍を退かんとすれど、放たざるを例の事とて仲働は見ぬ風し

つつ、器具と壜（ボトル）とをテエブルに置きて、直に退り出でぬ。かく執念く愛せらるるを、宮はなかな

か憂くも浅ましくも思ふなりけり。
雪は風を添へて撹乱し撹乱し降頻りつつ、はや日暮れなんとするに、楽き夜の漸く来れるが最も辱き唯継の目尻なり。

「近頃はお前別して鬱いでをるやうぢやないか、俺にはさう見えるがね。さうして内にばかり引籠んでをるのが宜くないよ。この頃は些とも出掛けんぢやないか。益す陰気になって了ふのだ。この間も鳥柴の奥さんに会つたら、さう言つてゐたよ。何為近頃は奥さんは些ともお見えなさらんのだらう。芝居ぐらゐにはお出掛になつても可ささうなものだが、全然影も形もお見せなさらん。なんぼお大事になさるって、そんなに仕舞込んでお置きなさるものぢやございません。慈善の為に少しは衆にも見せてお遣んなさい、なんぞと非常に遣られたぢやないか。それからね、知つてをる通り、今度の選挙には実業家として福積が当選したらう。俺も大いに与つて尽力したんさ。それで近日当選祝があつて、それが済次第に慰労会と云ふやうな名で、格別尽力した連中を招待するんだ。その席へは令夫人携帯といふ訳なんだから、是非お前も出なければならん。驚くよ。俺の社会では富山の細君と来たら評判なもんだ。会つたことの無い奴まで、お前の事は知つてをるんさ。そこで、俺は実は自慢でね、さう評判が好いけれど、然し、近頃のやう軽々しく出行かれるのも面白くない。余り顔を見せん方が見識が好いけれど、然し、近頃のやうに籠つてばかり居るのは、第一衛生におまへ良くない。実は俺は日曜毎にお前を連れて出たいんさ。おまへの来た当座はさうであつたぢやないかね。子供を産んでから、さう、あれから半年ば

かり経つてからだよ。余り出なくなつたのは。それでも随分彼地此地出たぢやないかね。

善し、珈琲出来たか。うう熱い、旨い。お前もお飲み、これを半分上げやうか。沢山だ？それだからお前は冷淡で可かんと謂ふんさ。ぢや、酒の入らんのを飲むと可い。寄鍋は未か。うむ、彼方に支度がしてあるから、来たら言ひに来る？それは善い、西洋室の寄鍋なんかは風流でない、あれは長火鉢の相対に限るんさ。

可いかね、福積の招待には吃驚させるほど美くして出て貫はなけりやならん。それで、着物だ、何か欲ければ早速拵へやう。おまへが、これならば十分と思ふ服装で、隆として推出すんだね。さうしてお前この頃は余り服装にかまはんぢやないか、可かんよ。いつでもこの小紋の羽織の疵恍けたのばかりは恐れるね。何為あの被風を着ないのかね、あれは好く似合ふにな。

明後日は日曜だ、何処かへ行かうよ。その着物を見に三井へでも行かうか。いや、さうさう、柏原の奥さんが、お前の写真を是非欲いと言つて、会ふ度に酷く催促するんで克はんよ。明日は用が有つて行かなければならんのだから、持つて行かんと捗いて。未だ有つたね、無い？そりや可かん。一枚も無いんか、そりや可かん。それぢや、明後日写しに行かう。直と若返つて二人で写すなんぞも可いぢやないか。

善し、寄鍋が来た？　さあ行かう」

夫に引添ひて宮はこの室を出でんとして、思ふところありげに姑く窓の外面を窺ひたりしが、

「どうしてこんなに降るのでせう」

「何を下らんことを言ふんだ。さあ、行かう行かう」

第　三　章

宮は既に富むと裕なるとに饜きぬ。抑も彼がこの家に嫁ぎしは、惑深き娘気の一図に、栄耀栄華の欲するままなる身分を願ふを旨とするなりければ、始より夫の愛情の如きは、有るも善し、有らざるも更に善しと、殆ど無用の物のやうに軽めたりき。今やその願足りて、しかも饜き足る彼は弥よ賷らるる愛情の煩きに堪へずして、寧ろ影を追ふよりも儚き昔の恋を思ひて、私に楽むの味あるを覚ゆるなり。

かくなりてより彼は自ら唯継の面前を厭ひて、寂く垂籠めては、随意に物思ふを懌びたりしが、図らずも田鶴見の邸内に貫一を見しより、彼のさして昔に変らぬ一介の書生風なるを見しより、一度は絶えし恋ながら、なほ冥々に行末塁あるが如く、さるは、彼が昔のままの容なるを、今もその独を守りて、時の到るを待つらんやうに思做さるるなりけり。宮は躬の心の底を叩きて、答を得るに泪みつつも、さすがに又己にも知れざる秘密の潜める心地して、一面には覚束なくも、又一面にはとにもかくにも信ぜらるるなり。

その時は果して到るべきものなるか。宮は躬の心の底を叩きて、答を得るに泪みつつも、さすがに又己にも知れざる秘密の潜める心地して、一面には覚束なくも、又一面にはとにもかくにも信ぜらるるなり。

便ち宮の夫の愛を受くるを難堪く苦しと思知りたるは、彼の写真の鏡面の前に悶絶せし日より

にて、その恋しさに取迫めては、いでや、この富めるに竪き、裕なるに倦める家を棄つべきか、棄てよとならば遅しと思へるも屡々なりき。唯敢てこれを為せざるは、窃に望は繋けながらも、行くべき方の怨を解かざるを虞るる故のみ。

素より宮は唯継を愛せざりしかど、決してこれを憎むとにはあらざりき。されど今はしも正にその念は起れるなり。自ら謂へらく、售るべくもあらざりし恋を奪ひけるよ、と悔の余はかかる恨をも他に彼せて、

彼は己を過りしをば、全く夫の罪と為せり。

この心なる宮はこの一月十七日に会ひて、いとどしく貫一が事の忍ばるるに就けて転た悪人の夫を厭ふこと甚かり。無辜の唯継はかかる今宵の楽を授くるこの美き妻を拝するばかりに、有程の誠を捧げて、蜜よりも甘き言の数々を呟きて止まざれど、宮が耳には人の声は聞えずして、雪の音のみぞいと能く響きたる。

その雪は明方になりて歌みぬ。乾坤の白きに漂ひて華麗に差出でたる日影は、漲るばかりに暖き光を鋪きて終日輝きければ、七分の雪はその日に解けて、はや翌日は往来の妨碍もあらず、処々の泥濘は打続く快晴の天に曝されて、刻々に乾き行くなり。

この雪の為に外出を封ぜられし人は、この日和とこの道とを見て、皆悴にかねて昨日より出でしも多かるべし。まして今日となりては、手置の宜からぬ横町、不性なる裏通、屋敷町の小路などの氷れる雪の九十九折、或は捏返せし汁粉の海の、差掛りて難儀を極むるとは知らず、見渡す

町通の乾々干に固へたりし人の出でざるはあらざらんやうに、往来の常よ
り頻なる午前十一時といふ頃、屈み勝に疲れたる車夫は、泥の粉衣掛けたる車輪を可悩しげに転
して、黒綾の吾妻コオト着て、鉄色縮緬の頭巾を領に巻きたる五十路に近き賤からぬ婦人を載せ
たるが、南の方より芝飯倉通に来かかりぬ。

これは富山唯継が住居にて、その女客は宮が母なり。主は疾に会社に出勤せし後にて、例刻に来
れる髪結の今方帰行きて、まだその跡も掃かぬ程なり。紋羽二重の肉色鹿子を掛けたる大円髷よ
り水は滴るばかりに、玉の如き喉を白絹のハンカチイフに巻きて、風邪気などにや、連に打咳き
つつ、宮は奥より出迎に見えぬ。その故とも覚えず著き面贏は、唯一目に母が心を驚せり。

唯有る横町を西に切れて、某の神社の石の玉垣に沿ひて、だらだらと上る道狭く、繁き木立に
南を塞かれて、残れる雪の鈴多きが泥交に踏散されたるを、件の車は曳々と挽上げて、取着に土
塀を由々しく構へて、門には電燈を掲げたる方にぞ入りける。

閑ある身なれば、宮は月々生家なる両親を見舞ひ、母も同じほど訪ひ音づるをば、此上無き
隠居の保養と為るなり。信に女親の心は、娘の身の定りて、その家栄え、その身安泰に、しかも
いまじう出世したる姿を見るに増して楽まさるる事はあらざらん。彼は宮を見る毎に大なる手柄
をも成したらんやうに吾が譃れるほどの親といふ親は、皆才覚無く、仕合薄くて、有様は気の毒
なる人達哉、と漫に己の誇らるるなりけり。されば月毎に彼が富山の門を入るは、正に人の母た
る成功の凱旋門を過る心地もすなるべし。

可懐きと、嬉きと、猶今一つにて、母は得々と奥に導れぬ。久く垂籠めて友欲き宮は、拯を得たるやうに覚えて、有るまじき事ながら、或は密に貫一の報を齎せるにはあらずやなど、枉げても念じつつ、せめては愁に閉ぢたる胸を姑くも寛うせんとするなり。

母は語るべき事の日頃蓄へたる数々を措きて、彼はさまでに己の贏れたるを懼れつつも、先づ宮が血色の気遣く衰へたるを詰りぬ。同じ事を夫へ問れしを思合せて、彼はさまでに己の贏れたるを懼れつつも、先づ宮が血色の気遣く衰へたるを詰りぬ。

「さう？　でも、何処も悪い所なんぞ有りはしません。余り体を動かさないから、その所為かも知れません。けれども、この頃は時々気が鬱いで鬱いで耐らない事があるの。あれは血の道と謂ふんでせうね」

「ああ、それは血の道さ。私なんぞも持病にあるのだから、やっぱりさうだらうよ。それでも、それで痩せるやうぢや良くないのだから、お医者に診てもらふ方が可いよ、放つて措くから畢竟持病にもなるのさ」

宮は唯頷きぬ。

母は不図思起して、さも慌忙しげに、

「後が出来たのぢやないかい」

宮は打笑みつ。されども例の可羞しとにはあらで傍痛さ余を微見せしやうなり。

「そんな事はありはしませんわ」

「さう何日までも沙汰が無くちや困るぢやないか。本当に未だそんな様子は無いのかえ」

「有りはしませんよ」

「無いのを手柄にでもしてゐるやうに、何だね、一人はもう無くてどうするのだらう、先へ寄つて御覧、後悔を為るから。本当なら二人ぐらゐ有つて好い時分なのに、あれきり後が出来ないところを見ると、やつぱり体が弱いのだね。今の内養生して、丈夫にならなくちや可けないよ。お前はさうして平気で、いつまでも若くて居る気なのだらうけれど、本宅の方なんぞでも後が欲しがつて、どんなに待兼ねてお在だか知れはしないのだよ。内ちや又阿父さんは、あれはどうしたと謂ふんだらう、情無い奴だ。子を生み得ないのは女の恥だつて、慍りきつてゐるなさるくらゐのに、当人のお前こそ、可厭に落着いてゐるから、憎らしくてなりはしない。さうして、お前は先の内は子供が所好だつた癖に、自分の子は欲くないのかね」

宮もさすがに当惑しつゝ、

「欲くない事はありはしませんけれど、出来ないものは為方が無いわ」

「だから、何でも養生して、体を丈夫にするのが専だよ」

「体が弱いとお言ひだけれど、自分には別段ここが悪いと思ふところも無いから、診てもらふのも変だし……けれどもね、阿母さん、私は疾から言はう言はうと思つてゐたのですけれど、実は気に懸る事があつてね、それで始終何だか心持が快くないの。その所為で自然と体も良くないのかしらんと思ふのよ」

母のその目は瞪り、その膝は前み、その胸は潰れたり。

「どうしたのさ！」

宮は俯きたりし顔を寂しげに起して、

「私ね、去年の秋、貫一さんに逢つてね……」

「さうかい！」

己だに聞くを憚る秘密の如く、母はその応ふる声をも潜めて、まして四辺には油断もあらぬ気勢なり。

「何処で」

「内の方へも全然齎来の様子は知れないの？」

「ああ」

「些も？」

「ああ」

「どうしてゐると云ふやうな話も？」

「ああ」

かく纔に応ふるのみにて、母は自ら湧せる万感の渦の裏に陥りてぞゐたる。

「さう？　阿父さんは内証で知つてお在ぢやなくて？」

「いいえ、そんな事は無いよ。何処で逢つたのだえ」

宮はその梗概を語れり。　聴ゐる母は、彼の事無くその場を遁れ得てし始末を詳かにするを俟ち

て、始めて重荷を下したるやうに哱と息を吐きぬ。実に彼は熱海の梅園にて膩汗を搾られし次手、悪さを思合せて、憂き目を重ねし宮が不幸を、不憫とも、惨しとも、今更に親心を傷むるなりけり。されども過ぎしその事よりは、為に宮が前途に一大障礙の或は来るべきを案じて、母はなか／＼心穏ならず、

「さうして貫一はどうしたえ」

「お互に知らん顔をして別れて了つたけれど……」

「ああそれから？」

「それきりなのだけれど、私は気になつてね。それも出世して立派になつてゐるのなら、さうも思はないけれど、つまらない風采をして、何だか大変痩れて、私も極が悪かつたから、能くは見なかつたけれど、気の毒のやうに身窄い様子だつたわ。それに、聞けばね、番町の方の鰐淵とかいふ、地面や家作なんぞの世話をしてゐる内に使はれて、やつぱり其処に居るらしいのだから、好い事は無いのでせう、ああして子供の内から一処に居た人が、あんなになつてゐるかと思ふと、昔の事を考へ出して、私は何だか情無くなつて……」

彼は襦袢の袖の端に窃と眶を拭りて、

「好い心持はしないわ、ねえ」

「へええ、そんなになつてゐるのかね」

母の顔色も異き寒さにや襲はるると見えぬ。

「それまでだつて、憶出さない事は無いけれど、去年逢つてからは、毎日のやうに気になつて、可厭な夢なんぞを度々見るの。阿父さんや、阿母さんに会ふ度に、今度は話さう、今度は話さうと思ひながら、私の口からは何と無く話し難いやうで、実は今まで言はずにゐたのだけれど、その事が初中終苦になる所為で気を傷めるから体にも障るのぢやないかと、さう想ふのです」

思凝せるやうに母は或方を見據ゑつつ、言は無くて頷きゐたり。

「それで、私は阿母さんに相談して、貫一さんをどうかして上げたいの――あの時にそんな話も有つたのでせう。さうして依旧鳴沢の跡は貫一さんに取して下さいよ、それでなくては私の気が済まないから。今までは行方が知れなかつたから為方がないけれど、聞合せれば直に分るのだから、それを拋つて措いちや此方が悪いから、阿父さんにでも会つて貰つて、何とか話を付けるやうにして下さいな。さうして従来通に内で世話をして、どんなにもあの人の目的を達しさして、立派に吾家の跡を取して下さい。私はさうしたら兄弟の盃をして、何処までも生家の兄さんで、末始終力になつて欲いわ」

宮がこの言は決して内に自ら欺き、又敢て外に他を欺かざりき。影とも儚く隔の関の遠き恋人として余所に朽さんより、近き他人の前に己を殺さんぞ、同く受くべき苦痛ならば、その忍び易きに就かんと冀へるなり。

「それはさうでもあらうけれど、随分考へ物だよ。あのひとの事なら、内でも時々話が出て、何処にどうしてゐるかしらんつて、案じないぢやないけれど、阿父さんも能くお言ひのさ、如何に

何だつて、余り貫一の仕打が憎いつて。成程それは、お前との約束ね、それを反古にしたと云ふので、齢の若いものの事だから腹も立たう、立たうけれど、お前自分の身の上も些は考へて見るが可いわね。子供の内からああして世話になつて、全く内のお蔭でともかくもあれだけにもなつたのぢやないか、その恩も有れば、義理も有るのだらう。そこ所を些と考へたら、あれぎり家出をして了ふなんて、あんなまあ面抵がましい仕打振をするつてが有るものかね。

それぢやあの約束を反古にして、もうお前にどうでも独で勝手に為るが可いと云ふやうな不人情なことを仮初にも為たのぢやなし、鳴沢の家は譲らうし、所望なら洋行も為せやうとまで言ふのぢやないか。それは一時は腹も立たうけれど、好く了簡して前後を考へて見たら、万更訳の解らない話をしてるのぢやないのだもの、私達の顔を立ててくれたつて、そんなに罰も当りはしまいと思ふのさ。さうしてお剰に、阿父さんから十分に訳を言つて、頭を低げないばかりにして頼んだのぢやないかね。だから此方には少しも無理は無い筈だのに、貫一が余り身の程を知らなゐ過ると。

それはね、阿父さんが昔あの人の親の世話になつた事があるさうさ、その恩返しなら、行処の無い軀を十五の時から引取つて、高等学校を卒業するまでに仕上げたから、それで十分だらうぢやないか。

全く、お前、貫一の為方は増長してゐるのだよ。それだから、阿父さんだつて、私だつて、あされて見ると決して可愛くはないのだからね、今更此方から捜出して、とやかう言ふほどの事ないか。

はありはしないよ。それぢや何ぼ何でも不見識とやらちやないか」

その不見識とやらを嫌ふよりは、別に嫌ふべく、懼るべく、警むべき事あらずや、と母は私に慮れるなり。

「阿父さんや阿母さんの身になつたら、さう思ふのは無理も無いけれど、どうもこのままぢや私が気が済まないんですもの。今になつて考へて見ると、貫一さんが悪いのでなし、阿父さん阿母さんが悪いのでなし、全く私一人が悪かつたばかりに、貫一さんには阿父さん阿母さんを恨ませるし、阿父さん阿母さんには貫一さんを悪く思はせたのだから、やつぱり私が仲へ入つて、元々通に為なければ済まないと思ふんですから、貫一さんの悪いのは、どうぞ私に免じて、今までの事は水に流して了つて、改めて貫一さんを内の養子にして下さいな。若しさうなれば、私もそれで苦労が減るのだから、きつと体も丈夫になるに違無いから、是非さう云ふ事に阿父さんにも頼んで下さいな、ねえ、阿母さん。さうして下さらないと、私は段々体を悪くするわ」

かく言出でし宮が胸は、ここに尽くその罪を懺悔したらんやうに、多少の涼きを覚ゆるなりき。

「そんなに言ふのなら、還つて阿父さんに話をして見やうけれど、何もその所為で体が弱くなると云ふ訳も無かりさうなものぢやないか」

「いいえ、全くその所為ですもの、この間逢ふ前まではそんなでもなかつたのだけれど、あれから急にるることがあるんですもの。始終そればかり苦になつて、時々考込むと、実に耐らない心持にな

──さうね、何と謂つたら可いのだらう──私があんなに不仕合な身分にして了つたとさう思つて、さぞ恨んでゐるだらうと、気の毒のやうな、可恐いやうな、さうして、何と無く私は悲しくね。外には何も望は無いから、どうかあの人だけは元のやうにして、末始終阿父さんや阿母さんの世話をして貰つたら、どんなに嬉しからうと、そんな事ばかり考へては鬱いでゐるのです。いづれ私からも阿父さんに話をしますけれど、差当阿母さんから好くこの訳をさう言つて、本当に頼んで下さいな。私二三日の内に行きますから」

されども母は投首して、

「私の考量ぢや、どうも今更ねえ……」

「阿母さんは！　何もそんなに貫一さんを悪く思はなくたつて可いわ。折角話をして貰はうと思ふ阿母さんがさう云ふ気ぢや、とても阿父さんだつて承知をしては下さるまいから……」

「お前がそれまでに言ふものだから、私は不承知とは言はないけれど……」

「可いの、不承知なのよ。阿父さんもやつぱり貫一さんが憎くて、大方不承知なんでせうから、私は毫末にはしないから、不承知なら不承知でも可いの」

私は涙含みつつ宮が焦心になれるを、母は打惑ひて、

「まあ、お聞きよ。それは、ね、……」

「阿母さん、可いわ──私、可いの」

「可かないよ」

「可かなくつても可いわ」

「あれ、まあ、……何だね」

「どうせ可いわ。私の事はかまつてはおくれでないのだから……」

我にもあらで迸る泣声を、つと袖に抑へても、宮は急来る涙を止めかねたり。

「何もお前、泣くことは無いぢやないか。可笑しな人だよ、だからお前の言ふことは解つてゐるか
ら、内へ帰つて、善く話をした上で……」

「可いわ。そんなら、さうで私にも了簡があるから、どうとも私は自分で為るわ」

「自分でそんな事を為るなんて、それは可くないよ。かう云ふ事は決してお前が自分で為ること
ぢやないのだから、それは可けませんよ」

「………」

「帰つたら阿父さんに善く話を為やうから、……泣くほどの事は無いぢやないかね」

「だから、阿母さんは私の心を知らないのだから、頼効が無い、と謂ふのよ」

「多度お言ひな」

「言ふわ」

真顔作れる母は火鉢の縁に丁と煙管を撃けば、他行持の暫く乾されて弛みし雁首はほつくり脱
けて灰の中に舞込みぬ。

第　四　章

頭部に受けし貫一が挫傷は、危くも脳膜炎を続発せしむべかりしを、肢体に数個所の傷部ととも
に、その免るべからざる若干の疾患を得たりしのみにて、今や日増に康復の歩を進ひて、可懼
しげにも自ら起居を扶け得る身となりければ、一日一夜を為す事も無く、ベッドの上に静養を勉
めざるべからざる病院の無聊をば、殆ど生きながら葬られたらんやうに倦み困じつつ、彼は更に
この病と相関する如く、関せざる如く併発したる別様の苦悩の為に侵さるるなりき。

主治医も、助手も、看護婦も、受附も、小使も、乃至患者の幾人も、皆目を側めて
彼と最も密なる関係あるべきを疑はざるまでに、満枝の頻繁病を訪ひ来るなり。三月にわたる久
きをかの美き姿の絶えず出入するなれば、噂は自から院内に播りて、博士の某さへ終に喫されて、
垣間見の歩をここに枉げられしとぞ伝へ侍る。始の程は何者の美形とも得知れざりしを、医員の
中に例の困められしがありて、名著の美人クリイムと洩せしより、いとど人の耳を驚かし、目を
悦ます種とはなりて、貫一が浮名もこれに伴ひて唱はれけり。

さりとは彼の暁るべき由無けれど、何の廉もあらむに足近く訪はるるを心憂く思ふ余に、一度
ならず満枝に向ひて言ひし事もありけれど、見舞といふを陽にして訪ひ来るなれば、理として好
意を拒絶すべきにあらず。さは謂へ、こは情の掛罠と知れば、又甘んじて受くべくにもあらず、

しかのみならで、彼は素より満枝の為人を悪みて、その貌の美きを見ず、その思切なるを汲まんともせざるに、猶かつ主ある身の謗りて仇名をも立たばなど気遣はるるに就けて、貫一は彼の入り来るに会へば、冷き汗の湧出づるとともに、創所の遽に疼き立ちて、唯異くも己れなる者の全く痒らさるるに似たるを、吾ながら心弱しと尤むれども効無かりけり。実に彼は日頃この煩を逃れん為に、努めてこの敵を避けてぞ過せし。今彼の身は第二医院の一室に密封せられて、しかも隠るる所無きベッドの上に横はれれば、宛然俎板に上れる魚の如く、空く他の為すに委するのみなる仕合を、掻拗らんとばかりに悶ゆるなり。

かかる苦き枕頭に彼は又驚くべき事実を見出しつつ、覰へつて己を顧れば、測らざる累の既に逮べる迷惑は、その薬蒲団の内に針の包れたる心地して、今なほ彼の病むと謂はば、恐くは外に三分を患ひて、内に却つて七分を憂ふるにあらざらんや。貫一もそれをこそ懸念せしが、果して鰐淵は彼と満枝との間を疑ひ初めき。彼は又鰐淵の疑へるに由りて、その人と満枝との間をも略し推し得たるなり。

例の煩き人は今日も訪ひ来つ、しかも仇ならず意を籠めたりと覚き見舞物など持ちて。はや一時間余を過せども、彼は枕頭に起ちつ、居つして、なかなか帰り行くべくも見えず。貫一は寄付けじとやうに彼方を向きて、覚めながら目を塞ぎていと静に臥したり。附添婆の折から出行きしを候ひて、満枝は椅子を躙り寄せつつ、

「間さん、間さん。貴方、貴方」

と枕の端を指もて音なへど、眠れるにもあらぬ貫一は何の答をも与へず、満枝は起ちてベッドの彼方へ廻り行きて、彼の寐顔を差覗きつ。

「聞さん」

猶答へざりけるを、軽く肩の辺を撼せば、貫一はさるをも知らざる為はしかねて、始めて目を開きぬ。彼はかく覚めたれど、満枝はなほ覚めざりし先の可懐しげに差寄りたる態を改めずして、その手を彼の肩に置き、その顔を彼の枕に近けたるまま、

「私、貫方に些とお話をして置かなければならない事があるのでございますから、お聞き下さいまし」

「あ、まだ在らしつたのですか」

「いつも長居を致して、さぞ御迷惑でございませう」

「…………」

「外でもございませんが……」

彼の隔無く身近に狎るるを可忌しと思へば、貫一はわざと寐返りて、椅子を置きたる方に向直り、

「どうぞ此方へ」

この心を暁れる満枝は、飽くまで憎き事為るよと、持てるハンカチイフにベッドを打ちて、かくまでに遇はれながら、なほこの人を慕はでは已まぬ我身かと、効無くも余に軽く弄ばるるを可

愧うて佇みたり。されども貫一は直に席を移さざる満枝の為に、再び言を費さんとも為ざりけり。

気嵩なる彼は胸に余して、聞えよがしに、

「唉、貴方には軽蔑されてある事を知りながら、何為私腹を立てることが出来ないのでせう。

実に貴方は！」

満枝は彼の枕を捉へて顱ひしが、貫一の寂然として眼を閉ぢたるに益苛ちて、

「余り酷うございますよ。間さん、何とか有仰つて下さいましな」

彼は堪へざらんやうに苦りたる口元を引歪めて、

「別に言ふ事はありません。第一貴方のお見舞下さるのは難有迷惑で……」

「何と有仰います！」

「以来はお見舞にお出で下さるのを御辞退します」

「貴方、何と……!!」

満枝は眉を昂げて詰寄せたり。貫一は仰ぎて眼を塞ぎぬ。

素より彼の無愛相なるを満枝は知れり。彼の無愛相の己に対しては更に甚きを加ふるをも善く知れり。満枝が手管は、今その外に顕せるやうに決して内に怐へかねたるにはあらず、かくしてその人と静ふも、また慊はざる恋の内に聊か楽む道なるを思へるなり。涙微紅めたる眶に耀き

て、いつか宿せる暁の葩に露の津々なる。

「お内にも御病人の在るのに、早く帰つて上げたが可いちやありませんか。私も貴方に度々来て

戴くのは甚だ迷惑なのですから」

「御迷惑は始から存じてをります」

「いいや、未だ外にこの頃のがあるのです」

「ああ！　鰐淵さんの事ではございませんか」

「まあ、さうです」

「それだから、私お話が有ると申したのではございませんか。それを貴方は、私と謂ふと何でも鬱陶しがつて、如何に何でもそんなに作るものぢやございませんよ。その事ならば、貴方が御迷惑遊ばしてゐらつしやるばかりちやございません。私だつてどんなに窮つてをるか知れは致しません。この間も鰐淵さんが可厭なことを有仰つたのです。私些もかまひは致しませんけれど、さうでもない、貴方がこの先御迷惑あそばすやうな事があつてはと存じて、私それを心配致してをるくらゐなのでございます」

聴かざるにはあらねど、貫一は絶えて応答だに為ざるなり。

「実は疾からお話を申さうとは存じたのでございますけれど、そんな可厭な事を自分の口から吹聴らしく、却つて何も御存じない方が可からうと存じて、何も申上げずにをつたのでございますが、鰐淵様のかれこれ有仰るのは今に始つた事ではないので、もう私実に窮つてをるのでございます。始終好い加減なことを申しては遁げてをるのですけれど、鰐淵さんは私が貴方をこんなに……と云ふ事は御存じなかつたのですから、それで済んでをりましたけれど、貴方が御入院あそ

ばしてから、私かうして始終お訪ね申しますし、鰐淵さんも頻繁いらつしやるので、度々お目に懸るところから、何とかお想ひなすつたのでございませう。それで、この間は到頭それを有仰つて、訳が有るなら有るで、隠さずに話をしろと有仰るのぢやございませんか。私為方がありませんから、お約束をしたと申して了ひました」

「え！」と貫一は繃帯したる頭を掻けて、彼の有為顔を赦し難く打目成れり。満枝はさすが過を悔いたる風情にて、やをら左の袂を膝に掻載せ、牡丹の苦の如く揃へる紅絹裏の振を弄りつつ、彼の咎を懼るる目遣してゐたり。

「実に怪しからん！　誑なことを有仰つたものです」

「もう可いから、早くお還り下さい」

彼を喝せし怒に任せて、半起したりし体を投倒せば、腰部の創所を強く抵てて、得堪へず呻き苦むを、不意なりければ満枝は殊に惑ひて、

「どう遊ばして？　何処ぞお痛みですか」

手早く夜着を揚げんとすれば、払退けて、

「もうお還り下さい」

言放ちて貫一は例の背を差向けて、遽に打鎮りゐたり。

「私還りません！　貴方がさう酷く有仰れば、以上還りません。いつまでも居られる軀でははな

いのでございますから、順く還るやうにして還して下さいまし」

いとはしたなくて立てる満枝は闇の啓くに驚かされぬ。入来れるは、附添婆か、あらず。看護

婦か、あらず。国手の回診か、あらず。小使か、あらず。あらず！

胡麻塩縮紗の地厚なる二重外套を絡へる魁肥の老紳士は悠然として入来りしが、内の光景を見

ると斉く胸悪き色はつとその面に出でぬ。満枝は心に少く慌てたれど、さしも顕さで、雍かに小

腰を屈めて、

「おや、お出あそばしまし」

「ほ、ほ、これは、毎度お見舞下さつて」

同く慇懃に会釈はすれど、疑も無く反対の意を示せる金壺眼は光を違う女の横顔を瞥見せり。

静に臥したる貫一は発作の来れる如き苦悩を感じつつ、身を起して直行を迎ふれば、

「どうぢゃな。好え方がお見舞に来てをつて下さるで、可えの」

打付に過ぎし言を二人ともに快からず思へば、頓に答は無くて、その場の白けたるを、さこそ

と謂はんやうに直行の独り笑ふなりき。如何に答ふべきか。如何に言釈くべきか、如何に処すべ

きかを思へる貫一は難しげなる顔を稍内向けたるに、今はなかなか悪怯れもせで満枝は椅子の

前なる手炉に寄りぬ。

「然しお宅の御都合もあるぢゃらうし、又お忙しいところを度々お見舞下されては痛入ります。そ

れにこれの病気も最早快うなるばかりじゃで御心配には及ばんで、以来お出で下さるのは何分お

断り申します」

言黒めたる邪魔立を満枝は面憎がりて、

「いいえ、もうどう致しまして、この御近辺辺まで毎々次手がありますのでございますから、その御心配には及びません」

直行の眼は再び輝けり。貫一は愁に彼を窘めじと、傍より言を添へぬ。

「毎度お訪ね下さるので、却つて私は迷惑致すのですから、どうか貫方から可然御断り下さるやうに」

「当人もお気の毒に思うてあの様に申すで、折角ではありますけど、決して御心配下さらんやうに、のう」

「お見舞に上りましてはお邪魔になりまする事ならば、私差控へませう」

満枝は色を作して直行を打見遣りつつ、その面を引廻して、やがて非ぬ方を目成りたり。

「いや、いや、な、決して、そんな訳ぢや……」

「余りな御挨拶で！女だと思召して有仰るのかは存じませんが、それまでのお指図は受けませんで宜うございます」

「いや、そんなに悪う取られては甚だ困る、畢竟貴方の為を思ひますじやに因つて……」

「何と有仰います。お見舞に出ますのが、何で私の不為になるのでございませう」

「それにお心着が無い？」

その能く用ゐる微笑を弄して、直行は巧に温顔を作れるなり。

満枝は稍急立ちぬ。

「ございません」

「それは、お若いでさう有らう。甚だ失敬ながら、すいぢや申して見やう。な。貴方もお若けり

や間も若い。若い男の所へ若い女子が度々出入したら、そんな事は無うても、人がかれこれ言ひ

易い、可えですか、そしたら、間はとにかくじや、赤樫様と云ふ者のある貴方の軀に疵が付く。

そりや、不為ぢやありますまいか、ああ」

陰には己自ら更に、甚き不為を強ひながら、人の口といふものの かくまでに重宝なるが可笑

し、と満枝は思ひつつも、

「それは御深切に難有う存じます。私はとにかく、間さんはこれからお美い御妻君をお持ち遊ば

す大事のお躯でむらつしやるのを、私のやうな者の為に御迷惑遊ばすやうな事が御座いまして

は何とも済みませんですから、私自今慎みますでございます」

「これは太い失敬なことを申しましたに、早速お用ゐのなさつて難有い。然し、間も貴方のやうな

方と嘘にもかれこれ言るるんぢやから、どんなにも嬉いぢやらう、私のやうな老人ぢやつたら、

死ぬほどの病気したて、赤樫さんは訪ねても下さりや為まいにな」

貫一は苦々しさに聞かざる為めしてゐたり。

「そんな事が有るものでございますか、お見舞に上りますとも」

「さやうかな。然し、こんなに度々来ては下さりやすまい」

「それこそ、御妻君が在つしやるのですから、余り頻繁上りますと……」

後は得言はで打笑める目元の媚、ハンカチイフを口蔽にしたる羞含しさなど、直行はふと目を奪はれて、飽かず覚ゆるなりき。

「はッ、はッ、はッ、すぢや細君が無いで、ここへは安心してお出かな。私は赤樫さんの処へ行つて言ひますぞ」

「はい、有仰つて下さいまし。私此方へ度々お見舞に出ますことは、宅でも存じてをるのでございますから、唯今も貴方から御注意を受けたのでございますが、私も用を抱へてをる体でかうして上りますのは、お見舞に出なければ済まないと考へまする訳がございますからで、その実、上りますれば、間さんは却つて私の伺ふのを懊悩く思召してゐらつしやるのですから、それは私のやうな者が余り参つてはお目障か知れませんけれど、外の事ではなし、お見舞に上るのでございますから、そんなに作らなくても宜いではございませんか。

然し、それでも私気に懸つて、かうして上るのは、でございます、宅へお出になつた御帰途にこの御怪我なんでございませう。それに、未だ私済みません事は、あの時大通の方をお帰りあそばすと有仰つたのを、津守坂へお出なさる方がお近いとさう申してお勧め申すと、その途でこの御災難でございませう。で私考へるほど申訳が無くて、宅でも大相気に致して、勉めてお見舞に出なければ済まないと申すので、その心持で毎度上るのでございますから、唯今のやうな御忠告

を伺ひますと、私実に心外なのでございます。そんなにして上れば、間さんは間さんでお喜びが無いのでございませう」

彼はいと辛しとやうに、恨しとやうにも、さては悲しとやうの情に堪へざらんとする満枝が顔をば、窃に金壺眼の一角を溶しつつ眺入るにぞありける。

その辛し、恨し、悲しとやうの情に堪へざらんとする満枝が顔をば、窃に金壺眼の一角を溶しつつ眺入るにぞありける。

「さやうかな。如何さま、それで善う解りましたじや。太い御深切な事で、間もさぞ満足ぢやらうと思ひます。又私からも、そりや厚うお礼を申しますのじや、で、な、お礼はお礼、今の御忠告は御忠告じや、悪う取つて下さつては困る。貴方がそんなに念うて、毎々お訪ね下さると思や、私も実に嬉しで、折角の御好意をな、どうか卻るやうな、失敬なことは決して言ひたうはないんじや、言ふのはお為を念ふからで、これもやつぱり年寄役なんぢやから、捨てて措けんで。貴方もやつぱり年寄はお嫌ひぢやらう。ああ、どうですか、ああ」

赤髯を拈り拈りて、直行は女の気色を偸視つ。

「さやうでございます。お年寄は勿論結構でございますけれど、どう致しても若いものは若い同士の方が気が合ひまして宜いやうでございますね」

「すぢやて、お宅の赤樫さんも年寄でせうが」

「それでございますから、もうもう口喧くてなりませんのです」

「ちや、口喧うも、気難うもないうたら、どうありますか」

「それでも私好きますんでございますね」

「それでも好かん？　太う嫌うたもんですな」

「尤も年寄だから嫌ふ、若いから一概に好くと申す訳には参りませんでございます。いくら此方から好きましても、他で嫌はれましては、何の効もございませんわ」

「さやう、な。けど、貴方のやうな方が此方から好いたと言うたら、どんな者でも可厭言ふ者は、そりや無い」

「あんな事を有仰つて！　如何でございますか、私そんな覚はございませんから、一向存じませんでございます」

「さやうかな。はッはッ。さやうかな。はッはッはッ」

椅子も傾くばかりに身を反して、彼はわざとらしく揺上げ揺上げて笑ひたりしが、

「間、どうぢやらう。赤樫さんはああ言うてをらるるが、さうかの」

「如何ですか、さう云ふ事は」

「誰か烏の雌雄を知らんとやうに、貫一は冷然として嘯けり。

「お前も知らんかな、はッはッはッ」

「私が自分にさへ存じませんものを、間さんが御承知有らう筈はございませんわ。ほほほほほほほ」

そのわざとらしさは彼にも遜らじとばかり、満枝は笑ひ囃せり。

直行が眼は誰を見るともなく無くて独り耀けり。

「それでは私もうお暇を致します」

「ほう、もう、お帰去かな。私もはや行かん成らんで、其所まで御一処に」

「いえ、私些と、あの、西黒門町へ寄りますでございますから、甚だ失礼でございますが……」

「まあ、宜い。其処まで」

「いえ、本当に今日は……」

「まあ、宜いが、実は、何じゃ、あの旭座の株式一件な、あれがつい纏りさうぢやで、この際お打合をして置かんと、『琴吹』の収償が面白うない。お目に掛つたのが幸ぢやから、些とそのお話を」

「では、明日にでも又、今日は些と急ぎますでございますから」

「そんなに急にお急ぎにならんでも宜いがな。商売上には年寄も若い者も無い、さう嫌はれてはどうもならん」

姑く推問答の末彼は終に満枝を拉し去れり。迹に貫一は悪夢の覚めたる如く連に太息吐いたり。

しが、やがて為ん方無げに枕に就きてよりは、見るべき物もあらぬ方に、止だ果無く目を奪れるたり。

第五章

檜葉、樅などの古葉貧しげなるを望むべき窓の外に、庭ともあらず打荒れたる広場は、唯麗なる日影のみぞ饒に置く余して、そこらの梅の点々と咲初めたるも、自ら怠り勝に風情作らずと見ゆれど、春の色香に出でたるは憐むべく、打霙める空に来馴るる鴨のいとどしく鳴頻りて、午後二時を過ぎぬる院内の寂々たるに、たまたま響くは患者の廊下を緩う行くなり。

枕の上の徒然は、この時人を圧して殆ど重きを覚えしめんとす。書見せると見えし貫一は辛うじて夢を結びたり。彼は実に夢ならでは有得べからざる怪き夢に弄ばれて、躬も夢と知り、夢と覚さんとしつつ、なほ睡の中に囚れしを、端無く人の呼ぶに驚されて、漸く慵き枕を欹てつ。

愕然として彼は瞳を凝せり。ベッドの傍に立てるは、その怪き夢の中に顕れし、終始相離れざりし主人公その人ならずや。打返し打返し視れども訪来れる満枝に紛らあらざりき。とは謂へ、彼は夢か、あらぬかを疑ひて止まず。さるはその真ならんよりなほ夢の中なるべきを信ずるの当れるを思へるなり、美しさも常に増して、夢に見るべき姿などのやうに四辺も可輝く、五六歳ばかりも若ぎて、その人の妹なりやとも見えぬ。まして、六十路に余れる夫有てる身と誰かは想ふべき。

髪を台湾銀杏といふに結びて、飾とてはわざと本甲蒔絵の櫛のみを挿したり。黒縮緬の羽織に

夢想裡に光琳風の春の野を色入に染めて、納戸縞の御召の下に濃小豆の更紗縮緬、紫根七糸に楽器尽の昼夜帯して、半襟は色糸の縫ある肉色なるが、頸の白きを匂はすやうにて、化粧などもやや濃く、例の腕環のみは燦爛と煩し。今日は殊に推して来にけるを、得堪へず心の尤むらん風情にて佇める姿限無く嬌きて見ゆ。

「お寝のところを飛んだ失礼を致しました。　私上る筈ではないのでございますけれど、是非申上げなければなりません事がございますので、些と伺ひましたのでございますから、今日のところはどうか御堪忍あそばして」

彼の許を得んまでは席に着くだに憚る如く、満枝は漂しげになほ立てるなり。

「はあ、さやうですか。一昨々日あれ程申上げたのに……」

内に燃ゆる憤を抑ふるとともに貫一の言は絶えぬ。

「鰐淵さんの事なのでございますの。　私困りまして、どういたしたら宜いのでございませう』

聞さん、かうなのでございますよ」

「いや、その事なら伺ふ必要は無いのです」

「あら、そんなことを有仰らずに……」

「失礼します。　今日は腰の傷部が又痛みますので」

「おや、それは、お劇いことはお在なさらないのでございますか」

「いえ、なに」

「どうぞお楽に在しつて」

貫一は無雑作に郡内縞の掻巻引被けて臥しけるを、疎略あらせじと満枝は勤篤に冊きて、やがて己も始めて椅子に倚れり。

「貴方の前でこんな事は私申上げ難いのでございますけれど、実は、あの一昨々日でございますね、ああ云ふ訳で鰐淵さんと御一処に参りましたところが、御飯を食べるから何でも附合へと有仰るので、湯島の天神の茶屋へ寄りましたのでございます。さう致すと、案の定厭い事をもう執濃く有仰るのでございます。さうして飽くまで貴方の事を疑つて、始終それを有仰るので、私一番それには困りました。あの方もお年効の無い、物の道理がお解りにならないにも程の有つたもので、一体私を何と思召してゐらつしやるのか存じませんが、客商売でもしてをる者に戯れるやうな事を、それも一度や二度ではないのでございますから、私残念で、一昨々日なども泣いたのでございます。で、この後二度とそんな事の有仰れないやうに、私その場で十分に申したことは申しましたけれど、変に気を廻してゐらつしやる方の事でございますから、取んだ八当で貴方へ御迷惑が懸りますやうでは、何とも私申訳がございませんから、どうぞそれだけお含み置き下さいまして、悪からず……。

今度お会ひあそばしたら、鰐淵さんが何とか有仰るかも知れません。さぞ御迷惑でゐらつしやいませうけれど、そこは宜いやうに有仰つて置いて下さいまし。それも貴方が何とか些でも思召してゐらつしやる方とならば、そんな事を有仰られるのもまた何でございませうけれど、嫌抜い

てお在あそばす私のやうな者と訳でもあるやうに有仰しやられるのは、さぞお辛くてゐらつしやいま
せうけれど、私のやうな者に見込れたのが因果とお諦め遊ばしまし。かう云ふのが実に因果と謂ふの
貴方も因果なれば、私も……私は猶因果なのでございます。
でございませうね」

金煙管の莨の独り杳眇と燻るを手にせるまま、満枝は儚さの遣方無げに萎れぬたり。さるをも
見向かず、答へず、頑として石の如く横はれる貫一。

「貴方もお諦め下さいまし、全く因果なのでございますから、切てさうと諦めて下され
ば、それだけでも私幾分か思が透つたやうな気が致すのでございます。
間さん。貴方は過日私がこんなに思つてゐることを何日までもお忘れないやうにと申上げた
ら、お志は決して忘れんと有仰いましたね。お覚えあそばしてゐらつしやいませ。ねえ、貴方、
よもやお忘れは無いでせう。如何なのでございますよ」

勢ひて問詰むれば、極めて事も無げに、

「忘れません」

満枝は彼の面を絶に怨視て瞬も為ず、その時人声して闥は徐に啓きぬ
案内せる附添の婆は戸口の外に立ちて請じ入れんとすれば、客はその老に似気なく、今更内の
様子を心惑せらるる体にて、彼にさへ可慎み小声に言付けつつ名刺を渡せり。

満枝は如何なる人かと瞥と見るに、白髪交りの鬢は長く胸の辺に垂れて、篤実の面貌瘠せたれ

ども賤からず、長は高しとにあらねど、素より腹にもあらざりし肉の自ら齢の衰へに削れたれ
ば、冬枯の峰に抽けるやうに聳えても見ゆ。衣服などさる可く、程を守りたるが奥幽くて、誰と
も知らねどさすがに疎ならず覚えて、彼は早くもこの賓の席を設けて待てるなりき。

貫一は婆の示せる名刺を取りて、何心無く打見れば、鳴沢隆三と誌したり。色を失へる貫一は
その塲へかぬる驚愕に駆れて、忽ち身を飜して其方を見向かんとせしが、幾ど同時に又枕して、
終に動かず。狂ひ出でんずる息を厳しく閉ぢて、燃ゆばかりに瞋れる眼は放たず名刺を見入りたり
しが、さしも内なる千万無量の思を籠める一点の涙は不覚に滲び出でぬ。こは怪しと思ひつつも

婆は、
「此方へお通し申しませうで……」
「知らん！」
「はい？」
「こんな人は知らん」

人目あらずば引裂き寰つべき名刺よ、濳しと投返せば床の上に落ちぬ。彼は強ひて目を塞ぎ、
身の顫ふをば吾と吾手に抱窘めて、恨は忘れずとも憤は忍ぶべしと、撻たんやうにも己を制すれ
ば、髪は逆竪ち蠢きて、頭脳の裏に沸騰る血はその欲するままに注ぐところを求めて、心も狂へ
と乱蕩すなり。彼はこれと争ひて猶も抑へぬ。面色は漸く変じて灰の如し。婆は懼れたる目色を
客の方へ忍ばせて、

「御存じないお方なので？」

「一向知らん。人違だらうから、断つて返すが可い」

「さやうでございますか。それでも、貴方様のお名前を有仰つてお尋ね……」

「ああ、何でも可いから早く断つて」

「さやうでございますか、それではお断り申しませうかね」

(五) の 二

　婆は鳴沢の前にその趣を述べて、投棄てられし名刺を返さんとすれば、手を後様に束ねたるまゝに受取らで、強ひて面を和ぐるも苦しげに見えぬ。

「ああ、さやうかね、御承知の無い訳は無いのだ。ははは、大分久い前の事だから、お忘れになつたのか知れん、それでは宜い。私が直にお目に掛らう。この部屋は間貫一さんだね、ああ、それでは間違無い」

　屹と思案せる鳴沢の椅子ある方に進み寄れば、満枝は座を起ち、会釈して、席を薦めぬ。

「貫一さん、私だよ。久う会はんので忘れられたかのう」

　室の隅に婆が茶の支度せんとするを、満枝は自ら行きて手を下し、或は指図もし、又自ら持来りて薦むるなど尋常の見舞客にはあらじと、鳴沢は始めてこの女に注目せるなり。貫一は知らざる如く、彼方を向きて答へず。仔細こそあれとは覚ゆれど、例のこの人の無愛想よ、と満枝は傍

に見つつも憫れに可笑かりき。

「貫一さんや、私だ。疾にも訪ねたいのであつたが、何にしろ居所が全然知れんので。一昨日ふと聞出したから不取敢かうして出向いたのだが、病気はどうかのう。何か、大怪我ださうではないか」

「睡をりますですかな」

猶も答のあらざるを幸に、満枝の居るを幸に、

「はい、如何でございますか」

彼はこの長者の窘めるを傍に見かねて、急上げ急上げ肩息してゐたり。何事とも覚えず驚されしを、色にも見せず、怪まるるをも言に出さず、些の心着さへあらぬやうに擬して、

「お客様がいらつしやいましたよ」

「今も言ひました通り、一向識らん方なのですから、お遣し申して下さい」

彼は面を伏せて又言はず、満枝は早くもその意を推して、また多くは問はず席に復りて、

「お人違ではございませんでせうか、どうも御覚が無いと有仰るのでございます」

長き鬢を推揉みつつ鴫沢は為方無さに苦笑して、

「人違とは如何なことでも！　五年や七年会はんでも私は未だそれほど老耄はせんのだ。然し覚が無いと言へばそれまでの話、覚もあらうし、人違でもなからうと思へばこそ、かうして折角会

ひにも来たらうと謂ふもの。老人の私がわざわざかうして出向いて来たのでのう、そこに免じて、些とでも会うて貫ひませう」

挨拶如何にと待てども、貫一は音だに立てざるなり。

「それぢや、何かい、こんなに言うても不承してはくれんのかの。ああ、さやうか、是非が無い。

然し、貫一さん、能う考へて御覧、まあ、私たちの事をどう思うてゐらるるか知らんが、お前さんの爾来の為方、又今日のこの始末は、ちと妥当ならんではあるまいか。とにかく鳴沢の翁に対してかう為たものではなからうと思ふが、どうであらうの。成程お前さんの方にも言分はあらう、それも聞きに来た。私の方にも少く言分の無いではない。それも聞かせたい。然し、かうしてわざわざ尋ねて来たものであるから、此方では既に折れて出てゐるのだ。さうしてお前さんに会うて話と謂ふは、決して身勝手な事を言ひに来たのぢやない、やはり其方の身の上に就いて善からうと計ひたい老婆心切。私の方ではその当時に在つてもお前さんの方に思ひ込んれと謂ひたい老婆心切。私の方ではその当時に在つてもお前さんを棄てた覚は無し、又今日も五年前も同じ考量で居るのだ。それを、まあ、若い人の血気と謂ふのであらう。唯一図に思ひ込んで誤解されたのか、私は如何にも残念でならん。今日までも誤解されてゐるのは愈よ心外で、お前さんの住所の知れ次第早速出掛けて来たのだ。凡そ此方の了簡を誤解されてゐるほど心苦しい事は無い。で、ああして睦う一家族で居つて、恩に被せうとて謀つたではないが、人の為に謀つて、さうして僅の行違から恨まれる、恩に被せうとて謀つたではないが、恨まれやうとは誰にしても思はん。僅の行違から音信不通の間になつて了ふと謂ふは、何ともはや浅ましい次ふ意であつたものを、私たちも死水を取つて貫

第で、私も誠に寝覚が悪からうと謂ふもの、実に姨とも言暮してゐるのだ。私の方では何処までも旧通りになつて貰うて、早く隠居でもしたいのだ。それも然しお前さんの了簡が釈けんでは話が出来ん。その話は二の次としても、差当り誤解されてゐる一条だ。会うて篤と話をしたら直に訳は分らうと思ふで、是非一通りは聞いて貰ひたい。その上でも心が釈けん事なら、どうもそれまで。私はお前さんの親御の墓へ詣つて、のう、抑もお前さんを引取つてから今日までの来歴を在様陳べて、鴫沢はこれこれの事を為、かうかう思ひまする、けれども成行でかう云ふ始末にもなりましたのは、残念ながら致方が無い、と丁とお分疏を言うて、そして私は私の一分を立ててから立派に縁を切りたいのだ。のう。はや五年も便を為んのだから、お前さんは縁を切つた気であらうが、私の方では未だ縁は切らんのだ。

私は考へる、たとへばこの鴫沢の翁の為た事が不都合であらうか知れん、けれども間貫一たる者は唯一度の不都合ぐらゐは如何にも我慢をしてくれんければ成るまいかと思ふのだ。又その我慢が成らんならば、も少し妥当に事を為てもらひたかつた。私の方に言分のあると謂ふのは其処だ。言はせればその通り私にも言分はある。然し、そんな事を言ひに来たではない、私の方にも如何様手落があつたで、その詫も言はうし、又昔も今も此方には心持に異変は無いのだから、それが第一に知らせたい。翁が久しぶりで来たのだ、のう、貫一さん、今日は何も言はずに清う会うてくれ」

曾て聞かざりし恋人が身の上の秘密よ、と満枝は奇き興を覚えて耳を傾けぬ。

我強くも貫一のなほ言はんとはせざるに、漸く恍へかねたる鳴沢の翁はやにはに、椅子を起ちて、強ひてもその顔見んと歩み寄れり。事の由は知るべきやう無けれど、この客の言を尽せるにも理聞えて、無下に打も棄てられず、されども貫一が唯涙を流して一語を出さず、いと善く識るらん人をば覚無しと言へる、これにもなかなか所謂はあらんと推測るれば、一も二も無く満枝は恋人に与してこの場の急を拯はんと思へるなり。

枕頭を窺ひつつ危む如く眉を攅めて、鳴沢の未だ言出でざる時、

「私看病に参つてをります者でございますが、何方様でもらつしやいますか存じませんが、この一両日病人は熱の気味で始終昏々いたして、時々譫語のやうな事を申して、泣いたり、懊つたり致すのでございますが、……」

頭を捻向けて満枝に対せる鳴沢の顔の色は、この時故に解きたりと見えぬ。

「はあ、は、さやうですかな」

「先程から伺ひますれば、年来御懇意でもらつしやるのを人違だとか申して、大相失礼を致してをるやうでございますが、やつぱり熱の加減で前後が解りませんのでございますから、どうぞお気にお懸け遊ばしませんやうに。この熱も直に除れますさうでございますから、又改めてお出しますでございます」

「はあ、それはそれは」

今日は私御名刺を戴いて置きまして、お軽快なり次第私から恐くお話を致しますでございます」

「はあ、それはそれは」

「実は、何でございました。昨日もお見舞にお出で下すつたお方に変な事を申掛けまして、何も病気の事で為方もございませんけれど、私弱りきりましたのでございます。今日は又如何致したのでございますか、昨日とは全で反対であの通り黙りきつてをりますでございますが、却つて無闇なことを申されるよりは始末が宜いでございます」

かくても始末は善しと謂ふかと、翁は打毀むべきを強ひて易へたるやうの笑を洩せば、満枝はその言了せしを喜べるやうに笑ひぬ。彼は婆を呼びて湯へ、更に熱き茶を薦めて、再び客を席に着かしめぬ。

「さう云ふ訳では話も解りかねる。では又上る事に致しませう。手前は鴫沢隆三と申して——名刺を差上げて置きまする、これに住所も誌してあります——貴方は失礼ながらやはり鰐淵さんの御親戚ででも？」

「はい、親戚ではございませんが、鰐淵さんとは父が極御懇意に致してをりますので、それに宅がこの近所でございますもので、ちよくちよくお見舞に上つてはお手伝を致してをります」

「はは、さやうで。手前は五年ほど掛違うて間とは会ひませんので、どうか去年あたり嫁を娶うたと聞きましたが、如何いたしましたな」

彼はこの美き看病人の素性知らまほしさに、あらぬ問をも設けたるなり。

「さやうな事はついに存じませんですが」

「はて、さうとばかり思うてをりましたに」

容儀人の娘とは見えず、妻とも見えず、しかも絢爛しう装飾れる様は色を売る儔にやと疑はれざるにはあらねど、言辞行儀の端々自らさにもあらざる、畢竟これ何者と、鳴沢は容易にその一斑をも推し得ざるなりけり。されども、懇意と謂ふも、手伝と謂ふも、皆詐ならんとは想ひぬ。

正き筋の知辺にはあらで、人の娘にもあらず、又貫一が妻と謂ふにもあらずして、深き訳ある内証者なるべし。若しさもあらば、貫一はその身の境遇とともに堕落して性根も腐れ、身持も頽れたるを想ふべし、とかくは好みて昔の縁を繋ぐべきものにあらず。如此き輩を出入せしむる鳴沢の家は、終に不慮の禍を招くに至らんも知るべからざるを、と彼は心中遽に懼を生じて、さては彼の恨深く言を容れざるを幸に、今日は一先立遅りて、尚ほ一層の探索と一番の熟考とを遂げて後、来る可くは再び来らんも晩からず、と失望の裏別に幾分の得るところあるを私に喜べり。

「いや、これはどうも図らずお世話様に成りました。いづれ又近日改めてお目に掛りますので、失礼ながらお名前を伺つて置きたうございますが」

「はい、私は」と紫根塩瀬の手提の中より小形の名刺を取出だして、

「甚だ失礼でございますが」

「はい、これは。　赤樫満枝さまと有仰いますか」

この女の素性に於ける彼の疑は　益暗くなりぬ。　夫有てる身の我は顔に名刺を用意せるも似気無し、まして裏面に横文字を入れたるは、猶可慎からず。　応対の雍にして人馴れたる、服装など

の当世風に貴族的なる、或は欧羅巴的女子職業に自営せる人などとならずや。が、又さる際には相応からずも覚えて、これ終に一題の麗き謎を彼に与ふるに過ぎざりき。鳴沢の翁は貫一の冷遇に悩むるをも忘れて、この謎の為に苦められつつ病院を辞し去れり。

客を送り出でて満枝の内に入来れば、ベッドの上に貫一の居丈高に起直りて、痩尽れたる拳を握りつつ、咄々、言はで忍びし無念に堪へずして、独り疾視の瞳を凝すに会へり。

第六章

数日前より鰐淵が家は燈点る頃を期して、何処より来るとも知らぬ一人の老女に訪るるが例となりぬ。その人は齢六十路余に傾きて、顔は皺みたれど膚清く、切髪の容などなかなか由ありげにて、風俗も見苦からず、唯異様なるは茶微塵の御召縮緬の被風をも着ながら、更紗の小風呂敷包に油紙の上掛したるを矢筈に負ひて、薄穢き護謨底の運動靴を履いたり。

所用は折入つて主に会ひたしとなり。生憎にも来る度他出中なりけれど、本意無げにも見えで急ぎ帰り、飽きもせずして通ひ来るなりけり。お峯は漸く怪しと思初めぬ。

彼のあだかも三日続けて来れる日、その挙動の常ならず、殊には眼色凄く、憚も無く人を目成りては、時ならずに独り打笑む顔の坐寒きまでに可恐しきは、狂人なるべし、しかも夜に入るを候ひ、時をも差へず訪ひ来るなど、我家に祟を作すにはあらずや、とお峯は遽に懼を抱きて、とて

も一度は会ひて、又と足踏せざらんやう、ひたすら直行にその始末を頼みければ、今日は用意して、四時頃にはや還り来にけるなり。

「どうも貴方、あれは気違ですよ。それでも品の良いことは、些とまああ旗本か何かの隠居さんと謂つたやうな、然し一体、鼻の高い、目の大きい、痩せた面長な、怖い顔なんですね。戸外へ来て案内する時のその声といふものが、実に無いんですよ。毎でも極つて、『頼みます、はい頼みます』とかう雍に、絞り二声言ふんで。もうもうその声を聞くと悚然として、ああ可厭だ。何だつて又あんな気違なんぞが来出したんでせう。本当に縁起でもない！」

お峯は柱なる時計を仰ぎぬ。燭の点るには未だ間ありと見るなるべし。直行は可難しげに眉を寄せ、唇を引結びて、

「何者か知らんで、一向心当と謂うては無い。名は言はんて？」

「聞きましたけれど言ひませんの。あの様子ぢや名なんかも解りは為ますまい」

「さうして今晩来るのか」

「来られては困りますけれど、きつと来ますよ。あんなのが毎晩々々来られては耐りませんから、貴方本当に来ましたら、篤り説諭して、もう来ないやうに作つて下さいよ」

「そりや受合へん。他が気違ぢやもの」

「気違だから私も気味が悪いからお頼申すのぢやありませんか」

「幾多頼まれたとて、気違ぢやもの、俺も為やうは無い」

頼める夫のさしも思はで頼み無き言に、お峯は力落してかつは尠からず心慌るなり。

「貴方でも可けないやうだつたらば、巡査にさう言つて引渡して遣りませう」

直行は打笑へり。

「まあ、そんなに騒がんとも可え」

「騒ぎはしませんけれど、私は可厭ですもの」

「誰も気遣の好えものは無い」

「それ、御覧なさいな」

「何じや」

知らず、その老女は何者、狂か、あらざるか、合力か、物売か、将主の知人か、正体の顕るべき時はかかる裏にも一分時毎に近くなりき。

終日灰色に打曇りて、薄日をだに洩さざりし空は漸く暮れんとして、弥増す寒さは怪からず人に遇れば、幾分の凌ぎにもと家々の戸は例よりも早く鎖されて、なほ稍明くその色厚氷を懸けたる如き西の空より、隠々として寂き余光の遠く来れるが、遽に去るに忍びざらんやうに彷徨へる巷の此処彼処に、軒ランプは既に点じ了りて、新に白き焔を放てり。

一陣の風は砂を捲きて起りぬ。怪しの老女はこの風に吹出されたるが如く姿を顕はせり。切髪は乱れ逆竪ちて、披払と飄される裾袂に行きつ留りつ、町の南側を辿り辿り、鰐淵が住へる横町に入りぬ。鋺槍の忍返を打ちたる石塀を盜れて一本の梅の咲誇れるを、斜に

軒ラムプの照せるがその門なり。

彼は殆ど我家に帰り来れると見ゆる態度にて、倖々と寄りて戸を啓けんとしたれど、啓かざりければ、かの雍しと謂ふ声して、

「頼みます、はい、頼みます」

風は飃々と鳴りて過ぎぬ。この声を聞きしお峯は竦みて立たず。

「貴方、来ましたよ」

「うん、あれか」

実に直行も気味好からぬ声とは思へり。小鍋立せる火鉢の角に猪口を措き、燈を持て来よと婢に命じて、玄関に出でけるが、先づ戸の内より、

「はい、何方ですな」

「旦那はお宅でございませうか」

「居りますが、何方で」

答はあらで、呟くか、小声ながら頻に物言ふが聞ゆるのみ。

「何方ですか、お名前は何と有仰るな」

「お目に掛れば解ります。何に致せ、おおお、まあ、梅が好く咲きましたぢやございませんか。当日の挿花はやつぱりこの梅が宜からうと存じます。さあ、どうぞ此方へお入り下さいまし、御遠慮無しに、さあ」

啓けんとせしに啓かざれば、彼は戸を打叩きて劇しく案内す。さては狂人なるよと直行も迷惑したれど、このままにては遂ふとも立去るまじきに、一度は会うてとにもかくにも為んと、心ならずも戸を開けば、聞きしに差はぬ老女は入来れり。

「鰐淵は私じやが、何ぞ用かな」

「おお、おまへが鰐淵か！」

つと乗出してその面に瞳を据ゑられたる直行は、鬼気に襲はれて忽ち寒く戦けるなり。熟くと見入る眼を放つと共に、老女は皺手に顔を掩ひて潜々と泣出せり。呆れ果てたる直行は金壺眼を凝してその泣くを眺むる外はあらざりけり。

彼は泣きて泣きて止まず。

「解らんな！　一体どう云ふんか、ああ、私に用と云ふのは？」

朽木の自ら頽れ行くらんやうにも打萎れて見えし老女は、猛然として振仰ぎ、血声を搾りて、

「この大騙め！」

「何ぢやと！」

「大、大悪人！　おのれのやうな奴が懲役に行かずに、内の……内の……雅之のやうな孝行者が……先祖を尋ぬれば、甲斐国の住人武田大膳太夫信玄入道、田夫野人の為に欺かれて、このまま断絶する家が誰か嫁が来る。柏井の鈴ちやんが、お嫁に来てくれれば、私の仕合は言ふまでもない、雅之もどんなにか嬉からう。子を捨てる藪は有つても、懲役に遣る親は無いぞ。二十七には

なっても世間不見のあの雅之、能うも能うもおのれは瞞したな！　さあ、さあさ讐を討つから立合ひなさい」

直行は舌を吐きて独語ちぬ。

「あ、いよいよ気違じやわい」

見る見る老女の怒は激して、形相漸くおどろおどろしく、物怪などの憑いたるやうに、一挙一動も全くその人ならず、足を踏鳴し踏鳴し、白歯の疎なるを牙の如く露して、一念の凝れる眸は直行の外を見ず、

「殺られた良人から懇々も頼まれた秘蔵の秘蔵の一人子、それを瞞しておのれが懲役に遣つたのだ。此方を女と侮つてさやうな不埒を致したか。長刀の一手も心得てゐるぞよ。恐入つたか」

彼は忽ちさも心地快げに笑へり。

「さうあらうとも、赦します。内には鈴ちやんが今日を曠と着飾つて、その美しさと謂ふものは！　ほんにまああんな縹致と云ひ、気立と云ひ、諸芸も出来れば、読、書、針仕事、そんなことは言つてゐるところではない。頸を長くして待つてお在だのに、早く帰つて来ないと云ふ法が有るものですか。大きにまあお世話様でございましたね、さあさ、馬車を待たして置いたから、おまへ私はね、漆車で行くから訳は無いとも」

履物はここに在るよ。なあに、かく言ふ間も忙しげに我が靴を脱ぎて、其処に直すと見れば、背負ひし風呂敷包の中結を釈きて、直行が前に上掛の油紙を抛げたり。

「さあさ、お前の首をこの中へ入れるのだ。ころっと落して。直に落ちるから、早く落してお了ひなさい」

さすがに持扱ひて直行の途方に暮れたるを、老女は目を繊めて、何処より出づらんやとばかり世にも奇き声を発ちて緩く笑ひぬ。彼は謂知らぬ凄気に打れて、覚えず肩を聳かせり。

懲役と言ひ、雅之と言ふに因りて、彼は始めてこの狂女の身元を思合せぬ。彼の債務者なる飽浦雅之は、私書偽造罪を以つて彼の被告としてこの十数日前、罰金十円、重禁錮一箇年に処せられしなり。実にその母なり。その母はこれが為に乱心せしか。

爾思へりしのみにて直行はその他に猶も思ふべき事あるを思ふを欲せざりき。雅之の私書偽造罪をもて刑せられしは事実の表にして、その罪は裏面に彼の謀りて陥れたるなり。

彼等の用ゐる悪手段の中に、人の借るを求めて連帯者を得るに窮するあれば、その一判にても話合の上は貸さんと称へて先づ誘ひ、然る後、但し証書の体を成さしめんが為、例の如く連帯者の記名調印を要すればとて、仮に可然き親族知己などの名義を私用して、在合ふ印章を捺さしめ、固より懇意上の内約なればその偽なるを知るといへども、一は焦眉の急に迫り、一は期限らしむるなり。借方もかかる所業の不義なるを咎めず、と手軽に持掛けて、実は法律上有効の証書を造内にだに返弁せば何事もあらじと姑息して、この術中には陥るなりけり。

期に迫びて還さざらんか、彼は忽ち爪牙を露し、陰に告訴の意を示してこれを脅し、散々に不当の利を貪りて、その肉尽き、骨枯るるの後、猶は驚く無き慾は、更に件の連帯者に対して寝

耳に水の強制執行を加ふるなり。これを表沙汰にせば債務者は論無う刑法の罪人たらざるべからず、ここに於て誰か恐慌し、狼狽し、悩乱し、号泣し、死力を竭して七所借の調達を計らさん。この時魔の如き力は喉を扼してその背を掩つ、人の死と生とは渾て彼が手中に在りて緊握せらる、欲するところとして得られざるは無し。

雅之もこの罠に繫りて学友の名を仮りて連印者に私用したりき。事の破綻に及びて、不幸にも相識れる学友は折から海外に遊学して在らず、しかも父なる人は彼を識らざりしより、その間の調停成らずして、彼の行為は終に第二百十条の問ふところとなりぬ。

法律は鉄腕の如く雅之を拉し去りて、剰さへ杖に離れ、涙に暗ふ老母をば道の傍に蹴返して顧ざりけり。噫、母は幾許この子に思を繫けたりけるよ。親に仕へて、此上無う優かりしを、柏井の鈴とて美き娘をも見立てて、この秋には妻すべかりしを、又この歳暮には援く方有りて、新に興るべき鉄道会社に好地位を得んと頼めしを、事は皆休みぬ、彼は人の歯せざる国法の罪人となり了れり。恥辱、憤恨、悲歎、憂愁、心を置惑ひてこの母は終に発狂せるなり。

「ああ宜いが。この首が欲いか、遣らうとも遣らうとも、ここでは可かんから外へ行かう。さあ無益に言を用ゐんより、唯手柔に搦み出すに如かじと、直行は少しも逆はずして、

「一処に来た」

狂女は苦々しげに頭を掉りて、

「お前さんの云ふことは皆妄だ。その手で雅之を瞞したのだらう。それ、それ見なさい、親孝行

の、正直者の雅之を瞞着して、散々金を取つた上に懲役に遣つたに相違無いと云ふ一札をこの通り入れたぢやないか、これでも未だ晶しい顔をしてゐるのか」

打披げたりし油紙を取りて直行の目先へ突付くれば、何を包みし移香にや、胸悪き一種の腥気ありて、夥く鼻を撲ちぬ。直行は猶ほ逆はで巳む無く面を背けたるを、狂女は目を瞪りつつ雀躍して、

「おおおお、あれあれ！　これは嬉しい、自然とお前さんの首が段々細くなつて来る。ああ、それ」

「おおおお、あれあれ！　今にもう落ちる」

地には落さじとやうに慌て悸き、油紙もて承けんと為る、その利腕をやにはに捉へて直行は格子の外へ攫さんと為たり。彼は推れながら突落す気たな。この老婦を騙討に為るのだな」

「ええ、おのれは他をこの崖から突落す気たな。この老婦を騙討に為るのだな」喚きつつ身を捻返して、突掛けし力の怪き強さに、直行は踏止らして尻居に倒るれば、彼は囃し立てて笑ふなり。忽ち起上りし直行は彼の衿上を掻摑みて、力まかせに外方へ突遣り、手早く雨戸を引かんとせしに、軋みて動かざる間に又駈戻りて、狂女はその凄き顔を戸口に顕はせり。余りの可恐しさに直行は吾を忘れてその顔をはたと撲ち、痩むところを得たりと戸を鎖せば、外より割るるばかりに戸を叩きて、

「さあ、首を渡せ。大事な証文も取上げて了つたな、大事な靴も取つたな。靴盗坊、大騙り！　首を寄来せ」

　直行は佇みて様子を候ひぬたり。　抜足差足忍び来れる妻は、後より小声に呼びて、

「貴方、どうしました」

　夫は戸の外を指してなほ去らざるを示せり。　お峯は土間に護謨靴と油紙との遺散れるを見付け

て、由無き質を取りけるよと思ひ煩へる折しも、

「頼みます、はい、頼みますよ」

と例の声は聞えぬ。　お峯は胴顫して、　長くここに留るに堪へず、夫を勧めて奥に入りにけり。

飛雪の如く乱点して、燈火の微に照す処その影は見えざるなりき。

　次の日も例刻になれば狂女は又訪ひ来れり。　主は不在なりとて、婢をして彼の遺せし二品を返

さしめけるに、前夜の暴れに暴れし気色はなくて、殊勝に聞分けて帰り行きぬ。　又試に婢を

出して不在の由を言はしめしに、こたびは直に立去らで、

「それぢやお帰来までここでお待ち申しませう。　実はね、是非お受取申す品があるので、それを

持つて帰りませんと都合が悪いのですから、幾日でもお待ち申しますよ」

　彼は戸口に蹲りて動かず。　婢は様々に言作へて賺しけれど、一声も耳には入らざらんやうに、

石仏の如く応ぜざるなり。　彼は已む無くこれを奥へ告げぬ。　直行も為ん術あらねば棄措きたりし

に、やや二時間も居て見えずなりぬ。

お峯は心苦がりて、この上は唯警察の手を借らんなど囃ぐを、直行は人を煩すべき事にはあらずとて聴かず。さらば又と来ざらんやうに逐払ふべき手立のありやと責むるに、害を為すにもあらねば、宿無犬の寝たると想ひて意に介するなとのみ。意に介くまじき如きを故に夫には学ばじ、と彼は腹立く思へり。この一事のみにあらず、お峯は常に夫の共に謀ると謂ふこと無くて、女童と侮れるやうに取合はぬ風あるを、口惜くも可恨くも、又或時は心細さの便無き余に、神を信ずる念は出でて、夫の頼むに足らざるところをば神明の冥護に拠らんと、天尊教と称ふるあり。差別無く敬神せるが中にも、ここに数年前より新に神道の一派を開きて、八百万の神といふ神は神体と崇めたるは、その光紫の一大明星にて、御名を大御明尊と申す。天地渾沌として日月も未だ成らざりし先高天原に出現ましましに因りて、天上天下万物の司と仰ぎ、諸の足らざるを補ひ、総て欠けたるを完うせしめんの大御誓をもて国土百姓を寧く恵ませ給ふとなり。彼は夙に起信して、この尊をば一身一家の守護神と敬ひ奉り、事と有れば祈念を凝して偏に頼み聞ゆるにぞありける。

この夜は別して身を浄め、御燈の数を献げて、災難即滅、怨敵退散の祈願を籠めたりしが、翌日の点燈頃ともなれば、夫は出でて未だ帰らざれば、今日若し罵り囃ぎて、内に躍入ることもやあらばと、如何せんと、前後の別知らぬばかりに動顛して、取次には婢を出し遣り、躬は神棚の前に駈着け、顔声を打揚げ、丹精を抽でて祝詞を宣りぬたり。狂女は不在と聞きて敢て争はず、昨日の如く、ここにて帰来を待たんとて、同き処に同き形して蹲れり。婢は格子を

鎖し固めて内に入りけるが、暫くは音も為ざりしに、遽に物語る如き、或は罵る如き声の頻に聞ゆるより主の知らで帰来て、捉へられたるにはあらずや、と台所の小窓より差覗けば、彼の外には人も在らぬに、在るが如く語るなり。その語るところは婢の耳に聞分けかねたれど、我子がこの主に欺かれて無実の罪に陥されし段々を、前後不揃に泣いつ怒りつ訴ふるなり。

第　七　章

子の讐なる直行が首を獲んとして夕々に狂女の訪ひ来ること八日に迫べり。浅ましとは思へど、逐ひて去らしむべきにあらず、又門口に居たりとて人を騒がすにもあらねば、とにもかくにも手を着けかねて棄措るなりき。

直行が言へりし如く、縮緬の被風着たる人の形の黄昏るる門の薄寒きに踞ひて、犬の寝たると太だ択ばざるべけれど、畢竟彼は何等の害をも加ふるにあらざれば、灰色の剪髪を掻乱し、妖星の光にも似たる眼を睨反して、笑ふかと見れば泣き、泣くかと見れば憤り、己の胸のやうに際も知らず黒く濁れる夕暮の空に向ひてその悲と恨とを訴へ、腥き油紙を拉りては人の首を獲んを待つなる狂女！　よし今は何等の害を加へずとも、終にはこの家に祟を作るべき望を繋くるにあらずや。人の執着の一念は水をも火と成し、山をも海と成し、鉄を鑠き、巌を砕くの例、ましてや家を滅し、人を蠱にすなど、塵を吹くよりも易かるべきに、可恐しや事無くてあれかしと、お峯は独り誾知らず心を傷むるなり。

夫は決して雅之の私書偽造を己の陥れし巧なりとは彼に告げざれば、悪は正く狂女の子に在り
て、此方に恨を受くべき筋は無く、自らかかる事も出来るは家業の上の勝負にて、又一方には貸
倒の損耗あるを思へば、所詮仕し、仆さるるは商の習と、お峯は自ら意を強うして、この老女の
狂を発せしを、夫の為せる業とは毫も思ひ寄らぬにあらざりき。さは謂へ、人の親の切なる情を思
へば、実にさぞと肝に徹ふる節無きにもあらざるめり。大方かかる筋より人は恨まれて、奇しき
殃にも遭ふなればと唯思過されては窮無き恐怖の募るのみ。

日に日に狂女の忘れず通ひ来るは、陰ながら我等の命を絶たんが為にて、多時門に居て動かざ
るは、その妄執の念力を籠めて夫婦を呪ふにあらずや、とほとほと信ぜらるるまでにお峯が夕暮
の心地は譬へん方無く悩されぬ。されば狂女の門に在る間は、大御明尊の御前に打頻り祝詞を
唱ふるにあらざれば凌ぐ能はず。かかる中にも心に些の弛あれば、煌々と輝き遍れる御燈の影
に晦み行きて、天尊の御像も朧に消失せなんと吾目に見ゆるは、納受の恵に泄れ、擁護の綱も切
れ果つるやと、彼は身も世も忘るるばかりに念を籠め、烟を立て、汗を流して神慮を驚かすにぞ
ありける。槍は降りても必ず来べし、と震摺れながら待たれし九日目の例刻になりぬれど、如何
にしたりけん狂女は見えず。鋭く返りたるこの日の寒気は鍼も背に膚に霜を種うらんやうに覚え
しめぬ。外には烈風怒り号びて、樹を鳴らし、屋を撼し、砂を捲き、礫を飛して、曇れる空なら
ねど吹揚げらるる埃に蔽れて、一天晦く乱れ、日色黄に濁りて、殊に物可恐き夕暮の気勢なり。
鰐淵が門の燈は硝子を二面まで吹落されて、火は消え、ランプは覆りたり。内の燈火は常より

鮮かに主が晩酌の喫台を照し、火鉢に架けたる鍋の物は沸々と薫じて、はや一銚子更へたるに、未だ狂女の音容はあらず。お峯は半危みつつも幾分の安堵の思を弄び喜ぶ風情にて、

「気違さんもこの風には弱つたと見えますね。もう毎もきつと来るのに来ませんから、今夜は来やしますまい、何ぼ何でもこの風ぢや吹飛されて了ひませうから。ああ、真に天尊様の御利益があつたのだ」

夫が差せる猪口を受けて、

「お相をしませうかね。何は無くともこんな好い心持の時に、戴くとお美いものですね。いいえ、さう続けてはとても……まあ、貴方。おやおやもう七時廻つたんですよ。そんなら断然今晩は来ないと極りましたね。ちや、戸締を為して了ひませうか、真に今晩のやうな気の霽々した、心の底から好い心持の事はありませんよ。あの気違さんぢやどんなに寿を短めたか知れはしません。もうこれきり来なくなるやうに天尊様へお願ひ申しませう。はい、戴きませう。御酒もお美いものですね。なあにあの婆さんが唯怖いのぢやありませんよ。それは気味は悪さうございますけれど、あれが来ると、慄然と、惣毛竪つて体が疎むのですもの、唯の怖いとは違ひますわね。それが、何だか、かう執着ればでもするやうな気がして、あの、それ、能く夢で可恐い奴なんぞに追懸けられると、逃げるには逃げられず、声を出さうとしても出ないので、どうなる事かと思ふ事がありませう、とんとあんなやうな心持なんで。ああ、もうそんな話は止しませう。私は少し酔ひました」

銚子を更へて婢の持来れば、

「金や、今晩は到頭来ないね、気違さんさ」

「好い塩梅でございます」

「お前には後でお菓子を御褒美に出すからね。貴方、これはあの気違さんとこの頃懇意になって

了ひましてね。気違の取次は金に限るのです」

「あら可厭なことを有仰いまし」

吹来り、吹去る風は大浪の寄せては返す如く絶間無く轟きて、その劇きは柱などをひちひちと

鳴揺がし、物打倒す轟き、引断る音、圧折る響は此処彼処に聞えて、唯居るさへに胆は冷されぬ。

長火鉢には怠らず炭を加へ加へ、鉄瓶の湯気は雲を噴くこと頻なれど、直行は後を牽きて已まず、お峯も心

鉄板などや負はさるるかと、飲めども多く酔ひ成さざるに、更に背面を圧する寒は

祝の数を過して、その地顔の赭きをば仮漆布きたるやうに照り耀して陶然たり。

狂女は果して来ざりけり。歓び酔へるお峯も唯酔へる夫も、褒美貰ひし婢も、十時近き比には

皆寐鎮りぬ。

風は猶も邪に吹募りて、高き梢は箒の掃くが如く撓められ、疎に散れる星の数は終に吹下され

ぬべく、層々凝れる寒は殆ど有らん限の生気を吸尽して、さらぬだに陰森たる夜色は益す冥く、

益す凄からんとす。忽ちこの黒暗々を劈きて、鰐淵が裏木戸の辺に一道の光は揚りぬ。低く発り

て物に遮られたれば、何の火とも弁へ難くて、その迸発の朱く烟れる中に、母家と土蔵との影は

朧に顕るるともなく奪はれて、瞬くばかりに消失せしは、風の強きに吹敷れたるなり。やや有り

て、同じほどの火影の又映ふと見れば、早くも薄れ行きて、こたびは燃えも揚らず、消えも遣ら

で、少時明を保ちたりしが、風の僅の絶間を偸みて、閃々と納屋の板戸を伝ひ、始めて騰れる焔

は炳然として四辺を照せり。塀際に添ひて人の形動くと見えしが、なほ暗くて了然ならず。

数息の間にして火の手は縦横に簷りつつ、納屋の内に乱入れば、噴出づる黒煙の渦は或は類

れ、或は畳みて、その外を引輻むとともに、見え遣り家も土蔵も堆き黯靆の底に没して、闇は

焔に破られ、焔は烟に採立られ、烟は更に風の為に砕かれつつ、蒸出す勢の夥ければ、猶

ほ所狭く漲りて、文目も分かず攪乱れたる中より爆然と鳴りて、天も焦げよと納屋は一面の猛火

と変じてけり。かの了然ならざりし形はこの時明に輝かされぬ。宵に来べかりし狂女の佇める

なり。躍り狂ふ烟の下に自若として、面も爛れんとすばかりに照されたる姿は、この災を司る鬼

女などの現れ出でにけるかと疑はしむ。実に彼は火の如何に焚え、如何に燬くや、と厳に監るが

如く皆を裂きて、その立てる処を一歩も移さず、風と烟と焔との相雑り、相争ひ、相勢ひて、力

の限を互に奮ふをば、妙くも為たりとや、漫笑を洩せる顔色はこの世に匹ふべきものありとも知

らず。

風の暴頻る響動に紛れて、寝耳にこれを聞着る者も無かりければ、誰一人出て噪がざる間に、

火は烈々と下屋に延きて、厨の燃立つ底より一声叫喚せるは誰、狂女は嘻々として高く笑ひぬ。

（七）の二

人々出合ひて打騒ぐ比には、火元の建物の大半は烈火となりて、土蔵の窓々より焰を出し、はや如何にとも為んやうあらざるなり。さしもの強風なりしかど、消防力めたりしに拠りて、三十幾戸を焼きしのみにて、午前二時に迫びて鎮火するを得たり。雑踏の裏より怪き奴は早くも拘引せられしと伝へぬ。かの狂女の去りも遺ざりしが捕れしなり。

火元と認定せらるる鰐淵方は塵一筋だに持出さずして、憐むべき一片の焦土を遺したるのみ。家族の消息は直ちに警察の訊問するところとなりぬ。婢は命辛々迸了せけれども、目覚むると斉く頭面は一面の火なるに仰天し、二声三声奥を呼捨にして走り出でければ、主たちは如何にかなりけん、知らずと言ふ。夜明けぬれど夫婦の出で来ざりけるは、過など有りしにはあらずやと、警官は出張して捜索に及べり。

熱灰の下より一体の屍の半焦爛れたるが見出されぬ。目も当てられず、浅ましう慘き限を尽したれど、主の妻と輙く弁ぜらるべき面影は焚残れり。さてはとその邁くを限無く搔起しけれど、酔ひて遁憊ひし他に見当るものは無くて、倉前と覚き辺より始めて焦壊れたる人骨を掘出せり。故か、貪りて身を忘れし故か、とにもかくにも主夫婦はこの火の為に落命せしなり。家屋も土蔵も一夜の烟となりて、鰐淵の跡とては赤土と灰との外に覓むべきものもあらず、風吹迷ふ長烟短焔の紛紅する処に、独り無事の形を留めたるは、主が居間に備へ付けたりし金庫のみ。

別居せる直道は旅行中にて未だ還らず、貫一はあだかもお釜の死体の出でし時病院より駈着け
たり。彼は三日の後には退院すべき手筈なりければ、今は全く癒えて勤を執るをも妨げざれど、
事の極めて不慮なると、急激なる、瑣小ならざるとに心惑のみせられて、病後の身を以てこれ
に当らんはいと苦かりけるを、尽瘁して万端を処理しつつ、ひたすら直道の帰京を待てり。

枕をも得挙げざりし病人の今かく健に起きて、常に来ては親く慰められし人の頭にも強かりし
を、空く爐余の断骨に相見て、弔ふ言だにあらざらんとは、貫一の遽にその真をば真とし能はざ
るところなりき。人は皆死ぬべきものと人は皆知れるなり。されどもその常に相見る人の死ぬべ
きを思ふ能はず。貫一はこの五年間の家族を迫めての一人も余さず、家倉と共に焚尽されて一夜
の中に儚くなり了れるに会ひては、おのれが懐裡の物の故無く消失せにけんやうにも頼み難く覚
えて、かくては我身の上の今宵如何に成りなんをも料られざるをと、無常の愁は頻に腸に沁む
なりけり。

住むべき家の痕跡も無く焼失せたりと謂ふだに、見果てぬ夢の如し、まして併せて頼めし主夫
婦を喪へるをや、音容幻を去らずして、ほとほと幽明の界を弁ぜず、剰へ久く病院の乾燥せる
生活に困じて、この家を懐ぶこと切なりければ、追慕の情は極りて迷執し、迫めては得るところ
もありやと、夜の晩きに貫一は市ヶ谷なる立退所を出でて、杖に扶けられつつ程遠からぬ焼跡を
弔へり。

連日風立ち、寒かりしに、この夜は遽に緩みて、朧の月の色も暖に、曇るともなく打霞める町

筋は静に眠れり。燻臭き悪気は四辺に充満ちて、踏荒されし道は水に繋り、爐に埋れ、焼杭焼瓦など所狭く積重ねたる空地を、火元とて板囲も得爲ず、それとも分かぬ焼原の狼藉として、鰐淵が家居は、全く形を失へるなり。

盛りたるは土蔵の名残と踏み行けば、灰燼の熱気は未だ冷めずして、微に面を撲つ。黒焦に削れたる幹のみ短く残れる一列の立木の傍に、塊々堆く挂いて慘然として佇めり。その立てる二三歩の前は直行が遺骨を発せし所なり。恨むと見ゆる死顔の月は、肉の片の棄てられたるやうに朱く敷ける満地の瓦を照して、目に入るものは皆伏し、四望の空く寥々たるに、黒く点せる人の影を、彼は自ら物凄く顧らるるなりき。

立尽せる貫一が胸には、在りし家居の状の明かに映じて、縈く光れるお峯が顔も、苦き口付せる主が面も眼に浮びて、歴々と相対へる心地もするに、始くはその境に己を忘れたりしが、やて徐に仰ぎ、徐に俯して、さて徐に一歩を行きては一歩を返しつつ、いとど思に沈みては、折々涙をも推拭ひつ。彼は転た人生の凄涼を感じて禁ずる能はざりき。苟くもその親める者の半にして離れ乖かざるはあらず。見よ或はかの棄てられし恨を遺し、或はこの奪はれし悲に遭ひ、前の恨の消えざるに又新なる悲を添ふ。棄つる者は去り、棄てざる者は逝き、亡きが故に悼むべきか、在る者は積憂の中に活き、亡き者は非命の下に在るが故に慶ぶべきか、亡きが故に悼むべきか、在る者は積憂の中に活き、亡き者は非命の下に斃る。

吾は煩悶の活を見るに、彼等が惨憺の死と相同からざるなし、但殊にするところは去ると留とのみ。

彼等の死ありて聊か吾が活の苦きをも慰むべきか、吾が活ありて、始めて彼等が死の抑もこの活とこの死とは孰を哀み、孰を悲まん。

傷ましきを弔ふに足らんか。吾が腸は断たれ、吾が心は壊れたり、彼等が肉は爛れ、彼等が骨は砕けたり。活きて爾苦しめる身をも、なほさすがに魂も消ぬべく打駭かしつる彼等が死状なるよ。産を失ひ、家を失ひ、猶も身を失ふに尋常の終を得ずして、極悪の重罪の者といへども未だ曾て如此き虐刑の辱を受けず、犬畜生の末までも箇様の業は曝さざる者と為すなかれ。人情は暗中に刃を揮ひ、世路然れども独り吾が直行をもて世間に善を作さざるはなし。若し吾が直行の行ふところは到る処に陥穽を設け、陰に陽に悪を行ひ、不善を作さざるはなし。しかも猶甚きを為して天も憎まず、命をもて咎むべしと為さば、誰か有りて咎められざらん。彼等の惨死を辱むるなかれ、適ま奇も薄んぜず、応報もこれを避るもの有るにあらずや。禍を免れ得ざりしのみ。

かく念へる貫一は生前の誼深かりし夫婦の死を歎きて、この永き別を遺方も無く悲み惜むなり。さて何時までかここに在らんと、主の遺骨を出せし辺を拝し、又妻の屍の横はりし処を拝して、心佗く立去らんとしたりしに、彼は怪くも遽に胸の内の掻乱るる心地するとともに、失せし夫婦の弔ふ者もあらで闇路の奥に打棄てられたるを悲く、あはれ猶少時留らずやと、いと迫めて乞ひ縋ると覚ゆるに、行くにも忍びず、又立還りて積みたる土に息へり。

実に彼も家の内に居て、遺骸の前に限知られず思ひ乱れんより、ここには亡き人の傍にも近く、遺言に似たる或る消息をも得るらん想して、立てたる杖に重き頭を支へて、夫婦が地下に窃せし念々を冥捜したり。やがて彼は何の得るところや有りけん、繁き涙は滂沱と頬を伝ひて零れぬ。

夜陰に轟き車ありて、一散に飛し来りけるが、焼場の際に止りて、翩と下立ちし人は、直ちに鰐淵が跡の前に尋ね行きて歩を住めたり。

焼瓦の踏破かるる音に面を擡げたる貫一は、件の人影の近く進来るをば、誰ならんと認むる間も無く、

「間さんですか」

「おお、貴方は！　お帰来でしたか」

その人は待ちに待たれし直道なり。貫一は忙く出迎へぬ。向ひて立てる両箇は月明に面を見合ひけるが、各口吃して卒に言ふ能はざるなりき。

「何とも不慮な事で、申上げやうもございません」

「はい。この度は留守中と云ひ、別してお世話になりました」

「私は事の起りました晩は未だ病院に居りまして、かう云ふ事とは一向存じませんで、夜明になつて漸く駈着けたやうな始末、今更申したところが愚痴に過ぎんのですけれど、私が居りましたらまさかこんな事にはお為せ申さんかつたと、実に残念でなりません。又お二人にしても余り不覚な、それしきの事に狼狽される方ではなかつたに、これまでの御寿命であつたか、残多い事を致しました」

直道は塞ぎし眼を怠げに開きて、

「何もかも皆焼けましたらうな」

「唯一品、金庫が助りました外には、すつかり焼いて了ひました」

「金庫が残りました？　何が入つてゐるのですか」

「貨も少しは在りませうが、帳簿、証書の類が主でございます」

「貸金に関した？」

「さやうで」

「ええ、それが焼きたかつたのに！」

口惜しとの色は絶かにその面に上れり。　貫一は彼が意見の父と相容れずして、年来別居せる内情を詳かに知れば、迫めてその喜ぶべきをも、却つてかく愛と為す故を暁れるなり。

「家の焼けたの、土蔵の落ちたのは差支無いのです。寧ろ焼いて了はんければ成らんのでしたから、それは結構です。両親の歿つたのも、私であれ、貴方であれ、かうして泣いて悲しむは、ここに居る二人きりで、世間に誰一人……さぞ衆が喜んでゐるだらうと思ふと、唯親を喪したのが情無いばかりではないのですよ」

されども堰敢へず流るるは恩愛の涙なり。　彼を憚りし父と彼を畏れし母とは、決して共に子として彼を慈むを忘れざりけり。その憚られ、畏れられし点を除きては、彼は他の憚られ、畏れられざる子よりも多く愛を被りき。生きてこそ争ひし父よ。亡くての今は、その聴れざりし恨より、親として事へざりし不孝の悔は直道の心を責むるなり。

生暖き風は急に来りてその外套の翼を吹捲りぬ。こはここに失せし母の賜ひしを、と端無く

彼は憶起して、さばかりは有のすさびに徳とも為ざりけるが、世間に量り知られぬ人の数の中に、誰か故無くして一紙を与ふる者ぞ、我は今聘せられし測量地より帰来れるなり。この学術とこの位置とを与へて恩と為ざりしは誰なるべき。外にこれを求むる能はず、重ねてこれを得べからざる父と母とは、相携へて杳に遐に隔つる世の人となりぬ。

炎々たる猛火の裏に、その父と母とは苦み悶えて援を呼びけんは幾許ぞ。彼等は果して誰をか呼びつらん。思ここに到りて、直道が哀咽は渾身をして涙に化し了らしめんとするなり。

「喜ぶなら世間の奴は喜んだが可いです。こんな事を申上げては実に失礼ですけれども、貴方が今日まで御両親をお持ちになつてゐら れたのは、私などの身から見ると何よりお可愛いので、この世の中に親子の情愛ぐらゐの詐の無いものは決して御座いませんな、私は十五の歳から孤児になりましたのですが、それは、親が附いてをらんと見縊られます。余り見縊られたのが自棄の本で、遂に私も真人間に成損つて了つたやうな訳で。固より己の至らん罪ではありますけれど、抑も親の附いてをらんかつたのが非常な不仕合で、そんな薄命な者もかうして在るのですから、それはもう幾歳になつたから親に別れて可いと謂ふ理窟はありませんけれど、聊か慰むるに足ると、まあ、思召さなければなりません」

貫一のこの人に向ひて親く物言ふ今夜の如き例はあらず、始より畜生視して、得べくば撲つて殺さんとも念ずるなりければ、今彼が言の端々に人がましき響あるを聞きて、いと異しと思へり。故に、彼こそ父が不善の助手なれと、この人の悪

「それでは、貴方真人間に成損つたとお言ひのですな」

「さうでございます」

「さうすると、今は真人間ではないと謂ふ訳ですか」

「勿論でございます」

直道は俯きて言はざりき。

「いや貴方のやうな方に向つてこんな太腐れた事を申しては済みません。さあ、参りませうか」

彼はなほ俯き、なほ言はずして、頷くのみ。

夜は太く更けにけれど、さらでだに音を絶てる寂静はここに澄徹りて、深くも物を思入る苦しさに直道が蹈躙る靴の下に、瓦の脆く割るるが鋭く響きぬ。地は荒れ、物は毀れたる中に一箇は立ち、一箇は優ひて、言あらぬ姿の侘しげなるに照すとも無き月影の隠々と映添ひたる、既に彷彿として悲の図を描成せり。

かくて暫く有りし後、直道は卒然言を出せり。

「貴方、真人間に成つてくれませんか」

その声音の可愁き底には情も籠れりと聞えぬ。貫一は粗彼の意を暁れり。

「どうですか」

「はい、難有うございます」

「どうですか」

「折角のお言ではございますが、私はどうぞこのままにお措き下さいまし」

「それは何為ですか」

「今更真人間に復る必要も無いのです」

「さあ、必要は有りますまい。私も必要から貴方にお勧めするのではない。もう一度考へてから挨拶をして下さいな」

「いや、お気に障りましたらお赦し下さいまし。貴方とは従来浸々お話を致した事もございませんで私といふ者はどんな人物であるか、御承知はございますまい。私の方では毎々お噂を伺つて、能く貴方を存じてをります。極深いお方なので、精神的に傷いたところの無い御人物、さう云ふ方に対して我々などの心事を申上げるのは、実際恥入る次第で、言ふ事は一々曲つてゐるのですから、正しい、直なお耳へは入らんところではない。逆ふのでございませう。で、深い貴方と、拗けた私とでは、始からお話は合はんところですから、それでお話を為る以上は、どうぞ何事もお聞流しに願ひます」

「ああ、善く解りました」

「真人間になつてくれんかと有仰つて下すつたのが、私は非常に嬉しいのでございます。こんな商売は真人間の為る事ではない、と知つてゐながらかうして致してゐる私の心中、辛いのでございます。そんな思をしつつ何爲してゐるか！　曰く言難しで、精神的に酷く傷けられた反動と、先づ思召して下さいまし。私が酒が飲めたら自暴酒でも呃つて、体を毀して、それきりに成つたのかも知れませんけれど、酒は可かず、腹を切る勇気は無し、究竟は意気地の無いところから、こ

んな者に成つて了つたのであらうと考へられます」

彼の潔しと謂ふなる直道が深き心の同情は、彼の微見したる述懐の為に稍動されぬ。

「お話を聞いて見ると、貴方が今日の境遇になられたに就いては、余程深い御様子が有るやう、どう云ふのですか、悉く聞して下さいませんか」

「極愚な話で、到底お聞せ申されるやうな者ではないのです。又自分もこの事は他には語るまい、と堅く誓つてゐるのでありますから、どうも申上げられません。究竟或事に就いて或者に欺かれたのでございます」

「はあ、それではお話はそれで措きませう。で、貴方もあんな家業は真人間の為べき事ではない、と十分承知してゐらるる、父などは決して愧づべき事ではない、と謂つて剛情を張り通した。実に浅ましい事だと思ふから、或時は不如父の前で死んで見せて、最後の意見を為るより外は無い、と決心したことも有つたのです。父は飽くまで聴かん、私も飽くまで棄てては措かん精神、どんな事をしても是非改心させる覚悟で居つたところ、今度の災難で父を失つた、残念なのは、改心せずに死んでくれたのだ、これが一生の遺憾で。一時に両親に別れて、死目にも逢はず、その臨終と謂へば、気の毒とも何とも、謂ひやうの無い。愈よ残念で、早く改心さへしてくれか、察し給へ。それに就けても、改心せずに死なしたのが、凡そ人の子として これより上の悲が有らう たらば、この災難は免れたに違無い。いや私はさう信じてゐる。今貴方が改心して下されば、私は父が改心した いから、父の代りに是非貴方に改心して貰ひたい。然し、過ぎた事は今更為方が無

も同じと思つて、それで満足するのです。さうすれば、必ず父の罪も滅びる、私の念も霽れる、貴方も正い道を行けば、心安く、楽く世に送られる。

成程、お話の様子では、こんな家業に身を墜されたのも、已むを得ざる事情の為とは承知してをりますが、父への追善、又その遺族の路頭に迷つてゐるのを救ふのと思つて、金を貸すのは罷めて下さい。父に関した財産は一切貴方へお譲り申しますからそれを資本に何ぞ人をも益するやうな商売をして下されば、この上の喜は有りません。父は非常に貴方を愛してゐつた、貴方も父を愛して下さるでせう。愛して下さるなら、父に代つて非を悔めて下さい」

聴ゐる貫一は露の晨の草の如く仰ぎ視ず。語り訖れども猶仰ぎ視ず、如何にと問ゐるにも仰ぎ視ざるなりけり。

忽ち一閃の光ありて焼跡を貫く道の畔を照しけるが、その燈の此方に向ひて近くは、巡査の見尤めて寄来るなり。両箇は一様に瞑へて、待つともなく動かずゐたりければ、その前に到れる巡査は如何に驚きけんよ、かれもこれも各惨として蒼き面に角燈の光は隈無く彼等を曝しぬ。

涙垂れたり——しかもここは人の泣くべき処なるか、時は正に午前二時半。

続金色夜叉

与紅葉山人書

学　海　居　士

紅葉山人足下。僕幼嗜読稗史小説。当時行於世者。京伝三馬一九。及曲亭柳亭春水数輩。雖有文辞之巧麗。搆思之妙絶。多是舐古人之糟粕。拾兎園之残簡。聊以加己意焉耳。独曲亭柳亭二子較之余子。学問該博。熟慣典故。所謂換骨奪胎。頗有可観者。如八犬弓張狭史伝。及田舎源氏諸国物語類是也。然在当時。読此等書者。不過閭巷少年。畧識文字。間有渉猟史伝者。識見浅薄。不足以判其巧拙良否焉。而文学之士斥為鄙猥。禁子弟不得縦読。其風習可以見矣。」年二十二。稍読水滸西遊金瓶三国紅楼諸書。兼及我源語竹取宇津保俊蔭等書。乃知稗史小説。亦文学之一途。不必止游戯也。而所最喜。在水滸金瓶紅楼。及源語。能尽人情之隠微。世態之曲折。用筆周到。渾思巧緻。而源氏之能描性情。文雅而思深。金瓶之能写人品。筆密而心細。蓋千古無比也。近時小説大行。少好文辞者。莫不争先攘臂其間。然率不過陋巷之

談。鄙夫之事。至大手筆如金瓶源氏等者。寥乎無聞何也。僕及読足下所著諸書。所謂細心邃思
者。知不使古人専美於上矣。多情多恨金色夜叉類。殆与金瓶源語相似。僕反覆熟読不能置也。
惜範囲狭。而事跡微。地位卑而思想偏。未足以展布足下之大才矣。盡借一大幻境。以運思馳
筆。必有大可観者。僕老矣。若得足下之一大著述。快読之。是一生之願也。足下以何如。

第　一　章

時を錢なりとしてこれを換算せば、一秒を一毛に見積りて、壹人前の睡量凡そ八時間を除きた
る一日の正味十六時間は、実に金五円七拾六銭に相当す。これを三百六十五日の一年に合計すれ
ば、金弐千壱百〇弐円四拾銭の巨額に上るにあらずや。さればここに二十七日と推薄りたる歳末
の市中は物情恟々として、世界絶滅の期の終に宣告せられたらんもかくやとばかりに、坐りし
人は出でて歩み、歩みし人は走りて過ぎ、走りし人は足も空に、合ふさ離るさの気立く、肩相摩し
ては傷き、轂相撃ちては砕けぬべきをも覚えざるは、心々に今を限ると慌て騒ぐ事ありて、不狂人
も狂せるなり。彼等は皆過去の十一箇月を虚に送りて、一秒の塵の積める弐千余円の大金を何処
にか振落し、後悔の尾に立ちて今更に血眼を瞪き、草を分け、瓦を探しても、その行方を尋ねん
と為るにあらざるなし。かかる間にも常は止一毛に値する一秒の壱銭乃至拾銭にも暴騰せる貴々
重々の時は、速射砲を連発にするが如く飛過るにぞ、彼等の恐慌は更に意言も及ばざるなる。

その平生に怠無かりし天は、又今日に何の変易もあらず、悠々として蒼く、昭々として闊く、浩々として静に、しかも確然としてその覆ふべきを覆ひ、終日北の風を下し、夕付く日の影を耀して、師走の塵の表に高く澄めり。見遍せば両行の門飾は一様に枝葉の末広く寿山の翠を交し、十町の軒端に続く注連縄は、福海の霞揺曳して、繁華を添ふる春待つ景色は、転た旧り行く歳の魂を驚かす。

かの人々の弐千余円を失ひて馳違ふ中を、梅提げて通るは誰が子、猟銃担げ行くは誰が子、妓と車を同うするは誰が子、楊枝して好き衣着たるは誰が子、或は二頭立の馬車を駆る者、結納の品々担する者、雑誌など読みもて行く者、五人の子を数珠繋にして勧工場に入る者、彼等は各若干の得たるところ有りて、如此く自ら足れりと為るにかあらん。これ等の少く失へる者は喜び、彼等の多く失へる輩は憂ひ、又稀には全く失はざりし人の楽めるも、皆内には麒麟として、盈てるは虧けじ、虧けては盈たんと、孰がその求むるところに急ならざるはあらず。人の世は三の朝より花の昼、月の夕にもその思の外はあらざれど、勇怯は死地に入りて始て明なる年の関を、物の数とも為ざらんほどを目にも見よとや、空臚の酔を踏み、鉄鞭を曳き、一巻のブックを懐にして、嘉平治平の袴の焼海苔を綴れる如きを穿ち、フラネルの浴衣の洗ひ曝して垢染にしたるに、二重外套は何の冬誰が不用をや譲られけん、尋常よりは寸の薄りたるを、身材の人より豊なるに文目も分かぬ木綿縞の布子を襲ねて、ジョンソン帽の瓦色に化けたるを頂き、焦茶地の縞羅紗の絡ひたれば、例の袴は風にや吹断れんと危くも閃きつつ、その人は齢三十六七と見えて、形癯せ

たりとにはあらねど、寒樹の夕空に倚りて孤なる風情、独り負ふ気無く麗くも富める髭鬚は、下には乳の辺まで髯々と垂れて、左右に拊りたるは八字の髯を巻きて耳の根にも遶びぬ。打見れば面目爽に、稍傲れる色有れど峻くはあらず、しかも今陶々然として酒興を発し、春の日長の野辺を辿るらんやうに、西筋の横町をこの大路に出で来らんとす。

「瓢空く夜は静にして高楼に上り、酒を買ひ、籠を巻き、月を邀べて酔ひ、酔中剣を払へば光月を射る」

彼は節をかしく微吟を放ちて、行く行くかつ楽むに似たり。打晴れたる空は瑠璃色に夕栄えて、俄に冴え勝る颶の目口に沁みて磨鐵を打つらんやうなるに、烈火の如き酔顔を差付けては太息噓いて、右に一歩左に一歩と踉きつつ、

「往々悲歌して独り流涕す、君山を剗却して湘水平に桂樹を砍却して月更に明ならんを、丈夫志有りて……」

と唱ひ出づる時、一隊の近衛騎兵は南頭に馬を疾めて、舞立つ砂煙の中に魁の花を装へる健児の参差として推行く後影をば、壮なる哉と謂まほしげに看送りて、

「我四方に遊びて意を得ず、陽狂して薬を施す成都の市」

と漫にその詩の首をば小声朗に吟じゐたり。さては往来の遣る目も皆率れて、この節季の修羅場を独り天下に吃ひ酔へるは、何者の暢気か、自棄か、豪傑か、悟か、酔生児か、と異き姿を見

て過る有れば、面を識らんと窺ふ有り、又はその身の上など思ひつつ　行くも有り。彼は太く酔へれば総て知らず、町の股脈を眺め遣りて、何方を指して行かんとも心定らず姑く立てるなりけり。

さばかり人に怪まるれど、彼は今日のみこの町に姿を顕したるにあらず、折々散歩すらんやうに出来ることもあれど、筍様の酔態を認むるは、兼て注目せる派出所の巡査も希しと思へるなり。やがて彼は鉄鞭を曳鳴して大路を右に出でしが、二町ばかりも行きて、乾の方より狭き坂道の開きたる角に来にける途端に、風を帯びて馳下りたる俥は、生憎其方に踊ける酔客の膝の辺を一衝撞てたりければ、彼は邜含を打つて二間も彼方へ撥飛さると斉く、大地に横面擦つて僵れたり。不思議にも無難に踏留り車夫は、この鹵忽に気を奪れて立ちたりしが、面倒なる相手と見たりけん、そのまま轅を回して逃れんとするを、俥の上なる黒綾の吾妻コオト着て、素鼠縮緬の頭巾被れる婦人は樺色無地の絹膓虎の膝掛を推除けて、駐めよ、返せと悶ゆるを、猶聴かで曳々

「待て、こら！」と喝する声に、行く人の始て事有りと覚れるも多く、はや車夫の不情を尤むる語も聞ゆるに、耐りかねたる夫人は強て其処に下車して返り来りぬ。例の物見高き町中なりければ、この忙き際をも忘れて、寄来る人数は蟻の甘きを探りたるやうに、一面には遭難者の土に蹻べる周辺を擁し、一面には婦人の左右に傍ひて、目に物らんと揉立てたり。婦人は途を来つつ被物を取りぬ。紋羽二重の小豆鹿子の手絡したる円髷に、鼈甲脚の金

七宝の玉の後簪を斜に、高蒔絵の格子櫛を翳して、粧は実に塵をも怜れぬべき人の謂ひ知らず思惑へるを、可痛しの嵐に堪へぬ花の顔や、と群集は自ら声を飲めて肝に徹するなりき。

いと更に面の裏もほしきこの場を、頭巾脱ぎたる彼の可羞しさと切なさとは、幾許なりけん、打棚めたる顔は措き所あらぬやうに、人堵の内を急足に辿りたり。帽子も鉄鞭も、懐にせしブックも、薩摩下駄の髪も投散されたる中に、酔客は半ば身を擡げて血を流せる右の高頬を平手に掩ひつつ寄来る婦人を打見遣りつ。彼はその前に先づ懦れず会釈して、何とも相済みませんでございます。おや、お顔を！　お目を打ちましたか、まあどうも……」

「どうも取んだ麁相を致しまして、何とも相済みませんでございます。おや、お顔を！　お目を

「いや太した事は無いのです」

「さやうでございますか。何処ぞお痛め遊ばしましたでございませう」

腰を得立てずゐるを、婦人はなほ気遣へるなり。

車夫は数次腰を屈めて主人の後方より進出でけるが、

「どうも、旦那、誠に申訳もございません、どうか、まあ平に御勘弁を願ひます」

眼を其方に転じたる酔客は悲れるとしもなけれど声粛に、

「貴様は善くないぞ。麁相を為たと思うたら何為車を駐めん。逃げやうとするから呼止めたんじや。貴様の不心得から主人にも恥を掻する」

「へい恐入りました」

「どうぞ御勘弁あそばしまして」
倅の主の身を下して辞を添へれば、彼も打頷きて、

「以来気を着けい、よ」

「へい……へい」

「早う行け、行け」

やをら彼は起たんとすなり。さては望外なる主従の喜に引易へて、見物の飽気無さは更に望外なりき。彼等は幕の開かぬ芝居に会へる想して、余に落着の蛇尾振はざるを悔みて、はや忙々に踵を回すも多かりけれど、又見栄あるこの場の模様に名残を惜みつつ去り敢へぬもありけり。

車夫は起ち悩める酔客を扶けて、履物を拾ひ、鞭を拾ひて宛行へば、主人は帽を清め、ブックを取上げて彼に返し、頭巾を車夫に与へて、懇に外套、袴の泥を払はしめぬ。疚きに堪へぬ心は、なほ為すべき事あるを呑ぬべきも、歴々と挫傷のその面に残れるを見れば、免されし罪は消えみて私せるにあらずやと省られて、彼はさすがに見捨てかねたる人の顔を始めは可傷しと眺めたりしに、その眼色は漸く鋭く、かつは疑ひかつは怪むらんやうに、忍びては瞑りつつ便無げに佇みけるに、いでや長居は無益とばかり、彼は暗跟と踏出せり。

婦人はとにもかくにも遣過せしが、又何とか思直しけん、遽に追行きて呼止めたり。　頭を捻向けたる酔客は耗れる眼を屹と見据ゑて、自か他と訝しさに言も出さず。

「もしお人違でございましたら御免あそばしまして。　貴方は、あの、もしや荒尾さんではあらっ

しやいませんですか」

「は？」彼は覚えず身を回して、丁と立てたる鉄鞭に仗り、こは是白日の夢か、空華の形か、正体見んと為れど、酔眼の空く張るのみにて、益す霽れざるは疑なり。

「荒尾さんでのらつしやいましたか！」

「はあ？」荒尾です、私荒尾です」

「あの間貫一を御承知の？」

「おお、間貫一、旧友でした」

「私は鳴沢の宮でございます」

「何、鳴沢……鳴沢の……宮と有仰る……？」

「はい、間の居りました宅の鳴沢」

「おお、宮さん！」

奇遇に驚かされたる彼の酔は頓に半は消えて、せめて昔の俤を認むるや、とその人を打眺むるより外はあらず。

「お久しぶりで御座いました」

宮は懐び勇みて犇と寄りぬ。

今は美き伜の主ならず、路傍の酔客ならず名宣合へるかれとこれとの思は如何。間貫一が鳴沢の家に在りし日は、彼の兄の如く友として善かりし人、彼の身の如く契りて怜かりし人にあらず

や。その日の彼等は又同胞にも得べからざる親を以て、膝をも交へ心をも語りしにあらずや。その日の彼等は多少の転変を覚悟せし一生の中に、今日の奇遇を算へざりしなり。よしさりとも、一たび同胞と睦合へりし身の、弊衣を飄して道に酔ひ、流車を駆りて富に驕れる高下の差別の自ら種有りて作せるに似たる如此きを、彼等は更に更に夢ざりしなり。その算へざりし奇遇と夢ざりし差別とは、咄々、相携へて二人の身上に逼れるなり。女気の脆き涙ははや宮の目に湿ひぬ。

「まあ大相お変り遊ばしたこと！」

「貴方も変りましたな！」

さしも見えざりし面の傷の可恐きまでに益す血を出すに、宮は持たりしハンカチイフを与へて拭はしめつつ、心も心ならず様子を窺ひて、

「お痛みあそばすでせう。少しお待ちあそばしまし」

彼は何やらん吩咐けて車夫を遣りぬ。

「直この近くに懇意の医者が居りますから、其処までいらしつて下さいまし。唯今俥を申附けました」

「何の、そんなに騒ぐほどの事は無いです」

「あれ、お始うございますよ。さうして大相召上つてゐらつしやるやうですから、ともかくもお俥でお出あそばしまし」

「いんや、宜い、大丈夫。時に間はその後どうしましたか」

宮は胸先を刃の透ゆるやうに覚ゆるなりき。

「その事に就きまして色々お話も致したいので御座います」

「然し、どうしてゐますか、無事ですか」

「はい……」

「決して、無事ぢやない筈です」

生きたる心地もせずして宮の恕ち慄ける傍に、車夫は見苦からぬ一台の辻車を伴ひ来れり。漸く面を挙れば、いつ又寄りしとも知らぬ人立を、可忌くも巡査の怪みて近くなり。

第二章

鬢深き横面に貼薬したる荒尾譲介は既に蒼く酔醒めて、煌々たる空気ランプの前に變積もあらぬ袴の膝を丈六に組みて、接待茣の葉巻を燻しつつ意気粛に、打萎れたる宮と熊の敷皮を斜に差向ひたり。こはこれ、彼の識れると謂ひし医師の奥二階にて、畳敷にしたる西洋造の十畳間なり。物語ははや緒を解きしなるべし。

「間が影を隠す時、僕に遺した手紙が有る、それで悉い様子を知つてをるです。その手紙を見た時には、僕も顫へて腹が立つた。直に貴方に会うて、是非これは思返すやうに飽くまで忠告し

て、それで聴かずば、もう人間の取扱は為ちやをられん、腹の癒ゆるほど打踏して、一生結婚の成らんやう立派な不具にしてくれやう、と既にその時は立上つたですよ。然し、間が言を尽して貴方が聴かんと云ふ、僕の言を容れやう道理が無い。又間が富山への売物じや。他の売物に疵を附けちや済まん、とさう思うて、そりや実に矢も楯も耐らん胸を挙つて了うたんです」

宮が顔を推当てたる片袖の端より、連に眉の顰むが見えぬ。

「宮さん、僕は貴方はさう云ふ人ではないと思うた。あれ程互に愛してをつた間さへが欺かれんちやから、僕の欺れたのは無理も無いぢやらう。僕は僕として貴方を怨むばかりでは慊らん、間に代つて貴方を怨むですよ、いんや、怨む、七生まで怨む、きつと怨む！」

終に宮が得堪へぬ泣音は洩れぬ。

「間の一身を誤つたのは貴方が誤つたのぢや。それは又間にしても、高が一婦女子に棄てられたが為に志を挫いて、命を抛つたも同然の堕落に果てる彼の不心得は、別に間として大いに責めんけりやならん。然し、間が如何に不心得であらうと、貴方の罪は依然として貴方の罪ぢや、のみならず、貴方が間を棄てた故に、彼が今日の有様に堕落したのであつて見れば、貴方は女の操を破つたのみでない。併せて夫を刺殺したも……」

宮は慄然として振仰ぎしが、荒尾の鋭き皆は貫一が怨も憑りたりやと、その見る前に身の措所無く打竦みたり。

「同じですよ。さうは思ひませんか。で、貴方の悔悟されたのは善い、これは人として悔悟せん
けりやならん事。けれども残念ながら今日に及んでの悔悟は業に晩い。間の堕落は間その人の死
んだも同然、貴方は夫を持つて六年、なあ、水は覆つた。盆は破れて了うたんじや。かう成つた
上は最早神の力も逮ぶことではない。お気の毒じやと言ひたいが、やはり貴方が自ら作せる罪の
報で、固よりかく有るべき事ぢやらうと思ふ」

宮は俯きてよよと泣くのみ。

「吁、吾が罪！　さりとも知らで犯せし一旦の吾が罪！　その吾が罪の深さは、あの人ならぬ人
さへかくまで憎み、かくまで怨むか。さもあらば、必ず思知る時有らんと言ひしその人の、争で
争で吾が罪を容すべき。吁、吾が罪は終に容されず、吾が恋人は終に再び見る能はざるか。

宮は胸潰れて、涙の中に人心地をも失はんとすなり。

おのれ、利を見て愛無かりし匹婦、憎しとも憎しと思はざるにあらぬ荒尾も、当面に彼の悔悟
の切なるを見ては、さすがに情は動くなりき。宮は際無く顔を得挙げずるなり。

「間が容さんでも、又僕が容さんでも、貴方はその悔悟に因つて自ら
容されたんじや」

由無き慰藉は聞かじとやうに宮は俯しながら頭を掉りて更に泣入りぬ。

「自にても容さるるのは、誰にも容されんのには勝つてをる。又自ら容さるるのは、終には人
に容さるるそれが始ぢやらうと謂ふもの。僕は未だ未だ容し難く貴方を怨む、怨みは為るけれど、

今日の貴方の胸中は十分察するのです。貴方のも察するからには、他の者の間の胸中もまた察せにやならん、可いですか。さうして孰が多く憐むべきであるかと謂へば、間の無念は抑どんなちやらうか、なあ、僕はそれを思ふんです。それを思うて見ると、貴方の苦痛を傍観するより外は無い。

かうして今日図らずお目に掛った。僕は婦人として生涯の友にせうと思うた人は、後にも先にも貴方ばかりじや。いや、それは段々お世話にもなつた、忝いと思うた事も幾度か知れん、その嫒友に何年ぶりかで逢うたのぢやから、僕も実に可懐う思ひました」

宮は泣音の迸らんとするを咬緊めて、濡浸れる袖に粲々と面を擦付けたり。

「けれど又、円齧に結うて、立派にしてゐらるるのを見りや、決して可愛うはなかった。幸ひ貴方が話したい事が有ると言るる、善し、あの様に間を詐つた貴方じや、又僕を幾何ほど詐ること ちやらう、それを聞いた上で、今日こそは打詰してくれやうと待つてをつた。然るに、貴方の悔悟、僕は陰に喜んで聴いたのです。今日の貴方はやはり僕の友の宮さんぢやつた。好う貴方悔悟なすつた！さも無かつたら、貴方の顔にこの十倍の疵を附けにや還さんぢやつたのです。なあ、自ら容されたのは人に赦さるる始──解りましたか。

で、間に取成してくれれい、詫を言うてくれれい、とのお嘱ぢやけれど、それは僕は為ん。為んのは、間に対してどうも出来んのぢやから。又貴方に罪有りと知つてをりながらその人から頼まる僕でない。又僕が間であつたらば、断じて貴方の罪は容さんのぢやから。

かうして親友の敵に逢うてからに、指も差さずに別るる、これが荒尾の貴方に対する寸志と思うて下さい。いや、久しぶりで折角お目に掛りながら、可厭な言ばかり聞せました。それぢや、まあ、御機嫌好う、これでお暇します」

会釈して荒尾の身を起さんとする時、

「暫く、どうぞ」宮は取乱したる泣顔を振挙げて、重き瞼の露を払へり。

「それではこの上どんなにお願ひ申しましても、貴方はお詫を為つては下さらないので御座いますか。さうして貴方もやはり私を容さんと有仰るので御座いますか」

「さうです」

忙しげに荒尾は片膝立ててゐたり。

「どうぞもう暫くゐらしつて下さいまし、唯今直に御飯が参りますですから」

「や、飯なら欲うありませんよ」

「私は未だ申上げたい事が有るのでございますから、荒尾さんどうかお坐り下さいまし」

「いくら貴方が言うたつて、返らん事ぢやありませんか」

「そんなにまで有仰らなくても、……少しは、もう堪忍なすつて下さいまし」

火鉢の縁に片手を翳して、何をか打案ずる様なる目を翳しつつ荒尾は答へず。

「荒尾さん、それでは、とてもお聴入はあるまいと私は諦めましたから、貫一さんへお詫の事はもう申しますまい、又貴方に容して戴く事も願ひますまい」

咄嗟に荒尾の視線は転じて、猶語り続る宮が面を掠め去りぬ。

「唯一目私は貫一さんに逢ひまして、その前でもって、私の如何にも悪かった事を思ふ存分謝りたいので御座います。唯あの人の目の前で謝りさへ為たら、それで私は本望なのでございます。素より容してもらはうとは思ひません。貫一さんが又容してくれやうとも、ええ、どうせ私は思ひは致しません。容されなくても私はかまひません。私はもう覚悟を致し……」

宮は苦しげに涙を呑みて、

「ですから、どうぞ御一所にお伴れなすって下さいまし。貴方がお伴れなすって下されば、貫一さんはきっと逢ってくれます。逢ってさへくれましたら、私は殺されましても可いので御座います。貴方と二人で私を責めて責め抜いた上で、貫一さんに殺さして下さいまし。私は貫一さんに殺してもらひたいので御座います」

感に打れて霜置く松の如く動かざりし荒尾は、忽ちその長き髯を振りて頷けり。

「うむ、面白い！　逢うて間に殺されたいとは、宮さん好う言れた。さうなけりゃならんじゃ。

然し、なあ、然しじゃ、貴方は今は富山の奥さん、唯継と云ふ夫の有る身じゃ、滅多な事は出来んですよ」

「私はかまひません！」

「可かん、そりゃ可かん。間に殺されても辞せんと云ふその悔悟は可いが、それぢゃ貴方は間有るを知って夫有るのを知らんのじゃ。夫はどうなさるなあ、夫に道が立たん事になりはせまいか、

そこも考へて貰はにやならん。

して見りや、始には富山が為に間を欺き、今又間の為に貴方は富山を欺くんじや。一人ならず二人欺くんじや！　始には富山が為に間を欺き、今又間の為に貴方は富山を欺くんじや。一人ならず二人欺くんじや！　一方には悔悟して、それが為に又一方に罪を犯したら、折角の悔悟の効は没つて了ふ」

「そんな事はかまひません！」

無慙に唇を咬みて、宮は抑へ難くも激せるなり。

「かまはんぢや可かん」

「いいえ、かまひません」

「そりや可かん！」

「私はもうそんな事はかまひませんのです。私の体はどんなになりませうとも、疾から棄ててをるので御座いますから、唯もう一度貫一さんにお目に掛つて、この気の済むほど謝りさへ致したら、その場でもつて私は死にましても本望なのですから、富山の事などは……不如さうして死んで了ひたいので御座います」

「それそれさう云ふ無考な、訳の解らん人に僕は与することは出来んと謂ふんじや。一体さうした貴方は了簡ぢやからして、始に間をも棄てたんじや。不埒です！　人の妻たる身で夫を欺いて、それでかまはんとは何事ですか。そんな貴方が了簡であつて見りや、僕は寧ろ富山を不憫に思ふです、貴方のやうな不貞不義の妻を有つた富山その人の不幸を憫まんけりやならん、いや、憫む、

貴方よりは富山に僕は同情を表する、愈よ憎むべきは貴方じや」

四途乱に湿べる宮の目は焚ゆらんやうに輝けり。

「さう有仰つたら、私はどうして悔悟したら宜いので御座いませう。荒尾さん、どうぞ助けると思召してお誨へなすつて下さいまし」

「僕には誨へられんで、貴方がまあ能う考へて御覧なさい」

「三年も四年も前から一日でもその事を考へません日と云つたら無いのでございます。それが為に始終悒々と全で疾つてるやうな気分で、憶もうこんなら、いつそ死んで了はう、と熟くさうは思ひながら、唯もう一目、一目で可うございますから貫一さんに逢ひませんでは、どうも死ぬにも死なれないので御座います」

「まあ能う考へて御覧なさい」

「荒尾さん、貴方それでは余りでございますわ」

独に余る心細さに、宮は男の袂を執りて泣きぬ。理切めて荒尾もその手を払ひかねつつ、吾ならぬ愁に胸塞れて、実にもと覚ゆる宮が衰容に眼を凝しゐたり。

「荒尾さん、こんなに思つて私は悔悟してをるのぢやございませんか、昔の宮だと思召して頼に成つて下さいまし。どうぞ、荒尾さん、どうぞ、さあ、お誨へなすつて下さいまし」

涙に昏れてその語は能くも聞えず、階子下の物音は膳運び出づるなるべし。果して人の入来て、夕餉の設とて少時紛されし後、二人は謂ふべからざる侘き無言の中に相

対するのみなりしを、荒尾は始て高く咳きつ。

「貴方の言るる事は能う解つてをる、決して無理とは思はんのじや。如何にも貴方に誨へて上げたい、誨へて貴方の身の立つやうな処置で有るなら、誨へて上げんぢやないです。けれどもじや、それが誨へて上げられんのは、僕が貴方であつたらかう為ると云ふ考量に止るので……いや、いや、そりや言れん。言うて善い事なら言ひます、人に対して言ふべき事でない、況や誨ふべき事ではない、止だ僕一箇の了簡として肚の中に思うたまでの事、究竟荒尾的空想に過ぎんのぢやから、空想を誨へて人を誤つてはどうもならんから、僕は何も言はんので、言はんぢやない、実際言得んのじや、然し猶能う考へて見て、貴方に誨へらるる方法を見出したら、更にお目に掛つて申上げやう。折が有つたら又お目に掛ります。は、僕の居住？　居住は、まあ言はん方が可い、蝸が子なれば宿も定めずじや。言うても差支は無いけれど、貴方に押掛けらるると困るから、まあ言はん。は、如何にも、こんな態をしてをるので、貴方は吃驚なすつたか、さうでせう。自分にも驚いてをるのぢやけれどもどうも為方が無い。僕の身の上に就ては段々子細が有るですけども、それもお話したいけれど、又この次に。

酒は余り飲むな？　はあ、今日のやうに酔うた事は希です。忝い、折角の御忠告ぢやから今後は宜い、気を着くるです。

力に成つてくれと言うたとて、義として僕は貴方の力には成れんぢやないですか。貴方の胸中も聴いた事ぢやから、敵にはなるまい、けれど力には成られんですよ。

間にもその後逢はんのですとも。一遍逢うて聞きたい事も言ひたい事も頗る有るのぢやけれども。訪ねもせんので。それにや一向意味は無いですとも。明日訪ねてくれい？ さうは可かん、僕もこれでなかなか用が有るのぢやから。ああ、貴方も浮世が可厭か、僕も御同様じや。世の中と云ふものは、一つ間違ふと誠に面倒なもので、ああ、貴方も今日の有様では生効の無い方じやけれど、このままで空く死ぬるも残念でな、さう思うて生きてはをるけれど、苦しみつつ生きてをるなら、死んだ方が無論勝ですさ。何故命が惜いのか、考へて見ると頗る解なくなる」

語りつつ彼は食を了りぬ。

「嗚呼、貴方に給仕して貰ふのは何年ぶりと謂ふのかしらん。間も善う食うた」

宮は差含む涙を啜れり。尽きせぬ悲しみを何時までか見んとやうに荒尾は俄に身度して、

「こりや然し却つてお世話になりました。それぢや宮さん、お暇」

「あれ、荒尾さん、まあ、貴方……」

はや彼は起てるなり。宮はその前に遮りて立ちながら泣きぬ。

「私はどうしたら可いのでせう」

「覚悟一つです」

始て誨ふるが如く言放ちて荒尾の排け行かんとするを、彼は猶も縋りて、

「覚悟とは？」

「読んで字の如し」

驚破、彼の座敷を出づるを、送りも行かず、坐りも遣らぬ宮が姿は、寂くも壁に向ひて動かざりけり。

第　三　章

門々の松は除かれて七八日も過ぎぬれど、なほ正月機嫌の失せぬ富山唯継は、今日も明日もと行処を求めては、夜を昼に継ぎて打廻るなりけり。宮は毫かもこれも咎めず、出づるも入るも唯彼の為すに任せて、あだかも旅館の主の為らんやうに、形ばかりの送迎を怠らざると謂ふのみ。

この夫に対する仕向は両三年来の平生を貫きて、彼の性質とも病身の故とも許さるるまでに目慣されて又彼方よりも咎められざるなり。それと共に唯継の行も曩日とは漸く変りて、出遊に耽らんとする傾も出で来しを、浅瀬の波と見し間も無く近き頃より俄に深陥して浮るると知れたるを、宮は猶しも措きて咎めず。他は如何にとも為よ、吾身は如何にとも成らば成れと互に咎めざる心易さを愉みて、戛き女夫の契を繋ぐにぞありける。

かかれども唯継はなほその妻を忘れんとはせず。始終の愛に瘠れたる宮は決して美き色を減ぜざりしよ。彼がその美しさを変へざる限は夫の愛は齷くべきにあらざりき。抑もここに嫁ぎしより一点の愛だに無かりし宮の、今に到りては啻に愛無きに止らずして、陰に厭ひ憎めるにあらず

や。その故に彼は漸く家庭の楽からざるをも感ずるにあらずや。その故に彼は外に出でて憂を霽すに忙しきにあらずや。されども彼の忘れず時に帰り来るは、又この妻の美き顔を見んが為のみ。既にその顔を見了れば、何ばかりの楽のあらぬ家庭は、彼をして火無き煖炉の傍に処しむるなり。彼の凍えて出でざること無し。出づれば幸ひにその金力に頼りて勢を得、媚を買ひて、一時の慾を肆まにし、其処には楽むとも知らず楽み、苦むとも知らず苦みつつ宮が空き色香に溺れて、内にはかかる美きものを手活の花と眺め、外には到るところに当世の翩して推廻すが、此上無き紳士の願足れりと心得たるなり。

いで、その妻は見るも厭き夫の傍に在る苦を片時も軽くせんとて、彼の繁き外出を見赦して、十度に一度も色を作さざるを風引かぬやうに召しませ猪牙とやらの難有き賢女の志とも戴き喜びて、いと堅き家の守とかつは等閑ならず念ひにけり。さるは独り夫のみならず、本家の両親を始め、親属知辺に至るまで一般に彼の病身を憫みて、おとなしき嫁よと賞め揚さぬはあらず。実に彼は某の妻のやうに出行かず、くれがしの夫人のやうに気儘ならず、又は誰々の如く華美を好まず、強請事せず、しかもそれ等の人々より才も容も立勝りて在りながら、常に内に居て夫に事ふるより外を為さざるが、最恰しと見ゆるなるべし。宮が褒める秘密は知る者もあらず、躬も絶えて異まるべき穂を露さざりければ、その夫に事へて排々しからぬ偽も偽とは為られず、却りて人に憫まるるなんど、その身には量無き幸を享くる心の内に、独り遣方無く苦める不幸は又量無しと為ざらんや。

十九にして恋人を棄てにし宮は、昨日を夢み、今日を嘆ちつつ、過せば過さるる月日を倦ねて、ここに二十あまり五の春を迎へぬ。この春の癡せしものは痛悔と失望と憂悶と、別に空くその身を老しむる齢なるのみ。彼は釈れざる囚にも同かる思を悩みつつ、元日の明るよりいとど懊悩の遺る方無かりけるも、年の始といふに臥すべき病ならねば、起きゐるままに本意ならぬ粧も、色を好める夫に勧められて、例の美しと見らるる浅ましさより、猶甚き浅ましさをその人の陰に陽に恨み悲むめり。

宮は今外出せんとする夫の寒凌ぎに葡萄酒飲む間を暫く長火鉢の前に佃くなり。二鉢の梅の影を帯びて南縁の障子に上り尽せる日脚は、袋棚に据ゑたる福寿草の五六輪咲揃へる蕋に輝きつつ、更に唯継の身よりは光も出づらんやうに、彼は昼眩き新調の三枚襲を着飾りてその最も珍と為る里昻製の白の透綾の絹領巻を右手に引攫ひ、左に宮の酌を受けながら、

「あ、拙い手付……ああ零れる、零れる！　これは恐入った。これだからつい余所で飲む気にも

なりますと謂つて可い位のものだ」

「ですから多度上つていらつしやいまし」

「宜いかい。宜いね。宜い。今夜は遅いよ」

「何時頃お帰来になります」

「遅いよ」

「でも大約時間を極めて置いて下さいませんと、お待ち申してをる者は困ります」

「遅いよ」

「それぢや十時には皆寝みますから」

「遅いよ」

又言ふも煩らはしくて宮は口を閉ちぬ。

「遅いよ」

「…………」

「驚くほど遅いよ」

「…………」

「おい、些と」

「…………」

「おや。お前悩つたのか」

「…………」

「悩らんでも可いぢやないか、おい」

彼は続け様に宮の袖を曳けば、

「何を作るのよ」

「返事を為んからさ」

「お遅いのは解りましたよ」

「遅くはないよ、実は。だからして、まあ機嫌を直すべし」

「お遅いなら、お遅いで宜うございますから……」

「遅くはないと言ふに、お前は近来直に慍るよ、どう云ふのかね」

「一つは病気の所為かも知れませんけれど」

「一つは俺の浮気の所為かい。恐入つたね」

「………」

「お前一つ飲まんかい」

「私沢山」

「ぢや俺が半分助けて遣るから」

「いいえ、沢山なのですから」

「まあさう言はんで、少し、注ぐ真似」

「欲くもないものを、貴方は」

「まあ可いさ。お酌は、それかう云ふ塩梅に、愛子流かね」

姐の名を聞ける宮の如何に言ふらん、と唯継は陰に楽み待つなる流晒を彼の面に送れるなり。

「宮は知らず貌に一口の酒を啣みて、眉を顰めたるのみ。

「もう飲めんのか。ぢや此方にお寄来し」

「失礼ですけれど」

「この上へもう一盃注いで貰はう」

「貴方、十時過ぎましたよ、早くいらつしやいませんか」

「可いよ、この二三日は別に俺の為る用は無いのだから。それで実はね今日は少し遅くなるのだ」

「さうでございますか」

「遅いと云つたつて怪いのぢやない。この二十八日に伝々会の大温習が有るといふ訳だらう、そこで今日五時から糸川の処へ集つて下温習を為るのさ。俺は、それ お特得の、「親々に誘はれ、難波の浦を船出して、身を尽したる、憂きおもひ、泣いてチチチチあかしのチントン風待にテチンチンツン……」

厭しげに宮の余所見せるに、乗地の唯継は愈よ声を作りて、

「たまたま逢ひはア——ア逢ひイ——ながらチンチンチンチンつれなき嵐に吹分けられエエエエエ、ツンツンツンテツテツトン、テツトン国へ帰ればアアアアア父イイイイ母のチチチチンチンチンチンチンチイン「思ひも寄らぬ夫定……」

「貴方もう好加減になさいましよ」

「もう少し聴いてくれ、「立つる操を破ら…」

「又寛り伺ひますから、早くいらつしやいませ」

「然し、巧くなつたなら、ねえ、些と聞けるだらう」

「私には解りません」

「これは恐入つた、解らないのは情無いね。少し解るやうに成つて貰はうか」

「解らなくても宜うございます」

「何、宜いものか、浄瑠璃の解らんやうな頭脳ぢや為方が無い。お前は一体冷淡な頭脳を有つてゐるから、それで浄瑠璃などを好まんのに違無い。どうもさうだ」

「そんな事はございません」

「何、さうだ。お前は一体冷淡さ」

「愛子か、あれはあれで冷淡でないさ」

「愛子はどうでございます」

「それで能く解りました」

「何が解つたのか」

「解りました」

「些も解らんよ」

「まあ可うございますから、早くいらつしやいまし、さうして早くお帰りなさいまし」

「うう、これは恐入つた、冷淡でない。ぢや早く帰る、お前待つてるか」

「私は何時でも待つてをりますぢや御座いませんか」

「これは冷淡でない！」

　漸く唯継の立起れば、宮は外套を着せ掛けて、不取敢彼に握手を求めぬ。こは決して宮の冷淡

ならざるを証するに足らざるなり、　故は、　この女夫の出入に握手するは、　夫の始より命じて習せし躾なるをや。

（三）の二

　夫を玄関に送り出でし宮は、やがて氷の窖などに入るらん想しつつ、是非無き歩を運びて居間に還りぬ。彼はその夫と偕に在るを謂はんやう無き累と為なれど、又その独りてこの家に処るるをも堪へ難く悒きものに思へるなり。必しも力むるとにはあらねど、夫の前には自ら気の張ありて、とにかくにさるべくは振舞へど恣まなる身一箇となれば、遽に慵く打労れて、心は整へん術も知らず紊れに乱るるが常なり。

　火鉢に倚りて宮は、我を喪べる体なりしが、如何に思入り、思回し思窮むればとて、解くべきにあらぬ胸の内の、終に明けぬ闇に彷徨へる可悲しさは、在るにもあられず身を起して彼は障子の外なる縁に出でたり。

　麗し迂えたる空は遠く三四の凧の影を転じて、見遍す庭の名残無く冬枯れたれば、浅露なる日の光の眩きのみにて、啼狂ひし柟の鴨の去りし後は、隔てる隣より憂々と羽子突く音して、なかなかここにはその寒さを忍ぶ値あらぬを、彼はされども少時居て、又空を眺め、又冬枯を見遣り、同き日の光を仰ぎ、同き羽子の音を聞きて、抑へんとはしたりけれども難さの竟に苦く、再び居間に入ると見れば、其処にも留らで書斎の次なる寝間に入るより、身を抛ちてベットに伏し

たり。

厚き蓐の積れる雪と真白き上に、乱畳める幾重の衣の彩を争ひつつ、妖なる姿を意も介かず横はれるを、窓の日の帷を透して隠々照したる、実に匂も零るるやうにして彼は浪に漂ひし人の今打揚げられたるも現ならず、ほとほと力竭きて絶入らんとするが如く、止だ手枕に横顔を支へて、力無き眼を瞪れり。竟には溜息吻きてその目を閉づれば、片寝に倦める面を内向けて、裾の寒さを佗しげに身動したりしが、猶も底止無き思の淵は彼を沈めて遁さざるなり。

隅棚の枕時計は突と秒刻を忘れぬ。益す静に、益す明かなる閨の内には、空しとも空き時の移るともなく移るのみなりしが、忽ち差入る鳥影の軒端に近く、俯したる宮が肩頭に打連りて飜きつ。

やや有りて彼は嬾くベットの上に起直りけるが、鬢の縺れし頭を傾けて、帷の隙より僅に眺めらるる庭の面に見るとしもなき目を遣りて、当所無く心の彷徨ふ蹤を追ふなりき。

久からずして彼はここをも出でて又居間に還れば、直に箪笥の中より友禅縮緬の帯揚を取出し、心に籠めたりし一通の文とも見ゆるものを抜きて、こたびは主の書斎に持ち行きて机に向へり。その巻紙は貫一が遺せし筆の跡などにはあらで、いつかは宮の彼に送らんとて、別れし後の思の丈を窃に書聯ねたるものなりかし。

往年宮は田鶴見の邸内に彼を見しより、いとど忍びかねたる胸の内の訴へん方もあらぬ切なさに、唯心寛の仮初に援りける筆ながら、なかなか口には打出し難き事を最好く書きて陳けも

為しを、あはれかのひとの許に送りて、思ひ知りたる今の悲しさを告げばやと、一図の意をも定めしが、又案ずれば、その文は果して貫一の手に触れ、目にも入るべきか。よしされぱとて、憎み怨める怒の余に投返されて、人目に曝さるる事などあらば、徒に身を滅す疵を求めて終りなんをと、遣れば火に入る虫の危く、捨つるは惜くも、やがて好き首尾の有らんやうに拠無き頼を繋ぎつつ、彼は懊悩に堪へざるまでに写し易ふる傍ら、或は書添へ、或は改めなどして、この文に向へば自らその人に取出でては写し易ふる夢をも結ぶに似たる快きを覚ゆるなりき、止これに因りて欲するままの夢をも結ぶに似たる快きを覚ゆるなりき。かくして得送らぬ文は写せしも灰となり、反古となりて、彼の帯揚に籠められては、いつまで草の可哀や用らるる果も知らず、宮が手習は実に久うなりぬ。

些箇に慰められて過せる身の荒尾に邂逅ひし嬪しさは、何に似たりと謂はんも愚にて、この人をこそ仲立ちて、積る思を遂げんと頼みしを、仇の如く与せられざりし悲しさに、さらでも切なき宮が胸に撹乱れて、今は漸く危きを懼れざる覚悟も出で来て、いつまで草のいつまでかくてあらんや、文は送らんと、この日頃思ひ立ちてけり。

紙の良きを択び、筆の良きを択び、墨の良きを択びて、彼は意してその字の良きを殊に択びて、打顫ふ手に十行余認めしを、つと裂きて火鉢に今日の今ぞ始めて仮初ならず写さんと為なる。焔の急に炎々と臆るを、可疎しと眺めたる折しも、紙門を啓けてその光に惧えし婢は、覚えず主の気色を異みつつ、

「あの、御本家の奥様がお出で遊ばしました」

第 四 章

主夫婦を併せて焼亡せし鰐淵が居宅は、さるほど貫一の手に頼りてその跡に改築せられぬ、有形よりは小体に、質素を旨としたれど専ら旧の構造を摸して差はざらんと勉めしに似たり。

間貫一と陶札を掲げて、彼はこの新宅の主になれるなり。家督たるべき直道は如何にせし。彼は始よりこの不義の遺産に手をも触れざらんと誓ひ、かつこれを貫一に与へて、その物は正業の資たれ。その人は改善の人たれと冀しを、貫一は今この家の主となれるに、なほ先代の志を継がずして、益々盛に例の貪を営むなりき。然れば彼と貫一との今日の関繋は如何なるものならん。絶えてこれを知る者あらず。凡そ人生箇々の裏面には必ず如此き内情若くは秘密とも謂ふべき者ありながら、幸に他の穿鑿を免れて、曖昧の裏に葬られ畢んぬる例尠からず。二代の鰐淵なる間のこの一件もまた貫一と彼との外に洩れざるを得たり。

かくして今は鰐淵の手代ならぬ三番町の間は、その向に有数の名を成して、外には善く貸し、善く飲むれども、内には事足る老婢を役ひて、僅に自炊ならざる男世帯を張りて、なほも奢らず、楽まず、心は失意の書生の如く依然たる変物の名を失はでゐたり。

趣は昔日の手代にして、出でてはさすがに労れて日暮に帰り来にける貫一は、彼の常として、吾家ながら人気無き居間

の内を、旅の木蔭にも休へる想ひつつ、稍興冷めて坐りも遣らず、物の悲しき夕を特に独の感じぬ

れば、老婢はランプを持ち来りて、

「今日三時頃でございました、お客様が見えまして、明日又今頃来るから、是非内に居てくれる

やうにと有仰つて、お名前を伺つても、学校の友達だと言へば可い、とさう有仰つてお帰りにな

りました」

「学校の友達？」

臆測にも知る能はざるはこの藪から棒の主なり。

「どんな風の人かね」

「さやうでございますよ、年紀四十ばかりの蒙茸と髯髯の生えた、身材の高い、剛い顔の、全で

壮士みたやうな風体をしてお在でした」

「…………」

些の憶起す節もありや、と貫一は打案じつつも半は怪むに過ぎざりき。

「さうして、まあ大相横柄な方なのでございます」

「明日三時頃に又来ると？」

「さやうでございますよ」

「誰か知らんな」

「何だか誠に風の悪さうな人体で御座いましたが、明日参りましたら通しませうで御座いますか」

「ちや用向は言つては行かんのだね」

「さやうでございますよ」

「宜い、会つて見やう」

「さやうでございますか」

起ち行かんとせし老婢は又居直りて、

「それから何でございました、間もなく赤樫さんがいらつしやいまして」

貫一は懌ばざる色を作してこれに応へたり。

「神戸の蒲鉾を三枚、見事なのでございます。それに藤村の蒸羊羹を下さいまして、私まで毎度又頂戴物を致しましたので御座います」

彼は益す不快を禁じ得ざる面色して、応答も為で聴きゐたり。

「さうして明日、五時頃些とお目に掛りたいから、さう申上げて置いてくれと有仰つてで御座いました」

可しとも彼は口には出さで、寧ろ止めよとやうに忙く頷けり。

（四）の 二

学校友達と名宣りし客はその言の如く重ねて訪ひ来ぬ。不思議の対面に駭き惑へる貫一は、迅雷の耳を掩ふに違あらざらんやうに劇く吾を失ひて、頓にはその惘然たるより覚むるを得ざるな

りき。荒尾譲介は席の温る間の手弄に放らぬ下鬚の、長く忘れたりし友の今を如何にと観るに忙しかり。

「殆ど一昔と謂うても可い程になるのぢやから話は沢山ある、けれどもこれより先に聞きたいのは、君は今日でも僕をぢや、この荒尾を親友と思うてをるか、どうかと謂ふのぢや」

答ふべき人の胸はなほ自在に語るべくもあらず乱れたるなり。

「考へるまではなからう。親友と思うてをるなら、をる、さうなけりや、ないと言ふまでで是か否かの一つぢや」

「そりや昔は親友であつた」

彼は覚束無げに言出せり。

「さう」

「今はさうぢやあるまい」

「何為にな」

「その後五六年も全く逢はずにゐたのだから、今では親友と謂ふことは出来まい」

「なに五六年前も一向親友ではありやせんぢやつたではないか」

貫一は目を側めて彼を訝りつ。

「さうぢやらう、学士になるか、高利貸になるかと云ふ一身の浮沈の場合に、何等の相談も為んのみか、それなり失踪して了うたのは何処が親友なのか」

その常に懇ちかつ悔る一事を責められては、癒えざる瘍をも割るる心地して、彼は苦しげに容を歛め、声をも出さでゐたり。

「君の情人は君に負いたぢやらうが、君の友は決して君に負かん筈ぢや。その通り棄てられた僕ぢやけれど、かうして又訪ねて来たのは、未だ君を実は棄てんのぢやと思ひ給へ」

学生たりし荒尾！　参事官たりし荒尾！！　尾羽打枯せる今の荒尾の姿は変りたれど、猶一片の変らぬ物ありと知れる貫一は、夢とも消えて、去りし、去りし昔の跡無き跡を悲しと偲ぶなりけり。

「然し、僕が棄てても棄てんでも、そんな事に君は痛痒を感ずるぢやなからうけれど、僕は僕で、友の徳義としてとにかく一旦は棄てんで訪ねて来た。で、断然棄つるも、又棄てんのも、唯今日にある意ぢや。

今では荒尾を親友とは謂へん、と君の言うたところを以つて見ると、又今更親友であることを君は望んではをらんやうぢや。さうであるならば僕の方でも敢て望まん、立派に名宣つて僕も間貫一を棄つる！」

貫一は頭を低れて敢て言はず。

「然し、今日まで親友と思うてをつた君を棄つるからには、これが一生の別になるのぢやから、その餞行として一言云はんけりやならん。

　間、君は何の為に貨を殖ゆるのぢや。かの大いなる楽とする者を奪れた為に、それに易へる者として金銭といふ考を起したのか。それも可からう、可いとして措く。けれどもじや、それを獲る為に不義不正の事を働く必要が有るか。君も現在他から苦められてゐる軀ではないのか。さうなれば己が又他を苦むるのは尤も用捨すべき事ぢやらうと思ふ。それが他を苦むると謂うても、難儀に附け入つて、さうしてその血を搾るのが君の営業、殆ど強奪に等い手段を以つて金を殖えつつ、君はそれで今日慰められてをるのか。如何に金銭が総ての力であるか知らんけれど、人たる者は悪事を行つてをつて、一刻でも安楽に居らるるものではないのぢや。それとも、君は怡然として楽んでをるか。長閑な日に花の盛を眺むるやうな気持で催促に行つたり、差押を為たりしてをるか。どうかい、間」

　彼は愈よ口を閉ぢたり。

　「恐くじや。さう云ふ気持の事は、この幾年間に一日でも有りはせんのぢやらう。　君の顔色を見い！　全で罪人じやぞ。獄中に居る者の面じや」

　別人と見るまでに彼の浅ましく瘁れたる面を眺りて、譲介は涙の落つるを覚えず。

　「間、何で僕が泣くか、君は知つてをるか。今の間ぢや知らんぢやらう。病が有るからと謂うて毒を飲んで、その病で、君はその分では到底慰めらるる事はありはせん。　幾多貨を殖へたところで、君はあたかも薬を飲む事を知らんやうなものじやぞ。僕の友であつた間はそんな痴漢ぢやなかつた、して見りや発狂したのじや。発狂してからに馬鹿な事を為居る奴は尤む
が痊るぢやらうか。　君はあたかも薬を飲んやうなものじやぞ。

るに足らんけれど、一婦人の為に発狂したその根性を、彼の友として僕が懸ぢざるを得んのじ
や。間、君は盗人と言れたぞ。罪人と言れたぞ、狂人と言れたぞ。少しは腹を立てい！　腹を立
てて僕を打つとも蹴るとも為て見い！」

彼は自ら言ひ、自ら憤り、尚自ら打ちも蹴も為んずる色を作して速々答を貫一に逼れり。

「腹は立たん！」

「腹は立たん？　それぢや君は自身に盗人とも、罪人とも……」

「狂人とも思つてゐる。一婦人の為に発狂したのは、君に対して実に面目無いけれど、既に発狂
して了つたのだから、どうも今更為やうが無い。折角ぢやあるけれど、このまま棄置いてくれ給
へ」

貫一は縒にかく言ひて已みぬ。

「さうか。それぢや君は不正な金銭で慰められてをるのか」

「未だ慰められてはをらん」

「何日慰めらるるのか」

「解らん」

「娶はん」

「さうして君は妻君を娶うたか」

「娶はん」

「何故娶はんのか、かうして家を構へてをるのに独身ぢや不都合ぢやらうに」

「さうでもないさ」

「君は今では彼の事をどう思うてをるな」

「彼とは宮の事かね。あれは畜生さ！」

「然し、君も今日では畜生ぢやが、高利貸などは人の心は有つちやをらん、人の心が無けりや畜生じや」

「さう云ふけれど、世間は大方畜生ぢやないか」

「僕も畜生かな」

「…………」

「間、君が彼が畜生であるのに激してやはり畜生になつたのぢやな。若し彼が畜生であつたのを改心して人間に成つたと為たら、同時に君も畜生を罷めにやならんじやな」

「彼が人間に成る？　能はざる事だ！　僕は高利を貪る畜生だけれど、人を欺く事は為んのだ。詐つて人の誠を受けて、さうしてそれを売るやうな残忍な畜生は決して為んのだ。始から高利と名宣つて貸すのだから、否な者は借りんがよいので、借りん者を欺いて貸すのぢやない。宮の如き畜生が何で再び人間に成り得るものか」

「何為成り得んのか」

「何為成り得るのか」

「さうなら君は彼の人間に成り得んのを望むのか」

「望むも望まんも、あんな者に用は無い！」

寧ろその面に唾せんとも思へる貫一の気色なり。

「そりや彼には用は無いぢやらうけれど、君の為に言ふべきことぢやと思ふから話すのぢやが、彼は今では大いに悔悟してをるぞ。君に対して罪を悔いてをるぞ！」

貫一は吾を忘れて嘲笑ひぬ。彼はその如何に賤むべきか、謂はんやうもあらぬを念ひて、更に嘲笑ひ猶嘲笑ひ、過めんとして嘲笑ひぬ。

「彼も さうして、悔悟してをるのぢやから、君も悔悟するが可からう、悔悟する時ぢやらうと思ふ」

「彼の悔悟は彼の悔悟で、僕の与る事は無い。畜生も少しは思知つたと見える、それも可からう」

「先頃計らず彼に逢うたのじや、すると、僕に向うて涙を流して、そりや真実悔悟してをるのじや。さうして僕に詫を為てくれ、それが成らずば、君に一遍逢せてくれ、と縋つて頼むのじやな、けれど僕も思ふところが有るから拒絶はした。又君に対しても、彼がその様に悔悟してをるから容して遣れと勧めは為ん、それは別問題じや。但僕として君に言ふところは、彼は悔悟して独り苦んでをる。即ち彼は自ら罰せられてをるのぢやから、君は君として怨を釈いて可からうと思ふ。君がその怨を釈いたなら、昔の間に復るべきぢやらうと考へるのじや。

君は今のところ慰められてをらん、それで又、何日慰めらるるとも解らんと言うたな、然しじ や、彼が悔悟してからにその様に思うてをると聞いたら、君はそれを以つて大いに慰められればせ

んかな。

君がこの幾年間に得た金銭、それは幾多か知らんけれど、その寡からん金銭よりは、彼が終に悔悟したと聞いた一言の方が、遙に大いなる力を以つて君の心を慰むるであらうと思ふのじやが、どうか」

「それは僕が慰められるよりは、宮が苦まなければならん為の悔悟だらう。宮が前非を悟つた為に、僕が失つた者を再び得られる訳ぢやない、さうして見れば、僕の今日はそれに因つて少しも慰められるところは無いのだ。憎いことは飽くまで憎い、が、その憎さに僕が慰められずにゐるのではないからして、宮その者の一身に向つて、僕は棄てられた怨を報いやうなどとは決して思つてをらん、畜生に響を復す価は無いさ。

今日になつて彼が悔悟した、それでも好く悔悟したと謂ひたいけれど、これは固よりさう有るべき事なのだ。始にあんな不心得を為さなかつたら、悔悟する事は無かつたらうに――不心得であつた、非常な不心得であつた！」

彼は黯然として空く懐へるなり。

「僕は彼の事は言はんのじや。又彼が悔悟した為に君の失うた者が再び得らるる訳でないから、それぢや慰められんと謂ふのなら、それで可いのじや。要するに、君はその失うた者が取返されたら可いのぢやらう、さうしてその目的を以つてゐるのぢやらう、なあ、さうりやその貨さへ得られたら、好んで不正な営業を為る必要は有るまいが。君が失うた者が有る事は知つてをる。それが為に常に楽まんのも、同情を表してゐる、そこで金銭の力に頼つて慰めら

れやうとしてゐる、に就いては君の考に委する。貨を殖ゆるも可い、可いとする以上は大いに富むべしじや。貨を殖ゆるも可い、可いとする以上は大いに富むべしじや。つて聚めんけりや貨は得られんのではない、不正な手段を用んでも、富む道は幾多も有るぢやらう。君に言ふのも、な、その目的を変へようではない、止だ手段を改めよじや。路は違へても同じ高嶺の月を見るのじやが」

「辱ないけれど、僕の迷は未だ覚めんのだから、間は発狂してゐる者と想つて、一切かまひ付けずに措いてくれ給へ」

「さうか。どうあつても僕の言は用られんのぢやな」

「容してくれ給へ」

「何を容すのじや！　貴様は俺を棄てたのではないか、俺も貴様を棄てたのじやぞ、容すも容さんも有るものか」

「今日限互に棄てて別れるに就いては、僕も一箇聞きたい事が有る。それは君の今の身の上だが、どうしたのかね」

「見たら解るぢやらう」

「見たばかりで解るものか」

「貧乏してをるのよ」

「それは解つてゐるぢやないか」

「それだけじや」

「それだけの事が有るものか。何で官途を罷めて、さうしてそんなに貧乏してゐるのか、様子が有りさうぢやないか」

「話したところで狂人には解らんのよ」

荒尾は空嘯きて起たんと為なり。

「解つても解らんでも可いから、まあ話すだけは話してくれ給へ」

「それを聞いてどう為る。ああ貴様は何か、金でも貸さうと云ふのか。No thank じや、赤貧洗ふが如く窮してをつても、心は恰然として楽んでをるのじや」

「それだから猶、どう為さう窮して、それを又楽んでゐるのか、それには何か事情が有るのだらう、から、それを聞せてくれ給へと言ふのだ」

荒尾は故らに哈々として笑へり。

「貴様如き無血虫がそんな事を聞いたとて何が解るものでぞ。人間らしい事を言ふな」

「さうまで辱められても辞を返すことの出来ん程、僕の軀は腐つて了つたのだ」

「固よりじや」

「かう腐つて了つた僕の軀は今更為方が無い。けれども、君は立派に学位を取つて、参事官の椅子にも居た人、国家の為に有用の器であることは、決して僕の疑はんところだ。で、僕は常に君の出世を予想し、又陰にそれを禱つてをつたのだ。君は僕を畜生と言ひ、狂人と言ひ、賊と言ふ

けれど、君を懐ふ念の僕の胸中を去つた事はありはせんよ。今日まで君の外には一人の友も無いのだ。一昨年であつた、君が静岡へ赴任すると聞いた時は、嬉しくもあり、可懐くもあり、又考へて見れば、自分の身が悲しくもなつて、僕は一日飯も食はんでゐた。それに就けても、久し振で君に逢つて慶賀も言ひたいと思つたけれど、どうも逢れん僕の軀だから、切て陰ながらでも君の出世の姿が見たいと、新橋の停車場へ行つて、君の立派に成つたのを見た時は、何もかも忘れて僕は唯嬉しくて涙が出た」

さてはと荒尾も心陰に頷きぬ。

「君の出世を見て、それほど嬉かつた僕が、今日君のそんなに零落してゐるのを見る心持はどんなであるか、察し給へ。自分の身を顧ずにかう云ふ事を君に向つて言ふべきではないけれど、僕はもう己を棄ててゐるのだ。一婦女子の詐如きに慣つて、それが為に一身を過つたと知りながら、自身の覚悟を以て匡正することの出来んと謂ふのは、全く天性愚劣の致すところと、自ら恨むよりは無いので、僕は生きながら腐れて、これで果てるのだ。君の親友であつた間貫一は既に亡き者に成つたのだ、とさう想つてくれ給へ。であるから、これは間が言ふのではない。君の親友の或者が君の身を愛んで忠告するのだと聴いてくれ給へ。どう云ふ事情か、君が話してくれんから知れんけれど、君の軀は十分自重して、社会に立つて壮なる働を作して欲しいのだ。君はさうして窮迫してゐるやうだけれど、決して世間から棄てられるやうな君でない事を僕は信ずるのだから、一箇人として己の為に身を愛みたまへと謂ふのではなく、国家の為に自重し給へと願

ふのだ。君の親友の或者は君がその才を用ゐる為に社会に出やうと為るならば、及ぶ限の助力を為る精神であるのだ」

貫一の面は病などの忽ち癒えけんやうに輝きつつ、如此く潔くも麗き辞を語れるなり。

「うう、それぢや君は何か、僕のかうして落魄してをるのを見て気毒と思ふのか」

「君が謂ふほどの畜生でもない！」

「其処じや、間。世間に貴様のやうな高利貸が在る為に、あつぱれ用ゐらるべき人才の多くがじや、名を傷け、身を誤られて、社会の外に放逐されて空く朽つるのじやぞ。国家の為に自重せい、と僕の如き者にでもさう言うてくるるのは忝ないが、同じ筆法を以つて、君も社会の公益の為にその不正の業を罷めてくれい、と僕は又頼むのじや。今日の人才を減す者は、曰く色、曰く高利貸ぢやらう。この通り零落れてをる僕が気毒と思ふなら、君の為に艱されてをる人才の多くを一層不敏と思うて遣れ。

君が愛に失敗して苦むのもじや、或人が金銭の為に苦むのも、苦むと云ふ点に於ては差異は無いぞ。で、僕もかうして窮迫してをる際ぢやから、憂を分つ親友の一人は誠欲しいのじや、昔の間貫一のやうな友が有つたらばと思はん事は無い。その友が僕の身を念うてくれて、世間に最も打つて出て壮に働け、一臂の力を仮さうと言うのであつたら、僕は如何に嬉からう！世間に最も喜ぶべき者は友、最も悪むべき者は高利貸ぢや。如何に高利貸の悪むべきかを知つてをるだけ、僕は益す友を懐ふのじや。その昔の友が今日の高利貸——その悪むべき高利貸！吾又何をか言は

んじや」

彼は口を閉ぢて、貫一を疾視せり。

「段々の君の忠告、僕は難有い。猶自分にも篤と考へて、この腐れた軀が元の通潔白な者に成り得られるなら、それに越した幸は無いのだ。君もまた自愛してくれ給へ。僕は君には棄てられても、君の大いに用ひられるのを見たいのだ。又必ず大いに用ひられなければならんその人が、さうして不遇で居るのは、残念であるよりは僕は悲い。そんなに念つてもゐるのだから一遍君の処を訪ねさしてくれ給へ。何処に今居るかね」

「まあ、高利貸などは来て貰はん方が可い」

「その日は友として訪ねるのだ」

「高利貸に友は持たんものな」

雍かに紙門を押啓きて出来れるを、誰かと見れば満枝なり。彼如何なれば不躾にもこの席には顕れけん、と打駭ける主よりも、荒尾が心の中こそ更に匹ふべくもあらざるなりけれ。いでや、彼は窘みてその長き髯をば痛に拈りつつ。されど狼狽へたりと見られんは口惜しとやうに、遽にその手を胸高に挟きて、動かざること山の如しと打控へたる様も、自らわざとらしくて、また見好げにはあらざりき。

満枝は先づ主に挨拶して、さて荒尾に向ひては一際礼を重くし、しかも躬は手の動き、目の視るまで、専ら貴婦人の如く振舞ひつつ、笑むともあらず面を和げて炊く辞を出さず。荒尾はこの際

なかなか黙するに堪へずして、

「これは不思議な所で！　成程間とは御懇意かな」

「君はどうして此方を識つてゐるのだ」

左瞻右視して貫一は呆るるのみなり。

「そりや少し識つてをる。　然し、長居はお邪魔ぢやらう、大きに失敬した」

「荒尾さん」

満枝は遒さじと呼留めて、

「かう云ふ処で申上げますのも如何で御座いますけれど」

「ああ、そりや此で聞くべき事ぢやない」

「けれど毎も御不在ばかりで、お話が付きかねると申して弱り切つてをりますで御座いますから

「いや、会うたところでからに話の付けやうもないのぢや。遁げも隠れも為んから、まあ、時節

を待つて貰はうさ」

「それはどんなにもお待ち申上げますけれど、貴方の御都合の宜いやうにばかり致してはをられ

ませんで御座います。そこはお察しあそばせな」

「うう、随分酷い事を察しさせられるのぢやね」

「近日に是非私　お願ひ申しに伺ひますで御座いますから、どうぞ宜く」

「そりや一向宜くないかも知れん」

「ああ、さう、この前でございましたか、あの者が伺ひました節、何か御無礼な事を申上げまし
たとかで、大相な御立腹で、お刀をお抜き遊ばして、斬って了ふとか云ふ事が御座いましたさう
で」

「有つた」

「あれ、本当にさやうな事を遊ばしたので？」

満枝は彼に恥ぢよとばかり嘲笑ひぬ。さ知つたる荒尾は飽くまで真顔を作りて、

「本当とも！　実際那奴斫却つて了はうと思うた」

「然しお考へ遊ばしたで御座いませ」

「まあその辺ぢや。あれでも犬猫ぢやなし、斬捨てにもなるまい」

「まあ、怖い事ぢや御座いませんか。私なぞは滅多に伺ふ訳には参りませんで御座いますね」

そは誰が事を言ふならんとやうに、荒尾は頂を反して嘆き笑ひぬ。

「僕が美人を斬るか、その目で僕が殺さるるか。どれ帰つて、刀でも拭いて置かう」

「荒尾君、夕飯の支度が出来たさうだから、食べて行つてくれ給へ」

「それは折角ぢやが、盗泉の水は飲まんで」

「まあ貴方、私お給仕を勧めます。さあ、まあお下にのらしつて」

満枝は荒尾の立てる脚下に褥を推付けて、実に遜さじと主にも劣らず最惜む様なり。

「全で御夫婦のやうじやね。これは好一対じや」

「そのお意で、どうぞお席にゐらしつて」

固より留らざるべき荒尾は終に行かんとしつつ、

「間、貴様は……」

「…………」

「…………」

彼は唇の寒かるべきを思ひて、空く鬱抑して帰り去れり。その言はざりし語は直に貫一が胸に響きて、彼は人の去にける迹をも、なほ聴くに苦き面を得挙げざりけり。

（四）の 三

程も有らずランプは点されて、止だ在りけるままに煉みゐたる彼の傍に置くるとともに、その光に照さるる満枝の姿は、更に粧をも加へけんやうに怪しからず妖艶に、宛然色香を擅にせる牡丹の枝を咲撓めたる風情にて、彼は親しげに座を進めつ。

「間さん、貴方どうあそばして、非常にお鬱ぎ遊ばしてゐらつしやるぢや御座いませんか」

貫一は怠くも纔に目を移して、

「私よりは、貴方があの方の御朋友でゐらつしやるとは、実に私意外で御座いますわ」

「一体貴方はどうして荒尾を御存じなのですか」

「貴方はどうして御存じなのです」

「まあ債務者のやうな者なので御座います」

「債務者？　荒尾が？　貴方の？」

「私が直接に関係した訳ぢや御座いませんのですけれど」

「はあ、さうして額は若干なのですか」

「三千円ばかりでございますの」

「三千円？　それでその直接の貸主と謂ふのは何処の誰ですか」

満枝は彼の遽に捩向きて膝の前むをさへ覚えざらんとするを見て、御自分のお聴きになりたい事は熱心にお成りで、歪むる口角に笑を忍びつつ、平生私が

「貴方は実に現金でゐらつしやるのね。御自分のお聴になりたい事は熱心にお成りで、歪むる口角に笑を忍びつつ、平生私が

「お話でも致すと、全で取合つても下さいませんのですもの」

「まあ可いです」

「些とも可い事はございません」

「うう、さうすると直接の貸主と謂ふのが有るのですね」

「存じません」

「お話し下さいな、様子に由つてはその金は私から弁償しやうとも思ふのですから」

「私貴方からは戴きません」

「上げるのではない、弁償するのです」

「いいえ、貴方とは御相談になりません。又貴方が是非弁償なさると云ふ事ならば、私あの債権

を棄てて了ひます」

「それは何為ですか」

「何為でも宜方御座いますわ。ですから、貴方が弁償なさらうと思召すなら、私に債権を棄てて了へと有仰つて下さいまし、さう致せば私喜んで棄てます」

「どう云ふ訳ですか」

「どう云ふ訳で御座いますか」

「甚だ解らんぢやありませんか」

「勿論解らんので御座いますとも。私自分で自分が解らんくらゐで御座いますもの。然し貴方も、聞さん、随分お解りに成りませんのね」

「いいや、僕は解つてゐます」

「ええ、解つてゐらつしやりながら些ともお解りにならないのですから、私も益す解らなくなりますですから、さう思つてゐらつしやいまし」

満枝は金煙管に手炉の縁を丁と拍ちて、男の顔に流眄の怨を注ぐなり。

「まあさう云ふ事を言はずに、ともかくもお話をなすつて下さい」

「御勝手ええ、貴方は」

「さあ、お話し下さいな」

「唯今お話致しますよ」

満枝は遽に煙管を索めて、さて傍に人無き若く綾に煙を吹きぬ。

「貴方の債務者であらうとは実に意外だ」

「…………」

「どうも事実として信ずる事は出来んくらゐだ」

「…………」

「三千円！　荒尾が三千円の負債を何で為たのか、殆ど有得べき事でないのだけれど、……」

「…………」

唯見れば、満枝はなほも煙管を放たざるなり。

「さあ、お話し下さいな」

「こんなに遅々してをりましたら、さぞ貴方憤ったくてゐらっしゃいませう」

「憤ったいのは知れてゐるぢゃありませんか」

「憤ったいと云ふものは、決して好い心持ぢゃございませんのね」

「貴方は何を言つてお在なのです！」

「はいはい恐入りました。それぢや早速お話を致しませう」

「どうぞ」

「蓋か御承知でゐらっしゃいましたら。前に宅に居りました向坂と申すの、あれが静岡へ参つて、今では些と盛に遣つてゐるので御座います。それで、あの方は静岡の参事官でお在なのでし

た。さやうで御座いましたらう。その頃向坂の手から何したので御座います。究竟あの方もその件から諭旨免官のやうな事にお成なすつて、又東京へお遣りにならなければ為方が無いので、彼方を引払ふのに就いて、向坂から話が御座いまして、宅の方へ始は委任して参つたので御座いましたけれど、丁度去年の秋頃から全然此方へ引継いで了ふやうな都合に致しましたの。

然し、それは取立に骨が折れるので御座いましてね、ああして止と遊んでお在も同様で、𤏋訳か何か少ばかり為さる御様子なのですから、今のところではどうにも手の着けやうが無いので御座いますわ」

「はあ成程。然し、あれが何で三千円と云ふ金を借りたかしらん」

「それはあの方は連帯者なので御座います」

「はあ！　さうして借主は何者ですか」

「大館朔郎と云ふ岐阜の民主党員で、選挙に失敗したものですから、その運動費の後肚だとか云ふ話でございました」

「うむ、　大館朔郎……それぢや事実でせう」

「御承知でゐらつしやいますか」

「それは荒尾に学資を給した人で、あれが始終恩人と言つてをつたその人だ」

はやその言の中に彼の心は急に傷みぬ。己の敬愛せる荒尾譲介の窮して戚々たらず、真に義の為に功名を擲ち、恩の為に富貴を顧ざりし故にあらずや。彼の貧きは万

むと言ひしは、天命を楽

万人の富めるに優れり。君子なる吾友よ。さしも深き志を抱ける者にして、その酬らるる薄倖の

彼の如く甚く酷なるを念ひて、貫一は漫ろ涙の沸く目を閉ぢたり。

第五章

遽に千葉に行く事有りて、貫一は午後五時の本所発を期して車を飛せしに、咄嗟、一歩の時を

遅れて、二時間後の次回を待つべき倒懸の難に遭へるなり。彼は悄々停車場前の休憩処に入りて

奥の一間なる縞毛布の上に温茶を啜りたりしが、門を出づる折受取りし三通の郵書の鞄に打込み

しままなるを、この時取出せば、中に一通の M. Shigis—— と裏書せるが在り。

彼はこれのみ開封せずして、やがて他の読売と一つに投入れし鞄を礑と閉づるや、枕に引寄せ

て仰臥すと見れば、はや目を塞ぎて睡を促さんと為るなりき。されども、彼は能く睡るを得べき

か。さすがにその人の筆の蹟を見ては、今更に憎しとも恋しとも、絶えて念には懸けざるべしと

誓へる彼の心も、睡らるるまでに安かる能はざるなり。

いで、この文こそは宮が送りし再度の懇にて、その始めて貫一を驚かせし一札は、約そ二週間前

に彼の手に入りて、一字も漏れずその目に触れしかど、彼は夙に荒尾に答へしと同様の意を以て

その自筆の悔悟を読みぬ。こたびとてもまた同き繰言なるべきを、何の未練有りて、徒に目を汚

し、懐を傷けんやと、気強くも右より左に搔遣りけるなり。

宮は如何に悲しからん！　この両度の消息は、その苦き胸を剖き、その切なる誠を吐きて、世をも身をも忘れし自白なるを。事若し誤らば、この手証は生ながら葬らるべき罪を獲るに余有るものならずや。さしも覚悟の文ながら、彼はその一通の力を以て直に貫一の心を解かんとは思設けざりき。

故に幾日の後に待ちて又かく聞えしを、この文にもなほ験あらずば、彼は弥増す悲の中に定めて三度の筆を援るなるべし。知らずや、貫一は再度の封をだに切らざりしを——三度、五度、七度重ね重ねて十百通に及ばんとも、貫一は断じてこの愚なる悔悟を聴かじと意を決せるを。

静に臥したりし貫一は忽ち起きて鞄を開き、先づかの文を出し、一片の焰は烈々として、白く颺るものは宮の思の何か、黒く壊落つるものは心の何か、彼が幾年の悲と悔とは嬉くも今その人の手に在りながら、すげなき烟と消えて跡無くなりぬ。

その端に火を移しつつ、火鉢の上に差翳せり。

貫一は再び鞄を枕にして始の如く仰臥せり。

間有りて婢どもの口々に呼邀ふる声して、入来し客の、障子越なる隣室に案内されたる気勢に、

彼等は若き人のやうにもあらず顔る沈寂に座に着きたり。

「まだ沢山時間が有るから寛り出来る。さあ、鈴さん、お茶をお上んなさい」

こは男の声なり。

「貴方本当にこの夏には是非一度帰んなさいますのですか」

「盆過には是非一度帰ります。然しね、お話をした通り尊父さんや尊母さんの気が変つて了つてお在なのだから、鈴さんばかりそんなに思つてるてゐれでも、これがどうして、円く納るものぢやない。この上はもう唯諦めるのだ。私は男らしく諦めた！」

「雅さんは男だからさうで々せうけれど、私は諦めません。さうぢやないとお言ひなさるけれど、雅さんは阿父さんや阿母さんの為方を慍つてお在なのに違無い。それだから私までが憎いので、いいえ、さうよ、私は何でも可いから、若し雅さんが引取つて下さらなければ、一生何処へも適きはしませんから」

女は処々聞き得ぬまでの涙声になりぬ。

「だつて、尊父さんや尊母さんが不承知であつて見れば、幾許私の方で引取りたくつても引取る訳に行かないぢやありませんか。それも、誰を怨む訳も無い、全く自分が悪いからで、こんな躰に疵の付いた者に大事の娘をくれる親は無い、くれないのが尤だと、それは私は自分ながら思つてゐる」

「阿父さんや阿母さんがくれなくても、雅さんさへ貰つて下されば可いのぢやありませんか」

「そんな解らない事を言つて！　私だつてどんなに悔いか知れはしない。それは自分の不心得から、あんな罪にも陥ちたのだけれど、実を謂へば、高利貸の罠に罹つたばかりで、自分の躰には生

涯の疵を付け、隻の母親は……殺して了ひ、又その上に……許婚は破談にされ、……こんな情無い思を為す位なら、不如私は牢の中で死んで了った……方が可かった！」

「あれ、雅さん、そんな事を……」

両箇は一度に哭き出せり。

「阿母さんがあん畜生の家を焼いて、夫婦とも焼死んだのは好い肚癒ぢやあるけれど、一旦私の軀に附いたこの疵は消えない。阿母さんも来月は鈴さんが来てくれると言って、朝晩にそればかり楽にして在すった……のだし」

女はつと出でし泣音の後を怺へて嗚上げぬ。

「私も破談に為る気は少も無いけれど、これは私の方から断るのが道だから、必ず悪く思って下さるな」

「いいえ……いいえ……私は……何も……断られる訳はありません」

「私に添へば、鈴さんの肩身も狭くなって、生涯何のかのと人に言れなけりやならない。それがお気毒だから、私は自分から身を退いて、これまでの縁と諦めてゐるので、然し、鈴さん、私は貴方の志は決して忘れませんよ」

女は唯愈よ咽びのたり。音も立てず臥したりし貫一はこの時忍び起きて、障子の其処此処より男を隙見せんと為たりけれど、竟に意の如くならで止みぬ。かの男は鰐淵の家に放火せし狂女の子にて、私書偽造罪を以て一年の苦役を受け

し飽浦雅之ならずと為んや。さなり、女のその名を呼べるにても知らるるを、と独り頷きつつ貫一は又潜りて聴耳立てたり。

「嘘にもさうして志は忘れられないなんて言つて下さる程なら、やつぱり約束通り私を引取つて下さいな。雅さんがああ云ふ災難にお遭なので、それが為に縁を切る意なら、私は、雅さん、……一年が間……塩断なんぞ為はしませんわ」

彼は自らその苦節を憶ひて泣きぬ。

「雅さんが自分に悪い事を為てあんな訳に成つたのぢやなし、高利貸の奴に瞞されて無実の罪に陥ちたのは、雅さんの災難だと、私は倶共に悔し……悔し……悔いとは思つてゐても、それで雅さんの軀に疵が附いたから、一処になるのは迷惑だなんと何時私が思つて！　雅さん、私はそんな女ぢやありません、そんな女ぢや……ない！

この心を知らずや、と情極りて彼の悶え慨くが手に取る如き隣には、貫一が内偸に頭を擦付けて、巻蔦の消えしを擎げたるままに横はれるなり。

「雅さんは私をそんな女だとお思ひのは、貴方がお留守中の私の事を御存じないからですよ。私は三月の余も疾つて……そんな事も雅さんは知つてお在ぢやないのでせう。それは、阿父さんや阿母さんは雅さんのところへ上げる気は無いにしても、若しああ云ふ事が有つたので雅さんの肩身が狭くなるやうなら、私は猶更雅さんのところへ適かずにはゐられない。さうして私も雅さんと一処に肩身が狭くなりたいのですから、さうでなけりや、子供の内からあん

なに可愛がつて下すつた雅さんの尊母さんに私は済まない。

親が不承知なのを私が自分の了簡通に為るのは、そりや不孝かも知れませんけれど、私はどうしても雅さんのところへ適きたいのですから、お可厭でなくば引取つて下さいましな。私の事はかまひませんから雅さんが貰つて下さるお心持がお有なさるのか、どうだか唯それを聞して下さいな」

貫一は身を回して臂枕に打仰ぎぬ。彼は己が与へし男の不幸よりも、添れぬ女の悲よりも、先づその娘が意気の壮なるに感じて、あはれ、世にはかかる切なる恋の焚る如き誠もあるよ、と頭は熱し胸は轟くなり。

さて男の声は聞ゆ。

「それは、鈴さん、言ふまでもありはしない。私もこんな目にさへ遭はなかつたら、今頃は家内三人で睦く、笑つて暮してゐられるものを、と思へば猶々の事、私は今日の別が何とも謂れないほど情無い。かうして今では人に顔向も出来ないやうな身に成つてゐる者をそんなに言つてくれるのは、この世の中に鈴さん一人だと私は思ふ。その優い鈴さんと一処に成れるものなら、こんな結構な事は無いのだけれど、尊父さん、尊母さんの心にもなつて見たら、今の私には添されないのは、決して無理の無いところで、子を念ふ親の情は、何処の親でも差違は無い。そこを考へれば こそ、私は鈴さんの事は諦めると云ふので、子として親に苦労を懸けるのは、不幸どころではない、悪事だ、立派な罪だ！

私は自分の不心得から親に苦労を懸けて、それが為に阿母さんも

ああ云ふ事に成つて了つたのだから、実は私が手に掛けて殺したも同然。その上に又私ゆゑに鈴さんの親達に苦労を懸けては、それぢや人の親まで殺すと謂つたやうな者だから、私も諦められないところを諦めて、これから一働して世に出られるやうに成るのを楽に、やつぱり暗い処に入つてゐる気で精一杯勉強するより外は無い、と私は覚悟してゐるのです」

「それぢや、雅さんや内の阿父さんや阿母さんの事はそんなに思つて下すつても、私の事は些も思つては下さらないのですね。私の軀なんぞはどうならうと、雅さんはかまつては下さらないのね」

「そんな事が有るものぢやない！　私だつて……」

「いいえ、可うございます。もう可いの、雅さんの心は解りましたから」

「鈴さん、それは違つてゐるよ。それぢや鈴さんは全で私の心を酌んではおくれでないのだ」

「それは雅さんの事よ。阿父さんや阿母さんの事をさうして思つて下さるなら、本人の私の事だつて思つて下さりさうな者ぢやありませんか。雅さんのところへ適くと極つて、その為に御嫁入道具まで丁と調へて置きながら、今更外へ適れますか、雅さんも考へて見て下さいな。阿父さんや阿母さんが不承知だと謂つても、そりや余り酷いわ、余り勝手だわ！　私は死んでも他へは適きはしませんから、可いわ、可いわ、私は可いわ！」

「そんな事をお言ひだつて、それぢやどう為うと云ふのです」

女は身を顫して泣沈めるなるべし。

「どう為ても可う御座います、私は自分の心で極めてゐますから」

歪いで男の声は為さりしが、間有りて誰じの、語り出でしとも分かず、又一時密々と話声の洩れけれど、調子の低かりければ此方には聞知られざりしは、互にその意に逆ふところ無かりしなるべし。

の間一たびも高く言を出さざりしは、互にその意に逆ふところ無かりしなるべし。彼等は久くこの細語を息めずして、そ

「きつと？　きつとですか」

始て又明かに聞えしは女の声なり。

「さうすれば私もその気で居るから」

かくて彼等の声は又低うなりぬ。されど益す絮々として飽かず語れるなり。貫一は心陰に女の計らず洩聞えけんやうに、憂かる己をも忘れんとしつ。

成効を祝し、かつ雅之たる者のこれが為に如何に幸ならんかを想ひて、あたかも妙なる楽の音の

今かの娘の宮ならば如何ならん、吾か雅之ならば如何ならん。吾は今日の吾たるを択ぶ可き

か、将かの雅之たるを希はんや。　貫一は空うかく想へり。

宮も嘗て己に対して、かの娘に遜るまじき誠を抱かざるにしもあらざりき。彼にして若し金剛

石の光を見ざりしならば、また吾をも刑余に慕ひて、その誠を全うしたらんや。唯継の金力を以て彼女を脅したらんには、またかの雅之を入獄の先に棄てたりけんや。　耀ける金剛石と汚れたる

罪名とは、孰か愛を割くの力多かる。

彼は更にかく思へり。

唯その人を命として、己も有らず、家も有らず、何処の野末にも相従はんと誓へるかの娘の、竟に利の為に志を移さざるを得べきか。利と争ひて打勝れたると、他の愛と争ひて敗れたると、吾等の恨は孰に深からん。

彼は又かくも思へるなり。

それ愛の最も篤からんには、利にも惑はず、他に又易ふる者もあらざる可きを、仮初もこれの移るは、その最も篤きにあらざるを明せるなり。凡そ異性の愛は吾愛の如く篤かるを得ざる者なるか、或は己の信ずらんやうに、宮の愛の特に己にのみ篤からざりしなるか。吾は彼の不義不貞を憤るが故に世上の恋なる者を疑ひ、かつ渾てこれを斥けぬ。されどもその一旦の憤は、これを斥けしが為に消ゆるにもあらずして、その必ず得べかりし物を失へるに似たる快々は、吾心を食尽し、終に吾身を斃すに至らざれば、得やは去るまじき悪霊の如く執念く吾を苦むるなり。かかれば何事にも楽むを知らざりし心の今日偶ま人の相悦ぶを見て、又躬も怡びつつ、楽の影を追ふらんやうなりしは何の故ならん。よし吾は宮の愛ならずとも、これに易ふる者を得て、とかくはこの心を慰めしむ可きや。

彼はいよいよ思廻せり。

宮はこの日頃吾に篤からざりしを悔いて、その悔を表せんには、何等の事を成さんも唯吾命の儘ならんとぞ言来したる。吾はその悔の為にはかの憤を忘るべきか、任他吾恋の旧に復りて

再び完かるを得るにあらず、彼は彼の悔の悔のみ、吾が失意の恨は終に吾が失意の恨なるのみ。

この恨は富山に数倍せる富に因りて始て償はるべきか、或はその富を獲んとする貪欲はこの恨を移すに足るか。

彼は苦き息を嘘きぬ。

吾恋を壊りし唯継！

或は壊らんと為るにあらざる無きか。彼等の恋を壊らんと為しは誰ぞ、その吾の今千葉に赴くも、又或は壊り、

吾が狂疾を医すべき特効剤なりや。かの妨げられし恋は、破鏡の再び合ふを得て楽み、吾が割れし愛は落花の復る無くして畢らんのみ！　いで、吾はかくて空く埋るべきか、風に因りて飛ぶべ

きか、水に落ちて流るべきか。

貫一は船橋を過る 燈 暗き汽車の中に在り。

第　六　章

千葉より帰りて五日の後 M., Shigis —— の書信は又来りぬ。貫一は例に因りて封のまま火中してけり。その筆の跡を見れば、忽ち浮ぶその人の面影は、唯継と並び立てる梅園の密会にあらざる無きに、彼は殆ど当時に同き憤を発して、先の二度なるよりはこの三度に及べるを、径廷く も廻らぬ筆の力などを以て、旧に返し得べき未練の吾に在りとや想へる、愚なる精衛の来りて大

海を填めんとするやと、却りて頑に自ら守らんとも為なり。

さりとも知らぬ宮は蟻の思を運ぶに似たる片便も、行くべき方には音づるるを、さてかの人の如何に見るらん、書綴れる吾誠の千に一つも通ずる事あらば、掛けても願へる一筋の緒ともなりなんと、人目あらぬ折毎には必ず筆採りて、その限無き思を写してぞ止まざりし。

唯継は近頃彼の専ら手習すと聞きて、その善き行を感ずる余に、良き墨、良き筆、良き硯、良き手本まで自ら求め来ては、この難有き心掛の妻に遣りぬ。宮はそれ等を汚はしとて一切用ゐること無く、後には夫の机にだに向はずなりけり。かく怠らず綴られし文は、又六日を経て貫一の許に送られぬ。彼は四度の文をも例の灰と棄てて顧ざりしに、日を経ると思ふ程も無く、五度の文は来にけり。よし送り送りて千束にも余れ、手に取るからの烟ぞと侮れる貫一も、曾て宮には無かりし執着のかばかりなるを謂知らず異みつつ、今日のみは直にも焚かざりしその文を、一度は披き見んと為たり。

「然し……」

彼は輙く手を下さざりき。

「赦してくれと謂ふのだらう。その外には、見なければ成らん用事の有る訳は無い。若し有ると為れば、それは見る可からざる用事なのだ。赦してくれなら赦して遣る、悔悟したで、それで可い。悔悟したから、又赦さんでも既に赦れてゐるのではないか。悔悟したなら、悔悟したで、それで可い。悔悟したから、赦したからと云つて、それがどうなるのだ。それが今日の貫一と宮との間に如何なる影響を与へるのだ。悔悟し

たからあれの操の疵が愈えて、又赦したから、富山の事が無い昔に成るのか。その点に於ては、貫一は飽くまでも十年前の貫一だ。宮！　貴様は一生汚れた宮ではないか。ことの破れて了つた今日になつて悔悟も赦してくれも要つたものか、無益な事だ！　少も汚れん宮であるから愛してをつたのだ、それを貴様は汚して了つたから怨んだのだ。さうして一遍汚れた以上は、それに対する十倍の徳を行つても、その汚れたのを汚れざる者に改めることは到底出来んのだ。

　であるから何と言つた！　熱海で別れる時も、お前の外に妻と思ふ者は無い、一命に換へてもこの縁は切られんから、俺のこの胸の中を可憐と思つて、十分決心してくれ、と実に男を捨てて頼んだではないか。その貫一に負いて……何の面目有つて今更悔悟……晩い！」

　彼はその文を再三柱に鞭ちて、終に縄の如く引捩りぬ。

　打続きて宮が音信の必ず一週に一通来ずと謂ふこと無くて、披れざるに送り、送らるるに披かざりしも、はや算ふれば十通に上れり。さすがに今は貫一が見る度の憤も弱りて、待つとにはあらねど、その定りて来る文の繁きに、自ら他の悔い悲める宮在るを忘るる能はずなりぬ。されど、その忘るる能はざるも、遽に彼を可懐むにはあらず、又その憤の弱れるも、彼を赦し、彼を容れんと為るにあらずして、始に恋ひしをば棄てられ、後には棄てしを悔らるる身の、その古き恋はなほ己に存し、彼の新なる悔は切に貧るも、徒に凍えて水を得たるに同かるこの両の者の、相対して相拯ふ能はざる苦艱を添ふるに過ぎざるをや。ここに於て貫一は披かぬ宮が文に向へば、その幾倍の悲きものを吾と心に読みて、かの恨ならぬ恨も生じ、かの憤ならぬ憤も発して、憂身独

の儚き世をば如何にせんやうも知らで、唯安からぬ昼夜を送りつつ、出づるに入るに茫々として、彼は履ばその貪るをさへ忘るる事ありけり。

貫一は、新緑の雨に暗き七時の闇に靄るる夢の苦く頻に呻きしを、再び彼に揺起れて驚けば、劇く物思ひて寝ねざりし夜の明方近く疲睡を催せしりつつ現ならず又睡りけるを、老婢に喚れて、覚めたりと知

「お客様でございます」

「お客？　誰だ」

「荒尾さんと有仰いました」

「何、荒尾？　ああ、さうか」

「お通し申しますで御座いますか」

主の急ぎ起きんとすれば、

「おお、早くお通し申して。さうしてな、唯今起きましたところで御座いますから、暫く失礼致しますとさう申して」

貫一はかの一別の後三度まで彼の隠家を訪ひしかど、毎に不在に会ひて、二度に及べる消息の返書さへあらざりければ、安否の如何を満枝に糺せしに、変る事無く其処に住めりと言ふに、さては真に交を絶たんとすならんを、姑く強て追はじと、一月余も打絶えたりしに、彼方より好くこそ来つれ、吾がこの苦を語るべきは朋の来れるも、実にかくばかり楽きはあらざらん。今日は酒を出して一日彼を還さじなど、心忙きまでに歓ばれぬ。

絶交せるやうに疎音なりし荒尾の、何の意ありて卒に訪来れるならん。貫一はその何の意なりやを念はず、又その突然の来叩をも怪まずして、畢竟彼の疎音なりしはその飄然主義の拘らざる故、交を絶つとは言ひしかど、誼の吾を棄つるに忍びざる故と、彼はこの人のなほ己を友として来れるを、有得べからざる事とは信ぜざりき。

手水場を出来しは貫一は腫眠の赤きを連瞬きつつ、羽織の紐を結びも敢へず、つと客間の紙門を排けば、荒尾は居らず、かの荒尾譲介は居らで、美う装へる婦人の独り羞含ひ控へたる、可疑き女客も未だ背けたる面を回さず、細雨静に庭樹を撲ちて滴る打惑ひて入りかねたる彼の目前に、可疑き女客も未だ背けたる面を回さず、細雨静に庭樹を撲ちて滴る翠は内を照せり。

「荒尾さんと有仰るのは貴方で」

彼は先づかく会釈して席に着きけるに、婦人は猶も面を示さざらんやうに頭を下げて礼を作せり。

しかも彼は軽くその下げたる頭とを拄へたる手とを挙げざるなりき。始に何者なりやと驚されし貫一は、今又何事なりやと弥よ呆れて、彼の様子を打瞠れり。乍ち有りて貫一の眼は慌忙く覓むらん色を作して、婦人の俯けるを佗と窺ひたりしが、

「何ぞ御用でございますか」

「…………」

「どう云ふ御用向でございますか。伺ひませう」

彼は益す急に左瞻右視して窺ひつ。

「…………」

露置く百合の花などの仄に風を迎へたる如く、その可疑き婦人の面は術無げに挙らんとして、又悲ち懼れたるやうに遅疑ふ時、

「宮!?」　と貫一の声は筒抜けて走りぬ。

宮は嬉し悲しの心味みて、身も世もあらず泣伏したり。

「何用有つて来た！」

怒るべきか、この時。恨むべきか、この時。辱むべきか、悲むべきか、号ぶべきか、罵るべきか、責むべきか、彼は一時に万感の相乱れて急なるが為に、吾を吾とも覚ゆる能はずして打顔ひのたり。

「貫一さん！　どうぞ堪忍して下さいまし」

宮は漸う顔を振挙げしも、凄く色を変へたる貫一の面に向ふべくもあらで萎れ俯しぬ。

「早く帰れ！」

「…………」

「宮！」

幾年聞かざりしその声ならん。宮は危みつつも可懐しと見る目を覚えず其方に転せば、鋭く瞬ふる貫一の眼の湿へるは、既に如何なる涙の催せしならん。

「今更お互に逢ふ必要は無い。又お前もどの顔で逢ふ意か。先達而から頻に手紙を寄来すが、あ

れは一通でも開封したのは無い、来れば直に焼棄てて了ふのだから、以来は断じて寄来さんやう
に。私は今病中で、かうしてゐるのも太儀でならんのだから、早く帰つて貰ひたい」

彼は老婢を召して、

「お客様のお立だ、お供にさう申して」

取附く島もあらず思悩める宮を委きて、貫一は早くも独り座を起たんとす。

「貫一さん、私は今日は死んでも可い意でお目に掛りに来たのですから、貴方の存分にどんな目
にでも遭せて、さうしてそれでともかくも今日は勘弁して、お願ですから私の話を聞いて下さい
まし」

「何の為に!」

「私は全く後悔しました! 貫一さん、私は今になつて後悔しました!! 悪い事はこの間からの
手紙に段々書いて上げたのですけれど、全で見ては下さらないのでは、後悔してゐる私のどんな
切ない思をしてゐるか、お解りにはならないでせうが、お目に掛つて口では言ふに言れない事ば
かり、設ひ書けない私の筆でも、あれをすつかり見て下すつたら、些とはお腹立も直らうかと、
自分では思ふのです。色々お詫は為る意でも、かうしてお目に掛つて見ると、面目が無いやら、
悲いやらで、何一語も言へないのですけれど、貫一さん、とても私は来られる筈でない処へかう
して来たのには、死ぬほどの覚悟をしたのと思つて下さいまし」

「それがどう為たのだ」

「さうまで覚悟をして、是非お話を為たい事が有るのですから、御迷惑でもどうぞ、どうぞ、貫一さん、ともかくも聞いて下さいまし」

涙ながらに手を拄へて、吾が足下に額叩く宮を、何為らんとやうに打見遣りたる貫一は、

「六年前の一月十七日、あの時を覚えてゐるか」

「…………」

「さあ、どうか」

「私は忘れは為ません」

「うむ、あの時の貫一の心持を今日お前が思知るのだ」

「堪忍して下さい」

唯見る間に出行く貫一、咄嗟、紙門は鉄壁よりも堅く閉てられたり。宮はその心に張充めし望を失ひてはたと頷伏しぬ。

「豊、豊！」と老婢を呼ぶ声劇く縁続の子亭より聞ゆれば、直に走り行く足音の響きしが、やがて返し来れる老婢は客間に顕れぬ。宮は未だ頭を挙げずゐたり。可憐き東髪の頸元深く、黄蘗染の半衿に紋御召の二枚袷を重ねたる衣紋の綾先づ謂はんやう無く、肩状優う内俯したる脊に金茶地の東綴の帯高く、勝色裏の敷乱れつつ、白羽二重のハンカチイフに涙を掩へる指に赤く、白く指環の玉を耀したる、殆ど物語の画をも看るらん心地して、この美き人の身の上に何事の起りけると、豊は可恐きやうにも覚ゆるぞかし。

「あの、申上げますが、主人は病中の事でございますもので、唯今生憎と急に気分が悪くなりましたので、相済みませんで御座いますが中座を致しました。恐入りますで御座いますが、どうぞ今日はこれで御立帰を願ひますで御座います」

面を抑へたるままに宮は涙を啜りて、

「ああ、さやうで御座いますか」

「折角お出のところを誠にどうもお気毒さまで御座います」

「唯今些と支度を致しますから、もう少々置いて戴きますよ」

「さあさあ、貴方御遠慮無く御寛と遊ばししまし。又何だか降出して参りまして、今日はいつそお寒過ぎますで御座います」

彼の起ちし迹に宮は身支度を為るにもあらで、始て甦りたる人の唯在るが如くに打沈みてぞ居たる。やや久かるに客の起たんとする模様あらねば、老婢は又出来れり。宮はその時遽に身仕して、

「それではお暇を致します。些と御挨拶だけ致して参りたいのですから、何方にお寝つてお在ですか……」

「はい、あの何でございます、どうぞもうおかまひ無く……」

「いいえ、御挨拶だけ些と」

「さやうで御座いますか。では此方へ」

主の本意ならじとは念ひながら、老婢は止むを得ず彼を子亭に案内せり。昨夜の収めざる蓐の内に貫一は着のまま打伏れて、夜着も掻巻も裾の方に蹴放し、枕に辛うじてその端に幾度か置易られし頭を載せたり。

思ひも懸けず宮の入来るを見て、起回らんとせし彼の膝下に、早くも女の転び来て、立たんと為れば袂を執り、猶も犇と寄添ひて、物をも言はず泣伏したり。

「ええ、何の真似だ！」

突返さんとする男の手を、宮は両手に抱き緊めて、

「貫一さん！」

「何を為る、この恥不知！」

「私が悪かったのですから、堪忍して下さいまし」

「ええ、耻い！ ここを放さんか」

「貫一さん」

「放さんかと言ふに、ええ、もう！」

その身を楯に宮は放さじと争ひて益す放さず、両筒が顔は互に息の通はんとすばかり近く合ひぬ。一生又相見じと誓へるその人の顔の、おのれ眺めたりし色は疾く失せて、誰ゆゑ今の別に豔なるも、なほ形のみは変らずして、実にかの宮にして宮ならぬ宮と、吾は如何にしてここに逢へる！ 貫一はその胸の夢むる間に現ともなく彼を瞡れり。宮は殆ど情極りて、繊に狂せざるを得る！

たるのみ。

彼は人の頭より大いなるダイアモンドを把る手をば釈かざらん。

大いなるダイアモンドか、幾許大いなるダイアモンドも、宮は人の心の最も小き誠に値せざるを既に知りぬ。彼の持たるダイアモンドはさせる大いなる者ならざれど、その棄去りし人の誠は量無きものなりしが、嗟乎、今何処に在りや。その嘗て誠を恵みし手は冷かに残されり。空くその手を抱きて泣かんが為に来れる宮が悔は、実に幾許大いなる者ならん。

「さあ、早く帰れ！」

「ええ、煩い！」

「もう二度と私はお目には掛りませんから、今日のところはどうとも堪忍して、打つなり、殴くなり貫一さんの勝手にして、さうして少小でも機嫌を直して、私のお詫に来た訳を聞いて下さい」

「ええ、煩い！」

「それぢや打つとも殴くともして……」

身悶して宮の縋るを、

「そんな事で俺の胸が霽れると思つてゐるか、殺しても慊らんのだ」

「ええ、殺れても可い！　殺して下さい。私は、貫一さん、殺して貰ひたい、さあ、殺して下さい、死んで了つた方が可いのですから」

「自分で死ね！」

彼は自ら手を下して、この身を殺すさへ屑からずとまでに己を鄙むなるか、余に辛しと宮は唇を咬みぬ。

「死ね、死ね。お前も一旦棄てた男なら、今更見とも無い態を為さずに何為死ぬまで立派に棄て通さんのだ」

「私は始から貴方を棄てる気などは有りはしません。それだから篤りとお話を為たいのです。死んで了へとお言ひでなくても、私はもう疾から自分ぢや生きてゐるとは思つてゐません」

「そんな事聞きたくはない。さあ、もう帰れと言つたら帰らんか！」

「帰りません！　私はどんな事してもこのままぢや……帰れません」

宮は男の手をば益々弛めず、益す激する心の中には、夫もあらず、世間もあらずなりて、唯この命を易ふる者を失はじと一向に思入るなり。

折から縁に足音するは、老婢の来るならんと、貫一は取られたる手を引放たんとすれど、こは如何、宮は些も弛めざるのみか、その容をだに改めんと為ず。果して足音は紙門の外に遁れり。

「これ、人が来る」

「………」

宮は唯力を極めぬ。

不意にこの体を見たる老婢は、半啓けたる紙門の陰に顔引入れつつ、

「赤樫さんがお出になりまして御座います」

窮厄の色はつと貫一の面に上れり。

「ああ、今其方へ行くから。——さあ、客が有るのだ、好加減に帰らんか。ええ、放せ。客が有ると云ふのにどうするのか」

「ぢや私はここに待つてゐますから」

「知らん！　もう放せと言つたら」

用捨もあらず宮は捻倒されて、落花の狼藉と起き敢へぬ間に貫一は出行く。

（六）の二

座敷外に脱ぎたる紫裏の吾妻コオトに目留めし満枝は、嘗て知らざりしその内曲の客を問はで止む能はざりき。又常に厚く恵るる老婢は、彼の為に始終の様子を告るの労を客まざりしなり。

さてはと推せし胸の内は臆悪に燃えて、可憎き人の疾く出で来よかし、如何なる貌して我を見んと為らん、と焦心のいとどしう久かりしに、貫一はなかなか出で来ずして、しかも子亭のほとほと人気もあらざらんやうに打鎮れるは、我に忍ぶかと、弥よ満枝は怜へかねて、

「お豊さん、もう一遍旦那様にさう申して来て下さいな、私今日は急ぎますから、些とお目に懸りたいと」

「でも、私は誠に参り難いので御座いますよ、何だかお話が大変込入つてお在のやうで御座います……

「かまはんぢやありませんか、私がさう申したと言つて行くのですもの」

「ではさう申上げて参りますです」

「はあ」

老婢は行きて、紙門の外より、

「旦那さま、旦那さま」

「此方にお在は御座いませんよ」

かく答へては客の声なり。豊は紙門を開きて、

「おや、さやうなので御座いますか」

実に主は在らずして、在るが如くその枕頭に坐れる客の、猶悲の残れる面に髪をば少し打乱し、左の袷の二寸ばかりも裂けたるままに姿も整はずゐたりしを、遽に引枢ひつつ、

「今し方其方へお出なすつたのですが……」

「おや、さやうなので御座いますか」

「那裡のお客様の方へお出なすつたのでは御座いませんか」

「いいえ、貴方、那裡のお客様が急ぐと有仰つてで御座いますものですから、さう申上げに参つたので御座いますが、それぢやまあ、那辺へいらつしやいましたらう！」

「那裡にもゐらつしやいませんの！」

「さやうなので御座いますよ」

老婢はここを倉皇起ちて、満枝が前に、

「此方へもいらつしやいませんで御座いますか」

「何が」

「あの、那裡にもいらつしやいませんので御座いますが」

「旦那様が？　どうして」

「今し方這裡へ出てお在になつたのださうで御座います」

「嘘、嘘ですよ」

「いいえ、那裡にはお客様がお一人でゐらつしやるばかり……」

「嘘ですよ」

「いいえ、どういたして貴方、決して嘘ぢや御座いません」

「だつて、此方へお出なさりは為ないぢやありませんか」

「ですから、まあ、何方へいらつしやつたのかと思ひまして……」

「那裡にきつと隠れてでもお在なのですよ」

「貴方、そんな事が御座いますものですか」

「どうだか知れはしません」

「はてね、まあ。お手水ですかしらん」

随処尋ねんとて彼は又倉皇起ちぬ。

有効無きこの侵辱に遭へる吾身は如何にせん、と満枝は無念の遣る方無さに色を変へながら、些も騒ぎ惑はずして、知りつつ食みし毒の験を耐へ忍びゐたらんやうに、得も謂れず恟に苦め
り。宮はその人の遁れ去りしこそ頼の綱は切られしなれと、はや留るべき望も無く、まして立帰るべき力は有らで、罪の報は悲くも何時まで儚きこの身ならんと、打俯し、打仰ぎて、太息吐く
のみ。

颯と空の昏み行く時、軒打つ雨は漸く密なり。
戸棚、押入の外捜さざる処もあらざりしに、終に主を見出さざる老婢は希有なる貌して又子亭に入来れり。

「何方にもむらつしやいませんで御座いますが……」
「あら、さやうで御座ですか。ではお出掛にでも成ったのでは御座いませんか」
「さやうで御座いますね。一体まあどうなすつたと云ふので御座いませう、那裡にも這裡にもお客様を置去に作つてからに。はてね、まあ、どうもお出掛になる訳は無いので御座いますけれど、家中には何処にもむらつしやらないところを見ますと、お出掛になつたので御座いますかしらん。それにしても……まあ御免あそばしまして」
彼は又満枝の許に急ぎ行きて、事の由を告げぬ。
「いいえ、貴方、私は見て参りましたので御座いますよ。子亭にむらつしやりは致しません、それは大丈夫で御座います」

彼は遽に心着きて履物を検め来んとて起ちけるに、躍いで起てる満枝の庭前の縁に出づると見れば、従々と行きて子亭の入口に顕れたり。

宮は何人の何の為に入来れるとも知らず、先づ愕きつつも彼を迎へて容を改めぬ。吾が恋人の恋人を拝まんとてここに来にける満枝の、意外にも敵の己より少く、己より美く、己より可憐く、己より貴きを見たる妬さ、憎さは、唯この者有りて可怜しさ故に、他の情も誠も彼は打忘るるよとあはれ、一念の力を剣とも成して、この場を去らず刺殺さまほしう、心は躍り襲り、躍り襲らんと為るなりけり。

宮は稍羞ひて、葉隠に咲遅れたる花の如く、夕月の涼う棟を離れたるやうに満枝は彼の前に進出でて、互に対面の礼せし後、

「始めましてお目に掛りますで御座いますが、間様の……御親戚？」

「おや、さやうでむらつしやいますか。手前は赤樫満枝と申しまして、間様とは年来の御懇意で、もう御親戚同様に御交際を致して、毎々お世話になつたり、又及ばずながらお世話したり、始終お心易く致してをりますで御座いますが、ついぞ、まあ従来お見上げ申しませんで御座いました」

憎き人をば一番苦めんの満枝が底意なり。

「はい親類筋の者で御座いまして」

「御親戚？　でむらつしやいますで御座いますか」

「はい、つい先日まで長らく遠方に参つてをりましたもので御座いますから」

「まあ、さやうで。余程何でございますか、御遠方で？」

「はい……広島の方に居りまして御座います」

「はあ、さやうで。唯今は何方に」

「池端に居ります」

「へえ、池端、お宜い処で御座いますね。然し、夙て間様のお話では、御自分は身寄も何も無いから、どうぞ親戚同様に末の末まで交際したいと有仰るもので御座いますから、全くさうとばかり私、信じてをりましたので御座いますよ。それに唯今かうして伺ひますれば、御立派な御親戚がお有り遊ばすのに、どう云ふお意であんな事を有仰つたので御座いませう。何も親戚のお有りあそばす事をお隠しになるには当らんぢや御座いませんか。あの方は時々さう云ふ水臭い事を一体作るので御座いますよ」

疑の雲は始て宮が胸に懸りぬ。父が甞て病院にて見し女の必ず訳有るべしと指せしはこれならん。さては客来と言ひしも詐にて、或は内縁の妻と定れる身の、吾を惜めて邪魔立せんとか、但は彼人のこれ見よとてここに引出せしかと、今更に差はざりし父が言を思ひて、宮は仇の為に病めるを答たるやうにも覚ゆるなり。いよいよ長く居るべきにあらぬ今日のこの場はこれまでと潔く座を起たんとしたりけれど、何処にか潜めるる彼人の吾が還るを待ちて忽ち出で来て、この者と手を把り、面を並べて、可哀なる吾をば笑ひ罵りもやせんと想へば、得堪へず口惜くて、如

何にせば可きと心苦く遅ひ為たり。

「お久しぶりで折角お出のところを、生憎と余儀無い用向の使が見えましたもので、お出掛になつたので御座いますが、些と遠方でございますから、お帰来の程は夜にお成りで御座いませう、近日どうぞ又御寛りとお出で遊ばしまして」

「大相長座を致しまして、貴方の御用のお有り遊ばしたところを、心無いお邪魔を致しまして、相済みませんで御座いました」

「いいえ、もう、私共は始終上つてをるので御座いますから、些とも御遠慮には及びませんで御座います。貴方こそさぞ御残念でみらつしやいませう」

「はい、誠に残念でございます」

「さやうで御座いませうとも」

「四五年ぶりで逢ひましたので御座いますから、色々昔話でも致して今日は一日遊んで参らうと楽に致してをりましたのを、実に残念で御座います」

「大きに」

「さやうなら私はお暇を致しませう」

「お帰来で御座いますか。丁度唯今小降で御座いますね」

「いいえ、幾多降りましたところが倅で御座いますから」

互に憎し、口惜しと鎬を削る心の刃を控へて、彼等は又相見ざるべしと念じつつ別れにけり。

第七章

し貫一は、我家ながらも身を容るる所無き苦紛れに、裏庭の木戸より傘も携さで忍び出でけるなり。

家の内を隈無く尋ぬれども在らず、さては今にも何処よりか帰来んと待てど暮せど、姿を晦せり。

されど唯一目散に脱れんとのみにて、卒に志す方もあらぬに、生憎降頻る雨をば、辛くも人の軒などに凌ぎつつ、足に任せて行くほどに、近頃思立ちて折節通へる碁会所の前に出でければ、ともかくも成らんとて、其処に躍入りけり。

客は三組ばかり、各静に窓前の竹の清韻を聴きて相対せる座敷の一間奥に、主は乾魚の如き親仁の黄なる髯を長く生したるが、兀然として独り盤を磨きゐる傍に通りて、彼は先づ濡れたる衣を炙らんと火鉢に寄りたり。

異み問はるるには能くも答へずして、貫一は余りに不思議なる今日の始末を、その余波は今も轟く胸の内に痛み思回して、又空く神は傷み、魂は驚くといへども、我や怒る可き、事や哀む可き、或は悲む可きか、恨む可きか、抑も喜ぶ可きか、慰む可きか、彼は全く自ら弁ぜず。五内渾て燃え、四肢直に氷らんと覚えて、名状すべからざる感情と煩悶とは新に来りて彼を襲へるなり。

主は貫一が全濡の姿よりも、更に可訝きその気色に目留めて、間はでも椿事の有りしを疑はざりき。ここまで身は迸れ来たれど、なかなか心安からで、両人を置去に為し跡は如何、又我が為んやうは如何など、彼は打惑へり。沸くが如きその心の騒しさには似で、小暗き空に満てる雨声を破りて、三面の盤の鳴る石は断続して甚だ幽なり。主はこの時窓際の手合観に呼れたれば、貫一は独り残りて、未だ乾ぬ袂を翳しつつ、愈よ限無く惑ひめたり。遽に人の騒立つるに愕きて顔を挙れば、座中尽く頸を延べて己が方を眺め、声々に臭しと喚はるに、見れば、吾が羽織の端は火中に落ちて黒煙を起つるなり。直に揉消せば人は静るとともに、彼もまた前の如し。

少頃有りて、門に入来し女の訪ふ声して、

「宅の旦那様はもしや這裡へいらっしやりは致しませんで為たらうか」

主は忽ち彼の顔を回して、

「ああ、奥にお在で御座いますよ」

豊かと差覗きたる貫一は、

「おお、傘を持つて来たのか」

「はい。此方にお在なので御座いましたか、もう方々お捜し申しました」

「さうか。客は帰つたか」

「はい、疾にお帰になりまして御座います」

「四谷のも帰つたか」

「いいえ、是非お目に掛りたいと有仰いまして」

「居る？」

「はい」

「それぢや見付からうと言つて措け」

「ではお帰りに成りませんので？」

「も少し経つたら帰る」

「直にもうお中食で御座いますが」

「可いから早く行けよ」

「未だ旦那様は朝御飯も」

「可いと言ふに！」

老婢は傘と足駄とを置きて悄々遣りぬ。

程無く貫一も焦げたる袂を垂れて出行けり。

彼はこの情緒の劇の紛乱せるに際して、可煩き満枝に賞らるる苦悩に堪へざるを思へば、その帰去らん後までは決して還らじと心を定めて、既に所在を知られたる碁会所を立出でしが、いよいよ指して行くべき方は有らず。はや正午と云ふに未だ朝の物さへ口に入れず、又半銭をも帯びずして、如何に為んとするにか有らん、猶降りに降る雨の中を茫々然として彷徨へり。

初夏の日は長かりけれど、纔に幾局の勝負を決せし盤の上には、殆ど惜き夢の間に昏れて、折

から雨も霽れたれば、好者どもも終に碁子を歛めて、惣立に帰るをあたかも送らんとする主の忙々しく燈ともす比なり、貫一の姿は始て我家の門に顕れぬ。

彼は内に入るより、

「飯を、飯を！」と婢を叱して、颯と奥の間の紙門を排けば、何ぞ図らん燈火の前に人の影在り。

彼は立てるままに目を瞪りつつ。されど、その影は後向に居て動かんとも為ず。満枝は未だ往かざるか、と貫一は覚えず高く舌打したり。女は尚も殊更に見向かぬを、此方もわざと言を掛けずして子亭に入り、膳を呼びて衣を更へ、豊を其処に取寄せしが、何とか為けん、必ず入来べき満枝の食事を了るまでも来ざるなりき。却りて仕合好しと、貫一は打労れたる身を暢かに、障子の月影に肱枕して、姑く喫烟に耽りたり。

敢て恋しとにはあらねど、苦しげに嬴れたる宮が面影の幻は、頭を回れる一蚊の声の去らさらんやうに襲ひ来て、彼が切なる哀訴も従ひて憶出でらるれば、なほ往きかねて那辺に忍ばずやと、風の音にも幾度か頭を挙げし貫一は、婆娑として障子に揺るる竹の影を疑へり。

宮は何時までここに在らん。彼は悔いたり、我より容さば容さるべきを、さは容さずして堅く隔つる思ひも、又怪しまでに貫一は侘くて、その釈き難き怨に加ふるに、或種の哀に似たるを感ずるなりき。いと淡き今宵の月の色こそ、その哀にも似たるやうに打眺めて、他の憎しとよりは転

思ふに、彼の悔いたるとは誠ならん、我の死を以て容さざるも誠なり。彼は例の孤なり。

た自を悲しと思続けぬ。彼は竟に堪へかねたる気色にて障子を推啓れば、涼き空に懸れる片割月は真向に彼の面に照りて、彼の愁ふる眼は又痛かにその光を望めり。

「間さん」

居たるを忘れし人の可疎き声に見返れば、はや背後に坐れる満枝の、常は人を見るに必ず笑を帯びざる無き目の秋波も乾き、顔色などは殊に橋れて、などかくは浅ましきと、心陰に怪む貫一。

「ああ、未だ御在でしたか」

「はい、居りました。お午前から私お待ち申してをりました」

「ああ、さうでしたか、それは大きに失礼しました。さうして何ぞ急な用でも」

「急な用が無ければ、お待ち申してをつては悪いので御座いますか」

語気の卒に厲きを駭ける貫一は、空く女の顔を見遣るのみ。

「お悪いで御座いませう。お悪いのは私能く存じてをります。第一お待ち申してをりましたのよりは、今朝ほど私の参りましたのが、一層お悪いので御座いませ。飛だ御娯のお邪魔を致しまして、間さん、誠に私相済みませんで御座いました」

その眼色は怨の鑓を露して、男の面上を貫かんとやうに緊く見据ゑたり。

貫一は苦笑して、

「貴方は何を読な事を言つてゐるのですか」

「今更お戻しなさるには及びませんさ。若い男と女が一間に入つて、取付き引付きして泣いたり

笑つたりしてをれば、訳は大概知れてをるぢや御座いませんか。私あれに控へてをりまして、様
子は大方存じてをります。七歳や八歳の子供ぢや御座いません、それ位の事は誰にだつて直に解
りませうでは御座いませんか。

爾後貴方がお出掛になりますと私直にここのお座敷へ推掛けて参つて、あの御婦人にお目に掛
りましたので御座います」

架しと聞流せし貫一も、ここに到りて耳を欹でつ。

「さうして色々お話を伺ひまして、お二人の中も私能く承知致しました。あの方も又有仰らなく
ても可ささうな事までお話を作らいますので、それは随分聞難い事まで私伺ひました」

為失したりと貫一は密に術無き拳を握れり。満枝は猶も言足らで、

「然し、間さん、遂に貴方で御座いますのね、私敬服して、了ひました。失礼ながら貴方のお腕
前に驚きましたので御座います。ああ云つた美婦人を御娯びに遊ばしてゐながら、世間へは
偏人だ事の、一国者だ事の、その方へ掛けては実に奇麗なお顔を遊ばして、今日の今朝まで何
年が間と云ふの秘隠に隠し通してゐらつしたお手際には私実に驚入つて一言も御座いません。
能く凄いとか何とか申しますが、貴方のやうなお方の事をさう申すので御座いませう」

「もうつまらん事を……、貴方何ですか」

「お口ぢやさう有仰つても、実はお嬉いので御座いませう。あれ、ああしちや考へてゐらつしや
る！　そんなにも恋くてゐらつしやるのですかね」

されば我が出行きし迹をこそ案ぜしに、果してかかる孽は出で来にけり。由無き者の目には触れけるよ、と貫一はいと苦く心跼りつつ、物言ふも憂き唇を閉ぢて、唯月に打向へるを、女は此方より熟々と見透して目も放たず。

「間さん、貴方さう黙つてゐらつしやらんでも宜いでは御座いませんか。ああ云ふお美いのを御覧に成つた後では、私如き者には口をお利きに成るのもお可厭なのでゐらつしやいませう。私お察し申してをります。ですから私決して絮い事は申上げません。少し聞いて戴きたい事が御座いますのですから、庶かそれだけ言して下さいまし」

貫一は冷に目を転して、

「何なりと有仰い」

「私もう貴方を殺して了ひたい！」

「何です?!」

「貴方を殺して、あれも殺して、さうして自分も死んで了ひたく思ふのです」

「それも可いでせう。可いけれど何で私が貴方に殺されるのですか」

「間さん、貴方はその訳を御存無いと有仰るのですか、どの口で有仰るのですか」

「これは怪からん！　何ですと」

「怪からんとは、貴方も余りな事を有仰るでは御座いませんか」

既に恨み、既に瞋りし満枝の眼は、ここに到りて始て泣きぬ。いと有るまじく思掛けざりし貫

は寧ろ可恐しと念へり。

「貴方はそんなにも憎くてゐらつしやるのですか。何で又さうお憎みなさるのですか。その訳をお聞せ下さいまし。私それが何ひたい、是非伺はなければ措きません」

「貴方を何日私が憎みました。私それが何ひたい、是非伺はなければ措きません」

「では、何で怪からんなどと有仰います」

「怪からんぢやありませんか、貴方に殺される訳が有るとは。私は決して貴方に殺される覚は無い」

満枝は口惜しげに頭を掉りて、

「有ります！ 立派に有ると私信じてをります」

「貴方が独で信じても……」

「いいえ、独で有らうが何で有らうが、自分の心に信じた以上は、私それを貫きます」

「私を殺すと云ふのですか」

「随分殺しかねませんから、覚悟をなすつてゐらつしやいまし」

「はあ、承知しました」

いよいよ昇れる月に木草の影もをかしく、庭の風情は添すけれど、軒端なる芭蕉葉の露 鴬 く夜気の侵すに墻へで、やをら内に入りたる貫一は、障子を閉てて燈を明うし、故に床の間の置時計を見遣りて、

「貴方、もうお帰りに成つたが可いでせう、余り晩くなるですから。ええ？」

「憚り様で御座います」

「いや、御注意、御座いますのです」

「その御注意が憚り様ですと申上げるので」

「ああ、さうですか」

「今朝のあの方なら、そんな御注意なんぞは遊ばさんで御座いませう。如何ですか」

憎さげに言放ちて、彼は吾矢の立つを看んとやうに、姑く男の顔色を候ひしが、

「一体あれは何者なので御座います！」

犬にも非ず、猫にも非ず、汝に似たる者よと思ひけれど、言争はんは愚なりと勘弁して、彼は才に不快の色を作せしのみ。満枝は益す独り慣れて、

「旧いお馴染ださうで御座いますが、あの恰好は、商売人ではなし、万更の素人でもないやうな、貴方も余程不思議な物をお好み遊ばすでは御座いませんか。然し、間さん、あれは主有る花で御座いませう」

「妄に言へるならんと念へど、如何にせん貫一が胸は陰に轟けるを。

「どうですか、なあ」

「さう云ふ者を対手に遊ばすと、別してお楽が深いとか申しますが、その代に罪も深いので御座いますよ。貴方が今日まで巧に隠し抜いてゐらしつた訳も、それで私能く解りました。こればか

りは余り御公に御自慢は出来ん事で御座いますもの、秘密に遊ばしますのは実に御尤で御座います。

その大事の秘密を、人も有らうに、貴方の嫌ひの嫌ひの大御嫌ひの私に知られたのは、どんなにか御心苦しからつしやいませう。私十分御察し申してをります。然し私に取りましては、これ程幸な事は無いので御座います。貴方が余り片意地に他を苦めてばかりゐらつしつたから、今度は私から思ふ様これで苦めて上げるのです。さう思召してゐらつしやい！」

聞訖りたる貫一は吃々として窃笑せり。

「貴方は気でも違ひは為んですか」

「少しは違つてもをりませう。誰がこんな気違には作すつたのです。私気が違つてゐるなら、今朝から変に成つたので御座いますよ。お宅に詣つて気が違つたのですから、元の正気に復してお還し下さいまし」

彼は擦寄り、擦寄りて貫一の身近に逼れり。浅ましく心苦かりけれど迯ぐべくもあらねば、臭き物に鼻を擦へる心地しつつ、貫一は身を側め側め居たり。満枝は猶も寄添はまほしき風情にて、

「就きましては、私一言貴方に伺ひたい事が有るので御座いますが、これはどうぞ御遠慮無く貴方の思召す通を丁と有仰つてお聞せ下さいまし、宜う御座いますか」

「何ですか」

「なんですかでは可厭です、宜いと截然有仰つて下さい。さあ、さあ、貴方」

「けれども……」

「けれどもぢや御座いません。私の申す事だと、貴方は毎も気の無い返事ばかり遊ばすのですけれど、何も御迷惑に成る事では御座いませんのです、私の申す事に就て貴方が思召す通を答へて下されば、それで宜いのですから」

「勿論答へます。それは当然の事ちやないですか」

「それが当然でなく、極打明けて少しも褒まずに言つて戴きたいのですから」

善と貫一は頷きつ。

「では、きつと有仰つて下さいまし。　間さん、貴方は私を慾い奴だと思召してゐらつしやるで御座いませう。私始終さう思ひながら、貴方の御迷惑もかまはずにやつぱりかうして附纏つてゐるのは、自分の口から簡様な事を申すのも、甚だ可笑いので御座いますけれど、私、実に貴方の事は片時でも忘れは致しませんのです。それは如何に思つてをりましたところが、元来私と云ふ者を嫌ひ抜いて御在なのですから、あの歌が御座いますね、行く水に数画くよりも儚きは、思はぬ人を思ふなりけりとか申す、実にその通り、私の願の悸な事は到底無いので御座いませうとも、行く水に数画くやうな者で、もうさうと知りながら、それでも、間さん、私こればかりは諦められんので御座います。

こんな者に見込れて、さぞ御迷惑ではゐらつしやいませうけれども私がこれ程までに思つてゐるのですから、貴方も御存でゐらつしやいませ。私が熱心に貴方の事を思つてゐると云ふ事は、貴方も御存でゐらつしやいませ。

御座います、それはお了解に成つてゐるで御座いませう」

「さうですな……そりや或はさうかも知れませんけれど……」

「何を言つてみらつしやるのですね、貴方は、或はもさうかもないでは御座いませんか！ さも無ければ、私何も貴方に慈がられる訳は御座いませんさ、貴方も私を慈いと思ふすのが、現に何よりの証拠で。漆膠くて困ると御迷惑してゐらつしやるほど、承知を遊ばしてお在のでは御座いませんか」

「それはさう謂へばそんなものです」

「貴方から嫌はれ抜いてゐるにも関らず、こんなに私が思つてゐると云ふ事は、十分御承知なので御座いませう」

「さう」

「で、私従来に色々申上げた事が御座いましたけれど、些とでもお聴き遊ばしては下さいませんでした。それは表面の理窟から申せば、無理なお願かも知れませんけれど、私は又私で別に考へるところが有つて、決して貴方の有仰るやうな道に外れた事とは思ひません。よしんばさうでありましても、こればかりは外の事とは別で、お互にかうと思つた日には、其処に理窟も何も有るのでは御座いません。究竟貴方がそれを口実にして遁げてゐらつしやるのは、始から解り切つてゐるので。然し、貴方も人から偏屈だとか、一国だとか謂れてゐらつしやるのですから、それで私

成程儀剛な片意地なところもお有なすつて、色恋の事なんぞには貪着を遊ばさん方で、それで私

うに存じてをつたので御座います……ところが！」

の心も汲分けては下さらんのかと、さうも又思つたり致して、実は貴方の頑固なのを私歯痒いや

と言ひも敢へず煙管を取りて、彼は貫一の横膝をば或る念力強く痛か推したり。

「何を作るのです！」

払へば取直すその煙管にて、手とも云はず、膝とも云はず、当るを幸に満枝は又打ち被る。

こは何事と駭ける貫一は、身を避る暇もあらず三つ四つ撃れしが、遂に取つて抑へて両手を働

かせじと為れば、内俯に引据ゑられたる満枝は、物をも言はで彼の股の辺に面を擦付けて咽泣に泣くなりき。怪から

ぬ女哉、と怒の余に手暴く撥放せば、なほ辛くも縋れるままに面を擦付けて咽泣に泣くなりき。怪から

貫一は唯不思議の為体に呆れ惑ひて言も出でず、漸く泣ゐる彼を推斥けんと為たれど、膠の附

きたるやうに取縋りつつ、益々泣いて泣止まず。涙の湿は単衣を透して、この難面き人の膚

に沁みぬ。

捨置かば如何に募らんも知らずと、貫一は用捨無く攀放して、起たんと為るを、彼は虚さず貫

りて、又泣顔を擦付れば、怺へかねたる声を励す貫一、

「貴方は何を為るのですか！　好い加減になさい」

「…………」

「さうして早くお帰りなさい」

「帰りません！」

「帰らん？　帰らんけりや宜い。もう明日からは貴方のここへ足踏の出来んやうに為て了ふか

ら、さうお思ひなさい」

「私死んでも参ります！」

「今まで我慢をしてゐたですけれど、もう抛つて置かれんから、私は赤樫さんに会つて、貴方の

事をすつかり話して了ひます」

満枝は始て涙に沾へる目を挙げたり。

「はあ、お話し下さい」

「…………」

「赤樫に聞えましたら、どう致すので御座います」

貫一は歯を鳴らして急上げたり。

「貴方は……実に……驚入つた根性ですな！　赤樫は貴方の何ですか」

「間さん、貴方は又赤樫を私の何だと思召してゐらつしやるのですか」

「怪からん！」

「彼は憎き女の頬桁をば撃つて撃つて打割る能はざるを憾と為るべし。

「定てあれは私の夫だと思召すので御座いませうが、決してさやうでは御座いませんです」

「そんなら何ですか」

「往日もお話致しましたが、金力で無理に私を奪つて、遂にこんな体にして了つた、謂はば私の

讐(かたき)も同然なので。成程人は夫婦とも申しませうが私の気では何とも思つてをりは致しません。さうですから、自分の好いた方に惚れて騒ぐ分は、一向差支(さしつか)の無い独身も同じので御座います。

間さん、どうぞ赤樫にお会ひ遊ばしたら、満枝の奴が惚れてゐる為方が無いから、さう思へと、貴方が有仰(おっしゃ)つて下さいまし。私豊(とよ)の手伝でも致して、此方(こなた)に一生奉公を致します。

貴方は大方赤樫に言ふと有仰つたら、震へ上つて私が怖がりでも為ると思召すのでせうが、私驚きも恐れも致しません、寧(むし)ろ勝手なのですけれど、赤樫がそれは途方に昧れるで御座いませう」

貫一はほとほと答ふるところを知らず。満枝も然(しか)こそは呆(あき)れつらんと思へば、

「それは実際で御座います。若し話が一間違つて、面倒な事でも生じましたら、私が困りますよりは余程赤樫の方が困るのは知れてゐるのですから、私を遠けやう為にお話をなさるのなら、徒爾(いたづ)らな事で御座います。赤樫は私を恐れてをりませんとも、私些(わたしち)ともあの人を恐れてはをりません。けれども、折角さう思召すものなら、物は試で御座いますから、間さん、貴方、赤樫にお話し遊ばして御覧なさいました。

私も貴方の事を吹聴致します。ああ云ふ主有る婦人と関係遊ばして、始終人目を忍んで逢引(あひびき)してゐらつしやる事を触散(ふれち)らしますから、それで何方が余計迷惑するか、比較事(くらべっこ)を致しませう。如何(いか)で御座います」

「男勝りの機敏な貴方にも似合はん、さすがは女だ」

「何で御座います？」

「お聞きなさい。男と女が話をしてゐれば、それが直ちに逢引ですか。又妙齢の女でさへあれば、必ず主有るに極つてゐるのですか。浅膚な邪推とは言ひながら、人を誣ふるも太甚い！　失敬千万な、気を着けて口をお利きなさい」

「間さん、貴方、些と此方をお向きなさい」

手を取りて引けば、振釈き、

「ええ、もう貴方は」

「お怒いでせう」

「勿論」

「私向後もつと、もつともつと怒くして上げるのです。さあ、貴方、今何と有仰つたので御座います、浅膚な邪推ですつて？　貴方こそ少し気を着けてお口をお利き遊ばせな、貴方も男子であらつしやるなら、何為立派に、その通だ。情婦が有るのがどうしたと、かう打付けて有仰らんのです。間さん、私貴方に向つてそんな事をかれこれ申す権利は無い女なので御座います。それに、何も私の前を憚つて、さう向に成つてお隠し遊ばすには当らんでは御座いませんか。貴方が余所外に未だ何百人愛してゐらつしやるのです。間さん、私貴方に向つてそんな事をかれこれ申す権利を有ちたくても、有つ事が出来ずにゐるので御座います。多さう云ふ権利を有ちたくても、私実を申しませうか、箇様なので御座います。貴方が余所外に未だ何百人愛してゐらつしやる

方が有りませうとも、それで愛相を尽して、貴方の事を思切るやうな、私そんな浮気な了簡ではないのです。又貴方の御迷惑に成る秘密を洩しましたところで、悧はない願が悧ふ訳ではないので御座いませう。どう思召してもいらつしやるか存じませんけれど、私それ程卑怯な女ではないやうで御座います。

世間へ吹聴して貴方を困らせるなどと申したのは、あれは些の其の場の憎まれ口で、私決してそんな心は微塵も無いので御座いますから、どうかその御積で、お心持を悪く遊ばしませんやうに。つい口が過ぎましたのですから、御勘弁遊ばしまして。私この通お詫を致します」

満枝は惜まず身を下して、彼の前に頭を低ぐる可憐しさよ。貫一は如何にとも為る能はずして、窃に首を掻いたり。

「就きましては、私今から改めて折入つた御願が有るので御座いますが貴方も従来の貴方ではないしに、十分人情を解してもいらつしやる間さんとして宣告を下して戴きたいので御座います。そのお辞次第で、私もう断然何方に致しても了簡を極めて置きますから、間さん、貴方も庶か歯に衣を着せずに、お心に在る通りをそのまま有仰つて下さいまし。宜う御座いますか。

今更新しく申上げませんでも、私の心は奥底まで見通しに貴方は御存でいらつしやるのです。従来も随分数々申上げましたけれど、貴方は一図に私をお嫌ひ遊ばして、些でも私の申す事は取上げては下さらんのです——さやうで御座いませう。貴方からそんなに嫌はれてゐるのですから、私さう申すから何もさう何時まで好い恥を掻かずとも、早く立派に断念して了へば宜いのです。私さう申すから何

で御座いますけれど、これでも女子にしては極未練の無い方で、手短に一か八か決して了ふ側な
ので御座います。それがこの事ばかりは実に我ながら何為かう意気地が無からうと思ふ程、……
これが迷つたと申すので御座いませう。自分では物に迷つた事と云ふは無い積の私、それが貴方
の事ばかりには全く迷ひました。

ですから、唯その胸の中だけを貴方に汲んで戴けば、私それで本望なので御座います。これ程
に執心致してをる者を、徹頭徹尾貴方がお嫌ひ遊ばすと云ふのは、能く能くの因果で、究竟貴方
と私とは性が合はんので御座いませうから、それはもう致方も有りませんが、そんなに為れてま
でもやつぱりかうして慕つてをるとは、如何にも不敏な者だと、設ひその当人はお気に召しませ
んでも、その心情はお察し遊ばしても宜いでは御座いませんか。決してそれをお察し遊ばす事の
出来ない貴方ではないと云ふ事は、私今朝の事実で十分確めてをります。

御自分が恋く思召すのも、人が恋いのも、恋いに差は無いで御座いませう。増して、貴方、片
思に思つてゐる者の心の中はどんなに切ないでせうか、間さん、私貴方を殺して了ひたいと申し
たのは無理で御座いますか。こんな不束な者でも、同じに生れた人間一人が、貴方の為には全で
奴隷のやうに成つて、しかも今貴方のお辞を一言聞きさへ致せば、それで死んでも惜くないとま
でも思込んでゐるので御座います。其処をお考へ遊ばしたら、如何に好かん奴であらうとも、雫
ぐらゐの情は懸けて遣らう、と御不承が出来さうな者では御座いませんか。

私もさう御迷惑に成る事は望みませんです、せめて満足致されるほどのお辞を、唯一言で宜い

のですから、今までのお馴染効にどうぞ間さん、それだけお聞せ下さいまし」

終に近く益す顔へる声は、竟に平生の調をさへ失ひて聞えぬ。彼は正くその一言の為には幾千円の公正証書を挙げて反古に為るも、なかなか客からぬ気色を帯びて遍れり。息は凝り、面は打蒼みて、その袖よりは劔を出さんか、その心よりは笑を出さんか、と胸跳らせて片時も苦く待つなりき。

切なりと謂はば実に極めて切なる、可憐しと謂はば又極めて可憐き彼の心の程は、貫一もいと善く知れけれど、他の己を愛するの故を以て直ちに蛇蝎に親まんや、と却りてその執念をば難堪く浅ましと思へるなり。

されど又情として厲く言ふを得ざるこの場の仕儀なり。貫一は打悩める眉を強て拔かせつつ、

「貴方もまあ何を有仰つてゐらつしやるのでせう。御自分の有仰る事を他にお聞き遊ばしたつて、誰が存じてをりますものですか」

「それはさうですけれど、私にも解らんから」

「さうして貴方が満足するやうな一言?……どう云ふ事を言つたら可いのですか」

「解るも解らんも無いでは御座いませんか。それが貴方は何か巧い遁口上を有仰らうとなさるから、急に御考も無いので、貴方に対する私、その私が満足致すやうな一言と申したら、間さん、外には有りは致しませんわ」

「いや、それなら解つてゐます……」

「解つてゐらつしやるなら些と有仰つて下さいましな」

「それは解つてゐるますけれど、貴方の言れるのはかうでせう。段々お話の有つたやうな訳であるから、とにかくその心情は察しても可からう、それを察してゐるのが善く解るやうな挨拶を為てくれと云ふのぢやありませんか。実際それは余程難い、別にどうも外に言ひ様も無いですわ」

「まあ何でも宜う御座いますから、私の満足致しますやうな御挨拶をなすつて下さいまし」

「だから、何と言つたら貴方が満足なさるのですか」

「私のこの心を汲んでさへ下されば、それで満足致すので御座います」

「貴方の思召は実に難有いと思つてゐます。私は永く記憶してこれは忘れません」

「間さん、きつとで御座いますか、貴方」

「勿論です」

「きつとで御座いますね」

「相違ありません！」

「きつと？」

「ええ！」

「その証拠をお見せ下さいまし」

「証拠を？」

「はあ。口頭ばかりでは私可厭で御座います。貴方もあれ程確に有仰つたのですから、万更心に

無い事をお言ひ遊ばしたのでは御座いますまい。さやうならそれだけの証拠が有る訳です。その

証拠を見せて下さいますか」

「みせられる者なら見せますけれど」

「見せて下さいますか」

「見せられる者なら。然し……」

「いいえ、貴方が見せて下さる思召ならば……」

鶯破、障子を推開きて、貫一は露けき庭に躍り下りぬ。つとその迹に顕れたる満枝の面は、斜

に葉越の月の冷き影を帯びながらなほ火の如く燃えに燃えたり。

第　八　章

家の内には己と老婢との外に、今客も在らざるに、女の泣く声、訴る声の聞ゆるは甚だ謂無し、

我或は夢むるにあらずやと疑ひつつ、貫一は枕せる頭を擡げて耳を澄せり。

その声は急に嘆き、相争ふ気勢さへして、はたはたと紙門を挙かすは、愈よ怪しと夜着排却け

て起ち行かんとする時、ばつさり紙門の倒るると斉く、二人の女の姿は貫一が目前に転び出で

ぬ。

苛まれしと見ゆる方の髪は浮藻の如く乱れて、着たるコートは雫するばかり雨に濡れたり。そ

の人は起上り様に男の顔を見て、嬉しや、可懐しやと心も空なる気色。

「貫一さん」と匐ひ寄らんとするを、薄色魚子の羽織着て、夜会結に為たる後姿の女は躍り被つ
て引据れば、

「あれ、貫、貫一さん!」

拯を求むるその声に、貫一は身も消入るやうに覚えたり。彼は念頭を去らざりし宮ならずや。
七生までその願は聴かじと邨けたる満枝の、我の辛さを彼に移して、先の程より打ちも詬りもし
たりけんを、猶慊らで我が前に責むるかと、貫一は怜へかねて顔ひるめたり。満枝は縦まに宮を据

へて些も動かせず、徐に貫一を見返りて、

「間さん、貴方のお大事の恋人と云ふのはこれで御座いませう」

頸髪取つて宮が面を引立てて、

「この女で御座いませ」

「貫一さん、私は悔う御座んす。この人は貴方の奥さんですか」

「私、奥さんならどうしたのですか」

「貫一さん!」

彼は足擦して叫びぬ。満枝は直ちに推伏せて、

「ええ、睨い! 貫一さんは其処に一人居たら沢山ではありませんか。貴方より私が間さんには
言ふ事が有るのですから、少し静にして聴いてお在なさい。

間さん、私想ふのですね、どんなに申しても
私の言は取上げては下さらんので御座いませう。元こ
の女は貴方を棄てて、余所へ嫁に入つて了つたやうな、実に畜生にも劣つた薄情者なのでは御座
いませんか。——私善く存じてゐるますわ。
お可愛いのか存じませんけれど、一旦愛想を尽して逃げて行つた女を、いつまでも思込んで遅々
してゐらつしやるとは、まあ何たる不見識な事でせう！　貴方はそれでも男子ですか。　私ならこ
んな女は一息に刺殺して了ふのです」

宮は跛返さんと為しが、又抑へられて声も立てず。

「間さん、貴方、私の申上げた事をば、やあ道ならぬの、不義のと、実に立派な口上を有仰いま
したでは御座いませんか、それ程義のお堅い貴方なら、何為こんな淫乱の人非人を阿容活けてお
置き遊ばすのですか。それでは私への口上に対しても、貴方男子の一分が立たんで御座いませ
う。何為成敗は遊ばしません。さあ、私決してもう二度と貴方には何も申しませんから、貴方も
この女を見事に成敗遊ばしまし。さもなければ、私も立ちませんです。

間さん、どう遊ばしたので御座いますね、早く何とか遊ばして、貴方も男子の一分をお立てな
さらんければ済まんところでは御座いませんか。私ここで拝見致してをりますから、立派に遣つ
て御覧あそばせ。卒と云ふ場で貴方の腕が鈍つても、決して為損じの無いやうに、私好い刃物を
お貸し申しませう。さあ、間さん、これをお持ち遊ばせ」

彼の懐を出でたるは蝋塗の晃く一口の短刀なり。　貫一はその殺気に撲れて一指をも得動かさ
ず、空く眼を輝して満枝の面を睨みたり。　宮ははや気死せるか、推伏せられたるままに声も無
し。

「さあ、私かうして抑へてをりますから、吭なり胸なり、ぐつと一突に遣つてお了ひ遊ばせ。え
え、もう貴方は何を遅々してゐらつしやるのです。刀の持様さへ御存じ無いのですか、かうして
抜いて！」

と片手ながらに一揮揮れば、鞘は発矢と飛散つて、電光袂を廻る白刃の影は、忽ち飜つて貫
一が面上三寸の処に落来れり。

「これで突けば可いのです」

「…………」

「さては貴方はこんな女に未だ未練が有つて、息の根を止めるのが惜くてゐらつしやるので御座
いますね。殺して了ふと思ひながら、手を下す事が出来んのですね。私代つて殺して上げませ
う。何の雑作も無い事。些と御覧あそばせな」

言下に勿焉と消えし刃の光は、早くも宮が乱鬢を掠めて顕れぬ。啊呀と貫一の号ぶ時、妙くも
彼は跂起ざまに突来る鎧を危く外して、

「あれ、貫一さん！」

と満枝の手首に縋れるまま、一心不乱の力を極めて撥伏せ撥伏せ、仰様に推重りて仆したり。

「貫、貫一さん、早く、早くこの刀を取つて下さい。さうして私を殺して下さい――貴方の手に掛けて殺して下さい。私は貴方の手に掛つて死ぬのは本望です。さあ、早く殺して、私は早く死にたい。貴方の手に掛つて死にたいのですから、後生だから一思に殺して下さい！」

この恐るべき危機に瀕して、貫一は謂知らず自ら異くも、敢て拯の手を藉さんと為るにもあらで、しかも見るには塔へずして、空く悶えに悶えたり。必死と争へる両箇が手中の刃は、或は高く、或は低く、右に左に閃々として、あたかも一鈎の新月白く風の柳を縫ふに似たり。

「貫一さん、貴方は私を見殺になさるのですか。どうでもこの女の手に掛けて殺すのですか！ 私は命は惜くはないが、この女に殺されるのは悔い！ 悔い!! 私は悔い!!」

彼は乱せる髪を夜叉の如く打振り打振り、五体を揉みて、唇の血を噴きぬ。彼も殺さじ、これも傷けじと、貫一が胸の廻るが若くなれど、如何にせん、その身は内より不思議の力に緊縛せられたるやうにて、逃れど、躁れど、寸分の微揺を得ず、せめては声を立てんと為れば、吭と塞りて、銃丸を啣める想。

力も今は絶々に、はや危しと宮は血声を揚げて、

「貴方が殺して下さらなければ、私は自害して死にますから、貫一さん、後生です、さ、さ、さあ取つて下さい！ 早く、貫一さん、この刀を取つて、私の手に持せて下さい。さ、早く、貫一さん、さあ取つて下さい！」

又激く揉合ふ郤舎に、短刀は憂然と落ちて、貫一が前なる畳に突立つたり。宮は虚さず躍り被りて、我物得つと手に為れば、遣らじと満枝の組付くを、推隔つる腕の下より後突に、棚も透れ

と刺したる急所、一声号びて仰反る満枝。鮮血！　兇器！　殺傷！　死体！　乱心！　重罪！

貫一は目も眩れ、心も消ゆるばかりなり。

「もうこの上はどうで私は無い命です。お願ですから、貫一さん、貴方の手に掛けて殺して下さい。私はそれで貴方に赦された積で喜んで死にますから。貴方もどうぞそれでもう塙忍して、今までの恨は霽して下さいまし、よう、貫一さん。私がこんなに思つて死んだ後までも、貴方が塙忍して下さらなければ、私は生替死替して七生まで貫一さんを怨みますよ。さあ、それだから私の迷はないやうに、貴方の口からお念仏を唱へて、これで一思ひに、さあ貫一さん、殺して下さい」

朱に染みたる白刃をば貫一が手に持添へつつ、宮はその可懐き拳に頻回頻擦したり。

「私はこれで死んで了へば、もう二度とこの世でお目に掛ることは無いのですから、せめて一遍の回向をして下さると思つて、今はの際で唯一言赦して遣ると有仰つて下さい。生きてゐる内にそどんなにも憎くお思ひでせうけれど、死んで了へばそれつきり、罪も恨も残らず消えて土に成つて了ふのです。私はかうして前非を後悔して、貴方の前で深く命を捨てるのも、その御詫が為たいばかりなのですから、貫一さん、既往の事は水に流して、もう好い加減に塙忍して下さいまし。よう、貫一さん、貫一さん！

今思へばあの時の不心得が実に悔くて悔くて、私は何とも謂ひやうが無い！　貴方が涙を零して言つて下すつた事も覚えてゐます。後来きつと思中るから、今夜の事を忘れるなとお言ひの声

も、今だに耳に付いてゐるわ。私の一図の迷とは謂ひながら何為あの時に些少でも気が着かなかつたか。愚な自分を責めるより外は無いけれど、死んでもこんな回復の付かない事を何で私は為ましたらう！　貫一さん、貴方の罰が中つたわ！　私は生きてゐる空が無い程、貴方の罰が中つたのだわ！　だから、もうこれで堪忍して下さい。よ、貫一さん。

さうしてとてもこの罰の中つた軀では、今更どうかうと思つても、願なんぞの悋ふと云ふのは愚な事、未だ未だ憂目を見た上に思死にでも為なければ、私の業は滅しないのでせうから、この世に未練は沢山有るけれど、私は早く死んで、この苦艱を埋めて了つて、さうして早く元の浄い軀に生れ替つて来たいのです。さう為たら、私は今度の世には、どんな艱難辛苦を為ても、きつと貴方に添遂げて、この胸に一杯思つてゐる事もすつかり善く聴いて戴き、又この世で為遣した事もその時は十分為てお目に掛けて、必ず貴方にも悦ばれ、自分も嬉い思を為て、この上も無い楽い一生を送る気です。今度の世には、貫一さん、私は決してあんな不心得は為ませんから、貴方も私の事を忘れずにゐて下さい。可うござんすか！　きつと忘れずにゐて下さいよ。人は最期の一念で生を引くと云ふから、私はこの事ばかり思窮めて死にます。貫一さん、この通だから堪忍して！」

声震はせて縋ると見れば、宮は男の膝の上なる鉞
(きつさき)
目掛けて岸破
(がば)
と伏したり。

「や、行つたな！」

貫一が胸は劈
(つんざ)
けて始めてこの声を出せるなり。

「貫一さん！」

無残やな、振仰ぐ宮が喉に血に塗れて、刃の半を貫けるなり。　彼はその手を放たで苦き眼を瞬きつつ、男の顔を視んと為るを、貫一は気も漫に引抱へて、

「これ宮、貴様は、まあこれは何事だ！」

大事の刃を抜取らんと為れど、一念凝りて些も弛めぬ女の力。

これを放せ、よ、これを放さんか。　さあ、放せと言ふに、ええ、何為放さんのだ」

「貫、貫一さん」

「おお、何だ」

「私は嬉しい。もう……もう思遺す事は無い。　堪忍して下すつたのですね」

「まあ、この手を放せ」

「放さない！　私はこれで安心して死ぬのです。貫一さん、ああ、もう気が遠く成つて来たから、早く、早く、赦すと言つて聞せて下さい。赦すと、赦すと言つて！」

血は滾々と益す流れて、末期の影は次第に黯くなる気色。　貫一は見るにも堪へず心乱れて、

「これ、宮、確乎しろよ」

「あい」

「赦したぞ！　もう赦した、もう堪……堪……堪忍……した！」

「貫一さん！」

「宮！」

「嬉い！　私は嬉い！」

貫一は唯胸も張裂けぬ可く覚えて、言は出でず、抱き緊めたる宮が顔をば紛れ下つる熱湯の涙に浸して、その冷たき唇を貪り吮ひぬ。宮は男の唾を口移に辛くも喉を潤して、

「それなら貫一さん、私は、吁、苦いから、もうこれで一思ひに……」

と力を出して剥らんと為るを、緊と抑へて貫一は、

「待て、待て待て！　ともかくもこの手を放せ」

「いいえ、止めずに」

「待てと言ふに」

「早く死にたい！」

漸く刀を挽放せば、宮は忽ち身を回して、輾けつ転びつ座敷の外に脱れ出づるを、

「宮、何処へ行く！」

遣らじと伸べし腕は逮ばず、苟つて起ちし貫一は唯一摑と躍り被れば、生憎滿枝が死骸に躓き、一間ばかり投げられたる其処の敷居に膝頭を砕けんばかり強く打れて、踏りしままに起きも得ず、身を竦めて呻きながらも、

「宮、待て！　言ふことが有るから待て！　豊、豊！　豊は居ないか。早く追掛けて宮を留めろ！」

　呼べど号べど、宮は返らず、老婢は居らず、貫一は阿修羅の如く憤りて起ちしが、又仆れぬ。仆れしを漸く起回りて、忙々に四下を眴せど、はや宮の影は在らず。その歩々に委せし血は莩環の糸を曳きたるやうに長く連りて、畳より縁に、縁より庭に、庭より外に何処まで、彼は重傷を負ひて行くならん。

　磐石を曳くより苦く貫一は膝の疼痛を怺へて、とにもかくにも塀外に踊ひ出づれば、宮は未だ遠くも行かず、有明の月冷かに夜は水の若く白みて、ほのぼのと狭霧罩めたる大路の寂として物の影無き辺を唯独り覚束無げに走れるなり。

「宮！待て！」

　呼べば弥は返せども、雲は幽にして彼は応へず。歯咬を作して貫一は後を追ひぬ。

　固より間は幾許も有らざるに、急所の血を出せる女の足取、引捉ふるに及べき何程の事有らんと、侮りしに相違して、彼は始の如く走るに引易へ、此方は漸く息疲るるに、距離は竟に依然として近く能はず。こは口惜しく、と貫一は満身の力を励し、僵るるならば僵れよと無二無三に走りたり。宮は猶脱るるほどに、帯は忽ち飆と靡けて脚に絡ふを、右に左に踢払ひつつ、跌きては進み、行きては蹌き、彼もはや力は竭きたりと見えながら、如何に為ん、其処に伏して復起きざる時、躬も終に及ばずして此処に絶入せんと思へば、貫一は今に当りて総に声を揚ぐるの術を余すのみ。

「宮！」と奮つて呼びしかど、懊むべし、その声は苦き喘の如き者なりき。

　我と吾肉を喫はん

と想ふばかりに躁れども、貫一は既に声を立つべき力をさへ失へるなり。さては効無き己に憤を作して、益す休まず狂呼すれば、彼の吭は終に破れて、泪然として一滴の鮮紅を嘔出せり。心晦みて覚えず倒れんとする耳元に、松風蕭然と吹起りて、吾に復れば、眼前の御塔端。只看る、宮

は行き行きて生茂る柳の暗きに分入りたる、入水の覚悟に極れりと、貫一は必死の声を搾りて連に呼べば、咳入り咳入り数口の咯血、斑爛として地に委ちたり。何思ひけん、宮は千条の緑の陰より、その色よりは稍白き面を露して、追来る人を熟と見たりしが、竟に疲れて起きも得ざる貫

一の、唯手を抗げて遥に留むるを、宛し給へと伏拝みて、つと茂の中に隠れたり。

彼は己の死ぬべきを忘れて又起てり。駛寄る岸の柳を潜りて、水は深きか、宮は何処に、と葎の露に踏滑る身を危くも淵に臨めば、轡轕と鴉く早瀬の水は、駸く浪の体を尽し、乱るる流の文を捲いて、眼下に幾個の怪き大石、かの鰲背を聚めて丘の如く、その勢を拒がんと為れど、触

るれば払ひ、当れば翻りへ、長波の邁くところ滔々として破らざる為き奮迅の力は、両岸も為に震ひ、坤軸も為に轟き、蹈居る土も今にや崩れなんと疑ふところ、衣袂の雨濃に灑ぎ、鬢髪の風転た急なり。

あな凄じ、と貫一は身毛も弥竪ちて、縋れる枝を放ちかねつつ、看れば、叢の底に秋蛇の行くに似たる径有りて、ほとほと逆落に懸崖を下るべし。危き哉と差覗けば、茅葛の頻に動きて、小

笹棘に見えつ隠れつ段々と辿り行くは、求むる宮なり。その死を止めんの一念より他あらぬ貫一なれば、かくと見るより心も空に、足は地を踏む遑も

あらず、唯遅れじと思ふばかりよ、空間の嵐の誘ふに委せて、蓦直に身を堕せり。

或は掉けて死ぬべかりしを、恙無きこそ天の佑なれ、彼は数歩の内に宮を追ひしが、流に浸れる巌を渉りて、既に渦巻く滝津瀬に生憎！　花は散りかかるを、

り。

「宮！」

と後に呼ぶ声残りて、前には人の影も在らず。

咄嗟の遅を天に叫び、地に号き、流に悶え、巌に狂へる貫一は、血走る眼に水を射て、此処や彼処と恋き水屑を覓むれば、正く浮木芥の類とも見えざる物の、十間ばかり彼方を揉みに揉んで、波間隠に推流さるるは、人ならず哉、宮なるかと瞳を定むる折しもあれ、水勢其処に一段急なり、在りける影は弦を放れし箭飛を作して、行方も知らずと胸潰るれば、忽ち遠く浮き出でた

嬉しやと貫一は、道無き道の木を攀ぢ、崖を伝ひ、或は下りて水を蹴え、石を踏み、巌を廻り、心地死ぬべく跟蹌として近き見れば、緑樹蔭愁ひ、潺湲声咽びて、浅瀬に繋れる宮が骸よ！

貫一は唯その上に泣伏したり。

吁、宮は生前に於て総に一刻の前なる生前に於て、この情の熱き一滴を幾許かは恙なみけん。

今や千行垂るといへども効無き涙は、徒に無心の死顔に濺ぎて宮の魂は知らざるなり。

貫一の悲は窮りぬ。

「宮、貴様は死……死……死んだのか。自殺を為るさへ可哀なのに、この浅ましい姿はどうだ。

刃（やいば）に貫き、水に溺（おぼ）れ、貴様はこれで苦くはなかつたか。可愛（かはい）い奴（やつ）め、思迫（おもひつ）めたなあ！

宮、貴様は自殺を為（な）た上身を投げたのは、一つの死では慊（あきた）らずに、二つ命を捨てた気か。さう

思つて俺は不敏（ふびん）だ！

どんな事が有らうとも、貴様に対するあの恨は決して忘れんと誓（ちか）つたのだ。誓つたけれども、

この無残な死状を見ては、罪も恨も皆消えた！　赦（ゆる）したぞ、宮！　俺は心の底から赦したぞ！

今はの際（きは）に赦したと、罪が一言云（ひとこと）つたらば、あの苦い息の下から嬉しと言つたが、宮、貴様は

俺に赦されるのがそんなに嬉いのか。好く後悔した！　立派な悔悟（くわいご）だぞ!!

余り立派で、貫一は恥入つた！　宮、俺は面目（めんぼく）無い！　これまでの精神とは知らずに見殺（みごろ）しに為（し）

たのは残念だつた！　俺が過だ！　宮、赦してくれよ！　可いか、宮、可いか。

嗚呼（ああ）死んで了つたのだ!!!」

貫一は彼の死の余りに酷（むご）く、余りに潔きを見て、不貞（ふてい）の血は既に尽く沃（そそ）がれ、旧悪の膚（はだ）は全く

洗れて、残れる者は、悔の為に、誠の為に、己（おの）れの為めたる亡骸（なきがら）の、実に憐みても憐むべく、

悲みても猶及ばざる思の、今は唯極めて切なる有るのみ。

かの烈々たる怨念の跡無く消ゆるとともに、一旦涸（か）れにし愛慕の情は又泉の涌（わ）くらんやうに起

りて、その胸に漲（みなぎ）りぬ。苦からず哉（や）、人亡（な）き後の愛慕は、何の思かこれに似る者あらん。彼はな

かなか生ける人にこそ如何なる恨をも繋（つな）ぐるの忍び易きを今ぞ知るなる。

貫一は腸（はらわた）断ち涙連（つれ）りて、我を我とも覚ゆる能（あた）はず。

「宮、貴様に手向けるのは、俺のこの胸の中だ。これで成仏してくれ、よ。この世の事はこれまでだ、その代り今度の世には、貴様の言った通り、必ず夫婦に成つて、百歳までも添へ、添、添遂げるぞ！　忘れるな、宮。俺も忘れん！　貴様もきっと覚えてゐろよ！」

氷の如き宮が手を取り、犇と握りて、永く眠れる面を覗かんと為れば、涙急にして文色も分かず、推重りて、怜しやと身を悶えつつ少時泣いたり。

「然し、宮、貴様は立派な者だ。一び罪を犯しても、かうして悔悟して自殺を為たのは、実に見上げた精神だ。さうなりや成らん、天晴だぞ。それでこそ始めて人間たるの面目が立つのだ。

然るに、この貫一はどうか！　一端男と生れながら、高が一婦の愛を失つたが為に、志を挫いて一生を誤り、餓鬼の如き振舞を為て恥とも思はず、非道を働いて暴利を貪るの外は何も知らん。

その財は何に成るのか、何の為にそんな事を為るのか。凡そ人と謂ふ者には、人として必ず尽すべき道が有る。己と云ふ者の外に人の道と云ふ者が有るのだ。俺はその道を尽してゐるか、尽さうと為てゐるか、思つた女と添ふ事が出来ん。唯それだけの事に失望して了つて、その失望の為に、苟くも男と生れた一生を抛たうと云ふのだ。人たるの効は何処に在る、人たる道はどうしたのか。

噫、誤つた！

宮、貴様が俺に対して立派に悔悟したのを見て、俺は実に愧入りも為りや、可羨くもある。当初貴様に貴様がかうして立派に悔悟したのを見て、俺は人たるの道に対して悔悟しなけりや済まん躰だ。

棄てられた為に、かう云ふ堕落をした貫一ならば、貴様の悔悟と共に俺も速かに心を慘めて、人たるの道に負ふところのこの罪を贖はなけりや成らん訳だ。

嗟乎、然し、何に就けても苦い世の中だ！

人間の道は道、義務は義務、楽は又楽で、それも無けりや立たん。俺も鴫沢に居て宮を対手に勉強してをつた時分は、この人世と云ふ者は唯面白い夢のやうに考へてゐた。あれが浮世なのか、これが浮世なのか。

爾来、今日までの六年間、人らしい思を為た日は唯の一日でも無かつた。それで何が頼で俺は活きてゐたのだ。死を決する勇気が無いので活きてゐたやうなものだ！　活きてゐたのではないない、死損つてゐたのだ！！

鰐淵は焚死に、宮は自殺した、俺はどう為るのか。俺のこの感情の強いのでは、又向来宮のこの死顔が始終目に着いて、一生悲い思をなければ成らん のだらう。して見りや、今までよりは一層苦しを受けるのは知れてゐる。その中で俺は活きてゐて何を為るのか。

人たるの道を尽す？　人たるの行を為る？　ああ、懲い、懲い！　人として をればこそそんな義務も有る、人でなくさへあれば、何も要らんのだ。自殺して命を捨てるのは、一の罪悪だと謂ふ。或は罪悪かも知れん。けれども、茫々然と呼吸してゐるばかりで、世間に対しては何等の益するところも無く、自身に取つてはそれが苦痛であるとしたら、自殺も一種の身始末だ。増して、俺が今死ねば、忽ち何十人の人が助り、何百人の人が懌ぶか知れん。

俺も一箇の女故に身を誤つたその余が、盗人家業の高利貸とまで堕落してこれでやみやみ死ん
で了ふのは、余り無念とは思ふけれど、当初に出損つたのが一生の不覚、あれが抑も不運の貫一
の誷は、もう一遍鍛直して出て来るより外為方が無い。この世の無念はその時霽す！」看々涙の頬の乾け

さしも遣る方無く悲めりし貫一は、その悲を立ちに抜くべき術を今覚れり。

る辺に、異く昻れる気有りて青く耀きぬ。

「宮、待つてゐろ、俺も死ぬぞ！　貴様の死んでくれたのが余り嬉いから、さあ、貫一の命も貴
様に遣る！　来世で二人が夫婦に成る、これが結納だと思つて、幾久く受けてくれ。貴様も定め
て本望だらう、俺も不足は少しも無いぞ」

さらば往きて汝の陥りし淵に沈まん。沈まば諸共と、彼は宮が屍を引起して背に負へば、その
軽きこと一片の紙に等し。怪しと見返れば、更に怪し！　芳芬鼻を撲ちて、一朶の白百合大さ人
面の若きが、満開の蓝を垂れて肩に懸れり。

不思議に愕くと為れば目覚めぬ。覚むれば暁の夢なり。

続続 金色夜叉

第 一 章

　貫一が胸は、益苦く成り愈りぬ。彼を念ひ、これを思ふに、生きて在るべき心地はせで、寧ろかの怪しき夢の如く成りなんを、快からずやと疑へるなり。

　彼は空しく万事を抛ちて、懊悩の間に三日ばかりを過しぬ。

　これを語らんに人無く、愬へんには友無く、しかも自ら拯ふべき道は有りや。有りとも覚えず、無しとは知れど、煩ふ者の煩ひ、悩む者の悩みて縦まなるを如何にせん。彼は実にこの昏迷乱擾せる一根の悪障を抉去りて、猛火に燬かんことを冀へり。その時彼は死ぬべきなり。生か、死か。

　貫一の苦悶は漸く急にして、終にこの問題の前に首を垂るるに至れり。

　値無き吾が生存は、又同く値無き死亡を以つて畢へしむべき者か。悔に堪へざる吾が生の値無かりしを結ばんには、これを償ふに足る可き死を以て為ざる可からざるか、或は、ここに過多き半生の最期を遂げて、新に他の値ある後半の復活を明日に計るべきか。

彼は強ちに死を避けず、又生を厭ふにもあらざれど、両ながらその値無きを、私に屑しと為ざるなり。　当面の苦は彼に死を勧め、半生の悔は恥を責めて仮令す。　苦を抜かんが為に、我は値無き死を辞せざるべきか、過を償はんが為に、我は楽まざる生を忍ぶべきか。　碌々の生は易し、死は即ち難し。　碌々の死は易し、生は則ち難し。　我は悔いて人と成るべきか、死してその愚を完うすべきか。

貫一は活を求めて得ず、死を覓めて得ず、居れば立つを念ひ、立てば臥すを想ひ、臥せば行くを懐ひ、寐ぬれば覚め、覚むれば思ひて、夜もあらず、日もあらず、人もあらず、世もあらで、唯憂ひ惑へる己一個の措所無く悩乱せり。

あだかもこの際抛ち去るべからざる一件の要事は起りぬ。　先に大口の言込有りし貸付の綬々急に取引迫りて、彼は些の猶予も無く、自ら野州塩原なる畑下と云へる温泉場に出向き、其処に清琴楼と呼べる湯宿に就きて、密に云々の探知すべき必要を生じたるなり。　行懸の是非無く、かつは難得き奇景の地と聞及べば、少時の憂を忘るる事も有らんと、自ら努めて結束し、かの日より約一週間の後、彼はほとほと進まぬ足を曳きて家を出でぬ。　その晨横雲白く明方の空に半輪の残月を懸けたり。　一番列車を取らんと上野に向ふ俥の上なる貫一は、この暁の眺矓に撲れて、覚えず悚然たる者ありき。

(一)の二

車は駛せ、景は移り、境は転じ、客は改まれど、貫一は易らざる他の憫鬱を抱きて、遣る方無き五時間の独に倦み憊れつつ、始て西那須野の駅に下車せり。

直ちに西北に向ひて、今尚茫々たる古の那須野原に入れば、天は潤く、地は遅に、唯平蕪の迷ひ、断雲の飛ぶのみにして、三里の坦途、一帯の重巒、塩原は其処ぞと見えて、行くほどに跡は窮らず、漸く千本松を過ぎ、進みて関谷村に到れば、人家の尽る処に潺々の響有りて、これに架れるを入勝橋と為す。

輙ち橋を渡りて僅に行けば、日光冥く、山厚く畳み、嵐気冷に壁深く陥りて、幾廻せる葛折の、後には密樹に声々の鳥呼び、前には幽草歩々の花を発き、いよいよ躋れば、遙に木隠の音のみ聞えし流の水上は浅く露れて、驚破や、ここに空山の雷白光を放ちて頽れ落ちたるか凄じかり。道の右は山を劃りて長壁と成し、嶺上の松の調も、石幽に群碧うして、幾条とも白糸を乱し懸けたる細瀑小瀑の珊々として瀁げるは、定てこの緒よりやと見捨て難し。

倐を駆りて白羽坂を踰えてより、回顧橋に三十尺の飛瀑を躋みて、山中の景は始て奇なり。これより行きて道有れば、水有り、水有れば、必ず橋有り、全渓にして三十橋、山有れば巌有り、巌有れば必ず瀑有り、全嶺にして七十瀑。地有れば泉有り、泉有れば必ず熱有り、全村にして四十五湯。猶数ふれば十二勝、十六名所、七不思議、誰か一々探り得べき。

抑も塩原の地形たる、塩谷郡の南より群峰の間を分けて深く西北に入り、綿々として箒川の流

に沿る片岨の、四里に岐れ、十一里に亘りて、到る処巉巌の水を夾まざる無きは、宛然青銅の薬

研に瑠璃末を砕くに似たり。　先づ大網の湯を過れば、根本山、魚止滝、児ヶ淵、左靫の険は

古りて、白雲洞は朗に、布滝、竜ヶ鼻、材木石、五色石、船岩なんどと眺行けば、鳥井戸、前山

の翠衣に染みて、福渡の里に入るなり。

途すがら前面の崖の処々に躑躅の残り、山藤の懸れるが、甚だ興有りと目留まれば、又この辺

殊に谿浅く、水澄みて、大いなる古鏡の沈める如く、深く蔽へる岸樹は陰々として眠るに似たり。

貫一は覚えず踏止りぬ。

かの逆巻く波に分け入りし宮が、息絶えて浮び出でたりし其処の景色に、似たりとも酷だ似た

る岸の布置、茂の状況、乃至は漾ふる水の文も、透徹る底の岩面も、広さの程も、位置も、趣も、

子細に看来ればいよいよ差はず。

彼は此を決きて寒慄せり。

怪むべき哉、曾て経たりし塲をそのままに夢むる例は有れ、所拠も無く夢みし跡を、歴々とか

く目前に見ると云ふも有る事か。宮の骸の横はりし処も、又は己の追来し筋も、彼処よ、此処よ

と、陰に一々指しては、限無く駭けるなり。

車夫を顧みて、処の名を問へば、不動沢と言ふ。

物可恐しげなる沢の名なるよ。　げに思へば、人も死ぬべき処の名なり。　我も既に死なんとせし

がと、さすが現の身にも沁む時、宮にはあらで山百合の花なりし怪異を又懐ひて、彼は肩頭寒く顔ひぬ。

卒に踵を回して急げば、行路の雲間に塞り、咄々、何等の物か、と先驚かさるる異形の屏風巌、地を抜く何百丈と見挙る絶頂には、はらはら松も危く立竦み、幹竹割に割放したる断面は、半空より一文字に垂下して、炭々たるその勢、幾ど眺むる眼も留らず。

貫一は憫然として佇めり。

彼が宮を追ひて転び落ちたりし谷間の深さは、正にこの天辺の高きより投じたらんやうに、冉として虚空を舞下る危惧の堪難かりしを想へるなり。

我未だ嘗て見ざりつる絶壁！危しとも、可恐しとも、夢ならずして争か飛下り得べき。又この人並ならぬ雲雀骨の粉微塵に散つて失せざりしこそ、洵に夢なりけれと、身柱冷かに瞳を凝す彼の傍より、これこそ名にし負ふ天狗巌、と為たり貌にも車夫は案内す。

貫一はかの夢の奇なりしより、更に更に奇なるこの塩原の実覚をば疑ひ懼れつつ立尽せり。

既に如此くなれば、怪は愈々怪に、或は夢中に見たりし跡の猶着々 活現し来りて、飽くまで我を脅かさざれば休まざらんと為るにあらずや、と彼は胸安からずも足に信せて、かの巌の頭上に聳ゆる辺に到れば、谿急に激折して、水これが為に鼓怒し、咆哮し、噴薄激盪して、奔馬の乱れ競ふが如し。この乱流の間に横はりて高さ二丈に余り、その頂は平に潤りて、寛に百人を立たしむべき大磐石、風雨に歳経る膚は死灰の色を成して、鱗も添はず、毛も生ひざれど、状可恐し

げに蹲りて、老木の蔭を負ひ、急湍の浪に漬りて、夜な夜な天狗巖の魔風に誘はれて吼えもしぬべき怪しの物なり。

その古、蒲生飛驒守氏郷この處に野立せし事有るに因りて、野立石とは申す、と例のが説出すを、貫一は頷きつつ、目を放たず打眺めつ、独り窃に舌を巻くのみ。

彼は実に窟間の宮を尋ぬる時、この大石を眼下に窺ひ見たりしを忘れざるなり。

又は流るる宮を追ひて、道無きに困める折、左右には水深く、崖高く、前には攀づべからざる石の塞りたるを、攀ぢて半に到りて進退谷りつつ、その石もこれなりけん、と肩は自と聳えて、久しく留るに堪へず。

数歩を行けば、宮が命を沈めしその淵と見るべき處も、彼が釈けたる帯を曳きしその巌も、歴然として皆在らざるは無し！　貫一が髪毛は針の如く竪ちて戦げり。　彼の思は前夜の悪夢を反復すに等しき苦悩を辞する能はざればなり。

夢ながら可恐くも、浅ましくも、悲しくも、可傷くも、分く方無くて唯一図に切なかりしを、事もし一塲の夢にして止らざらんには、抑も如何！　今や塩原の実景は一々夢中の見るところ、然らばこの景既に夢ならず！　思掛けずもここに来にける吾身もまた夢ならず！　但夢に欠く者とては宮一箇のみ。　縦に彼のここに来らざるのみ!!

貫一はかく思到りて、我又夢に入りとも為つ。夢ならずと為ば、我は由無き処に来にけるよ。幸に夢に似る事無くてあれかし。　異しとも甚だ異し！　疾く往きて、

疾く還らんと、遽に率し伸び車に乗りて、白倉山の麓、塩釜の湯、高尾塚、離室、甘湯沢、兄弟滝、玉簾瀬、小太郎淵、路の頭に高きは寺山、低きに人家の在る処、即ち畑下戸。

第二章

一村十二戸、温泉は五箇所に涌きて、五軒の宿あり。ここに清琴楼と呼べるは、南に方りて箒川の綏く廻れる磧に臨み、俯しては、水石の粼々たるを弄び、仰げば西に、富士、喜十六の翠巒と対して、清風座に満ち、袖の沢を落来る流は、二十丈の絶壁に懸りて、素練を垂れたる如き吉井滝あり。

東北は山又山を重ねて、琅玕の玉簾深く夏日の凛るべきを遮りたれば、四面遊目に足りて丘壑の富を擅にし、林泉の奢を窮め、又有るまじき清福自在の為に幾度か魂飛び肉銷して、理むる方無く搔乱されし胸の内は靄然として頓に和ぎ、恍然として総て忘れたり。

貫一はこの絵を看る如き清穏の風景に値ひて、かの途上険き巌と峻き流との為の別境なり。

彼は以為らく。

誠に好くこそ我は来つれ！　なんぞ来るの甚だ遅かりし。山の麗しと謂ふも、壌の堆き者のみ、川の暢しと謂ふも、水の逝くに過ぎざるを、牢として抜く可からざる我が半生の痼疾は、争で壌と水との医すべき者ならん、と歯牙にも掛けず侮りたりし己こそ、先づ侮らるべき愚の者ならずや。

看よ、看よ、木々の緑も、浮べる雲も、秀る峰も、流るる渓も、峙つ巌も、吹来る風も、日の

光も、鶏の鳴く音も、空の色も、皆自ら浮世の物ならで、我はここに憂を忘れ、悲を忘れ、苦を忘れ、労を忘れて、身はかの雲と軽く、心は水と淡く、希はくは今より如此くして我生を了らん哉。

恋も有らず、怨も有らず、金銭も有らず、権勢も有らず、名誉も有らず、野心も有らず、栄達も有らず、堕落も有らず、競争も有らず、執着も有らず、得意も有らず、失望も有らず、止だ天然の無垢にして、形骸を安くのみなるこの里、我思を埋むるの里か、吾骨を埋るの里か。

性来多く山水の美に親まざりし貫一は、殊に心の往くところを知らざるばかりに愛で悦びて、始より滝に向へる欄干に倚りて、偶ま人中を迷ひたりし子の母の親にも逢ひけんやうに、少時はその傍を離れ得ざるなりき。

楼前の緑は漸く暗く、遠近の水音泫えて、はや夕暮るる山風の身に沁めば、先づ湯浴などせばやと、何気無く座敷に入りたる彼の眼を、又一個驚かす物こそあれ。

鞄を置きたる床間に、山百合の花のいと大きなるを唯一輪棒挿に活けたるが、茎形に曲り傾きて、あたかも此方に向へるなり。

貫一は覚えず足を踏止めて、その瞠れる眼を花に注ぎつ。宮ははやここに居たりとやうに、彼は卒爾の感に衝れたるなり。

既に幾処の実景の夢と符合するさへ有るに、またその殊に夢の夢なる一本百合のここに在る事、畢竟偶合に過ぎずとは謂へ、さりとては余りにかの夢とこの旅との照応急に、因縁深きに似

て、などかくは我を驚かすの太甚き！

奇を弄して益出づる不思議に、彼は益懼を作して、或はこの裏に天意の測り難き者有るなからんや、とさすがに惑ひ苦めり。

やがて傍近く寄りて、幾許似たると眺むれば、打抜ける蕾は凛として玉を割いたる如く、濃香芬々と迸り、葉色に露気有りて緑鮮に、定て今朝や剪りけんと覚き花の勢なり。

少く楽まされし貫一も、これが為に興冷めて、俄に重き頭を花の前に支へつつ、又かの愁を徐に喚起さんと為つ。

「お風呂へ御案内申しませう」

その声に彼は姉を見返りて、

「ああ、姐さん、この花を那裏へ持つて行つておくれでないか」

「はあ、その花で御座いますか。旦那様は百合の花はお嫌ひで？」

「いや、匂が強くて、頭痛がして成らんから」

「さやうで御座いますか。唯今直に片付けますです。これは唯一つ早咲で、珍う御座いましたも

んですから、先程折つてまゐつて、徒に挿して置いたんで御座います」

「うう、成程、早咲だね」

「さやうで御座います。来月あたりに成りませんと、余り咲きませんので、これが唯一つ有りま

したんで、紛れ咲なので御座いますね」

「うう紛れ咲、さうだね」

「御案内致しませう」

　風呂場に入れば、一箇の客先在りて、未だ燈点さぬ微黯の湯槽に漬りけるが、何様人の来るに驚けると覚く、甚だ忙しげに身を起しつ。貫一が入れば、直に上ると斉く洗場の片隅に寄りて、色白き背を此方に向けたり。

　年紀は二十七八なるべきか。やや孱弱なる短軀の男なり。頰に左頬右胆すれども、明々地ならぬ面貌は定かに認め難かり。されども、自ら見識越ならぬは明なるに、何が故に人目を避るが如き態を作するすらん。華車なる形成は、ここ等辺の人にあらず、何人にして、何が故になど、貫一は徒に心牽れてゐたり。

　やがて彼が出づれば、待ちけるやうに男は入替りて、なほ飽くまで此方を向かざらんと為つつ、蕭索に浴を行ふ音を立つるのみ。

　その膚の色の男に似気無く白きも、その骨軀に肉の痩せたるも、又はその擧動の打湿りたるも、その人を懼るる気色なるも、総じて自ら尋常ならざるは、察するに精神病者の類なるべし。さては何の怪むところ有らん。節は初夏の未だ寒き、この寥々たる山中に来り宿れる客なれば、保養鬱散の為ならずして、彼は病客なるべきと心釈けては、湯治の目的なるを思ふべし。誠にさなり、彼は病客なるべきと心釈けては、はや目も遣らずなりける間に、男は浴み果てて、貸浴衣引給ひつつ出で行きけり。

　暮色はいよいよ濃に、転激き川音の寒さを添ふれど、手寡なればや燈も持来らず、湯香高く蒸

膿る煙の中に、独り影暗く蹲るも、少く凄き心地して、程無く貫一も出でて座敷に返れば、床の間には百合の花も在らず煌々たる燈火の下に座を設け、膳を据ゑて傍に手焙を置き、茶器食籠など取揃へて、この一目さすがに旅の労を忘るべし。

先づ衣桁に在りける褞袍を被ぎ、夕冷の火も恋く引寄せて蒀を吃しのれば、天地静に石走る水の響、楢を渡る風の声、颯々凉々と鳴りて、幽なること太古の如し。

乍ちはたはたと跫音長く廊下に曳いて、先のにはあらぬ小婢の夕餉を運び来れるに引添ひて、其処に出でたる宿の主は、

「今日は好うこそ御越し下さいまして、さぞ御労様でむらつしやいませうで御座います。ええ、又唯今程は格別に御茶料を下し置れまして、甚だ恐入りました儀で、難有う存じまして、厚く御礼を申上げまするで御座います。

ええ前以てお詫を申上げまするのは、召上り物のところで御座りまして一向はや御覧の通何も御座りませんで、誠に相済みませんで御座いますが、実は、未だ些と時候もお早いので、自然お客様のお越も御座りませんゆゑ、何分用意等も致し置きませんやうな次第で、然し、一両日中にはお麁末ながら何ぞ差上げまするやうに取計ひまするで御座います。どうぞ、まあ今明日のところは御勘弁を下さいまして、御覧と御逗留下さいますやうに。――これ、早う御味噌汁をお易へ申して来ないか」

主の辞し去りて後、貫一は彼の所謂何も無、椀も皿も皆黄なる鶏子一色の膳に向へり。

「内にはお客は今幾箇有るのだね」

「這箇の外にお一方で御座りやす」

「一箇？　あのお客は単身なのか」

「先に湯殿で些と遇つたが、男の客だよ」

「さよで御座りやす」

「はい」

「あれは病人だね」

「どうで御座りやすか。——そんな事無えで御座りやせう」

「さうかい。何処も不良いところは無いやうかね」

「無えやうで御座りやすな」

「どうも病人のやうだが、さうでないかな」

「ああ、旦那様はお医者様で御座りやすか」

貫一は覚えず噴飯せんと為つつ、

「成程、好い事を言ふな。俺は医者ぢやないけれど、どうも見たところが病人のやうだから、さうぢやないかと思つたのだ。もう長く来てゐるお客か」

「いんえ、昨日お出になりやしたので」

「昨日来たのだ？　東京の人か」

「はい、日本橋の方のお方で御座りやす」

「それぢや商人か」

「私能く知りやせん」

「どうだ、お前達と懇意にして話をするか」

「そりやなさりやす」

「俺と那箇が為る」

「旦那様とですけ？　そりや旦那様のやうにはなさりやせん」

「うむ、さうすると、俺の方がお饒舌なのだな」

「あれ、さよぢや御座りやせんけれど、那裏のお客様は黙つてゐらつしやる方が多う御座りやす。さうして何でもお連様が直にいらしやる筈で、それを、まあ酷う待つてお在なさりやす」

「おお、伴が後から来るのか。いや、大きに御馳走だつた」

「何も御座りやせんで、お粗末様で御座りやす」

婢は膳を引きて起ちぬ。貫一は顧然と臥たり。

二十間も座敷の数有る大構の内に、唯二人の客を宿せるだに、寂寥は既に余んぬるを、この深山幽谷の暗夜に蔽れたる孤村の片辺に倚れる清琴楼の間毎に亘る長廊下は、星の下行く町の小路より、幾許心細くも可恐き夜道ならんよ。戸一重外には、山嵐の絶えずおどろおどろと吹廻りて、早瀬の波の高鳴るは、真に放鬼の名をも懐ふばかり。

折しも唾壺打つ音は、二間ばかりを隔てて甚だ蕭索に聞えぬ。貫一は何の故とも知らで、その念頭を得放れざるかの客の身の上をば、独り様々に案じ入りつつ、彼既に病客ならず、又我が識る人ならずと為ば、何を以つて人を懼るるや。抑も彼は何者なりや。又何の尤むるところ有りて、さばかり人を懼るるや。

貫一はこの秘密の鑰を獲んとして、左往右返に暗中摸索の思を費すなりき。

(二) の 二

明る朝の食後、貫一は先づこの狭き畑下戸の隅々まで一遍見周りて、略ぼその状況を知るとともに、清琴楼の家格を考へなどして、礒に出づれば、浅瀬に架れる板橋の風情面白く、渡れば喜十六の山麓にて、十町ばかり登りて須巻の滝の湯有りと教へらるるままに、遂に其処まで往きて、午近き頃宿に帰りぬ。

汗を流さんと風呂場に急ぐ廊下の交互に、貫一はあたかもかの客の湯上りに出会へり。こたび彼は面を見せじとやうに、慌忙く打背きて過行くなり。則ち人を懼るるなり。故は、自ら尤るなり。彼は果して何者ならん、と貫一は愈よ深く怪みぬ。

今は疑ふべくもあらず、彼は正く人目を避けんと為るなり。昨日こそ誰乎彼の黯黮にて、分明に面貌を弁ぜざりしが、今の一目は、躬も奇なりと思ふばかり奇くも、彼の不用意の間に速写機の如き力を以てして、その映じ来りし形を総て脱さず捉へ得り寄くも、

たりしなり。

貫一はその相貌の瞥見に縁りて、直ちに彼の性質を占はんと試るまでに、いと善く見極めたり。されども、いかにせん、彼の相するところは始に疑ひしところと頗る一致せざる者有り。若し実に人を懼るると為らば、彼の人を懼るる所以と、我より彼の人を懼るる所以とは、或は稍趣を異にせざらんや。又想ふに、彼は決して自ら尤るところなど有るに非ずして、止だその性の多羞なるが故のみか、未だ知るべからず。この二者の前のをも取り難く、さすがに後のにも領きかねて、彼は又新に打惑へり。

午飯の給仕には年嵩の姆出でたれば、余所ながらかの客の事を問ひけるに、箸をも取らで今外に出で行きしと云ふ。

「はあ、飯も食はんで？　何処へ行つたのかね」

「何でも昨日あたりお連様がお出の筈になつてをりましたので御座いませう。それを大相お待ちなすつてゐらつしやいましたところが、到頭お着が無いもんで御座いますから、今朝から御心配遊して、停車場まで様子を見がてら電報を掛けに行くと有仰いまして、それでお出ましに成つたので御座います」

「うむ、それは心配だらう。能く有る事だ。然し、飯も食はずに気を揉んでゐるとは、どう云ふ伴なのかな。――年寄か、婦ででもあるか」

「如何で御座いますか」

「お前知らんのか」

「私存じません」

彼は覚えず小首を傾くれば、

「旦那も大相御心配ぢや御座いませんか」

「さう云ふ事を聞くと、俺も気になるのだ」

「ぢや旦那も余程苦労性の方ですね」

「大きにさうだ」

「それぢやお連様がいらしつて見て、お年寄か、お友達なら宜う御座いますけれど、もしも、ね
え、貴方、お美い方か何かだつた日には、それこそ旦那は大変で御座いますね」

「どう大変なのか」

「又御心配ぢや御座いませんか」

「うむ、大きにこれはさうだ」

風恬に草香りて、唯居るは惜き日和に奇痒く、貫一は又出でて、塩釜の西南十町ばかりの山中
なる塩の湯と云ふに遊びぬ。還れば寂く夕暮るる頃なり。例の如く湯に入りて、上れば直に膳を
持出で、燈も漸く耀きしに、かの客、未だ帰り来ず、

「閑寂なのも可いけれど、外に客と云ふ者が無くて、全でかう独法師も随分心細いね」

託言がましく貫一は言出づれば、

「さやうでゐらつしやいませう、何と申したつてこの山奥で御座いますから。全体旦那がお一人でゐらつしやると云ふお心懸が悪いので御座いますもの、それは為方が御座いません」

婢はわざとらしう高笑しつ。

「成程、これは恐入つた。今度から善く心得て置く事だ」

「今度なんて仰有らずに、旦那も明日あたり電信でお呼寄になつたら如何で御座います」

「五十四になる老婢を呼んだつて、お前、始らんぢやないか」

「まあ、旦那はあんな好い事を言つてゐらつしやる。その老婢さんの方でないのをお呼びなさいましよ」

「気の毒だが、内にはそれつきりより居ないのだ」

「ですから、旦那、づつと外にお在んなさるので御座いませう」

「そりや外には幾多でも在るとも」

「あら、御馳走で御座いますね」

「なあに、能く聴いて見ると、それが皆人の物ださうだ」

「何ですよ、旦那。貴方、本当の事を有仰るもんですよ」

「本当にも嘘にもその通だ。私なんぞはそんな意気な者が有れば、何為にこんな青臭い山の中へ遊びに来るものか」

「おや！　どうせ青臭い山の中で御座います」

「青臭いどころか、お前、天狗巌だ、七不思議だと云ふ者が有る、可恐い山の中に違無いぢやないか。そこへ彷徨、閑さうな貌をして唯一箇で遣つて来るなんぞは、能々の間抜と思はなけりやならんよ」

「それぢや旦那は間抜なのぢや御座いませんか。そんな解らない事が有るものですか」

「間抜にも大間抜よ。宿帳を御覧、東京間抜一人と附けて在る」

「その傍に小く、下女塩原間抜一人と、ぢや附けさせて戴きませう」

「面白い事を言ふなあ、おまへは」

「やっぱり少し抜けてゐる所為で御座います」

彼は食事を了りて湯浴し、少焉ありて九時を聞きけれど、かの客は未だ帰らず。寝床に入りて、程無く十時の鳴りけるにも、水声空く楼を繞りて、松の嵐の枕上に落つる有るのみなり。

始よりその人を怪まざらんにはこの答むるに足らぬ瑣細の事も、大いなる模糊の影を作りて、いよいよ彼が疑の眼を遡り来らんとするなりけり。貫一はほとほと疑ひ得らるる限疑ひて、躬も其の妄に過るの太甚きまでに至りて、始て罷めんと為たり。

これに亜いで、彼は抑も何の故有りて、肥瘠も関せざるかの客に対して、かくばかり軽々しく思を費し、又念を懸るの固執なるや、その訓無き己をば、敢て自ら解かんと試みつ。貫一は抑へて怪まざらんと為ば、理されども、人は往々にして自ら率いるその己を識る能はず。又幻視せるが如きその大いなる影の冥想の間に纏に於て怪まずしてあるべきを信ずるものから、

綿して、或は理外に在る者有る無からんや、と疑はざらんと為る傍より却りて惑しむるなり。表階子の口に懸れる大時計は、病み憊れたるやうの鈍き響を作して、廊下の闇に彷徨ふを、数ふれば正に十一時なり。

かの客はこの深更に及べども未だ帰り来ず。

彼は帰り来らざるなるか、帰り得ざるなるか。今や十二時にも成りなんにと心に懸けながら、その音は聞くに及ばずして遂に眠を催せり。日高き朝景色の前に起出づれば、座敷の外を小婢は雑巾掛してゐたり。

「お早う御座りやす」

「睡さうな顔をしてゐるな」

「はい、昨夜那裏のお客様がお帰になるかと思つて、遅うまで待つてをりやしたで、今朝睡うござりやす」

「ああ、あのお客は昨夜は帰らずか」

「はい、お帰が御座りやせん」

貫一はかの客の間の障子を開放したるを見て、咥楊枝のまま欄杆伝ひに外を眺め行く態して、その前を過れば、床の間に小豆革の手鞄と、浅黄キャリコの風呂敷包とを並べて、傍に二三枚の新聞紙を引捏ね、衣桁に絹物の袷を懸けて、その裾に紺の靴下を畳置きたり。

さては少く本意無きまでに、座敷の内には見出すべき異状も有らで、彼は宿帳に拠りて、洋服

仕立商なるを知くところ有りとも覚えざるなりき。

拍子抜して返れる貫一は、心私にその臆測の鑿なりしを娯ぢざるにもあらざれど、又これが為に、直ちにその濡衣を剝去るまでに釈然たる能はずして、好し、この上はその待人の如何なる者なるかを見て、疑は決すべしと、やがてその消息を齎し来るべき彼の帰来の程を、陰ながら最更に遅しと待てり。

夜は山精木魅の出でて遊ぶを想はしむる、陰森凄幽の気を凝すに反してこの霽朗なる昼間の山容水態は、明媚争か画も如かん、天色大気も殆ど塵境以外の感無くんばあらず。黄金を織作せる羅にも似たる麗き日影を蒙りて、万斛の珠を鳴す谷間の清韻を楽みつつ、欄頭の山を枕に恍惚として消ゆらんやうに覚えたりし貫一は、急遽き跫音の廊下を動じ来るに駭されて、起回りさまに頭を捻向れば、何事とも知らず、年嵩の婢の駈着るなり。

「些と旦那、参りましたよ」

「何が来たのだ」

「何でも可いんですから、早くいらつしやいましよ」

「何だ、何だよ」

「早く階子の所へいらしつて御覧なさい」

「おゝ、あの客が還つたのか」

彼ははや飛ぶが如くに引返して、貫一の言は五間も後に残されたり。彼が注進の模様は、見る

べき待人を伴ひ帰れるならんをと、直ぐに起ちて表階子の辺に行く時、既に晩し両箇の人影は欄の上に顕れたり。

鍔広なる藍鼠の中折帽を前斜に冠れる男は、例の面を見せざらんと為れど、かの客なり。引連れたる女は、二十歳を二つ三つも越したる可し。堆朱彫の玉根掛をして、髷の一髪をも乱さず、極めて快く結ひ做したり。葡萄茶の細格子の縞御召に勝色裏の袷を着て、羽織は小紋縮緬の一紋、阿蘭陀模様の七糸の袱紗帯に金鎖子の繊きを引入れて、嬌き友禅染の襦袢の袖して口元を拭ひつつ、四季袋を紐短かに挈げたるが、弗と此方を見向ける素顔の色蒼く、口の紅も点さで、やや裏寂くも花の咲過ぎたらんやうの蕭寞を帯びたれど、美目の盻たる色香尚濃にして、漫ろ人に染むばかりなり。

両箇は彼の見る目の顕露なるに打惑ひて、なかなか精く看るべき違あらざりけれど、その女は万々彼の妻なんどにはあらじ、と独り合点せり。

銀杏返を引約めて、本甲蒔絵の挿櫛根深に、大粒の淡色瑪瑙に金脚の後簪、

第三章

かの男女は娚しさに堪へざらんやうに居寄りて、手に手を交へつつ密々に語れり。

「さうなの、だから私はどんなに心配したか知れやしない。なかなか貴方がここで想つてゐるや

うな訳には為されませんとも。そりや貴方の心配もさうでせうけれど、私の心配と云つたら、本
当に無かつたの。察しるが可いつて、そりや貴方、お互ちやありませんか。吁、私は今だに胸が
悸々して、後から追掛けられるやうな気持がして、何だか落着かなくて可けない」

「まあ何でも、かうして約束通り逢へりや上首尾なんだ」

「全くよ。一昨日の晩あたりの私の心配と云つたら、こりやどうだかと、さう思つたくらゐ、今
考へて見れば、自分ながら好く出られたの。やつぱり尽きない縁なのだわ」

些
と男の顔を聳りて、濡るる瞼を軽く拭へり。

「その縁の尽きないのが、究竟彼我の身の窮迫なのだ。俺もかう云ふ事に成らうとは思はなかつ
たが、成程、悪縁と云ふ者は為方の無いものだ」

女は尚窃に泣きゐる面を背けたるまま、

「貴方は直に悪縁だ、悪縁だと言ふけれど、悪縁ならどうするんです!」

「悪縁だからかうなつたのぢやないか」

「かう成つたのがどうしたんですよ!」

「今更どうするものか」

「当然さ!　貴方は一体水臭いんだ!!」

「おい、お静、水臭いとは誰の事だ」

色を作せる男の眼は、つと湧く涙に輝けり。

「貴方の事さ！」

女の目よりは潸々と零れぬ。

「俺の事だ?!　お静……手前はそんな事を言つて、それで済むと思ふのか」

「済んでも済まなくても、貴方が水臭いからさ」

「未だそんな事を言やがる！　さあ、何が水臭いか、それを言へ」

「はあ、言ひますとも。ねえ、貴方は他の顔さへ見りや、直に悪縁だと云ふのが癖ですよ。彼我の中の悪縁は、貴方がそんなに言なくたつて善く知つてゐるんちやありませんか。それを貴方がさもさも迷惑さうに、何その端には悪縁だとお言ひなさるけれど、聞される身に成つて御覧なさいな。余り好い心持は為やしません。それも不断ならともかくもですさ、この場になつてまでも、さう云ふ事を言ふのは、貴方の心が水臭いからだ──何がさうでない事が有るもんですか」

「悪縁だから悪縁だと言ふのちやないか。何も迷惑して……」

「悪縁でも可ござんすよ！」

彼等は相背きて姑く語無かりしが、女は忍びやかに泣きぬたり。

「おい、お静、おい」

「貴方きつと迷惑なんでせう。貴方がそんな気ちや、私は……実に……つまらない。私はどうせう。情無い！」

お静は竟に顔を掩うて泣きぬ。

「何だな、お前も考へて見るが可いぢやないか。それを迷惑とも何とも思はないからこそ、世間を狭くするやうな間にも成りさ、又かう云ふ……なあ……訳なのぢやないか。それを嘘にも水臭いなんて言れりや、俺だつて悔いだらうぢやないか。余り悔くて俺は涙が出た。お静、俺は何も芸人ぢやなし、お前に勤めてゐるんぢやないのだから、さう思つてゐてくれ」

「狭山さん、貴方もそんなに言はなくたつて可いぢやありませんか」

「お前が言出すからよ」

「だつて貴方がかう云ふ場になつて迷惑さうな事を言ふから、私は情無くなつて、どうしたら可からうと思つたんでさね。ぢや私が悪かつたんだから謝ります。ねえ、狭山さん、些と」

お静の顔を打囁りつつ、男は茫然たるのみなり。

「狭山さんてば、貴方何を考へてゐるのね」

「知れた事さ、彼我の身の上をよ」

「何だつてそんな事を考へてゐるの」

「………」

「今更何も考へる事は有りはしないわ」

狭山は徐々に目を転じて、太息を嘘いたり。

「もうそんな溜息なんぞを嘘くのはお舎しなさいつてば」

「お前二十……二だつたね」

「それがどうしたの、貴方が二十八さ」

「あの時はお前が十九の夏だつけかな」

「ああ、さう、何でも袷を着てゐたから、丁度今時分でした。湖月さんのあの池に好いお月が映してゐて、暖い晩で、貴方と一処に涼みに出たんですよ、善く覚えてゐる。あれが十九、二十、二十一、二十二と、全三年に成るのね」

「おお、さうさう。昨日のやうに思つてゐたが、もう三年に成るなあ」

「何だか、かう全で夢のやうね」

「吁、夢だなあ！」

「夢ねえ！」

「お静！」

「狭山さん！」

両箇は手を把り、膝を重ねて、同じ思を猶悲く、

「ゆ……ゆ……夢だ！」

「夢だわ、ねえ！」

声立てじと男の胸に泣附く女。

「かう成るのも皆約束事ぢやあらうけれど、那奴さへ居なかつたら、貴方だつて余計な苦労は為

はしまいし。私は私で、ああもかうも思つて、末始終の事も大概考へて置いたのだから、もう少しの間時節が来るのを待つてゐられりや、曩日の御神籤通な事に成れるのは、もう目に見えてゐるのを、那奴が邪魔して、横紙を裂くやうな事を為やがるばかりに大事に為なけりや成らない貴方の体に、取つて返しの付かない傷まで附けさせて、私は、狭山さん、余り申訳が無い！ 墻……

「忍……して下さい」

「そりやなあに、お互の事だ」

「いいえ、私がもう少し意気地が有つたら、かうでもないんだらうけれど、胸には色々在つても、それが思切つて出来ない性分だもんだから、ついこんな破滅に成つて了つて、私は実に済まないと、自分の身を考へるよりは、貴方の事が先に立つて、さぞ陰ぢや迷惑もしてお在なんだらうに、逢ふ度に私の身を案じて、毎も優くして下さるのは仇や疎な事ぢやないと、私は嬉いより難有いと思つてゐます。だものだから、近頃ぢや、貴方に逢ふと直に涙が出て、何だか悲くばかりなるのが不思議だと思つてるたら、果然かう事になる識だつたんでせう。

貴方にはお気の毒だ、お気の毒だ、と始終自分が退けてゐるのに、悪縁だなんぞと言れると、私は体が縮るやうな心持がして、ああ、さうでもない、貴方が迷惑してゐるばかりなら未だ可いけれど、取んだ者に懸り合つた、ともしや後悔してお在なんちやなからうかと思ふと、私だつて好い気持はしないもんだから、つい向者はあんなに言過ぎて、私は誠に済みませんでした。それはもう貴方の言ふ通り悪縁には差無いんだけれど、後生だからそんな可厭な事は考へずにゐて下

さい。私はこれで本望だと思つてゐる」

「生木を割いて別れるよりは、まあ愈だ」

「別れる？　吁！　可厭だ！　考へても慄然とする！　切れるの、別れるのなんて事は、那奴が来ない前には夢にだつて見やしなかつたのを、切れろ切れろぢや私もどの位内で責められたか知れやしない。さうして挙句がこんな事に成つたのも、想へば皆那奴のお蔭だ。ええ、悔い！　私はきつと執着いても、この怨は返して遣るから、覚えてゐるが可い！」

女は身を顫せて罵るとともに、念入りて呪ぶが如き血相を作せり。

不知、この恨み、罵り、呪はるる者は、何処の誰ならんよ。

「那奴も好加減な馬鹿ぢやないか！」

男は歯咬しつつ苦しげに嘲笑せり。

「馬鹿も大馬鹿よ！　方図の知れない馬鹿だわ。畜生！　所歓の有る女が金で靡くか、靡かない
か、些は考へながら遊ぶが可い。来りや不好な顔を為て遣るのに、それさへ解らずに、もう慾く
附けつ廻しつして、了局には人の恋中の邪魔を為やがるとは、那奴も能く能くの芸無猿に出来
ゐるんだ。憎さも憎し、私はもう悔くて、悔くて、狭山さん、実はね、私はこの世の置土産に、
那奴の額を打割つて来たんでさね」

「ええ、どうして！」

「なあにね、貴方に別れたあの翌日から、延続に来てゐやがつて、ちつとでも傍を離さないんぢ

やありませんか。這箇は気が気ぢやないところへ、もう悪漆膠くて耐らないから、病気だと謂つて内へ遁げて来りや、直に追懸けて来て、附綿つてゐるんでせう。さうすると寸法は知れてまさね、丁と渉が付いてゐるんだから、阿母さんは傍から『ちやほや』して、そりや貴方、真面目ぢや見ちやゐられないお手厚さ加減なんだから、那奴は図に乗つて了つて、やあ、風呂を沸せだ事の、ビイルを冷せだ事のと、あの狭い内へ一個で幅を為やがつて、なかなか動きさうにも為ないんぢやありませんか。

私は全で生捕に成つたやうなもので、出るには出られず、這箇の事が有るから、さうしてゐる空は無し、あんな気の揉めた事は有りはしない──本当にどうせうかと思つた。ええ、なあに、あんな奴は打抛出して措いて、這箇は掻巻を引被つて一心に考へてゐたんですけれど、もう慣れたくて耐らなくなつて来たから、不如かまはず飛出して了はうかと、余程さう念つたものの、丹子の事も、ねえ、考へて見りや可哀さうだし、あの子を始め阿母さんまで、私ばかりを頼りに為てゐるものを、さぞや私の亡い後には、どんなにか力も落さうし、又あの子も為ないでも好い苦労を為なけりやなるまいと、そればかりに牽されて、色々話も有るものだから、あの子の阿母さんにも逢つて遣りたし、それに、私も出るに就いちや、為て置かなけりやならない事も有るし為るので、到頭遅々して出損つて了つたんです。

さうすると、どうでせう、まあ、那奴はその晩二時過までうで付いてゐて、それでも不承々々に遣つたのは可い。すると翌日は半日阿母さんのお談義が始まつて、好加減に了簡を極めろでせ

う。さう言つちや済まないけれど、育てた恩も聞飽きてゐるわ。それを追繰返し、引繰返し、悪体交りには、散々聴せて、了局は口返答したと云つて足蹴にする。なあに、私は足蹴にされたつて、撲れたつて、それを悔いとは思やしないけれど、這箇だつて貴方と云ふ者が有ると思ふから、もう一生懸命に稼いで、為るだけの事は丁と為てあるのに、何ほ慾にきりが無いと謂つても、自分の言条ばかり通さうとして、他には些でも楽を為せない算段を為る。私だつて金属で出来た機械ちやなし、さうさう駆使はれてお為にばかり成つてゐられ嫌や、這箇の身が立ちはしない。

別にどうしてくれなくても、訳さへ解つてゐてくれりや、辛いぐらゐは私は辛抱する。所歓は堰いて了ふし、旦那取は為ろと云ふ。そんな不可な真似を為なくても、立派に行くやうに私が稼いであるんぢやありませんか。それをさう云ふ無理を言つてからに、素直でないの、馬鹿だのと、足蹴に為るとは……何……何事で……せう！

それぢや私も赫として、もう我慢が為切れなく成つたから、物も言はずに飛出さうと為る途端に、運悪く又那奴が遣つて来たんぢやありませんか。さあ、捉つて了つて、其処の場図で迯るには迯られず、阿母さんは得たり賢しなんでせう、一処に行け行けと啀く言ふし、那奴は何でも来いと云つて放さない。私も内を出た方が都合が好いと思つたから、まあ言ふなりに成つて、例の処へ拐られて行つたとお思ひなさい。あの長尻だから、さあ又遂らない、さうして何か所思でも有つたんでせうよ、何だか知らないけれど、その晩に限つて無闇とお酒を強るんでさ。這箇も鬱勃肚で、飲めも為ないのに幾多でも引受けたんだけれど、酔ひさうにも為やしない。

その内に漸々又お極りの気障な話を始めやがつて、這箇が柳に受けて聞いてゐて遣りや、可いかと思つて増長して、呆れた真似を為やがるから、性の付く程罵々さう言つて遣つたら、さあ自棄に成つて、それから毒吐き出して、やあ店番の埃被だの、冷飯吃ひの雇人がどうだのと、聞いちやゐられないやうな腹の立つ事を言やがるから、這箇も思切つて随分た悪体を吐いて遣つたわ、私は。

さうすると、了局に那奴は何と言ふかと思ふと、幾許七顛八倒しても金で縛つて置いた体だなんぞ、と利いた風な事を言ふんぢやありませんか。だから、私はさう言つて遣つた、お気の毒だが、貴方は大方目が眩んで、そりやお袋を縛つたんだらうつて」

聴るゝ狭山は小気味好しとばかりに頷けり。

「それで那奴は全然悩つて了つて、それからの騒擾でさ。無礼な奴だとか何とか言つて、私は襟を持つて引摺り仆された。随分飲んでゐたから、やつぱり酔つてゐたんでせう。その時はもう全で夢中で、唯那奴の憎らしいのが胸一杯に込上げて、這畜生と思ふと、突如其処に在つたお皿を那奴の横面へ叩付けて遣つた。丁度それが眉間へ打着つて血が淋漓流れて、顔が半分真赤に成つて了つた。これは居ちや面倒だと思つたから、家中大騒を遣つてゐる隙を見て、窃と飛出した事は飛出したけれど、別に往所も無いから、丹子の阿母さんの処へ駆込んだの。

ところが、好かつた事には、今旅から帰つたと云ふところなんで、時間を見ると、十時余程廻つてゐるんでせう。滊車はもう出ず、気ばかりは急くけれど、若箇道間に合ふんぢやなし、それ

に話は有るし為るもんだから、一晩厄介に成る事にして、髪なんぞを結んでもらひながら、些と訳が有つて、貴方と一処に当分身を隠すのだと云やうに話を為てね、それから丹子の事も悪く言置いて遣りましたら——善い人ね、あの阿母さんは——おいおい泣出して、自分の子の事はふつつりとも言はずに、唯私の身ばかりを案じて、ああのかうのと色々言つてくれたその実意と云つたら……噫、同じ人間でありながら、内の阿母さんは、実に、あなた、鬼ですわ！　私もある子の阿母さんのやうな実の親が有つたらば、こんな苦労は為やしまいし、又貴方のやうな方の有るのを、さぞかし力に念つて、喜びも為やうし、大事にも為る事だらうと思つたら、もうもう悲くなつて、悲しくなつて、如何に何でも余り情無くて、私はどんなに泣きましたらう。

それに、私をばあんなに為つてゐた阿母さんの事だから、当分でも田舎へ行つて了ふと云ふのを、それは心細がつて、力を落したの何のと云つたら、私も別れるのが気の毒に成るくらゐで、先へ落付いたら、どうぞ一番に住所を知せてくれと、初中終旅を出行いてゐる体だから、直に御機嫌伺ひに出ると、その事をあんなに懇々も頼んでゐましたから、後で聞いたら、さぞ吃驚して……きつと疾病でも為るでせうよ。考へて見りや、丹子も可愛し、あの阿母さんも怜いし、吁、吁！」

歔欷して彼は悶えつ。

「さう云ふ訳ぢや、猶更内ぢや大騒をして捜してゐる事だらう」

「大変でせうよ」

「それだと余り遅々しちやゐられないのだ」

「どうで、狭山さん、先は知れてるの……」

「さうだ」

「だからねえ、もう早い方が可ござんすよ」

女は咽びて其処に泣伏しぬ。狭山は涙を連瞬きて、

「お静、おい、お静や」

「あ……あい。狭山さん！」

憐むべし、情極りて彼等の相擁するは、畢竟尽きせぬ哀歓を抱くが如き者ならんをや。

(三) の 二

両箇は此方にかつ泣きかつ語れる間、彼方の一箇は徒然の柱に倚りて、やうやう傾く日影に照されゐたり。

その待人の如何なる者なるかを見て、疑は決すべしと為せし貫一も、かの伴ひ遯りし女を見るに迫びて、その疑はいよいよ錯雑して、しかも新なる怪訝の添はるのみなり。如何なればや、女の顔色も甚だ勝れず、その点の男といと善く似たるは、同じ憂を分つにあらざる無からんや。我聞く、犯罪の底には必ず女有りと、若し信なりとせば、彼は正く彼女ゆゑに如何なる罪をも犯せるならんよ。その罪の故に男は苦み、その苦の故に女は憂ふると為れば、彼等は誠に相愛するの堅き者ならず哉。

知らず、彼等は何の故に相率てこの人目稀なる山中には来れる。その罪を遁れんが為か、その苦と憂とを忘れんが為か、或はその愛を全うせんが為か、明に彼等は夫婦ならず、又は、女の芸者風なるも、決して尋常の隠遊にあらずして、自から穂に露るるところ有り。さては何等の密会ならん。

貫一は彼を以て女を偸みて奔る者ならずや、と先推しつつ、尚ほ如何にやなど、飽かず疑へる間より、忽ち一片の反映は閃きて、朧にも彼の胸の黯きを照せり。

彼はこの際熱海の旧夢を憶はざるを得ざりしなり。

世上貫一の外に愛する者無かりし宮は、その貫一と奔るを諾はずして、僅に一瞥の富の前に、百年の契を蹂躙りて咨まざりき。嗚呼が当時の恨、彼が今日の悔！　今彼女は日夜に栄の街ひ、利の誘ふ間に立ち、守るに難き節を全うして、世の容れざる愛に随つて奔らんと為るか。爾思へる後の彼は、陰にかの両個の先に疑ひし如き可忌き罪人ならで、潔く愛の為に奔る者たらんを、禱るばかりに糞へり。若しもあらば、彼は具に彼等の苦き身の上と切なる志とを聴かんと念ひぬ。

心永く瘁きて恋に敗れたる貫一は、殊更に他の成敗に就いて観るを欲せるなり。彼は己の不幸の幾許不幸に、人の幸の幾許幸ならんかを想ひて、又己の失敗の幾許無残に、人の成効の幾許十分ならんかを想ひて、又己の契の幾許薄く、人の縁の幾許深からんかを想ひて、又己の受けし愛の幾許浅く、人の交せる情の幾許篤からんかを想ひて、又己の恋の障碍の幾許強く、人の容れら

れぬ世の幾許狭からんかを想ひて。

嗟呼、既に己の恋は敗れに破れたり。　知るべからざる人の恋の末終に如何ならんかを想ひて。

昼間の程は努めて籠りゐしかの両個の、夜に入りて後打連れて入浴せるを伺ひ知りし貫一は、例の益す人目を避るならんよと念へり。

還り来て多時酒など酌交す様子なりしが、高声一つ立つるにもあらで、唯障子を照す燈のみい、内の寂しさは露をも置きけんやうにて、さてはかの吹絶えぬ松風に、彼等は竟に酔を成さざるならんと覚ゆばかりなりき。

為す事もあらねば、貫一は疾く臥内に入りけるが、僅に眠むと為れば直に、寤めて、そのまゝに睡は失るとともに、様々の事思ひゐたり。

夜の静なるを動かして、かの男女の細語は洩れ来ぬ。甚だ幺微なれば聞知るべくもあらねど、娚々として絶えず枕に打響きては、なかなか大いなる声にも増して耳煩はしかり。

さなきだに寝難かりし貫一は、益す気の澄み、心の亙え行くに任せて、又徒にとやかくと、彼等の身上を推測り推測り思回らすの外はあらず。彼方もその幺微なる声に語り語りて休まざるは、思の丈の短夜に余らんとするなるか。

貫一は愕然として枕を欹てつ。女は遽に泣出せるなり。

その時男の声音は全く聞えずして、唯独り女の縦まに泣音を洩すのみなる。寤めたる貫一は弥

が上に窘めて、自ら故を知らざる胸を轟せり。

少焉泣きたりし女の声は漸く鎮りて、又湿り勝にも語り初めしが、一たび情の為に激せし声音は、自から始よりは高く響けり。されどなほその言ふところは聞知り難くて、男の声は却りて前よりも仄なり。

貫一は咳きも遣らで耳を澄せり。

或は時に断ゆれども、又続ぎ、又続ぎて、彼等の物語は蚕の糸を吐きて倦まざらんやうに、限も知らず長く亘りぬ。げにこの積る話を聞きも聞せもせんが為に、彼等はここに来つるにやあらん。されども、日は明日も明後日も有るを、甚だ忙くも語るもの哉。さばかり間遠なりし逢瀬なるか、言はでは裂けぬる胸の内か、かく有らでは懐らぬ恋中か、など思ふに就けて、彼はさすがに我身の今昔に感無き能はず、枕を引入れ、夜着引被ぎて、寝返りたり。

何時罷みしとも覚えで、彼等の寝物語は漸く絶えぬ。

貫一も遂に短き夢を結びて、常よりは蚤かりけれど、目覚めしままに起出でし朝冷を、走り行きて推啓けつる湯殿の内に、人は在らじと想ひし眼を驚して、かの男女は浴しゐたり。

貫一ははたと閉して急ぎ返りつ。

第四章

両箇はやや熱かりしその日も垂籠めて夕に抵りぬ。むづかしげに暮山を繞りし雲は、果して雨と成りて、冷々と密下るほどに、宵の燈火も影更けて、壁に映ふ物の形皆寂く、懲ひに起きて在るべき夜頃ならず。さては貫一も枕に就きたり。

ランプを細めたる彼等の座敷も甚だ静に、宿の者さへ寐急ぎて後十一時は鳴りぬ。凄き谷川の響に紛れつつ、小歇もせざる雨の音の中に、かの病憊れたるやうの柱時計は、息も絶気に半夜を告ぐわたる時、両箇が閨の燈は乍ち明かに耀けるなり。

彼等は倶に起出でて火鉢の前に在り。

「膳を持って来ないか」

「ええ」

女は幺微なる声して答へけれど、打萎れて、なかなか立ちも遣らず。

「狭山さん、私は何だか貴方に言残した事が未だ有るやうな心持がして……」

「呀、もうかう成つちやお互に何も言はないが可い。言へばやつばり未練が出る」

彼は熟と内向きて、目を閉ぢたり。

「貴方、その指環を私のと取替事して下さいね」

「さうか」

各その手に在るを抜きて、男は実印用のを女の指に、女はダイアモンド入のを男の指に、摂し了りてもなほ離れかねつつ、物は得言はでゐたり。

颯と鳴りて雨は一時繁く濺ぎ来れり。

「ああ、大相降つて来た」

「貴方は不断から雨が所好だつたから、きつとそれで……暇……乞に降つて来たんですよ」

「好い折だ。あの雨を看に……お静、それぢや私も……覚……悟したわ」

「あ……あい。狭山さん、それぢや私も……覚悟を為ろよ！」

「あい」

お静も今は心を励まして、宵の程誂へ置きし酒肴の床間に上げたるを持ち来て、両箇が中に膳を据れば、男は手早く燗して、その間に各服を更むる忙しさは、忽ち衣の擦り、帯の鳴る音高く繚繞と乱れ合ひて、転た雨濃なる深夜を驚かせり。

「酒を持つて来な」

「あい」

「ええ、もう好かない！」

帯緊めながら女はその端を振りて身悶せるなり。

「どうしたのだ」

「なあにね、帯がこんなに結ばつて了つて」

「帯が結ばつた？」

「ああ！　あなた釈いて下さい、よう」

「何か言い事が有るのだ」

「私はもしも遣損つて、耻でも曝すやうな事が有つちやと、それが苦労に成つて耐らなかつたん
だから、これでもう可いわ」

「それは大丈夫だから安心するが可い。けれど、もしもだ、お静、そんな事は無いとは念ふけれ
ど、運悪く遅れたら、俺はきつと後から往くから——どんなにしても往くから、恨まずに待つ
てゝくれ。よ、可……可いか」

つと俯したるお静は、男の膝を咬みて泣きぬ。

「その代り、偶としてお前が後になるやうだつたら、俺は死んでも……魂はおまへの陰身を離れ
ないから、必ず心変を……す、するなよ、お静」

「そんな事を言はないで、一処に……連れて……往つて……下さいよ」

「一処に往くとも！」

「一処に！　一処に往きますよ！」

「さあ、それぢやこ、この世の……別に一盃飲むのだ。もう泣くな、お静」

「泣、泣かない」

「さあ、那裏へ行つて飲まう」

　男は先づ起ちて、女の手を把れば、女はその手に縋りつつ、泣く泣く火鉢の傍に座を移しても、なほ離難なに寄添ひぬたり。

「猪口でなしに、その湯呑に為やう」

「さう。ぢや半分づつ」

　熱燗の酒は烈々と薫じて、お静が顕ふ手元より狭山が顕ふ湯呑に為がれぬ。

　女の最も悲かりしは、げにこの刹那の思なり。彼は人の為に酒を佐るに嫋ひし手も、などや今宵の恋の命を、儚き夢か、うたたの水盃のみづからに、酌取らんとは想の外の外なりしを、唄にも似たる身の上哉と、漫に遍る胸の内、何に譬へん方もあらず。

　男は燗の過ぎたるに口を着けかねて、少時手に せるままに眺めをれば、よし今は憂くも苦くも、久く住慣れしこの世を去りて、永く返らざらんとする身には、僅に一盃の酒に対するも、又哀別離苦の感無き能はざるなり。

　念へ、彼等の逢初めし夕、互に意有りて衝みしもこの酒ならずや。吉き事積りし後の凶の凶なる今夜の末期に酬ゆるの、情の必ず濃なれば、必ず芳かりしもこの酒ならずや。その恋中の楽を添へて、三歳の宴を霽せしもこの酒ならずや。彼はその酒を取りて、更に両個の影に伴ひて、人可哀に余り、可悲きに過るを観じては、口にこそ言はざりけれど、玉成す涙は点々と散りて零れぬ。

「おまへの酌で飲むのも……今夜きりだ」

「狭山さん、私はこんなに苦労を為て置きながら、到頭一日でも……貴方と一処に成れずに、芸者風情で死んで了ふのが……悔い、私は！」

聞くも苦しと、男は一息に湯呑の半を呷りて、

「さあ、お静」

女は何気無く受けながら、思へば、別の盃かと、手に取るからに胸潰れて、

「狭山さん、私は今更お礼を言ふと云ふのも、異な者だけれど、貴方は長い月日の間、私のやうなこんな不束者の我儘者を、能くも愛相を尽かさずに、深切に、世話をして下すつた。

私は今まで口には出さなかつたけれど、心の内ぢや、狭山さん、嬉いなんぞと謂ふのは通り越して、実に難有いと思つてゐました。その御礼を為たいにも、知つてゐる通の阿母さんが在るばかりに唯さう思ふばかりで、どうと云ふ事も出来ず、本当に可恥かしいほど行届かないだらけで、さうしたら一度にこの恩返しれぢや余り済まないから、一日も早く所帯でも持つやうに成つて、さうしたら一度にこの恩返しを為ませうと、私は、そればかりを楽に、出来ない辛抱も為てゐたんだけれど、もう、今と成つちや何もかも水……水……水の……泡。

つい心易立から、浸々お礼も言はずにゐたけれど、狭山さん、私の心は、さうだつたの。もうこれぎりで、貴方も……私も……土に成つて了へば、又とお目には掛れ、ないんだから、せめて

は、今改めて、狭山さん、私はお礼を申します」

男は身をも搾らるるばかりに怜へかねたる涙を出せり。

「もうそ、そ、そんな事……言つて……くれるな！　冥路の障だ。両箇が一処に死なれりや、そ

れで不足は無いとして、外の事なんぞは念はずに、お静、お互に喜んで死なうよ」

「私は喜んでゐますとも、嬉いんですとも。嬉くなくてどうしませう。このお酒も、祝つて私は

飲みます」

涙諸共飲干して、

「あなた、一つお酌して下さいな」

注げば又呷りて、その余せるを男に差せば、受けて納めて、手を把りて、顔見合せて、抱緊め

て、惜めばいよいよ尽せぬ名残を、いかにせばやと思惑へる互の心は、唯それなりに息も絶えよ

と祈る可かめり。

男は抱ける女の耳のあたかも唇に触るる時、現ともなく声誘はれて、

「お静、覚悟は可いか」

「可いわ、狭山さん」

「可けりや……」

「不如もう早く」

狭山は直に枕の下なる袱紗包の紙入を取上げて、内より出せる一包の粉剤こそ、正に両個が絶

命の刃に易ふる者なりけれ。

女は二つの茶碗を置並ぶれば、玉の如き真白の粉末は封を披きて、男の手よりその内に頒たれ

ぬ。

「さあ、その酒を取つてくれ。お前のには俺が酌をするから、俺のにはお前が」

「ああ可うござんす」

雨はこの時漸く霽れて、軒の玉水絶々に、怪禽鳴過る者両三声にして、跡松風の音颯々たり。狭山はやがて銚子を取りて、一箇の茶碗に酒を注げば、お静は目を閉ぢ、合掌して、聞えぬほどの忍音に、

「南無阿弥陀仏、南無阿弥陀仏」

代りて酌する彼の想は、吾手男の胸元に刺違ふる鋩を押当つるにも似たる苦しさに、自から洩出づる声も打震ひて、

「南無阿弥陀仏、南無阿弥陀仏、南無……阿弥陀……南無阿弥……陀……仏、南無……」

と両個は心も消入らんとする時、俄に屋鳴震動して、百雷一処に堕ちたる響に、男は顚れ、女は叫びて、前後不覚の夢か現の人影は、乍ち顕れて燈火の前に在り。

「貴下方は、怪からん事を！　可けませんぞ」

男は漸く我に復りて、慄ぢ慴ける目を睜き、

「ああ！　貴方は」

「お見覚ありませう、あれに居る泊客です。無断にお座敷へ入つて参りまして、甚だ失礼ぢや御座いますけれど、実に危い所！　貴下方はどうなすつたのですか」

悄然として面を挙げざる男、その陰に半ば身を潜めたる女、貫一は両個の姿を胸しつつ、彼の答を待てり。

「勿論これには深い事情がお有んなさるのでせう。ですから込入つたお話は承はらんでも宜い、但何故に貴下方は活きてをられんですか、それだけお聞せ下さい」

彼は又黙せり。

「お二人が添ふに添れん、と云ふやうな事なのですか」

男は甚だ微に頷きつ。

「さやうですか。さうしてその添れんと云ふのは、何故に添れんのです」

「…………」

「その次第を伺つて、私の力で及ぶ事でありましたら、随分御相談合手にも成らうかと、実は考へるので。然し、お話の上で到底私如きの力には及ばず、成程活きてをられんのは御尤だ、他人の私でさへ外に道は無い、と考へられるやうなそれが事情でありましたら、私は決してお止め申さん。ここに居て、立派に死なれるのを拝見もすれば、介錯もして上げます。貴下方を拯ふ事が出来るか、空く手を退く訳には行かんのです。私もこの間に入つた以上は、幸に拯ふ事が出来たら、私は命の親。又出来なかつたら、貴下方はこの世に亡い人。この世に亡い人なら、如何なる秘密をここで打明けたところが、一向差支無からう

と私は思ふ。若し命の親とすればです。猶更その者に喪み隠す事は無いぢやありませんか。私は

何も洒落に貴下方のお話を聴かうと云ふのぢやありません、可うございますか、顕然と聴くだけの覚悟を持つて聴くのです。さあ、お話し下さい！」

第五章

　貫一は気を厳粛にして遍れるなり。さては男も是非無げに声出すべき力も有らぬ口を開きて、

「はい御深切に……難有う存じます……」

「さあ、お話し下さい」

「はい」

「今更お褒みなさる必要は無からう、と私は思ふ。いや、つい私は申上げんでをつたが、東京の麹町の者で、間貫一と申して、弁護士です。かう云ふ場合にお目に掛るのは、好々これは深い御縁なのであらうと考へるのですから、決して貴下方の不為に成るやうには取計ひません。私も出来る事なら、人間両個の命を拯ふのですから、どうにでもお助け申して、一生の手柄に為て見たい。私はこれ程までに申すのです」

「はい、段々御深切に、難有う存じます」

「それぢや、お話し下さるか」

「はい、お聴に入れますで御座います」

「それは忝ない」

彼は始めて心安う座を取れば、恐る惶る狭山は先づその姿を偸見て、

「何からお話し申して宜いやら……」

「いや、その、何ですな、貴下方は添ふに添れんから死ぬと有仰る——！　何為添れんのですか」

「はい、実は私は、恥を申しませんければ解りませんが、主人の金を大分遣ひ込みましたので御座います」

「はあ、御主人持ですか」

「さやうで御座います。私は南伝馬町の幸菱と申しまする。又これは新橋に勤をしてをります者で、柏屋の愛子と申しまする名宜られし女は、消えも遣らでのたりし人陰の闇きより僅に躍り出でて、面伏にも貫一が前に会釈しつ。

「はあ、成程」

「然るところ、昨今これに身請の客が附きまして」

「ああ、身請の？　成程」

「否でもその方へ参らんければ成りませんやうな次第。又私はその引負の為に、主人から告訴致されまして、活きてをりますれば、その筋の手に掛りますので、如何にとも致方が御座いませんゆゑ、無分別とは知りつつも、つい突迫めまして、面目次第も御座いません」

彼等はその無分別を悲ちたりとよりは、この死失ひし見苦しさを、天にも地にも曝しかねて、俯しも仰ぎも得ざる頃を竦め、尚も為さん方無さの目を閉ぢたり。

「ははあ。さうするとここに金さへ有れば、どうにか成るのでせう！　貴方の費消だつて、その金額を弁償して、宜く御主人に詫びたら、無論内済に成る事です。婦人の方は、先方で請出すと云ふのなら、此方でも請出すまでの事。さうして、貴方の引負は若干ばかりの額に成るのですか」

「三千円ほど」

「三千円。それから身請の金は？」

狭山は女を顧みて、二言三言小声に語合ひたりしが、

「何やかやで八百円ぐらゐは要りますので」

「三千八百円、それだけ有つたら、貴下方は死なずに済むのですな」

打算し来れば、真に彼等の命こそ、一人前一千九百円に過ぎざるなれ。

「それぢや死ぬのはつまらんですよ！　三千や四千の金なら、随分そこらに滾つてゐやうと私は思ふ。就いては何とか御心配して上げたいと考へるのですが、先づとにかく貴下方の身の上を一番悉く御話し下さらんか」

かかる際には如何ばかり嬉き人の言ならんよ。彼はその偽と真とを思ふに違あらずして、遣る方も無き変身の憂きを、冀くば跡も留めず語りて竭さんと、弱りし心は雨の柳の、漸く風に揺れたる勇を作して、

「はい、ついに一面識も御座いません私共、殊に痴情の果に箇様な不始末を為出しました、何ともはや申しやうも無い燗死蛆に、段々と御深切のお心遣、却つて恥入りまして、実に面目次第も御座いません。

折角の御言で御座いますから、思召に甘えまして、一通りお話致しますで御座います。

実は、只今申上げました三千円の費消と申しますのは、究竟遊蕩を致しました為に、店の金に手を着けましたところ、始の内はどうなり融通も利きましたので、それが病付に成つて、段々と無理を致しまして、長い間に惷々穴を開けましたのが、積り積つて大分に成りましたので御座います。

然るところ、もう八方塞つて遣繰は付きませず、いよいよ主人には知れますので、苦紛れに相場に手を出したのが怪我の元で、ちよろりと取られますと、さあそれだけ穴が大きく成りましたものですから、愈よ為方御座いません、今度はどうか、今度はどうかで、もうさう成つては私も死物狂で、無理の中から無理を致して、続くだけ遣りましたところが、到頭逐倒されて了ひまして、三千円と申上げました費消も、半分以上はそれに注込みましたので御座います。

然し、これだけの事で御座いますれば、主人も従来の勤労に免じて、又どうにも勘弁は致してくれましたので現にこの一条が発覚致しまして、主人の前に呼付けられました節も、この度の事は格別を以つて赦し難いところも赦して遣ると、箇様に申してはくれましたので

「成程?!」

「と申すのには、少し又仔細が御座いますので。それは、主人の家内の姪に当ります者が、内に引取つて御座いまして、これを私に妻せやうと云ふ意衷で、前々からその話は有りますので御座いますが、どうも私は気が向きませんものて、何と就かずに段々言延して御座いましたのを、決然どうかと云ふ手詰の談に相成りましたので。究竟、費消は赦して遣るから、その者を家内に持て、と簡様に主人は申すので御座います」

「大きに」

「其処には又千百事情が御座いまして、私の身に致しますと、その縁談は実に辞りるにも辞りかねる義理に成つてをりますので、それを不承知だなどと吾儘を申しては、なかなか済む訳の者ではないので御座います」

「ああ、さうなのですか」

「そこへ持つて参つて、此度の不都合で御座います、それさへ大目に見てくれやうと云ふので御座いますから、全で仇をば恩で返してくれますやうな、申分の無い主人の所計。それを乖きましては、私は罰が中りますので御座います。さうとは存じながら、やつぱり私の手前勝手で、如何にともその気に成れませんので、已むを得ず縁談の事は拒絶を申しましたので御座います」

「うむ、成程」

「それが為に主人は非常な立腹で、さう吾儘を言ふのなら、費消を償へ、それが出来ずば告訴す

る。さうしては貴様の体に一生の疵が附く事だから、思反して主人の指図に従へと、中に人まで入れて、未だ未だ申してくれましたのを、何処までも私は剛情を張通して了つたので御座います」

「吁！　それは貴方が悪いな」

「はい、もう私の善いところは一つでも有るのぢや御座いません。その事に就きまして、主人に書置も致しましたやうな次第で、既に覚悟を極めました際まで、心懸と申すのは、唯そればかりなので又その最中にこれの方の身請騒が起りましたので」

「成程！」

「これの母親と申すのは養母で御座いまして、私も毎々話を聞いてをりますが、随分それは非道な強慾な者で御座います。まあ悪く申上げれば、長いお話も御座いますが、これも娘と申すのは名のみで、年季で置いた抱も同様の取扱を致して、為め遣る事は為ないのが徳、稼げるだけ稼がせないのは損だと云つたやうな了簡で、長い間無理な勤を為せまして、散々に搾り取つたので御座います。

で、私の有る事も知つてはをりましたが、近頃私が追々廻らなく成つて参つたところから、さあ聘く言出しまして、毎日のやうに切れろ切れろで責め抜いてをります際に、今の身請の客が附いたので御座います。丁度去年の正月頃から来出した客で、下谷に富山銀行といふのが御座います、あれの取締役で」

「え!?　何⋯⋯何⋯⋯何ですか!」

「御承知で御座いますか、あの富山唯継と云ふ⋯⋯」

「富山?　唯継!」

　その面色、その声音！　彼は言下に赫怒して、その名に躍り被らんとする勢を示せば、愛子は驚き、狭山は懼れて、何事とも知らず狼狽へたり。貫一は轟く胸を推鎮めても、なほ眼色の燃ゆるが如きを、両個が顔に忙く注ぎて、

「その富山唯継が身請の客ですか」

「はい、さやうで御座いますが、貴方は御存じでゐらつしやいますので」

「知つてるます!　好く⋯⋯知つてるます!」

　狭山の打惑ふ傍に、女は密に驚く声を放てり。

「那奴が身請の?」

　問はるる愛子は、会釈して、

「はい、さやうなんで御座います」

「で、貴方は彼に退かされるのを嫌つたのですな」

「はい」

「さうすると、去年の始から貴方はあれの世話に成つてをつたのですか」

「私はあんな人の世話なんぞには成りは致しません!」

「はあ？　さうですか。　世話に成つてゐたのぢやないのですか」

「いいえ、貴方。　唯お座敷で始終呼れますばかりで」

「ああ、さうですか！　それぢや旦那に取つてをつたと云ふ訳ぢやないのですか」

女は聞くも穢しと、さすが謂ふには謂れぬ尻目遣して、

「私には、さう云ふ事が出来ませんので、今までついにお客なんぞを取つた事は、全然無いんで御座います」

「ああ、さうですか！　うむ、成程……成程な……解りました、好く解りました」

狭山は俯きゐたり。

「それではかう云ふのですな、貴方は勤を為てをつても、外の客には出ずに、この人一個を守つて——さうですね」

「さやうです」

「さうして、余所の身請を辞つて——富山唯継を振つたのだ！　さうですな」

「はい」

倏忽に瞳を凝せる貫一は、愛子の面を熟視して止まざりしが、やがてその眼の中に浮びて、輝くと見れば露ひて出づるものあり。

「嗚呼……感心しました！　実に立派な者です！　貴方は命を捨てても……この人と……添ひたいのですか！」

何の故とも分かず彼の男泣に泣くを見て、両個は空く呆るるのみ。

貫一が涙を見るなるか。彼はこの色を売るの一匹婦も、知らず誰か爾に教へて、死に抵るまで尚この頼り難き義に頼り、守り難き節を守りて、終に奪はれざる者あるに泣けるなり。

其の泣く所以なるか。彼はこの人の世に、さばかり清く新しくも、崇く優しくも、高く麗しくも、又は、完くも大いなる者在るを信ぜざらんと為るばかりに、一度は目前暗きを得て、その倒懸の苦を寛うせん、と心燃くが如く望みたりしを、今却りて浮漂の底に沈める泥中の光に値へる卒爾の欲極まれればなり。

「勿論さう無けりや成らん事！　それが女の道と謂ふもので、さう有るべきです、さう有るべき事です。今日のこの軽薄極つた世の中に、とてもそんな心掛のある人間は、私は決して在るものではないと念つてをつた。で、もし在つたらば、どのくらゐ嬉からうと、さう念つてをつたのです。私は実に嬉しい！　今夜のやうに感じた事は有りません。私はこの通泣いてゐる――涙が出るほど嬉しいのです。私は人事とは思はん、人事とは思はん訳が有るので、別して深く感じたのです」

かく言ひて、貫一は忙々く鼻涙打擤みつ。

「ふむ、それで富山はどうしました」

「来る度に何のかのと申しますのを、体好く辞るんで御座いますけれど、もう慇く来ちや、一頼なんぞは毎日揚詰に為られるんで、私はふつふつ不好なんで御座います。それに、あの人があれで大の男自慢で、さうして独で利巧ぶつて、可恐い意気がりで、二言目には金々と、金の事さへ言

へば人は難有がるものかと思つて、俺がかうと思や千円出すとか、ここへ一万円積んだらどうするとか、始終そんな有余るやうな事ばかり言ふのが癖だもんですから、衆が『御威光』と云ふ仇名を附けて了つて、何処へ行つたつて気障がられてゐる事は、そりや太甚いんで御座います」

「ああ、さうですか」

「そんな風なんですから、体好く辞つたくらゐぢや、なかなか感じは為ませんので、可けもしない事を不相変執煩く、何だかだ言つてをりましたけれど、這箇も剛情で思ふやうに行かないもんですから、了局には手を易へて、内のお袋へ親談をして、内々話は出来たんで御座んせう。どうもそんなやうな様子で、お袋は全で気違のやうに成つて、さあ、私を責めて責めて、もう箸の上下には言れますし、狭山と切れろ切れろの啼くて成りましたのも、それからなので、私は辛さは辛し、熟くこんな家業は為る者ぢやないと、何も解らずに面白可笑く暮してゐた夢も全く覚めて、もうどうしたら可いんだらう、と鬱ぎ切つてゐる矢先へ、今度は身請と来たんで御座います」

「うむ、身請——けれども、貴方を別にどう為たと云ふ事も無くて、直に身請と云ふのですか」

「さうなので」

「変な奴な！　さう云ふ身請の為方が、然し、有りますか」

「まあ御座いませんです」

「さうでせう。それで、身請をして他へ囲つて置かうとでも云ふのですか」

「はい、これまで色々な事を申しても、私が聴きませんもんで、末始終気楽に暮せるやうにして遣つたら、言分は無からうと云つたやうな訳で、まあ身請と出て来たんで。何ですか、今の妻君は、あれはどうだから、かう為るとか、ああ為るとか、好いやうな嬶がらせを言つちやをりましたけれど」

眉を昂げたる貫一、なぞ彼の心の裏に震ふものあらざらんや。

「妻君に就いてどう云ふ話が有るのですか」

「何んですか知りませんが、あの人の言ふんでは、その妻君は、始終寐てゐるも同様の病人で、小供は無し、用には立たず、有つても無いも同然だから、その内に隠居でもさせて、私を内へ入れてやるからと、まあさう云つたやうな口気なんで御座います」

「さうして、それは事実なのですか、妻君を隠居させるなどと云ふのは」

「随分ちやらつぽこを言ふ人なんですから、なかなか信にはなりは致しませんが、妻君の病身の事や、そんなこんなで余り内の面白くないのは、どうも全くさうらしいんで御座んす」

「ははあ」

彼は遽に何をや打案ずらん、夢むる如き目を放ちて、

「折合が悪いですか！……病身ですか！……隠居をさせるのですか！……ああ……さうですか！」

宮の悔、宮の恨、宮の歎、宮の悲、宮の苦、宮の愁、宮が心の疾、宮が身の不幸、噫、竟にこ

れ宮が一生の惨禍！　彼の思ひは今将たこの憐むに堪へたる宮が薄命の影を追ひて移るなりき。

貫一はかの生ける宮よりも、この死なんと為る女の幾許か幸にかつ愚ならざるかを思ひて、躬の、先には己の愛する者を拯ふ能はずして、今却りて得知らぬ他人に恵みて余有る身の、幾許幸無くも又愚なるかを思ひて、謂ふばかり無く悲めるなり。

時に愛子は話を継ぎぬ。

「そんな押懸最中に、狭山さんの方が騒擾に成りましたんで、私の事はまあどうでも、ここに三千円と云ふお金が無い日には、訴へられて懲役に遣られると云ふんですから、私は吃驚して了つて、唯もう途方に昧れて、これは一処に死ぬより外は無いと、その時直にさう念つたんで御座います。けれども、又考へて、背に腹は替へられないから、これは不如富山に訳を話して、それだけのお金をどうにでも借りるやうに為やうかとも思つて見まして、狭山さんに話しましたところ、俺の身はどうでも、お前の了簡ぢや、富山の処へ行くのが可いか、死ぬのが可いか、とかう申すので御座いませう」

「うむ、大きに」

「私はあんな奴に自由に為れるのはさて置いて、これまでの縁を切るくらゐなら死んだ方が愈だと、初中終言つてをりますんですから、あんな奴に身を委せるの、不好は知れてゐます」

「うむ、さうとも」

「さうなんですけれど金ゆゑで両個が今死ぬのも余り悔いから、三千円きつと出すか、出さない

か、それは分りませんけれど、もし出したらば出さして、なあに私は那裏へ行つたつて、直に迯げて来さへすりや、切れると云ふんちやなし、少の間不好な夢を見たと思へば、それでも死ぬよりは愈ましだらう、と私はさう申しますと、狭山さんは、それは詐取だ……」

「それは詐取だ！　さうとも」

あだかも我名の出でしままに、男はこれより替りて陳べぬ。

「詐取で御座いますとも！　情婦を種に詐取を致すよりは、費消の方が罪は遙に軽う御座います。そんな悪事を働いてまでも活きてゐるやうとは、私は決して思ひは致しません。又これに致しましても、あれまで振り通した客に、今と成つて金ゆゑ体を委せるのは、如何なる事にも、余り意気地が無さ過ぎて、それぢや人間の皮を被つてゐる効が御座りません。私は金に窮つて心中なんぞを為た、と人に嘲りましても、やうやう那奴等は助つてゐるのだ、と一生涯言はれますのは不好で御座います。そんな了簡が出ます程なら、死ぬより外は無い！　私は死ぬと覚悟を為たが、お前の了簡はどうか、と実は私が申しましたので」

ここに活きてゐるやうと云ふには、どうでもこの上の悪事を為なければ成りませんので、とても死ぬより外は無い！

「成程。そこで貴方が？」

「私は今更富山なんぞにどうしやうと申したのも、究竟私ゆゑにそんな訳に成つた狭山さんが、

ける方は外に幾多も御座いますので。両個の命ぐらゐの助

どうにでも助けたいばかりなんで御座いますから、その人が死ぬと言ふのに、私一箇残つてた
つて、為様が有りは致しません。貴方が死ぬなら、私も死ぬ——それぢや一処にと約束を致して、
ここへ参つたんで御座います」

「いや、善く解りました！」

貫一は宛然我が宮の情急に、誠壮に、凛たるその一念の言を、かの当時に聴くらん想して、独
り自ら胸中の躍々として痛快に堪へざる者あるなり。

正にこれ、垠も知らぬ失恋の沙漠は、濛々たる眼前に、麗き一望のミレヱジは清絶の光を放ち
て、甚だ饒に、甚だ明かに浮びたりと謂はざらん哉。

彼は幾どこの女の宮ならざるをも忘れて、その七年の憂憤を、今夜の今にして始て少頃も破除
するの間を得つ。信に得難かりしこの間こそ、彼が宮を失ひし以来、唯これに易へて望みも望み
たりし者ならずと為んや。

嗚呼麗きミレヱジ！

貫一が久渇の心は激く動されぬ。彼は声さへやや震ひて、

「さう申しては失礼か知らんが、貴方の商売柄で、一箇の男を熟と守つて、さうしてその人の落
目に成つたのも見棄てず、一方には、身請の客を振つてからに、後来花の咲かうといふ体を、男
の為には少しも惜まずに死なうとは、　実に天晴なもの！　余り見事な貴方のその心掛に感じ入つ
て、私は……涙が……出ました。

貴方は、どうか生涯その心掛を忘れずにゐて下さい！　その心掛は、貴方の宝ですよ。又狭山さんの宝、則ち貴下方夫婦の宝なのです！

今後とも、貴方は狭山さんの為には何日でも死んで下さい。可う御座いますか。

きっと持ってゐて下さい。

千万人の中から唯一人見立てて、この人はと念つた以上は、勿論その人の為には命を捨てるくらゐの了簡が無けりや成らんのです。その覚悟が無いくらゐなら、始から念はん方が可いので、一旦念つたら骨が舎利に成らうとも、決して志を変へんと云ふのでなければ、色でも、恋でも、何でもないです！　で、若し好いた、惚れたと云ふのは上辺ばかりで、その実は移気な、水臭い者とも知らず、逗箇は一心に成つて思窮めてゐる者を、いつか寝返を打れて、突放されるやうな目に遭つたと為たら、その棄てられた者の心の中は、どんなだと思ひますか」

彼の声音は益す震へり。

「さう云ふのが有ります！　私は世間にはさう云ふの方が、多いと考へる。そんな徒爾な色恋は、為た者の不仕合、棄てられた者も、互に好い事は無いのです。私は現にさう云ふのを賭てゐるから今貴下方がかうして一処に死ぬまでも離れまいと云ふまでに思合つた、その満足はどれ程で、実に謂ふに謂はれん程の者であらう、と私は思ふ。

それに就けても、貴方のその美い心掛、立派な心掛、どうかその宝は一生肌身に附けて、どん

な事が有らうとも、決して失はんやうに為て下さい！——可う御座いますか。貴下方はお二人とも末長く、です、毎も今夜のやうなこの心を持つて、睦く暮して下さい、私はそれが見たいのです！

今は死ぬところでない、死ぬには及びません、三千円や四千円の事なら、私がどうでも為て上げます」

聞訖りし両個が胸の中は、諸共に潮の如きものに襲はれぬ。

未だ服さざりし毒の俄に変じて、この薬と成れる不思議は、喜ぶとよりは愕かれ、愕くとよりは打惑はれ、惑ふとよりは怪まれて、鬼か、神か、人ならば、如何なる人かと、彼等は覚えず貫

一の面を見据ゑて、更にその目を窃に合せつ。

四辺も震ふばかりに八声の鶏は高く唱へり。

夜すがら両個の運星蔽ひし常闇の雲も晴れんとすらん、隠約と隙洩る曙の影は、玉の緒長く座に入りて、光薄るる燈火の下に並べるままの茶碗の一箇に、小き蛾有りて、落ちて浮べり。

新続金色夜叉

第一章

生れてより神仏を頼み候事とては一度も無御座候へども、此度ばかりはつくづく一心に祈念致し、吾命を縮め候代に、必ず此文は御目に触れ候やうにと、それをば力に病中ながら筆取りまゐらせ候。幸に此の一念通じ候て、ともかくも御披せ被下候はば、此身は直ぐ相果て候とも、つゆ憾には不存申候。元より御憎悪強き私には候へども、何卒是は前非を悔いて自害いたし候一箇の愚なる女の、御前様を見懸けての遺言とも思召し、せめて一通り御判読被下候はば、未来までの御情と、何より嬉う嬉う存上げまゐらせ候。

抔とや、先頃に久々とも何とも、御生別とのみ朝夕に諦め居り候御顔を拝し、飛立つばかりの御懐しさやら、言ふに謂れぬ悲しさやらに、先立つものは涙にて、十年越し思ひに思ひまゐらせ候事何一つも口には出ず、あれまでには様々の覚悟も致し、また心苦き御目もじの恥をも忍び、女の身にてはやうやうの思にて参じ候効も無く、誠に一生の無念に存じまゐらせ候。唯其折の

形見には、涙の隙に拝しまゐらせ候御姿のみ、今に目に附き候て旦暮忘れやらず、あらぬ人の顔

までも御前様のやうに見え候て、此頃は心も空に泣暮し居りまゐらせ候。

久う御目もじ致さず候中に、別の人のやうに総て御変り被成候も、私には何とやら悲しく、又

殊に御顔の羸、御血色の悪さも一方ならず被為居候は、如何なる御疾に候や、御見上げ申すも心

細く存ぜられ候へば、折角御養生被遊、何は措きても御身は大切に御厭ひ被成候やう、くれぐ

れも念じ上候。それのみ心に懸り候、余、悲き夢などをも見続け候へば、一入御案じ申上まゐら

せ候。

　私事恥を恥とも思はぬ者との御さげすみを顧ず、先頃推して御許まで参し候胸の内は、なかな

か御目もじの上の辞にも尽し難くと存候へば、まして廻らぬ筆には故と何も記し申さず候まゝ、

何卒々々宜く御汲み下度候。さやうに候へば、其節の御腹立も、罪ある身には元より覚悟の

前とは申しながら、余とや本意無き御別に、いとど思は懲り候て、帰りて後は頭痛み、胸裂るや

うにて、夜の目も合はず、明る日よりは一層心地悪く相成、物を見れば唯涙こぼれ、何事とも無

きに胸塞り、ふとすれば思迫めたる気に相成候て、夜昼と無く劇しく悩み候ほどに、四日目には最

早起き居り候事も大儀に相成、午過より夢に就き候まゝ、今日まで臥々致し候て、唯々懐しき御

方の事のみ思続け候ては、みづからの儚き儚き身の上を慨き、胸は愈よ痛み、目は見苦しく腫起

り候て、今日は昨日より痩衰へ申候。

かやうに思迫め候気にも相成候上に、日毎に闇の奥に引入れられ候やうに段々心弱り候へ

ば、疑も無く信心の誠顕れ候て、此の蕾に就き候が元にて、はや永からぬ吾身とも存候まゝ、何卒これまでの思出には、たとひ命ある内こそ如何やうの御恨は受け候とも、今はの際には御前様の御膝の上にて心安く息引取り度くと存候へども、それは叶はぬ罪深き身に候上は、もはや再び懐ひ懐き御顔も拝し難く、猶又前非の御ゆるしも無くて、此儘相果て御事かと、諦め候より外無く存じながら、とてもとても諦めかね候苦しさの程は、此心の外に知るものも、喩ふるものも無御座候、是のみは御憎悪の中にも少は不愍と思召被下度、かやうに認め居り候、涙こぼれ候て致方無く、覚えず麁相いたし候て、かやうに紙を汚し申候。御容し被下度候。

さ候へば、私事如何に自ら作りし罪の報とは申ながら、かくまで散々の責苦を受け、かくまで十分に懺悔致し、此上は唯死ぬるばかりの身の可哀を、つゆほども御前様には通じ候はで、これぎり空く相成候が、余に口惜く存候事、一生に一度の神仏にも縋り候て、此文には私一念を巻込め、御許しまゐらせ候。

返す返すも悔き熱海の御別の後の思、又いつぞや田鶴見子爵の邸内にて図らぬ御見致し候。而来の胸の内、其後途中にて御変り被成候荒尾様に御目に懸り、しみじみ御物語致し候事など、先達而中冗うも冗うも差上申候。毎度の文にて細に申上候へども、一通の御披せも無之やうに仰せられ候へば、何事も御存無きかと、誠に御恨う存上候。百度千度繰返し候ても、是非に御耳に入れまゐらせ度存候へども、今此の切なく思乱れ居候折から、又仮初にも此上に味気無き昔を偲び候事は堪難く候故、ここには今の今心に浮び候まゝを書続けまゐらせ候。

何卒余所ながらも承はり度存じ上候は、長々御信も無く居らせられ候御前様の是迄如何に御過し被遊候や、さぞかし暴き憂世の波に一方ならぬ御艱難を遊ばせられしと、思ふも可恐しやうに存じ

上候を、ようもようも御めでたう御障無う居らせられ候、悲き中にも私の喜は是一つに御座候。御前様の数々御苦労被遊候間に、私とても始終人知らぬ愛思を重ね候て、此世には苦みに

生れ参り候やうに、唯儚き儚き月日を送りまゐらせ候。吾身ならぬ者は、如何なる人も皆可歎く、

朝夕の雀鴉、庭の木草に至る迄、それぞれに幸ならぬは無御座、世の光に遠き囹圄に繋れ候悪人にても、罪ゆり候日の楽は有之候、ものを、命有らん限は此の苦艱を脱れ候、事慚はぬ身の

悲しさは、如何に致し候はば宜きやら、御推量被下度。申すも異な事に候へども、抑も始より我心には何とも思はぬ唯継に候へば、夫婦の愛情と申候ものは、十年が間に唯の一度も起り申

さず、却つて憎き仇のやうなる思も致し、其傍に居り候も口惜く、僐く疎み果て候へば、三四年前よりは別居も同じ居候始末にて、私事一旦の身の潰れ、漸く今は浄く相成、益々堅く心

の操を守り居りまゐらせ候。先頃荒尾様より御諭も受け、さやうな心得は、始には御前様に不実の上、今又唯継に不貞なりと仰せられ候へども、其の始の不実を唯今思知り候ほどの愚なる私が、

何とて後の不貞や何やら弁へ申すべきや。愚なる者なればこそ人にも勾引され候て、帰りたき空さへ見えぬ海山の果に泣倒れ居り候を、誰一箇も憫みて救はんとは思召し被下候はずや。御前

様にも其の愚なる者を何とも思召し被下候はずや。愚なる者の致せし過も、並々の人の過も、罪

は同きものに御座候や、重きものに御座候や。

愚なる者の癖に人がましき事申上候やうにて、誠に御恥し存候へども、何とも何とも心得難

く存上候は、御前様唯今の御身分に御座候。天地は倒に相成候とも、御前様に限りては、今

猶私は疑ひ居り候ほど驚入まゐらせ候。世に生業も数多く候に、優き優き御心根にもふさはしか

らぬ然やうの道に御入り被成候までに、世間は兎やしく御前様を苦め申候か。田鶴見様方にて

御姿を拝し候後始めて御噂承はり、私は幾日も幾日も泣暮し申候。これには定て深き仔細も御

座候はんと存候へども、玉と成り、瓦と成るも人の一生に候へば、何卒昔の御身に御立返り被遊、

私の焦れ居りまゐらせ候やうに、多くの人にも御慕れ被遊候 御出世の程をば、偏に偏に願上

まゐらせ候。世間には随分賢からぬ者の好き地位を得て、時めかし居り候も少からぬを見るにつ

け、何故御前様には然やうの善からぬ業を択に択りて、折角の人に優れし御身を塵芥の中に御捨

て被遊候や、残念に残念に存上まゐらせ候。

愚なる私の心得違さへ無御座候はば、始終御側にも居り候事とて、さやうの思立も御座候節

に、屹度御諫め申候遣さや叶ひまゐらせ候ものを、返らぬ愚痴ながら私の浅はかより、みづからの一生を誤

り候のみか、大事の御身までも世の廃り物に致させ候かと思ひまゐらせ候へば、何と申候私の罪

の程かと、今更御申訳の致しやうも無之、唯そら可恐しさに消えも入度く存まゐらせ候。御免し

被下度、御免し被下度、御免し被下度候。

私は何故富山に縁付き申候や、其気には相成申候や、又何故御前様の御辞には従ひ不申候や、

唯今と相成候て考へ申候へば、覚めて悔き夢の中のやうにて、全く一時の迷とも可申、我身なが

ら訳解らず存じまゐらせ候。二つ有るものの善きを捨て、悪しきを取り候て、好んで箇様の悲しき身の上に相成候は、よくよく私に定り候運と、思出しては諦め居り申候。

其節御前様の御腹立一層強く、私をば一打に御手に懸けられ被下候はば、なまじひに今の苦娘は有之間敷、又さも無く候はば、いつそ御前様の手籠にいづれの山奥へも御連れ被下候はば、今頃は如何なる幸を得候事やらんなど、愚なる者はいつまでも愚に、始終愚なる事のみ考へ居り申候。

嬉くも御赦を得、御心解けて、唯二人熱海に遊び、昔の浜辺に昔の月を眺め、昔の哀しき御物語を致し候はば、其の心の内は如何に御座候やらん思ふさへ胸轟き、書く手も震ひ申候。今も彼の熱海に人は参り候へども、そのやうなる楽を持ち候ものは一人も有之まじく、其代には又、私如き可憐の跡を留め候て、其の一夜を今だに歎き居り候ものも決して御座あるまじく候。

世をも身をも捨て居り候者にも、猶肌身放さず大事に致候宝は御座候。それは御遺置の三枚の御写真にて何見ても楽み候はぬ目にも、是のみは絶えず眺め候て、少しは憂さを忘れ居りまゐらせ候。いつも御写真に向ひ候へば、何くれと当時の事憶出し候中に、うつつとも無く十年前の心に返り候て、苦き胸も暫は涼く相成申候。最も所好なるは御横顔の半身のに候へども、あれのみ色褪め、段々薄く相成候が、何より情無く存候へども、長からぬ私の宝に致し候間は仔細も有るまじく、亡き後には棺の内に歛めもらひ候やう、母へは其を遺言に致候覚悟に御座候。

ある女世に比無き錦を所持いたし候処、夏の熱き盛とて、差当り用無く思ひ候不覚より、人の望むままに貸与へ候後は、いかに申せども返さず、其内に秋過ぎ、冬来り候て、一枚の曠着さ

へ無き身貧に相成候ほどに、いよいよ先の錦の事を思ひに思ひ候へども、今は何処の人手に渡り候とも知れず、日頃それのみ苦に病み、慨き暮し居り候折から、さる方にて計らず一人の美き女に逢ひ候処、彼の錦をば華かに着飾り、先の持主とも知らず貧き女の前にて散々ひけらかし候上に、恥まで与へ候を、彼女は其身の過と諦め候て、泣く泣く無念を忍び申候事に御座候が、其錦に深き思の繋り候ほど、これ見よがしに着たる女こそ、憎くも、悔くも、恨くも、謂はうやう無き心の内と察せられ申候。

先達而は御許しにて御親類のやうに仰せられ候御婦人に御目に掛りまゐらせ候。毎日のやうに御出で被成候て、御前様の御世話万事被遊候。御方の由に候へば、後にて御前様さぞさぞ御大抵ならず御迷惑被遊候御事と、山々御察し申上候へども、一向さやうに御内合とも存ぜず、不躾に参上いたし候段は幾重にも、御詫申上まゐらせ候。

尚数々申上度存候事は胸一杯にて、此胸の内には申上度事のみくだくだしく相成候ていくらも、書くとも書くとも尽き申間敷、殊に拙き筆に候へば、よしなき事のみくだくだしく相成候、いつの限無く手に致し大切の事をば書洩し候が思残に御座候。惜き惜き此筆止めかね候へども、後にて御前様はやはや恋き御名居り候事も叶ひ難く、折から四時の明近き油も尽き候て、手元暗く相成候ままはやはや恋き御名を認めて、これまでの御別と致しまゐらせ候。

ただし、明日は今日よりも病重き事と存候。明後日は唯今の此の気分苦く、何とも難堪き様子にては、筆取る事相叶ひ候間は、臨終までの胸の内御許に通じ猶重くも相成可申、さやうには候へども、

まゐらせ度存候へば、覚束無くも何なりとも相認め可申候。

私事空く相成候とも、決して余の病にては無之、御前様御事を思死に死候、ものと、何卒々々御愍み被下、其段はゆめゆめ詐にては無御座、みづから堅く信じ居候事に御座候。

明日は御前様御誕生日に当り申候へば、わざと陰膳を供へ候て、私事も共に御祝ひ可申上、嬉きやうにも悲きやうにも存候。猶くれぐれも朝夕の御自愛御大事に、幾久く御機嫌好う明日を御迎へ被遊、ますます御繁栄に被為居候やう、今は世の望も、身の願も、それのみに御座候。

まづはあらあらかしこ。

　　　　　　五月二十五日

　　　　　　　　　恋し恋き
　　　　　　　　　生別の御方様

　　　　　　　　　　　　　まゐる

　　　　　　　　　　　　　　　　おろかなる女より

第　二　章

隣に養へる薔薇の香の烈く薫じて、颯と座に入る風の、この読尽されし長き文の上に落つると

見れば、紙は冉々と舞延びて貫一の身を縈り、猶も跳らんとするを、彼は徐に敷据ゑて、その膝に怖げなる面杖掛きたり。

にしてこたびばかりは終に打拆きけん、彼はその手にせし始に、又は読去りし後に、自らその故を譲めて、自ら知らざるを愧づるなりき。

彼はやがて屈めし身を起ししが、又直ちに重さに堪へざらんやうの頭を支へて、机に倚れり。

緑濃かに生茂れる庭の木々の軽々なる燥気と、近き辺に有りと有る花の薫とを打雑ぜたる夏の

初の大気は、太だ慢く動きて、その間に旁午する玄鳥の声 朗に、幾度か返しては遂に往きける

跡の垣穂の、さらぬだに燃ゆるばかりなる満開の石榴に四時過の西日の 夥く輝けるを、彼は

煩しと目を移して更に梧桐の涼き広葉を眺めたり。

文の主はかかれと祈るばかりに、命を捧げて神仏をも驚かししと書けるにあらずや。貫一は又、

自ら何の故とも知らで、独りこれのみ抜くべくもあらぬ者を抜き見たるにあらずや。彼を絡へる

文は猶解けで、厳に浪の澹ぐが如く懸れり。

そのままに専と思入るのみなりし貫一も、漸く悩く覚えて身動ぐとともに、この文殻の垤無

き様を見て、やや慌てたりげに左肩より垂れたるを取りて二つに引裂きつ。さてその一片を手繰

らんと為るに、長きこと帯の如し。好きき程に裂きては累ね、累ぬれば、皆積みて一冊にも成りぬ

べし。

かかる間も彼は自と思に沈みて、その動す手も怠く、裂きては一々読むかとも目を凝しつつ。

やや有りて裂了りし後は、あだかも劇き力作に労れたらんやうに、弱々と身を支へて、長き頂を垂れたり。

されど久きに勝へずやありけん、卒に起たんとして、かの文殻の委せたるを取上げ、庭の日陰に歩出でて、一歩に一たび裂き、二歩に二たび裂き、木間に入りては裂き、花壇を続りては裂き、留りては裂き、行きては裂き、裂きて裂きて寸ろに作しけるを、又引捉りては歩み、歩みては引捥りしが、はや行くも苦しく、後様に唯有る冬青の樹に寄添へり。

折から縁に出来れる若き女は、結立の円髷涼しげに、襷掛の惜くも見ゆる真白の濡手を弾きつつ座敷を覗き、庭を窺ひ、人見付けたる会釈の笑をつと浮べて、

「旦那様、お風呂が沸きましたが」

この姿好く、心信かなるお静こそ、僅にも貫一がこの頃を慰むる一の唯一の者なりけれ。

（二）の 二

浴すれば、下立ちて垢を流し、出づるを待ちて浴衣を着せ、鏡を据ゆるまで、お静は等閑ならず手一つに扱ひて、数ならぬ女業の効無くも、身に称はん程は貫一が為にと、明暮を唯それのみに委ぬるなり。されども、彼は別に奥の一間に己の助くべき狭山あるをも忘るべからず。そは命にも、換ふる人なり。又されども、彼と我との命に換ふる大恩をここの主にも負へるなり。如此く孰れも疎ならぬ主と夫とを同時に有てる忙しさは、盆と正月との併せ来にけんやうなるべきをも、

彼はなほ未だ覚めやらぬ夢の中にて、その夢心地には、如何なる事も難しと為るに足らずと思へ
るならん。寔に彼はさも思へらんやうに勇み、喜び、誇り、染める色あり。彼の面は為に謂ふば
かり無く輝ける程に、常にも愈して妖艶に見えぬ。

暫し浴後を涼みゐたる貫一の側に、お静は習々と団扇の風を送りゐたりしが、彼の面は縁柱に靠れて、物
をも言はず劬れたる彼の気色を左瞻右視て、

「貴方、大変にお顔色がお悪いぢや御座いませんか」

貫一はこの言に力をも得たらんやうに、萎え頽れたる身を始て揺りつ。

「さうかね」

「あら、さうかねぢや御座いませんよ、どうあそばしたのです」

「別にどうも為はせんけれど、何だかかう気が閉ぢて、惺然せんねえ」

「惺然あそばせよ。麦酒でも召上りませんか、ねえ、さうなさいまし」

「麦酒かい、余り飲みたくもないね」

「貴方そんな事を有仰らずに、まあ召上つて御覧なさいまし。折角私が冷して置きましたので
すから」

「それは狭山君が帰つて来て飲むのだらう」

「何で御座いますつて?!」

「いや、常談ぢやない、さうなのだらう」

「狭山は、貴方、麦酒なんぞを戴ける今の身分ぢや御座いませんです」

「そんなに堅く為んでも可いさ、内の人ぢやないか。もつと気楽に居てくれなくては困る」

「この上の気楽が有つて耐えるものぢや御座いません」

お静は益と涙含みし目を拭ひて、

「けれども有物だから、所好なら飲んでもらはう。お前さんも克くのだらう」

「はあ、私もお相手を致しますから、一盃召上りましよ。氷を取りに遣りまして――夏蜜柑でも

剝きませう――林檎も御座いますよ」

「お前さん飲まんか」

「私も戴きますとも」

「いや、お前さん独で」

「貴方の前で私が独で戴くので御座いますか。さうして貴方は？」

「私は飲まん」

「ちや見てゐらっしやるのですか。不好ですよ、馬鹿々々しい！　まあ何でも可いから、ともか

くも一盃召上ると成さいましよ、ね。唯今直に持つて参りますから、其処にゐらっしやいまし」

気軽に走り行きしが、程無く老婢と共に齎せる品々を、見好げに献立して彼の前に陳ぶれば、

さすがに他の老婆子が寂き給仕に義務的吃飯を強ひらるるの比にもあらず、やや難捨き心地もし

て、コップを取挙れば、お静は慣れし手元に噴溢るるばかり酌して、

「さあ、呷とそれを召上れ」

貫一はその半を尽して、先づ息へり。林檎を剥きみるお静は、手早く二片ばかり剥ぎて、

「はい、お肴を」

「まあ、一盃上げやう」

「まあ、貴方——いいえ、可けませんよ。些とお顔に出るまで二三盃続けて召上れよ。さうすると幾らかお気が霽れますから」

「そんなに飲んだら倒れて了ふ」

「お倒れなすたつて宜いぢや御座いませんか。本当に今日は不好な御顔色でゐらつしやるから、それがかう消えて了ふやうに、奮発して召上りましょ」

彼は覚えず薄笑して、

「薬だつてさうは利かんさ」

「どうあそばしたので御座います。何処ぞ御体がお悪いのなら、又無理に召上るのは可う御座いませんから」

「体は始終悪いのだから、今更驚きも為んが……ぢや、もう一盃飲まうか」

「へい、お酌。ああ、余りお見事ぢや御座いませんか」

「見事でも可かんのかい」

「いいえ、お見事は結構なのですけれど、余り又——頂戴……ああ恐入ります」

「いや、考へて見ると、人間と云ふものは不思議な者だ。今まで不見不知の、実に何の縁も無いお前さん方が、かうして内に来て、狭山君はああして実体の人だし、お前さんは優しく世話をしてくれる、私は決して他人のやうな心持は為んね。それは如何なる事情が有つてかう成つたにも為よ、那裏で逢はなければ、何処の誰だかお互に分らずに了つた者が、急に一処に成つて、貴方がどうだとか、私がかうだとか、……や、不思議だ！　どうか、まあ漁らず一生かうしてお附合を為たいと思ふ。けれども私は高利貸だ。世間から鬼か蛇のやうに謂れて、この上も無く擯斥されてゐる高利貸だ。お前さん方もその高利貸の世話に成つてゐられるのは、余り栄でも無く、さぞ心苦しく思つてゐられるだらう、と私は察してゐる。のみならず、人の生血を搾つてまでも、非道な貸を殖へるのが家業の高利貸が、縁も所因も無い者に、設ひ幾らでも、それほど大事の金をおいそれと出して、又体まで引取つて世話を為ると云ふには、何か可恐い下心でもあつて、それもやつぱり慾徳渾成で恩を被せるのだらうと、内心ぢやどんなにも無気味に思つてゐられる事だらう、とそれも私は察してゐる。

「さあ、コップを空けて、返して下さい」

「召上りますの？」

「飲む」

酒気は稍彼の面に上れり。

「お静さんはどう思ふね」

「私共は固より命の無いところを、貴方のお蔭ばかりで助つてをりますので御座いますから、私共の体は貴方の物も同然、御用に立ちます事なら、どんなにでも遊してお使ひ下さいまし。狭山もそんなに申してをります」

「忝ない。然し、私は天引三割の三月縛と云ふ躍利を貸して、暴い稼を為てるのだから、何も人に恩などを被せて、それを種に銭儲を為るやうな、暴い迂い事を為る必要は、まあ無いのだ。だから、どうぞ決してそんな懸念は為さるな。又私の了簡では、元々此の酔興で二人の世話を為るのだから、究竟そちらの身さへ立つたら、それで私の念は届いたので、その念が届いたら、もう剰銭を貰はうとは思はんのだ。と言つたらば、情無い事には、私の家業が家業だから、鬼が念仏でも言ふやうに、お前さん方は愈よ怪く思ふかも知れん――いや、きつとさう思つてゐられるには違無い。残念なものだ！」

彼は長吁して、

「それも悪木の蔭に居るからだ！」

「貴方、決して私共がそんな事を夢にだつて思ひは致しません。けれども、そんなに有仰いますなら、何か私共の致しました事がお気に障りましたので御座いませう。かう云ふ何も存じません粗才者の事で御座いますから」

「いいや、……」

「いいえ、私は始終言はれてをります狭山に済みませんですから、どうぞ行届きませんところ

は」

「いゝ、いゝ、さう云ふ意味で言つたのではない。今のは私の愚痴だから、さう気に懸けてくれては甚だ困る」

「ついにそんな事を有仰つた事の無い貴方が、今日に限つて今のやうに有仰ると、日頃私共に御不足がお有なすつて」

「いや、悪かつた、私が悪かつた。なかなか不足どころか、お前さん方が陰陽無く実に善く気を着けて、親身のやうに世話してくれるのを、私は何より嬉しく思つてゐる。往日話した通り、私は身寄も友達も無いと謂つて可いくらゐの独法師の体だから、気分が悪くても、誰一人薬を飲めと言つてくれる者は無し、何かに就けてそれは心細いのだ。さう云ふ私に、鬱いでゐるから酒でも飲めと、無理にも勧めてくれるその深切は、枯木に花が咲くやうな心持が、いゝえ、嘘でも何でも無い。さあ、嘘でない信に一献差すから、その積で受けてもらはう」

「はあ、是非戴かして下さいまし」

「あゝ、もうこれには無い」

「無ければ嘘なので御座いませう」

「未だ半打の上有るから、あれを皆注いで了はう」

「可うございますね」

貫一が老婢を喚ぶ時、お静は逸早く起ち行けり。

（二）の　三

話頭は酒を更むるとともに転じて、

「それはまあ考へて見れば、随分主人の面でも、友達の面でも、踏躙つて、取る事に於ては見界なしの高利貸が、如何に虫の居所が善かつたからと云つて、人の難儀――には附込まうとも――それを見かねる風ぢやないのが、何であんな格にも無い気前を見せたのかと、これは不審を立てられるのが当然だ。

けれども、ねえ、いづれその訳が解る日も有らうし、又私といふ者が、どう云ふ人間であるかと云ふ事も、今に必ず解らうと思ふ。それが解りさへしたら、この上人の十人や二十人、私の有金の有れたけは、助けやうが、恵まうが、少しも怪む事は無いのだ。かう云ふと何か酷く偉がるやうで、聞辛いか知らんけれど、これは心易立に、全く奥底の無いところをお話するのだ。

いやさう考込まれては困る。陰気に成つて可かんから、話はもう罷に為う。さうしてもつと飲み給へ、さあ」

「いいえ、どうぞお話をお聞せなすつて下さいまし」

「肴に成るやうな話なら可いがね」

「始終狭山ともさう申してゐるので御座いますけれど、旦那様は御病身と云ふ程でも無いやうにお身受申しますのに、いつもかう御元気が無くて、お険いお顔面ばかりなすつてゐらつしやるの

は、どう云ふものかしらんと、陰ながら御心配申してをるので御座いますが、

「これでお前さん方が来てくれて、内が賑かに成つただけ、私も旧から見ると余程元気には成つ
たのだ」

「でもそれより御元気がお有なさらなかつたら、まあどんなでせう」

「死んでゐるやうな者さ」

「どうあそばしたので御座いますね」

「やはり病気さ」

「どう云ふ御病気なので」

「鬱ぐのが病気で困るよ」

「どう為てさうお鬱ぎあそばすので御座います」

貫一は自ら嘲りて苦しげに哂へり。

「究竟病気の所為なのだね」

「ですからどう云ふ御病気なのですよ」

「どうも鬱ぐのだ」

「解らないぢや御座いませんか！　鬱ぐのが病気だと有仰るから、どう為てお鬱ぎ遊すのですと
申せば、病気で鬱ぐのだつて、それぢや何処まで行つたつて、同じ事ぢや御座いませんか」

「うむ、さうだ」

「うむ、さうだちやありません、緊りなさいましよ」

「ああ、もう酔つて来た」

「あれ、未だお酔ひに成つては可けません。お横に成ると御寮に成るから、お起きなすつてゐらつしやいまし。さあ、貴方」

お静は寄りて、彼の肘杖に横はれる背後より扶起せば、為ん無げに柱に倚りて、女の方を見返りつつ、

「ここを富山唯継に見せて遣りたい！」

「ああ、舍して下さいまし！　名を聞いても慄然とする？」

「名を聞いても慄然とする。さう、大きにさうだ。けれど、又考へて見れば、あれに罪が有る訳でも無いのだから、さして憎むにも当らんのだ」

「ええ、些の太好かないばかりです！」

「それぢや余り差はんぢやないか」

「あんな奴は那箇だつて可いんでさ。第一活きてゐるのが間違つてゐる位のものです。本当に世間には不好な奴ばかり多いのですけれど、貴方、どう云ふ者でせう。三千何百万とか、四千万とか、何でも太した人数が居るのぢや御座いませんか、それならもう少し気の利いた、肌合の好い、嬉しい人に撞見しさうなものだと思ひますのに、一向お目に懸りませんが、ねぇ」

「さう、さう、さう！」

「さうして富山みたやうなあんな奴がまあ紛々然と居て、番狂はせを為て行くのですから、それです

から、一日だつて世の中が無事な日と云つちや有りは致しません。どうしたらあんなにも気障に、

太好かなく、厭味たらしく生れ付くのでせう」

「おうおう、富山唯継散々だ」

「ああ、もうあんな奴の話をするのは馬鹿々々しいから、貴方、舍しませうよ」

「それぢやかう云ふ話が有る」

「はあ」

「一体男と女とでは、だね、那箇が情合が深い者だらうか」

「あら、何為で御座います」

「まあ、何為でも、お前さんはどう思ふ」

「それは、貴方、女の方がどんなに情が」

「深いと云ふのかね」

「はあ」

「信にならんね」

「へえ、信にならない証拠でも御座いますか」

「成程、お前さんは別かも知れんけれど」

「可う御座いますよ！」

「いいえ、世間の女はさうでないやうだ。それと云ふが、女と云ふ者は、慮が浅いからして、どうしても気が移り易い、これから心が動く――不実を不実とも思はんやうな了簡も出るのだ」

「それはもう女は浅掉な者に極つてゐるますけれど、気が移るの何のと云ふのは、やつぱり本当に惚れてゐないからです。心底から惚れてゐたら、些も気の移るところは無いぢや御座いませんか。善く女の一念と云ふ事を申しますけれど、思窮めますと、男よりは女の方が余計夢中に成つて了ひますとも」

「大きにさう云ふ事は有る。然し、本当に惚れんのは、どうだらう、女が非いのか、それとも男の方が非いのか」

「大変難く成りましたのね。さうですね、それは那箇かが非い事も有りませう。又女の性分にも由りますけれど、一概に女と云つたつて、一つは齢に在るので御座いますね」

「はあ、齢に在ると云ふと？」

「私共の商賈の者は善くさう申しますが、女の惚れるには、見惚に、気惚に、底惚と、かう三様有つて、見惚と云ふと、些と見たところで惚込んで了ふので、これは十五六の赤襟盛に在る事で、唯奇麗事でありさへすれば可いのですから、全で酸いも甘いもあつた者ぢやないのです。それから、十七八から二十そこそこのところは、少し解つて来て、生意気に成りますから、顔の好いのや、扮装の奇なのなんぞには余り迷ひません。気惚と云つて、様子が好いとか、気合が嬉しいとか、何とか、そんなところに目を着けるので御座いますね。ですけれど、未だ未だやつぱり浮

気なので、この人も好いが、又あの人も万更でなかつたりなんぞして、究竟お肚の中から惚れると云ふのぢやないのです。何でも二十三四からに成らなくては、心底から惚れると云ふ事は無いさうで。それからが本当の味が出るのだとか申しますが、そんなものかも知れませんよ。この齢に成れば、曲りなりにも自分の了簡も据り、世の中の事も解つてゐると云つたやうな勘定ですから、いくら洒落気の奴でも、さうさう上調子に遣つちやゐられるものぢやありません。其処は何と無く深厚として来るのが人情ですわ。かうなれば、貴方、十人が九人までは滅多に気が移るの、心が変るのと云ふやうな事は有りは致しません。あの『赤い切掛け島田の中は』と云ふ唄の文句の通、惚れた、好いたと云つても、若い内はどうしたつて心が一人前に成つてゐないのですから、やつぱりそれだけで、為方の無いものです。と言つて、お婆さんに成つてから、やいのやいの言れた日には、殿方は御難ですわ」

お静は一笑してコップを挙げぬ。貫一は連に頷きて、

「誠に面白かつた。見惚に気惚に底惚か。齢に在ると云ふのは、これは大きにさうだ。齢に在る！

「大相感心なすつてゐらつしやるぢや御座いませんか」

「大きに感心した」

「ぢやきつと胸に中る事がお有なさるので御座いますね」

「ははははははは。何為」

「でも感心あそばし方が凡で御座いませんもの」

「ははははははは。愈よ面白い」

「あら、さうなので御座いますか」

「ははははははは。さうなのとはどうなの？」

「まあ、さうなのですね」

彼は故に瞠れる眼を凝して、貫一の酔ひて赤く、笑ひて綻べる面の上に、或者を索むらんやうに打瞻れり。

「さうだつたらどうかね。はははははは」

「あら、それぢや愈よさうなので御座いますか！」

「ははははははは」

「可けませんよ、笑つてばかりゐらしつたつて」

「ははははははは」

第　三　章

惜くもなき命は有り候ものにて、はや其より七日に相成候へども、猶日毎に心地苦く相成候や、今以つて此世を去らず候へば、未練の程の御つもらせも然ぞかしと、口惜うに覚え候のみにて、今以つて此世を去らず候へば、未練の程の御つもらせも然ぞかしと、口惜

くも御恥く存上參らせ候。御前様には追々暑に向ひ候へば、いつも夏まけにて御悩み被成　候

事とて、此頃は如何に御暮し被遊候やと、一入御案じ申上參らせ候。

私事人々の手前も有之候故、儀ばかりに医者にも掛り候へども、もとより薬などは飲みも

致さず、皆打捨て申候。御存じの此疾は決して書物の中には載せて在るまじく存候を、医者

は訳無くヒステリイと申候。是もヒステリイと申候外は無きかは不存申　候へども、自分には広

き世間に比無き病の外の病とも思居り候ものを、さやうに有触れたる名を附けられ候は、身に取

りて誠に無念に御座候。

昼の中は頭重く、胸閉ぢ、気疲劇く、何を致候も大儀にて、別けて人に会ひ候が億く、誰にも

一切口を利く事も不申、誰独り引籠り居り候て、空く時の経ち候中に、此命の絶えず些づつ弱り候

て、最期に近く相成候が自から知れ候やうにも覚え申候。

夜に入り候ては又気分変り、胸の内俄に百々と相成、なかなか眠り居り候空は無之、かかる折

に人は如何やうの事を考へ候ものと思召被成候や、又其人私に候はば何と可有之候や、今更申

上候迄にも御座候はねば、何卒宜く御判じ被遊度、夜一夜其事のみ思続け候て、毎夜寝もせず明

しまゐらせ候。

さりながら、何程思続け候とても、水を覓めて遽し焔に燃かれ候に寄き苦艱の募り候のみにて、

いつ此責を免るるともなく存へ候は、層弱き女の身には余に余に難忍き事に御座候。猶々此の

やうの苦き思を致し候て、惜むに足らぬ命の早く形付き不申るやうにも候はば、いつそ自害致候

てなりと、潔く相果て候が、迥に愈と存付き候へば、万一の場合には、然る
覚悟極めまゐらせ候。

さまざまに諦め申し候へども、此の一事は迚も思絶ち難く候へば、私　相果て
是非一度、如何に致候ても推して御目もじ相願ひ可申と、此頃は唯其事のみ一心に考居り申し候。
昔より信仰厚き人達は、現に神仏の御姿をも拝み候やうに申し候へば、私とても此の一念の力なら
ば、決して恔はぬ願にも無御座と存参らせ候。

　　（三）の　二

昨日は見舞がてらに本宅の御母様参られ候。是は一つは唯継事近頃不機嫌にて、とかく内を外
に遊びあるき居り候処、両三日前の新聞に善からぬ噂出で候より、心配の余様子見に参られ候
次第にて、　其事に就き私へ懇々の意見にて、唯継の放蕩致し候は、畢竟内の　おもしろからぬ故
と、日頃の事一々誰が告げ候にや、可恥き迄に皆知れ候て、此後は何分心を用ゐく候やうにと
被申候。　私事其節一思ひに不法の事を申掛け、愛想を尽され候やうに致し、離縁の沙汰にも
相成候はば、　誠に此上無き幸と存付き候へども、此姑と申　候人は、評判の心掛善き御方に
て、殊に私をば娘のやうに思ひ、日頃の厚き情は海山にも喩へ難きほどに候へば、なかなか辞を
返し候段にては無之、心弱しとは思ひながら、涙の零れ候ばかりにて、無拠身の不束をも詫び
申候。　次第に御座候。

此命御前様に捨て候ものに無御座候はば、外には此人の為に捨て可申と存候。此の御方を母とし、御前様を夫と致候て暮し候事も相叶ひ候はば、私は土間に寐ね、蓆を絡ひ候ても、其楽は然ぞやと、常に及ばぬ事を恋く思居りまゐらせ候。私事相果て候はば、他人にて真に悲みくれ候は、此世に此の御方一人に御座あるべく、第一然やうの人を欺き、然やうの情を余所に致し候

私は、如何なる罰を受け候事かと、悲く悲く存候に、はや浅ましき死様は知れたる事に候へば、外に私の願の障とも相成不申やと、始終心に懸り居り申候。

思へば、人の申候ほど死ぬる事は可恐きものに無御座候。私は今が今此儘に息引取り候はば、何よりの仕合と存参らせ候。唯後に遣し候親達の歎を思ひ、又我身生れ効も無く此世の縁薄く、かやうに今在る形も直に消えて、此筆、此硯、此指環、此燈も此居宅も、此夜も此夏も、此の蚊の声も、四囲の者は皆永く残り候に、私独り亡きものに相成候て、人には草花の枯れたるほどにも思はれ候はぬ儚さなどを考へ候へば、返す返す情無く相成候て、心ならぬ未練も出で申候。

注　解

（一）　銀梨子地　蒔絵の一種。銀粉を蒔き、上に梨子地漆を塗って研ぎだしたもの。銀粉が漆を通して斑に浮き出た様が、梨のはだに似ている。

（二）　八朶　八挺ともいう。国の八つのはて。極遠の地。

（三）　二重外套　身ごろにケープがついた、そでなしの外套。わが国には明治初期に洋服とともに輸入されたが、男子の和服用外套として独特の形が考案され、二重回し・とんびなどの名で親しまれた。

（四）　茶微塵　茶色の微塵縞。経・緯ともに二色の糸を一本置きに織り合せて作ったきわめて細かな縞。

（五）　奉書紬　羽二重に似た上質の紬。福井県の産出。

（六）　五十目掛　蠟燭の大きさを、製造に要した蠟の分量で〈何匁目掛〉と呼んだ。ここでは五十匁（一八七・五グラム）の重さの蠟燭。

（七）　空気ランプ　石油の燃焼をよくするために空気の供給をくふうしたランプ。

（八）　三綱五常　儒教で説く、人の守るべき道。君臣・父子・夫婦の道と、仁・義・礼・智・信をいう。

（九）　糸瓜の皮　何の役にもたたぬものの喩。

（一〇）　夜会結　束髪の一種。鬢からねじりあげて、左右に輪をつくり、銀杏返しをおしつぶしたようにしたもの。明治十六年の鹿鳴館建設により西欧風俗の模倣が流行して、従来の日本髪

（一一）紫根　紫草の根を乾したもの。濃紫色の皮がついていて、紫染めの染料に用いられるときもあった。

（一二）七糸　繻珍　経緯子に数種の色緯糸をもちいて浮きもようを織り出した布地。明治から大正初期にかけて婦人の帯地の王座をしめていた。

（一三）縒金　金箔を糸によりつけたもの。

（一四）布袋　布袋和尚（?～917）支那後梁の禅僧。円満の福相が、古来好画材として多く描かれた。わが国の七福神の一つである〈布袋〉は布袋和尚を神格化したものという。

（一五）黒塩瀬（塩瀬）は厚地の畝緯のある羽二重のこと。明治十年から二十年頃にかけて装身工芸品が発達、普及していった。

（一六）金剛石　明治三、四年頃毛利家でカマボコ形のダイヤモンド入り指環を作らせたのが、わが国最初の石入り指環だという。重々しい質感と張りが喜ばれ、男子の紋付羽織に用いられた。

（一七）三百円　当時では、約二カラットのダイヤの値段。そのころ、米価は一升約十銭であった。これから割りだせば、いまの六十万円程度にあたる。

（一八）社会党　資本主義社会の矛盾を批判し、社会主義の実現をめざす大衆政党。わが国では明治十五年に東洋社会党・車会党などが結成され、本格的政党としては明治三十四年片山潜らにより社会民主党が結成されている。

（一九）高等中学　明治十九年の学制で、尋常中学（五年制）と高等中学（二年制）があった。明治二十七年高等中学は高等学校となり、同三十二年尋常中学は中学校になった。高等中学は帝国大学への準備教育機関としての性格が強かった。

(一〇)　奏任　奏任官の略称。もと三等以下の高等官。旧制の官吏で、天皇が内閣総理大臣・主任大臣・宮内大臣の奏薦で任命したもの。

(一一)　帚木の好運　『源氏物語』の「帚木」の巻に、紀伊守の後妻が、たまたま方違えで立ち寄った源氏に見初められ一夜の契りを結ぶ話がある。ここでは、そのようにしてふとした機会に貴人の目にとまり縁を得ることをさしている。また、信州薗原中に、遠くからよく見え、近寄ると消えるという帚木の伝説があり、これを源氏の帚木にかけた洒落。

(一二)　君に勧む……枝を折ることとなかれ　中国唐時代の詩人杜牧(803―852)の『杜秋娘詩』に〈秋〉持白玉璧醉　興唱金縷衣　とある。その注に〈勸君莫惜金縷衣……(略)……李錡長唱此辞〉とあり、李錡の愛妾、杜秋が〈金縷の衣を惜しまれるより、過ぎ去る時を大切になさいまし〉とうたったのを、李錡がよく口ずさんでいたということである。また、全体の形が直立し端正なものを〈真〉と呼ぶ場合もある。

(一三)　真　いけ花の用語で、中心をなす軸をいう。

(一四)　鋏鐮切　鋏鐮型。あくび型。竹製の花器のひとつ。

(一五)　裁片畳　「畳」は「畳紙」の略。厚紙に渋や漆を塗り、折目をつけ畳むようにしたもの。結髪の道具や衣類などを入れる。ここでは布入れ。

(一六)　八犬伝　南総里見八犬伝。江戸時代末期の作家滝沢馬琴(1767―1848)作の読本。仁義礼智忠信孝悌の文字を彫った八つの玉のもとに、八人の勇士が活躍して里見家をおこすという長編伝奇小説。

(一七)　浜路　『八犬伝』の登場人物。弥々山蟇六は、幼少から養い育てた犬塚信乃を、養女浜路の聟にするつもりでいたが、陣代籠山逸東太が浜路に求婚したことから信乃が邪魔になり策を講ずる。それを逃れた信乃は浜路の哀願を退けて旅に出る。その後浜路は信乃に節をたてて悪

漢に殺される。

（二八）　粧奩　婦人の用いる化粧道具。嫁入り道具。ここでは宮の持参金（鴫沢家の財産七千円）を
さす。

（二九）　森々　水面の広々として限りないさま。

（三〇）　一生の苦楽他人に頼る　女の一生の苦楽は夫次第できまる。唐の詩人白居易（772―846）の
『太行路』に〈人生莫＝為〔婦人身〕、百年苦楽由＝他人〕とある。

（三一）　精縷　セルジ（serge＝仏）の略。サージ。

（三二）　黒餅　定紋を描くべきところを白抜きにして染めあげた衣服地。

（三三）　立沢瀉　紋所の一。おもだか科の多年生草本オモダカを、図案化したもの。一種。中央に箭
形・長葉柄の葉を立て、左右に花をあしらっている。

（三四）　仙台平　精巧な絹袴地のひとつ。本練り平と精巧平とがある。貞享のころ伊達政宗（1565
―1636）が仙台藩の絹織物奨励のため、京都の織師小松弥右衛門を招いて織らせたのを始め
とする。

（三五）　遊仙窟　中国唐代の小説で、張文成（660？―740？）作。文成が命を奉じて、黄河の河源
（青海地方）に赴く途中、神仙の窟に迷いこみ、崔十娘や嫂の両女仙の歓待を受けた情
事を描いている。

（三六）　美人クリイム　美人の高利貸の意。クリイムはアイスクリイムのことで、〈氷菓子〉に同音
の〈高利貸〉をかけた隠語。

（三七）　鬼神のお松　三世桜田治助作、世話物歌舞伎脚本。『新版越白波』の通称。嘉永四年九月江
戸市村座初演。越後国笠松峠で旅の武士が女賊にあざむかれて道連れとなり、谷川を渡る
途中刺殺された話を脚色。この女賊は実在したともいわれる。

（三八）　藝妓　はしため。下女と妾を兼ねた者。

（三九）　中銭　芝居・見世物などの興行物で、木戸銭・下足料などのほかに、場内で見物人から取る
　　　銭。ここでは話の途中で請求された葡萄酒のことを洒落れていったもの。

（四〇）　ハヴァナ〔Havana〕　キューバの首都ハバナで製造される葉巻タバコ。

（四一）　一朶の梨花海棠を圧して　一枝の清楚な白い梨花が、艶麗な薄紅色の海棠花を圧倒する。意
　　　外の相手を征服するたとえ。

（四二）　アルフレッド大王〔Alfred the Great (849?─901)〕　古代イギリス、西サクソン人の王。イ
　　　ングランド侵入のデーン人（ノルマンの一派）を破って和を結び、デーン人のイングランド
　　　東北部の支配を認め、南部の領土を確保。軍事・法制・文教に意を用いた。

（四三）　黒楞文絹〔楞文絹〕は〔Chaul（絹）〕のこと。あるいはインドの国名 Chaul のなまりともい
　　　う。オランダ・広東あたりから輸入された。甲斐絹に似て、木目のあやのある絹織物。

（四四）　三十間堀　現在の銀座東一丁目より新橋川にいたる間の堀。戦後埋め立てられた。

（四五）　一炷　香のひとくゆり。〈炷〉は線香などを数える数詞に添える語。

（四六）　百和香　種々の香を合せて練った香。

（四七）　麻蝦夷　地糸に麻を用いた蝦夷錦織。〈蝦夷錦〉は紺地・花色地・赤地などに金糸・銀糸と
　　　染糸とで雲竜の模様を織り出す。もと中国産で、満州・樺太・蝦夷を経て日本に渡った。

（四八）　御主殿持〔御主殿〕は〈御守殿〉が正しい。江戸時代に、諸大名に嫁した将軍の娘の敬称
　　　で、御守殿に仕えた女中の使用した道具類を御守殿持と呼んだ。転じて、一般に女性用の品
　　　品の総称、ここでは後者の意である。

（四九）　羅宇〔ラオ〔laos〕。ラオスから渡来した黒斑竹を用いたからいう。　煙管の火皿と吸い口と
　　　をつなぐ竹の管。

（五〇）写真　写真機の渡来については、天保十二年に長崎の上野常定が、オランダよりの輸入品を島津斉興に献上したという説がある。一種の芸術写真が世に認められるようになってきたのは、紅葉・露伴らの提唱で作られた東京写友会がクラブ展を開いたころからである。

（五一）比翼　二羽の鳥が、たがいにその翼をならべること。転じて、男女の契りの深いのにたとえる。

（五二）スプレイ〔spray（英）〕霧。

（五三）米屋町に出入し〈米屋町〉は取引所用語で、米穀取引所隈の内のこと。現在の中央区日本橋蠣殻町あたり。ここでは、米相場によって生活したこともあるの意。

（五四）牛頭馬頭　牛頭人身、馬頭人身の地獄の獄卒。

（五五）三悪道　仏教用語で、人が生前の悪業によって、死後におもむくとされる三つの世界。餓鬼道・畜生道・地獄道をいう。

（五六）羝羊の乳　〈羝羊〉は牡羊。牡羊が子を生む。決してありえないことのたとえ。

（五七）べいろしゃ　毘盧遮那は大日如来、べいろしゃ゠（酒に酔って）舌が回らなくなること。訳のわからぬことを嘲り笑うのにもち「おん・あぼきゃ・べい・ろしゃ・のう」の上下略。いる語。

（五八）心火　やきもち。

（五九）塗籠　周囲を厚く壁で塗りこめ、明取を付け、妻戸から出入りするようにした部屋。衣服・調度を納め、または寝所とする。今の納戸の類。

（六〇）変裏　衣服の裏地の裾回しの部分だけをちがった色の布で仕立てたもの。

（六一）冷艶　麗艶。うるわしくあでやかなこと。

（六二）装束切摸の色紙散　古代装束の布地を摸写した色紙を散りばめた模様。

（六三）　女四書の内訓　〈女四書〉は中国清時代に王晋升が女子の読むべき書物として編集した『女誡』『女論語』『内訓』『女範』の四書。『内訓』は明の成祖の皇后が書いたものだが、その他もすべて女性の手になる教訓書。江戸時代、明暦二年に辻原元甫が和刻し、『女大学』とともに女子の修養書として重んじられた。明治時代には若江薛蘭・嘉悦孝子らの注釈や評釈がでている。

（六四）　片截、片切彫り。金属彫刻の一。金属面に絵模様を陰刻するのに、絵柄をあらわす線の片側を垂直に、他の一方を斜めに彫ったもの。

（六五）　黒麦酒　明治五年ごろから新聞雑誌にビールの記事や広告がみられ、同九年十月の『家庭叢談』には〈此節頻りに流行する麦酒の如きも日本製品多し〉とある。三十二年七月の諸新聞には、はじめてビアホールの広告があった。

（六六）　罐詰　明治七年、アメリカ人教師に雇われていた日本人が野菜の罐詰を作ったのが最初で、十年ごろから果実や魚獣肉も使われだした。十三年ごろより広告も多くなる。日清戦争後に一般化した。

（六七）　一ゲエム　〈撞球〈玉突き〉〉をさす。嘉永二年ごろ日本に輸入され、

（六八）　てう　〈貂〉足らず、続くにフロックを以つて為るとある。これを踏まえて、動物の貂と、ゲームの得点の点をかけた洒落。『晋書・趙王倫伝』に〈貂不ᵣ足狗尾続〈ちょうたらずしてくびつぐ〉〉がある。

（六九）　フロック〈fluke〈英〉〉　まぐれ当り。

（七〇）　チョオク　球棒の先に塗って、球のすべりどめにする。

（七一）　白馬は馬に非ず　中国の戦国時代の末期に、公孫龍の説いた認識論のひとつに、白馬非馬論がある。白い馬という概念と、馬という概念は同一ではないとし、概念の厳密さを求めたもの。

（七二）　一ヒ深く探る蛟鰐の淵　斎藤監物の詩「題児島高徳書桜樹図詩」に見える詩句。〈一ヒ〉は、一本の短刀。〈蛟〉は、みずち。蛇に似て角と四脚とを具え、毒気を吐いて人を害するという想像上の動物。〈鰐〉は、わに。

（七三）　身支度に婦人の心添　堀部安兵衛が高田馬場で叔父の仇を討ったおり、いあわせた婦人からたすきの紐を借りたという伝説をさしている。

（七四）　轍鮒　わだちにたまった水のなかの鮒の意で、危急に瀕したもののたとえ。荘子の故事に拠る。

（七五）　嘉納流　嘉納治五郎（1860—1938）の創始した講道館柔道。今日の柔道の発達はこれによるところが大きい。

（七六）　水滸伝　中国の長編小説。作者は明の羅貫中とも伝えられるが諸説あって不明。首領の宋江を中心に一〇八人の遊侠が政府に反抗して武勇をふるい、民衆の喝采を博するという大盗物語。

（七七）　日済金　日済金の略。毎日、少しずつ返すという約束で貸す金。

（七八）　地鞴を踏み　〈地鞴〉は、〈地蹈鞴〉、転じて〈じだんだ〉のこと。〈効無き地鞴を踏みて〉は、意のままにならぬじれったさの形容。

（七九）　壮士芝居　明治初期に壮士と呼ばれた政治青年が、自由民権思想を民衆に訴えようとする目的ではじめた素人演劇。明治二十一年に角藤定憲が創始し、二十四年には川上音二郎の一座ができた。現在の新派劇の前身。

（八〇）　樽爼　出典は『晏子春秋』。酒を入れる器と爼をのせる机。転じて公の酒宴、談判の意。「樽爼折衝」は、武力を用いぬ交渉によって相手を挫くことをいう。

（八一）　勧工場　勧工場は明治・大正時代に多くの商店が組合をつくり、ひとつの建物のなかに種々

の商品を陳列して販売した場所。現代のデパートにあたる。

（八二）黄海大海戦　日清戦争の海戦のひとつ、明治二十七年九月、日本の連合艦隊が黄海で清国艦隊を撃破した戦いをいう。

（八三）檳榔子　正しくは〈ビロウ〉。ヤシ科の常緑高木。高さ五〜十メートル。頂部にシュロに似た大羽状複葉をつける。材で傘の柄・ステッキ・たばこ盆を作る。〈ビンロウ〉と混同されやすい。

（八四）黒一楽　〈一楽〉は、一楽織りのこと。綾織りにした精巧な絹織物。

（八五）紋緞子　〈緞子〉は、紋織物の一種。生糸または練糸をもちいた繻子組織の絹織物で、地が厚く光沢がある。

（八六）コニャック〔cognac（仏）〕フランス・コニャック地方名産の酒。葡萄を原料として醸造し、楢材の樽に詰めてその香りを移す。

（八七）三井　三井呉服店。越後屋が明治二十九年に屋号を改めたもので、現在の三越の前身。翌年東京本店の階上を改造して陳列場とし、デパート風に客が自由に品物をえらべるようにするなど、経営の近代化をはかった。

（八八）吾妻コオト　長さが裾までである婦人用コート。明治二十三年ごろ、白木屋呉服店が、江戸時代の男合羽に似た折り衿のコートを作り、東コートの名で売り出した。

（八九）台湾銀杏　〈銀杏返し〉のこと。女子の髪型で、髻の上を両分し、左右に曲げて半円形に結んだもの。鹿鳴館時代、束髪に対抗して流行した。ここではその変り型の名。

（九〇）無想裏　〈無想〉は、無双とも書き、表服の表裏をおなじに作ること。〈夢想羽織〉は表裏が同色の羽織。のちには表裏の布地を同じにし、色を違えたものをもいうようになった。ここでは後者。

（九一）　光琳風　江戸時代の画家・工芸家尾形光琳（1658─1716）の画風。濃厚・鮮麗な色彩をもち
　　　　い、大胆な装飾化・図案化をほどこした。

（九二）　半襟は色糸の縫ある　半襟の刺繍は明治のはじめ頃、一部の人の贅沢品として愛用されてい
　　　　た。明治十年代に入ってから、半襟のおしゃれはいっそう凝ったものになり、刺繍も部分か
　　　　総縫いへとひろがった。

（九三）　第二百十条　旧刑法で、現刑法の一五九条「私文書偽造」に相当する罪。

（九四）　黯認　くもって明らかでないさま。ここでは周囲がすっかり煙につつまれたさまをいう。

（九五）　肩相摩して《肩摩轂撃》。車の轂（こしき）が撃ちあい、人の肩がふれあうという、市街の
　　　　繁華を形容する語。

（九六）　寿山《寿山福海》　はともにめでたい図柄。転じて、人の長寿を祝う語。

（九七）　嘉平治平　正しくは嘉平次平。銘仙織りの袴地。武蔵国（埼玉県）入間郡の人藤本嘉平治が
　　　　創始したという。

（九八）　君山　中国の安徽省盱眙県の東北にある。

（九九）　湘水　中国の中南区湖南省にある河。湘江。源を同区広西省北部の興安県下の海陽山に発し
　　　　て、洞庭湖に注ぐ。全長約一一五〇キロメートル。

（一〇〇）　砍却　《砍》は《カン・コン》と読み、切る意。切りけること。

（一〇一）　陽狂　狂気をよそおうこと。にせきちがい。

（一〇二）　政子櫛　鶴岡八幡宮に、北条政子（1157─1225）の遺品として伝わる櫛。径二寸八分・高さ
　　　　一寸二分で、青貝の螺鈿細工がほどこしてある。ここではそれを模して作った政子形櫛。

（一〇三）　空華　かすんだ目で天空を見る時に、ちらちら見える花のようなもの。煩悩からおこる種々
　　　　の妄想をいう。

（一〇五）、丈六に組み　あぐらを組むこと。

（一〇四）、水は覆った　覆水盆に返らず。『拾遺記』の故事による。いったん起ったことは取りかえしがつかぬの意。

（一〇六）、蟹が子なれば宿も定めず〈蟹が子〉は漁夫、または漁夫の子。『新古今集』（雑下）に〈白波の寄するなぎさに世をつくすあまの子なれば宿も定めず〉の歌がある。

（一〇七）、暑　かげ。はしらかげ。太陽の運行をはかるためにたてた竿が地上に投影する影。ここでは〈日〉と同意で使っている。

（一〇八）、里昴　リヨン〔Lyons〕。フランス東南部、ローヌ・ソーヌ両河に跨がる都市。絹工業の中心地。

（一〇九）、伝々会　〈でんでん〉は、太棹の三味線の音。転じて、義太夫節の俗称、ここではその愛好者のつどい。

（一一〇）、親々に誘はれ……思ひも寄らぬ夫定　近松徳叟（1751—1810）作、翠松園主人補訂の浄瑠璃義太夫節『生写朝顔話』の「宿屋の段」に見える詩句。盲になった深雪が恋人の前で、それとは気づかずに琴を弾く場面。

（一一一）、藤村　いまの文京区本郷三丁目にある和菓子屋。寛永三年創業の老舗として有名。

（一一二）、盗泉の水は飲まん　盗泉、中国の山東省泗水県にある泉。どんなに飢渇していようとも、名が盗泉というだけでその水は飲まないの意。『淮南子』に〈渇すれど盗泉の水は飲まず〉とある。転じて不義の財を恥むことをいう。

（一一三）、倒懸　手足を縛ってさかさまにかけること。転じて、非常な苦しみのたとえ。

（一一四）、破鏡　夫婦の離別すること。『神異経』に、夫婦別れをしたものが、鏡をわって各々その一片を持っていたという故事がある。

（一五）　愚なる精衛の……填めんとするやと　〈精衛〉は、中国の伝説上の鳥。炎帝の女が、東海に溺れ死してこの鳥に化し、西山の木や石を口にふくんで運び、東海を埋めようとしたという故事がある。

（一六）　蟻の思を運ぶ　諺に〈蟻の思いも天まで通る〉とある。微弱な者でも、一念が強ければ望みを達することができるの意。

（一七）　黄蘗染　黄蘗の皮から製した染料で染めた布地。

（一八）　東綴　明治末年に栃木県の足利市から織り出された模造の綴れ錦。女の帯地に用いる。

（一九）　行く水に……思ふなりけり　『古今集』〈恋一〉にある歌。〈数画〉は、涅槃経より出た語で、水にものの数を書く、つまり、はかないこと、つまらないことのたとえ。

（二〇）　薄色魚子〈薄色〉は、経は紫で、緯は白の織り出し。薄紫色。〈魚子〉は魚子織りのこと。織り目が方形で、魚卵のように打違いに粒だって見える。

（二一）　鼇背　鼇は鼈の俗字。大ウミガメの背。また、その形をしたもの。

（二二）　秋蛇の行くに似たる径　委蛇（うねうねと曲りくねったさま）という言葉がある。折れまがった道のこと。

（二三）　野州塩原〈野州〉は、下野（いまの栃木県）の別称。塩原は栃木県北部、塩谷郡にある温泉町。箒川の渓流に沿い、大網・福渡・塩釜・畑下・門前・須巻・古町・袖が沢、高原山北斜面の塩の湯・新湯・元湯などがあり、総称して塩原温泉という。

（二四）　巉巌　きりたてたような、けわしい岩石。

（二五）　薬研　主として漢方の製薬にもちいる金属製の器。舟型で細長く、なかが窪んでいる。ここに薬種を入れ、車型の道具で、押しくだいて細かくする。

（二六）　瑠璃末　瑠璃の粉末。〈瑠璃〉は七宝のひとつ。色は深青や、緑青をおびたものなど。

（二七）　雲雀骨　やせて骨ばっているさま。

（二八）　噴薄激盪　〈噴薄〉は、水がふきあげて岸にせまること。〈激盪〉は、激しくゆれること。

（二九）　蒲生飛騨守氏郷　蒲生氏郷（1556─1595）。安土桃山時代の武将。織田信長・豊臣秀吉に仕

（三〇）　丘壑　丘と谷。転じて隠者の住居、またその楽しみをいう。
　　　　　会津百万石を領した。

（三一）　玉根掛　〈根掛〉は婦人が日本髪の髻に飾りとして巻くもの。明治時代には金・銀・さんご・
　　　　　ガラス玉などの加工品に紐を通したり、また幅広の鎖形にして用いた。ここではそれが堆朱
　　　　　彫りの玉でできているもの。

（三二）　ミレエジ　［mirage（英）］空中楼閣。空想。

（三三）　旁午　縦横にいりみだれること。往来のはげしいこと。

（三四）　林檎　慶応四年四月の『中外』十八号に、田中芳男が外国から持ち帰った品として〈苹果も
　　　　　方今は許多の菓を結ぶに至れり。苹果元和産なし。西洋名アップル俗称オホリンゴといふ。
　　　　　林檎の属にして実大に且甜美なり〉とある。苗木がはじめて輸入されたのは明治五年ごろと
　　　　　伝えられる。

（三五）　躍利　高利貸などからの借金が期限になっても返済できない時、借金を継続して、その切替
　　　　　えの日の利息を二重にとられること。

（三六）　三千何百万　明治三十五年の日本の総人口は約四千五百万人である。

（三七）　赤襟　少女。または、まだ一人前でない芸妓。

　　　三好行雄

解説

1

　作者の尾崎紅葉は本名徳太郎、慶応三年（一八六八）十二月十六日（一説二十七日）江戸芝中門前町に生れた。雅号は芝の紅葉山に因む。父惣蔵は武田姓も名のり、谷斎と号し牙彫の名人、奇人癖があって身を幇間の群れに投じていた。世間から彼が緋ちりめんの羽織を常用して花街に出没したので「赤羽織の谷斎」と呼ばれた。紅葉はこれを恥じ秘密にしていた。しかし芸に打込むエ芸家の血は紅葉の文学に濃い影響がある。紅葉六歳の折、母庸が亡くなったので、芝神明町の母の実家漢方医荒木舜庵方で養育された。府立二中（後の一中、現日比谷高校）を中退、岡鹿門、石川鴻斎に漢学、漢詩文を学び、また三田英学校で大学予備門入学準備をした。明治十六年東京大学予備門入学、十八年山田美妙、石橋思案、丸岡九華等と硯友社を起し、五月から回覧雑誌『我楽多文庫』を発行した。初めは文筆愛好者の遊戯的な営みにすぎなかったが、社会の新文学要求に誌友も増し、ついに印刷公売するまでに発展した。紅葉も初め大学は法科を選んでいたが、二十二年九月には国文学科に転じ文学へ専心進む決意をつけた。

吉岡書籍店の『新著百種』第一号（明治二十二・四）の『二人比丘尼色懺悔』を出世作に文壇に登場、なお二十二年十二月には、読売新聞に入社、ここを地盤として、『伽羅枕』『紅白毒饅頭』『三人妻』『心の闇』『紫』『不言不語』『青葡萄』『多情多恨』『金色夜叉』等の力作はすべて同紙に掲げた。

その人柄、文学的才能によって、紅葉は広津柳浪、川上眉山、江見水蔭、石橋思案、大橋乙羽等の同人を擁する硯友社の頭目と仰がれ、またその門から泉鏡花、徳田秋声、小栗風葉、柳川春葉を初め多くの作家を輩出せしめた。そして自然主義以前の明治文壇に幸田露伴と並んで輝かしい位置を占めたが、明治三十六年十月三十日、三十七歳で永眠した。

2

『金色夜叉』は紅葉の代表作であり、また明治の小説で最も大衆に愛読されたものである。読売新聞には明治三十年一月一日から三十五年五月十一日まで断続しながら六年間にわたって連載され、単行本初版は春陽堂から前編（三十一年七月）中編（三十二年一月）後編（三十三年一月）続編（三十五年四月）続々編（三十六年六月）、なお続々編七版（三十八年七月）には新続編が含まれて刊行された。

読売連載が断続した理由には作者生来の鏤骨の文章表現の苦心とこれとからみあった病苦のせいであった。

この小説のストーリイは、たとえ原作を読まないでも演劇、映画化等で主人公貫一、宮の名と共に多く大衆に知られている。すなわち、明治時代の閉ざされた男女交際機関の一つの有力な窓ともいうべき正月のカルタ会で、銀行家の子、富山唯継に見染められた鳴沢宮には、許嫁第一高等中学校生間貫一がいた。貫一は身よりがなく、鳴沢家に同居していた。しかし富山の宮に対する求婚を宮の両親は承知し、その償いとして貫一を将来洋行させようと云った。貫一はそれを不本意として、熱海の海岸で、宮の本心を確認しようとした。ところが意外にも宮の心も富山にかたむいていたことを知って、貫一は絶望し、その行方をくらました。貫一はすっかり金銭の鬼と化してしまい、高利貸し鰐淵直行の手代となっていた。同業の赤樫満枝に恋されたこともあったが動じない。一方、富山と結婚した宮は夫を愛しえない。貫一の親友であった豪放な荒尾譲介によって貫一の住所をたしかめ詫びたが貫一はうけつけない。このように冷酷な金銭の鬼となった貫一であったが、塩原の宿で偶然富山に身請けされることを嫌い、その愛人と死のうとしている芸者をその愛情にうたれて助ける心は保っている。悔恨の宮からは詫び状がとどくが貫一は開封しようともしない。しかし、ある日、またとどいた手紙をふと開いてみると、死を願うあわれな宮の現状が記されてあった。

『金色夜叉』はここで未完に終って紅葉は完成することなく亡くなったのであるが、全体の構想はどうであったか。またその素材は何によったか。

門下生篠山吟葉・星野麦人編集の『紅葉遺文』に『如是畜生』と題し、

「恋ゆゑの高利貸。

黄金不足の為に失恋して世の中は黄金以外ならずと妄断し、我寧ろ魔道に落ちむと強慾一点の非道を行ふこと十年。二万余円の富を累ねて一朝忽ち大悟し、金の為に死に逼る情死を救ひ発心して情死救済の広告をなして五十余人の命を助け一文無しになる」

とある。紅葉の腹案筋書きがあり、これに「編者曰く金色夜叉の趣向はこれを敷衍せしめしもの乎」とある。　別に『如是畜生』以外の遺稿断片を勝本清一郎が整理した「金色夜叉腹案覚書」（中央公論社版『尾崎紅葉全集』第六巻所載）がある。未完以後の構想を要約すると、宮は憂悶して、ついに発狂し、別家に幽せられる。本家にその姿をいれた唯継に、ついに宮は棄てられる。そこで貫一は心が解けて、宮を引取り、高利貸しも廃業する。また貫一は負債に困っている旧友荒尾のため償主を探して借金を返してやり、荒尾は後でこれを知って驚くといった筋で『如是畜生』より自然性がある。

なお紅葉は作品の構想とそれを作品化するについて、後藤宙外編の『唾玉集』中で次のように語っている。

「私は始め極漠然とした事柄……いや概念も概念も非常に疎い概念を先に拵へましてね、例を取

れば『金色夜叉』で云ふと、ラブの為に性質が一変してしまつて激烈なる高利貸しになる、と云ふ考へをきめ、それから始まりと真中と収結とをきめて、つまり初中終の三つをきめて又その小割を更に三つ位にする」とその創作技法を説明している。

紅葉はこの構想を何でえたか。　江見水蔭は『自己中心明治文壇史』中、明治二十九年七月、当時、相州片瀬にいた水蔭を紅葉が訪れた時、紅葉はその恋愛観を説き、最近読んだある米国女流作家の『ホワイト・リリイ』という小説の梗概を話した。それは主人公の若者が失恋する。相手の女は財産家の方に傾いてそれと結婚する。その結婚式の日、教会の鐘の音の聞えぬ所まで主人公は逃げて行くという筋で、これにヒントを得て近々読売に小説を書くといった、翌年一月から読売に出始めたのが『金色夜叉』であったと述べている。

なお木村毅によれば、この米国女流作家はバーサ・エム・クレー（Bertha M. Clay）であろう、しかし彼女には『ホワイト・リリー』という作はなく、それは白百合という言葉が、しばしば現われる『ドラ・ソオーン』でないか、なおこの作は末松謙澄の『谷間の姫百合』の原本であり、菊池幽芳の『乳姉妹』もこの翻案だという。そして、『金色夜叉』構想の若干の種本となったかも知れないが、同じ作者の "When the Bell is Ringing" はなお筋が似ているとて、次のような筋を記している。

それは女に捨てられた男は、女の冷淡を怒って、かえって人命救済の大悲願をおこして医者になる。『金色夜叉』の主人公と愛憎が逆でありながら筋は似ており、その医者を見すてた女が、か

えって不幸になり、瀕死の病軀をその男の病院に収容され、ついに息をひきとるが、その時鐘が鳴っていたというのである。筋が似ていると思う。

こうした構想のほか貫一のモデルとして、その失恋という点から巌谷小波説が一般に流布している。すなわち小波は若い日川田甕江の塾にあり、その次女綾子を恋し求婚した。しかし当時巌谷家の家産がかたむき、小波の不安定な作家という職業からこれが拒絶された。また小波は、硯友社同人も時々出かけていた芝の紅葉館の女中須磨子を思慕していたが、彼女は博文館主大橋新太郎に見初められ結婚した。大橋の父佐平は、一流の出版社を持つほか、勧業銀行他五十社ほどの重役を兼ねた財閥でもあった。友情に厚かった紅葉の義憤と共に財が愛にいちおう勝ったもののやはり愛に人生の幸福はあるというこの作のテーマのモデルにしたと思われる。また貫一が高利貸しになるという設定には、硯友社仲間の川上眉山や中村花痩が同じように高利貸しに苦しめられている話をしばしば聞いていたので、そのことが頭にあって貫一の失恋からの転身をそこに求めることを思いついたのであろう。

4

この長編は新聞連載中から非常に愛読された。泉鏡花は、老若婦女、桃割れの娘もべっこうぶちの目鏡をかけた隠居も、それを耽読したのは、紅葉の苦心の章句調律が、自ら微妙な音楽となって、風は蕭々として紙上に鳴り、水は潺々として筆意に濡いで、直ちに読者の心胸に響いたせい

であろうという。それもあろうが、更に宮の運命に、その筋の展開に心ひかれたせいであろう。命旦夕にせまったある令嬢は、死後墓前に花や水を供えるより『金色夜叉』掲載の読売を毎朝供えてほしいと遺言したというほどであった。

宮の美貌は、経済的な理由で男性の従属物であった明治期の女性の男性へ対抗する唯一の支柱であり武器であった。たとえ学士という当時のエリートで、将来は保証されたにせよ、経済的に不安定な貫一より、銀行家という財閥へ宮の心は移ったが、心中貫一を思う心はなお残っていた。それが富山の冷酷さにあってなおさら貫一へひかれている。それを貫一は許そうとしない。読者は宮の運命に次第に同情し、また貫一の行動、心理の変化に強く関心を持ったのである。なお宮は一度富山にとついで、財産をえて貫一に復帰する計算であったと熱海の海岸での会話から解釈する説もあるが、賛成することはできない。

紅葉はここに明治の世相、社会を大きく截断してみせた。発表当時愛読されたこの作は、その後多く演劇、映画、流行歌、放送等で一般化したため、極めて通俗小説視されるきらいがあるが、紅葉文学の集大成として、一大ロマンとして、明治文学の代表作たる価値は長く保ちつづけるだろう。

昭和四十四年九月

福田清人